NEW ZEALAND NURSES

New Zealand Nurses
Caring for our people
1880–1950

PAMELA WOOD

OTAGO UNIVERSITY PRESS
Te Whare Tā o Te Wānanga o Ōtākou

*To New Zealand nurses
everywhen and everywhere.*

Published by Otago University Press
Te Whare Tā o Te Wānanga o Ōtākou
533 Castle Street
Dunedin, New Zealand
university.press@otago.ac.nz
www.otago.ac.nz/press

First published 2022
Copyright © Pamela Wood
The moral rights of the author have been asserted.

ISBN 978-1-99-004832-6

A catalogue record for this book is available from the National Library of New Zealand. This book is copyright. Except for the purpose of fair review, no part may be stored or transmitted in any form or by any means, electronic or mechanical, including recording or storage in any information retrieval system, without permission in writing from the publishers. No reproduction may be made, whether by photocopying or by any other means, unless a licence has been obtained from the publisher.

Published with the assistance of Creative New Zealand

Editor: Erika Bűky
Index: Lee Slater
Author photograph: Jeremy Bright, Grabb Photography, Taupō

Printed in China through Asia Pacific Offset

Contents

Acknowledgements 7

Introduction 11

1   Narrating a history of New Zealand nursing 21

2   Nurse training in New Zealand 47

3   Becoming a New Zealand nurse 67

4   Brightening sunless lives – district nursing 91

5   The 'intrepid nurse' in the backblocks 111

6   Nursing Māori, Māori nurses 133

7   Caring in conflict – the emotional labour of wartime nursing 161

8   Virus and tremor – nursing in disasters 185

9   Contesting 'the modern nurse' 207

10   Building a nursing community and culture 223

11   Nursing at the southern edge of empire 249

Conclusion 271

Abbreviations 278

Notes 279

Bibliography 347

Index 364

Acknowledgements

The research for this book depended entirely on accessing historical primary sources, so I am very grateful to the numerous archivists and librarians who helped make it possible. In particular, I thank Anne Jackman, regional director, and the team at the Dunedin Office of Archives New Zealand who organised a smooth process for accessing many records; the consistently helpful staff in the Manuscripts Collection of the Alexander Turnbull Library, as well as Linda Evans, oral history curator, for the valuable collection of recordings and virtual access system; Anna Blackman, head curator, and staff at the Hocken Collections, University of Otago, Dunedin; Cathy Dunn and Linda Macan, MTG Archives, Napier; and the splendid team at the Taupō Library, who were always very obliging and supportive.

For sending me or providing access to other historical material, I need to thank Viv Kerr, librarian, Hawke's Bay District Health Board, Hastings; Lindsey Seaton, administrator, Taupō Museum; Jana Uhlrova, curator and manager, Central Hawke's Bay Museum, Waipawa; Eloise Wallace, director, and Christine Page, archivist, Tairāwhiti Museum, Gisborne; Professor Kay Morris Matthews, Napier; Merian Litchfield, Wellington; Rachel Hurd, archivist, Presbyterian Research Centre (Archives), Knox College, Dunedin; Mike Gooch and Lucy Macfarlane, Puke Ariki, New Plymouth; Alyce Stock, Dunedin City Library; and the family of Mavis Attree, Wellington.

Dr Judith Clare, Hastings, provided information about a nurse's grave; Dr Maxine Alterio, Dunedin, sent me books; Terri Foley and colleagues of the Lake Taupō Branch of the New Zealand Society of Genealogists gave advice about Māori death records; Helen Sweet, UK, gave information about the training of Indigenous African women as nurses and confirmed the year the first Indigenous African nurse was registered; and Bill McKay, University of Auckland, provided information about octagonal buildings used as influenza wards in New Zealand military camp hospitals. My thanks go to numerous nurses who have given their time and memories in oral history interviews. I am also grateful to Nadia Munir, at the Royal College of Nursing, London, and Rose Brown, at the Barts Health Archives, London, for checking information. Derek Maddock, archivist, Sudeley Castle and Gardens, Winchcombe, UK, understood an odd request, very generously sent me precisely the material I needed and did so under difficult circumstances in 2020.

In accessing historical images, I had patient help from Trish McCormack, Archives New Zealand, Wellington; Adam Simpson, Wairarapa Archive, Masterton; Susan Tolich, Auckland War Memorial Museum; Keith Giles, Research, Heritage and Central Library, Auckland; Dolores Ho, National Army Museum, Waiōuru; Jennifer Jeffery, Presbyterian Research Centre (Archives), Dunedin; Heather Woods, New Zealand Nurses' Organisation Library, Wellington; Viv Kerr, Hawke's Bay District Health Board Library, Hastings; Dudley Meadows, Tairāwhiti Museum, Gisborne; Clare Ashton, Kokatahi; and Glenn Coster and colleagues, Christchurch City Library. I am grateful for their permission to reproduce selected images in this book. Jeremy Bright, Grabb Photography, Taupō, worked marvels with images from my historical collection and prepared them for publication. And I owe special thanks to Susan Elijas, who provided timely IT expertise.

Several people gave me generous permission to draw significantly from their publications. In particular, I need to thank Professor Linda Bryder, Dr Felicity Barnes, Dr Raeburn Lange, Colleen Williams, and Ian and Diane Grant of Fraser Books, Masterton. I am grateful for their permission to summarise scholarly arguments, use several short extracts as quotations or retell stories. Every effort has been made to contact copyright holders of material referred to in the text, but if representatives of authors' estates could contact us if necessary, we would be grateful. I would like to acknowledge the contribution all sources have made to this work. Anne Manchester and co-editors of *Kai Tiaki: Nursing New Zealand*, continued the generous permission they have granted over several years for me to quote from numerous articles and relate stories published in historical issues of the journal. I owe thanks to Heather Woods, New Zealand Nurses Organisation, for permission to reproduce some of the material in the Nursing Education and Research Foundation Oral History Collection recordings, and to Radio New Zealand for permission to quote from two *Spectrum* programmes. The Executive of the New Zealand Federation of Women's Institutes, through Colleen Dryden, executive officer, kindly permitted me to retell the story that starts the book.

Acknowledgements

Family and friends gave me practical help and encouragement. In particular, I thank my sons, Linden, Cameron and David Wilkie; Laraine and Warwick Lash, who listened to endless stories; Barbara Benson, who provided much-needed gardening expertise; and Doreen Gordon's Thursday group, who always took an interest in progress. Dr Annette Huntington and Dr Janice McDrury provided welcome hospitality during several research trips to Wellington and Dunedin, and always asked good questions. I am grateful to Dr Barbara Mortimer, Edinburgh, for the generous gifts of historical books from her collection, the wonderful conversations on nursing history, and her hospitality on research trips, over many years. Professor Christine Hallett, University of Huddersfield, has also kindly provided hospitality and always given valuable perspectives on historical wartime nursing.

Finally, I am grateful to Rachel Scott, Sue Wootton and the excellent team at Otago University Press, and to Erika Bűky for her editing expertise. Their interest, encouragement and belief in the book made the publishing process a heartening experience.

Introduction

On the morning of Christmas Eve 1911, a nurse at the small hospital in the Otago goldfields town of Naseby went to borrow some vases. Friends had sent her a large basket of flowers to decorate her ward, and she had planned a 'delicate colour scheme in pink, blue and mauve'. As she walked to the township, Mr James Crawford was sitting at his gate. The old man was a veteran of the 1853–56 Crimean War. He treasured a memory of holding Florence Nightingale's hand as he helped her down the ship's gangway when she arrived at Scutari. His pride in this recollection meant he took a personal interest in the Naseby hospital and would often sit in the sun outside his cottage to offer fruit or flowers to the nurses as they passed. The nurse loved listening to his stories of Nightingale. As she passed his cottage, he asked her to wait a minute while he went into the house. When he came back, he presented her with three posies of flowers tied with garter grass and cut with very short stems. They were 'homely, every-day flowers – sweet william, marigolds, mignonette, moss roses, pansies, four o'clocks, fat little pink and white daisies, with bits of geranium' from his wife's window. 'These are for your ward to-morrow, Nurse.' He and his wife would be down to see it in the afternoon.

She thought with dismay of her planned colour scheme; then, recalling Florence Nightingale, she decided to use the homely posies. She arranged the short-stemmed flowers to their best advantage in little jars filled with moist sand and placed them in the ward. Among her patients were five very old men, pioneers of the Hogburn gold rush. When they saw the flowers on Christmas morning, they loved them. One man over 80 enjoyed the scent of the sweet williams, and the sight of a geranium reminded him of his mother's kitchen window display in the 'old country'. A snowy-haired Highlander's eyes became misty as he lifted from his locker a pot with three moss rosebuds. He had placed moss roses in his sweetheart's hands when she died, sixty-four years before. 'The scent o' these bring far thoughts to me.'

'No long stemmed flowers arranged in tall vases could have awakened such memories,' the nurse recalled. 'That afternoon the veteran and his wife visited the hospital. The quiet look of pride on their faces more than repaid me for side-tracking my colour scheme.'[1]

This story connects a nurse at the southernmost edge of the British Empire with Florence Nightingale at its centre. A year after her death, Nightingale's enduring influence on nursing practice is clear. She believed that good nursing was 'doing a number of small things well.'[2] A touch of flowers could make a difference. She said in 1859: 'I remember (in my own case) a nosegay of wild flowers being sent me, and from that moment recovery became more rapid.'[3] In December 1864 Emma Dent of Sudeley Castle sent Nightingale, now confined to bed, some dried flowers that she had gathered at Scutari. On Christmas Eve, Nightingale wrote to Dent that the gift had filled her eyes with 'grateful tears of joy' and would make her 'Christmas a day of thanksgiving ... Your Scutari flowers are standing, and always will stand, opposite my bed, to which I am now a complete prisoner.' The flowers were 'a pledge' to the spirit of 'our heroes lying at Scutari whose uncomplaining endurance I always labour to be worthy of'. She added: 'I used to have a foolish wish that my body might be taken back to Scutari to lie beside them. But your flowers are a better earnest of the same thing.'[4]

New Zealand nursing training instilled respect for the work and leadership of Nightingale and other notable international nurses. Pageants of nursing history, with nurses dressed in appropriate costumes, always featured Nightingale, the 'Lady with the Lamp', who was frequently acknowledged as the founder of modern nursing.[5] Annie Matheson's 1913 biography is typical of the reverent tone of early Nightingale biographies: 'Florence Nightingale would have enriched our calendar of uncanonised saints even if her disciplined high-hearted goodness had exercised an unseen spell by simply *being*, and had, by some limitation of body or of circumstance, been cut off from much active *doing*.'[6] Sir Edward Cook's weightier two-volume biography, also published in 1913, was less hagiographic but proved popular.[7] In her review of the work for New Zealand's only nursing journal, *Kai Tiaki*, Hester Maclean said, 'We personally could not part with the copy sent from the book-sellers (Messrs Mackay & Sons, Wellington), we wish to read it again, and keep it to dip into again and yet again.'[8] And so she did. On the wartime voyage of the 'First Fifty' nurses from New Zealand to Egypt in April 1915, Sister Edna Pengelly noted: 'Very cold last night. Miss Maclean and I did some French translation. In the evening we read *Florence Nightingale* and retired early.'[9]

Any association with Nightingale merited notice. Newspapers identified former Crimean casualties and women who had nursed with Nightingale at the Scutari military hospital. One was Mrs A. Evans of Hāwera, in her eighties in 1913 (and still the lessee of the Hāwera railway refreshment rooms 'to the satisfaction of all concerned'). She had nursed a Mr Neville Thornton of Whanganui at Scutari after he was wounded . Both 'liked a glass of beer or toddy'.[10] The two had met again with a 'warm greeting' in 1910.[11] Mr J. Furman of Christchurch, another Crimean soldier, had been admitted to the Scutari hospital with cholera. He remembered Nightingale as kind and cheerful; she had given him a brandy stimulant and asked him not to tell the doctor.[12] Mary Tattersall, who went with Nightingale to the Crimea after her fiancé was killed in action, later came to New Zealand, where she continued nursing. She was buried in the Greymouth cemetery in 1895. In 1944 a former Greymouth resident, William Noy, wrote to the matron of Greymouth's hospital to tell her about the grave. As a result, the Registered Nurses' Association took steps to restore it.[13] Nurse Lyons, who had been sent to the Edinburgh Infirmary by Nightingale as one of its first trained nurses, cherished the letters Nightingale wrote to her in the 1870s, before she emigrated to New Zealand. They were eventually given to the Post Graduate School for Nurses, where the students bound them into a volume and presented them to the library.[14]

Alfred H. Reed, a Dunedin publisher, wrote a small book about Nightingale to 'strengthen the resolve of some who may feel a call to enter this humanitarian profession'. He noted that the Dunedin Public Hospital held a letter from Nightingale.[15] In 1939 Masterton schoolchildren made a snow statue of Nightingale (though it was trumped by Form III's 'perfectly marvellous' statue of Queen Victoria, 12ft or 3.6m high).[16]

Any physical object connected with Nightingale could also be treasured. The professional association displayed a probe that Nightingale allegedly used at Scutari. In the foundation stone of the new nurses' home at Southland Hospital was a brick from a hospital associated with Nightingale, secured by Ruth Bridges when she was at Bedford College in London in 1936.[17] A similar brick was obtained by Emily Nutsey, Auckland Hospital's retired lady superintendent (matron). The *Evening Post* reported in 1943: 'This brick, mounted in a glass case, has since been a treasured relic in the nurses' common room at the hospital, and some concern was expressed last week that it had been removed, a bright red one having been put in its place, apparently for a joke. It has now been restored to its place of honour.'[18]

Florence Nightingale therefore had an acknowledged place in the New Zealand nursing culture, and her legacy connected nurses at the empire's periphery with its centre. In 1860, using funds provided by a grateful nation in recognition of her work in the Crimea, Nightingale established a school of nursing at St Thomas's Hospital in London. This marked the emergence of modern nursing. Nightingale was not directly involved in running the school but took a keen interest in it, writing frequent letters to the probationers and reading their case notes. Other hospitals in Britain and elsewhere sought its graduates to be their matrons and establish similar schools. Nightingale even responded to requests for teams of nurses, including the team Lucy Osburn led to the Sydney Infirmary in 1868.[19] Nurses who had trained in the Nightingale system, either at St Thomas's or at hospitals led by its graduates, gradually spread around the world. This was the late-nineteenth-century British nursing diaspora, and New Zealand was its southernmost landfall.[20]

From the 1880s onward, New Zealand hospitals similarly recruited these nurses to be their matrons and formalise nurse training. Was a British nursing culture simply transplanted into New Zealand with these arrivals, or did a distinctly New Zealand culture emerge? What was the nurse's role in New Zealand's self-image as a modern colony and dominion? Were nurses agents of empire? And how did nurses at the empire's periphery view themselves in relation to the empire and the wider nursing world?

This book answers these questions by exploring three kinds of nursing narratives. First, it draws on a rich collection of nurses' personal stories of caring for the sick and promoting health in a range of settings – hospitals, homes, rural backblocks, urban slums, Māori communities, clinics, factories, schools, war zones and disaster areas. Second, it examines a range of opinions, from nurses and others, of what a modern New Zealand nurse should be and do. Narratives of nursing were written by interested onlookers as well as nurses. And third, it examines the emergence of a nursing culture, with its specialised knowledge, values, history, traditions, symbols, rites of passage, sense of community, gossip, folklore and myths.

Discussions of the nature of nursing appear in diaries, letters, memoirs, autobiographies, reminiscences, oral histories, professional journals, popular magazines, newspaper articles, letters to the editor, official records, textbooks, procedure manuals, lecture notes, marginalia, archival manuscripts, ephemera, recruitment booklets, examination questions and answers, student nurses' magazines, scrapbooks, parliamentary debates, speeches, eulogies and formal histories. Films, photographs, mementos and memorial windows and plaques also tell stories. Few personal narratives survive from the nineteenth century, though the voices of nurses of this period were occasionally heard in public inquiries into 'hospital troubles'. One exception is Mary Fraser, who was one of the first nurses to train at Dunedin Hospital from 1884. Recounting her experiences at a public celebration of the hospital's diamond jubilee in 1926, she told of the hard work, hospital conditions, the matrons and doctors she worked with, and the porter, Dryburgh, who wore on his watch chain a gold guinea that the ailing Nightingale gave him when he helped carry her aboard the ship that would take her back from the Crimea.[21]

Important historical sources include professional nursing journals and nurses' letters, autobiographies and memoirs. Hester Maclean founded the journal *Kai Tiaki* in 1908 to connect nurses scattered throughout the country and keep them up to date with changes in practice and the profession. When she retired as chief nurse in 1923, she sold the journal to the New Zealand Trained Nurses' Association but remained its editor until her death in 1932. It was published quarterly until 1930, when its name changed to the *New Zealand Nursing Journal* and it was published every second month. From 1939 until 1948 it was a monthly journal, and then it reverted to bimonthly publication. Maclean was justifiably proud of the 'little paper' and was delighted when full sets were requested for the International Council of Nurses (ICN) headquarters in Geneva, the National Council of Trained Nurses of Great Britain and Ireland, and the Imperial War Museum in London.[22] In 1926 Maclean was appointed as the Australasian representative of the ICN's five-member Publication Committee.[23]

For nurses far from home, either on wartime service or in isolated rural regions, letters connected them with their friends and colleagues and created a sense of professional community. Letter writing enabled nurses to portray themselves as adventurous, courageous and effective in these diverse new roles. Accounts from New Zealand nurses in the South African (Boer) War were published in newspapers. Nurses in overseas service in World War I wrote to Hester Maclean, who was not only New Zealand's chief nurse but also matron-in-chief of the New Zealand Army Nursing Service. In her separate role as *Kai Tiaki* editor, she published around 350 nurses' letters in full or as excerpts or summaries. Similarly, she published letters she received as chief nurse from nurses in the backblocks and Māori health services.

Nurses' personal stories convey the reality of New Zealand nursing in rural areas and towns, hospitals and homes, disasters and war. These accounts not only documented their experiences but also helped the nurses to make sense of them.[24] This book draws as much as possible from the nurses' own reflections, both contemporary and retrospective, on what nursing was and what it meant to be a New Zealand nurse. The common elements of these narratives contributed to a nursing folklore, with each account and anecdote reinforcing shared professional values. This folklore informed and was informed by the cultural beliefs, attitudes, political processes, art, literature and films of the time.[25] New Zealand nursing also developed its own myths. In cultural history, the term *myth* denotes not a fantastic story but an enduring and powerful narrative with special meaning for the people who create it, heed it and pass it on. Its function is to reinforce values, to help explain contradictions or to create a charter for action.[26]

The veracity of personal reminiscence can, of course, be questioned. But facts can be verified, and these narratives give a vivid immediacy to the past. Bridget Ristori, who trained at Masterton Hospital in the early 1920s, was a prolific writer, publishing articles and books about her own nursing experiences in many countries, information about nursing as a career, and health advice and home nursing, as well as articles and short stories on many topics. She pasted copies into a scrapbook. When she was interviewed by journalists, she was extremely disgruntled at the errors in their articles and listed them on the scrapbook page. One, from the *Dannevirke Evening News* in 1958, had the notation alongside: 'This just shows you can't believe half you read. It is full of errors!' And she listed them. Another, from the *Northland Age* the same year, received similar treatment: 'Another example of NOT believing all you read – there are at least 10 mistakes in this article.' Again, all were listed.[27]

This book explores the culture of New Zealand nursing, what it meant to be 'a modern nurse' in New Zealand in the time of empire. It takes 1880 as its starting point – the time when hospital reforms began to formally introduce Nightingale's vision of 'modern nursing' into New Zealand – and ends in 1950, three years after New Zealand ceased to be a dominion of the British Empire and became an independent realm within the Commonwealth.

In 1908, Britain's *Nursing Mirror* published an article on nursing's contribution to the imperial project. The writer was proud that England was the birthplace of modern nursing and that its nurses had spread its teaching, traditions and civilising influence to 'many quarters of the Empire'.[28] Her viewpoint was distinctly from the empire's centre, looking outward to the spread of imperial power and influence throughout the world.

New Zealand nurses had a different view. In just a few years, between 1895 and 1909, New Zealand nursing showed the Old Country how nimbly a relatively young colony could innovate. This view was strengthened when nurses compared themselves with those from other countries in wartime service. It faltered a little with nervousness around reciprocity of registration when Britain finally instituted a state nursing register, and was bolstered again with the leadership provided by New Zealanders in international nursing organisations. Historians who have examined the relationship between the 'local' and the 'global' argue that the two are co-constituted: processes and people at the local level shape the global, and global changes in turn affect local lives.[29] In exploring the influence of the British way of nursing in New Zealand, and the ways New Zealand nurses developed their own culture and influence, this book explores both global and local aspects of nursing.

To present a history of the New Zealand nursing culture does not imply that there was a single view of what it meant to be a New Zealand nurse. The idea was contested both within and outside the profession. Citizens expressed their opinions of nurses in various practice settings and with respect to the profession overall. Their views are also reflected in depictions of the nurse in literature and film. As a cultural group, nurses did have an explicit set of expected qualities and values – but some nurses bucked against this 'code of virtues', and their actions sometimes created problems for their hospitals, colleagues and superiors. The notion of the modern nurse also changed, though one constant was that each generation of nurses believed that the previous generation had been more devoted, and the older generation thought the current one more interested in nursing as a career than as a vocation.

Nursing was not a one-sided undertaking: it was co-constructed by nurses and patients.[30] But patients' perspectives are harder to discover. They appear occasionally in letters to newspaper editors and testimony in hospital inquiries, or are revealed secondhand in nurses' narratives, as in the Naseby nurse's story. Nurses' narratives of their own illnesses and their time as patients offer intriguing insights into nursing practice. As patients, nurses gave their colleagues a particular view and often pertinent advice.

This book focuses on general nursing and not psychiatric nursing, which was considered a separate form of practice, with its own training and qualifications.[31] Maternity nursing and midwifery are discussed only in relation to nurses' career development or particular practice settings, such as the rural backblocks where nurses provided care in sickness, childbirth and accidents. From 1905 in New Zealand, as a result of the Midwives Act 1904, St Helens hospitals, which provided care for working-class women during childbirth, offered midwifery training, with a shorter course available to registered nurses. However, as many nurses did not intend to practise midwifery but needed a qualification in this field for career advancement, health authorities introduced a separate course and registration in maternity nursing with the Nurses and Midwives Registration Act 1925. Many nurses had a range of post-registration specialty qualifications. Plunket nursing (providing mothers with advice and help in caring for infants and young children) was one, and some nurses focused on this as their career. It is considered here particularly in relation to views of empire.[32]

During these years the New Zealand general nursing profession was largely Pākehā. It is difficult to determine the number of Māori women who became registered nurses, as ethnicity was not usually recorded in the nurses' personal training records. However, Māori nurses are identified wherever possible, as their work was significant. Ākenehi Hei, for example, was an exemplary nurse who in 1910 published a valuable article on the tensions of being a Māori nurse in a Māori setting.[33] Māori nurses also experienced tensions in the Pākehā-dominated health system. These are examined here, as well as the support given to Māori women to train, qualify and practise. Crossing these cultural boundaries was complex.

This book focuses on the experiences of women, because the profession in these years was overwhelmingly female. Provision for registering male nurses was made only with the Nurses and Midwives Act 1945. In discussing the proposed legislation, the minister of health, Arnold Nordmeyer, still kept to a gendered view of nursing, noting that male nurses would be able to relieve female nurses of 'onerous and difficult duties' in 'certain wards'. (He was probably referring to venereal disease wards, where the presence of a female nurse was always troubling to the public.) Some cases, he said, were also beyond the nurses' strength. And male nurses would be able to serve for a lifetime, which was not the case with women whose 'term of service was comparatively short on account of marriage'.[34] The first state examination for male nurses was held in 1947, but few hospitals were able to initiate the required two-year training course. Separate arrangements were required for men, who were not allowed to attend lectures on female anatomy or conditions or to nurse women. The Auckland Hospital Board was large enough to accommodate a special course for men, which started in 1948. Men trained mostly at the Cornwall geriatric hospital, with further experience at Greenlane Hospital. The attrition rate was high: just under a third of the 90 men who started training there between 1948 and 1952 completed the course by 1954.[35] The number of male nurses remained very small.

Chapter 1 of the book offers an overview of New Zealand nursing history, following the chronological structure adopted by the chief nurse, Mary Lambie, in the nursing history she produced in 1939 as part of the country's centennial celebration.

(She produced expanded versions in 1946 and 1950.) This chapter identifies elements of the emerging nursing culture, gives historical background not highlighted by Lambie, and uses ordinary nurses' stories to show the effect of policy changes.[36] Chapter 2 describes the culture of nurse training as envisaged by authorities, and chapter 3 examines the experiences of nurse trainees, particularly in adopting or challenging a nursing code of virtues and continuing a significant folklore. Chapter 4 examines the work and culture of district nursing in people's homes, and nurses' role in addressing the effects of poverty. Chapter 5 turns to nursing in the rural backblocks, where nurses provided an essential service for settlers and thus contributed to the project of empire. Chapter 6 explores the nursing culture that evolved in connection with providing a health service to support rural Māori and examines the training, experience and contribution of Māori nurses.

Because the experiences of New Zealand nurses in wartime have been explored by other writers, chapter 7 focuses on a particular aspect of the work – emotional labour – for nurses serving overseas in the South African (Boer) War and World War I, and at home in New Zealand in World War II.[37] Chapter 8 describes the experience and culture of nursing in and after disasters, focusing on the 1918 influenza pandemic and the 1931 Hawke's Bay earthquake.

Chapter 9 shows how the idea of the modern nurse was contested both by nurses and by those outside the profession, in particular during dramatic inquiries into 'hospital troubles'. Chapter 10 examines more general elements of the nursing culture, including delineation of its spheres of knowledge and practice, and the creation and preservation of culture through traditions, symbols, commemoration, social events, obituaries, farewells and gossip. Chapter 11 considers New Zealand nurses' view of themselves and their profession with respect to the British Empire and the rest of the world, and it examines various forms of nurses' international engagement.

New Zealand nurses had collective but sometimes conflicting understandings of their professional identity and a complex sense of themselves in relation to the empire and wider nursing world. Despite the clamour of competing ideas from those outside the profession, nurses found their own way of being. They defined a new female occupation within a relatively new country that needed them to help implement its emerging health system and support its image as a modern and influential society.

Mary Lambie, chief nurse from 1931 to 1949, wrote an official history of New Zealand nursing in 1939. Mary Lambie, *My Story: Memoirs of a New Zealand nurse* (Christchurch: N.M. Peryer, 1963), frontispiece

CHAPTER 1

Narrating a history of New Zealand nursing

In December 1939 Mary Lambie, New Zealand's chief nurse, wrote a historical account of New Zealand nursing, beginning in 1840. As a nurse in the school medical service in Christchurch, she had been involved in research on standards of living, the impact of an open-air classroom on children's health, and the effectiveness of iodine in treating goitre, which was endemic in the Canterbury region.[1] In 1925 she was sent to Canada to take a postgraduate course in public health nursing at the University of Toronto. Later, as chief nurse, she led the New Zealand Registered Nurses' Association's Nursing Education Committee in conducting nationwide surveys into nursing procedures. She was directly involved in the International Council of Nurses' research into nurses' health, was co-author of its report and presented it at its congress in London in 1937.[2] At the end of 1939, just prior to New Zealand's centennial celebration, all division directors in the Department of Health were asked to include a short historical account in their sections of the departmental annual report. Lambie brought her inquiring mind and broad experience to bear on this topic and devoted half of her 17-page report to it.[3]

This was the first official history of New Zealand nursing, and it was written by a nurse.[4] Expanded versions appeared in 1946 and 1950, and the Department of Health published it separately to 'meet the many requests from overseas, and for use in the training schools', as Lambie noted in the preface to the later editions. She hoped it would 'encourage a study of the history of our system of nursing so that every nurse will have an intelligent understanding of the origin and trend of service of which she has the honour to be a member'.[5] Its significance was reinforced in 1960, when the original 1939 account was reprinted in the *New Zealand Nursing Journal*, presented as a 'wealth of information, facts relating to our nursing history which every nurse should know'.[6]

Lambie's history, written from the point of view of a nursing leader, provides valuable insights into the emerging culture of professional nursing. It is supplemented here by additional information and accounts of the experiences and careers of nurses working in other capacities throughout the country.

1840–1900

Lambie opened the first chronological section of her history by observing that the first example of hospital nursing in New Zealand came with the establishment of a military hospital in Auckland, and that hospitals were later established throughout the country in response to local needs. She noted four significant changes during the 1880s and 1890s: the shift to a trained, all-female nursing staff in hospitals; Grace Neill's appointment to the Department of Hospitals; the establishment of the country's first district nursing service by Sibylla Maude (although this ascription is disputable); and New Zealand nurses' service in the South African (Boer) War. Lambie also mentioned the introduction of an eight-hour day and a three-shift system for probationer nurses. This was 'another step forward' at a time when the condition was 'still unheard of in the majority of hospitals in the Old World'.[7]

From 1840, families and friends cared for the sick in their homes and communities. Through these experiences, many women developed nursing skills that they used as a means of employment. Among them, as Catherine Bishop's study of businesswomen in colonial New Zealand shows, were midwives and monthly nurses (those who cared for women in the first month following childbirth).[8] Many women, however, also advertised their services as a 'sick nurse' in newspapers. In the 1860s, for example, Mrs Barrows of Napier frequently advertised as a sick nurse charging moderate rates.[9] Often these women were willing to take on other duties, such as that of monthly nurse, housekeeper or lady's companion. One described herself in 1879 as a respectable woman available for 'office-cleaning, or will Sick Nurse'.[10] Another offered to take washing.[11] Some left their particulars at the local chemist shop[12] or responded to calls from local employment agencies advertising for sick nurses in addition to general servants, shop girls, barmaids, housemaids, waitresses, cooks, clerks and laundresses.[13] As they were untrained, these women relied on patients' and medical men's testimonials to build their reputation for nursing. Although many gained the confidence of doctors, who recommended them to patients, in the 1880s and 1890s they faced increasing competition from professional nurses with hospital training.

From the beginning of his term in 1845, Governor George Grey advocated and facilitated the establishment of public hospitals in the main emerging towns. In contrast to Britain's dual system of Poor Law hospitals and 'voluntary' hospitals supported by donations and subscriptions, there was one system for all citizens. At first, most of the patients were accident cases or the elderly infirm, attended by untrained wardsmen and female domestic staff under the control of the hospital master and the untrained matron, whose role was primarily that of hospital housekeeper. Convalescent patients also provided care to others. This system of staffing continued in main hospitals until the 1890s, and longer in smaller hospitals.

Some hospitals had diligent wardsmen who won the appreciation of medical staff and patients. When Hāwera's cottage hospital opened in 1894, for example, Andrew Farrar was chosen from 28 applicants for the wardsman's position, and a trained nurse, Rose Tyers, was appointed matron. The next year, Farrar was recognised as a 'diligent suitable attendant' and transferred to New Plymouth Hospital, where he received an annual salary of £75 plus board. In 1899 Farrar declared he was worth £100, as his work involved 'every kind of personal service to helpless patients', was unending and required some skill. He would, however, settle for an increase of £10. A hospital board member pointed out that this would bring his salary within £5 of the matron's, and his request was declined. The local newspaper editor thought the decision shortsighted. Farrar had earned the medical staff's confidence through his skill and trustworthiness, patients were grateful for his 'unvarying kindness and sympathetic attention', and 'no more efficient and capable wardsman' would be found throughout the country.[14] The board was unmoved, and Farrar went to Nelson.

Farrar's replacement at Hāwera was unsatisfactory: when he got into a 'drunken frenzied state' and threatened to burn the hospital down, Tyers dismissed him and called the local policeman for assistance. The next replacement was also 'totally unsuited'. He had never been in a hospital before, admitted he could not stand the work and cleared out.[15] Such reports of wardsmen were not unusual. Wellington Hospital, for example, dismissed wardsmen for 'drunkenness, rough conduct and inattention to duty'.[16] Drunkenness was also a problem at Dunedin Hospital in the 1870s and 1880s, and the house surgeon in charge, Dr W.S. Roberts, requested 'more intelligent' wardsmen.[17] Nevertheless, whenever a public complaint was made about wardsmen, other citizens would respond with praise of their care.[18]

Lambie's history focused on the untrained women, rather than the wardsmen, employed in hospitals between 1840 and 1880. She stated simply that the women were 'uneducated, rough, and uncouth' and that these traits were 'reflected in the state of the wards and care of the patients'.[19] This was a rather harsh assessment. Dr George Grabham, appointed in November 1882 as the government's first inspector of hospitals, immediately inspected the country's 38 hospitals and gave detailed accounts of both good and poor care in his first report in 1883.[20] Lambie's assessment was perhaps intended to serve as a contrast to the rapid change over the next few years to an all-female staff, trained in the system devised by Florence Nightingale.

Senior medical men in New Zealand had visited hospitals in other countries, and at intercolonial medical conferences doctors discussed the change to employing trained female nurses. They were aware of the difference professional nursing could make not only for the welfare of their patients but also for their professional reputations. In the 1880s they began urging hospital trustees to make this change.

From 1883, hospitals gradually introduced a system of formal training for nursing probationers. Unlike the British system, in which at the major hospitals a higher tier of 'lady probationers' paid for their training, in New Zealand's system all probationers were paid. They learned mainly from working with other nurses in the wards, ward sisters' instruction, and lectures by matrons and doctors. Lambie quoted Grabham's remarks in 1884 that a 'very excellent system' was in place at Wellington and Auckland Hospitals, where 'well-educated ladies may be seen serving their apprenticeship'.[21] He recommended this as an example to other hospitals. In 1887, Dr Duncan MacGregor, who succeeded Grabham, reported that the Wellington nursing staff 'struck me as being particularly satisfactory. They are well trained, intelligent, and lady-like, being evidently drawn from a class very much superior to the old-fashioned hospital-nurse of former times'.[22]

Most of the first matrons employed to set up nurse-training systems were recruited from among qualified nurses in Britain and Australia. Some were already in New Zealand. Annie Crisp, Auckland's matron from 1883 to 1888, was appointed shortly after her arrival in New Zealand. Mrs Bernard Moore, who instituted training at Wellington Hospital in 1883, had been offering home nursing courses in Auckland before her appointment.[23] Several nurses who trained at Wellington Hospital in the 1880s and 1890s became matrons elsewhere by 1910.[24]

The shift to an all-female trained staff was a radical idea, however, and hospitals were cautious. In Dunedin, the shift was part of a raft of reforms promoted by a faction of the honorary medical staff in the late 1880s.[25] Patricia Sargison has noted that in a colony without the hereditary and (in early years) landed elite that existed in Britain, doctors enjoyed an elevated social and political standing, which gave them

Four of the six probationers in New Zealand's first nurse training programme, at Wellington Hospital, in 1883. Author's collection

the power to bring about this change. This, she said, was one of the key characteristics that distinguished the colony's nursing reform from that in Britain.[26] In 1890, after further urgent demands, the hospital trustees sent circulars to medical men throughout the country asking for opinions on the matter. Of the 29 replies, 26 were in favour of the change to female nurses. A Wellington doctor with a military background, Morgan Grace, favoured the change on the grounds that colonial wardsmen were 'part broken-down, sickly, disappointed men, who loathe neatness and order'. If they were to work as nurses, they needed military discipline. Eighteen respondents remained in favour of male attendants for patients with delirium tremens and the 'vilest diseases' (venereal) – for both the patients' and nurses' benefit. A journalist commented on the survey's responses: 'Men may have the strength, and may easily acquire the skill required; but after all, the patience, which is one of the requisites of a good nurse, is more likely to be found in women.'[27] This observation foreshadowed the explicit inculcation of an enduring 'code of virtues' based on womanly qualities in nurse training and culture.

Having confirmed the general feeling, the Dunedin Hospital trustees agreed and recruited Edith Mawe as matron. She arrived from Britain in 1891 but resigned at the end of 1892, having tried to implement changes too quickly for the comfort of the hospital trustees.[28] As Sargison noted, the transition to female nursing was 'enmeshed in a power struggle within hospitals from which doctors emerged victorious'. This was often a three-way struggle, as 'administrators, doctors and matrons jostled for supremacy within the rapidly growing empires these institutions represented.'[29] Isabella Fraser succeeded Mawe in 1893 and remained matron of Dunedin Hospital for nearly 20 years. Fraser had trained at the Edinburgh Infirmary, which had employed St Thomas's–trained nurses since 1873.[30] She had subsequently worked in Glasgow, Hobart and Melbourne.

Following the 1890 hospital reforms, the somewhat haphazard training offered in the 1880s was organised and strengthened. New probationers had to be aged between 21 and 30 when they applied, They were required to 'live in' at the hospital and undertake a two-year course, with examinations twice a year. Under Fraser's influence, in 1894 the course was extended to three years, and the minimum age of entry was raised to 23.[31]

Amelia Bagley started her training as a probationer at Dunedin Hospital in 1892 when she was 22 years old. She was no doubt pleased that a new nurses' home, built with public donations, had opened that year, so that nurses no longer had to sleep in rooms off the hospital wards. In the probationer's uniform of a long navy serge dress worn with starched white cuffs, collar, cap and apron, Bagley cared for patients anywhere in the hospital except the venereal ward, which continued to be staffed by wardsmen. The work was hard. She worked mostly 12-hour shifts, probably grateful for the help that convalescent patients usually provided. In these ways her training and nursing experience were similar to those of probationers in other large hospitals. Bagley completed her training in 1895.[32]

Some British-trained nurses emigrated to New Zealand for personal reasons,

Amelia Bagley during her training at Dunedin Hospital, from 1892 to 1895. Nurses often struggled with the starched collars and removed their cuffs while tending patients.

F.S. Maclean, *Challenge for Health: A history of public health in New Zealand* (Wellington: R.E. Owen, Government Printer, 1964), facing p. 192.

seeking adventure, new nursing opportunities or a better life. Among them was Eva Godfray. Born in Jersey in 1865, she started training at the London Hospital in 1888 under the notable matron Eva Lückes, who was considered a 'great maker of matrons'.[33] On completing the two-year training, she remained another year; then, in January 1892, she arrived in New Zealand with a friend from the hospital, Anne

Matron Eva Godfray with her nurses outside the nurses' cottage at Waipawa Hospital, Waipukurau, Hawke's Bay, about 1904.

Waipawa Hospital Board, *Waipukurau Hospital Centennial Souvenir Booklet 1879–1979* (Waipukurau: Waipawa Hospital Board, 1979). Reproduced with permission of Hawke's Bay District Health Board.

Hesk. 'In search of health', Godfray 'rested from her arduous labours for a year' before starting work in Wellington at the private hospital in Grant Road, Thorndon, established by Hesk in 1893. The hospital combined 'skilled nursing with the comfort and quiet of a private house'. By 1897 Godfray was its lady superintendent.[34] That year she was the successful candidate among five applicants for the position of matron at the small rural Waipawa Hospital in Waipukurau, Hawke's Bay.[35] Her younger brother, Sidney Charles Godfray, a surgeon who had arrived in New Zealand in the 1870s, was the hospital's medical superintendent. MacGregor reported that the new matron was a 'great acquisition', as it was evident 'even to the casual observer' that the hospital was a 'well managed institution'.[36]

Lambie singled out two nurse leaders for special mention in this period: Grace Neill and Sibylla Maude. Neill, born Elizabeth Grace Campbell in 1846, was a tall, red-headed Scot with a 'springy walk' who had trained as a nurse and midwife in England. In 1886 she and her ailing husband, a doctor, went with their young son to

Queensland, Australia. When her husband died, Neill worked in journalism and ran a typewriting business to support herself and her son. Because of her connections and undoubted ability, she was appointed to a Queensland commission of inquiry into working conditions in shops and factories. She came to New Zealand in 1893, and her experience and capability led to her appointment as New Zealand's first female factory inspector. MacGregor recognised her talents and soon arranged her transfer to his Department of Hospitals and Charitable Aid, and in May 1895, aged 49, Neill became assistant inspector of hospitals.[37] MacGregor explained that because of political and social developments, there were 'numerous and delicate questions affecting women ... that ought to be handled in the first instance by a woman'. He believed that Neill combined 'in a very high degree the ability, knowledge, and sympathy required for this position'.[38] Lambie similarly situated Neill's appointment in the context of the changing social and political position of women, particularly their expanded opportunities for higher education and the legislation enacted by Premier Richard Seddon's Liberal government, including women's franchise in 1893.

Neill was the first woman appointed to a senior position in the public service. Her modest salary and constant travelling to inspect hospitals, asylums and charitable institutions led her to dress in a hard-wearing coat and skirt and nondescript hat. She was a keen smoker (but not in public).[39]

Neill was closely involved in the writing of MacGregor's annual reports and advised on all nursing matters. As a nurse with a role in a central government department, Neill was, in effect, New Zealand's (and the world's) first chief nurse. Her position gave rise to some unique aspects of early New Zealand nursing culture. Although she was part of the British nursing diaspora, Neill had a pioneering spirit. In a young colony used to social innovation, and unfettered by the divided nursing factions that impeded progress in Britain, she could swiftly implement her vision for New Zealand nursing.[40]

In 1899 Neill attended the International Women's Congress in London, which included a

From 1895 to 1906, Grace Neill was New Zealand's first chief nurse. Her professional innovations drew international admiration and respect.

Lavinia L. Dock, ed., *A History of Nursing*, vol. 4 (New York: G.P. Putnam's Sons, 1912), facing p. 216.

section on nursing. Attendees were keen to discuss the state registration of nurses. Neill, the principal speaker, shared her vision of nursing as a service to patients, her ideas on nursing registration and the importance of women's suffrage. The world's first state registration of nurses was instituted in the Cape Colony, South Africa, through a late inclusion in the Medical and Pharmacy Act 1891. Neill was keen to see registration in place in New Zealand to protect the public from untrained or poorly trained 'sick nurses' and to ensure consistent training among the country's scattered hospitals. She envisaged a three-year apprenticeship-style training concluding with an examination by independent examiners and documented by a certificate of competence and a register of qualified nurses. Once that system was in place, she said, 'we may leave the rest to a discriminating public' who could check a nurse's credentials.[41] Mrs (Ethel) Bedford Fenwick, the British nurse leader who chaired the meeting that day, and Lavinia Dock, the American nurse leader who led the ensuing discussion, both openly admired Neill's clear vision, her position in a government department, and her privileged situation as both an enfranchised woman and nurse. In fact, Dock ignored the barely descriptive second paper, given by the Cape Colony delegate, and mentioned only Neill's.[42] Through her presentation, Neill could demonstrate that despite, or perhaps because of, New Zealand's distance from the centre of empire, significant advances in nursing could be achieved there.

The London gathering of nurses decided to establish an International Council of Nurses (ICN), and Neill was directly involved in its creation. Engagement with the ICN quickly broadened the gaze of New Zealand nursing from the centre of empire to the wider nursing world.

Back in New Zealand, after consulting widely, Neill drafted the world's first Nurses Registration Act, which was passed in 1901. Although the Cape Colony had initiated state registration, New Zealand was the first country to enact separate and specific legislation for this purpose. It established the legal basis for the recognition of this emerging women's occupation as a profession, a status it did not achieve in Britain until 1919. To become registered, a nurse required a certificate from a three-year training course at an approved hospital.

According to Sargison, New Zealand doctors controlled nurse training and 'defined the limits of nursing knowledge by preparing the syllabus, giving most of the lectures, writing the textbooks and setting and marking the examinations'.[43] In fact, it was Grace Neill who wrote the syllabus used in all New Zealand training hospitals and designed the examination system. She and her successors, working

Front and back of the star medal belonging to Ellen Dougherty, the first nurse to register in New Zealand, in January 1902. Author's collection

from 1925 with regulatory authorities, chose the examiners and monitored their approach to setting and marking examination papers. Matrons and ward sisters did most of the teaching, and the textbooks prescribed in syllabuses were written by both nurses and doctors. Under the regulations drafted by Neill governing nurses' practice and the approval of hospitals as training schools, chief nurses and their nurse assistants inspected training hospitals and assessed the training provided. Doctors' influence was therefore far less than that of nurses themselves. Neill also designed the five-pointed star medal that became the emblem of New Zealand registered nurses.

The register opened in 1902, and Neill was the seventh nurse listed. The first was Ellen Dougherty, matron of Palmerston North Hospital. As Eva Godfray had completed only a two-year period of training in London, she did not qualify (despite the fact that Eva Lückes, the London Hospital matron, believed two years at her hospital were worth three anywhere else).[44] In order to be registered, Godfray had to provide additional evidence of competence.

Neill had an excellent working relationship with MacGregor, another Scot. As her friend Dr Agnes Bennett later remarked, hearing their lively conversations, with their 'clash of opinion and wit, mellowed by an obvious mutual respect and friendship, made it a never-to-be-forgotten occasion'.[45] Neill knew how to work with politicians, including Seddon and, in fact, with anyone in a senior position. As she said: 'I love to bully the male if he be placed in the position of superior officer. It was real plums to twist & twiddle Ministers and Premiers & make them think they were having their own way all the time. Catch me allowing any public official to treat me as "putty", however soft my outer coat might be. They knew I could take it off on occasions.'[46]

The second leader singled out by Lambie, Sibylla Maude, was born in Christchurch in 1862, went to England in 1889 to train as a nurse at Middlesex Hospital in London, and returned to New Zealand to become matron at Christchurch Hospital in 1893. She resigned in 1896 to set up a district nursing service to care for the poor in their own homes. Lambie described Maude as the pioneer of district nursing in New Zealand, a view that is disputable but was widely held. Echoing Nightingale's views on the nurse's dual role of caring for the sick and preventing illness, Maude believed that district nurses could teach family members how to care for the patient as well as the home so that further sickness might be avoided.

Maude began her service in Christchurch at the house of the Sisters of the Community of the Sacred Name in St Asaph Street, with 'the use of a telephone, and the space of a cupboard'.[47] Short and thick-set, and wearing her nurse's uniform, she became a familiar sight on Christchurch streets. Despite her forbidding, abrupt manner and stern expression, she drew admiration and affection from Christchurch citizens who recognised her kindness and dedication to their welfare.[48] By the end of the first year she had 'paid 1,100 visits on foot, and found it no easy matter trudging through all weathers with a heavy bag'.[49] She soon found she needed an office in a central position to store donated clothing and nursing requisites and to see people seeking advice. An office was eventually found in Durham Street, which was her headquarters for many years.

Maude held firm to the ideal that district work needed the best nurses – those who were 'thoroughly trained' in surgical and medical nursing and in midwifery, and 'above all, women of tact, judgment and resources'.[50] District nurses' stories, taken up by newspaper reporters to support fundraising for their voluntary agencies, formed a folklore focusing on 'brightening sunless lives'. This folklore challenged Seddon's claim that no poverty existed in New Zealand, fostered public awareness that district nursing could remedy an Old World evil in the New and reinforced nursing values.[51]

The final topic Lambie covered in this section of the report was the role of New Zealand nurses in the South African (Boer) War. This, she observed, was the first time a body of nurses from New Zealand had 'served in any capacity overseas', and their service was 'favourably commented upon'.[52] About 30 nurses served in South Africa, about half of whom travelled there independently at their own expense. The others were funded by donations.[53] James Henry Coleman of Napier, who proposed to sponsor two nurses, received ten applications from trained nurses.[54] One of the successful applicants was Eva Godfray. The other was Margaret Carston from Timaru Hospital, who had previously worked at the hospital in Waipukurau. They left for South Africa in March 1900.[55]

Godfray and Carston served at Portland Hospital in Bloemfontein, a marquee field hospital that was financed largely by the Duke of Portland but under general army control, and then at Pretoria. Writing from Bloemfontein, Carston described the alien land and its dust, flies, ants and cold. On night duty, she sat in a hospital tent that was 'flip-flapping with the wind' and could hardly hold her pen for the cold. Large convoys of soldiers arrived sick with enteric (typhoid) fever. Many lived only for another day or two. Despite her disappointment at nursing mostly sick rather than wounded soldiers, she was glad to be there.[56]

In a converted school building in Pretoria, Carston got her wish to nurse the wounded, probably more than she anticipated. After receiving one convoy of wounded, within a few days the hospital had to make room for even more casualties.[57] Carston's letters foreshadowed those of nurses from later wars, which together formed an enduring folklore of the nurse 'caring in conflict'.

Carston and Godfray returned to New Zealand in 1901. Godfray went back to the Waipawa Hospital at Waipukurau but resigned in 1904, as she wanted to 'give up nursing for a time'.[58] Two years later she successfully applied to be the first matron of the new Dannevirke Hospital using, in a rather unnecessary social onslaught, letters of reference from the notable surgeon Sir Frederick Treves, whom she knew from the London Hospital, and the Duke of Portland from her South African service. When she resigned, she was succeeded by Carston, who had taken a series of positions, including that of matron of the small Pahiatua Hospital, in the interim. Carston's nurses saw her as 'quick in speech and movement', 'fair and just'. She taught them 'manners as well as nursing skills' and demanded a high standard of nursing but gave praise when due. She had a lively sense of humour and was a keen gardener.[59]

1900–1919

Lambie opened her discussion of nursing in the new century with Grace Neill's second legislative achievement, the Midwives Act 1904, which set in place the registration of midwives and the establishment of four St Helens hospitals, named after Seddon's birthplace in Lancashire, to train midwives and provide childbirth care for working-class women. Although the inspector-general of hospitals was officially the registrar of nurses and midwives, Neill did the actual work. To these responsibilities were now added midwifery state examination arrangements, supervision of midwives throughout the country and inspection of the St Helens hospitals.

In 1906, when Neill retired, Hester Maclean was appointed the new chief nurse. Lambie commented on Maclean's 'unusually wide and varied experience'. Born in Australia, she trained at the Royal Prince Alfred Hospital in Sydney. After midwifery training in England, she returned to Australia, where she worked in a private hospital, in district nursing, and as matron of a cottage hospital, a mental hospital and finally the Melbourne Women's Hospital. Lambie described her as 'a woman of strong character with a forceful personality who was interested in people as individuals, which made her well known and beloved by those with whom she came in contact'.[60] Her manner might have appeared abrasive to some, especially to those who opposed her ideas, but comments by nurses showed that many held her in great affection.

Maclean's leadership shaped the nursing culture in important ways. In 1908 she founded the nursing journal *Kai Tiaki*, which she edited outside her working hours. The following year, she encouraged the four nurses' associations in Auckland, Wellington, Christchurch and Dunedin to combine to form the New Zealand Trained Nurses' Association, and she became its first president. As Lambie commented: 'Looking back it can be seen how much these two steps meant in the moulding of nursing opinion and of developing a unity of thought and purpose.'[61] The innovations were crucial for developing an emerging nursing community and culture. Maclean also had a good working relationship with Dr Thomas Valintine, the inspector-general of hospitals and, from 1909, chief health officer. *She* found *him* a 'forceful personality' who would come back victorious from meetings with politicians and 'tell us all about it with a school-boy glee'. Afterwards, she would 'remonstrate with him, and beg him to be more careful'.[62]

When the Private Hospitals Act 1906 brought private institutions under the Department of Hospital's supervision, more nurse inspectors were needed. Maclean took the opportunity of a work visit to Ōamaru to meet Jessie Bicknell, whom Neill

Hester Maclean, New Zealand's chief nurse from 1906 to 1923, was the founder and editor of the *Kai Tiaki* nursing journal.

Lavinia L. Dock, ed., *A History of Nursing*, vol. 4 (New York: G.P. Putnam's Sons, 1912), facing p. 216.

had mentioned as a potential matron for a St Helens hospital. Maclean was impressed enough to ensure she was appointed as a nurse inspector instead.[63] Bicknell trained at Nelson Hospital, became a registered nurse in 1903 and subsequently nursed at Wairau Hospital in Blenheim and the Waipawa Hospital under Carston. She trained in midwifery at the Dunedin St Helens Hospital in 1906 and started as a nurse inspector in May 1907. The second inspector appointed was Amelia Bagley, who by that time had shifted from Dunedin and was private nursing in Wellington.[64] Private hospital authorities exerted continuing pressure to permit their hospitals to be training schools – pressure that Maclean consistently resisted, as she believed they could not give probationers a sufficiently broad experience.

In this period Lambie also highlighted the training of Māori nurses, an initiative undertaken in co-operation with the Education Department in 1905. 'This was a new move and it must have been a great effort for these Maori girls who were required to follow the same course of training and pass the same examinations as their European sisters,' she said.[65] The 'new move' was actually the extension of an earlier scholarship scheme that the Department of Education had set up in 1898, enabling senior Māori schoolgirls to spend an extra year taking a nursing course to prepare them for nursing in their own communities and becoming 'efficient preachers of the gospel of health'.[66] Hāmiora Hei introduced the idea at the Te Aute College Students' Association conference of past pupils in December 1897.[67] He and James Pope, the inspector of Native schools who also attended the association's gatherings, then developed a proposal for the training, which was soon approved by the government and put in place. Its rapid establishment reflected government concerns about Māori health and its alignment with other trade apprenticeship and university scholarship schemes already in place for young Māori men.[68] In September 1898 two senior pupils at St Joseph's Catholic School and Hukarere Anglican School in Napier were awarded the first scholarships. They attended Napier Hospital as day pupils while still boarding at their schools and therefore being supported by a familiar community. The student from Hukarere School gave up her scholarship after six months, as she 'found the work irksome'.[69] The matron requested a further year for the other student, Ema Mitchell, to complete her training. Mitchell worked for two years at Waipawa Hospital under Eva Godfray before marrying and living at Pakipaki. Married nurses were required to leave nursing employment, but William Bird, who succeeded Pope, reported that she was 'doing a great deal of good for her people'.[70]

The scholarship's extension in 1905 was intended to assist Māori women to carry on and undertake the full training to become registered nurses. Despite considerable difficulty at times in finding both hospital training places and Māori women to take up the scholarships, the scheme continued for many years.

Lambie did not identify the first two Māori nurses to qualify as registered nurses under the extended scholarship scheme. They were Hēni Whangapirita, who trained at Wellington Hospital, and Ākenehi Hei, who trained at Napier Hospital. Both registered in July 1908.[71] In addition, other Māori women trained outside the scholarship scheme, even before Whangapirita and Hei completed their training. It is difficult to determine the precise number, as historical records do not usually identify nurses' ethnicity, and names are not always reliable indicators. Ethel Watkins Taylor, for example, first trained as a midwife and then undertook her nurse training at Hawera Hospital, completing it in December 1910.[72] In 1911 she became a ward sister at Gisborne Hospital, where Eva Godfray had become matron two years earlier.

During these two decades, nursing roles expanded beyond the hospital as the profession became a key component of the developing public health system. Lambie noted the 'new conception of social and public-health services' arising from the realisation that 'prevention was better than cure'.[73] New forms of nursing practice emerged to fulfil these roles. Plunket Society nurses visited homes to support mothers with new babies and young children, and eventually ran clinics which mothers could visit.[74] Nurses joined the school medical service in 1917. Under the Child Welfare Act 1907, a few nurses also worked in the state supervision of the 'backward and unwanted child',[75] who might be fostered or cared for in a 'home'. New nursing services also supported isolated rural settlers and Māori in rural communities.

Stories from nurses in the new rural services created a strong folklore centred on the figure of the 'intrepid nurse'. Margaret Bilton was the first nurse in the Backblocks Nursing Service, stationed at Urutī in Taranaki from 1909. Her stories, published in *Kai Tiaki*, depicted the challenges of caring for settlers in their rudimentary homes in cases of sickness, childbirth and accidents, and getting about on foot or horseback or, when luckier, in someone's gig. The same trope appeared in stories of nursing in Māori communities. From 1909 a sporadic nursing service for Māori started under the Department of Native Affairs. As the ideal had been to have Māori nurses serving Māori communities, Ākenehi Hei and Hēni Whangapirita were the first appointed in 1909. They nursed in several epidemics and advised communities on health and sanitation.

In 1911, with the return of responsibility for Māori health to the Department of Public Health (established in 1901), more determined organisation of a nursing service for Māori began. As there were so few Māori nurses, it was recognised that the service needed to be open to Pākehā nurses as well. The first nurse appointed to the new service was Mary Purcell, who had trained at Wellington Hospital and in midwifery at the Wellington St Helens Hospital. The year before her appointment she had visited England, where she had gained sanitation knowledge that would be of 'great value'. She was sent to relieve Amelia Bagley, who was temporarily nursing

Māori with typhoid at Ahipara in the Far North. Bagley then went to Auckland and was responsible for establishing and overseeing additional Māori health nursing stations in remote areas.[76]

In summing up the beginning of the Māori health service, Lambie commented: 'These early nurses experienced great difficulties as they had to live very isolated lives, often under great hardships ... Several laid down their lives in attempting the establishment of this important branch of our nursing services. Probably no one will ever fully realise the heroic deeds these women carried out so quietly and devotedly.'[77] This captured the trope of the dedicated and self-sacrificing 'quiet heroine', one trope more commonly used by people outside the nursing profession, unless there were nursing deaths.

Lambie's final topics in this section were World War I and the 1918 influenza pandemic. Nurses had to argue strongly to be sent overseas to care for sick and wounded New Zealand soldiers. Apart from a small group of nurses sent to Samoa in 1914, the first contingent of the newly formed New Zealand Army Nursing Service to go overseas, known as the 'First Fifty', went at short notice in April 1915 on the *Rotorua* to Egypt. Among them were two from Gisborne – Māori nurse Ethel Taylor and Agnes (Peggy) Williams. Williams had trained under Eva Godfray at Gisborne Hospital, becoming a registered nurse in 1910, and had been in charge of the men's surgical ward for four years.[78] Another in the First Fifty was Margaret Rogers, who had completed her training at Christchurch Hospital in June 1913 and trained in midwifery in preparation for mission work in the New Hebrides (now Vanuatu). Her plans were disrupted when a volcanic eruption and earthquake destroyed the mission hospital at Ambrym. Instead, she joined Sibylla Maude's district nursing service and was working there when she enlisted.[79] More than 550 New Zealand nurses served overseas during the war.

Lambie commented: 'The work of these women brought great distinction to New Zealand. They proved themselves very adaptable, confident, intelligent, and ready to expend themselves to the utmost in the care of their patients.' Many were awarded the Royal Red Cross, but Lambie considered that the 'best record of their work ... lay in the excellent reputation they left in England concerning the value of the New Zealand nurses' ability.'[80] Not all returned. On 23 October 1915, as the troopship *Marquette* was transporting troops and the No. 1 New Zealand Hospital from Alexandria to Salonika, a German torpedo sank the ship. Ten nurses died, including Rogers. The professional and public reaction to the nurses' sacrifice and the bravery of those who survived contributed to the trope of the quiet heroine.

Just as the country was welcoming soldiers back from the war, the influenza pandemic struck New Zealand, peaking in November 1918. As nearly a quarter of the nursing workforce was still overseas, the depleted number at home was inadequate to manage the disaster. Many nurses fell ill with the disease, and 42 died.[81] Volunteers were urgently needed in emergency and main hospitals. In 1919, a commission of inquiry into New Zealand's management of the pandemic deplored the scarcity of women who knew the basics of nursing the sick. This prompted a proposal to provide basic nursing training for women to prepare the country for future emergencies. Hester Maclean vehemently resisted conducting such training in hospitals, as she feared it would open the way to 'two grades of nursing' and undermine the status of probationers training to be registered nurses. This argument highlighted nurses' claim to professional knowledge and practice. It was a complex situation. While Maclean fought that battle, she accommodated the intent of the proposal by employing nurses returning from the war to give community lectures in home nursing. Nurses willingly shared their knowledge, even writing home nursing books.[82] The commission of inquiry also led to the Health Act 1920 and a reorganised Department of Health.

1920–1935

In the new Department of Health, Maclean's position became Director of the Division of Nursing (DDN). The country now had four health districts, each with a nurse inspector responsible for supervising private hospitals, midwives and maternity nurses. As Maclean was nearing retirement, Jessie Bicknell was identified as a potential successor and sent to study developments in Britain. She was appointed the new DDN in 1923, the first New Zealand-trained nurse to become chief nurse.

One of Bicknell's priorities was postgraduate education for nurses. The first proposal for extended training, suggested by Dunedin nurses, was a five-year programme at Otago University, established in 1923. Students would spend two years at the School of Domestic Science, then two in a hospital (after which they were eligible for nursing registration). In the fifth year they would undertake studies to prepare them for leadership roles. In preparation for teaching the fifth year, Lambie was sent to do a course in public health nursing at Toronto University, and Janet Moore, a Dunedin-trained nurse who was matron of the Waikato Hospital, was sent to Bedford College in London to study hospital administration and the management of nursing schools. Although this programme was never fully implemented, the planned fifth year was used as the basis for a postgraduate diploma course for nurses, established in Wellington in 1928. Lambie and Moore became its two Department of Health instructors.

Regulatory control over the profession also changed in the 1920s. The Nurses and Midwives Registration Act 1925 set up the Nurses and Midwives Registration Board (NMRB), which shifted more control from the medical to the nursing profession. Lambie noted that this change was partly spurred by the fact that England's new General Nursing Council had a majority of nurse members. Although the NMRB's chair and another member were medical men, Bicknell as DDN was its registrar, and the New Zealand Trained Nurses' Association was empowered to nominate two nurses (one also a midwife) as members. An amendment in 1930 increased the membership to three nurses in addition to the registrar, as well as a lay member who was nominated by the Hospital Boards Association.

These regulatory changes constituted a recognition that the nursing profession could manage its own affairs. The board approved training schools, supervised training, arranged examinations, managed nurses' and midwives' registration and regulated their practice. As many of the nurses who trained as midwives did not practise midwifery but just needed a qualification in that field for career advancement, the board created a new course for them in maternity nursing, keeping midwifery separate. Following 'considerable agitation', another amendment empowered the board, with provisos, to approve private hospitals as training schools. Although Lambie did not say so, Bicknell was against this idea, just as Maclean had been. Lambie remarked in 1939 with apparent satisfaction that 'to date only one hospital has qualified'.[83] This was the Mater Misericordiae Hospital in Auckland.[84]

Lambie noted superannuation for nurses as an important achievement in this period. The professional association had for many years agitated for a nurses' superannuation scheme. Nurses earned a modest salary and had little opportunity to save adequately for retirement. Communities recognised this difficulty and often farewelled a matron on her retirement with a purse of sovereigns to compensate.[85] The Nurses' Memorial Fund, set up as a living memorial for the *Marquette* nurses, also helped nurses in straitened circumstances. The National Council of Women took up the cause at their conference in 1924. They recognised that nurses worked long hours and were 'scandalously paid' for their trying work. The quiet heroine trope was brought to bear: 'The career of a nurse was one of self-sacrifice,' said a speaker, 'and she frequently had matters of life and death in her hands. The salary of a nurse would not provide her with bread and butter when she retired … and she was

The first postgraduate nursing class, Wellington, 1928. The two instructors were Janet Moore and Mary Lambie (seated at centre, left and right).

M.I. Lambie, *My Story: Memoirs of a New Zealand nurse* (Christchurch: N.M. Peryer, 1956)), facing p. 72.

entitled to something more than that.'[86] The Superannuation Act 1926 set up a fund for nurses engaged in hospital board work.

The majority of trained nurses, however, worked outside the hospital board system. They nursed in small private hospitals or were self-employed and stayed in private homes to care for patients who were sick, having an operation at home or convalescing after illness or surgery. Amy Rickman found private case nursing a good way to gain experience and earn her passage home to England. She had come to New Zealand in 1919 to care for a child of the Campbell family, who had a sheep station in the Cheviot Hills. After two years she started training at Auckland Hospital and registered in 1924. In between private cases she lived at the Nurses' Club in Mountain Road. However, her first three patients died within three days of her arriving to care for them, causing her friends to ask, 'Rick, have you got shares in an undertaker's business?'[87]

Many nurses established or bought small private hospitals as a business venture.[88] Peggy Williams, who was one of the First Fifty, married a Scot, William Wood, while she was serving overseas. At the end of the war her husband was posted to Basra, Mesopotamia, and as she did not want to raise their son there, she returned to New Zealand with the boy in 1920. She purchased Cairnsmore Hospital in Invercargill to support herself and her son and ran it with her friend Lily Eddy. Her pre-nursing experience as a bookkeeper was an asset. In 1935 she sold the hospital and retired to Havelock North in a home across the paddock from Eva Godfray, her former matron at Gisborne Hospital, who had retired in 1916.[89]

This period saw other significant changes. On the professional front, the association bought *Kai Tiaki* from Maclean on her retirement in 1923, though Maclean continued as editor until her death in 1932. It dramatically increased its number of branches and in 1932 changed its name to the New Zealand Registered Nurses' Association (NZRNA). In nursing practice, as preventive health measures rapidly expanded, more nurses were employed in Plunket, Māori health, public health and school work, as well as in industry, children's health camps and in clinics for tuberculosis and venereal disease.

On 3 February 1931 a magnitude 7.8 earthquake struck Hawke's Bay. As Lambie worked as a department inspector during the months that the Post Graduate School was closed, she was sent to organise relief efforts in an emergency hospital set up on a racecourse in Napier. One month later Bicknell retired, and Lambie became DDN. Almost immediately, she said, she was faced with the effects of the economic depression. Unemployment among nurses was high. Ironically, the Depression to some extent helped both the reorganisation of the department's work and nursing employment. Under the new director-general of health, Dr Michael Watt, large health districts were broken up into health units, each with a supervising nurse, and again into smaller areas, each with a district health nurse responsible for all its public health services. Similarly, when the department rescinded many small hospitals' approval as training schools, registered nurses were needed at the hospitals to replace the nurse trainees.

Amy Rickman became one of the new district health nurses. She had saved the fare for her trip home to England in 1926 and worked as a private case nurse there and in France, spending a year with the family of Madame la Baronne Henri de Rothschild, whose son was a French diplomat. (When Madame was not in Paris, Rickman recounted, her 'silk stockings and accordion pleated pink, crêpe de chine French knickers were sent in the [diplomatic] bag to Paris for laundering'.) Rickman returned to New Zealand in 1928. She trained in midwifery in Christchurch and in 1929 went back to Auckland to take up private case nursing until she could gain a position as a district health nurse. In 1933 she was successful and was posted to Houhora in the Far North, where she spent six years. The advertisement had said applicants needed to be able to ride a horse. 'I couldn't, of course!' She soon learned. With long distances to cover, she was reliant on her horse, Tartan, lent by the local hotel owner, Bill Evans. She was no expert in horse management, however. Sometimes on the long trek home from Te Hāpua and Te Kao, she would take a break at Ngataki and have a meal and game of bridge with the schoolmaster and his wife, who lived in a two-roomed 'corrugated iron shed'. She would tie Tartan to a fence, only to find him later 'grazing happily with the fence post trailing at the end of his bridle'.[90]

1935–1950

In 1935 the first Labour Government came into power. The Social Security Act 1938, which introduced health benefits, had a profound effect on nursing. The maternity and free hospital service benefits introduced in 1939, as well as doctors' greater dependence on tests that were possible only in hospitals, increased demand for hospital beds. More nurses and trainees were needed.[91] In the 1940s the NZRNA, Hospital Boards' Association and Health Department joined together in a recruitment campaign. Their advertising, broadcast appeals and promotional films focused on nursing as a career with many opportunities.[92] This recruitment strategy reflected the change many saw in the nursing culture, with the modern nurse deemed more commercial and career-oriented than the devoted nurse of the past. The campaign had only limited success, perhaps because it did not match the image of the nurse in the public mind or in the imagination of potential recruits. To them, the old virtues were still at the core of what it meant to be a nurse.

To gain a clear picture of the nursing workforce, the nursing register needed to be purged, as it was cumulative and included names of nurses who were no longer working or who had died. The annual practising certificate, introduced in 1939, enabled an accurate picture of the actual nursing workforce. Just over 3000 nurses on the register were 'active' – 53 per cent worked in public or private hospitals, 21 per cent in private case nursing, 11 percent in public health or Pacific services and the remainder overseas.[93] To boost staffing numbers further, a two-year course was introduced in 1939 for registered nursing aids. This was the first recognition in the nursing culture of the possibility of different categories, or 'levels', of nurses. Lambie explained that the course was intended to appeal to girls who might not pass the registered nurses' examination or who wanted to earn money before they were old enough to enter nurse training. If they chose later to train for full registration, they would receive a time concession of one year. With the general expansion of work opportunities, however, it was difficult to attract the numbers needed, and many did not remain for their second year. As a result, the course was shortened to 18 months and the concession to six months.

As the number of nurses in hospitals increased, so did the demand for accommodation in nurses' homes. Authorities therefore encouraged trained staff to 'live-out' and gave them an allowance to do so. Lambie's comment that 'the majority learned to enjoy this freedom from institutional life' was perhaps an understatement.[94] Student nurses, however, were required to 'live-in', as they apparently still needed the control of a nurses' home sister to maintain standards of behaviour.

In 1939 Amy Rickman was still in the Far North. Lambie was aware of the hardships of isolated rural living and on her annual visits used to bring books for her. Rickman was happy there and did not want to leave, but Lambie thought it was time she 'got back to civilisation', so late that year Rickman returned to Auckland and became district health nurse in the Papakura district. This area had a similarly large Māori population, as well as a number of Chinese market gardeners. After her nursing visits, the leather seats in the back of Rickman's large black official car would be 'filled with cauliflower, cabbages and everything you could think of'. She shared the bounty with her landlady and a girl in the top flat. 'I couldn't use it all myself, but I had to take it or they would have been offended.'[95]

In 1944 new benefits under the Social Security Act 1938 enabled hospital boards to employ more district nurses. In urban areas, nurses and voluntary agencies needed to rationalise their overlapping services. In rural areas, nurses juggled the need to provide bedside care as well as to run clinics. Through the new benefits, hospital boards now subsidised two-thirds of agencies' district nursing costs, and government grants helped with particular expenses, such as buying a car for the nurse's rounds. While the rural district health nurses' stories sustained the trope of the intrepid nurse, the role of urban district nurses in 'brightening sunless lives' disappeared from newspapers as the need for fundraising lessened.

The Post Graduate School for Nurses prepared teachers and supervisors to provide the expanding services, and scholarships offered opportunities for international study. In 1936, a scholarship from the Florence Nightingale Memorial Committee enabled E. Ruth Bridges to spend 18 months on a study tour of Britain, Europe and the United States before returning to take over the school from Janet Moore, who retired in 1937. Flora Cameron was awarded a Rockefeller Foundation fellowship and spent a year in Canada and the United States, returning to the school in 1940.

When World War II was declared in September 1939, hundreds of nurses were eager to join the military nursing services. This time a system was put in place to ensure that civilian staff numbers were not depleted in any particular hospital or area. By May 1940 more than 1200 nurses had volunteered to serve overseas.[96] Around 640 did so. Again, Lambie was pleased that military authorities gave New Zealand nurses the 'highest praise', which 'reflected great credit on New Zealand nursing'.[97]

After the war, regulation of the profession changed again. The Nurses and Midwives Act 1945 set up a new regulatory authority, the Nurses and Midwives Board (NMB). Responsibility for psychiatric nurses was transferred to the new board, and a separate registration in this field was established. Hospitals could also opt to train male nurses, who now had their own register. They were granted a time concession in recognition of service as army medical orderlies or hospital attendants. The profession remained, however, overwhelmingly female. The NMB approved the expansion of training opportunities for registered nurses and issued certificates, first in Plunket nursing and then for courses such as plastic surgery and neurosurgery nursing. The NZRNA offered bursaries and loans for further training and formed a Student Nurses' Association. It continued working with Lambie to undertake surveys in nursing techniques and ran essay competitions for student nurses. These activities helped develop nursing scholarship, strengthened nursing's claim to a professional sphere of knowledge and practice, and were precursors to developing a research culture in the later twentieth century.[98] And through its NMB membership the association took, as Lambie remarked, an active interest in legislation and all matters affecting the profession.[99]

From the 1920s the nursing profession had been a sphere in which New Zealand asserted leadership in the Pacific region. After the war, nurses took on expanded leadership roles in public health services and education. Amy Rickman, working in the Papakura district, mentioned to Helen Comrie, the nurse inspector, that she would love to work in the Pacific. 'It was arranged very quickly', and in early 1940 she took up a two-year contract in Rarotonga. The hospital was small, with just a matron and one nurse. Rickman took over from a nurse she had trained with in Auckland, Elizabeth (Beth) Paora. When Paora heard Rickman was coming to replace her, she wrote: 'Rick, there's a big spider in your bedroom, in the wardrobe, don't kill it. It eats all the mosquitos!'[100] Next, Rickman accepted a two-year posting to Niue as matron. In the small, open wooden hospital, patients' relatives slept beside them on the floor and brought them food. Rickman went on district nursing rounds in the doctor's car, which was as hot as an oven. 'When I got back, various parts of my body would be raw. I needed several showers to cool down.'[101] After two years back in New Zealand, Rickman served a second term in Niue from the end of 1946.

Lambie noted that after the war, many nurses were 'unwilling to remain settled in one place', resulting in 'a great deal of exchange of nurses between countries'. She commented that 'this world-wide movement of nurses has resulted in a fresh interest in the training of nurses and a pooling of ideas as never formerly'. She hoped the new approach would reduce the number of students who left during training, but sounded a cautionary note: 'The future ahead is one of promise provided the standard of training is maintained and adapted to the needs of the country and that the ethical principles of service are maintained.'[102] This was Lambie's final comment in the revised reports. She retired at the end of 1949. According to one matron, Marjorie Chambers, she was 'an outstanding and competent person ... as well as being a most interesting and lovable personality.'[103]

***

Lawrence Jones has described the myths of progress and heroic pioneers in literary and historical responses to New Zealand's centenary.[104] Lambie's narration of a century of New Zealand nursing history was a typically progressivist account in this vein, depicting a steady and admirable advancement of nursing in response to emerging needs. Written from the viewpoint of a nurse leader, it focused on the achievement of nurse leaders of the past. It left out, understandably, the conflicts between matrons and hospital boards and the enquiries into hospital management that affected nurses, briefly mentioning just two relating to small rural hospitals and private hospitals agitating to be approved as training schools. Nevertheless, Lambie's account was a good representation of the significant changes in the nursing profession over more than 100 years. The experiences of nurses affected by the changes show how nurses' working lives were interwoven in different places over time. These connections helped to maintain a community and therefore a basis for a nursing culture.

CHAPTER 2

Nurse training in New Zealand

When Louise Renouf (later Fleming) started her nurse training at Napier Hospital on 1 January 1900, she was sent directly to a ward. 'My first duty introduced me to a scrubbing brush and bucket.' In the little dayroom she was also shown how to take temperatures and so 'started ward work at the bedside'. She worked 11 hours one day and 12 the next, with a half day off a week once she had worked eight hours on the ward. Each week she attended two lectures by a doctor and one by the matron. These were held in the evenings after the long duty, 'so naturally we were jaded'. For the first three months' trial period trainees supplied their own cotton uniforms and were unpaid. After that, if deemed suitable, they were supplied with uniforms and initially earned 5 shillings a week, a wage that was raised to 10 shillings for most of their three years' training.

Applicants had to be at least 21 years old, and there was a long waiting list. They worked for three months in each ward, including night duty, and when in the isolation ward for patients with infectious diseases they were on duty for 24 hours. 'We worked hard, studied hard and lived hard.' In 1903 she was the first nurse trained at Napier Hospital to gain her registered nurse medal. After six months she successfully applied for the position of head nurse and acting matron at Timaru Hospital, 'the attraction being an eight-hour duty and £52 per annum', which reduced her hours by a third and doubled her salary.[1]

Colleen Turbet (later Williams) was 18 years old when she started training at Auckland Hospital in February 1949. She had been living in Ceylon (Sri Lanka), as her father was in the British Colonial Service. She applied for nursing training at Perth, Sydney and Auckland Hospitals, all of which offered her a place. She visited each city and, like Goldilocks, decided that Auckland was 'not too hot, not too big, just right'. Instead of starting in a ward on the first day like Louise Renouf, she had seven weeks in the Preliminary Training School (PTS), learning hospital etiquette, anatomy and physiology, bacteriology and basic nursing procedures that were practised on 'Mrs Chase' the demonstration mannequin, or classmates. She had never swept a floor before, so it was 'a complete surprise' to find that there was a system for it. The skill was to sweep away from the feet with overlapping strokes, tapping the broom at the end of each stroke to knock off the dust. In the wards, nurses first strewed damp tea leaves from an old jam tin onto the floor, 'as if we were sowing seeds', to gather up the dust as they swept.[2]

While in the PTS, Turbet studied from 8.30am to 4.30pm during the week and worked from 7am to 3pm in a hospital ward on Saturdays. When she completed PTS, she worked either a 7am–3pm or 3pm–11pm duty, with a month of 11pm–7am night duty every three months. She had one rostered day off a week. In addition, a scheduled study day away from the ward each week was dedicated to further lectures, demonstrations and practising techniques. A rotation in each kind of ward, and at Greenlane, Middlemore and Cornwall Hospitals for different specialties, ensured a broad experience. She was paid £3 8s a fortnight in her first year. In December 1952 she passed the state final examination and left to get married. Her certificate of service noted she had been a 'capable, methodical and dependable nurse'.[3]

These two nurses' experiences mark the changes in nurse training over five decades. Grace Neill set down the first syllabus, in place from 1902.[4] In the three-year apprenticeship-style training, ward sisters ensured probationers learned by working with more experienced nurses on the wards. Doctors and matrons gave lectures, which probationers were expected to attend even if off-duty. With the establishment of the first PTS in 1923, a more systematic course of instruction was established. Christchurch Hospital appointed the first tutor sister whose sole responsibility was teaching nurses, and other hospitals gradually followed this lead. The PTS was in place in larger training hospitals by the end of the 1930s, and the system of study blocks or days was introduced in the 1940s to release nurses from ward duty in order to attend classes throughout their training.[5]

Competing needs of service and training

In 1888 Dunedin Hospital had just five female nurses, who worked only on the women's and children's wards. They worked every day for 12 hours, except for Saturday, when they worked a half day and made up the time by working four additional hours on Sunday. For their efforts they received £12 a year and the promise of lectures and training. After a short time, they realised the hospital trustees were not keeping their promise. The matron, Mrs Burton, was a housekeeper and not a trained nurse. In her broad Scottish accent, she scorned their request for lectures – she had not had any and had got on all right. 'Lectures! Umph!' The nurses spoke to their friend Andrew Burns, the house steward, who made their case to the trustees, with the result that the hospital doctors began a series of lectures, delivered after the nurses' 12-hour duty, with an examination at the end of the year.[6] The lectures were sporadic, and it was not until 1891 that more formal training was put in place. The nurses' challenge to the trustees was, ironically, possible only because they were not yet subject to the rigid discipline that formalised training would bring.

Debates over the competing priorities of a hospital's service needs and the training of nurses showed how different parties contested the right to define what a nurse should be and do. Several commissions of inquiry investigated this tension. The commission at Auckland Hospital in 1904, for example, upheld one complaint (among others) that Dr J. Clive Collins, the medical superintendent, had failed to provide sufficient and regular lectures to the nurses.[7] Dr Duncan MacGregor, the inspector-general of hospitals, reported that the proper training of nurses had been 'almost neglected' there for the past years, and he was relieved that Dr E. McKellar had resumed the teaching.[8]

This tension was also evident at the centre of empire. Service needs took precedence over training and delayed the establishment of PTSs in England in all hospitals but the London Hospital, where Eva Lückes had used her powers of persuasion to establish one in 1895. Although the first PTS had been established at the Glasgow Infirmary under Rebecca Strong in 1893, Scotland lagged further behind, and even the Royal Infirmary of Edinburgh did not have a PTS until 1924, a year after the first was established in New Zealand.[9]

Hospital authorities and others justified nurses' poor pay on the grounds that they were receiving training. At Dunedin Hospital in 1907, domestic servants earned more than the majority of nurses. The local newspaper editor contested this status quo, arguing that too much was made of the 'boon conferred on nurses in the way of training'. The colony's hospitals were 'worked by cheap labour'. The 'very generous impulse' that induced young women to become nurses was 'in a measure exploited, making the life of hospital nurses all too much one of underpaid drudgery'.[10] His argument had little effect. In 1919 Hester Maclean, the chief nurse, asserted that as probationers were receiving valuable training, they should receive 'merely pocket-money'; but, in return for their service, she believed, the teaching should be brought up to a 'uniform high standard'.[11] The 1926 census statistics showed that nurses in training (probationers) were the lowest paid of all female workers. They earned £52 annually (plus board), whereas a pupil-teacher earned £100 for fewer hours of work. An 'office girl' earned £70, and a charwoman and waitress £100.[12] Dorothy Scammell (later Ford), at Wairoa Hospital from 1929, earned £3 a month, an amount that bought 'a pair of shoes or a very ordinary winter dress'.[13]

Although nurses' low pay went largely unchallenged, in 1909 the government legislated for an eight-hour day for probationers. Maclean had vehemently opposed the initial proposal for all nurses to work shorter shifts, as she considered it went against the vocational nature of nursing, disrupted the continuity of care and would degrade the profession 'to the level of a trade'.[14] As her civil service position prevented her from opposing the department's position too publicly, she rallied the New Zealand Trained Nurses' Association (NZTNA) to do so. As a result of her influence, the legislation introduced the eight-hour day for probationers only.[15] This was still a 56-hour week as nurses had no day off, and the directive was barely observed in reality. Nurses on morning duty stayed on after the end of their shift to complete their allotted tasks, especially cleaning, and in many hospitals those on afternoon duty were also expected to work in the operating theatre in the mornings.[16] A day off a week was suggested at different times in the 1920s but, largely because of the cost of arranging nursing cover, even the training school matrons at their first conference in 1927 would agree only that a minimum of two days' leave a month was desirable, where possible.[17] It was not in place throughout the country until the 1940s.

In times of nursing shortages, service needs were prioritised over training policies. Selection processes were loosened to increase the number of entrants, with the idea that unsuitable probationers would be 'weeded out' during training.[18] The minimum age of registration was lowered from 23 so that nurses could enter training sooner after leaving school and not be lost to other occupations or to marriage.[19] Classroom work was arranged in study days or blocks to make nursing a more attractive occupational choice,[20] and several hospitals extended their training contract to four years under the guise of preparing 'thoroughly trained nurses'.[21]

In 1938 Mary Lambie, the chief nurse, after a seven-month tour to compare New Zealand's conditions of training with those in other countries, reported to the government that few people in New Zealand realised that nurses paid for their education by their labours and that very often authorities did not appreciate that their hospitals were 'educational bodies'.[22] But the issue of competing staffing and training needs remained. Nursing shortages meant nurses in training were overworked. Colleen Turbet wrote to her parents that in her Auckland Hospital men's medical ward they were 'hectically busy with 32 patients and some mornings there are only two of us on'. Most were cardiac patients on full bedrest, so the two nurses had to fully sponge 20 of them each morning. Although overworked, she said, 'I wouldn't give it up. I really feel as if I am doing something worthwhile.'[23] Perhaps hospital authorities relied on this.

Despite the tensions around competing service and training needs, from 1902 the aim of training was consistent – to produce efficient, effective and biddable nurses who could provide care for a patient with any disease or condition. Nurse training therefore included experience in all wards of a hospital and a curriculum organised around the ideas of dirt, body and duty.

Dealing with dirt

Dirt in any form was not to be tolerated. It endangered the patient and was the visible sign of nursing incompetence. This aversion to dirt shaped nursing practice.

Dirt has been defined as 'matter out of place' that is problematic, often disgusting, slimy, sticky, difficult to remove and associated with decomposition and decay.[24] In the nursing culture, material that exuded from the body, such as sputum, was matter out of place and problematic until disposed of effectively. The effort to control the chaos of illness entailed maintaining scrupulous cleanliness in the wards. As Ward Sister Florence Gill pointed out at the NZTNA conference in 1929, the junior nurse's role in removing dust from a lampshade was as important as the senior nurse's correct aseptic treatment of a wound.[25]

As nurses gained seniority, they engaged with smaller forms of dirt. Junior nurses were taught to remove visible dirt from the ward environment and patients' bodies in what was called 'medical asepsis' or 'medical cleanliness'. Senior nurses learned 'surgical asepsis' or 'surgical cleanliness', the removal of the invisible microbe.

A British general nursing textbook used in New Zealand made it clear that an 'untidy and a slovenly ward generally signifies slovenly and bad work'.[26] When Margaret Macnab started her training at Christchurch Hospital in the early 1920s, she, like Louise Renouf two decades earlier, went straight onto a ward where a nurse immediately introduced her to 'the mops and brooms'.[27] Mary Clark, starting at the small Taumarunui Hospital in 1933, was also 'thrown in the deep end, straight into the world of bedpans and cleaning sluices'.[28] Even when a hospital had a PTS, cleaning was the first task nurses learned. Marjorie Chambers' class at Christchurch Hospital in 1936 had to clean the entire school each morning. 'Everything was moved, every inch of floor space was swept and polished, all ledges were wet dusted, and polished, and every surface dealt with in a suitable way.'[29]

On the ward each morning, junior nurses carried out the same duties. They scrubbed the grooved kauri sluice-room bench and whitened it with sandsoap. Later, out of the ward sister's sight but to gain her approval, they surreptitiously shined stainless steel benches with methylated spirits. Nurses cleaned and sterilised bedpans, urinals and bowls at the end of the morning duty and could not leave the ward until the cleaning was done. Once a week the junior 'pro' had to do 'high dusting' using a 'long-handled, duster-covered brush that would reach window tops, door jambs, cupboard tops, and all other tiresome, high ledges'.[30] Floors had to be spotless and shiny. Semi-liquid polish was splashed on with a stick and rubbed in with a mop 'with great gusto'.[31] Others polished floors with 'heavy padded things on long handles called "bonzers"'.[32] One citizen wrote to a newspaper in 1924 about this apparent prioritising of 'work of a charring nature, scrubbing and polishing'. 'It is no wonder,' he said: 'that patients have been heard to remark that they envy the attention the floors and lockers receive.'[33]

Dealing with dirt required diligence and discipline – and visible effort. Bridget Ristori, based at Masterton Hospital in the early 1920s, was sent for her turn at the small rural Pahiatua Hospital. After she had polished the floor of the men's ward on her hands and knees, the matron ordered her to do it again. 'You can't have done it properly,' the matron said: 'you aren't even perspiring.'[34]

Matrons and ward sisters had sharp eyes. Rose Muir, lady superintendent (or matron) at Christchurch in the 1920s, 'could spot dust a mile away, well, half a ward away anyhow. She would stand at the entrance to the ward and, with an accusing finger, point to what seemed an invisible place behind a heater halfway down the ward.' She was nicknamed 'Rosie Manure'.[35] Another matron would 'run her finger along ledges and suchlike to make sure there wasn't any dust – woe-betide you if there was.'[36] Dorothy Scammell had a ward sister who was 'ever-alert, keeping everything under control with a seeming radar eye for the slightest evidence of muddle or untidiness.'[37] In the 1940s Sonja Davies, who was training at Christchurch Hospital, had a 'martinet' of a ward sister. Davies had never seen so much brass – toilet chains and hinges, bath chains and plugs, door handles and finger plates. It all had to be polished. 'Sister's standards were so exacting. Her inspections were excruciating and she was never completely satisfied.'[38]

According to Dorothy Scammell, 'Cleanliness was rated higher than godliness for patients and their beds and surroundings.'[39] Maintaining the cleanliness and orderliness of the ward also required rigidly straightening beds – and patients – before doctors' rounds each morning. Beds were made with a specified length of sheet turnover at the top, counterpane corners were neatly mitred, pillows plumped and their openings positioned away from the ward entrance, and bed wheels were turned at right angles to the wall.

The dirt and detritus exuded by the patients had to be dealt with as well. Bathing patients or sponging those who were on bedrest but not critically ill, doing bedpan rounds, and emptying vomit bowls and sputum mugs were part of the junior nurse's role, and they required a strong stomach. Sputum mugs had a hinged lid and a paper lining. Nurses emptied them by tipping the lining down the sluice, 'hoping it came away neatly and didn't leave slime of greenish-yellow sputum on the lip'. Knowing the sputum was 'alive with bugs' made one nurse feel 'particularly squeamish', but nurses were not permitted to show any revulsion.[40] 'Emptying and sterilising sputum mugs was one revolting task.'[41]

On surgical wards, professional relationships were shaped by the war against microscopic forms of dirt.[42] In the mid-nineteenth century doctors regarded wound sepsis (infection) as inevitable, as they believed it was caused by miasma (vapours) always present in the hospital. The presence of pus was 'laudable', as it was seen as evidence that a wound was healing. However, in Britain in the 1860s, Joseph Lister argued that contamination of wounds was caused by airborne microbes that could be combatted through a system of 'antisepsis', particularly the use of a carbolic spray that covered everyone in the operating theatre (and, alarmingly, turned their urine green from carbolic poisoning), and by using antiseptics in instrument sterilisation and wound care. In the late nineteenth century this approach was countered by the idea of asepsis. Microbes were not ever-present in the air but could be eliminated by thoroughly cleaning the environment and using heat and steam to sterilise instruments. By the turn of the century, most hospitals had ceased using the carbolic spray but were sterilising the theatre and instruments with the combined approach of antiseptics and heat or steam.[43] Surgeons could now anticipate a wound healing without sepsis. Preventing it was regarded as the surgical ward nurse's responsibility, regardless of anything that might have happened during the operation to cause it. A skilled surgical nurse was therefore vital not only to a patient's recovery but also to the surgeon's professional reputation. Septic wounds could cause septic relations.

Some historians have depicted the nurse as an obedient, subservient handmaiden to the doctor.[44] Contemporary narratives of nursing in international publications throughout the period show a more complex professional relationship. At least one

British surgeon acknowledged that mistakes occurred and were to be learned from, and did not single out the nurse for blame.[45] Most, however, saw a nurse's negligence as the likeliest cause of postoperative complications. Her 'carelessness or neglect may nullify the most stringent precautions adopted'.[46] Any 'slackness' meant that unless she had 'a conscience', she was 'unfit to undertake surgical work', otherwise suspicion could fall unjustly on others (presumably surgeons) 'who have faithfully done their duty'.[47] By the 1930s the nurse was more often regarded as a member of the surgical team, with success seen as dependent on combined efforts.[48] However, in 1937 one British nurse still warned that a surgeon's 'skilled work' could be 'rendered of no avail' by some careless or unconscientious action on the part of a nurse.[49]

The British and Australian textbooks used in New Zealand showed collegial relationships between doctors and nurses.[50] The strongest local opinion came from Dr Joseph McNaughton Christie, a gynaecologist, who told nurses at the Wellington Branch of the NZTNA in 1914 that in preventing sepsis 'the surgeon has to depend absolutely on the co-operation and care of the nurse. If one wishes a good result from his operation (and who does not?), then one must have careful antisepsis during the preparation before the operation, during the operation, and in the after treatment.'[51] And Guy Hallwright, the surgeon at Wairoa Hospital, despite his 'puckish sense of humour' and 'a deceptively cherubic expression', had a 'testy temper'. He was proud of being Lister's godson.[52] Louisa Corkill, who trained at Wairoa from January 1918, wrote: 'He was eagle eyed in watching our techniques & he could wither us with his scorn if he thought we were not being *ALERT* enough.'[53]

Nurses were taught bacteriology and given detailed instructions on the prevention and management of various forms of sepsis. The subject was also discussed in their professional journal.[54] Sepsis was the most frequently occurring topic in the surgical nursing paper of the state final examination for registration.[55]

Senior nurses were responsible for presenting a thoroughly cleaned and antiseptic-swabbed patient to the operating theatre, and for attending afterwards to their wound. If wounds became septic, to avoid cross-infection the nurse did all the 'clean dressings' on the ward first and left the 'dirty dressings' (septic wounds) till the end. In 1933 Mary Lambie and the association's Nursing Education Committee (NEC) carried out a survey of handwashing technique before dressings in all training schools, which showed considerable variations in the stipulated time and the disinfectants used. They recommended that when preparing to do a dressing, a nurse should scrub her hands for 10 minutes and immerse them in biniodide of mercury for two minutes (a potentially toxic procedure).[56] Nurses kept their hands wet with disinfectant while doing the dressing. These measures led to cracked skin and irritated and infected fingers among nurses. According to Mavis Borthwick (later Hunter), who worked at Stratford Hospital from 1939 to 1943, 'We were always scrubbing up to our elbows with a nail brush and soap, and then putting our arms into a bowl of cyllin (a derivative of coal tar). My arms used to be raw during the winter time because of course we couldn't dry them.'[57]

By the time of the 1933 survey, two hospitals had introduced the use of gloves, which reduced the frequency of skin damage and infection.[58] The rubber gloves had to be patched if torn and were difficult to obtain during World War II, but a survey report in 1942 recommended their use for all septic dressings. Other procedures also changed. Hands were now to be scrubbed for just three minutes, 'timed by a clock, watch or sand glass', and dried before donning the gloves. The same gloves were worn for a series of dressings, with the nurse washing her gloved hands 'as though bare' and rubbing them with Lysol or Dettol in between dressings.[59] A survey in 1944, however, showed that the problem of septic fingers persisted. Apart from the discomfort it caused to nurses, it led to the loss of 1600 days of nursing care at a cost to hospitals of £600 in wages, plus the nurses' keep.[60] By 1948, the use of disinfectants after handwashing was no longer advocated, as authorities realised that 'any substance which is strong enough to destroy bacteria is irritating to the skin' and rendered the nurse's hands liable to cracking and infection.[61] Dealing with dirt therefore had repercussions for hospital economy, patients' recovery and nurses' efficiency and health.

By 1950 the introduction of penicillin into general hospital use had radically altered the management of infection. The role of the nurse, however, remained one of scrupulous attention to dirt.

Nursing the body

Nursing was an embodied art for both patient and nurse. The patient's body was minutely monitored, described and regularly treated. The nurse's body was enlisted in the hard physical work of positioning helpless patients, many of whom were confined to bed for weeks, and carrying equipment and heavy wooden screens to the bedside. Matrons declined applicants who seemed too short or not sufficiently strong.[62] From the 1930s, during their time in the PTS nurses attended physical culture (exercise) classes, usually led by a hospital masseuse (physiotherapist). One nurse at Wellington Hospital in 1936 explained that as this class was accompanied by 'suitable music', they enjoyed it.[63] The nurse was trained to be deft with her hands, and her senses were fine-tuned to monitor minute signals of the patient's physical condition. (Although the patient was seen as a person, the curriculum did not include mental and social aspects of illness or psychology.)[64]

Scientific attention to the patient's body required precise monitoring of vital signs. Taking temperatures was one of the first skills acquired by new nurses. They soon learned to shake the thermometer's mercury down with an 'experienced flick and click of the wrist'.[65] As one nurse noted in an examination paper, to avoid breaking thermometers, 'small flicks of the wrist are much more effective than great muscular thrusts from the whole arm'.[66] The nurse learned to use her senses to monitor the patient's signs of pain, bowel motions, urine, vomitus and sputum. Her touch was needed to discern whether a patient's pulse was slow, rapid, regular, intermittent, hard, soft, full and bounding, or thready. She listened to hear if respirations were deep and sighing, shallow, difficult, stertorous, stridulous (or crowing, as in croup), or in the Cheyne-Stokes pattern that foreshadows death.[67] (Or, as one examination candidate put it, 'chained stoats'.)[68]

Nurses also paid close attention to the colour, texture and smell of patients' excreta. As textbooks instructed them, sputum could be mucoid (thin and colourless), muco-purulent (thick, tenacious, greenish-yellow and sometimes with a faintly sweet odour, in cases of pneumonia and tuberculosis), purulent (yellow, thick, with an offensive smell and composed of pus, as with a lung abscess), rusty (pneumonia), mummular (coin-like, in tuberculosis) or bright red (a sign of a ruptured blood vessel in the lung). Comparisons with food were enlisted. Sputum could resemble prune juice (in cases of severe pneumonia) or redcurrant jelly (considered indicative of cancer). Urine could be orange-red (signalling excess pigment), smoky (blood), porter-coloured (bile), milky (pus) or with a pink sediment (urates). A 'light flocculent cloud' floating in the urine, despite its pleasant-sounding description, indicated the presence of mucus.[69]

More senior nurses were responsible for testing urine from patients with diabetes, adding a reagent to a test tube of urine and holding it over a Bunsen burner flame to watch for a colour change indicating the level of glucose. Colleen Turbet felt it was 'worth doing when you had a lovely reaction to chemicals'.[70] Louisa Dixon at Greenlane Hospital in the early 1940s, however, found it a difficult procedure. The urine was 'vigorously boiled' for two minutes and the 'trick was to point the open end of the test tube away from yourself because the hot liquid would spurt out, and not to drop the tube when it got hot. It was not a favourite procedure.'[71]

Good health and fitness were important for the hard physical work of nursing. Here Wellington Hospital nurses are led in a physical fitness class, about 1944.
ABRR 7563 W4 990/13, Archives New Zealand

Tolerating these sights and smells required fortitude. Abdominal wounds drained through tubes into the glass bottles of Wangensteen suctions, 'truly smelly things, filled with evil looking fluids'.[72] Nurses worried the bottles might overflow. Dorothy Scammell felt sick when cleaning faeces from a bed or skimming pus off the bath water where a badly burnt man was submerged except for his face. 'However, I never let on that I'd vomited'.[73]

Training a useful all-rounder nurse required rotating her through different wards to gain experience with a range of conditions, which were sometimes imprinted on the memory through smells. In the 1930s Scammell nursed patients (often children) with rheumatic fever who had their 'painful swollen joints wrapped in flannel bandages soaked in oil of wintergreen', and its pungent smell years later vividly brought to her mind these 'beds of little sufferers'. Patients with bronchitis were nursed in a steam tent, with Friars' Balsam added to the water in the steam kettle – another smell that always conjured up 'dramas in the side ward' at Wairoa.[74] Nurses at Stratford associated its smell with children sick with bronchitis, as the steam bubbled from the long-spouted kettle on a cooking ring in the middle of the room. 'You could smell it all over the ward'.[75]

Patients with infectious diseases such as diphtheria and scarlet fever were treated in the isolation ward, which reeked of disinfectant. 'The first thing that hit you as you arrived was the smell of disinfectant; it was unforgettable and stayed with you even when you went off duty.'[76] An 'Iso' rotation meant literal isolation for the nurse too. The ward was usually in a separate building at the far end of the hospital grounds. Nurses were confined there for the whole of their rotation, which might last several weeks, and were on duty for 24 hours a day unless two nurses could be assigned. At the isolation ward at Wairau Hospital in Blenheim, there was no means of communication with the main hospital until a speaking tube was installed in 1899, thankfully replaced by a telephone in 1901.

In the late 1920s, if patients in isolation were well enough to be left for a short time, the nurse collected meals from the hospital – but only through the kitchen window.[77] When Mavis Borthwick nursed in the isolation ward at Stratford Hospital in the early 1940s, the meals were brought over from the hospital. 'I got so sick of stew,' she said. 'One Thursday when I knew the nurses would be having bacon and eggs I called out to poor Daisy Hosking bringing my tray, "If it's stew again you can take it away," and I watched her turn round and go back.' Borthwick was lonely and had no radio there, so perhaps she regretted the missed chance of a chat, even if only through a door. Emily O'Callaghan (later Collingwood) spent six weeks at the small isolation hospital in the large grounds of Wellington Hospital during her training, between 1915 and 1918, and 'did not leave the place AT ALL'. The isolation unit had its own nurses' home, from which she went to the ward 'in uniform which you changed (even shoes) and worked duty. After, on the way out you bathed in disinfectant and put on uniform again. The doctors didn't do all that!' Disinfection to prevent cross-infection seemed an arbitrary process.[78] Nurses at Stratford Hospital stayed in the isolation building even when off duty. Borthwick noted: 'When I finally was able to leave the building after the month I had to have a disinfectant bath down there, leave all my uniforms down there and get another nurse to bring my own clothes.'[79] Disinfectant was therefore the first and last smell of isolation nursing.

With no appliances like hoists yet introduced, nursing was embodied in another way. Nurses singlehandedly lifted patients out of bed and into and out of baths and wheelchairs, and paired up to reposition an inert patient up the bed using a shoulder lift. Orthopaedic nursing was especially taxing. Beverly Barker, who became matron of Middlemore Hospital in 1951, said that as it was predominantly an orthopaedic hospital, 'it was heavy nursing which took its toll on the nurses' backs'.[80] Embodiment of nursing was also represented in the high standard of personal hygiene required.

As a standard nursing textbook instructed, the nurse should be 'an example of perfect neatness and cleanliness'. As she had a responsibility to educate the public up 'to a scientific standard of cleanliness', she should 'practise cleanliness as a matter of honour. Every vestige of dirt, whether visible or not, must be removed.'[81]

Although training was intended to produce an all-rounder nurse, one illness was regarded as the measure of an excellent nurse: being able to bring a patient through the 'crisis' of pneumonia.[82] This was the most frequent topic in the state final examination medical paper.[83] When the 'crisis' was expected, usually around the seventh day, the nurse got ready with hot water bottles, hot blankets, oxygen, stimulants such as brandy or a syringe of strychnine, and a warm, dry garment for the patient, who would sweat profusely. A successful outcome depended on 'vigilant and careful nursing.'[84] 'It was distressing to nurse a very ill lobar pneumonia case,' said Dorothy Scammell. The restless, often delirious patients fought for breath, their faces flushed and cyanosed. 'It almost seemed a miracle when what was called "the crisis" had passed; the patient broke out in a profuse sweat, the temperature fell, breathing eased, and a whispered voice asked for something to eat!'[85] Joan Boyle (later Loeber) at Wellington Hospital in the 1930s assisted a final-year nurse, Audrey Webster, in successfully nursing a young man with pneumonia who had not been expected to live. Webster was the 'most talented, skilled and caring nurse' Loeber ever knew. Loeber 'watched her, her movements' and saw 'poetry in nursing'.[86] Once antibiotics were in general hospital use, however, the importance of nursing patients through a pneumonia crisis faded.

The most damning sign of a poor nurse was a patient who developed bedsores – ulceration and sloughing resulting from pressure, often over a bony prominence where the flesh was thin. 'The nurse must look upon bed-sores as a reproach,' said one textbook, 'for they rise from insufficient nursing, and are only rarely unavoidable.'[87] Nurses soon learned that allowing a patient to develop a bedsore was 'a crime,'[88] or 'almost a capital offence'. 'I have always felt great satisfaction that none of the typhoids, diabetics, or paralysed patients in my care ever did so,' said Scammell.[89] In addition to preventing pressure by frequently turning patients in bed, and avoiding friction by removing crumbs and creases, the nurse washed body areas at risk, particularly the patient's back, with hot, soapy water as often as four times a day, massaged it with her palm lathered in soap, allowed the lather to dry on the patient's back, and applied methylated spirits to dry and harden the skin. Rubbing was seen as of 'paramount importance' to restore the circulation and was to be 'gently performed with the palm of the hand' until the area was 'pink and warm'.[90] Nurses called a ward

By the 1940s nurses in training were given study days or blocks away from the wards to attend classroom lectures, rather than attending in their own time after ward duty. Here Dr John Cairney delivers a lecture to Wellington Hospital nurses.
ABRR 7563 W4990/13, Archives New Zealand

round of this procedure 'doing the backs'. Incipient bedsores were treated with an antiseptic powder, red lotion (containing zinc sulphate), or a soothing ointment of castor oil mixed with zinc or Friars' Balsam. If the area ulcerated it was treated like a wound, with an ointment or paraffin wax dressing, and if it became infected, the slough could be removed with warm carbolic surgical fomentations.[91] These were made of lint, placed in a small wringer frame and boiled in a saucepan or steriliser, wrung out, held with forceps and shaken to ensure that the steam was removed before applying.[92]

All these procedures needed to be carried out not only with skill but also with diligence, economy and gentleness, three qualities that were part of the definition of a nurse's duty.

Defining duty

Nurse training defined duty in terms of etiquette, ethics and a code of behaviour based on virtues. Neill listed these requirements in the general section of the first nursing syllabus and expanded them in the 1908 version.[93] Textbooks and lectures made them explicit, nurses recorded them in the first pages of their notebooks, and nursing practice reinforced them. They were what Jan Rodgers called 'the persistence of the Nightingale ethos'.[94]

Etiquette was a rigid system of deference to seniority. 'Etiquette was strongly instilled into us; one didn't go through a door before anybody more senior. Since everybody was more senior at first we had to wait till last. Hands behind the back when talking to a senior was de rigueur, and in a body we stood up when senior staff came into the room.'[95] A nurse's notebook from Wellington Hospital in the 1940s added: 'Do not use colloquial expressions such as: Righto, alright, O.K. Instead say either yes or very well, followed by Sister or nurse as the case may be. Excuse yourself if passing a senior in the corridor. Stand back if necessary. Never stand talking in groups in the corridor.'[96] Clearly some nurses forgot. A memo was circulated around the hospital reminding nurses that they 'must walk *quietly* through the Hospital Corridors. There must be no talking, laughing or loitering whilst in the corridors. This applies particularly to large groups when coming to and returning from Lectures, and when returning to the Nurses' Home via the Main Corridor after attending Pictures and other places of entertainment in the late evening.'[97]

Rules of etiquette also applied within the nurses' home. At many hospitals nurses were seated at meals according to seniority. Sandra Chisholm (later Main), who started at Waikato Hospital in 1929, noted: 'There would be two sittings and you'd have to get your meal finished in 20 minutes because as soon as the seniors rose everyone had to go too. That was where I learned to eat quickly. Unless you ate quickly, you left the table hungry.'[98] At Wairoa, Dorothy Scammell went to second breakfast and dinner 'along with others of lowly status'. She enjoyed the informality. At breakfast it meant she had 'a good run-down of the hospital scene and learned a few things not to do'. In the half-hour allotted, however, she also had to make her bed and tidy her room, which would be inspected later by the home sister, and change her uniform. 'Everyone said, "You're late," when you returned to the ward.' Occasionally, though, the matron would come to the second tea. She enjoyed a captive, attentive audience for her war stories. 'We didn't mind, as she relaxed and told a story with plenty of gory detail, which turned one off the mutton stew even more.

Sometimes she got lost in the narrative, making us late getting back to the ward where, of course, we "stopped a blast" from Sister or Staff Nurse.'[99] Mealtimes were also a chance for inspection by the matron. Margaret Macnab at Christchurch noted that 'if anyone had failed to wash off her lipstick before getting into uniform she was sent back to do just that or to make some adjustment to her appearance or person if that was not considered suitable to her calling.'[100]

Nursing ethics in this period were the rules of conduct that guided nurses' relations with patients, doctors, hospitals, the public and the profession.[101] A patient's affairs should not be discussed. Nurses should be loyal to doctors, which meant carrying out their prescribed treatments correctly and promptly, accurately reporting the patient's condition, and not discussing doctors with others. A nurse was also expected to show loyalty to the hospital and conduct herself in a way that brought credit on it. To the public, who were her employers – especially in private case nursing – she should provide efficient service. High fees demanded a high standard. Responsibility to the profession meant she should be loyal and work to advance the cause of nursing through NZTNA membership.[102] A state final examination paper in 1921 asked candidates to write a brief essay on nursing ethics. One candidate's answer, later used as an exemplar, began by saying it could be summed up in three words – 'refinement, insight and common sense'. Similarly, an article in 1925 summarised it as 'refinement, understanding and common sense'. It is likely both were drawn from a common (but unidentified) source.[103]

Nurses' relations with colleagues were mixed. When Mary Clark started at Taumarunui Hospital in 1933, the matron was Mary O'Connor, who had been a hospital ship sister in World War I, so the hospital was 'run on military lines with the name of Florence Nightingale being often evoked'. The strict hierarchy meant that answering back to a senior was 'definitely out. One stood meekly with hands behind one's back and simply "took it". Doctors ... were half a degree behind God. Even Sisters and Matron had to stand respectfully with them.'[104] If the ward sister was unavailable, the most senior nurse had to accompany a doctor or matron on a ward round. Marjorie Chambers was 'pretty frightened' the first time she had to do this. 'It was essential to know every patient's name and condition. It was lucky we didn't have to do this duty when we were very junior – we would have been useless.'[105] When the sister of the children's ward came back from breakfast one day in 1947, she found a small boy with a 'large pillow stuffed down the front of his dressing gown, going from bed to bed'. When asked what he was doing, he said, 'I'm the Matron,

Sister', and did a round of the ward, 'stopping at the end of every bed to say "Good morning, little boy, and how are you this morning?"'[106]

The timing of the doctor's round was the goal for completing all the morning tasks. 'You would have thought God was coming,' said Joan Loeber.[107] Dorothy Scammell described the doctor's round as a 'ceremonious procession', with an attentive sister and two nurses following the doctor and holding the patients' charts. 'As soon as this daily royal procession was over, everyone heaved a sigh of relief. A general clamour for urgently needed bedpans followed immediately, then a general tidying up.'[108]

Most nurses appreciated the way doctors shared their knowledge, although some could be boring lecturers. Bridget Ristori said a poor one could make you fall asleep even if they were describing Florence Nightingale's adventures in the Crimean War.[109] The medical superintendent as Masterton Hospital was a 'brilliant man', but to keep awake during his lectures she read the romantic novel *The Sheik* under cover of her desk.[110] Some doctors went beyond lectures to help nurses learn, inviting them to their homes for extra group tutorials and, in Ristori's case, marking her answers to past examination questions published in *Kai Tiaki* as she prepared for her state final examination.[111]

The curriculum, textbooks and lectures also made explicit an expected code of behaviour, sometimes described as womanly qualities and elevated to 'virtues' by nurses' moral obligation to demonstrate them while attending the sick. In 1925, in the Christchurch Hospital magazine, a nurse addressed her colleagues: 'Recall to your mind the horror in which you first read over the "Nurse" chapter in your "Millicent". What a feeling of despair it evoked at the time … Even though you may be moderately virtuous, the list of added virtues which a woman, as a nurse, must possess is of terrifying length.' The 'Millicent' was the textbook *A Complete System of Nursing*, by Millicent Ashdown, which identified 21 virtues. However, in an address to the nurses at Wellington Hospital in 1926, Dr Malcolm MacEachern, director of the American College of Surgeons, said that from time to time he had 'jotted down' the qualities required for a 'perfect nurse', and after three years he had 65 on the list.[112] Thankfully, he did not recite them.

The most frequently identified virtues were punctuality, obedience, method, keen observance, loyalty and economy (mainly for the benefit of the hospital and management of nursing care), sympathy, gentleness, tact, courtesy, cheerfulness, kindness tempered with firmness and quietness (for the patient's benefit). Nurses were also exhorted to be even-tempered, dignified, truthful, reliable and careful. Other virtues included in some but not all textbooks were patience, generosity, tenderness, a sense of proportion and a sense of humour.[113] The public awareness of these expected qualities in nurses is evident from their frequent mention in letters of reference from teachers, doctors and ministers of religion for applicants for nursing training.[114]

Although this code of virtues was prominent in the nursing culture, these qualities were not tested in the final examinations, as Agnes Innes noted in 1928: 'There is no evaluation of the degree of sympathy, patience, tolerance of monotonous routine, punctuality, rectitude, economy,' she said. A nurse who possessed them could fail, while another who lacked them could pass well owing to 'greater self-assurance and facility of expression'. She thought the reports nurses received at the end of their rotation on each ward should form perhaps 75 percent of the final mark.[115] It was certainly the ward sister who assessed a nurse's demonstration, or lack, of any virtues and noted it in her report.

The reports were intended to help the nurse learn and correct her faults, but supervising nurses could be harsh. Rose Macdonald, matron at Napier Hospital from 1912 to 1930, noted in her register of the hospital's sisters that one was 'inclined to be rather hard with nurses', though she was 'a splendid manager'.[116] An anonymous critic of nurse training in 1936 said that 'in no other job, factory, school, office or shop are girls spoken to so rudely, unreasonably, even cruelly, as in nursing. A probationer in tears is a common sight'.[117] As one junior nurse said, 'Many a Nightingale has taken up work in a biscuit factory or an office because of the hectoring attitude of her seniors.'[118]

Introducing a New Zealand nursing culture

Nursing history reinforced the idea of a professional nursing culture. Edith Tennent, matron of Dunedin Hospital, called for its inclusion in the curriculum at a matrons' conference in 1929. She was already giving lectures based on an American history of international nursing.[119] From the mid-1930s, nursing history became a curriculum subject.

Studying nursing history, nurses were told, would save them from a narrow outlook that could blind them to significant current events which could affect their careers. It would help them recognise that the struggle of progress was centuries long, always hard and often bitter, and that history repeated itself and could have valuable lessons. And by studying the lives of nursing pioneers, they would gain a better understanding of the spirit and ideals of nursing.[120]

History lectures covered the 'primitive period' of nursing in Greek and Roman times (including mythological figures like Hygeia and Panacea, and 'early nursing saints' like Phoebe and Fabiola), medieval monastery hospitals and a 'dark period' that was the time of Charles Dickens' fictional Betsy Prig and Sairey Gamp, relieved only by Florence Nightingale and nursing reform. This narrative positioned New Zealand nurses as descendants of a long nursing lineage. The lectures also covered aspects of New Zealand nursing that were very much in line with those that Lambie had addressed in her historical account: the development of different branches of nursing, nursing registration and regulatory bodies, New Zealand's place in the international context, and key figures like Grace Neill, Hester Maclean, Jessie Bicknell and Mary Lambie.[121] The nurses' notebooks had notes obviously written from dictation (as indicated by spelling mistakes) but also contained cyclostyled pages, probably copied from material sent from the Department of Health. In 1945 the 10 curriculum hours assigned to nursing history remained the same, but the content was altered slightly to 'arouse interest in the growth of the profession and to develop ideals rather than merely give out facts'.[122]

Nurses often brought this history to life through pageants. The inspiration came from one staged in London in 1911 to highlight the importance of nursing and gain support for the (unsuccessful) bid for nursing registration legislation. The pageant featured a parade of figures who had nursed the sick through the ages, each addressing the central figure of Hygeia. The voluminous script was published in the *British Journal of Nursing* and reprinted over two issues of *Kai Tiaki*.[123] New Zealand nurses enthusiastically presented a much-abbreviated version with New Zealand features grafted on. Pageants were popular at graduation ceremonies, for recruitment drives and to raise funds for patriotic or other causes.[124] In 1940, when the graduating class of the country's Post Graduate School for Nurses performed a pageant, each nurse also presented the school with a large doll dressed to represent the figure she had played. These were circulated on request to any branch of the professional association to use for recruitment and were often displayed in the window of an obliging department store, along with a life-size mannequin of a modern nurse, as a 'Cavalcade of Nursing'.[125]

In 1936 the live pageant formed part of an international fair at the Auckland Town Hall. The newspaper reporter was impressed by the way it showed that nursing went further back than Nightingale, and that it included the New Zealand innovation of Plunket nursing. Coupled with the fact that New Zealand had the world's lowest infant mortality rate (an often-repeated claim), the pageant revealed 'that in some respects at least this small Dominion can lead the world'.[126]

Nurse training therefore inculcated and shaped a nursing culture that reflected both internationally accepted ideas about the modern nurse and distinctly New Zealand features. In this way it was both transnational and local.

CHAPTER 3

Becoming a New Zealand nurse

The experiences of two nurses who trained at Dunedin Hospital, both named Nancy, show the difference between ease and struggle in training as a nurse. Ward sisters' reports about them briefly mentioned skills and knowledge but focused mainly on their demonstration of the 'code of virtues' – the crux of *becoming* a nurse.

Nancy Scott came from the Tahora sheep station near Gisborne and started training at Dunedin Hospital on 1 November 1927, at the age of 19. She had had no previous occupation other than domestic duties and wanted a profession she could use in the future. She applied to Dunedin Hospital because her cousin had trained there. Her ward reports over the next three years consistently listed an exemplary range of virtues. She was professional, respectful, willing, interested, thorough, conscientious, utterly dependable, helpful to juniors and in the running of the ward, and she could be trusted to manage operating theatre cases by herself. She gave ungrudging service, and nothing seemed to be a trouble. She had a charming manner with patients, was cheerful, kind but firm, quiet and tactful, and unfailingly won their liking and confidence. She was clearly the ideal nurse.

Before a nurse could sit the state final examination, the matron had to write to the chief nurse to confirm that the candidate had completed the required training hours and rotations, passed the hospital final examination and shown that if she passed the state final examination she was worthy of being registered as a nurse. Edith Tennent, the Dunedin Hospital matron, began her report on Nancy Scott by saying: 'It would be impossible to speak too highly of Nurse Scott's nursing ability and manner of dealing with patients.' She summarised the ward sisters' comments and added: 'She is the most outstanding nurse that has passed through this hospital for some years.' Nancy Scott passed the examination with honours in December 1930 and became a registered nurse. After only a year as a staff nurse, she was promoted to ward sister. At the end of August 1933 she resigned as she was about to marry Dr Raymond Kirk.[1]

One month later Nancy Newman began her training at the hospital, also at the age of 19. She lived in South Dunedin with her two sisters, her mother and her father, who was a railway official. After leaving high school at the age of 15, she had studied at the Barth Pianoforte School of Music in Dunedin for four years and earned her piano teacher's diploma. Beatrice Barth, who ran the school with her three sisters, considered her conscientious, enthusiastic, painstaking and always anxious to do her best. These comments were not predictive of her progress through nurse training, in which she continually struggled but was determined to succeed. Each ward sister commented that her work when she started on the ward was not satisfactory but noted her improvement by the end. As in her piano training, she was willing and worked to the best of her ability – it was just that she required continual supervision and correction. This was partly due to her forgetfulness. She had to be reminded to do things but then did them in the way she had been taught. Overall, therefore, although she struggled, she showed determined and continual improvement.

From mid-1936 the Dunedin ward reports included a mark out of 100, with nursing technique worth 35 and the virtues of reliability, cheerfulness, willingness, helpfulness, interest, carefulness, economy and professional attitude to others worth the remaining 65. Of the total 100 marks, Newman's hovered between 64 and 69, which was considered fair to good, but in June 1937 she failed the state final examination. In the next few weeks, however, everything seemed to gel. In July, although she lacked confidence, her work was generally regarded as satisfactory. In October, she was assigned to the isolation ward, which demanded scrupulous attention to detail to avoid cross-infection. Her report said she carried out her duties well and showed a keen interest in her work. Her mark was a resounding 80.

Significantly, throughout her training, the main virtues mentioned in her reports related to the patients' care. Ward sisters consistently noted that she was cheerful, pleasant, kind, considerate, very good to patients and very popular among them. This was the core of becoming a nurse, and Newman achieved her goal. In December 1937 she reattempted and passed the state final examination and became a registered nurse. Her subsequent appointment as a staff nurse in the Casualty Department was a vote of confidence. Jessie Tomlinson, who succeeded Tennent as matron, noted that Newman's work there was very satisfactory: she was orderly, showed attention to detail and was capable in emergencies. Newman resigned in April 1938 to take up private nursing.[2]

Starting training

The reasons applicants gave for wanting to train as a nurse reflected the public perception of the nursing culture as well as their individual motives.[3] Nurses gave service to others. Nursing was noble, unselfish work that relieved the suffering of the sick. It was a worthy and useful life. Some applicants cited war as an impetus for training. Emily Mathias, who applied in 1915, noted that one of her brothers had 'given his life to his country', and three others were at the front. She was very keen to do her share. She felt she would be helping trained nurses get to Egypt by taking their place in the hospital.[4] Other applicants were following a family tradition, with mothers, aunts, cousins or sisters who were nurses. Many stated that they had wanted to be a nurse from childhood, sometimes because they had been in hospital themselves and had admired the nurses. A number had to wait a long time for home circumstances to change before they could apply, as they had been needed on the farm or in the family business, or helped at home with domestic work and cared for younger children or a sick mother. It was not until a younger sister finished her schooling that an older one could hand over the domestic duties and leave home. Conversely, Frances and Grace Bretherton of Wairere, Waipawa, aged 25 and 22, applied in March 1915 because there was no longer enough at home for three sisters to do. Two brothers had left home so there were fewer people to take care of, and another sister would soon finish her schooling. They thought it advisable to earn their own living. Grace said her brothers thought she was 'first class' at keeping house, a noteworthy point because 'brothers don't spare compliments on their sisters'. They applied to train in Dunedin as one brother worked in the Public Trust office there. He wrote to the matron that his sisters were good workers with 'brains and enthusiasm'. They were accepted.[5]

The application process was not always straightforward. Some applicants were considered too short and had to hope they would grow taller and be able to reapply. Some boosted their credentials by working in a private hospital first, even though this experience would not count towards their training time. During application interviews matrons made quick judgements about candidates' physical and social suitability. Rose Macdonald, the matron at Napier Hospital, jotted brief comments in her applications register. Applicants could be rejected as 'too delicate', 'not particularly tidy looking' or just 'unsuitable'. One in 1913 was rejected because she had 'for some years acted in the capacity of Barmaid in different hotels in N.Z.'. Those accepted were 'refined', looked 'strong and capable' or seemed 'bright'. Well over half of all applicants, both Māori and Pākehā, were accepted. Several had previously been employed as shop assistant, governess, office worker, lady's help, dressmaker, domestic servant, children's nurse or dental assistant.[6] Nurses' motives could sometimes be questioned. Janet Moore, who started at Dunedin Hospital in 1904, had to appear before the board as part of her application process. 'Can you work?' asked the chairman. 'If you think you are going there to eat chocolates and flirt with the [medical] students you are very much mistaken.'[7]

Applicants of course worded their statements to maximise their chances of acceptance. Nurses' memoirs and oral reminiscences often gave more personal reasons for entering the profession, which they would not have volunteered to their prospective matron. Edna Pengelly decided on nursing as a career because she had successfully 'splinted a rooster's leg and painted the throat of a hen which had croup' on the small poultry farm she and her mother ran near Levin. She was accepted at Wellington Hospital in 1904.[8] Sandra Chisholm (later Main) wanted to be a nurse because of the stories she heard from her aunt, Alexandra Keddie, who trained at Timaru Hospital from 1900 to 1904. Chisholm knew that her aunt used to get another nurse to look after her ward so she could slip out to the park with one of the doctors. By the time Chisholm started training at Waikato Hospital in 1929 her aunt was the matron, with a reputation as a disciplinarian. Perhaps Chisholm relished knowing those stories.[9]

Some applicants just wanted to get away from home. The fact that accommodation was provided in a nurses' home overcame some parental objections. Phyllis Wright (later Streeter) was captivated by the stories of the four nurses in her mother's family, to the extent that she went against her father's wish for her to become a teacher and in 1947, aged 20, started training at Christchurch Hospital.[10] Audrey Dawson (later Gilbert), who grew up on a farm near Kaitāia, greatly admired a local district health nurse, Ina Miller (later Ferguson). 'I would see this angel of mercy going about and oh, I wanted to be like her!' But it was the prospect of wartime manpowering that gave her the final nudge to apply. Manpowering, introduced in 1942, was a form of civilian conscription. Women could be directed to work in particular traditional and nontraditional occupations to ensure an adequate supply of labour in priority areas. Manpowering could also be used to prevent those already employed in essential work from changing to another occupation.[11] Dawson anticipated that if she started nurse training, she would not be forced into another line of work. She trained at Auckland Hospital.[12] In contrast, Mabel Kewene had not wanted to be a nurse at all, but in 1942 she was manpowered into working as a hospital aide at Costley Home (later part of Greenlane Hospital), and the matron saw her potential. Within six weeks she had started her nurse training.[13] It seemed to Joyce Speirs, who started at Southland Hospital in 1943, that many in her class of 16 would not have been there without the 'likelihood of being manpowered into some undesirable occupation'.[14]

Subterfuge was sometimes apparent in parts of the application process and was not always the nurse's doing. When Marian Thorp applied to Wellington Hospital in 1908, her father arranged for a testimonial from a fellow member of the Wairarapa Hospital Board, Alexander Hogg, MP for Masterton, who had never met her.[15] Bridget Ristori was able to start at Masterton Hospital in 1920 because her 'auntie', Mabel Beetham of the Brancepeth estate, had fibbed to the matron that Ristori was 20 years old, although she was barely 18. Ristori was willing to 'forfeit two years' of her life and skip to being 20 in order to start. The Beethams' doctor 'obligingly produced' the required medical certificate for her, sight unseen.[16] In Taumarunui, Mary Clark's doctor, Welby Fisher, checked her suitability for nursing in 1933 'in a somewhat unorthodox manner'. He had her hold a kidney dish while he lanced a patient's breast abscess and 'released a cascade of pus into the dish'. On the basis of her response to this unexpected event, he then wrote a 'good letter of recommendation'.[17]

The start of nurse training was a rite of passage. New trainees were suddenly separated from family and secluded in a nurses' home. They had to struggle with a strange uniform, strict etiquette, new language and the alien environment of a hospital ward. When Dorothy Scammell was offered a place at Wairoa Hospital in 1929, she was full of doubts about going so far away from her family. Her

Sister Edna Pengelly was in charge of the nurses' home at Wellington Hospital, 1910. Nurses learned (but did not always observe) clear rules of etiquette and discipline.
Author's collection

mother, who was 'made of sterner stuff', urged her to accept. A week later Scammell was in the 'back seat of a bone-shaking old service car, sandwiched between two large Maori men eating crayfish out of newspaper, on the long, dusty, hot, winding road over the hills to Wairoa.'[18] Ristori arrived at Masterton Hospital in grander style, in the Beethams' car, 'with family crest upon the door and chauffeur in uniform at the wheel'. With this ostentatious start, her new colleagues felt she would not last. They did not realise she was orphaned, penniless and obliged to work in order to live. She was shy and 'smoked cigarettes furiously all the first evening. I felt it was the smart thing to do. I was violently sick.' In her diary she noted: 'Moral – Don't try to swank.'[19]

New trainees were met by the home sister, shown to their rooms, instructed in the rules of the home and fitted for uniforms if they had not been required to bring them. Uniforms were worn for practical reasons but their design was a matter of nursing and hospital culture. Rank was signified by the uniform's colour, by stripes or stars added to cap, sleeve or epaulette, or by the style of cap or veil. From the 1880s the uniform dress was long, usually with deep pockets, covered with a full white apron and finished with a belt and a stiff white collar and cuffs. 'The collars were murderous things,' said Edna Pengelly, 'almost cutting our throats.'[20] Marjorie Chambers, starting at Christchurch in 1936, commented that new nurses 'didn't know how to fix a stiff collar so that it didn't chafe around the neck or stand out absurdly at the back, or how to arrange a flat thing into a nurse's cap. It had to be pulled up at the back with a tape and no-one told us to wet the tape first.'[21] Christchurch retained its traditional uniform, just shortening the hemline somewhat over time, but other hospitals changed to an all-in-one uniform without an apron. At Auckland Hospital in 1949, Colleen Turbet wore a short-sleeved, starched white duty uniform that opened with detachable buttons down the front left side, a wide starched belt (cinched in as much as possible, as 'tiny waists were much admired'), heavy white lisle stockings and white lace-up shoes. Her hair was completely covered with a white cloth triangle, knotted at the back or, in the style of Land Girls (wartime agricultural workers), knotted at the top of the head. For dress occasions and for walking to and from the ward she wore a long-sleeved blue uniform, a blue woollen cape and a starched white cap.[22]

Hair was supposed to be covered. In his 1906 report Dr Duncan MacGregor, inspector of hospitals, complained that the nurse's cap had 'shrunk into a small piece of starched linen crowning an edifice of pads and loose hair'. Wellington Hospital, under Matron Frances Keith Payne, was exempt from this criticism, as the nurses there were 'neat and tidy'.²³ A hairstyle was one way for nurses to express individuality despite the requirement of uniformity, and in ensuing decades Wellington nurses were also complicit in evading rules. In the wartime 1940s nurses favoured their screen idols' hairstyles. Circulated notices instructed them that 'dressing the hair in the style that prevails at present must be discontinued', as it was 'unprofessional and unhygienic'. Hair needed to be covered, and a hairnet could 'prevent it falling loosely about the neck'. The matron in chief, Blanche Clark, threatened that 'unless nurses themselves take more pride in adhering to this regulation other measures will have to be adopted'.²⁴ The problem seemed widespread. An editorial in the *New Zealand Nursing Journal* in 1943 noted that after an hour or so in a busy ward, the curls and drape of nurses' hair 'suffered disarrangement and the consequent untidiness has destroyed any impression there may have been of smartness and efficiency'.²⁵

The first day on the ward was another rite of passage, often a shocking one. The home sister at Christchurch in 1920 'prodded and poked' Margaret Macnab into her 'crackling uniform' and sent her off to Ward 10.²⁶ Dorothy Scammell at Wairoa in 1929 was greeted by a 'tall angular nurse in a blue uniform' who said, 'Come on, Pro. You're in my ward, and we're full as hell.' For the next hour she was in the ward kitchen, 'slicing and buttering unbelievably large piles of bread'. No one told her what to do with it until an ambulant patient ('those angels in disguise') came to her rescue, saying, 'I'll show you the ropes.' Feeling 'out of place and very new and self-conscious in the unfamiliar cap and uniform', she handed out the trays of food. The patients 'teased and chaffed good-naturedly, trying, I think, to make me feel at ease'.²⁷ Even for nurses starting in a preliminary training school, the first visit to a ward was sobering. Marjorie Chambers had not known what to expect: she had 'never before seen so many very ill-looking people all together', and it upset her 'considerably for quite a long time'.²⁸ Joan Boyle (later Loeber), also at Christchurch in the 1930s, felt the same. 'I was petrified! I'd never been in a hospital, I'd never seen anyone sick, and all of a sudden I began to wonder what I'd done. However, you were kept so busy, there was something happening all the time that you didn't have time, really, to worry.'²⁹

The camaraderie of the nurses' home also helped. Entertainment consisted of going to the shops, a film or a tea room; picnics, walks or bicycle rides; or visits to the local swimming pool. When Amy Rickman at Auckland Hospital came off night duty, she and a few friends would 'go to the Parnell Baths while we were waiting for breakfast'. There was also a tennis court on the nurses' home roof.³⁰ These were inexpensive activities that could be fitted into limited off-duty time. For quiet relaxation, nurses read novels reviewed in *Kai Tiaki*. Those featuring nurses received close scrutiny, not always to the author's advantage. 'We nurses can rarely recognise ourselves as we appear in fiction,' said one review.[31] Flirtations and free-and-easy use of nicknames in *The Night Nurse* between a senior nurse and doctor, said another review, would not be found in a well-disciplined and well-conducted hospital. 'It would more likely be the frivolous flighty nurse and the irresponsible junior resident who would so act.'[32] Nevertheless, Bridget Ristori enjoyed reading it.[33]

The nurses' home also provided opportunity to debrief after a hard duty. 'One of our greatest pleasures,' said Marjorie Chambers, 'was to collect in someone's room and talk our heads off. This with lots of laughter and a good giggle, was very good for us, if rather noisy for other people. It was a natural way to let off steam.'[34] Similarly, Colleen Turbet noted that they would 'pile into each other's rooms and let the worries of the evening go as we swapped stories and occasionally smoked a fag.'[35]

Nurses prized a cheap seat in the pit or 'the gods' at a concert, play or film. For Edith Lewis, who began training at Wanganui Hospital in 1904, entertainment when nurses were feeling 'very affluent' was 'a seat in the pit to see a play at the Opera House. When a benefactor invited us there, one evening dress between four of us and a black velvet cloak with a different lining which we could alternate by turning, rang a change.'[36] Dorothy Scammell at Wairoa noted that 'if you had time, had done your swot and lectures, were not on call, or just plain "fagged out", there was plenty going on', including 'shopping when payday came round, Saturday night dances, and "the pictures". Nurses flocked to any film with their favourite stars. 'We sat in the cheapest seats, munched lollies out of a bag, and drooled wide-eyed over Greta Garbo or Ronald Coleman.' Ristori went regularly to the Masterton cinema in the early 1920s and jotted brief comments in her diary. *Sporting Life*, *Bars of Iron* and *The Mark of Zorro*, for example, were 'absolutely top hole', *Peck's Bad Boy* was 'topping', Rudolph Valentino in *The Sheik* was 'lovely' and *Omar Khayyam* was 'ripping' and had 'most gorgeous scenery'. When she passed the state final examination as equal holder of the coveted Top of the Dominion position, she celebrated by seeing the play *My Lady's Dress* ('very good'). Dorothy Trim, who trained at Southland Hospital from 1941 to 1944, remembered 'the joy of sitting in the gods of the Civic Theatre listening to J.C. Williamson's drama and opera from Australia, and rushing out from tea to get the tram into the city, hoping that the queue for the gods would not be too long and that the rain should stay away.'[37] Invitations were also plentiful. At Wairoa, the nurses' home phone 'rang constantly as the local lads sought dates for Saturday night pictures.'[38]

Nurses took full advantage of their days off. Here a group pose as bathing belles at Lyall Bay, Wellington, in the 1930s. Mavis Attree album, author's collection

Nurses and doctors were out in full force on the opening night of *Exit Sir Derek* in Christchurch in October 1935. The play was Dr Henry Jellett's dramatisation of the novel *The Nursing Home Murder*, which the New Zealand detective fiction writer Ngaio Marsh had written in collaboration with Jellett, her gynaecologist, who supplied the medical details.[39] It featured the murder of a patient during an operation. The cast included three nurses – the competent matron, the victim's spurned lover and the 'bolshie' radical political activist (who helpfully 'proclaimed her "red" sympathies' by wearing a red check suit and red jumper and carrying a bright red umbrella).[40] While Marsh was producing the play, Jellett provided precise instructions in half-page, clipped-on additions to the script to show her how the actors should manage the surgical 'operation'.[41] He also placed a registered nurse in the wings to prepare the 'patient' and supervise the operation process, and he released sweet-smelling ether into the air for authenticity. Despite his perfectionist approach, the first performance had mishaps. A surgeon retrieved his dropped glove from the operating theatre floor in violation of aseptic protocols, and the operation's realism caused an audience member to scream and faint. She was carried out of the auditorium with difficulty.[42]

Nurse training could be overwhelming, and the attrition rate was high. When Audrey Dawson saw a surgical patient returning from theatre with 'wicked looking' tongue forceps in a bowl beside them, she was 'quite ready to make back for the farm'. Her Aunt Myrtle, who lived in Auckland, rebuked her. 'Goodness girl,' she said, 'go back and get on with it.' So she did.[43] However, according to Margaret McDougall's study of Wellington Hospital nursing registers for the years 1916–25, of the 375 nurses in training during that period, only 255 (68 percent) completed the course. This statistic was comparable with retention rates at other hospitals, including those in Britain. For 31 percent of those who left, no reason was recorded, but 23 percent left in order to get married, 18 percent because of ill-health, 9 percent failed examinations and 6 percent left for family reasons. The remainder left because they were going overseas, did not like the work or feel strong enough for it, were deemed unsuitable or not strong enough, were dismissed for dishonesty, or died.[44] Although Dunedin Hospital applicants had to sign a statement that they would be free from family responsibilities for four years, parents still expected a daughter to return to care for a sick family member. Many did, and had to make up the missed training time.[45]

Training folklore

The folklore of training was a strong feature of the nursing culture. Across different settings and different decades nurses told the same stories, which emphasised a loss of innocence through intimate tasks or shocking encounters with bodily dejecta, or they reinforced the virtues of efficiency and obedience by illustrating forgivable and unforgivable mistakes and misdemeanours.

A common story was of a very new trainee being asked for 'a bottle' by a male patient confined to bed. The naïve nurse did not realise he was using the colloquial term for a urinal, a metal or thick glass container. Instead, much to his surprise or annoyance, she brought a container of water or a hot water bottle. It was a story always told by the nurse against herself. Alexandra Keddie, for example, told her niece Sandra Chisholm about her mistake. It had taken her 15 minutes to fill and test the temperature of the hot water bottle. When she came back, the patient (by then probably desperate) had said, 'Oh, you fool of a girl.'[46] The story perhaps prevented Chisholm from making the same mistake. On Bridget Ristori's first day she wondered why the patient had asked for a bottle, as it was rather a hot day. She obligingly fetched him a hot water bottle. She thought his retort of 'not that sort' was rather rude, or perhaps he was being facetious. Was it a beer bottle he wanted? 'He assured me it was not. I was annoyed. I hadn't got all day to listen to foolish requests. I marched off and left him to call another nurse.'[47] Even when the request had been explained to them, some new trainees were embarrassed. 'It was many a day before I could deliver these articles, when requested, in an impersonal, nonchalant manner,' said Dorothy Scammell.[48]

Another jolt from innocence centred on nurses' unexpected and confronting encounters with bodily wastes. Dealing with faeces and sputum could be disgusting, but these tasks were commonplace. It was the unexpected encounter that formed the basis of this type of folktale. A tuberculosis patient's haemorrhage or haemoptysis from a coughing fit was sudden, spectacular and shocking. For Colleen Turbet it was 'sheer horror' being with a patient 'who suddenly coughed up huge amounts of blood all against the white sheets. How the ward went silent when it happened.'[49] Sonja Davies, nursing tubercular patients, 'never got used to the massive froth of red blood pouring from them in a seemingly endless tide.'[50] Elizabeth Will (later Woodward), on her first day on a ward at Waikato Hospital in 1949, was being shown the ropes by Gertie Rushton, who was 'a good nurse' but 'slightly hyper and enthusiastic and rushed round and chatted the whole time and pulled me hither and yon'. A patient had had a pulmonary haemorrhage and 'in the sluice room Gertie said, "Look at this!" and showed me a tumbler full of blood. She said, "Isn't that interesting? She coughed that all up from her lungs!"' For Will, the rest of the day was a daze.[51]

The contrast of red blood against white sheets created a superstition against placing red and white flowers in the same vase. When Colleen Turbet placed her attractive flower arrangement in the centre of another ward, the distressed ward sister ordered her to take it away at once, saying they would be sure to have a haemorrhage.[52]

Sonja Davies, on her first day in a ward at Wellington Hospital in November 1941, was shocked by the definition and disposal of waste. A busy senior nurse tending a patient thrust a kidney dish into Davies' hands and told her to wrap up the contents and take them to the incinerator. She reached the sluice room before realising that it was a foetus. 'It took me ages to find courage to wrap it in the Evening Post and start down the corridor on the way to the incinerator. I kept thinking, "I just can't do it." Finally, when I was a jabbering wreck, it was taken from me and I was pointed in the direction of the ward. Back there, I was descended on by Sister who bawled me out for wasting time when patients were needing bedpans.'[53] On another occasion Davies was the 'unlucky afternoon junior' who was told to bath an itinerant man just admitted to the medical ward. They 'eyed each other' while she filled the bath. 'As he undressed I saw a filthy bandage on his leg and on removing it found his varicose ulcers were alive with wriggling maggots. He watched them with fascination while I vomited into the sluice – and then pulled myself together and dealt with the situation.'[54]

One recurring tale involved a nurse being handed a patient's amputated leg in the operating theatre. The weight of the leg was startling. For Colleen Turbet it was an 'unnerving moment'.[55] Dorothy Scammell was told to hold a man's leg as it was amputated. 'When the saw went through the bone it was a near thing for me,' she said, 'and I still feel the leg as it dropped in the bucket.' This was an imprinted memory. While waiting to start her nurse training, Sue Coleman (later Greenstreet) worked as an aide in a private hospital in Grafton run by her mother's friend. The staff tried to help her understand what nursing was about, so she observed an amputation in the operating theatre. The sister handed her the leg in a towel and told her to take it away. 'She did not say where, so I went to the kitchen to ask the cook, who said perhaps the broom cupboard would be best until the matron came back.' When the matron returned and saw the leg, she told Coleman to bury it in the garden. Carrying it around the garden, she finally found a suitable spot behind the gladioli. For the rest of her life, seeing gladioli reminded her of burying the leg.[56] In a variation of this tale, Colleen Turbet, while working night duty, went to get an intravenous drip stand out of a cupboard and 'out rolled a leg. I thought it was part of a body and screamed at the top of my voice before I realised it was a wooden one.'[57]

Some folktales recounted mistakes. The story of the flooded steriliser was extremely common. As it was the result of overwork and therefore forgivable, the story was easily told by the nurse against herself. The sluice room steriliser was a large stainless steel tub-like contraption with a hinged lid and a heating element in the base. It was used to boil a load of bowls and kidney dishes, or bedpans and urinals. The junior nurse loaded the steriliser then turned on the water to fill it. As this took a long time, she would go to do another of her many tasks while it was filling or be called to help another nurse. The ensuing flood was not noticed until water seeped out into the ward or leaked through the floor into a ward below. The familiarity with this commonplace error is reflected in a tongue-in-cheek 'helpful hints' article in a hospital nurses' magazine, which said: 'When filling the sterilizer, depart to parts unknown. Someone undoubtedly needs exercise to mop up the result.'[58]

Another forgivable mishap occurred when an overburdened nurse carried a tray of food across the highly polished floors. The junior nurse would be hurrying to get meals out to a ward of 30 or so patients. Sandra Chisholm, for example, carried 'great, big, tin trays' which took 'six big porridge plates. Well, the floors in those wards were very slippery and took a bit of getting used to when you were starting. I hadn't been there very long and was taking out my porridge on my tray and I slipped under a bed. Fortunately, the tray and contents remained intact in my lap under the bed. I think the patients were more perturbed than I was.'[59] Joyce Speirs, starting at Dee Street Hospital in Invercargill in 1943, 'set off with about 12 glasses of milk on a large heavy wooden tray. Just inside the ward my feet went from under me and I was flat on my back with a lake of milk and glasses in all directions. The glasses were thick and only dignity was hurt.'[60] A variation of this tale was told by Anne McDonald, training at Wellington Hospital from 1945. For her the problem was carrying equipment to the bedside to wash patients before breakfast. To save time nurses partially filled a basin with hot water, put a tooth mug in a bowl, placed these items in the basin and stacked another two full sets on top. 'You learnt to carry two or three, all with hot water, you could stack them up. Sometimes you slipped, and it all went, you were saturated. Couldn't do anything about that. Just went on till you dried out. But it was like that, it was race, race, race, from start to finish.'[61]

A more serious mistake, one that signified inefficiency or even incompetence, related to dentures. As it depicted a failure of common sense, it was inevitably told about other nurses. Because so many patients in that period had dentures, the junior nurse on a busy ward would be scrambling to clean them each morning. In her haste she would collect them all in, scrub them all together in the sluice room sink, and then have the perturbing task of trying to determine which dentures formed a pair and which sets belonged to which patients. Some, in a cleaning fervour, even boiled them in the steriliser.

The commonest folktale involved the fire escape. Although trainees were relied on to act responsibly in caring for patients, even having sole charge of a ward at night, when off duty they were considered in need of supervision and constraint to ensure their health and readiness for duty. A curfew was imposed, and late passes for special occasions were restricted. For nurses, flouting this rule was an acceptable, enjoyable minor challenge to authority. Each nurses' home had its own system for sneaking in after curfew. The window to a bedroom off the fire escape was left ajar for a nurse to clamber in, a shoe was left dangling from a window so the late returner could attract the occupant's attention, or the nurse in a ground-floor bedroom would be woken up with a knock on her window to admit the latecomer. Sonja Davies regretted being allocated a room with another nurse at the end of a corridor. 'Night after night we were awoken by the muffled laughter of various colleagues being given a heave up on male shoulders into our open bedroom window. We learned to keep the space between our beds clear in order to facilitate the quiet passage of our nocturnal guests who then had to brave the corridor and avoid the night sister.'[62]

Another folktale featured the dead patient. The nurse's first encounter with death could be traumatic, but attending a dying patient, making them as comfortable as possible and laying out the body were the nurse's final acts of caring. Laying out meant carefully sponging and drying the body, lightly packing orifices if necessary, dressing the body in a long shroud with a high ruffled neck and long ruffled sleeves, lightly binding the knees and ankles together with a white gauze bandage and placing the arms at the sides or the hands on the chest. The body was then wrapped in a large mortuary sheet with the top turned down over the head, the end up over the feet and the sides tucked under in the middle, all secured with seven pins.[63] The folktale involved unexpected aspects of this process, such as the struggle to lay a body flat when the joints were stiffened by arthritis. The story of one nurse was typical. 'As she pushed his head down, his legs flew up. When she pushed his legs down his head came up. The Night Supervisor had to calm down a very unnerved

Nurses told many stories about evading curfew by means of the fire escape. These young women were at Wellington Hospital in the early 1930s. Mavis Attree is on the top step. Mavis Attree album, author's collection

young nurse and help her make the best of a very odd layout.'⁶⁴ Colleen Turbet and her friend Pat were laying out the body of an old man who had been in the merchant navy and was always cracking jokes. When they rolled his body on to its side, they were astounded to see 'on his backside a large tattooed eye complete with eyelashes and underneath the letters ICU'. They got the giggles. It was a nervous reaction, she said, and although they felt disrespectful they could not stop but tried to stifle their laughter. At least he had liked jokes and would have understood.⁶⁵

Other tales of this kind recounted trips to the morgue. Dorothy Scammell was holding the lantern while accompanying two orderlies carrying a dead body on a stretcher to the mortuary in another building. It was a 'very windy, dark night with high winds tossing the pines', so when a large branch tore off with a 'screeching wail', one frightened orderly dropped his end of the stretcher and fled. The lantern was knocked from Scammell's hand and went out, and the body rolled down the bank. Luckily the second orderly had matches, so between them they 'scrambled down the bank, retrieved the lantern and got it going again, then pulled and dragged the corpse up the slope and back onto the stretcher'. When they reached the mortuary, they found that they had lost the keys. 'There was nothing for it but to prise open the window, which was a narrow one. Being small, it was me who was hoisted up to break into a mortuary at night!'[66] At Stratford Hospital they called the mortuary trolley 'the go-cart'.[67]

Violating the code of virtues

Violations of the code of virtues could be unintentional, a form of mild boundary testing or deliberate defiance, and they were punished in proportion to intent. Unintentional mistakes were still penalised. Breaking a thermometer, for example, showed a lack of the virtues of economy and efficiency. The nurse had to present the broken instrument to the matron and often pay for a replacement, 'regardless of the carelessness of the patient'. It cost Louise Renouf, at Napier Hospital in the early 1900s, 2s 6d, which was a quarter of her week's wage.[68] Colleen Turbet committed a more personal gaffe in the operating theatre with a cantankerous surgeon who insisted upon a deadly hush. One day she broke it when one of the attachments on her suspender belt snapped and the sixpence she was using as its button rolled around and around on the floor. Under the surgeon's glare, she meekly apologised.[69]

Unwitting actions could be construed as demonstrating a lack of obedience or disrespect for the nursing hierarchy. Katharine Price at Christchurch Hospital in the 1930s felt that the newly instituted radio licences were too dear for nurses on their limited salary. She wrote to the postmaster general suggesting one licence for all radios in a building, such as a nurses' home. 'Unaware of any sword of Damocles' hanging over her head, she was called to the lady superintendent's office. Miss Grace Widdowson made it extremely clear that a mere junior nurse should not have the effrontery to write such a letter. The matter should have gone through the home sister, to the assistant matron, then to Widdowson herself, who would have referred it to the hospital board secretary for the board to discuss. Widdowson then handed her the reply letter that agreed to the single licence. Price did not recall leaving the office. In spite of Widdowson's 'withering comments', she thought that the lady superintendent 'was probably secretly much amused by the incident and admired the temerity and initiative of anyone who could take such a step and write so persuasive a letter'.[70]

The nurse who fell sick, especially if she caught a disease from a patient, was considered deficient in the virtues of efficiency, economy and carefulness. According to the 'culture of blame' in early twentieth-century nursing, the hospital nurse was responsible for her own health, and contracting an infectious illness was proof of carelessness in infection-prevention techniques. The ailing nurse was sickening, physically and figuratively. Hester Maclean, as chief nurse from 1906 to 1923, particularly blamed those who jeopardised their health through irresponsible uses of leisure time. Under Mary Lambie, chief nurse from 1931 to 1949, the culture increasingly recognised nursing as a 'hazardous profession'. Lambie's keen interest in public health, her concern about the incidence of tuberculosis among nurses and her direct involvement in international research on nurses' health led to measures to protect nurses, including regular health checks and chest X-rays. Under her leadership, a curriculum change in 1933 increased the emphasis on bacteriology, prevention of cross-infection and nurses' personal hygiene. In 1939 a new examination was introduced at the end of the first year of training to ensure nurses had gained this knowledge.[71]

Boundary testing, such as escapades involving the fire escape, was usually considered a misdemeanour. If a nurse was caught she was sent to the matron, and the punishment was usually loss of late pass privileges for a time or a stint in the sewing room making shrouds or mending sheets. If several

Nurses were at risk of contracting infectious diseases from their patients. Agnes Maud Snell died from scarlet fever and tuberculosis in 1908, before she finished her training at Wellington Hospital.
ABRR 7563 W4990/10f, Archives New Zealand

nurses were involved, however, punishment was harsher. In 1925, for example, six nurses at Wellington Hospital were dismissed when caught returning via the fire escape. They applied to the hospital board for reappointment. After a heated argument, six members felt the nurses should be reappointed as they were young and it was a first offence, but eight voted for their dismissal.[72] At the next meeting Major Edward Vine, a member who had championed the nurses' cause, argued that the curfew should be extended by an hour to 11pm. He believed that 'attendance at the picture shows was the daily curriculum of home life', as was having supper with friends in town, and besides, 'girls in New Zealand were to be trusted'.[73]

The matter was reported in many national and regional newspapers, and Hester Maclean conveyed her views in a *Kai Tiaki* editorial. The sympathy some board members had shown was 'greatly to be deprecated'. She could 'sympathise with the high spirits of youth' and realised that using the fire escape could be 'a mere exultation of spirits' that warranted only a reprimand. However, to Maclean the incident was less a matter of disobedience than proof of the dangers of too much leisure time, one of her frequent complaints about the changing conditions for nurses. How could a nurse do her work if she went on duty 'tired out by lack of proper rest?' It was disgraceful. 'Recreation is necessary but should not be indulged in to excess, and the work she has to do on duty should be the main object and interest of a nurse's day, not to be got over as quickly and easily as possible to make way for amusement.'[74]

Boundary testing also took the form of subverting the system. When the new list of ward rotation assignments came out at Christchurch Hospital, outgoing nurses supplied the new staff with a list of the next ward sister's foibles, even providing diagrams showing how she liked the table set and summing her up as a teacher, organiser and person.[75] Autoclaves, used for sterilising by pressurised steam, could also be pressed into service to make pavlovas, cook corn cobs perfectly, dry rugby jerseys and flatten buckled music records.[76] Dorothy Scammell and her friends at Wairoa Hospital in the early 1930s quickly learned how to distract their matron from disciplinary matters: she loved telling a wartime story, and the nurses 'exploited this aspect quite shamelessly to turn potential wrath away from themselves'. Scammell also used one lecture as an opportunity to gain better meals. When the medical superintendent was explaining nutrition and vitamins, one of his favourite subjects, Scammell commented that night nurses were deficient in these because they had to eat reheated leftover meals. The lecturer 'took the point enthusiastically', with the result that night nurses were supplied with fresh food.[77]

The pressure of ward work led to nurses learning shortcuts in procedures from more senior nurses. Elizabeth Will asked a colleague where she could get the dairy thermometer to test the temperature of a hot water bottle. She swiftly learned that no one ever followed this procedure. 'People were cutting corners the whole time.'[78] Marjorie Chambers at Christchurch knew that nurses learned most by 'watching and helping other people', but that sometimes they developed 'bad habits, short cuts in nursing techniques when we were all short of time and not being careful enough'.[79]

A deliberate violation of the code of ethics could be an act of defiance or sometimes a subversive act of caring. In 1940 Sonja Davies started work at Bowen Hospital in Wellington to gain experience until she was old enough to enter training. Working in a private hospital was a challenge to her 'emerging social and political conscience', and she was aware that some less well-off patients had made a real sacrifice to be there. 'When it came to flowers, the rich had many, others none. From time to time I redressed this situation, figuring that a person with fifty bouquets and posies would not miss two or three which I gave to those without any, always making sure that the original recipient had the donor's card among the huge pile on the dressing table.'[80]

Colleen Turbet disobeyed the rules in a more consequential way while at Middlemore Hospital for orthopaedic nursing experience. She nursed an elderly woman admitted from Oakley, a psychiatric hospital, who had a fractured hip that was not treated surgically. She 'lay in bed in awful pain, moaning and screaming out'. When she developed pneumonia, she was prescribed four-hourly injections of the new drug penicillin. Early forms of penicillin were difficult to press through the syringe needle into a muscle. 'It was fine for the doctor to order injections into the emaciated old lady but for us to actually give the injections was awful for we could only use one buttock. She screamed if we touched her and fought us off physically.' Turbet decided not to give the injections. 'I felt like a murderer.' Feeling unable to discuss the matter with the ward sister, she confessed to her friend, who was on night duty, and learned that she, too, had stopped giving the injections for the same reason. The patient died peacefully. 'We were full of guilt but pleased at the outcome.'[81] The nurses had acted on their own interpretation of the virtues of kindness and sympathy.

Turbet also recalled the occasion when she and her friend Pat were laying out the old seaman who had liked jokes and were overcome with giggles at the large tattooed eye on his backside. He had been full of life, regaling nurses with stories of his exploits, including romantic encounters, so as a tribute to him they used 'the rest of the gauze bandage to tie a pretty bow on his penis'. Once off duty, they 'came down to reality' and worried they would be reported for what others would see as an 'indignity' when discovered in the morgue. 'We waited in trepidation for days for the call to see Matron and our subsequent dismissal; it never came.'[82]

Some nurses deliberately violated the virtues code for their own gain. Serious offences were usually failings of obedience and honesty and were not tolerated. The cases of two particular nurses at Dunedin Hospital exemplify this view. The first involved a nurse who unsettled the ward sisters by her abruptness, lack of thoughtfulness and occasional signs of untrustworthiness. She once defied a summons to return to dust a ward after she had gone off duty, as it had been 'extremely badly done'. Instead she sent a junior with the message that she was dressed and going out. Tennent summoned her and identified this 'grave breach of discipline'. Two months later, when items and money went missing in the nurses' home, this nurse was suspected. When Tennent questioned her, she emphatically denied it. Police detectives were called in. Although they, too, felt there was strong circumstantial evidence that the nurse was responsible, they could not prove it, so could take no further action. When Tennent sent her report to the chief nurse prior to the state final examination, she relayed the situation factually but ended with the statement: 'I will be relieved when she leaves the staff though I am very vexed to think she will represent this training school. She has had a very severe warning. It may help her in the future.'[83]

The second nurse, after completing her training, became unwell with loss of weight, tiredness and malaise – signs suggestive of tuberculosis. Although her chest X-ray was clear, she was granted three months' sick leave on full salary. At the end of this period she sent in her resignation. Her doctor wrote to the Dunedin medical superintendent informing him that the nurse was pregnant. After the birth, Tennent refused to supply references for the nurse when she applied for maternity nurse training, saying she did not consider the nurse suitable for maternity work. A few months later Mary Lambie, the chief nurse, wrote to Tennent following up a maternity hospital matron's query about a missing reference for the same nurse, who was already partway through the training. Tennent was shocked. She replied to Lambie that although the nurse's work had been 'very good indeed', her conduct leading to the pregnancy was 'most discreditable' and had resulted in 'much unpleasant scandal', as the men involved 'treated the matter as a good joke and were not reticent about their conduct with her'. But in Tennent's view the nurse's most serious offence was to accept three months' salary for sickness 'knowing her condition was due to pregnancy'. She considered this 'false pretences'. Tennent added that it had never occurred to her that 'any matron would accept her without making enquiries' first. 'At that time,' she said, 'the present system of reporting unsatisfactory nurses and their names being circulated by you among the training schools was not in vogue. This case illustrates the value of the system.'[84] Lambie clearly had a blacklist scheme in place, of which Tennent approved.

Becoming a registered nurse

The final rites of passage in nurse training were sitting the state final examination, receiving results and graduating. Examinations were held twice a year and around 80 percent of candidates passed.[85] Nurses sat medical and surgical nursing papers in which all questions were usually compulsory and, from the 1940s, an additional paper on nursing technique. Their skills were assessed in an oral and practical examination.[86] Nurses from small hospitals had to travel to larger centres to sit the examination. Irene (Rene) Ancell, who trained at Cook Hospital in Gisborne under Eva Godfray, had to travel by sea to Napier for her examination in 1915 and pay for her return voyage and expenses. She was fortunate in having the £4 12s 6d reimbursed by the hospital board.[87] By the time Dorothy Scammell completed her training at Wairoa Hospital in the early 1930s, Gisborne was a larger centre, and she sat the examination there. Although Scammell felt that she and the oral examiner 'seldom agreed on my answers', she passed the whole examination with honours.[88]

Some hospitals had customs to mark the occasion. At Wellington Hospital in the 1930s, while a candidate sat her final paper the nurses from her ward would decorate her room with fruit, chocolate fish, crepe paper, balloons and flowers picked (with permission) from gardens in the hospital grounds and nearby homes. As Joan Loeber said, 'It just made it special for the nurses.'[89]

The announcement of results was usually also marked in some way. A few weeks after Bridget Ristori at Masterton sat her examination in 1923, she was walking down the ward with a bedpan when she saw the matron hurrying towards her. The matron flung her arms around her neck and congratulated her on being placed Top of the Dominion. Unusually, three candidates in the country were top equal that year. In her diary Ristori jotted: 'Glorious news … Can't believe it. Was so excited.' Training schools coveted this honour, and for a small hospital like Masterton, where nurses' clinical experience was limited, it was a significant achievement.[90] Hospital boards took pleasure in announcing results in the local newspapers and made special mention of any nurse who passed with honours. Top of the Dominion deserved particular notice. The New Plymouth Hospital Board, for example, wrote to Winifred Waite in 1915 congratulating her on this result.[91] Marjorie Chambers and her successful classmates, who were off duty when the results arrived by telegram, marked their pass in a simpler way. They 'rushed round the wards telling our friends of the results. It was against the rules to go to the wards in mufti, and as we were not in uniform, the breaking of that rule added to the fun.'[92]

A ceremony to mark the presentation of the five-pointed star medal to new registered nurses was slow to develop. In the early twentieth century nurses were simply sent their medal in the post. Edith Lewis at Whanganui in 1908 received hers in a matchbox. Others in the 1930s received theirs in tobacco tins.[93] Some of the large hospitals, however, established a ceremony at which a dignitary was invited to pin the medals on the graduating nurses. This was sometimes held on National Hospital Day, a fundraising event often held on Florence Nightingale's birthday, 12 May. Having a procession and formal ceremony was a way of not only acknowledging individual nurses' achievement but also presenting nursing as a special occupation with noble traditions, and thus recruiting new nurses. One of the earliest ceremonies was at Dunedin Hospital in 1924, with medals presented by Ellen (Nellie) Monson, one the five nurses working at the hospital in 1888 who had argued for their right to receive lectures in return for service.[94]

Nurses often realised at the end of their training just how little they knew. The first day Joan Loeber wore her medal, a ward sister said to her, 'Now, Nurse, you will begin to learn.' 'And that was true,' said Loeber. 'You began to learn.'[95]

***

Becoming a nurse was not just a process of acquiring the necessary knowledge and skills; in New Zealand and elsewhere, it also meant being enculturated into the profession's norms, values and beliefs about what it meant to be a nurse. Central to nursing identity was the code of virtues. Textbooks in Britain, Australia and the United States specified the qualities expected of a nurse, and lecturers made sure they were understood. The first trainees at St Bartholomew's Hospital in London in 1877, for example, were told to be truthful, even-tempered, punctual, clean and obedient.[96] As in New Zealand, nurses elsewhere copied the required virtues into their notebooks. Edwina Perkins, training in Wales from 1937 to 1941, noted the attributes of a good nurse as 'good health, truthfulness, obedience, punctuality, loyalty, observation and tactfulness'.[97] The folklore of training traversed not only hospital boundaries but also national borders and was repeated over time.⁹⁸ Like their counterparts in other countries, New Zealand nurses developed loyalty to their training hospital, learned its customs and proudly wore its uniform. The five-pointed star medal, unique to New Zealand nurses, was a valued symbol, whether delivered in a tobacco tin or pinned on in a public ceremony.

CHAPTER 4

Brightening sunless lives – district nursing

Annie Sexton found district nursing 'often wearisome, sometimes saddening, but always interesting'. She started work as a district nurse for the St John Ambulance Association in Wellington in 1905, nursing the sick poor in their own homes. Three years later she and her colleague, Mirian Macandrew, published a short narrative of their work in *Kai Tiaki*.[1] It was the first article on this new way of delivering patient care. Its publication probably irked Nurse Sibylla Maude, whose own article on the subject appeared in the following issue.[2]

To Sexton and Macandrew, district nursing was a 'labour of love'. They listed the necessary, familiar virtues of patience, cheerfulness and 'sound common sense', with the addition of courage and resourcefulness. They noted somewhat floridly that the 'ideal aspect' of their work was visible in a sunny-faced child's welcome, patients' grateful smiles, the help the poor gave to one another in times of distress, and the heroic patience of the sick. To convey the practical aspects of the work, they gave a fictionalised account of answering a call to a house in a back street 'usually surrounded with mud'. There a mother of seven children, aged from 3 weeks to 12 years, was suffering from 'nervous prostration' and an extensively ulcerated leg. They called a doctor to see her, then washed her, changed her bed with the fresh linen they provided (as none was available in the house) and hurried off to their many other cases.

The 'gleams of humour' in their work, they said, prevented it from being burdensome. When they asked another mother about her baby boy who had been taken to hospital with diphtheria, with 'a very sad sigh, and tears in her eyes' she informed them he must be 'awfully bad' because he was 'isolated'. They asked if she knew what that meant. She replied that a neighbour had told her it was 'small bits of ice that were put all over the baby'.[3]

This early narrative portrays several elements of the culture of district nursing apparent in nurses' stories through the next four decades – the required virtues and the tiring, sad but interesting work that was leavened by humour and rewarded by patients' gratitude. The district nursing folklore that developed in the early 1900s in New Zealand newspapers and in *Kai Tiaki* was a hybrid folklore, jointly constructed by journalists and nurses, usually to boost fundraising efforts. Vivid stories of district nursing cases and busy daily rounds were used to stimulate the public's interest and tug at heartstrings. Nurses' professional narratives contained similar literary flourishes, but they were also packed with nursing detail. This folklore portrayed the sick poor as vulnerable inhabitants of hovels whose misery was relieved only by the kindness of neighbours and district nurses' cheerful visits and skilled care.[4] Central to the folklore was the district nurse's role in brightening sunless lives.

Development of district nursing

District nursing services were inspired by services at the empire's centre. With Florence Nightingale's support, William Rathbone started a district nursing service in Liverpool after his wife's death in 1859. He had seen the benefit of having a nurse tend his wife during her illness and decided to extend this service to Liverpool's poorest citizens. Advocates for services in New Zealand towns also drew on examples from Australia – the Melbourne District Nursing Society, founded in 1885, and the District Trained Nursing Society, established in Adelaide in 1894.[5]

District nursing services were certainly needed. At the turn of the twentieth century, New Zealand hospital authorities were reluctant to care for patients with chronic conditions such as leg ulcers, abscesses, rheumatism, cancer and tuberculosis. The chronically ill, and acutely ill people who could not afford to pay for a private nurse, were left to struggle alone or depended on family and neighbours for rudimentary care. They were the 'sick poor'. Some religious organisations gave untrained care, like Mother Mary Joseph (Suzanne) Aubert's Sisters of Compassion in Wellington from 1899,[6] but most services began with a professionally trained nurse. Regardless of the governing body providing the service, district nursing was shaped by a strong belief that the sick poor had the right to highly competent care by qualified nurses, who would also teach household carers hygiene and simple nursing skills so that they could independently provide basic care and prevent further illness.

Existing organisations, specially formed voluntary community agencies and one church were the main New Zealand organisers. In these the nurse became the proxy for philanthropists' or local communities' benevolent efforts. A small number of services were set up by businesses like insurance companies or nurses' private enterprise in 'hourly nursing'. Hospital boards became responsible for district nursing in 1926, but many simply subsidised the voluntary agencies rather than starting their own services. From 1944 a new government benefit (under the Social Security Act 1938) enabled all hospital boards to introduce or expand their district nursing services or subsidise two-thirds of the cost of those provided by community agencies. Voluntary agencies could now also receive a government grant for major items, such as a car for the nurse's rounds. These changes meant that all patients in the community could receive free nursing care in their homes.

Professional district nursing began in Christchurch. It was not, however, started by Sibylla Maude, as is widely believed. It was Thomas Herrick at the City Mission Home who, in May 1895, employed the first qualified district nurse. Sibylla Maude began as a district nurse 18 months later, in November 1896.[7]

Thomas Herrick was born in Desford, Leicestershire, in 1862 and came to New Zealand as a young man. In June 1888 he resigned his position as secretary of the Prison Gate Mission in Christchurch as he had just opened his City Mission Home for destitute men.[8] In the economic Long Depression of the 1880s and 1890s, many men were unemployed and tramped the country as 'swaggers' looking for casual work. The Christchurch home provided transient men with a daily meal and a bed. It also took in recently discharged destitute patients from the hospital who were 'too weak to go on the road immediately'.[9] In addition, the home lent blankets and 'shakedowns' to the city's poor and gave them food and clothing.

Herrick relied on public subscriptions and fundraising events to support his charitable work and made frequent pleas for donations of money and items. Each month he sent the local newspaper a report of the work undertaken. Through his outreach work he had firsthand knowledge of the city's sick poor. In September that first year he reported: 'Among the sick there has been soup, milk, eggs and jellies kindly given by ladies.'[10] He arranged for ad hoc nursing help as far as funds permitted but believed strongly that the mission should employ its own fully qualified nurse.[11] From 1891 Herrick launched urgent fundraising appeals for the £50 per annum that this would cost. He did not meet the target, but in 1895 he announced that he had employed a nurse anyway. He believed that with 'this practical step' the funds would materialise.[12]

The nurse was Emily Lloyd Lees. She had trained at Wellington Hospital from 1886 to 1887 and was matron of Napier Hospital from 1888, earning an annual salary of £52. Dr Duncan MacGregor considered her 'a capital manager' who 'inspired her staff with her own spirit'.[13] After three months' district nursing she referred in her August report to 15 cases, with brief comments such as 'Wounds dressed, sores very painful'; 'In great poverty, children ill and mother sickly'; 'Very poorly, so prostrate and weak, cannot take any food'; 'Died this morning, husband in a muddled state through drink'; 'Widow over eighty, crippled and infirm though rheumatism'. Herrick included these remarks in his monthly newspaper report to illustrate the effects of the economic depression on the health and welfare of the poor. They were dealing with 'cases of poverty and distress, resulting from long illness of the breadwinner, be it father or mother', and 'every day there is some fresh case of trouble'.[14] On a practical level, he appealed directly for a folding chair for the nurse to use and received a new one, two worn ones, and 30 shillings towards 'nursing requisites'.[15] In seven months Lloyd Lees made 730 visits. Of these, 644 were for nursing or attending childbirth. She also distributed food, medical comforts, and blankets and quilts. The previous winter 'the distress was appalling,' she said, 'and more than fifty children slept with no other covering than sacking'.[16]

In his August 1896 report Herrick explained that the demand for the mission's services had increased but donations had fallen – not because the public had wearied of giving but because the continuing economic depression was affecting the middle classes and the smaller tradesmen who were its chief supporters. Many were in need of help themselves. The increase in benevolent organisations had also 'created a sort of competition' for donations. With the 'very many needy sick cases', all depending daily on the nurse, the need for a district nurse was obvious.[17]

In March 1897 Herrick died suddenly of a lung haemorrhage at the age of 34.[18] His widow struggled on with the home until 1909, but no further mention was made of Lloyd Lees or the district nursing service after Herrick's death. Lloyd Lees shifted to private case nursing and ran a residential club for private case nurses at 137 Salisbury Street, Christchurch.[19] She died in Christchurch on 17 August 1911 and was remembered by the public and profession as an enthusiastic, conscientious, respected and warmly regarded nurse.[20]

In contrast to Herrick's continual struggle to raise funds and requisites for Emily Lloyd Lees' work, Sibylla Maude had the advantage of wealthy and philanthropic friends. She started work as a district nurse 18 months after Lloyd Lees, and their work overlapped for four months. Both had been hospital matrons, but Maude was better known in Christchurch. Local newspapers publicised the work of both. In the first years Maude worked alone, just as Lloyd Lees had done, but she had the backing of a well-recognised wealthy elite, church dignitaries and city businessmen. The myth of the origin of district nursing therefore evolved around her.

Among Maude's supporters were Lady (Jessie) Rhodes, wife of Sir Heaton Rhodes, who was parliamentary representative for the rural Ellesmere electorate near Christchurch from 1899 to 1925. Maude's closest friend since childhood, Edie Rhodes, was Heaton's sister and married Jessie's brother, Alister Clark. Heaton's aunt by marriage was Sarah Ann Rhodes, a wealthy Wellington widow.[21] This tangle of personal and family connections facilitated the setting up of district nursing services in both Christchurch and Wellington. Jessie Rhodes was a strong supporter of Maude's early work, including the district nursing association in Christchurch that started in Maude's name in 1901, and also supported the Christchurch St John Ambulance Association. Her frequent visits to Wellington, accompanying her husband, probably sparked Sarah Rhodes' interest in and philanthropic support for the establishment of the Wellington St John district nursing service in 1903. Sarah Rhodes led its District Nursing Guild for the first decade, and Jessie Rhodes actively supported her fundraising work.[22]

Historian Margaret Tennant has noted that in the early twentieth century, individual or organisational benevolence in New Zealand was 'not necessarily hands-on, long term, or directed at poor relief'. Philanthropists preferred 'solid memorials with a name over the door' rather than 'the ongoing support of poor people living in their own homes'.[23] However, support for district nursing services was clearly an exception. The nursing culture of caring for all in times of illness, regardless of social standing, gave philanthropists a willing band of professionals to act as their proxies in providing care and relief to the sick poor. Tennant noted that as the century advanced, the focus of voluntary effort shifted from poverty relief to health initiatives.[24] Philanthropic support for district nursing at the start of the twentieth century foreshadowed this shift.

The founding myth continued to grow around Sibylla Maude because her district nursing service was a model for others in some New Zealand towns and cities, and because of its connections to other nursing services. For example, Mrs Annie Holgate, who was the first nurse in the Wellington St John Ambulance Association service in 1903,[25] had started training (as a widow) at Middlesex Hospital in London in 1892. She would have known Maude, who was in her final year there. Holgate was a district nurse in the London docklands before working with Maude in the

Christchurch service from 1902. Maude was invited to Dunedin in 1905 to speak at a public meeting on the need for a service in that city.[26] Potential sponsors and nurses visited the Nurse Maude service to see how a district nursing service could be put into practice.[27] Nurse L. Donohue, who worked for the Nurse Maude service, went to Hastings in 1926 to set up a similar service there before returning to Christchurch. And Maude Cassin, who also worked in the Christchurch service, was appointed as Hastings' district nurse.[28] Sibylla Maude's reputation as the founder of district nursing was entrenched at the time of her death. Her body lay in state at the Christchurch Cathedral, thousands lined the streets and paid their respects, and the newspapers lauded her as the 'pioneer of district nursing in New Zealand'.[29]

Delivering district nursing services

Dunedin provides good examples of the variety of ways district nursing care was delivered in New Zealand. A free service for the sick poor was set up in 1906 by an existing voluntary community agency, the St John Ambulance Association. Elizabeth Barclay was its first nurse.[30] Dunedin's second service, also free, was the only one in the country provided by a church. Jessie Torrance worked as the Knox Church nurse from 1919 after spending three years filling in for Barclay, who nursed overseas during World War I.[31] Torrance's practice was not limited to the Knox parish: she cared for people of any denomination anywhere in Dunedin.[32] In 1923 the Colonial Mutual Life (CML) Assurance Society started a free nursing service for policyholders, followed four years later by the Temperance & General (T&G) Mutual Life Assurance Society with Gertrude (Eva) Cheek as its Dunedin district nurse.[33] CML agents were exhorted to use the nursing service as a 'canvassing tool' in gaining new policyholders by providing informational postcards and leaflets titled 'Your Friend the Nurse' and 'Speeding Up Recovery'.[34] Beyond Dunedin, the Coal & Oil Company in the small rural town of Kaitangata also offered district nursing. Nurse Lakeman provided care free of charge in employees' homes, and at a moderate fee to other residents, during sickness, accident and childbirth. In 1925, however, the company could no longer afford the expense. It offered to subsidise a service if the South Otago Hospital Board employed Lakeman. Although a large number of workers petitioned the board to do so, they were unsuccessful.[35]

The economic depression of the 1930s created unemployment among nurses, and an 'hourly nursing' scheme evolved as a mutually beneficial enterprise that would keep nurses employed and make nursing care available to people who could afford a nurse only for a short time once or twice a day or week.³⁶ The Depression also spurred the creation of a new Dunedin service, this time offered by a voluntary community agency. The Roslyn District Nursing Association started in 1934, with Harriet Kinmont as its district nurse covering Roslyn, Māori Hill, Kaikorai and Wakari.³⁷ Much of her district was middle class, but it also included the 'new poor' created by the Depression. Most patients were treated free of charge, and a significant part of her initial work was welfare relief.³⁸

In the 1930s the new director-general of health, Dr Michael Watt, restructured public health services, and the chief nurse, Mary Lambie, urged overlapping services to rationalise their efforts. Voluntary agencies occasionally discussed forming a single, national co-ordinated service, with St John as the vehicle, but this did not eventuate.³⁹ Lambie was not in favour of nurses working for lay employers, as she believed such arrangements compromised the registered nurse's right to practise independently or to be supervised by

Jessie Torrance was the Knox Church district nurse in Dunedin from 1919, caring for people of any religious denomination across the city.

Torrance-Jessie-081, Presbyterian Research Centre (Archives), Dunedin

a senior registered nurse. She singled out insurance companies, telling students at New Zealand's Post Graduate School for Nurses in 1934 that at least the T&G company employed a supervising nurse in Sydney, but the nurses working for the CML company did not have even this distant professional supervision. Instead, they were responsible to laypeople who had very little knowledge of nursing. In England and America, she said, insurance companies did not employ their own nurses but paid a local district nursing service for each visit made to their policyholders.⁴⁰ Her criticism did not seem to extend to a lay community organisation like St John, presumably because it had a long history of providing home nursing courses, and those trained were able to provide the district nurse with practical assistance when needed. It would have been warranted, though, in the case of the Wanganui District Nursing League.

In 1909 the local Women's Branch of the National Defence League in Whanganui decided to start a district nursing service. As their name obscured their purpose, they became the Wanganui District Nursing League and raised funds to employ a nurse.[41] They engaged Beatrice Walton, who had trained in London and left her private hospital in Marton to take up the position. All went well until August 1911. By then the league membership had changed substantially, and perhaps new members did not understand the professional, independent status of a registered nurse. The custom in all district nursing services was for the nurse to provide her employing organisation with a monthly written report of the number of patients on the books, visits completed and calls made to the office, and to attend a monthly meeting to discuss any issues. The Wanganui League, however, now required Walton to phone the secretary at the end of each day and provide the names and addresses of any new patients. In addition, she was required to supply a weekly (rather than monthly) written report that gave each patient's name, address and disease, and their doctor's name, with a cross put beside the patient's name for each visit she made. The league's 'lady visitors', who were supposed to support the nurse's work by meeting patients' welfare needs, started checking on Walton's work. Patients told her that the visitors were asking if the reports were true, and whether she had, for example, visited twice on a particular day as noted in the report. Patients were upset by both the visitors' calls and the league's apparent distrust of its nurse. Walton felt humiliated. Added to the distrust, she later commented, she had 'the constant feeling of antipathy and dislike on the part of the majority of the Committee to swallow'.[42] She resigned. The flurry of letters and articles in the local newspaper showed the deep divide between those who supported her stand and praised her work and those who saw her reluctance to comply with the league's new procedures as unreasonable.[43] It was a perfect, if rare, example of Lambie's concern.

District nursing work and culture

Nursing narratives revealed the cultural values embedded in district nurses' work – courage, adaptability, resourcefulness, tact and patience. Courage was needed to venture into some of the grim and grimy city areas and squalid buildings that were beyond nurses' usual experience. Most New Zealand nurses had middle-class backgrounds: three-quarters of nurses beginning training at Christchurch Hospital between 1892 and 1910, for example, had fathers who were businessmen, professionals or wealthy farmers.[44] Courage was also needed to continue through the relentless daily round of visits, bear the heartache of helpless and hopeless cases, and continue caring for the occasional cantankerous patient.[45] When Jessie Torrance was working for the Dunedin St John service in 1917, she described the case of a man whose legs and feet were covered with a skin growth 'like the blighty excrescence that grows on fruit trees'. He was 'a mass of pain', and moving him meant slowly shifting one small part of his body at a time. 'This poor man's temper was as distorted as his body. We forgave him a good deal, but it was always a nurse with a flushed tired face that went out of that house.'[46] On a more practical level, courage was needed to return to houses known to be infested with fleas. As one district nurse noted, 'Our trusted friend Pyrethrum Powder must be freely used if there are too many inhabitants of a cottage.'[47] Jessie Torrance luckily had only one house with 'objectionable small company'. 'We would not have objected so much,' she said, 'if a number had not come away with us.' After the neighbour told her there were 'thousands of them', she said it 'took some courage' for the nurses to keep going there, but they did. When she was giving the patient a bath laced with Jeyes fluid, she disturbed the pile of clothes left in a heap on the floor. The old woman shouted, 'Dinna touch them; leave a' the critters together.'[48]

Unlike their British counterparts, New Zealand nurses did not have special training in district nursing.[49] Nursing patients in their homes and without the benefits of hospital equipment and supplies called for adaptability and resourcefulness.[50] Jessie Torrance told the story of a nurse tending a sick couple in one bed. To wash the husband, the nurse had to 'mount on the bed and manage the best she could, as he lay on the wall side. To make the bed required an original plan, but for a District Nurse resourcefulness and originality are a necessity.'[51] Bridget Ristori advised future district nurses: 'You must learn the art of improvisation – hot bricks or bags of hot sand in place of hot water bottles – the kitchen chair as a back rest for Pneumonias and Heart disease, the frying-pan for the baby's bath.'[52] In turn, district nurses drew on the resourcefulness of ladies' committees and of sewing, nursing and hospital guilds for support of their work. These organisations raised funds for air beds, air rings and appliances for nurses to lend to patients. They also arranged supplies of coal, wood, blankets, clothing and soup for nurses to distribute. These supplemented the medicines, liniments, lotions and dressing supplies the nurse kept in her consulting room.

Historian Bronwyn Labrum has described the material culture of welfare in New Zealand, focusing particularly on clothing in the encounters between families and state welfare workers.[53] In district nursing services, though, providing material welfare caused professional controversy. District nursing leaders overseas warned against complicating nursing service by providing welfare relief. Amy Hughes, superintendent of district nurses in the Queen Victoria's Jubilee Institute for Nurses, believed that nurses should work 'without suspicion of alms-giving' and not 'sow seeds of dependence on outside help when sickness and trouble invade the home'.[54] Grace Neill, chief nurse at the time district nursing services were set up in Christchurch, Wellington and Dunedin, held a similar view, regarding charitable aid from the state as encouraging pauperism. Women in particular could be 'brazen-faced beggars'.[55] The Auckland St John service, established in 1920, stipulated that 'no food, money or medicines' could be supplied by nurses.[56] For most New Zealand district nurses, however, alleviating the acute needs they encountered was part of the work,[57] and they were allocated an additional comfort fund to procure medicines or supplies for patients in need.[58] The material culture of district nursing was beyond the state's purview: it centred on items that supported nursing practice and relieved practical needs. As such, it represented the combined adaptability and resourcefulness of district nurses and their supporting agencies.

Funds to support these efforts were raised through collection boxes on street corners, special concerts, fairs and lectures by a variety of speakers. The girls at Columba College in Dunedin held a concert in August 1919 that raised £40 14s, sufficient to supply Jessie Torrance's initial equipment,[59] and in 1921 Mr D.K. Macdonald gave a lecture illustrated by 90 lantern slides on 'The Congo and its People' to raise funds for furnishing Torrance's consulting room in the Knox Church Sunday School Hall. He had been captain of a Congo steamer for many years and had travelled extensively for the British Consulate investigating 'rubber atrocities' in the 'Dark Continent'. He had also brought along examples of cloth, blacksmiths' work, spears and knives. After this thrilling yet disturbing (and perhaps eye-straining) lecture, the apparently relieved reporter noted that 'a pleasing degree of variety' was provided by solo musical items and a school choir.[60]

District nurses participated directly in fundraising. Annie Holgate supplied a two-page report for the substantial programme sold as an entry ticket to the bazaar held to raise funds for the Wellington St John service in August 1904. Her report, accompanied by her photograph in full nursing uniform, had a human appeal, and she supported the effort more personally by taking charge of the lucky-dip bran tubs.[61] Jessie Torrance gave a lecture at a fundraising concert for the Dunedin St John district nursing service in July 1920, a year after she had left it, and another at the Roslyn District Nursing Association's annual meeting in May 1938.[62] She assisted at a sweet stall for the St John Oriental Carnival in Dunedin and at the tearoom of the YWCA sale in 1924, was a member of the St John Ambulance Association executive from 1922 and assessed applications to the Mayor's Relief Fund in 1940.[63]

Resourcefulness and tact were especially important when nursing those who hid their poverty. People would 'keep up a nice garden, and struggle to maintain appearances, and no one passing would dream that they often go without the bare necessities of life'.[64] The district nurses, as 'gentle detectives', would 'discover the proud poor' and 'do good by the utmost stealth. Surreptitiously they leave behind a bottle of medicine or a shin of beef'.[65] Grace Nobbs, district nurse at Whanganui for just over a year until November 1912, made her own soup for patients. The Bristol and Caddy local butchers gave her 10 pounds of beef and marrow-bones twice a week. Patients sometimes gave her vegetables. She bought the remaining ingredients, such as pearl barley, salt and pepper, out of her patient comfort allowance, and her landlady allowed her to cook the soup on her stove. It took two days to make each batch. She lugged the nourishing concoction to patients in a quart billy-can.[66]

The virtue of patience was essential. Trying to overcome patients' abhorrence of fresh air, for example, took time. Sibylla Maude told a Dunedin audience in 1905 of the 'difficulty she experienced in the effort to persuade people to keep their windows open. The work of a district nurse … seemed to be principally teaching fresh air'.[67] As another district nurse said, opening a window during her visit always ensured that 'at least one blast of fresh air has entered that day'.[68] One elderly bedridden man in a country town refused to have his window open or to be washed, and when asked a question simply grunted. However, one day the nurses managed to give him a blanket bath, change his bed and make him comfortable. When they had finished, his wife came into the room, sat down, looked at him, then shook her head and said in a sad voice, 'My God, I never saw him look so nice in all his life.'[69]

Another challenge to district nurses' tempers was their patients' reluctance to follow instructions, heeding neighbours' advice instead. A district nurse advised a mother on the care of her sick boy but found his condition worse when she returned a few days later. He was 'the victim' of 'over the fence' advice, including home remedies.[70] Similarly, Sibylla Maude, tending a man with chronic rheumatism, found he had followed a remedy that a friend had suggested. He corked worms up tight in a stone bottle, buried it in manure for three weeks, then strained off the liquid and rubbed it into his joints. When she saw him he was covered in boils. 'It did just smell!' he said, 'but look, I can now use them freely, it is the phosphorous and electricity that does it.'[71] Sometimes nurses' advice could be misconstrued. When one nurse offered to bring an air cushion the next morning for an emaciated old man, the family said they had one. She suggested they position him on it when they next moved him. In the morning, they 'joyfully said he was on the air-ring', and he was. The poor man, she said, died later in the day 'after spending his last night on earth' sitting not on a 'soft and yielding' cushion but on one that had perished and was 'filled with tennis balls'.[72]

Patients particularly appreciated the core virtues of kindness and efficiency, as unsolicited letters to the CML Society show. In 1930 a woman in Mornington, Dunedin, wrote 'just a line to thank you for the very nice nurse you sent' who was 'very good and kind' and a 'help and comfort'. Another in Khandallah, Wellington, appreciated Florence Heany being 'capable and most kindly'.[73] A resident of Andersons Bay, Dunedin, in 1934 could 'truthfully say' that Nurse Lindsay was 'efficient in every way. She knows her work and knows how to go about it.' And his wife thought she was 'just lovely'. Similarly, a resident of Papanui, Christchurch, in 1934 thought his nurse was 'just splendid, everything one could wish for in a nurse'.[74]

The district nursing culture emphasised sharing knowledge and skills. Teaching someone in the household how to care for the patient's basic needs was just as important as the nurse carrying out a skilled procedure such as a wound dressing. 'Women are eager to learn,' said Jessie Torrance, 'and grateful for information. The nurse can teach them how to change sheets, prepare foments, and compresses – how to avoid bed-sores and manage paralytics, etc.'[75] Nurses also taught classes in home nursing to the general public at local halls or technical colleges, or through community organisations like the St John, Red Cross and Girl Guides associations, and gave public talks on health topics. Torrance also gave 12 lectures and demonstrations a year on 'the principles and detail of home nursing' to the students at the Training Missionary Institute at Knox Church.[76]

It is difficult to know what part religion played in district nurses' motives for nursing the sick poor. Historian Frank Prochaska argued that in nineteenth-century Britain, the work of Ellen Ranyard's Bible Nurses in London's slums clearly illustrated the role of Christian ideology in social welfare and medical philanthropy. But in the early twentieth century, even this nursing mission 'struggled to sustain the religious enthusiasm which had been its hallmark'.[77] Certainly Annie Sexton and Mirian Macandrew in the Wellington St John Service in the early 1900s had as their motto the biblical expression 'Inasmuch' (referencing Matthew 25:40: 'Inasmuch as ye have done it unto the least of these my brethren, ye have done it unto me').[78]

Nurse Maude's district nurses, shown here in 1914, cared for the 'sick poor' in their homes across Christchurch. Sybilla Maude is fourth from right. Webb, Stephano, 1880–1967: Collection of negatives, 1/1-005293-G, Alexander Turnbull Library, Wellington

Agnes Falconer also used it in 1934 when describing the Roslyn district nurse's day. The nurse herself, Harriet Kinmont, was the daughter of a Presbyterian minister.[79] Jessie Torrance, the Knox Church nurse, taught in the Knox Church Sunday School. Her father had been a hospital and prison chaplain and a church elder. But district nurses could also be motivated by a more general humanitarian spirit. As Torrance said, they might get 'blunted' from their difficult work and endless rounds, but 'from a humanitarian point we get sharpened'.[80]

The first, practical challenge was gaining entry to the homes of the sick poor. Doctors, lady visitors, ministers, neighbours and hospitals alerted a district nursing office to needy cases, and nurses walked, cycled or travelled by tram to reach them. Although from the 1930s several district nursing services raised funds for motor cars, many urban nurses continued to travel by public transport. The Auckland St John service set a district boundary of one mile from tramlines,[81] and services in different towns often arranged for nurses to be issued with tram passes.

The district nursing folklore

Venturing into parts of the city where the sick poor lived represented more than travel logistics: it was a powerful motif of the district nursing folklore. This hybrid folklore, jointly created by journalists and district nurses, emerged in the early twentieth century to describe and support district nursing. When district nursing services solicited funds, their narratives used the metaphors of darkness and light to portray the homes and lives of the sick poor and the district nurse's ministrations. An article about Annie Holgate's work in 1904, a year after the Wellington St John service began, was titled 'Sunless lives'. Another, on the work of Annie Sexton and Mirian Macandrew there four years later, was called 'In the shadow'.[82]

Journalists also used these tropes in describing their forays into the poorer city areas when they accompanied the district nurse on her rounds, portraying the venture as an exploration into an unknown sunless land, a terra incognita for both the journalist and newspaper readers. This rhetorical device would have been familiar to readers of Charles Dickens. 'One moment the explorer was in a main street,' said the reporter accompanying Annie Sexton in 1908. 'In the next instant he was in a dark slushy alley-way which got little of broad daylight.' He and the district nurse traversed a 'narrow dingy lane', a 'squalid thoroughfare' and 'a tunnel', into the 'dark land'.[83]

Historical geographer Robin Law showed that from the beginning of the twentieth century, changes in public transport led to shifts in the gendered use of the street as a social space and means of access to work.[84] The alleys, however, were still passageways, liminal spaces leading from the familiar public social space of a city, with its well-off citizens, to the hidden, cramped and often squalid quarters of the poor. In dense inner-city areas such as the Te Aro Flat in Wellington or the ill-drained harbour edge in Dunedin, the narrow lanes and back alleys were usually deep in filth.[85] They were also considered socially unsafe. Historian Mark Peel has pointed out that while Melbourne charity workers were familiar with such areas in their city, they did not live there.[86] In New Zealand, this was true of Jessie Torrance, for example, who lived in Royal Terrace in Dunedin. However, while Annie Holgate's Wellington home and consulting room was in an area of medical and other professional rooms in Willis Street, it was only a short step from the edge of the Te Aro Flat, and it is possible that Annie Sexton lived close to the service's Ghuznee Street office within the Te Aro district.[87] While the liminal space of the alley or lane could signify a dangerous transition, nurses felt protected by their uniform and professional standing.[88] The alley could also represent vibrancy and social activity. Jessie Torrance helped one old lady into a chair in the alley outside her door. Facing towards the street and happily watching people 'bobbing past the small spot at the foot of the lane', she said in her Irish brogue: 'I wouldn't call the queen me mother.'[89]

Historian Alan Mayne contended that the city slum was a journalistic construct that did not represent the reality of poorer inner-city areas.[90] Some early twentieth-century commentators also voiced the idea that slums did not exist, but the journalist who accompanied Annie Sexton firmly rebuffed this view. After spending three hours with her visiting 'the most desolate reaches' of South Wellington, a 'dreary region, a huddle of ramshackle houses, blind alleys, habitation as sick-looking as some of the inhabitants', he had seen enough to confirm that slums existed.[91] It was a surprise to many that the 'slum cancer' could be found even in New Zealand's capital.[92] Yet it remained a feature: in her 1922 story 'The Garden Party', Katherine Mansfield described the 'eyesore' of 'little mean dwellings' in 'smoky and dark' lanes.[93]

District nurses' narratives also provided evidence of slums. They did so not simply in order to elicit public donations but to show the practical challenges of nursing in this environment. Sibylla Maude described the 'sordid, dirty, forsaken looking homes' where 'there is nothing for it but to hang your cloak on the clothes line (the cleanest spot), roll up your sleeves, and look about for some cleansing utensils'.[94] Another nurse reported that she had fetched a patient bread and butter from a cupboard 'none of you would eat out of, if you went without food for a week'.[95] Again, these narratives deployed metaphors of darkness and light. As Sibylla Maude pointed out, at the end of her visit the district nurse could go 'out into the fresh air and sunshine thankful for her own healthy mind and body'.[96]

These tropes persisted in accounts of district nursing through to the 1930s. The person accompanying Elizabeth Barclay in Dunedin in 1909 entered a 'tenement of small cottages' with higher buildings behind 'shutting out the rays of the afternoon sun'. The nurse attended to an emaciated old man who 'brightened up considerably'.[97] In 1912 Whanganui residents were told that the district nurse's 'cheery presence' and help 'brighten many a saddened home'.[98] One 1928 newspaper account noted that district nurses 'lighten the sunless lives of their patients'.[99] In the 1930s nurses were 'radiating the sunshine of hope'; they 'shed the sunshine of their lives' and went like 'gleams of light' among their patients.[100] In the early 1940s the image shifted to one of bringing comfort, hope, cheer and confidence,[101] although an obituary for Jessie Torrance in the Presbyterian magazine in 1950 said she 'carried the sunshine of a cheery Christian influence' into patients' homes.[102]

The folklore tacitly acknowledged Old World evils in the new colony. Newspaper discussions of poverty, including Charles Booth's 1889–1903 survey of poverty in

London, were part of its context.[103] The author of the 1904 'Sunless lives' article directly challenged Premier Richard Seddon's claim that there was 'no poverty in New Zealand'. The poor led 'a sunless existence at the best of times' and always faced 'the menace of eclipse through sickness'.[104] In response to the Long Depression of the 1880s and 1890s, charitable aid legislation and practice made provision for the poor. The argument was around who deserved it. As historian John Stenhouse has pointed out, anti-church 'free thinkers' and eugenicists in the government and public service, including three premiers and Dr Duncan MacGregor, who oversaw charitable aid, viewed the poor as undeserving and dangerous.[105] This attitude contrasted with Prochaska's view of a Christian ideology underlying British social welfare.[106]

In addition to the fear that charitable aid spurred 'pauperism' or dependence on aid, there was a worry that some were falsely claiming it. Even Thomas Herrick at the Christchurch City Mission Home was aware of 'loaferism', as he termed it, and false claims.[107] This worry and reluctance continued under Dr Thomas Valintine, who succeeded MacGregor in 1906,[108] but journalists kept repeating the message that there was 'straight-out, unmistakable poverty, with no semblance of bluff about it'.[109] The hybrid folklore was therefore designed to persuade the public of the existence of poverty and need in order to gain support. It deliberately evoked the self-image of the colony and dominion as a place with a humanitarian spirit, which colonial settlers had brought with them, and which was manifest in the 'large-hearted' generosity of the country's citizens.[110]

To stimulate this humanitarian impulse, Jessie Torrance had a favourite (and elaborate) narrative device that she used from 1917 until her last published speech in 1938. This was to link local services with the history of the Order of St John. She borrowed its respected lineage and historical narrative to support district nursing in a relatively young country and to persuade potential donors that this was a worthy cause.[111] A Wellington reporter had dismissed this device in 1906, as he reckoned it made 'no great appeal' to people's sympathies or purses in 'a practical age'. Like light through the coloured panes of an old cathedral, it could only 'brighten' the painful features of a district nurse's work tending the sick poor.[112] But it appeared to work for Torrance.

Nurses noted that many patients existed on the old age pension of around 10 shillings a week when the rent for a room was 6 shillings; the price in Auckland for even 'the smallest shack in the city' was around 10s 6d a week.[113] They balanced these descriptions with accounts of patients' surprising resilience. In a speech in 1917, Jessie Torrance described one old woman who cooked 'on a smoky Beatrice stove'; another cooked on a spirit lamp while lying in bed and lived mostly on potatoes and grated cheese, and eggs when she could get them. Everything was in reach under or on top of the bed, or in a cupboard beside it. She leaned out to reach what she needed or hitched it up with a crooked stick.[114] In later speeches, Torrance consistently stressed patients' 'cheerful uncomplaining spirit' and desire to make the best of things.[115] As another nurse commented in 1927, 'In spite of all this poverty our patients on the whole are a cheery lot, and if it were not for this it would sometimes be hard to carry on.'[116]

Neighbours' kindness supported the nurses' efforts. Elizabeth Barclay, for example, cared for a young bedridden woman whose neighbours raised money to purchase a wheelchair, which they used each day to move her 'into the sunshine and fresh air'.[117] During the Depression of the 1930s neighbours provided practical help, and women in the community made soup and jellies, sewed or knitted clothing, and donated equipment and nursing requisites.[118]

In their efforts to remedy poverty-related sickness, district nurses acted as cultural mediators between public and private, blurring the boundaries between the spheres and interpreting one to the other. By revealing the existence of poverty and its effects on health to citizens who could be unaware or wilfully ignorant, they transformed health problems from private domestic matters into a public concern.

Another theme of district nursing folklore was the variety of duties in the nurse's relentless daily round. Sibylla Maude was known to 'expound the details (some of them minute) of her own daily round'.[119] Accomplishing all the day's tasks required endurance and efficiency. Bridget Ristori advised future district nurses: 'Every moment of the day counts; you do essentials and then move on.'[120] Another explained that 'a great deal of time is required to get through a day's work'.[121]

Demonstrating the diverse challenges of the daily round by telling stories about cases was tricky. It meant balancing patients' privacy against the need to stimulate donors' generosity. A Dunedin reporter noted in 1906 that Elizabeth Barclay 'very properly declined to discuss any particular cases' and gave only general statistics of conditions, but nevertheless later allowed an interested person to accompany her on her rounds.[122] The journalist reporting Jessie Torrance's speech on behalf of the Dunedin St John service in 1917 noted that it was hard to describe district nurses' work because the nurse was hemmed in between nursing etiquette and common kindness. To a great extent the 'personal element' had to be avoided, yet it was precisely that 'individual touch', he said, that would 'give life' to an account. He was therefore probably delighted to have Torrance's lively accounts of various patients and perhaps had a copy of her speech or her *Kai Tiaki* article to refresh his memory of what she had said. The journalist used less graphic imagery, however, as a 'detailed account' would have been 'harrowing or even repulsive'.[123]

In the article, Torrance described some of her cases in clinical detail. One old man had developed bedsores from lying on his back for months. When the district nurse was finally called, she found 'great holes' in his flesh, 'living with vermin'. Every day for three years the nurses dressed a boy's tubercular abscesses, draining copious and offensive-smelling discharge from his hip, thigh and abdomen. He was 'skin and bone' and moved with pain and difficulty. Two old ladies had gangrenous feet and legs. The flesh 'fell away bit by bit, until little was left, but the bone', and their death was a 'great release' to them both. The nurses had a 'back-breaking task' with an Assyrian family with 13 children when all broke out in sores. Every day for months the district nurses bathed several of them with Jeyes fluid, rubbed ointment on them, applied bandages and covered the areas with butter-muslin garments they made for the purpose. The nurses made this family's home the last call for the day and went straight home to a bath. And an Englishwoman with a heart condition, who had 'much agony' with her limbs twisted from chronic rheumatism, told the nurses her only relief was 'to yell, and yell she does, as the neighbours can testify'. The nurses had tried to persuade her to go into hospital but she was reluctant, as on a previous occasion the hospital nurses had objected to her yelling. As her pains were worse at night, the district nurses could quite believe her. When not in pain she was quite merry and sang along with her canaries. Her Chinese husband, Tommy, who looked after her, also became ill, so until a neighbour came to the rescue, the district nurse had to give breakfast to the husband and wife, the hens, the cat and two canaries.[124]

Journalists reported nurses' narratives of varied cases and continuous daily work until the end of the 1930s,[125] helping to convince the public of the need for district nursing services. From 1944, government support of district nursing services for all meant that fundraising was no longer an urgent need, and the hybrid folklore narratives disappeared.

Public perception of the district nurse

The district nursing culture of caring at first for the sick poor, and then also for those who could afford to pay a little, was understood, appreciated and supported by the public. In the early twentieth century the public perception of district nurses, shaped by and represented in newspapers, blended the symbolic with the practical to create an image of the ministering angel who was also a skilled professional.

The district nurse carried out a 'self-sacrificing mission'.[126] A Whanganui journalist described the situation of two homebound elderly sisters, one with rheumatism and the other with ulcerated legs, in order to encourage the public to contribute to the Sunday street collection for their local district nursing service. 'Is it any wonder that to them the nurse is a guardian angel, and that they watch for her coming as the one great event of each weary, pain-racked day? Worth giving to help a case like that, eh?'[127] Some journalists portrayed the nurse as an evangelical figure who carried the 'common-sense hygiene gospel' into the 'often squalid' homes of the sick poor, managed 'prejudice, untidiness and dirt'[128] and at her best was 'an angel carrying healing in her wings'. Even the least capable district nurse was an 'immeasurable improvement' on Dickens' fictional Sairey Gamp, the often drunk and unreliable nurse attending London's poor. Instead, she was the 'sweet-faced, neatly-uniformed, pleasant-spoken trained nurse' whose 'modest demeanour' hid a 'vast storehouse of knowledge'.[129] District nursing was 'more trying than ordinary nursing', so it needed an 'exceptional person' to do the work.[130] Florence Nightingale had also held this view, saying that 'a district nurse must be even a better trained nurse than a hospital nurse, because she has so much less help at hand'.[131]

In the 1930s, although the public perception of the district nurse sometimes included the trope of the quiet heroine, Jessie Torrance in 1938 was still thrilled at the 'heroisms' of the world's district nurses. St John nurses had been doing 'heroic work for so many years, helping, consoling, relieving wherever they go. I have often listened to eulogies of these nurses from some of their patients.'[132] Increasingly, however, such portraits emphasised the nurse's professional role and the practical challenges of the work. A Dunedin journalist in 1936 saluted Elizabeth Barclay as both heroic and professional, saying that she had done her work 'so quietly and unostentatiously that many citizens were scarcely aware that it was going on. But the duties of the district nurse are arduous and exacting.'[133] District nurses, wrote another reporter, were 'at the beck and call night and day of every resident in the district', which could extend 20 miles (32km) from their headquarters. However, 'in spite of, or possibly because of, the arduous nature of their duties the nurses are full of enthusiasm for their work.'[134] Nurses themselves in the 1930s told the public that district nursing benefited them professionally, as they could focus on the patient as a person and care for them over a longer time than in hospital, and it let them put their hospital training to practical use in entirely different circumstances. One, however, was concerned that her nurses had to do their paperwork in their off-duty hours.[135]

One possibly unexpected outcome of the early services was the symbolic role the district nurse unwittingly played in disciplining children. Sibylla Maude told nurses in 1908 that mothers warned their naughty children that the district nurse would give them 'a nasty dose of medicine' or put them 'in her black bag'.[136]

***

A complex interplay of philanthropic will, personal relationships and the newly professionalised occupation of nursing led to the establishment of a variety of district nursing services in New Zealand. It was a transnational nursing specialty. The establishment of district nursing in Liverpool and then throughout Britain inspired similar services elsewhere. Carrie Howse has asserted that a service in Boston, Massachusetts, was 'the reflection of England's light'.[137] Australian services similarly reflected the British example. In turn, those advocating for services in New Zealand pointed to examples in Melbourne and Adelaide. District nursing in New Zealand was not initially the responsibility of the chief nurse, but Hester Maclean, who was in that role from 1906 to 1923, had a working knowledge of its challenges and rewards, as she had been in charge of both the Melbourne service and the Sydney District Nursing Association before coming to New Zealand.[138]

New Zealand did not have the equivalent of Britain's co-ordinated system of the Queen Victoria's Jubilee Institute for Nurses (QVJIN), incorporated in 1889, with which many of the small rural and town services eventually amalgamated, or the specialised district nurse training provided by the QVJIN.[139] New Zealand district nurses themselves, however, had common work practices and cultural values. While lacking the extent of philanthropic patronage enjoyed by British services, New Zealand also thereby avoided the class-based conflicts between British district nurses and their untrained 'lady benefactor' employers.[140] The cultural interplay between lay philanthropy and professional nursing in New Zealand usually worked well. Its services also differed from others that were reluctant to involve nurses in providing welfare relief.[141] In New Zealand, nurses' stories and work served an additional function of revealing and addressing the confronting evidence of poverty and its effect on health in the new colony and dominion.

CHAPTER 5

The 'intrepid nurse' in the backblocks

On 24 May 1911 Amelia Bagley, a departmental nurse inspector, gave a lecture to the Wellington Branch of the New Zealand Trained Nurses' Association (NZTNA) titled 'The Nurse's Larger Sphere'. Among the available specialties she identified as nurses' career options were the government nursing services for Māori and backblocks settlers. The Backblocks Nursing Service started in 1909 for Pākehā settlers opening up farms. Country nursing, Bagley said, was a 'large and splendid sphere of nursing work'. Nurses' letters were 'full of descriptions of interesting cases, exciting adventures, and humorous incidents'.[1]

Nurses' letters, the core narratives of New Zealand rural nursing, reveal the central trope of the 'intrepid nurse'. Hester Maclean, editor of New Zealand's nursing journal *Kai Tiaki*, printed excerpts from the letters she received. As the country's chief nurse, this gave her a unique opportunity to attract more nurses to rural posts, which were often difficult to fill, and, in her role as journal editor, a supply of good human-interest stories.

The letters show that nurses enjoyed the work, despite the difficulty in getting about through dense bush or along rough roads and tracks, on foot or horseback, to care for settlers in their rudimentary homes. In 1912 Jessie Kennedy was the backblocks nurse at Urutī in Taranaki. She wrote that she had had some rough trips on bad roads and was glad she had been brought up in the country, where she had gained a fair knowledge of horses. Although her district was the 'true back-blocks', she felt she suffered no great hardships – after all, she had not been asked 'to bake bread or milk cows'. Charlotte Parker, an English-trained nurse newly stationed at Waipiro Bay in the East Coast's Waiapu district, had not had the same advantages: she had to learn to ride a horse.[2]

The narratives gave vivid accounts of the backblocks nurse's life and work. Maclean avoided presenting an overly romanticised notion of backblocks work by including accounts of difficult cases and other professional challenges. There were risks. Charlotte Parker contracted typhoid from patients and died in October 1912.[3] Two weeks before her death, she had written to Maclean that the work was right for her, adding: 'I like the country.'[4] When Maclean quoted this letter in a speech to the NZTNA conference the next month, she inflated it to: 'I love the country.'[5] It was certainly a necessary sentiment for all rural nurses.

Working in unfamiliar, rugged and remote parts of New Zealand, nurses never knew what challenges awaited them at the end of a long journey. They wrote of isolation, the expectation of being constantly available, long journeys over difficult but beautiful terrain, clinical challenges and the importance of community and professional relationships.

In 1930 the backblocks and Māori health nursing services were combined, restructured and renamed as district health nursing. To the narratives of long journeys were added the new challenges and advantages of mastering the motor car. In describing the new service, the main difference was the combined range of bedside and public health nursing that could be undertaken in one day. Versatility was key.

Backblocks nursing work and culture

In her 1961 celebratory history of New Zealand nursing, Joan Rattray gave a romantic account of the origin of the Backblocks Nursing Service in 1909. In Rattray's telling, Hester Maclean 'looked outwards to the vast tracts of swamplands, rugged mountain country, and wide, open plains that were being prepared for cultivation. Dense areas of bush were being cleared and turned into rich pasture land. Dusty, arid plains were awaiting their future harvests of grain, meat, and wool.' Maclean thought about the 'intrepid settlers, cradling New Zealand's economy of the future', who were 'fighting sickness without medical aid'. It was to assist these stalwart souls that the Backblocks Nursing Service began.[6] In fact, the service was the idea of Dr Thomas Valintine. He had been a rural general practitioner in Inglewood, Taranaki, before becoming inspector-general of hospitals in 1906 and also chief health officer in 1909. Maclean's role was to implement the idea.[7]

Maclean's view of the scheme was set in a wider international context. In 1910 she explained that a 'simultaneous wave of thought and care' for people in sparsely settled rural areas had arisen in many countries. 'This thought has concentrated itself in each place in some brain, and become the great object of work and schemes, not always on identical lines, but running always in the same direction and to the same end.' In the 'older Dominion' of Canada, the Victorian Order of Nurses service was 'a good scheme, but not, I think, quite so good and practical as that advanced' in New Zealand. And Australia was still only considering a bush nursing service.[8]

The idea for an Australian service was being promoted by Lady (Rachel) Dudley, wife of the new governor-general. She had little success, however, until Amy Hughes, lady superintendent of Britain's successful Queen Victoria's Jubilee Institute of Nurses (QVJIN), which included 'village nurses' in rural areas, arrived to sway local opinion. At the time of Maclean's comment, British services were supporting settlers in India, and the Grenfell Mission sent British and other nurses to sparsely settled areas of Newfoundland and Labrador. Red Cross and other outpost nursing stations were not established in Ontario until the 1920s and in Quebec until the 1930s.[9]

The Backblocks Nursing Service was a complex scheme but seemed to work well. Residents in an isolated rural locality, where the nearest doctor might be 50 miles (80km) away, could form a committee and apply to their hospital board or directly to the Department of Hospitals for a backblocks nurse. They had to guarantee half her salary, which was raised through subscriptions and patients' fees that went to the hospital board; the balance was subsidised by the department. The board or department recruited the nurse, who was approved by the department. Ideally, she had both nursing and midwifery qualifications. She could visit patients who needed only sporadic care, such as dressing an abscess, but would stay in settlers' homes when providing care in cases of sickness, accident and childbirth. She charged a scheduled fee for the scheme's subscribers and a higher fee for nonsubscribers. Often the local committee provided a horse, paddocking, saddle and bridle and, if the nurse was very lucky, a cottage. She made a monthly report to the hospital board, but her work was supervised at a distance by the department. She was therefore responsible to two authorities as well as having to maintain good relations with the local committee, the community and any doctor in the area, who might either value her work or object to her presence if he felt his income or authority were threatened.

It was no wonder that Maclean said that the scheme needed the 'very best' trained nurses, 'women of experience … with infinite tact to deal with all classes of the community; with resource to make the best of means available; with judgment to decide the best steps to take, and with force of character, to ensure those steps being taken'. In addition, the nurse needed 'geniality and sociability' and the ability to 'make herself one of the people among whom she lives; to share their amusements as well as to soothe their pain.'[10]

Maclean might have equated force of character with getting the job done, but it was evident too in nurses' determination to achieve the first essential task – getting about the district. Some areas of dense bush could be pushed through only on foot. Most committees could supply a horse, but many nurses, like Charlotte Parker, had to learn to ride. A gig or buggy made travelling easier if the state of the roads allowed it. Esther Gates at Pongaroa, east of Pahiatua in the Tararua district, managed the hard, dusty clay roads in summer but said that 'in winter, they defy description.' In the six months she had been there, she had covered 627 miles (close to 1000km), and the committee chairman said she was becoming 'as well known as a Bank of England note.' Backblocks nurses 'required a knowledge of riding and a strong nerve,' Gates said, as the roads made one 'quail inwardly', but 'the fact that one is urgently needed at the end of the journey helps one wonderfully on the road.' She had had 'many a good laugh over the difficulties and drawbacks encountered' in reaching her patients. Her greatest reward came when a settler told her, 'Nurse, I don't know what I shall do without you.'[11]

Some remote nurses had different transport challenges. In 1914 Fanny McDonald, called to an emergency birth at a bush sawmill, was transported on a motor jigger, 'just like a raft on small engine wheels, with a motor cycle fixed on top and a belt connecting to the wheels.' She gripped the kerosene box that was her seat as the jigger went 'full speed' along the rail lines leading into the bush.[12] Mrs Sara Somerville, the backblocks nurse on Stewart Island from 1912 to 1917, was conveyed to its numerous sawmills in a fishing boat, but if the tide was unfavourable she went ashore in a dinghy. Unfortunately, one day the dinghy tipped and no one could lift 'the rather large Nurse Somerville' back into it, so 'a bedraggled nurse with a keen sense of humour was towed to the beach.'[13] Gladys Peters, the Stewart Island nurse from 1933 to 1948, said this story, handed down over the years, had apparently made an impression: the fishermen made sure that she never got even her feet wet.[14]

Even in the 1930s when more roads were metalled or sealed, transport remained a challenge for district health nurses. Some still needed to learn to ride a horse, as Amy Rickman did in the Far North.[15] The nurse on Waiheke Island in 1937 wrote to the Auckland Hospital Board to request a better horse. On her recent visit to isolated sheep stations, she noted, 'I was away four days, and had a horse that was no good. I had to kick it all the way there and back, and walk up and down all the steep hills.' The account provoked 'facetious comments' among the members until Mrs M.M. Dreaver pointed out the seriousness of the nurse's situation. The other members still laughed, but the chairman, the Rev. W.C. Wood, 'assured her smilingly that a better horse would be provided.'[16] In 1944 when Helen Mackie took up her

Nurse P. Wharfe on Peter the Perfect, Te Kao, 1946. Even in the 1940s, some district health nurses in remote rural areas had to travel about their districts on horseback.
Margaret Macnab album, New Zealand Nurses' Organisation Library, Wellington

first position as a district health nurse based at the small community of Frasertown, her district extended from the outskirts of Wairoa to the east to big river valleys to the north and west, the bush-clad Urewera Ranges, Lake Waikaremoana and the Tuai power station. Beyond the shingle roads, 'the journey had to be either on horseback or on Shanks's pony! In a district with so many rivers, I had to visit several houses with access by a cage, pulled across the river by an overhead cable.' At other times she paddled a canoe across the river to a group of houses directly across from Frasertown to save a long journey to cross on the bridge at Wairoa and return.[17]

Getting about might have been challenging, but the scenery was rewarding. Nurses' narratives often reveal a keen sense of place. Esther Gates at Pongaroa said in 1913 that there were 'hills everywhere, glorious hills, "natural cathedrals" Ruskin calls them – and when one is weary, and is weighed down by a sense of failure, or at least only partial success, to "lift up one's eyes to the hills" is a very great help indeed'. There was 'infinite variety of shade and colouring, and a fresh view at every turn of the road'. Most of the bush there was 'left only in patches' as land had been cleared for farming, so 'the greater part of the country is covered with gaunt trunks of former giants whose roots lie exposed on the hillside like the tentacles of enormous octopi.'[18]

This scenery aided Maclean in recruiting nurses for remote districts. In 1914, she said the nurse who gained the position for the Waiuta gold-mining district south of Reefton should be very happy there, as it was 'in a beautiful locality on the top of a mountain surrounded by distant snow-clad mountains. The road to it runs alongside the mountain looking down on the most beautiful forest of black birch.' As additional (and more practical) attractions, it would not have the 'long journeys over rough roads as in some districts', and the residents would 'welcome a nurse into their midst'.[19] Similarly, in recruiting a nurse for the South Westland district in 1920, she said, 'The country is beautiful, and is gradually becoming more settled; rivers bridged and better roads.' She reminded nurses, though, that 'to be able to ride is essential'.[20] The Westland Hospital Board emphasised the scenery even more: 'For those who are fond of an outdoor life amongst some of the most remarkable and beautiful scenery in the world, and do not object to living and journeying in a very sparsely settled district, this affords a unique opportunity of gratifying such tastes.' And, as a further attraction, the 'open-hearted kindness and hospitality of the West Coast is proverbial'.[21]

Mabel Baker, the nurse appointed, soon perceived both advantages. She wrote to Maclean that on New Year's Eve she was called to see a child with suspected appendicitis 120 miles (193km) to the south. On her long trek, with three stops for refreshment and change of horse and one welcome hot bath, she saw the dawn of the new year by the shore of Lake Māpōurika, a 'pretty sight'. 'The scenery here is lovely,' she said. 'The Franz Joseph is a never-ending delight and wonder and ... I have never seen such beautiful bush country before.' The settlers were 'most kind', having a horse and meal waiting at each stage of the journey. During the whole of her time in South Westland she had received 'every consideration from the settlers'. Her case of suspected appendicitis was resolved easily with a dose of cod liver oil: the child had had 'too much Christmas fare'.[22]

The virtues of geniality and sociability that Maclean identified were vital both professionally and personally, as there was no anonymity or privacy in a rural community. The nurse was known to all, and always on call. Maclean noted that people expected 'besides the anxious nursing of the sick, too much from the nurses in work for the well'.[23] Most nurses, though, commented on the kindness, consideration and support they received and had great admiration for the settlers struggling on the land. In return, women in isolated places deeply appreciated the nurse's occasional company. Annie O'Callaghan at Urutī in Taranaki wrote to Maclean: 'I wish I could write an article for your nursing journal about the settlers away back here. One woman rode in fourteen miles [22km] ... to see me, she was not feeling well. She has no woman anywhere near her.'[24]

Nurses followed Maclean's advice to make settlers' amusements their own. One in the Far North in 1922 said she had 'made friends all over the country' and would be sorry when her year ended, though she was longing to go to Lambton Quay 'to buy some new dresses and a new hat'. In the meantime, she had been duck-shooting up the Hokianga River on a 'foggy, damp dawn'. Crouching behind the mangroves and rushes, with decoys bobbing a few feet away, she concluded after three hours that it was a 'very slow sport and worse than trying to spear flat fish'. The ducks 'refused to come and be shot', so the hunting party packed up and tramped over rough country in search of other quarry. 'Although the ducks jeered at us from distant mud flats on our way home,' she said, 'a plump pheasant, three quail and two rabbits had crossed our paths, to their sorrow.'[25] Amy Rickman, based at Houhora in the 1930s, was 'never lonely'. She would ride over to Ninety Mile Beach with friends and once saw Charles Kingsford Smith land his plane on it. Wearing her usual off-duty outfit of linen coat and riding breeches, she and others were photographed in front of the plane. 'I was looking like nothing on earth,' she said.[26]

Tact was another essential virtue in work and community life. It was needed in persuading mothers, for example, that it was injurious to feed their eight-month-old

Amy Rickman, the district health nurse at Houhora in the Far North, felt she looked 'like nothing on earth' when photographed with Charles Kingsford-Smith and the Southern Cross in 1934. Amy is seated (right). 1/2-030539-F, Alexander Turnbull Library, Wellington

infants bread, potatoes, cabbage, pudding and a saucerful of strong tea from their cup. The task was 'almost hopeless', the nurse said, as the mothers themselves had been brought up on this fare.[27] Tact was needed in managing committees' expectations. And it was needed in communicating with the few doctors who objected to a nurse suggesting a diagnosis or attending patients who would otherwise have paid the doctor a fee for attendance.[28]

The conflicting obligations of following a doctor's instructions when available by telephone but making their own treatment decisions when they were not, demanded judgement and force of character from nurses. Acting beyond the scope of their official role, as they frequently had to do, could make them anxious. A nurse on the East Coast in 1914 identified the worry and risk involved in maternity and emergency work but was pleased she had 'put up a child's leg, a fracture, quite successfully not long ago.'[29] Maclean acknowledged that nurses 'must be prepared to act on their own responsibility when confronted with an emergency and away from medical direction, but in no case to give advice or assume any such responsibility under other circumstances'. She would rather wait to obtain nurses with the necessary 'discretion' than fill a position too quickly.[30] Many nurses, however, appreciated the measure of independence they enjoyed working in isolation. Maclean, too, noted that backblocks nurses had 'more scope for individuality and initiative' than those in hospitals.[31]

This challenge persisted through the decades. Gladys Peters on Stewart Island said that a nurse's duty was not to diagnose, but in places like the island they had to do just that.[32] When Helen Mackie arrived in Frasertown in 1944, she recognised that the work was very different from the routine of hospital nursing, as there was no demarcation of being 'on or off duty', and nurses were on their own. 'There was no one else at one's side to rely on, or blame, or grizzle with. What was done was entirely one's own responsibility. We were out in the country depending solely on our training and our wits, and it was on our shoulders that much of the work rested.'[33]

Early backblocks nurses' accounts of caring for patients in rudimentary dwellings testify to their resourcefulness. Women at Flaxdown in Taranaki in 1911 gave birth in the small tents they lived in on the flax plantation.[34] One nurse attended a woman with a miscarriage in a dwelling with an 'earth floor, on a filthy shakedown at one end. The other end contained a pile of food stores, on which numerous fowls were perching, and a packing-case table under which a goat was reposing.'[35] In 1922 Nurse M.A. Reid attended the only woman living in a North Auckland railway public works camp near Mareretu, whose 'very rough and crude' dwelling comprised four small huts joined together with a large corrugated-iron chimney. The stove smoked badly, and there was only one kerosene tin to carry water and a small tub for washing clothes and bathing. The floorboards were so far apart that 'the black, sharp eye of a hen could be seen peering through'.[36]

Even when backblocks nursing was refashioned in 1930 into district health nursing, resourcefulness was essential. Those working in the Hokianga district in the 1930s and 1940s with Dr George Smith, the eccentric, visionary medical superintendent at Rāwene Hospital, learned how to make a splint out of the *Auckland Weekly News* magazine, which was found in most homes. Helen Mackie recalled, 'This big magazine was almost impossible to bend and made the perfect sling, rounding the limb and padding it with thick pages. It was not only readily available but also easy to apply and extremely comfortable.' Another innovation was his ointment made from castor oil and Vaseline. The dressings were 'smelly but could be left on a wound untouched for three days. When redressed, the wound would always be clean and well on the way to healing.'[37] Another Rāwene nurse wrote that this remedy had become 'routine treatment for all septic wounds, impetigo, carbuncles, boils, burns and scalds, ulcers, etc.'[38] Amy Rickman thought the ointment was 'wonderful'.[39]

Rural nurses needed to be resourceful and determined when responding to the many bush, mine, public works and railway accidents. For example, when a section of the partially constructed Ōtira Tunnel collapsed in 1910, Olive Drewitt and a junior doctor went from the small Greymouth Hospital to attend the trapped men. They had a 'most strenuous time of it' for 24 hours as men were rescued and transported to hospital.[40] In 1934 Doris Workman, the Whangamōmona nurse in Taranaki, examined a pig hunter brought to her cottage at 5.30am who had been rescued after falling more than 250 feet (76m) over a cliff. He was unconscious and suffering from shock and exposure but had no broken bones. She took him to Stratford Hospital, first by train, on a stretcher slung from the roof of the guard's van, and then by ambulance. That December, when two trains collided, she went by jigger through the railway tunnel and transported injured men back on the same jigger to Pohokura, where a waiting ambulance took them on to hospital.[41] In 1939 a miner suffered severe spinal injuries in a rockfall in a coal mine up the Mōkau River. His colleague got him out and rowed him 12 miles (19km) down the river to transfer him to a launch that took him two miles to a ferry and to the nurse's cottage at Mōkau across the river. Nurse I.M. Sinclair then had the anxious task of driving the severely injured man 70 miles (112km) to the hospital.[42]

Despite the vaunted attractions of backblocks nursing, recruitment was difficult, although nurses were recruited from Britain in only one year, 1912.[43] Retention was variable. A quarter of the nurses worked just their initial year's contract, but half stayed for two to five years. They left for further training, hospital positions, private nursing, wartime service, retirement or marriage, or because of ill health or accident.[44] The life was hard, but Nellie Nickless at Eketāhuna thought that if nurses only knew what a 'free, happy life' it was, more would go in for it.[45] Esther Gates at Pongaroa said: 'It is worth the wear and tear, it is worth being cut off, practically from all that one's soul loves in the way of pleasure and recreation, it is worth, even spending one's Christmas out-back, away from one's dear ones, with only the mail to keep one in touch.'[46]

Backblocks nursing folklore

The virtues Maclean identified as essential for backblocks nursing were revealed in narratives that gave rise to the folklore of the intrepid nurse. It began in January 1910 with a story from the first backblocks nurse, Margaret Bilton, stationed at Urutī in Taranaki from August 1909. She had just finished shifting from the general store to board in a resident's house when she was called to see a child with pneumonia. After giving the child initial care, she was almost immediately fetched by a man in 'dire distress' to see his wife, who was in danger after giving birth prematurely. Bilton explained to the pneumonia patient's mother how to care for the girl during the night, rang the hospital from the general store to arrange the girl's admission the next day, then rode with the new mother's husband over Mt Messenger. This was always a difficult journey, but this time it was brightened by moonlight and glow-worms 'like rows upon rows of electric lights'. She found the mother well but scolded the two neighbours who had attended her during the birth for 'not scrubbing up their grimy hands, and for not having the placenta for me to examine'. She administered Lysol douches to reduce the risk of infection. The baby, who did well initially, 'lost ground' on the seventh day and had to be taken to a doctor and on to a hospital. There Bilton handed over the baby, 'quite sorry to part with the little mite', but knowing she also had to go on to her next maternity case, who was due to give birth that day.[47]

The pioneers of this new form of nursing were keen to tell others about it. Versions of this story of answering the call were often published in *Kai Tiaki* until 1915 (when they were overtaken by nurses' wartime stories) and reappeared in accounts and memoirs of rural nursing from the 1920s to the 1940s. The consistent elements of the genre were a call to attend a patient, an arduous journey, the arrival and reconnaissance in an unfamiliar environment, the clinical challenge and its resolution.[48] Such efforts are characteristic of folklore focusing on a test of a hero's ability.[49] The intent of these narratives was to show the stark contrast between backblocks nursing and hospital nurses' experiences. The intrepid-nurse folklore engaged readers with its dramatic descriptions of nurses' isolation, difficult journeys in rugged but beautiful terrain, constant availability, and hard work in meeting nursing challenges.[50] At the same time, the clipped and concrete detailing of a patient's clinical presentation and treatment were characteristic of professional nursing notes and ensured the tales' credibility.

One example of the genre was contributed in 1911 by Sarah Warnock at Seddon in Marlborough, who was called to attend a woman in labour at Cape Campbell Lighthouse. On a dark night, with no lights, she was taken in a horse-drawn trap to the beach, where the rocks proved impassable. She was hoisted on to the unyoked draught horse, 'laden with midwifery bag and douche can, etc' and had 'an awful scramble of four miles' around the shore. She reached the lighthouse at 4am to find the baby alive but cold and the mother lying on piles of dusty, blood-soaked blankets. The woman was pallid from blood loss, as she was 'losing more than any case I had ever seen before. The uterus large and flabby; the blood coming away in a stream, accompanied by clots'. It was impossible to call the nearest doctor, 35 miles (56km) away, as the tide had come in. 'I massaged uterus without success, but managed to stop loss by long, hot douche, but not for some time. I had decided upon plugging, but fortunately it was not needed.' She warmed the baby with a hot water bottle and gave it brandy (as a stimulant), and over the next two days it 'came on beautifully'. She left on the eighth day but was going back for the christening and a picnic.[51]

Hester Maclean selected this story, published in *Kai Tiaki*, for the account of New Zealand nursing that she contributed to an international nursing history compiled by the American nurse leader Lavinia Dock.[52] The main test could sometimes be the journey. Annie O'Callaghan, who took Bilton's place at Urutī in 1911, told of being called to a maternity case seven miles (11km) away. She managed a difficult ride along the Moki Road, a cliffside track. It had been partially washed away and was only three feet wide in some places, with a 300-foot (90m) drop to the river.[53]

An account by Nora Kelly, the next Urutī nurse, drew sharp contrasts between relaxation and work, comfort and discomfort, safety and danger, warmth and cold, domestic and natural realms, light and dark, cleanliness and mud, mobility and immobility, ease and difficulty. Her peaceful Saturday night was disrupted by a knock at the door just as she had 'settled down by a good fire, with my writing materials all ready, hoping to get several letters answered'. A boy delivered a note saying there had been a bush accident and 'to come at once'. It was a very dark night. She and the boy cantered the first two miles (3km) but then had to 'climb up and up' to a razorback ridge where the sharp, narrow track was muddy and slippery, almost impassable with great slips. To 'make the ride more cheerful', the boy told her 'interesting facts', like the place where a man had been thrown from his horse and nearly killed, and where an old lady had rolled over a precipice, breaking her arm and being rescued only after several hours. When Kelly's horse refused to go farther, the boy said to hit it, so hit it she did, and horse and rider slid down a perpendicular bank together. But on they went, in the intense dark, with bush each side. At midnight they saw the lights of their destination. She was warmed by the greeting, 'Oh, nurse, how glad we are to see you,' and the 'cheerful fire and ever-welcome cup of tea', but this domestic haven was disrupted by the presence of a lad of 17 lying on a stretcher by the fire, whose leg had been broken by a falling tree. It was 'splendidly put up in temporary splints' cut from the bush and held in place with strips of sheeting. A doctor arrived at 4am and set the leg. At 11am they began the outward trek, with volunteers carrying the lad on the stretcher for the first seven miles (11km), and arrived at New Plymouth Hospital at midnight. 'No one but a nurse,' she said, 'can understand how lovely it feels to be in a hospital once more. The beds look so clean, and white, and you know that the patient could not be in a better place.'[54] The natural realm of the bush, cold at night and intensely dark, contrasted with the lights and cheerful fires of the domestic realms. The dangers of bush-felling work and both journeys were set against the safety of the hospital, and the rough stretcher contrasted with the clean, white hospital beds.

Difficult journeys with less successful outcomes were also recorded in memoirs and reported sympathetically in newspapers. The chairman of the Stratford Hospital Board in 1934, Mr W.L. Kennedy, noted that the backblocks nurse's position was 'no sinecure'. Doris Workman, having consulted the Stratford Hospital medical superintendent, carried a sick baby on horseback for nine miles (14km) from its home in the bush at the Moki Mill to a car waiting at Tahora to transport it to hospital. When she reached the Moki Saddle, just three miles from Tahora, the baby died.[55] And in 1936, the call came too late for Amy Rickman at Houhora to reach a man at Thom's Landing, an isolated gum-fields port 35 miles (56km) away. The man had mistaken a tin of yellow powder for brimstone (sulphur) and had mixed it with treacle to make the common brimstone-and-treacle 'blood purifier' or tonic. The powder was sheep dip. He took a spoonful of the mixture and gave another to his daughter. Both were violently ill and died.[56]

Another variant of the intrepid-nurse folktale emphasised the varied workload and relentless duty. In 1911, Annie O'Callaghan at Urutī again went down the dreaded Moki Road to a maternity case, where she stayed for a month before being called away to attend a five-month-old child who had developed pneumonia following whooping-cough. She was just getting the child settled when someone came galloping in to fetch her to an accident – a man had been thrown from his horse six miles (9km) away. She found him covered in blood, unconscious and with people throwing cold water on him and trying to give him 'the usual draught of whisky'. She swiftly stopped them and made a thorough assessment – 'found no indications of fracture; then could not find any traces of discharge from ears, nose, or mouth so thought it must be concussion'. She got a stretcher made from an old tarpaulin and two fence posts and had him carried a mile and a half to his bed. She telephoned a doctor, who agreed the man was suffering from concussion. He regained consciousness the next day and improved over the week. She ended by saying she hoped to 'get a few days' off after this.[57]

Her next story, which Maclean printed immediately after, showed that O'Callaghan was to be disappointed. It started with her leaving the concussion case to go to a man with appendicitis, a father of eight, who was miles away along the bridle track around the cliffs. Three pairs of men took turns carrying him eight miles (12km) on a stretcher while she walked beside him. They balanced the stretcher on a log to ford the river, then conveyed him in a trap to the hospital, the whole journey taking 12 hours. She had just returned to Urutī when she was called to a maternity case. The woman was haemorrhaging with placenta praevia.[58] She was taken to hospital, the baby was born the next morning, and both did well. In her first 10 weeks at Urutī, O'Callaghan had not had a day to herself at home. Since then, she said, she had been having a rest. Maclean added the postscript: 'From these accounts it is easy to see how much needed is this work in the backblocks.'[59]

In another account Maclean published the same year, a nurse reported: 'For three weeks I lived on bread and butter, frequently having no time to even boil my kettle, as I was going from early morning till night. One day I put my hat on at 4 a.m. and did not remove it till 11 p.m.' She made relentless duty a positive experience by adding: 'There is great work possible here for an enthusiastic nurse.'[60]

Fictionalised or composite accounts of a district health nurse's routine touched on the same themes. These narratives similarly emphasised the versatility needed for the varied work – bedside care, taking acute cases to hospital, maternity work and the public health work of inoculations, schoolchild health checks and health talks – and presented the nurse's day as far longer than a hospital nurse's shift. In Mary Lambie's account from 1930, the nurse worked from 6.30am till 8pm. Flora Cameron's account, published in 1945, started before 8am and ended with the nurse (and the reader) finally able to 'settle comfortably with our knitting' in the evening and listen to 'Officer Crosby' on the radio. Both authors were postgraduate nursing instructors and future chief nurses. Cameron had been a district health nurse herself, and Lambie had made visits as a nurse inspector. These accounts appeared in multiple publications, including an American journal on public health nursing, New

Department of Health nurse inspector Janet Moore on a tour of inspection in the Far North in the late 1920s, enjoying a picnic in the Waipoua bush – a chance for one district nurse to hand her over to the nurse in the next district. Margaret Macnab album, New Zealand Nurses' Organisation Library, Wellington

Zealand's *Public Service Journal*, the *New Zealand Nursing Journal* and newspapers such as the *Evening Post* and *Gisborne Times*.[61]

Under the challenging and isolating circumstances faced by backblocks nurses, the efforts to forge a community constituted another aspect of the professional narratives. Janet Moore gave an account of touring the Far North in 1929 as nurse inspector. She started with Mabel Vos, based at Dargaville in the Kaipara district, who had a nice cottage, a Māori assistant and a good Morris Cowley car.[62] Fortunately, good metalled roads were 'spreading fast all over the north', revealing that the 'recent terra incognita' was now desirable country. The narrative blended an appreciation of people and scenery. On Friday, Moore and Vos went to Hokianga with a hospital nurse who had saved her day off for the purpose. They diverted to meet a 'married ex-nurse, who is a power and a blessing to her neighbourhood, and incidentally stands by our district nurse with kind thoughtfulness in the shape of a hot meal and a helping hand, notwithstanding the full demands of her busy home and family'. Driving through a kauri forest with its 'great boles of trees, straight and stately', they reached the Waipoua River, where they 'prepared luncheon under the trees, using a fire-place made by the Public Works department staff while making the road'. Nurse Ella Leslie from Rāwene arrived in her own Dodge car,[63] and 'full justice was done to the contents of some peculiar shaped packages which had travelled with us, but were returned to the car much flatter and easier to handle'.

Moore then 'sped on' with Leslie towards Rāwene, meeting on the way Ngapori Naera, who had once worked as a health nurse for Māori.[64] Leslie's cottage at Rāwene was 'very tumbled-down and damp', but housing in the area was scarce. On Sunday Moore and Leslie picnicked at the Mangamuka Bridge with three ex-nurses who lived in the locality, and nurses Amy Jewiss from Kaitara and Mabel Mangakāhia, so 'a merry party sat down under the big bridge, sheltered from the passing showers'.[65] They crossed the narrows of the Hokianga River by punt and drove along the river, after which Moore and Leslie farewelled the Hokianga nurses, who took a long route home in order to visit patients. Travelling through the 'glorious' Mangamuka Gorge where the forest and scenery were superb, Moore and Leslie arrived at Kaitāia at 4pm. After tea they visited Sarah Polden, the former matron of Thames Hospital, who was now working as a mission sister among the Māori. After working at Kaitāia, on Monday they went to Peria to see another ex-nurse, then on to Mangōnui, and on Tuesday to Kawakawa to see Mary Hall, the Bay of Islands mission nurse.[66] This journey connected several current and former nurses who would in earlier years have been isolated. As Moore said, 'The bond of our calling is sweet and strong through all the years.'[67]

Reports of such gatherings came from various localities. Janet Moore toured the north again in 1931. The same nurses – Leslie, Jewiss, Hall and Vos – 'passed her on from one to another by their cars', with a picnic lunch at the Kaitāia district boundary.[68] Janie North, nurse inspector in the East Coast district in the 1930s, often connected with her district health nurses with 'a roadside picnic and time for a chat'.[69]

The backblocks nursing folklore shared characteristics of travel writing by women in the empire that emphasised exploration of terra incognita and 'ripping yarns'.[70] Women's travel writing stressed physical hardships to demonstrate their competence as explorers and representatives of empire.[71] As literary historian Lydia Wevers noted in describing New Zealand travel writing, travellers processed their journeys through text. Travel writing was also 'an act of control. By writing about their travels, tourists transformed them into a meaningful narrative and placed themselves at the centre of meaning.' Moreover, what 'occupies travellers' attention, and energises their narratives, is the action they are engaged on, the business of getting themselves about, the physical effort it takes'.[72]

The distinctive New Zealand bush was a significant attraction to overseas visitors and a strong feature of travel literature as well as of late-colonial novels, poetry and short stories. As environmental historian Julian Kuzma has pointed out, writers like Jane Mander and William Satchell left detailed, factual and accurate accounts of bush journeys. Travellers depicted the bush as a shaper of emotion and mood, a terrible antagonist, a rough antithesis of civilisation, as well as a resource to be exploited.[73] Similar tropes are evident in backblock nurses' narratives.

The clearance of the bush as a form of resource extraction and a necessary precursor to farming was a central tenet in New Zealand writing in the 1880–1914 period, which Jane Stafford and Mark Williams have described as 'Maoriland' literature, the beginnings of literary nationalism.[74] It chronicles the dramatic shift in the landscape from impenetrable bush to pasture through felling and burning. Blanche Baughan's short stories and poems, for example, focused on 'burnt bush' and a landscape strewn with 'long, prone, grey-black logs'.[75] Baughan, who immigrated to New Zealand in 1903, was British-born and influenced by John Ruskin, the British writer, literary critic, artist and art critic who saw moral value in landscape and taught her to see it 'in painterly, constructed terms'.[76] Esther Gates, the Pongaroa nurse, referred both to Ruskin's 'natural cathedral' of hills that supported her when downcast and to the cleared bushland with its exposed roots and 'gaunt trunks of former giants'.[77]

Gates' reference to Ruskin indicated that nurses could be well-read. Hester Maclean encouraged nurses to read widely, and in *Kai Tiaki* she featured poetry (usually inspirational) and semi-regular reviews of books, including novels. The majority of New Zealand nurses in the early twentieth century had a middle-class background, as far as class distinctions existed in New Zealand, and would have had some high school education.[78] Writing essays and studying English literature, including Shakespeare's plays and Victorian novels, were part of any high school syllabus for girls.[79] Nora Kelly, for example, studied at New Plymouth Girls' High School, and her father, a medically educated farmer and justice of the peace, wrote articles for the local newspaper.[80]

The folklore served a cultural purpose by reinforcing the core rural nursing virtues of resourcefulness, judgement, force of character, tact, geniality and sociability. The accounts in *Kai Tiaki*, representing backblocks nursing as an exciting new avenue of work, might have helped Maclean recruit new rural nurses, and tales of day-and-night duty reinforced her objection to the eight-hour day for registered nurses that had been unsuccessfully proposed in 1909.

Public and professional perception

In 1909 Dr Thomas Valintine believed that the nurse in rural districts would 'supply the link in the chain between the base hospital and the remote backblock'.[81] The nurse's complex positioning in relation to community, local committee, hospital board and department ensured her value in this role.

By the 1930s and 1940s, the rural nurse's role in preventive health measures had increased markedly. Dr Harold B. Turbott was medical officer of health in the East Coast region, established in 1928 to combine two isolated districts that were previously costly and difficult to manage. In 1933 he published an article in the *International Nursing Review* (printed in English, French and German) explaining the benefits of combining medical and nursing staff efforts. In Gisborne, the district's nine nurses were 'local preventive units'. They were supplied with cars, except in the remote Ūawa, Matakaoa and Waiapu counties, where the nurse still provided 'horseback coverage'. Nurses visited 100 schools each year, treating pediculosis, scabies and impetigo, identifying children needing particular attention at the annual school medical examination and following up with families about any health issues. They gave inoculations and health talks, supplied free medicine and ointments to Māori, provided maternity care, and identified and followed up cases of tuberculosis. Through the nurses, the district medical officer became 'acquainted with the amount and nature of sickness' in each area.[82]

Turbott's article testified to the value of district health nurses, but his relationship with individual nurses was more complex. He sometimes defended them against criticism from the Department of Health, but at other times he initiated it. When Mary Lambie, acting as a nurse inspector in November 1928, gave him an assessment of the nurses and their work,[83] Turbott responded that her criticism of Whakatāne nurse Susie Trewby's 'indifferent manner' and lack of frankness was 'really too harsh a summary'. She was a reserved but willing and conscientious nurse of good character and well-liked by those who got to know her.[84] Clearly, he believed Lambie's brief encounter was an insufficient basis for such a criticism. In contrast, the following year he objected to the way Isabel Banks, based at Frasertown, had gone directly to the Department of Health to complain about having to do work in schools in addition to her present 'extensive duties', saying that lack of time could mean she would not be able to do it properly.[85] Turbott said she had 'not been over-weighted with school work': she had spent only three separate days on follow-up work in the previous eight months. He asserted that she was responsible for the

Wairoa Hospital Board's opposition to preventive work. As he had now managed to persuade the board of its usefulness, Nurse Banks had evidently decided to 'secure her own way by personal appearance in Wellington'. She was almost entirely occupied in midwifery work, which she liked, and wanted to be 'left alone in it'. The preventive side was 'neglected almost entirely'.[86]

The backblocks nurse could therefore be a pawn in a tussle for authority between hospital board, local district health office and department;[87] and sometimes, as Banks' direct appeal shows, she could be an active agent. Power players could also engage in a more public debate about the nurse's role and how she performed it. In South Westland there was controversy over the cottage promised to the backblocks nurse. The issue kept arising in newspaper articles, letters to the editor and hospital board minutes. Should it be built first, or only when a nurse was appointed? Should it be a cottage hospital, with room for two patients? As the nurse had to travel so much, would it be a white elephant? Who should pay for it?[88] Mabel Baker took the position of nurse in December 1920. When she married Alick Gunn the next year, she continued as the backblocks nurse and rarely used the cottage that was finally built. The newspaper considered she did very good work, was well esteemed, had 'taken up her duties with a will' and readily went 'long distances at a moment's call'.[89] However, she did not have support from all the hospital board members. Mr J. Ritchie objected to her not living more often in the provided cottage.[90] A letter to the editor supported her, saying she was 'doing her duty, and doing it worthy of a pioneer'. As Ritchie well knew, it was 'no light task for a woman to surmount the difficulties of the 50 mile [80km] ride from Mahitahi to Okuru in bad weather or fine', but the nurse had done it many times.[91]

According to Gunn, the cottage's location made travel through the district difficult for her and her horse. The only remedy was to neglect her patients or get a caravan and a team of horses so that 'like a snail my residence may travel with me'. After a wet, tiring ride she found the damp, lonely and poorly provisioned cottage 'particularly uninviting' and naturally preferred to put up at the Waiho Hotel, 'where one receives a cheery welcome, a hot meal and dry bedding'. Furthermore, was Mr Ritchie aware that she had her daily bath there? According to 'a nurse's idea of cleanliness', this would require an eight-mile (12km) ride from the cottage each day.[92]

Ritchie also opposed her request for a salary increase and used financial figures to make a case against her. Gunn, indignant, responded that it was 'a gross insult' to her profession and herself to suggest that 'figures can show the operations of a nurse'. She strongly objected to 'his attempt to belittle and falsely represent' the financial value of her services to the hospital board and ratepayers, and gave figures from her register.[93] Ritchie replied that he had 'no animosity' against her and thought she owed him an apology.[94] Gunn remained determined not to be a pawn and continued to tackle issues head-on until the end of her time as the South Westland nurse in 1924.[95]

The different lay and professional understandings of rural nurses' status and role continued. Mary Lambie's strong objection to insurance companies or groups of laypeople (like the Wanganui District Nursing League) employing nurses was also aimed at the 'bush nursing' scheme of the Women's Division of the New Zealand Farmers Union (WDFU). This scheme was not, as historian Rosemarie Smith has claimed, based on the Australian Bush Nursing Service, which had a very different organisational model.[96] The WDFU bush nursing scheme was established in 1927, just two years after the formation of the Women's Division itself, with Catherine Blackie as its first nurse.[97] It initially aimed to support poorer rural women, but by 1930 had expanded to provide 'scientific and experienced nursing at a moderate cost to all people living in the outlying districts'. Apart from nursing and midwifery qualifications, the 'bush nurse' had to work wherever needed, understand country conditions and be prepared to help with housework.[98] This last expectation would have irked Lambie. She told the postgraduate nursing class in 1934 that the WDFU nurses were really 'subsidised private nurses' for country people, but the scheme was 'most unsatisfactory', as nurses were employed by laypeople.[99] In her view, the registered nurses working in the backblocks should answer only to professionals.

***

New Zealand rural nurses' narratives were similar to those from nurses in other countries but not necessarily influenced by them: apart from the occasional story from an Australian bush nurse, such accounts were not easily accessible in New Zealand.[100] Bridget Ristori, a New Zealand nurse who from 1929 worked for two years in the relatively new Frontier Nursing Service in the Kentucky mountains in the United States, wrote similar accounts in her memoir.[101] However, these stories had different purposes in different locales. New Zealand's backblocks nursing service, funded by subscriptions and fees from settlers and by the government, did not need the aristocratic patronage that underwrote rural nursing services in Canada, India, Ireland and Australia, and thus nurses did not have to tell their stories in order to support fundraising efforts, as rural nurses in Ireland did.[102] Nor did their description of scenery serve to attract tourists, like the letters from British nurses in the Colonial Nursing Service in the Caribbean.[103] New Zealand rural nurses' stories did, however, help Maclean demonstrate to health authorities and politicians the value nurses offered in the emerging health system by supporting settlers in the rural backblocks – settlers who were vital to New Zealand's positioning as a prosperous modern nation that contributed valuable resources to the empire. One nurse in a newly opened farming district in the King Country in 1913 was pleased that she had been able to help settlers get through their troubles in the strenuous 'beginnings'.[104] And Esther Gates at Pongaroa the same year said: 'I am grateful for the honour of being the pioneer of the great scheme of district nursing in this little corner of our Dominion.'[105] Backblocks nursing was well established by the time it was reorganised as district health nursing for both Pākehā and Māori in the 1930s and 1940s. Nurses' narratives then helped Mary Lambie, as chief nurse, show that nurses could effectively implement the department's demanding combination of bedside nursing and rural public health services.

CHAPTER 6

Nursing Māori, Māori nurses

In 1922 Nurse Mary Jane Cartwright wrote that she had just returned home from a 'strenuous ride up hills and down dales' around the Māori settlements in the Rāwene district, when a call came saying there was a 19-year-old Māori youth at Whangapē ill with typhoid fever. The journey to reach him entailed crossing the 'unbridged immense' Hokianga River by the 'cream launch', a guided horseback ride along a 12-mile (19km) track with many mud holes in a drenching thunderstorm, a ferry trip (free of charge) to Whangapē, a stretch in a 'pulling boat' up the Awaroa River, and a struggle on foot across a mudflat and along a muddy road to the whare. There the patient's condition filled her 'heart with pity, and a great desire to help him'. The whare was 'dirty in the extreme' and crowded with those waiting for the young man to die, as well as cats, dogs and 'relics of a poultry yard'. The patient enjoyed the 'cup of cold water and a "swim" (tepid sponge bath)' he begged for, and 'how the old folk peeped and chattered over the performance!' He had been ill for over four weeks, and as he had 'haemorrhage per rectum', was too weak to move to hospital. Next morning, she isolated him as best she could in a hillside hut she asked the family to repair. 'Didn't he revel in that fresh air and sunshine, quietness and view,' she said. And yes, he was still alive.

Food was scarce, so locals brought supplies. Two youths used sheet iron to rainproof a whare in the church grounds, where she camped with a Primus stove and enjoyed the Sunday choir. Everyone co-operated, but the patient's elderly father could not be persuaded to remove the animals from his whare, quoting the biblical Noah's ark story as justification.

The nurse had several visitors, including a couple with a baby son she had previously treated for sores. They had at first been reluctant for her to do so, as they believed in the faith healing of Tahupōtiki Wiremu Rātana, but they were proud now to show him healed.

As Cartwright's young typhoid patient began to mend, a telegram called her to investigate sickness at the other end of the county. After hurried preparations, she set off with her guide to ride 14 miles (22km) along the coast and then up the precipitous Golden Stairs Track, where all she could do was 'hold on – and hold my breath'. After a brief moment on the summit to enjoy the panorama, they descended to the sandy coast and traversed treacherous sandhills to arrive at Rangi Point, 'aching and sore', just in time to catch the cream launch. A Māori woman summoned a lad to help Cartwright onto the launch. 'Without any word of warning or time to look around', she was 'simply picked up, carried through the tide and hoisted aboard'. She ended her story by anticipating another journey that meant crossing the river 12 times to reach a beautiful valley where she had already 'seen a good deal of our Maori fellow-citizens', in sickness and health.[1]

This story captured elements familiar in nurses' narratives of caring for rural Māori between 1909 and 1950 – the challenges of reaching and caring for patients, Māori generosity, differing cultural views of cleanliness and nurses' sometimes frustrated yet willing struggle to understand and work with Māori life and customs. Their narratives included te reo Māori words and phrases such as kai, kōrero, ka pai, kei te pai, and neehi (nurse).[2] The major health concern was typhoid fever until the 1930s, when it was eclipsed by tuberculosis.

Māori health, nursing Māori

Historian Raeburn Lange has described the late nineteenth- and early twentieth-century popular and scholarly beliefs and attitudes shaping the government's Māori health policy and how these meshed with the Māori vision for their own future.[3] Fundamental to the government approach was a belief that Māori were a 'dying race'. Although collecting population statistics for Māori was problematic, the evidence for the decline in numbers was strong. Lange draws on Ian Pool's estimate of a Māori population of around 70,000 to 90,000 in 1840.[4] By the 1896 census it had declined to about 42,000. Lange notes that the 'dying race' prophecy had taken such a hold on popular opinion that subsequent evidence of the slowing rate or even reversal of Māori population decline went largely unnoticed.

Popular culture reflected a belief in continuing decline. A.A. Grace's 1901 short story collection was titled *Tales of a Dying Race*. Charles Goldie's Māori portraits deliberately portrayed 'poses of despondent weariness' and carried titles like *A Noble Relic of a Noble Race* and *The Last of Her Tribe*.[5] As Lange notes, although no doubt boosted by a desire for land, Pākehā responses to Māori decline (whether sorrowful or soulless) were only part of a complex array of attitudes at the time. The eighteenth-century European idea of the 'noble savage' had not entirely disappeared – Māori were seen as a 'superior' native race – but Pākehā were unsparing in their criticism of a Māori way of life that did not reflect their own standards. Nineteenth-century humanitarianism shaped a belief that Māori could be protected, preserved and gradually brought to a Christian, civilised standard of living through example and benign intervention. This view shaped a paternalistic policy of benevolent tutelage. State-run Native schools, for example, established from 1867 and eagerly sought by Māori communities, taught the primary school syllabus and emphasised health. James Pope, inspector of Native schools, strongly supported this emphasis and wrote *Health for the Maori,* a manual that promoted health reforms. It was widely distributed and used as a reader.[6]

In the late nineteenth century, Lange notes, the growing belief that governments could, and should, intervene to protect public health was matched by increasing confidence in public health knowledge and practices. Concern for Māori health was part of the Liberal government policy, but little was done until the plague scare of 1900 that was concentrated in Auckland but created national concern. This led directly to the Public Health Act 1900, which designated Māori settlements as special districts, and to the establishment of the Public Health Department the following year, with Dr Maui Pōmare appointed as Native health officer. Further legislation in 1900 set up Māori Councils in each settlement with a wide range of responsibilities, including sanitation, water supply and the registration of births, deaths and marriages. This system was eagerly adopted by Māori, who had long been agitating for self-government at least at the local level. Thanks to Pōmare's energetic programme of kāinga visits and persuasive argument, the komiti marae set up under the new Māori Councils were usually enthusiastic supporters of sanitary reforms. From the 1890s, young Māori leaders had supported the need for health reform. These included past pupils of Te Aute College, Pōmare among them, who had founded its Students' Association. John Thornton, the headmaster, consistently encouraged boys to develop pride in their Māori identity. These emerging leaders came to be known as the Young Māori Party. Older Māori also supported sanitary reform, as demonstrated by the 100-strong deputation of chiefs to the government in support of Te Piri Kiore, or the 'Rat Bill' – the Public Health Bill enacted in 1900.[7]

Before the development of a Māori nursing service, Māori suffering from illness in the late nineteenth century were attended to by whānau or community members, tohunga, Native school teachers (who dispensed government-provided medicines) and sisters in religious missions. Suzanne Aubert, who had gained some nursing and medical experience in France before coming to New Zealand in 1860, cared for Māori in Hawke's Bay, combining the herbal remedies she learned from them with her own. She established the Sisters of Compassion mission at Hiruhārama (Jerusalem) on the Whanganui River in 1883 before relocating her order to Wellington in 1899, where for a short time it provided basic care for the sick poor in their own homes.[8] Few religious sisters had nurse training, however, even in the early twentieth century.[9] Māori were often reluctant to go to Pākehā hospitals, which were impersonal and uncongenial, had unfamiliar customs, excluded visitors and were associated with death. Hospital authorities, moreover, were often reluctant to admit them, as they would often not pay their fees, and Māori land did not contribute financially to hospitals through the local rates levy.[10]

Initially, a government nursing service for Māori was envisioned as an initiative 'by Māori, for Māori', with Māori nurses serving their communities. The proposal by Hāmiora Hei and James Pope, following a Te Aute Association conference in December 1897, spurred the establishment of Department of Education scholarships to enable senior Māori pupils to extend their time at the (Anglican) Hukarere or (Catholic) St Joseph Schools in Napier and, as day pupils, gain a year's nursing experience at Napier Hospital, so that they could return to their communities as 'efficient preachers of the gospel of health'.[11] It became apparent, however, that Māori nurses needed to be fully qualified as nurses if they were to have the necessary 'mana and weight' to do their work effectively.[12] The scheme was therefore expanded in 1905 to enable participants to train as registered nurses.[13] By 1908 interdepartmental cooperation was formalised. The Education Department selected students and paid them an additional allowance for clothing and books, and the Department of Hospitals managed their hospital placements, where they received the same salary and training as other probationers. Other hospitals joined the full scholarship scheme, including Auckland Hospital, which also trained day pupils from Queen Victoria College.

Alexandra McKegg has argued that the significant obstacles to the success of the scholarship schemes were the cultural barriers and racism confronting Māori trainees, including hospital authorities' lack of confidence in their ability and racially segregated accommodation. However, this last point appears to be based on only one example, at Waikato Sanatorium.[14] Separate accommodation did not seem to be an issue elsewhere, and day pupils, still boarding at their schools, retained the daily support of their Māori school communities. Nevertheless, Māori trainees were entering and navigating a Pākehā-dominated health system with its inherent cultural biases and assumptions. Hospital board discussions on training Māori, whether in the scholarship scheme or applying independently, revealed that some members believed Māori were difficult to train, found the study difficult, made less efficient nurses and did not stay long once qualified. On the other hand, members recognised that having Māori nurses would be good for Māori and believed there should be no discrimination against Māori applicants. In 1915, for example, the Wanganui Hospital Board discovered that one applicant with 'a typically English name' was actually Māori. The chairman objected to accepting her, but one board member said the chairman was 'drawing the colour line', and Māori should have the same privileges as Pākehā.[15] The reluctance of some hospital boards and matrons to take scholarship holders was not necessarily an indication of the racism that McKegg claims: it was also engendered by a sense of fairness to the long list of applicants (Pākehā and Māori) who often waited months to start training and who would be displaced if scholarship holders were given priority in selection. In addition, Māori scholarship holders did not always meet the minimum age required for entering training.

Concerns that Māori probationers found the study too difficult were balanced by efforts to support them: for example, they could sit state examinations in te reo Māori if they wished.[16] Mary Lambie also reminded tutor sisters that a Māori nurse frequently thought in Māori and could therefore be slower to grasp new instructions given in English, and if she thought in English, her background and experience might be very different from those of her fellow nurses.[17] There were undoubtedly difficulties for Māori probationers, but the recognition of the need for Māori nurses and the assistance provided indicate that the situation was a complex mix of challenges and support.

The myth of the first Māori registered nurse

When the first nurses qualified from the full government scholarship scheme, in 1908, one was mistakenly identified as the first Māori woman to register as a nurse. This pioneering figure had symbolic significance both in newspaper stories and within the profession. The account that prevailed served its powerful mythic function of explaining contradictions, reinforcing values and providing a charter for action.

Ākenehi Hei was the first Māori woman to gain dual qualifications as a nurse and midwife, in 1908.

Lavinia L. Dock, ed., *A History of Nursing*, vol. 4 (New York: G.P. Putnam's Sons, 1912), facing p. 212.

At that time both Hēni Whangapirita and Ākenehi Hei were candidates for this title. They trained at Wellington and Napier Hospitals, respectively, but sat the same state final examination in June 1908. Both registered in July, but Whangapirita's name appeared well above Hei's on the register. Both completed their midwifery training, Hei by the end of 1908 and Whangapirita in mid-1909. Both were employed by the Native Department in 1909, nursing typhoid patients in remote fever camps and advising Māori communities on sanitation and health. They sometimes worked together. Both contracted typhoid fever. Whangapirita became ill in September 1910, recovered and left the service early in 1911 to marry. Hei contracted typhoid in November 1910 from nursing members of her own family and died on 28 November 1910.

Not only did Whangapirita technically register before Hei, but Māori women had registered as nurses before either of them. In 2001 Diana Masters identified Mereana Tangata as the first Māori registered nurse. She had completed three years' training at Auckland Hospital in 1896 under her Pākehā name of Mary Anne Leonard and registered in June 1902.[18] However, the first Māori registered nurse was not Tangata but Kate Wyllie, the daughter of James Wyllie and Keita Waere (née Halbert).[19] She started working as a nurse at Gisborne Hospital in 1894. In 1897 she was given a senior nurse position and often took on further responsibility in the absence of the matron, Caroline Stewart. When a formal training course began the next year, she was already considered a 'very competent nurse'.[20] Completing the course and gaining its certificate in December 1901 enabled her to show evidence of three years' formal training when the nursing register opened at the beginning of 1902.[21] She registered in February, the 26th nurse in the country to do so.[22] (Caroline Stewart provided leadership by being the second nurse on the register.)[23] At the end of April 1902 Wyllie married Edgar (Ted) George Stevens, left the profession and

Kate Wyllie appears to have been the first nurse to qualify at Gisborne Hospital, in 1901, and the first Māori woman to register as a nurse, in 1902. Kate Wyllie, 900-Wyllie-03-Wyllie-KateJnr, Tairāwhiti Museum

ran a rural accommodation house at Gray's Hill, Waimata. Two of their daughters – Flora and Tui – became nurses.[24]

Despite the facts, on her death Ākenehi Hei was hailed as the first Māori registered nurse.[25] The myth that evolved around Hei's very brief career was important in the nursing culture because it seemed to show that it was possible to live in both the Māori and Pākehā worlds. The myth also reinforced the virtues of courage, determination, adaptability and astuteness demonstrated by Hei, and provided a charter for action for future Māori women seeking to train and work as nurses.[26]

Māori women had to cross cultural boundaries and set aside any traditional health beliefs and practices while learning nursing based on Western medicine and science. They recrossed that cultural boundary to work in their own communities, bringing with them Western health beliefs and practices. Ākenehi Hei described the difficulties of negotiating these boundaries in an article in *Kai Tiaki* in 1910. It was true, she said, that her people did not extend their natural suspicions of European doctors and nurses to her. However, her work meant 'the dissolution of some time-honoured customs; the tearing down of ancestral habits and teachings; the alteration of Maori thoughts and ideas of living; in fact, a complete revolution in their socialistic, communistic and private life'. And besides, she asked, 'Who cares to have a stranger poking around his back door, condemning the hundred and one things which sanitarians know are detrimental to public health?'[27] Bringing new sanitary practices into the Māori world might require Māori nurses to counter elders' authority and teaching.

Development of Māori health nursing services

Although the full scholarship scheme struggled at times to find hospital places, or Māori probationers to fill them, six to 10 full scholarships were awarded each year even in the 1930s and 1940s.[28] In 1937 the day-pupil scholarship changed. Scholarship holders no longer completed the short course in a hospital but remained for a further two years at secondary school to provide a firmer educational foundation for nurse training and to prevent the two-year delay before reaching the required entry age.[29] The philanthropic McKenzie Trust Board also provided scholarships to Māori registered nurses in the 1940s to undertake Plunket training in Dunedin or the full postgraduate nursing course in Wellington.[30]

Despite this training support and the fact that other Māori women successfully trained outside the scholarship scheme, there were never enough Māori nurses to achieve the initial nineteenth-century idea of a 'by Māori' health service. Pākehā nurses were therefore also sought for the ad hoc service provided by the Native Department from 1909 and the Department of Health's new Native Health Nursing Service, which replaced it in 1911. Much of the work was caring for Māori in fever camps in remote areas during typhoid outbreaks. Department staff transported equipment and set up a tent camp, and one or two department nurses were left there to care for patients whose families could be persuaded to bring them. Besides Hei and Whangapirita, Nurse McElligot was employed by the Native Department

Registered Nurse Hēni Whangapirita and English-trained Nurse McElligot at an East Coast typhoid fever camp, about 1911.
7_A12380, Heritage Collection, Auckland Libraries

and worked with Whangapirita in East Coast fever camps. A photograph of them appeared, rather surprisingly, in the Education Department's annual report on Native schools in 1912, perhaps because Whangapirita had qualified from the department's day-pupil and probationer scholarship schemes.[31] As McElligot had completed only the two-year training programme at the London Hospital, she was not eligible to register as a nurse in New Zealand, which required a three-year hospital training certificate. Despite this, Hester Maclean, the chief nurse, was so impressed with her

Amelia Bagley, shown here around 1920, was superintendent of nurses in the health service for Māori until 1931, and established new nursing stations in remote rural areas.

Margaret Macnab album, New Zealand Nurses' Organisation Library, Wellington

work that when responsibility for Māori health was transferred back to the Health Department in June 1911, she allowed McElligot to continue working in the new Native Health Nursing Service.[32]

As Whangapirita had married and Hei had died, the Native Health Nursing Service started with Mary Purcell, Cicely Beetham and McElligot working under the supervision of Amelia Bagley.[33] The numbers continued to grow, and the scheme changed its name in 1923 to the Māori Health Nursing Service. As McKegg has shown, of its 63 nurses in the years 1909 to 1930, half stayed two to five years, a quarter 10–15 years, and the remainder up to 20 years.[34] The longest-serving was Amelia Bagley, who not only supervised all nurses in the service but also opened new remote nursing stations. She retired in 1931. In the 1930s, when district health nurses served both Māori and Pākehā populations, Māori represented 97 percent of patients treated. In the 1940s the numbers, though variable, were more evenly balanced.[35]

Only a few Māori nurses ever worked in the Native or Māori Health Services.[36] Maud Mataira nursed in the Northland, Rotorua and Whakatāne districts from 1911 to 1914 and, after a break, was reappointed in 1917 to the Hokianga region.[37] Eva Wi Repa worked briefly with Cicely Beetham in the Hāwera district in 1911, but Maclean reported that she was 'not able to manage the work and was not in sympathy with the people'.[38] The difficulties perhaps related to the issues that Hei had identified or to working with a different iwi from her own, but they may also have resulted from the fact that this nursing service had not been her first career choice. She took up private case nursing in Hawke's Bay.[39] Ellen Taare nursed in the Bay of Plenty and Northland regions from 1913 until 1915 when she resigned, exhausted from fever-camp nursing.[40] Ngapori Waitarehu Naera nursed in fever camps starting in 1915. She then worked in the Kaipara, Hokianga, Te Kaha, Wairoa and Tolaga Bay districts until 1923, when she took up private case nursing in the Hokianga.[41] Having qualified at Southland Hospital in December 1913, Rena

Te Au joined the service the next year and worked at Ōtaki while Ethel Lewis was on leave for overseas wartime service. She resigned in 1916 to return to Invercargill. Communities in both places enjoyed her concert singing, as she was known as the 'Maori Bellbird'.[42] Ngaro Ngapo joined in 1916, working in Northland, Waikato and the Bay of Plenty before resigning in 1923 to nurse at the Woodside Private Hospital in Auckland.[43] Ethel Watkins Taylor began in the service in 1919, stationed at Te Karaka in the East Coast district, and left in 1921 to marry. As Mrs Pritchard, living at Mātāwai, she worked unofficially in the area for 20 years, initially driving her red, six-cylinder, two-door Chevrolet with a door in the back for loading stretchers.[44] Rangi Wereta worked in the Ōtaki district from 1924.[45] In the 1930s, when the back-blocks and Māori services were combined, Māori district health nurses included Grace Ormsby, Elizabeth (Beth) Paora and Mabel Te Aowhaitini Mangakāhia, who was the first Māori nurse to achieve four qualifications.[46] Although the public and authorities expected Māori nurses to work in Māori communities, Mary Lambie recognised that they had the same right as any other nurses to work where they pleased.

Māori nurses serving Māori communities no doubt encountered challenges similar to those that Ākenehi Hei identified. According to McKegg another impediment was that health officials lacked confidence in Māori nurses' ability to exercise authority when placed in sole charge of a district.[47] Dr Thomas Valintine thought they were 'inclined to shirk responsibility', and it was better when a Pākehā nurse could 'stiffen up' the Māori nurse.[48] Hester Maclean similarly believed they lacked 'application and reliability', though not 'intelligence and adaptability'.[49]

Maclean and Valintine were perhaps misinterpreting deference and respect as lack of authority and responsibility. Māori nurses usually joined the service as soon as they registered and were first sent as assistants to Pākehā nurses.[50] In contrast, Pākehā nurses normally had (sometimes considerable) experience before joining. Sending newly graduated Māori nurses first to work with the more numerous and experienced Pākehā nurses could have been intended to ensure they had support and the chance to gain confidence in the new work and its responsibilities rather than a sign of biased assumptions about their abilities. Maud Mataira, for example, registered in July 1911 and went to work for a short time with Mary Purcell, the first Native health nurse, who had been a registered nurse for eight years. And Ellen Taare, who joined the service in 1913, as soon as she had registered, worked first in the Thames district with Lilian (Lily) Dawson, an Australian nurse who had 16 years' nursing experience before becoming a Native health nurse.[51]

Māori health nursing work and culture

Nurses' narratives of Māori health nursing both reflected and countered social attitudes and beliefs relating to Māori. Nurses certainly did not see their work as 'smoothing the pillow of a dying race', even though the idea persisted in popular culture for decades.[52] They saw themselves as actively working with Māori to improve their health. Nurses' narratives did reflect the widespread criticism of sanitation in Māori communities, but they did not portray this as endangering Pākehā health by spreading typhoid fever, as Dr Herbert Chesson, the medical officer of health for the Wellington region, complained in his reports.[53] Maclean's 1912 description of the nurse's intended duties reflected the humanitarian yet paternalistic philosophy of benign intervention,[54] leading a 'native race' to better standards by example and guidance. Apart from detecting illness, nursing patients and preventing the spread of disease, the nurse was to 'live among them, help them with advice and example to live a more hygienic life and to bring up their children in a healthy manner'.[55] Cicely Beetham, based at Ōkaiawa in 1912, said: 'To stay in the kaingas and nurse the sick, thereby demonstrating instructions, is a wonderful help towards the progress of this work … [T]he people clearly realize that the nurses have their welfare truly at heart and are deeply interested in the work and the people.'[56] In turn, Māori were among those providing support for the service, and nurses often commented that they could not have managed without this.[57] As historian Linda Bryder has noted, providing healthcare for Māori was 'always a two-way process'.[58]

Māori health nursing required the same virtues as backblocks nursing – tact, resourcefulness, judgment, force of character, geniality and sociability.[59] In addition, Maclean believed Māori health nurses needed initiative, a happy spirit and sense of humour, and dignity to balance their friendliness.[60] Mary Lambie considered they needed patience, perseverance, ingenuity and judgement.[61]

Resourcefulness and initiative were certainly evident in nurses' narratives. Bertha Whittaker wrote to Maclean in 1917 that she could now ride a horse, milk a cow, and garden. She had had vegetables all summer, had enough for winter, and was especially proud of 'two nice beds of celery'. Maclean commented that her letter showed 'great enterprise' and the 'right spirit'.[62] Two years later Maclean reported that Nurse Fergusson 'negotiates a very difficult district in a novel and interesting way, which does credit to her own initiative'. She had turned an old ambulance into a caravan, with two camp stretchers for herself and her assistant, Miss Kidner. It could stow medicines, nursing requisites, food and personal supplies for 'quite a long tour'. They travelled around the large Hokianga district, stopping and working where needed.[63]

Compelled by a scarcity of 'liveable quarters' in the area, Elizabeth Fergusson had built her own cottages, one at Kaitāia and another small one at Te Hāpua in the Far North.[64] She had even put on the roof and iron chimneys. Amelia Bagley commented after her supervision visit that these structures were 'an unequalled example of what a woman can accomplish if she so desires, and the need presents itself, in work that she is supposed to be incapable of doing'. In the 1930s Margaret Macnab had a small house with 'minimal linen and awful pillows' and no furniture. She made a settee out of orange boxes with a squab on top, and a friend made a chair out of boxes and a sack. It was only years later, when she was a nurse inspector, that she discovered she could have requisitioned furniture.[65]

Ingenuity was also needed in health teaching. Jane Minnie Jarrett showed it in giving talks – 'quite informal ones, no soap-box business at all in them' – particularly in one on a complication in childbirth when the membranes that had encapsulated the infant and amniotic fluid were retained in the uterus. Nurses often acknowledged that Māori did not need their attendance in normal childbirth,[66] but Jarrett commented that they were 'always a little afraid of the third stage of labour, and do their best to hurry matters – the result, retained membranes'. If the umbilical cord was pulled to remove the placenta, membranes could be left behind and cause postpartum haemorrhage. Jarrett used her cupped hands and a roped handkerchief to represent the delivery of the placenta and membranes. When the women practised this, there was always a 'big sigh of relief' when the handkerchief membranes came away.[67]

Resourcefulness helped manage communication. In the early 1900s nurses relied on being summoned by a message brought to their house. By the 1930s district health nurses considered telephones essential, but sometimes other means of communication were needed as well. At Te Kaha the local store was the telephone exchange, and if Lilian Hill took her Māori assistant out with her as interpreter, the storekeeper always knew where she was.[68] Amy Rickman at Houhora did not have a telephone, so people contacted the nearby hotel and messages were passed on to her.[69] When Helen Mackie shifted house in the Hokianga in the 1940s, the Health Department provided the porcelain caps and wire and the post office agreed to connect the phone. The owner organised a working bee one Sunday. The wire was strung across a valley to a cabbage tree in the distance, then took an enormous loop across the harbour to another tree and a third to a pole and was finally extended to the post office.[70] Barbara Ancott-Johnson, also in the Hokianga in the 1940s, had a party line. Even though four others shared the line, the only ring that roused her at night was her Morse call sign, 'K'.[71]

Mabel Vos, in the health service for Māori, getting about her district between Te Kaha and Cape Runaway in the Bay of Plenty in 1919. Margaret Macnab album, New Zealand Nurses' Organisation Library, Wellington

Nurses' force of character and determination were evident in their narratives of getting about their districts. Like backblocks nurses, those in the early Māori health services travelled on horseback or on foot, and the going was often difficult. Lily Dawson reported that the Hauraki swamp was 'simply appalling in the way of bad roads and mud'. Her horse got bogged, and she had to 'sit still and possess my soul in patience' until two Māori rescued her. 'I thought I knew all about mud before,' she said, 'but found I didn't even know the A B C of it till I started working on the Hauraki Plains.'[72] Work and travel could be relentless. As Jean Cormack at Te Karaka said: 'For the last three weeks I was riding from 18 to 30 miles [29–48km] every day – would just come in from one case to find a horse ready to take me to another. Really, I began to hate the sight of a horse.'[73]

When motor cars were introduced they created new challenges. At Frasertown, when Helen Mackie's car wheels 'slipped off the metal into soft slushy mud', she knew 'no feeling so forlorn as standing beside a car that won't move, gazing up and down a road in the depth of the country, with not a soul in sight!'[74] In Kāwhia in the

Nurses were glad of help in freeing cars from muddy roads. This vehicle was stuck at Cape Runaway in the Bay of Plenty in the 1930s. Margaret Macnab album, New Zealand Nurses' Organisation Library, Wellington

1930s, local Māori raised funds to enable Frances Hayman to buy an old Model T Ford. 'It was said of them that they would take you anywhere but into society, but I found that they had their disadvantages.' She was 'occasionally startled by the smell of burning shoe leather' when she held the pedal down too long climbing one of the 'endless hills'. On the whole, though, 'the car was a staunch friend and seemed capable of extraordinary feats, such as bridging ditches or climbing low hedges'. But in winter, 'rain and wind streamed in through its flapping sides and hood'. In short, the Model T had to be replaced. Hayman bought 'a Morris 8 of more recent vintage' but found there were dozens in the area, all looking alike. Coming out of the post office, she 'drove gaily off' towards the harbour before she saw a note: 'Darling, if you can't bring chops, get sausages, and *please* don't forget Fluffy's fish.' Realising with shock that she had 'converted a car', she quickly returned and handed it over to its irate owner, who was 'scowling fiercely' and berating her. As she drove off in her own car she could not resist retorting: 'And you'd better not forget Fluffy's fish.'[75]

Rides in butchers' carts and bakers' vans or on the back of motorbikes were all part of Margaret Macnab's transport when she worked as a relief nurse in North Auckland. When assigned to Te Kaha, she collected a baby Austin 'with no windows and a canvas roof' from Ōpōtiki, along with the nurse inspector, Ada (Janie) North. Macnab had rarely driven and had no licence but the road was almost empty, so she set off up the steep winding route to Te Kaha, with Miss North 'looking down the sheer drops and clutching the doorhandle for the full 40 miles [64km]'.[76]

Nurses' ingenuity and determination helped them overcome any lack of resources. At Whangapē in 1922, Mary Cartwright said, 'Up here the kerosene tin is ubiquitous. It turns up everywhere, and how we welcome it and its cases!' It served 'myriad purposes, from that of "copper" boiler to bath, toilet basin and steriliser, and [was] cut down into many sizes to suit its various missions'.[77] Another nurse working in the Te Araroa and Ruatōria area explained to others how to use discarded items when nursing typhoid patients in tents. She used kerosene tins to boil up excreta and sputum before burying them, to boil bedlinen with soap, and to save bath water for rinsing out bedpans. Old jam or fruit tins made good sputum mugs and pickle bottles were useful as urinals.[78]

Narratives often emphasised the need for tact, particularly in persuading people to allow a sick relative to be transferred to hospital or to follow unfamiliar sanitary measures.[79] Beth Paora wrote in 1940 that there was 'usually some solution to the problems of a health district when one remains tactful, patient and persevering'.[80] One measure in early years of the service where nurses' tact failed, though, was in persuading Māori to use privies. Māori were puzzled about their use, saw no reason to change their usual practices, or regarded them as useful for other purposes. One elderly man used the privy to hang meat.[81]

Māori health nursing folklore

The challenges of Māori health nursing gave rise to its own folklore. Fever-camp stories recounted tests of nurses' skill, resourcefulness and grit, often pitting the nurse against the forces of nature. The first example of this type of tale to appear in *Kai Tiaki* was a nurse's account of setting up a fever camp in a typhoid outbreak in the Far North in 1913.

Despite clear instructions, the shipping company landed the two nurses and two sanitary inspectors from Auckland without their equipment. They took a coach to within three miles (4km) of their patients and waited for their tents. When some of the equipment arrived the sanitary inspectors went ahead to spend the night under the stars and set up the camp early in the morning, while the nurses stayed in town and obtained other supplies, including a meat safe and their 'greatest boon and necessity – a portable boiler'. The camp was on a narrow ridge, approached by a dangerous and 'alarmingly rough track'. The only advantage of the site was good water from a spring, as the ground was 'terribly rough and dirty and there was no shelter from the blazing sun, although the bush was all around us in the gullies'.

In two tents erected in a gully, six very ill patients lay on mats on the ground. They were moved further up the ridge. Fern was cut to cover the dusty ground beneath their mattresses until camp stretchers arrived in the evening. Two patients were delirious, one violently. 'It was a trying day,' wrote the nurse, 'heat intense and no shade, everything looking in hopeless disorder. We had to hurry, and empty a packing case to serve as a table to put the patients' milk etc on … There was nothing to sit on, and nothing but the ground for anything.' They ate outside in the blazing heat, and 'nothing was ever more welcome than tea at that first luncheon'. When the camp stretchers arrived it was a relief to shift the patients onto them, sponge them and make them comfortable. The nurses did not mind placing patients on the clean Māori mats, but to 'crawl after them on our knees on that dirty ground was impossible'. They later found that the best uniform for camp life in the summer was 'a thin dark cambric dress, as few under garments as possible, a blue overall, shady panama hat, sandals, no stockings'.

Their own tent had not arrived, so they set up a camp stretcher at the end of the hospital tent and divided the night duty between them. 'Sleeping was of course out of the question with delirious patients, and much to do all night.'

The next evening brought a third nurse, the kitchen marquee and a bell tent, which they had hoped to sleep in themselves but in the end needed for a Pākehā patient. They made do with the fly of the kitchen tent, pitched down the hill in the bush. They would never forget the 'regiments of blow-flies, mosquitoes, crickets, and surely every tribe of the insect world in full force and array, that made our nights under that tent fly hideous' and the 'crawling, flapping things, coming at us, were more nerve-racking than our delirious patients'.

To accommodate more patients they placed Māori and Pākehā together and separated men and women, partitioning off an end of the hospital tent as a male ward. One girl believed a tohunga had told her she was going to die. Although very delirious, she had one or two quiet nights, which her mother attributed to an old Māori charm, but the girl's condition gradually worsened and she died. Some patients were 'very bad indeed' and all had complications – bronchopneumonia, cardiac symptoms, haemorrhage or diarrhoea – but hers was the only death.

They tried to give patients some relief from the excessive heat by moving them from one side of the tent to the other as the sun worked around, sponging them and plying them with drinks of cold boiled water. With the help of Sam, their Māori 'man of all work', and contributions from settlers and village tradespeople, they managed to make the camp more presentable and comfortable. The grocer had supplied as many candle boxes and cases as he could spare so they had 'tables' in the kitchen, ward and sleeping tents, covered with 'white American cloth'. Sam made shelves for crockery, a food cupboard and even a long bench seat and stools. Māori cut ferns and brought mats from their meeting house for the hospital tent. This 'greatly allayed the dust nuisance'. Sam managed firewood and carried all the water 'in an array of kerosene tins and buckets', and 'how he kept his eye on them!' He always left a boiler full of hot water for their baths before departing for the night. He was 'invaluable'.

At the end of the nurse's narrative, Maclean added a note to say the 'unfortunate sequel' was that the nurse herself had become ill. Two more patients were admitted at their worst, 'and a bad worst it was too'. Gales and storms wrecked their tents one night, endangering their lives. Of course, 'they made the best of it all', appreciating any comical situations, thankful to have succeeded in 'pulling the worst cases through' and bringing their very ill comrade 'back convalescent to her home'.[82]

In this tale nursing skills are brought to bear against the power of nature. Some measure of control is seen in the gradual shift from disorder to basic comfort in the camp, though the nurses and patients still had to contend with excessive heat, insects, gales and storms. A kind of professional compromise with nature is evident in the nurses' changes to their usual uniform in the interest of ease and practicality.

Although the tale reveals that Māori and Pākehā patients were initially segregated, it also illustrates the collaboration between Sam and the nurses. Camp life was bearable only because of Sam's skills, ingenuity, hard work and organisation. The nurse's own illness signalled a professional lapse, but both health and status were regained through her colleagues' careful nursing.

This tale had a sequel: Florence Gill's narrative of 11 weeks at the same fever camp, picking up from the end of the first tale and incorporating many of the same folkloric elements.[83] A storm she described as a 'Trojan' visited them one Saturday night. 'What a night it was!' she said. 'All our tents blew down but the

Nursing patients in remote fever camps required ingenuity and determination. Nurses had few resources and appreciated help and supplies from local Māori. Here Nurse McElligot is caring for patients with typhoid fever near Tūpāroa on the East Coast in 1911.
J. Enright, AWNS-19110608-2-4, Heritage Collection, Auckland Libraries

patients' marquee.' Fortunately only one patient, a convalescent, was at the camp. On Sunday morning the kitchen marquee presented a 'particularly dismal appearance'. The grocery cupboard had been knocked over and 'salt, sugar, soda, water, methylated spirits, oatmeal, Benger's Food [a milk-based powder] and tea were in hopeless confusion on the floor. We had Benger's Food and tea (mixed) for breakfast – nourishing, no doubt, but not very palatable.' Their treasured oil stove was lying disjointed on the floor in a pool of kerosene but was gently reconstructed and seemed none the worse. 'For a few nights after this gale,' Gill said, 'I went to bed with my boots on, so as to be ready for action when the next call came.' There were no more gales or patients except for their own nurse, who had developed a severe case of typhoid. When she was fit to move, they took her to stay at the doctor's home at Ōhaeawai until she was well enough for the homeward journey.[84]

Other fever-camp accounts from the same year depicted similar battles with nature, ingenuity in adapting to challenging conditions with few resources, generous Māori support, and long hours sharing day and night duty with their assistants. As one nurse said: 'This is camping with a vengeance, boxes and kerosene tins do duty for nearly everything, and I had no idea that so many things – things that one almost considers a necessity at ordinary times – could be done without.'[85] One nurse heated a tent with an old camp oven filled with glowing coals, replenished from an outside fire as needed. At the end of this narrative Maclean added an editorial comment noting that many other letters 'in this strain' showed that 'the spirit of nursing, so often deplored as dying out in this age of commercialism', was still alive. 'When the love of caring for the sick can so survive the discomfort, long hours and difficulties encountered during the last few epidemics of typhoid among the natives, that the nurses volunteer again and again for the work, and even after contracting the disease, write saying that they are nearly "ready again for the fray", we shall not despair of the future of the profession.'[86]

Although there were several narratives from typhoid fever camps, only one emerged from the camps caring for Māori during the smallpox epidemic of 1913. In this tale the test was threefold: first, managing the highly contagious disease in a tent hospital; second, working 'out of the usual routine', as nurses gave vaccinations, arranged provisions for isolated patients and their contacts, rode from kainga to kainga to check quarantine measures, and fumigated and disinfected; and third, finding ways to nurse patients covered with suppurating sores. The narrator explained in detail how they turned a patient by having one nurse manipulating the patient with the draw sheet while the other supported the shoulder and buttock with large swabs of wool soaked in warm Lysol and wrung out. The smell of a bad case, she said, was never to be forgotten.[87]

Another element of the Māori nursing folklore was cultural exchange and learning, which often occurred in the meeting house on a marae or in private homes. Several narratives describe nursing in meeting houses that were converted into temporary typhoid hospitals. Nurses quickly learned to shift dying patients out to the verandah or a tent so they did not die inside the wharenui, as this concerned Māori greatly, and the importance to Māori of having many visitors. Māori in turn acknowledged the nurses' need to limit the number of people visiting a sick patient. As one nurse said, their friends 'rolled up' on Sundays, and the verandah would be filled with 'squatting, smoking men and women', who seemed to enjoy themselves. 'Various were the kits they brought, some with eggs, some with pipes and such like dainties. If the patients were not allowed them, would I accept? But even I could not manage to use more than half-a-dozen eggs at a time.'[88]

Māori generosity was a constant theme. In this connection, many visitors were concerned about the fluid diet used with typhoid patients (initially consisting of milk or beef tea) to prevent solid food from perforating the ulcerated intestine and causing a haemorrhage or peritonitis. Māori visitors saw this diet as starvation, and nurses frequently had to stop them from giving the patients food.

Amelia Bagley's narrative of nursing in the typhoid outbreak in the Far North in 1911 describes another instance of cultural learning when she took the swabs she had used for cleaning a patient's mouth, wrapped them in paper and threw them into the fire. 'They did not like it,' she said, 'so I always refrain now from polluting the fire.'[89]

This stumbling discovery of Māori customs was a recurring theme through the decades. In an account from the 1940s, Barbara Ancott-Johnson observed that the three-week introductory course in public health nursing in Wellington had not prepared her for working with Māori. District health nurses were taught how to fill in forms, always to wear a hat and gloves, and never to put their brown bag on the floor. Since most of the houses she visited in the Kawakawa district had no furniture, the problem was where to put the bag. She could never master the art of weighing a baby in a sling on the end of a spring balance held in one hand while holding 'that wretched bag' in the other, so when she entered one house that had a table, she put the bag on it, not realising that a table should be used only for food. She suspected this was only one of the many blunders she felt she must have made through ignorance, but the courteous Māori 'forgave me for my gaffes'.[90] In another home an old woman stopped her from throwing 'a neat little parcel' of waste products into the fire, as she had been taught to do in the introductory course, and told her very quietly of 'many mistakes I had made or might make … I was overcome by gratitude for her tact and kindness'. When asked why she had taken so much trouble, the old woman said they both had the same name, Johnson (Hoanitana), and they must see that it was held in respect.[91] With guidance from patients and their whānau, Ancott-Johnson became more knowledgeable about Māori tikanga, and after many months 'sensed a change from doubt to trust'. Then, 'how the work moved!'[92]

She put her new understanding of the appropriate disposal of waste into practice when she went to the home of a Māori man who had an infected foot from trying to remove a pūriri splinter with a nail. Incising the taut purple mass with a scalpel released a tremendous spurt of blood and pus over the floor and furniture, with an appalling stench. When she had cleaned and dressed the wound, buried the drained pus and mopped up the mess with newspaper and Dettol, she wrapped the soggy waste and soiled equipment in her discarded gown and secured it with flax to the belt of her oilskin for the journey home.[93]

This nursing folklore reflected the prevailing attitudes and beliefs relating to Māori, with the significant exception of 'smoothing the pillow of a dying race'. The details of nursing practice in fever camps, meeting-houses and Māori homes would have made these stories credible to nurses. As with the backblocks folklore, the drama lay in the venture into literal and professional terra incognita, particularly the challenges of translating Pākehā health practices into a Māori world and learning to respect and work with Māori ways. The tales also enabled Maclean to promote the nurses as courageous, enterprising and representing the best ideals of the new profession.

Māori health nursing and Māori culture

In 1910 Ākenehi Hei said that even in the most Europeanised Māori families there lurked a secret attachment to old customs that were the result of centuries of experience, and that these customs deserved consideration. They would help Europeans understand the Māori mind, which would inspire deeper sympathy for Māori and abate the 'racial feeling'. This shift would do more to uplift Māori than all laws and health regulations. It was impossible, she said, for Māori to sever physical health from religious beliefs. 'Great discretion must be used not to offend the patient's beliefs, and at the same time uphold one's own mission,' she said. 'This is perhaps the greatest difficulty encountered by those who minister to the health of my people.'[94]

Even after the Tohunga Suppression Act 1907, nurses often reported that tohunga still held considerable influence and could make their work difficult.[95] Besides 'tohungaism', their main frustration was the influence of particular Māori religious leaders or faith healers. One was Rua Kēnana, a prophet, land rights activist and faith healer who in 1907 formed a settlement called Maungapōhatu in the Urewera. A nurse reported in 1915 that Rua's 'long-haired supporters' were still in Te Teko in the Bay of Plenty, though she mistakenly identified them as Hauhau (meaning the often-violent element subverting the quite separate Pai Mārire or Hauhau religion). Rua's people were 'more difficult to teach better ways, on account of their many superstitions', she said bluntly, but 'great headway' had been made, as they were not averse to anti-typhoid inoculation.[96] Janie North had a different view of Rua. When she worked in the Whakatāne district, Rua had shifted from the Urewera to Matahī. He was 'always very helpful in an intelligent and practical way', and his support was of 'the greatest value'.[97] Rua, in fact, understood the dangers of poor sanitation and ensured that his community followed the laws of health.[98]

By contrast, North considered another faith healer, Tahupōtiki Wiremu Rātana, a 'difficult proposition'. Following a vision in 1918, he founded the Christian Rātana movement and a separate Rātana Church in 1925. She recounted that after setting up his base at Pupuruhi, he announced that he was going to cure the blind and maimed. 'The people flocked to him,' she said. 'There was a big meeting at the church and Ratana's people put their arms across the entrance to stop me from entering.' Eventually she was able to go in. 'The business was a fiasco. The blind and the lame were not healed. They had to turn away without hope.'[99] His influence persisted, however. In 1929 a nurse reported hearing about an 18-year-old girl who had died in a settlement three miles (4km) away. When she investigated, she found the girl had been ill for two years. She had been shifted to three different homes, and no nurse or doctor had been called. She died of pulmonary tuberculosis. Her family were of the Rātana religion.[100] According to a 1955 history of public health nursing, the sick or maimed were brought to Rātana Pā for healing, even infectious cases that the Department of Health had to remove to Wanganui Hospital. When followers returned to their homes they ignored nurses' instructions and hid the sick from them. When Dr Peter Buck (Te Rangi Hīroa) interviewed Rātana, however, he said he believed in scientific medicine, took cough mixture himself and used boracic acid to bathe his eyes. It was his ardent followers, he said, who would not believe that scientific and spiritual methods should go hand in hand.[101]

Despite her frustration with Rātana, North considered leaders of the Ringatū Church, established by Te Kooti Arikirangi te Turuki (known as Te Kooti) in 1868, as the greatest stumbling block to progress. 'They would not allow hot water to be used even to wash wounds. Everything had to be cold.' When a nurse visited, 'the sick were hidden until someone would whisper a hint of where they were'.[102]

Nurses' responses to the influence of Māori beliefs and faith healers on health were therefore mixed and reflected societal attitudes toward some aspects of Māori culture. Nurses made positive efforts to understand the culture and align their nursing practice with Māori customs. They also acknowledged the effectiveness of some traditional Māori treatments. Lilian Hill, for example, working at Te Kaha in the 1930s, paid attention to Māori remedies such as using dock leaves on septic wounds. 'I tried them all out myself, for my own satisfaction,' she said, and was pleased with the result. She also used her willingness to learn as a means of gaining Māori confidence. If she watched their ways first, she could then suggest they watch hers.[103] Mary (Molly) O'Meara learned a lot from her colleague Isabel Banks, who was a 'very practical person, steeped in Maori medicine.'[104] But several nurses found that the medicines or ointments they left with Māori patients remained unused as patients believed they worked only if the nurse herself administered them.[105] Frances Hayman had an additional problem. She noticed that babies and children were not gaining weight, although the malt she had left for them disappeared rapidly. She discovered that parents were using it to make a 'particularly potent home brew'. Word had spread, and they had established a 'very profitable black market'.[106]

Nurses' inability to speak the Māori language was a hindrance. One nurse in 1911 acknowledged the difficulty but preferred to communicate through a Māori interpreter rather than risk misunderstanding by trying to speak Māori herself.[107] Jean Cormack at Te Karaka, on the other hand, made an effort to learn.[108] Janie North considered knowledge of the language the nurse's greatest asset. 'I tried hard to learn Maori. How they used to laugh. I used to say the most awful things I believe, trying to make myself understood. But when I could speak reasonably well, many barriers were broken down.'[109] Māori assistants helped nurses learn the language and explained Māori customs.[110]

In summing up the nurse's need to understand and work with the Māori culture, Minnie Jarrett told nurses attending a refresher course in Auckland in 1928 that where the newly appointed nurse 'falls in' was in failing to realise that they must respect religion and the tapu of all sects. They needed to be able to say a karakia for a sick person with sincerity and to 'see the other chap's point of view' while gently giving their own. They should be honest – no 'quibbling or evasions' – and say yes or no and stick to it. A keen sense of humour was the saving grace. Without it, they would review their day's work 'with a feeling akin to despair'.[111] Nurses understood that the results of their public health work would not be immediately evident, but the work was worthwhile. They often had to work beyond the scope of their usual role, which made them 'sharpen every faculty to do the very best possible', as Marky Minto Tait at Te Araroa said. She enjoyed Māori health nursing and encouraged all nurses to take it up, even if only for a year or so.[112]

Public and professional perception

Public acknowledgments of Māori health nurses came from both Pākehā and Māori perspectives. In 1912 a Native Land Court judge praised 'those brave and noble women' who took their lives in their hands and 'put up with hardships and discomforts' in nursing Māori. They did this 'ungrudgingly, and with a good moral effect on the natives whom they are continually schooling in the necessity and practice of sanitation'.[113] After the 1913 smallpox epidemic, Hautai Hohepa wrote to Dr Thomas Valintine, chief health officer, on behalf of Hokianga Māori, saying their love and gratitude to the nurses was 'boundless'. They enclosed a gift of money. Valintine explained that nurses could not accept gifts but asked whether nurses could use the money to buy luxuries for sick Māori. He assured them that the contributors' generosity and appreciation would be 'published far and wide in the Nurses' Journal'.[114] And in 1915, settlers and Māori at Tolaga Bay told the Gisborne Hospital Board that Jean Cormack had been 'indefatigable in her efforts', showing 'untiring energy and devotion to duty' and always working 'cheerfully and without complaint'. They recommended a salary raise.[115]

In 1921 Dr Peter Buck, director of the new Division of Māori Hygiene, reported that nurses were doing good work among the Māori people. They and the sanitary inspectors were really the department's 'watch-dogs' and the buffer between ill Māori and the general public, because they prevented the spread of disease. They made many sacrifices. Despite the rigours of travel between settlements in the dreadful winter months, they carried on and rendered 'most efficient service indeed'. He could not fully express his appreciation of their 'devoted services' in the interests of Māori health.[116]

Despite this praise the Health Department did not always provide adequate support to rural nurses in their lonely and isolated lives, as is evident from nurses' domestic situation. In the south Taranaki district in the 1930s, the intention was always to have the nurse based in the remote township of Manaia. But in the absence of a suitable cottage, Amy Jewiss, who began nursing there in 1934, was initially based in Ōpunake and was given £1 a week towards accommodation. If she wanted something better, she had to pay the difference herself.[117] The next year she thought Hāwera would give her more chances than Ōpunake of 'a little social life to snatch at between times', but in the end moved into a cottage in Manaia.[118] In 1936 several terse memos were exchanged between the department and the medical officer of health for her region over whether the nurse's broken crockery should be replaced.

District health nurse Mavis Attree at her rented cottage in Manaia, south Taranaki, in the late 1930s. Mavis Attree album, author's collection

In the end, Dr Michael Watt, director-general of health, ended the 'Tea-Set Tussle' by rather stingily decreeing that a teapot could be replaced but not teacups, as they were not part of the initial provision for the cottage.[119] On the other hand, Watt supported Mavis Attree, who held the position in 1937, when she wanted to shift to Hāwera, as on his visit he thought she was overworked, off-colour and not sleeping well.[120] (Attree changed her mind when she discovered that her intended Hāwera landlady was inclined to be interfering.)[121]

Two years later the medical officer of health pressed the department to urgently supply a bed as the Manaia nurse still had only a camp bed to sleep on.[122] In 1944, when new accommodation had to be found in Manaia, the house chosen for the nurse had an outside toilet consisting of an inverted gramophone trumpet in lieu of a pan, and an elaborate flushing arrangement that supplied water through a hose from a kerosene tin next to the seat. The waste drained into a pit where a dump of decaying vegetables masked the odour. The 'extraordinary affair' was 'rather reminiscent of Heath Robinson' but was deemed suitable.[123] A comfortable cottage, supplied with normal household items like beds and teacups, in a location that allowed social interaction, was clearly not regarded as important for nurses' well-being.

The Māori health nurse and empire

International studies of colonial nursing have focused on British nurses' work in the Colonial Nursing Association (CNA) and later the Colonial Nursing Service (CNS). These services originally provided care to limited numbers of isolated British settlers in far-flung colonies. Over time, they began to attend to the health of much larger numbers of Indigenous peoples who were needed to provide labour for the imperial enterprise, and they trained Indigenous nurses. CNA and CNS nurses were therefore agents of empire. At best, they have been portrayed as part of the 'civilising' mission, rescuing Indigenous peoples from the effects of the colonising process of which they were paradoxically a part. At worst, they supported a process of forced assimilation to imperial cultural standards.[124]

Were Māori health nurses agents of empire? McKegg has argued that they were, attempting to compel Māori communities to assimilate by adopting Pākehā health and sanitation methods.[125] Nurses' narratives, however, show that they did not regard themselves as imperial agents. Their narratives could, of course, be regarded as biased toward showing nurses in the best light, but in that case they would presumably have portrayed themselves as dutiful employees implementing official government policy, which was one of assimilation. Instead, nurses' narratives for the most part reveal sincere efforts to understand and work with Māori beliefs and customs. As historian Linda Bryder has similarly said, nurses soon learned that Māori health nursing was 'not a matter of foisting their own culture on others', and nurses should not be seen 'as simply agents of the State imposing Western values on colonial subjects'.[126]

In addition, Māori were active in seeking better health. They welcomed the chance for self-regulation through Māori Councils and komiti marae with responsibility for sanitation and health measures. If Pākehā methods demonstrated benefit, Māori readily – even enthusiastically – adopted them. At other times, their confidence in changes was hard-won and their support occasionally lacking. Nurses willingly adapted their approach in order to win co-operation through their respect for most Māori customs, beliefs and intelligence.

Nursing in New Zealand differed in significant ways from practices elsewhere in the British Empire. Unlike other countries, New Zealand did not have nurses sent by the CNA or CNS, and the Māori health service nurses were mostly trained in New Zealand. It was therefore a home-grown service with a New Zealand vision, rather than an imperial venture. The training of Māori women as nurses was also different from the training of Indigenous nurses elsewhere in the empire. The government scholarship scheme, which began as a Māori initiative, appears to have been the first in the world to support Indigenous women to train as nurses. New Zealand was also the first country with an Indigenous registered nurse, Kate Wyllie. The Cape Colony had state registration of nurses from 1892, but its first Indigenous registered nurse was Cecilia Makiwane, who trained at a mission hospital for Indigenous patients from 1903 and registered in January 1908.[127] And New Zealand was the first country to have Indigenous nurses with the right to vote.

When Jean Cormack left her Te Karaka community to serve overseas in World War I, a reporter at the farewell ceremony noted that in sending her, the district would be 'keeping up the tradition of giving its best for the help of the Empire'.[128] This observation underscores the fact that Māori health was not seen as an imperial project, and that if nurses were to serve the empire, they would do so outside New Zealand.

CHAPTER 7

Caring in conflict – the emotional labour of wartime nursing

In March 1900 Emily Jane Peter from Canterbury was nursing in the No. 1 Stationary Hospital at Ladysmith during the South African (Boer) War.[1] Many soldiers were sick with enteric (typhoid) fever. Sometimes five died each night, but in three weeks she had lost only one because she fought for her patients' food and stimulants. Her forcefulness had made her unpopular with the authorities. When sick officers were moved into a single ward with just one English sister, who simply told untrained orderlies what to do and left them to do it, Emily Peter was loath to have a particular 20-year-old patient transferred there. She had pulled him through the worst but he was still dangerously ill. She told the authorities plainly that if they insisted on moving him and he died, she would write to his people and tell them. They decided not to move him but put a black mark against her name. When another nurse was needed in Modder Spruit they tried to send her there, but she repeated her threat. Her patient continued to improve. After his temperature had been normal for just two mornings in a row, the authorities sent her on her way. Two days later the patient died. 'He was simply murdered,' she said. 'Hundreds here are murdered through carelessness and ignorance.'[2]

Sixteen years later, in World War I, Christian Maclean was on the 'Channel run', caring for sick and wounded soldiers transported on the *Maheno* from France to England. 'We brought over 1140 soldiers from Havre on our first trip,' she said in August 1916. 'The wounds are terrible, but all bear them bravely … One New Zealander in particular, who had half his face shot away, asked me to dress another's wound first, as it was more painful than his.'[3]

During World War II, Joyce Macdonald was at the tent hospital at Gerawla in Egypt in 1942 when exhausted men from the Libyan campaign arrived. 'There is no satisfaction greater in the nursing world than to work on a patient made almost unrecognizable by a week's growth and the dust of hundreds of miles, to put him clean and comfortable between cool sheets and to hear the muffled voice saying, "God, is this really me – this is sheer heaven!"[4]

Meanwhile, in New Zealand, nurses cared for soldiers preparing to go to war. (Elsie Leipst at Hastings used to cook them whitebait fritters.)[5] Theirs was mainly a 'war from afar'. It was brought home when mail arrived with desperate news of loved ones at war. Sonja Davies recalled that at Wellington Hospital 'it was a frequent occurrence to see a white-faced nurse slipping quietly away with her private sorrow'.[6]

These glimpses into wartime nursing show some of the effort and emotion nurses invested in their work, regardless of the setting. Emily Peter's anger, anguish and strong advocacy, Christian Maclean's admiration for a soldier's bravery, and Joyce Macdonald's satisfaction at the simple but profound relief she could provide were evident in other nurses' letters, diaries and later memoirs as well, but only as occasional comments. This emotional labour of wartime nursing was almost all hidden.

New Zealand nurses' motives for serving overseas in these wars undoubtedly included a desire for adventure and travel, but the main motivation was to care for 'their boys'. Around 30 New Zealand nurses served in the South African War.[7] Only four, all from Canterbury, were officially sanctioned by military authorities to go. Seven from Otago and Southland were funded by patriotic committees; others paid their own way or were supported by benefactors. Nurses made their own khaki uniforms and were later pleased that they 'did not show the dust'.[8] Once in South Africa, they were under military direction.

In World War I at least 550 nurses served overseas, mainly in the New Zealand Army Nursing Service (NZANS).[9] A few joined the Australian corps in 1915. Some who were already in Britain at the outbreak of war, and others who paid their own way from New Zealand, joined the Queen Alexandra's Imperial Military Nursing Service (QAIMNS) or its Reserve (QAIMNSR), or the Red Cross, French Flag Corps or Scottish Women's Hospitals, which worked in the field.

As Anna Rogers has provided a comprehensive history of New Zealand nurses' overseas wartime service from 1899 to 1948, this chapter focuses mainly on overseas service in just two wars and on a specific aspect of that service – emotional labour, the need for nurses to manage their emotions in order to work effectively.[10] Whenever nurses could find the time and energy, they wrote letters home. During the South African War, these often appeared in New Zealand newspapers. In World War I, Hester Maclean, as editor of *Kai Tiaki*, printed letters she received as matron-in-chief of the NZANS. In all these narratives, the emotional burden of wartime nursing was mentioned only briefly and in passing.

Rogers has noted that her overseas focus does 'not imply any lack of respect for the vital work done by women who nursed in New Zealand during wartime'.[11] The later oral history testimony and occasional life writing by nurses who had worked in New Zealand during World War II show that emotional labour was certainly part of their 'war from afar', and their role, too, is examined here.

Emotional labour in the culture and work of wartime nursing overseas

In both the South African War and World War I, nurses worked in tents, huts, converted buildings, trains and military hospitals. In South Africa they cared mostly for soldiers who were sick with typhoid fever. In Egypt, France, Britain and elsewhere in World War I, some similarly nursed 'medical' cases, but many cared for 'surgical' patients, those with horrendous wounds. Besides courage, the key qualities that were required for this work were stoicism and endurance. Stoicism was needed to maintain professional integrity while simultaneously caring with warmth and compassion for men laid low (needlessly) by rampant typhoid fever or mutilated by the machinery of war.

In both wars, narrative comments revealing nurses' emotional labour focus on the emotional investment and effects of caring for damaged soldiers, the critical need to care for themselves, and the energy required to manage sometimes difficult working relationships.

Caring for soldiers

Once overseas, nurses were keen to start work and impatient at delays, but the reality of the work hit hard. In South Africa they were shocked to find Bloemfontein a 'hot bed of fever', as Bessie Teape described it. Deaths were inevitable in the overcrowded and understaffed hospitals. Field hospitals meant to hold 500 soldiers had 1500 each but no extra nurses. 'It was heart-rending to see poor fellows dying all round, and still sadder to see fine fellows heaped up on a gun carriage under the Union Jack, and carted away to be buried, thirty in a trench, with only their blanket round them.'[12] Sarah Ross was also anguished. 'It seems positively cruel when one thinks of it,' she said. 'Really, it is too dreadful to see the poor fellows here, dying like sheep. To-day I saw six funerals leave our camp. I felt that I wanted a quiet corner to sit in for a few minutes.'[13] For Emily Peter, who fought for her patients' provisions, the battle was not over when she left South Africa. Once home, she was 'very outspoken as to the crying need for reform, root and branch.'[14]

In both wars, the number of sick or wounded men arriving at one time distressed nurses who wanted to do their best for each one. As Bessie Teape in Bloemfontein said, 'Men were being brought in in hundreds, fever-stricken, ragged and badly in need of a wash.'[15] In World War I, Cora Anderson wrote to her brother from Cairo in August 1915: 'We are right in the thick of things now, wounded and sick coming in faster that we can take them.' The previous night 91 men had arrived, adding to the influx of 150 two days before. 'Beds and mattresses are all round the corridors and verandahs. As every few patients go out a fresh batch is put in … The men say it is just like Heaven to be here, and one feels that one cannot do enough for them.'[16] Operating theatre sisters in 1916 'sat in a chair and dozed for an hour during the night' before hearing that another 100 badly wounded were coming in.[17] A nurse on the hospital ship *Marama* said she would 'never forget the sight of the seemingly endless stream of men … It makes one's heart bleed to see them coming on – all mud, clothes torn to pieces very often, and dried blood everywhere – all black, tired and hungry. They fall asleep the minute they get on the bed.'[18] Nurses' first priorities were making the patients secure, clean and comfortable, and giving them food, drink and a cigarette.[19] 'We feel that we are doing what we came for,' said Cora Anderson, 'and are all putting every available ounce of ourselves into the work.'[20]

Making connections with home was another form of emotional labour. Early in World War I, New Zealand nurses were not necessarily caring for New Zealand soldiers but for any evacuated from Gallipoli to hospitals in Egypt, or later on hospital ships carrying soldiers from France to Britain. Nurses made a point of visiting New Zealand patients if they knew of any in their hospital. In turn, the distinctive medal worn by all New Zealand registered nurses made them immediately identifiable to New Zealand soldiers. Edith Lewis said in 1917: 'If any of them are in the wards they always hail me when they see my badge, and we have quite a talk over where we each come from.'[21] Jean Cormack knew that Māori patients 'all seem pleased to have a korero with the "wahine pakeha"'. She had learnt to speak some te reo Māori in her work at Te Karaka.[22] And Ethel Watkins Taylor, the only Māori nurse in the NZANS, who was organising the nursing of up to 260 New Zealand patients under canvas on a football field in England, had a shelter made that was a boon in summer. She named it the 'Whare'.[23]

Nurses' compassion focused on the terrible effects of bullets, exploding shells and mustard gas, and months in cold muddy trenches. Frostbite, gangrene and gas

Otago and Southland nurses about to leave for service in the South African War in March 1900. From left they are Nellie Monson, Dora Harris, Janet Williamson (superintendent), Dora Peiper, Sarah Ross, Bessie Hay and Isabella Campbell. Nurses's contingent, Muir & Moodie, PH-CNEG-C30702, Auckland War Memorial Museum

gangrene caused permanent, often life-changing damage.[24] Nurses needed stoicism and endurance to stand at operating tables for hours and receive countless amputated limbs. 'Oh! how one realises the awfulness of war when one sees what the poor men have to suffer,' said Sister Lily Eddy, writing in August 1915 from the British Hospital in Alexandria.[25] Shrapnel from shells made jagged wounds, embedded with bits of khaki, dirt, mud, straw and sometimes the contents of pockets. One surgeon described extracting coins, buttons, a pencil and a piece from a miniature New Testament from thigh wounds.[26] Such wounds were highly susceptible to sepsis (infection). Once cleaned out under anaesthetic, they required lengthy, painful daily dressings. Nurses admired patients' courage in enduring both the wait for their dressings to be changed and the pain of the process. It made a sister on the *Maheno* in 1915 wish she had 'six pairs of legs and hands'.[27] The introduction of the revolutionary BIPP treatment (bismuth, iodoform and paraffin paste) brought great relief to both nurse and patient. Under anaesthetic the wound was cleaned, smeared with the paste, sutured and not dressed for at least a week. The patients suffered less pain, could sleep all night and were 'not living in constant apprehension of being daily tortured by having their dressings done'.[28] It gave far more comfort than the new Carrel-Dakin treatment, which required patients to lie still as an antiseptic solution was trickled into a wound through a series of perforated rubber tubes to keep it constantly moist.[29]

When Margaret Tucker's ship called at Port Said in August 1915, she visited the New Zealand hospital: 'How terrible it is to see these fine men so dreadfully injured, and how cheerful they are. It is marvellous to hear them joking with each other, and about their scratches; these latter we find on investigation to be ghastly wounds.'[30] Clara Cherry, in charge of a medical ward at the British 21st Military Hospital in Alexandria in 1915, had a verandah filled with noisy convalescent patients, 'all in the highest spirits'. They 'sing and play all day' and enjoy 'all the fun that boys can get up to'. They had no fear at all, she said. 'Tears are near their eyes only when they mention "home" – never when they talk of the firing line.' It made her heart ache to think of the mothers at home who suffered. She urged her friends to 'tell all the mothers of boys you know that they are happy'.[31]

Behind the jokes and cheerfulness, however, soldiers held bleak memories. Nurses bore witness to their grim stories as a way of offering the men temporary release from their horrors, but doing so added to their own burden of emotional labour. Sarah Ross at Bloemfontein said, 'Such wrecks some of them are; it made one's heart sore to look at them and hear their stories.'[32] Bessie Teape told friends in Christchurch, 'It is heartrending to see fine young fellows worn-out, half-starved, and some of them heart-broken over the loss of their comrades, ready to die for their Queen and their country.'[33] In World War I Laura James, a Wellington nurse working with the QAIMNS, said, 'The men tell us appalling stories of things that have happened. Surely this ghastly war cannot last for long.'[34] It was still 1914. Even in July 1916, Daphne (Rona) Commons commented from the Brockenhurst Hospital for New Zealand soldiers in Britain about the atrocities her colleague Ethel Lewis had seen when nursing in Serbia: 'What she has seen, and gone through! She doesn't talk much, except when one gets asking her questions, but some of the awful things she has actually seen would make you feel ill.'[35] Historian Christine Hallett has commented that World War I nurses 'acted as witnesses to trauma, listening to the stories of their patients, enabling them to make sense of, and even to normalise their often-outrageous experiences. The presence of women close to the battle lines enabled patients to feel "safe" and to believe that they might survive and reach home.'[36]

All tucked up. A photograph postcard conveying a calm and ordered ward in the military hospital at Walton-on-Thames in England, to send home to worried family. This one was sent by Jim Dunsmuir (on the extreme right) to his mother in Auckland in October 1917.
Ward No. 7 No. 2 NZSH Walton on Thames, PH-CNEG-C31774, call no. D570 M48 W241 p4, Auckland War Memorial Museum

The dreadful irony of wartime nursing was that nurses' successful efforts meant many soldiers were returned to the front. 'We sent off our first batch of wounded men to N.Z. today who have been injured in the fighting in France,' said Daphne Commons in October 1916. 'It is the only place we like to see them leave for.'[37] Soldiers felt relief when they got a 'Blighty', a wound debilitating enough for them to be sent to England. On the hospital ship *Oxfordshire* in 1917, Kate Barnitt's appreciation of the Tommies' excitement was tempered by the sad reason for their trip. 'I had the officers' ward and oh! the pitifulness of the maimed and wounded boy officers.'[38]

Even though nurses were well aware that some patients could not be saved, it still hurt. Sister Mabel Kittlety was nursing at the No. 15 General Hospital in Alexandria in 1915 when a 'New Zealand boy' died. She said: 'I wrote to his mother and sent her a ring off his finger. Our poor mothers, they are the ones who feel it most.'[39] 'Several poor boys have not got any further than here,' said Edith Lewis in 1918. 'Their wounds have proved fatal, and they now lie on a sunny hill facing the sea.'[40]

Caring for themselves

On her return to New Zealand from South Africa in 1900, Sarah Ross told a Dunedin audience that after her first depressing fortnight at Bloemfontein she would have 'given a lot if she could have run away'.[41] Bessie Teape confided: 'I can tell you I have seen sights which I shall never forget as long as I live.' Many of her colleagues were also falling ill with enteric fever. 'We are always wondering whose turn will come next.'[42] The Otago and Southland nurses prepared for the worst. 'We have just finished doing a rather cold-blooded thing. Each of us has taken a list of all our New Zealand addresses, to be kept in our writing cases in case anything should happen to us.'[43] It was typical of nurses' pragmatic way of dealing with matters. Daphne Commons, in World War I, dealt the same way with the subject of money, telling her family about her bank accounts and pay book. 'Don't think by this I am feeling ill! I am really remarkably well, but it just struck me today, I had better mention it.'[44]

For World War I nurses, working long hours, doing their best and witnessing severe or permanent damage to soldiers took its toll. It was a 'ghastly' war.[45] And as

World War I nurses in Cairo being inoculated against infectious diseases, 1915.
PH-2017-2-2-p24-5, Agnes (Peggy) Williams photograph album, Auckland War Memorial Museum

Lengthy delays in receiving mail made letters from home more precious. These nurses are reading their mail at the New Zealand military hospital at Brockenhurst in England in January 1918. 1992.1156.1, (detail), Kippenberger Military Archive, National Army Museum Te Mata Toa, Waiōuru

it went on the need for stoicism and endurance increased. Clare Jordan, with the QAIMNSR in Boulogne, said in 1915, in a lull between battles, 'One rather dreads the beginning of the ghastly business over again. It does not do to have time to stop and think in this kind of war.'[46] Another nurse, with the No. 1 Stationary Hospital in France in 1916, told Hester Maclean, 'The convoys the last three days have been most terrible – gas gangrene cases are too awful for words ... I never want to see another amputation while I live.'[47] And at the end of 1917 Margaret Davies' ability to endure was also coming to an end. 'We often wonder when we are all going to get home again; everybody is, to use that very expressive term, "fed up", and the cry from everyone is "when is it all going to end".'[48] For some nurses the toll was too great. Annie Holgate, well known in New Zealand for her district nursing work and professional activity, went independently to England in December 1914. She worked with the Red Cross in France for seven months until her health broke down. In the end, she lived as a semi-invalid in Bournemouth.[49]

Connecting with home was as important for nurses as for soldiers. The value of letters from family and friends was immeasurable, but in both wars mail was slow.[50] Nurses also relished brief visits by soldiers from home and made the most of caring for them.[51] Bessie Teape in Bloemfontein was delighted when Sergeant-Major Digby Cardale of the First New Zealand Contingent visited her. 'It was a God-send to see and talk to a New Zealander from Christchurch. He is going away to the front again to-morrow.'[52] Nurses had the same experience in World War I. 'Picture us with a brother or friend straight out of the line, and the pleasure we had in hunting up new socks and underwear for them. This was easily done owing to our plentiful supply of Red Cross goods, and the boys declared they were new men after a hot bath, change, and meal with us.'[53] But such pleasures were bittersweet for nurses who knew they might never see their friends and brothers again. Two of Sister Catherine Blackie's three serving brothers were dead.[54] And connections with home could sometimes add to wartime stress, as Daphne Commons learned in her relentless search for news of her missing brother, Kenneth.[55] She discovered that he had been 'awfully cut up' about a friend's death and evidently had this on his mind 'when he went into that last charge. Poor Kenneth, it was the first real grief he had ever had I suppose.'[56]

Nurses took every opportunity to rest or do something completely separate from the war and its horrors. When time, duties and energy allowed, they enjoyed bicycle rides and walks, paying particular attention to seasonal changes and flowers.[57] They also enjoyed seeing the distinctive sights of the places where they were stationed. Sarah Ross and Dora Harris in Cape Town had an opportunity one morning to visit Cecil Rhodes' home, where the house steward let them see a few rooms inside. They marvelled at the furnishings, including electric chandeliers, but the highlight was the bath, cut out of a solid piece of granite.[58]

World War I nurses in Cairo enjoyed tea at the popular Groppi's café or on the terrace of Shepheards Hotel or in the garden of the Red Cross club for nurses, where they could also play tennis and use the common rooms for reading, writing and receiving gentleman friends – until 6pm.[59] They enjoyed entertaining (though their published letters say nothing about relationships). They could relax at Aboukir, a 'delightful place' on the beach an hour's train journey from Alexandria. It was 'beautifully fitted up with everything to make life comfortable'.[60] There were also markets, sightseeing and sailing excursions on the Nile. Edith Lewis even took an early morning flight over Cairo in a Bristol biplane, wearing a leather suit and helmet.[61]

Nurses stationed in England at hospitals for New Zealand soldiers were delighted to see sights they had only heard or read about. They commented particularly on the green English countryside and the heathery moorland of Scotland. When one nurse toured the lakes of the Trossachs, she commented, 'It was all so fresh and peaceful everywhere.'[62] Clara Cherry, nursing in the tin huts of Codford, appreciated wandering the country lanes and picking cowslips, primroses, bluebells and lilac to decorate the huts.[63] Nurses could rest or recuperate at a large, beautiful house near

Sandwich in Kent, which the owners, the American Astor family, had 'left as they use it themselves. Any amount of comfy chairs, couches, etc, and books – well they are numerous and it is most luxurious.'[64] Lady Williams from Hastings, Hawke's Bay, lent another house near Barnstaple in Devon, 'quite in the country, surrounded by gloriously green fields and rolling downs'.[65] Nurses in France similarly enjoyed their rare opportunities for walks and sightseeing.[66] Eva Brooke, matron of the No. 1 New Zealand Stationary Hospital in France in June 1918, even planted a garden, but as the ground was 'very sour and rank', the vegetables either died or were eaten by rabbits. She had higher hopes for the potatoes.[67]

Working with others

Working with army orderlies, untrained women in the Voluntary Aid Detachment (VADs) and English nurses could be challenging.[68] With so few nurses in South African military hospitals, much of the work had to be left to orderlies, and New Zealand nurses felt this an odd way to work. Their views of orderlies were mixed. Emily Peter, not surprisingly, vehemently asserted that with few exceptions they were 'absolute rubbish' and 'utterly unfitted for their work'.[69] In contrast, Bessie Teape thought they were 'very willing' and gave 'a great deal of help'.[70] The difficulty was their inconsistency and lack of training. 'It is very awkward at times, as one has to trust so much to the orderly in many little ways. If he is a conscientious man it is all right, but if not the reverse.'[71] Patients with enteric fever needed extremely gentle handling to avoid perforating the ulcerated intestine, which could lead to haemorrhage or peritonitis and death. It was no wonder that Sarah Ross was worried. 'The orderlies I have,' she said, 'know nothing. Imagine putting a boy on as orderly to look after four enterics (very bad), who had not been in a ward before. It is really too dreadful.'[72] And some orderlies 'did not like being "bossed" by women'.[73]

New Zealand nurses made great efforts to train their orderlies. Ida Willis, reflecting 50 years later, said: 'We were always sad when the orderlies we had trained were taken for more forward duties, especially as we knew that they might never return, and also we were faced with having possibly untrained replacements.'[74] The situation was brought home personally to Daphne Commons at Brockenhurst in 1916. She wrote: 'We have been very much shocked today to hear how our orderlies had fared in France. It only seems such a little time since they were with us here, and now we hear that one of them ... has been killed; another has lost an arm and a leg, others are wounded and some are missing. Of course they have fared no worse than many others, but it has made us realise things more.'[75]

Nurses were frustrated not only by sketchily trained orderlies but also by the prospect of working with untrained volunteers. Hester Maclean, as both the NZANS matron-in-chief and the country's chief nurse, vehemently opposed the suggestion made 'in a persuasive manner' by 'a Christchurch woman' of sending untrained women as volunteer nurses in World War I.[76] She was referring to Ettie Rout who, despite government opposition, organised the Volunteer Sisterhood, a group of New Zealand women who went to Cairo to work in canteens, clubs and hospitals.[77] Maclean's stance was political as well as pragmatic. Nursing had only recently achieved professional status with the Nurses Registration Act 1901, and Maclean had worked hard to protect and advance this, establishing a professional journal, association and conferences. Sending untrained women to act in any nursing capacity would severely undermine the status of professional nurses.[78] Maclean also firmly believed that soldiers deserved the best, and that meant being cared for by registered nurses.

The British nursing profession also voiced objections to VADs, but without success. They had an unlikely but outspoken supporter in the unconventional Lady (Daisy) Greville, Countess of Warwick, who wrote a scalding piece on the 'butterfly sisterhood' of English socialites who volunteered as nurses merely to seek the latest sensation and who were, in her view, motivated by erotomania.[79] As Christine Hallett has pointed out, in the emotionally charged setting of the military ward, VADs considered nurses overly detached and impersonal, and nurses viewed VADs' overly familiar behaviour toward soldiers as a sign that they had volunteered to seek romance and adventure rather than to help the sick and wounded.[80]

New Zealand nurses who worked with untrained English VADs had mixed views of their worth.[81] Edna Pengelly was usually scathing. When yet another VAD died of dysentery at the Citadel Hospital in Cairo, she said: 'I don't think the V.A.D. helpers are a success in this climate. It is too trying and many of them are quite useless.'[82] Mrs Mildred Salt (formerly Sister Ellis) said that the sick nurses' quarters at Brockenhurst were 'rarely empty, but mostly occupied by V.A.D.s'. Climate was not the issue. She did not think that 'the English girl can work so hard as the Colonials'.[83]

New Zealand nurses also disparaged the tendency of trained, professional English nurses to eschew the hard, physical work of nursing, relying on orderlies instead. Ida Willis commented that in 1917, when the New Zealanders speedily set up another hospital at Amiens, there was 'confusion' over who was to be in charge: the New Zealanders, who had arrived first, or the English sisters. The New Zealanders ceded control to the English sisters and 'retired', but in a few days Ida Willis was urgently recalled. The sisters had discovered that untrained orderlies could not manage the care of very sick patients and, 'being used to supervising only, made no attempt to nurse the patients themselves as we New Zealand Sisters did, and so trained our orderlies to such excellence'. She had to explain to her English counterparts that 'they must do their share of the running or expect to be exchanged'. Eventually the English sisters 'recognised the need and settled down', but, Willis said, the few good New Zealand orderlies were relieved to be recalled to the New Zealand unit and its sisters.[84]

On their return from overseas, not all nurses stayed in the profession. Some married. Some did further training as masseuses before they left England and either worked in military hospitals in New Zealand or set up businesses at home. (Massage, which later evolved into physiotherapy, was considered a branch of medical nursing.)[85] Nurses who had gained specialist training and experience as nurse-anaesthetists during the war were frustrated that New Zealand authorities did not recognise their skills and expertise.[86] Others, physically and emotionally exhausted by the demands of wartime nursing, found themselves unable to continue in the profession. As Hester Maclean put it, some were 'war-worn and really not fit for duty'.[87] Clara Cherry, who had served overseas in hospitals in Egypt and England and on hospital trains and ships, returned to Auckland Hospital but found working in the noisy children's ward and sleeping in its basement too much. Her request for leave, which three doctors had advised, was declined. She resigned.[88] In 1927 Margaret Campbell disappeared from home during the night, and her body was discovered on an Auckland beach by a search party. Reports noted she had been in ill-health for some time as a result of her wartime service.[89]

Wartime nurses had the same eligibility as returning soldiers to apply for the land ballot under the soldier-settlement scheme, which enabled successful applicants to acquire government-purchased land and receive assistance in setting up farms.[90] Several turned to farming. One sister, who was invalided for some months after her return, was successful in the ballot. 'She got the very section she wanted' – four acres (1.6ha) in the old Caccia-Birch Estate near Palmerston North – and hoped to have 'pigs, cows, a horse and trap, and many fowls, also bees'.[91] Several trained at the Ruakura state farm where they could learn about horticulture and keeping poultry and bees. 'You would be surprised to see how quickly people improve here. I suppose it is the outdoor life, and we are all getting fat and sun-burned,' said one sister. 'Some of the sisters are very keen about bees, and are quite determined to be bee-farmers.'[92]

Nursing at home in World War II

At the outbreak of World War II in 1939, New Zealand nurses were as keen as their predecessors to serve overseas. The wartime Nursing Council, created to manage an orderly process of NZANS enlistment and ensure that domestic hospitals remained adequately staffed, worked hard to convince nurses that their service was just as valuable at home as on the war front.[93] Mary Lambie, the chief nurse, who also chaired the council, observed that there was 'no greater service at this present time than carrying on efficiently and uncomplainingly with the job in hand'. Every nurse needed 'to enter into the daily round with a whole-hearted zest and enthusiasm, confident that in doing so she is giving the best and noblest service.'[94]

Those who heeded the plea and remained in New Zealand experienced the emotional labour of dealing with 'war from afar'. In December 1939 Joan Boyle married Cyril Loeber; a fortnight later he was sent overseas with the army's dental unit. She did not see him again for three years. She was working in Wellington Hospital's Casualty Department, and men in uniform would come to say goodbye to staff they knew.[95]

Voluntary aids (VAs) assisted on the wards during the nursing shortage and received the same short course in basic nursing care and brief hospital experience that English VADs went through in World War I.[96] Occasionally the same mutual hostility arose. One VA complained in the nurses' journal that sisters had 'a cold precise manner' towards them, and they never knew if they gave satisfaction.[97] One nurse swiftly replied: 'Your intentions are probably excellent but you have a great distance to go to get beyond yourself.'[98] To Joan Loeber, however, they were 'like fresh air. They were energetic, quick, and learnt fast.' She was sorry to see them go. 'One old patient told me that it made him feel he was doing a bit for the war letting them learn on him!'[99]

Letter writing kept personal connections alive, but time was scarce. Because of the nursing shortage, Joan Loeber was suddenly promoted to be in charge of a men's surgical ward and had little time or energy for correspondence. And what should she write about? After twice going to see *Gone with the Wind* and falling asleep both times, and crying through Greer Garson's *Blossoms in the Dust*, she had given up on films. Her husband, serving in Egypt with the New Zealand Dental Corps, complained that her letters 'read like ward reports'. He would much rather know what she was doing. 'But it wasn't very easy to do, really.'[100]

In turn, receiving letters sustained connections with loved ones, but the news they brought could be devastating. Sonja Davies said the Wellington Hospital mail board was filled twice a day and 'anxiously scanned' by all.[101] When brothers, cousins and friends died, nurses were expected to carry on regardless. Elizabeth (Beth) Crawford was called one day to the Timaru Hospital matron's office to be told that her boyfriend had been killed in action. 'She was then sent back to work and had to continue her duty.'[102]

The need for leisure and laughter was keenly felt in wartime. Off-duty nurses 'spent hours round the piano singing the evocative songs of wartime'. From lunchtime onwards the Wellington Hospital nurses' home foyer was filled with servicemen, mostly American, calling for nurses or hoping to meet one. After the United States entered the war, American servicemen in the Pacific campaign on leave in New Zealand were seen as glamorous and attentive companions. Nurses became 'adept at negotiating' the fire escape when returning late to the nurses' home.[103]

In 1942 the war came suddenly closer. Sick and wounded servicemen flooded into New Zealand hospitals from the Pacific and the nation faced the prospect of Japanese air raids or invasion. Notices of new wartime regulations were circulated in hospitals, instructing staff on how to protect patients from splinters and flying glass, the flames of incendiary bombs and the effects of blast.[104] Mavis (Pat) Paton, who trained at Wellington Hospital during the war, said every nurse had to keep in her room a 'Jap Bag', a small suitcase holding immediate needs in readiness for emergency evacuation. Torch batteries were 'like gold', and 'the last glimmer of life was squeezed out … by warming them in the hot food press'. When blackout regulations were imposed, taped windows, opaque blinds, dim corridor lights, torchlight, and bed lights shrouded in red or blue cloth created a new, gloomy atmosphere that seemed symbolic of war. The sight of armed sentries outside a ward of Japanese prisoners of war conflicted with the nursing ideal of compassion for all patients.[105]

Alongside these sharp reminders of war came official expressions of concern about its effects on nursing discipline, including nurses' 'hair-dos'. 'Flopping curls and frizzing mops greet us on all sides … a mode no doubt influenced by the cinema and complicated by the permanent waving machine,' said an editorial in *Kai Tiaki*. 'A roll or group of curls drawn up from the forehead or a drape reaching down to the shoulders, with a patch of muslin perched on the crown of the head, may result in a certain allure and be suitable for the nurse-heroine of a cinema drama, but in actual practice it is another story.'[106] Similar concerns were voiced by Blanche Clark, the matron-in-chief of Wellington Hospital, for whom alluring curls and a languid drape of hair with its scanty covering perhaps symbolised her fears of nurses' behaviour with American servicemen.[107]

The emotional impact of the war from afar could be long-lasting. When Joan Loeber's husband returned, reconnecting was not simple. She found she had changed and matured, was self-reliant and used to making decisions. The slow process of reuniting required new emotional investment. 'We began to enjoy each other's company again, and although we couldn't bridge the years, we were at least bridging the gaps.'[108]

Wartime nursing folklore

The wartime culture of emotional labour engendered a small but powerful set of folktale motifs. Christmas Day brought a vivid connection with home. Nurses in field hospitals and general hospitals or aboard hospital ships strove to make the day as happy as possible for their homesick patients.

The folktale described re-creating familiar Christmas traditions in a profoundly alien setting. The stories depicted nurses' efforts to find presents for their patients and decorate a tree. Convalescent patients joined in, preparing decorations for their wards, fancy dress outfits and concert performances. If the men could find mistletoe, nurses went on alert. 'Poor Sister Lea declares this is "a dog's life"!' said Daphne Commons. 'You see she is young and pretty and the boys all like her, and I'm sure they are determined to catch her if they can.'[109] Christmas Eve was celebrated with a sumptuous supper and carol singing. On Christmas Day men woke to find small presents at their bedsides, enjoyed a festive midday dinner if their dietary regime allowed it, visited mates in other wards if they were ambulant, and had an elaborate afternoon tea or supper. The hospital might stage a fancy dress parade (with prizes) and a concert. Prizes were also awarded for the best-decorated ward, often commemorated with a picture postcard.[110] Christmas preparations meant extra work for nurses, but this, wrote Ida Willis, was 'well repaid by the sight of the happy faces.'[111]

Variations of the tale centred on the challenges of acquiring Christmas food or presents. Edith Lewis was preparing for Christmas at a camp hospital on the Sinai Peninsula when the railway link was suddenly disrupted, delaying arrival of the Christmas food. She was relieved when an Australian canteen offered tins of mincemeat and some dried fruit, and the nurses were soon at work making mince pies with the medical staff cutting out the pastry with scalpels. On Christmas morning the plum puddings arrived – by camel.[112] Ida Willis and another sister at Amiens at

Christmas 1916 'spent an afternoon in the small shops of back streets, hunting for cheap little toys costing threepence to sixpence. We bought engines, cars, ships, leaden soldiers, whistles, trumpets, mouth organs, as well as gifts of a more practical nature, and laden with these, we returned to the hospital grubby but triumphant.' They hung the toys on the tree. When it was wheeled around the ward in its tub in the morning, the tiny presents were handed to the patients, and the 'joy showing on their faces was lovely to see'. The men decided to send the toys home, so orderlies found paper, string and cardboard and took them to the post office. Ida Willis was given the 'tiny yellow-haired wooden doll decked out in a bright pink dress' that had been put atop the tree instead of a star.[113]

Such trinkets and toys were a frequent choice of gift, intended not to infantilise the patients but to evoke connections with family and home. The matron of the *Maheno* in 1915 said the toys 'brightened things up, and the boys had some fun out of it, that was the main thing. After all they had gone through on the Peninsula [Gallipoli] they deserved the best we could do.'[114] On more practical lines, men also received parcels containing 'an assortment of cigarettes, soap, shaving brush and cream, face cloth, socks, pipes, chocolates, handkerchiefs and other things dear to a man's heart. These were most welcome particularly as the men had lost all their personal belongings during the battle.'[115] These presents, 'something useful for the trenches',[116] symbolised the expectation that soldiers would return to the front line but also expressed a wish to make their lot easier.

Nurses, in their turn, received special Christmas gifts from New Zealand citizens that cheered them immensely. Like relief parcels for soldiers, gift parcels labelled 'To a Nurse' were organised by Red Cross branches, patriotic committees or local communities and sent overseas.[117] Mothers and others who were suffering the effects of the war from afar expressed their appreciation of the nurses caring for 'their boys'. Kate Stephenson, at the New Zealand hospital at Codford in England, thanked the Public Health Department for her Christmas parcel. 'And such a gift, just everything one requires, and then the N.Z. leather bag was just the finishing touch. I just had to swank that bag in London, when I went on my ten days' leave. Uniform or no uniform, that bag was not to be resisted.' Three weeks later she received another parcel, this time containing soap, handkerchiefs and powder, and she declared that 'as a result I shine and smell nice'.[118]

Nurses' narratives always emphasised Christmas food. Offering a sharp contrast to trench rations of bully beef and hard biscuits, it defied wartime privations.[119] Christmas dinner on the hospital ship *Maheno* in 1915 included 'chicken, ham, lamb, green peas, cabbage and potatoes. Then a grand plum pudding and sauce, jellies, fruit salads, nuts and sweets and ale – which the boys all enjoyed (and the chicken was tender).'[120] This ritual celebration of Christmas dinner provided more than a momentary distraction from war and wounds: it enabled patients and nurses to hold fast to the culture of home and show that war would not disrupt it. Stories of Christmas overseas reflected the ritual at home. And each year, *Kai Tiaki* carried nurses' narratives of Christmas celebrations in different hospitals in New Zealand.[121] It was a familiar tale.

Another form of wartime nursing folklore was personal encounters with the enemy – sometimes devastating experiences that forced nurses to confront the contradictions between their perception of the enemy and the reality of caring for a sick or wounded enemy soldier. Sarah Ross, at the Green Point Military Hospital in Cape Town in 1900, where many Boer prisoners were held, wrote of a man being shot trying to escape: 'Such an awful thing it seems to me to shoot a man down like that. The Boer was brought into one of my wards, and I had the pleasure of helping the surgeons and giving him some brandy, for which he was very grateful, and said "Thank you" so nicely. He spoke English very well. I did feel so sorry for him. He only lived twelve hours after.' For her, the sight of Boer prisoners 'standing about staring over the fence, and looking so miserable' was pitiful. 'Some of them are mere boys about fifteen; others, again, sixty or seventy years of age.'[122]

In World War I a variation of this story came from Ella Cooke, serving with the French Flag Nursing Corps at Bernay. She was surprised when 30 German soldiers she was nursing made a formal speech to her on New Year's Day, 1915, thanking her for her care. 'Of course I was quite taken aback and thanked them as best I could for their good wishes, and said that my greatest wish was that peace should reign. After which they gave three cheers for "Nurse Anglaise". I must say the Germans I have had to deal with, so far, have been very nice – the Prussian element seems much the worst.'[123]

During World War II, nurses at Wellington Hospital cared for around 30 Japanese prisoners of war. Joan Loeber was put in charge of their ward. As stories of the Japanese treatment of New Zealand prisoners had already 'filtered through', nurses cared for them only reluctantly. According to one nurse, the patients were arrogant, rude and 'didn't want to do anything, obey any rule. They did everything to be pests, to be annoying.'[124] Sonja Davies, who was training at the hospital at that time, had contradictory experiences with one Japanese patient, who made 'the most exquisite wind songs from coloured cellophane'. Neither could speak the other's language, but over a period of weeks she discovered that he had a wife and four children. This amity was sundered when he either misunderstood what she said or 'had a momentary brainstorm'. He grabbed her wrist and 'smashed it against the metal edge of his locker'. She received little sympathy from her father, who 'viewed the resultant broken wrist with distaste and said it served me right for fraternising with the enemy'.[125]

There were also direct hostile encounters. On 23 October 1915, the troopship *Marquette*, unprotected by the red cross symbol a hospital ship would carry, was conveying troops and the No. 1 New Zealand Stationary Hospital from Alexandria to Salonika. At 9am, nurses walking and chatting on deck heard a swishing sound. They looked down and saw a ray of green light streaming toward the ship. When the torpedo struck, nobody panicked. Everyone knew what to do. Nurses calmly donned lifebelts and assembled at their posts, 18 on each side of the ship. But the ship was already listing, making it difficult to lower lifeboats on the port side. One crashed down, crushing nurses in the lifeboat beneath. On the starboard side, a lifeboat tipped at one end, throwing nurses into the sea. The ship was rapidly sinking. Two nurses still on deck went to the gangway, held hands and jumped. They were not seen again. It took only 13 minutes for the *Marquette* to sink like 'a tiny cockle shell, and so quietly'. Nurses and men were in the water for up to eight hours, clinging to rafts or bits of wreckage, or clambering into repeatedly capsizing lifeboats. Nora Hildyard sang 'Tipperary' and the jaunty 'Are We Downhearted?' to boost spirits until she, too, died in the water. Others held their exhausted friends until they slipped away. In all, ten nurses died. French and British ships rescued the survivors, who were eventually taken to recuperate in Alexandria. Nurses who had not been on the *Marquette* waited anxiously to hear the casualty list and quietly grieved for friends who had died.[126]

When the news first reached New Zealand, newspapers portrayed the nurses as self-sacrificing heroines who had cheered the soldiers being loaded into lifeboats and 'of one accord' urged rescuers to 'Take the Fighting Men First!'.[127] Sarah Christie has explained how editing practices and the reprinting of metropolitan articles in regional newspapers helped construct a 'nationally homogenous version of events'. The reporting of this event adapted concepts of maternal sacrifice and British and colonial ideas of bravery to portray the nurses as imperial heroines.[128]

The continual public invocation of the trope of nurse as self-sacrificing, quiet heroine irritated nurses more interested in presenting themselves as professionals. As soon as possible, the surviving *Marquette* nurses put the record straight. Maclean

Edith Lewis served in both world wars. As matron of the Trentham Military Hospital in 1945, she cared for women liberated from internment in the Stanley Camp in Japanese-occupied Hong Kong.

Edith Lewis, *Joy in the Caring* (Christchurch: N.M. Peryer, 1963), frontispiece

confirmed that although nurses had indeed shown bravery, they could not have declared anything 'of one accord', as they were not in one group, and besides, she was relieved that the men had not allowed nurses to sacrifice themselves for the soldiers' sake. The origin of the story, she said, was wrapped in mystery.[129]

Nevertheless, the story was a boon for wartime propaganda. Newspaper references to the death of the *Marquette* nurses were often combined with accounts of the execution in Belgium of the British nurse Edith Cavell the following month, a story that captured an outraged public's imagination. Cavell had sheltered British and Allied soldiers and helped them to escape to Britain, but the execution of a woman and nurse drew international condemnation. Many countries raised or named memorials to her, including hospitals, rest homes for nurses, street names, bridges and even a mountain.[130] New Zealand nurses preferred to create a living memorial to their dead colleagues from the *Marquette* and set up a fund to assist any nurses suffering hardship. The *Marquette* story had permanent appeal. Hester Maclean repeated it in 1923 in her chapter on the history of New Zealand's war effort and in her memoir in 1932.[131] And the erroneous detail of nurses urging rescuers to save the men first persisted, even being used in an Anzac Day speech to children in 1936.[132] The wartime folklore was also embedded in stained glass and brass in hospitals and communities and in the construction of the Nurses' Memorial Chapel at Christchurch Hospital.

Overcoming damage caused by the enemy was a theme illustrated in Edith Lewis's wartime recollections. Near the end of World War II she was matron of the Trentham military hospital. In late 1945 the hospital received a group of British women who had been released after three years as civilian internees in the Stanley Camp in Japanese-occupied Hong Kong. The women had severe malnutrition and associated diseases and would stay until healthy enough to travel to Britain. Edith Lewis knew how to care *for* them as patients, but, having read of the Japanese treatment of internees, she and her nurses also planned to show the women that they were cared *about*. The nurses filled the wards with 'flowers in abundance', easy chairs and coloured cushions, 'lovely things to look at' and books with beautiful pictures. The women arrived debilitated and in rags. 'It was heartbreaking,' she said, 'to hear their stories of grim, humiliating treatment.' Despite their harsh experience in the Stanley Camp, they responded well to the nurses' care and caring. The power of beauty prevailed. When it was time for them to board the ship for their onward journey, Edith Lewis saw them off, returned to her quarters and was overwhelmed to find they had left her a tribute of their 'gratitude and esteem'. It was a Doulton china ornament of an elderly woman selling balloons of all colours. She recognised it: the women had treasured it through their three years of captivity as a surviving symbol of beauty, and Lewis treasured it in her turn.[133]

Public and professional perception

The cultural construct of the wartime nurse was both nurtured by and reflected in propaganda, popular literature and film. Children read tales of nurses' courage and daring in their annuals and newspaper columns, starting with the South African War.[134] During World War I, New Zealand's *School Journal* promoted wartime nurses as models of civilian courage and sacrifice, like Florence Nightingale before them.[135] Although the *School Journal* did not portray the impact of the war in harsh, unflinching terms until the mid-1920s,[136] it did publish a nurse's graphic account of the emotional impact of working on a hospital ship during the Gallipoli campaign. 'We nurses see heartbreaking sights,' she said. 'I remember vividly a New Zealander, badly burnt on the face by a bomb, his arm shattered, his two legs badly wounded ... The arm had to come off at once, and the gallant soldier died ... There are hundreds of such cases, and they wring our hearts.'[137]

Public references to trained nurses, such as news stories and eulogies, frequently invoked the trope of self-sacrificing devotion. Dr Percival Fenwick, after serving in South Africa, called Bessie Hay from Southland the 'New Zealand Angel'. Although overworked, she stubbornly refused to rest, leading a soldier-patient to say that 'she could not sit still, as it would crush her wings'.[138]

Propaganda posters, popular films and even songs like 'The Rose of No Man's Land' instead emphasised the trope of the self-sacrificing, untrained volunteer bearing the red cross symbol and living out an expectation, in Jane Potter's words, of 'devotional glamour'.[139] Audiences hurried to silent films like *Sweetheart of the*

Doomed, Satan in Sydney, Vive la France and *The Dark Silence* that featured Red Cross or other volunteers rather than trained nurses. Filmmakers believed it was the young, noble and courageous volunteer who would capture the imagination.[140] The exception was the romanticised film *The Martyrdom of Nurse Cavell*. When it was shown in Wellington in 1916, instead of the usual piano accompaniment for a silent film, the full matinee programme included 'special music' by an 'augmented orchestra', songs by a well-known vocalist and a recitation by Mr P.S. Latham of Martha Young's 'The Martyr'.[141]

The burgeoning international literature of the 1930s featured a grittier representation of war. It included *War Nurse* by the English writer Rebecca West (the pseudonym of Dame Cicily Fairfield) and Vera Brittain's memoir *Testament of Youth*.[142] *War Nurse* was ostensibly based on the diaries of an unidentified American volunteer nurse. While it gave accurate details of nursing procedures, it was, as Christine Hallett has explained, semi-fictionalised and highly sensationalist in its portrayal of the heroine's work and gradual disintegration.[143] Brittain's memoir of her experience as a VAD also amplified the drama and horror of war and showed her elitist contempt for qualified nurses.[144] VADs' memoirs were highly popular, more so than those of professional nurses, because in Britain VADs had a higher social profile.[145] In contrast, readers of the New Zealand novelist Nelle Scanlan's *Tides of Youth*, the second volume of her very popular Pencarrow saga about a New Zealand family, would have had to squint to find much on New Zealand's war efforts overseas.[146] Nevertheless, *Tides of Youth* and *Testament of Youth* were both in high demand at libraries.[147]

During World War II, the popular culture of literature and film shifted the focus from the romanticised volunteer to the professional army nurse. A film that merged the two was *Cry Havoc*, in which the main characters were two army nurses and 11 women volunteers on an island bombed and occupied by a Japanese force. Although the women were depicted as grubby and their clothing torn as a result of the hardships and perils they encountered, they were remarkably able to retain the elaborate 'hair-dos' that had so worried Blanche Clark.

Those who directly observed or received war nurses' professional attention were full of admiration and gratitude. Guy Farrell, an orderly on night duty on Lottie Le Gallais's ward on the *Maheno* in World War I, picked up a copy of *Kai Tiaki* on her desk, saw the nurses' published letters and decided to write to the editor about her. During their initial days in Anzac Cove he wrote, 'my poor sister worked like a Trojan, and it beats me how she kept up so long and with such frightful cases as we were getting.'[148] Soldier-patient Len Hart preferred the 'free and easy' manner of New Zealand and Australian nurses to that of the English, who were 'the limit'.[149] Alexander de Montalk wrote a poem acclaiming New Zealand nurses, comparing them favourably with Nightingale: 'Not even Florence, in the dark Crimea / Tending her stricken heroes, lamp in hand / Surpasses those who come from our dear land.' When the poem's anonymous publication in *Kai Tiaki* in July 1916 caught Daphne Commons's eye, she wrote to her mother about 'that rhyme of De Montalk's about Florence Nightingale and the nurses in Egypt! *How in the world* did it get there? A good thing no names were mentioned.'[150] Often nurses' professional efforts went unnoticed by patients. As Commons remarked: 'The sad part is that the really sick ones that one spends so much time over don't remember that part of it when they are better.' When nurses checked on convalescents, the patients often did not recognise them.[151]

For nurses themselves, World War I was one of the first opportunities to see how they measured up professionally against nurses from other countries in the empire. They considered themselves on a par with other 'colonial' nurses and readier to roll up their sleeves and work than their English colleagues. QAIMNS nurses, imbued with a military culture, were used to supervising orderlies. New Zealand nurses, experienced in civilian hospitals, expected to do the nursing themselves. When Maclean was overseas in 1915, a representative from the War Office told her that the New Zealand nurses should only supervise and that the actual nursing work should be done by orderlies, as in regular military hospitals. She told him sternly that untrained orderlies could not possibly nurse patients as they should be nursed. Moreover, 'New Zealand sent the nurses to care for the men themselves, to work, not to simply supervise'.[152]

New Zealand nurses were gratified and relieved to find that their training measured up well. Margaret Tucker declared, 'If we did not know it already we should soon be convinced that the New Zealand training is hard to beat.' She acknowledged the debt to nursing pioneers in England, but 'with a true Imperialistic spirit as a daughter of the Motherland', she thanked 'whatever Gods there be for my working colonial life'.[153] Hester Maclean was proud of the reputation of New Zealand nurses. 'They have worthily upheld the highest ideals of nursing and have shown the technical skill organised by careful training.'[154] Surgeon-General Robert Henderson, director-general of Medical Services, also recognised the standing of New Zealand nurses in a speech at a concert for the Nurses' Memorial Fund in October 1917. Even if he praised nurses to loosen purses, his view was based on evidence. He advised the audience that patients in New Zealand were receiving the 'scientific assistance of about the finest nurses in the world. (Applause.)' They were some of the 'most capably trained nurses' that could be found anywhere. He knew this from his own experience in New Zealand and from 'the testimony of matrons of our imperial hospitals' in Egypt and England, who repeatedly said they welcomed New Zealand nurses because they were 'so capable and so thoroughly well trained'.[155]

Nurses felt, however, that their colonial colleagues outshone them in the matter of uniforms. The New Zealand uniform was a long, dark-grey dress with full white apron, collar, cuffs and veil, and an outdoor uniform of a dark-grey coat with a scarlet-lined collar and grey bonnet. But the Canadian nurses' uniform was deemed the best. It was 'very smart – navy blue dresses and cloaks lined with scarlet, and gold buttons and navy blue felt hats',[156] although Daphne Commons sniffed that it had 'too many brass buttons etc for my fancy'.[157]

***

The narratives of nurses overseas offer glimpses of the emotional labour of wartime nursing. These are not long, stirring accounts like those of Vera Brittain and other, often upper-class English VADs. New Zealand nurses' narratives show the emotional toll of war in occasional, brief but heartfelt comments amid their prosaic, factual accounts of wartime work. Unable to show their feelings while working, nurses expressed them in letters home, but even then the terseness of the comments suggests a reluctance to let go. In every war they learned to contain their reactions. During the South African War one nurse said that she wanted to cry, as instead of the 'glory of war' she had to 'look upon the maimed limbs, the ghastly wounds, the suffering, the sad deaths, the after results of an engagement, be it a victory or a defeat'.[158] And nearly half a century later, in World War II, a returned nurse said that her saddest moment was 'seeing men with whom we'd gone over in the ship come into the hospital later, with a leg off, or wounded in some other way. Nurses don't get hardened to such things. They just get better at not showing their feelings.'[159]

CHAPTER 8

Virus and tremor – nursing in disasters

Dorothy Burgess left teaching to take up nursing in July 1917 when she had just turned 27. She was from Ōtāne, a small township just north of Waipawa in Hawke's Bay, and was the oldest daughter of Mary and Frederick Burgess, a timber sawmill owner.[1] Although the nearby hospital at Waipukurau had started taking a few probationers for training, she chose Napier Hospital. It commanded a striking view to the north over the harbour and the sea beyond, from a hilltop high above the town on the southern side. Dorothy's training progressed well, and in December that year she passed the hospital's junior examination.[2] But the following year, on 5 November, the deadly second wave of the 'Spanish flu' pandemic reached Napier. Dorothy seemed to contract a mild case. The virus spread across Hawke's Bay as it did through the rest of the country, taxing the hospital's ability to cope. Many nurses fell ill, and at one point Napier Hospital was left with only one trained nurse and 12 probationers.[3] In Napier West, where most of the city's deaths occurred, a relatively new school was converted into an emergency hospital that could take up to 45 patients. When it opened on 18 November, Dorothy had recovered enough to volunteer to work there. Thirteen days later, having suffered a relapse, she died.[4]

The nearby city of Hastings on the Hawke's Bay plain had no general hospital, so an emergency facility was swiftly set up at the racecourse. Ina Leech, a 26-year-old registered nurse who had trained at Christchurch Hospital and was in Hastings on holiday from Rangiora, immediately volunteered her services. She too succumbed to influenza, dying on 26 November.[5]

Thirteen years later, Nancy Thorne-George and her sister Margo were training at Napier Hospital. They were originally from Gisborne where they had won prizes for reading and history at Miss Aylmer's private school. They came to Napier in 1919 when their father George was made branch manager of the New Zealand Insurance

Company.[6] On the morning of 3 February 1931 they were chatting in the three-storey nurses' home, which had opened five years before. Without warning, at 10.47am a 7.8 magnitude earthquake struck. The ferro-concrete building collapsed 'like a pack of cards'.[7] Nancy, aged 24, was killed. Margo was 'hurled from the top floor'. Mr E.T. Rees, the hospital board secretary, found her 'staggering in the roadway'. As she was still in danger from falling debris, Rees guided her to safety before rescuing another nurse.[8] Margo was badly bruised and was sent with others by train to Palmerston North Hospital to recover.[9] Five other Napier nurses and one nursing sister were killed in the quake.

Individual nurses had responded admirably in other earthquakes. At Westport Hospital during the 7.3 Murchison earthquake in June 1929, despite being thrown to the ground by the quake, Edith Dunsford acted with 'courage, coolness and resource' to organise evacuation and patient care with 'the mountains positively leaping'.[10] But the Hawke's Bay quake was far more destructive.

The influenza pandemic and the 1931 earthquake were the most significant disasters that the New Zealand nursing profession had faced, with respect to both the demands on nurses and the number of nurses who died.

Pandemic nursing in 1918

Although outbreaks of infectious diseases had occurred before 1918, they were usually localised and comparatively manageable. New Zealand's remote location offered no protection against the global sweep of the deadly 1918–19 influenza pandemic. The disastrous second wave struck Auckland in late October 1918, just as people were welcoming soldiers home from war. It peaked throughout the country in November as people celebrated the armistice, and waned in early December. In less than eight weeks the virus had infected around 40 percent of New Zealand's population, then around 1.2 million, and killed around 8500 people.[11] A person could be asymptomatic in the morning, develop virulent symptoms during the day and be dead by nightfall.[12] Whole households could be affected. Sometimes only one person, perhaps just a child, was left to care for others.

Hospitals were unprepared for and overwhelmed by the rapid influx of cases. In 1918, 2195 qualified nurses were on the register but nearly a quarter were still on wartime service overseas. The remaining trained nurses in the hospitals, as well as probationers, struggled to care for the seriously ill patients who filled the wards.

The situation rapidly worsened when three-quarters of these nurses fell ill themselves.[13] The minister for public health, George W. Russell, declared that they 'went down like hay before the reaper's scythe'.[14] At Auckland Hospital, 160 of the 180 nursing staff contracted the disease, with 140 ill at one time.[15] Of the 305 admissions to Wellington Hospital in November, 96 were nurses.[16] Christchurch Hospital's complement of around 100 nurses was reduced to 38,[17] and at Dunedin Hospital, 82 of the 116 nurses fell ill.[18] Small hospitals were equally affected. In early December, six nurses at Wairoa Hospital contracted influenza, leaving one trained nurse and three probationers to provide 24-hour care for them and for 40 other seriously ill patients.[19] Hester Maclean, the country's chief nurse, noted that there was on average only one trained nurse for every 70 to 80 patients.[20] This was not enough to ensure even one qualified nurse for each ward or emergency hospital. She declared, 'It was a nightmare of a time.'[21]

Department of Health nurses were redeployed wherever possible. Mary Lambie, who was working in the School Medical Service in Christchurch, was sent to Cheviot. She found the school buildings unsuitable for an emergency hospital as there were only two small rain-water tanks, two lavatories at the bottom of a paddock and no cooking facilities. She therefore commandeered a local boarding house where 12 residents were already ill. At times they had 40 patients but very little help. She was glad to see another trained nurse and a midwife when they arrived from Christchurch. 'It was my first experience of emergency work,' she said, and one that taught her many things. She and her colleagues lost only one patient.[22]

The critical shortage of nurses led authorities to plead for volunteer help, and citizens rapidly responded. Trained nurses who had left the profession for marriage or retirement returned to work. Many took voluntary charge of emergency hospitals set up in schools, halls, racecourses and tents. Some, like Miss Bailey in Paeroa and Mrs Lovell in Auckland, set up emergency hospitals in their own homes.[23] Members of the public, religious sisters and others who had completed a St John or Red Cross home-nursing course volunteered for work in hospitals and homes. This took courage as well as commitment. The risks were clear. Many volunteers became ill, and several died.[24]

Three factors contributed to hospital nurses' staggering rate of illness – their exhaustion from long hours of taxing work, their minimal protection from droplet infection during their close contact with patients, and a lack of experience and supervision among probationers.

Exhaustion was recognised but ignored. As the number of available nurses plummeted, those still on their feet worked ever-longer hours. Before the pandemic qualified nurses usually worked a 12-hour duty, but probationers, by law, were supposed to work only eight hours a day. The pandemic required disregard for that law, and nurses frequently worked up to 17 hours a day. Grace Widdowson, training at Christchurch Hospital, came off duty 'so tired that the long corridor just waved in front of me. The staff was so denuded that we had to stay on and do the best that we could with the few that were there.' There was little time to eat or sleep before returning to the ward. With exhausted nurses rapidly falling ill, all were aware of the danger. As Widdowson said, 'It was a grim time. No one ever thought we would emerge alive … [W]e all expected to die, but some of us survived.'[25] Dorothy Palmer (later Reyburn), who fell ill while on night duty at Auckland Hospital, had been 'trying to do all sorts of things in two wards' because of lack of staff. When she knew she was sick, she thought, 'I can't go on, it's not fair to others.' She asked the night sister to send relief, but no nurses were available. She was told she would 'just have to carry on'. So she did. In the morning she was looking out the window and asked one of the patients whether there were two boats or only one. When he said one, she realised she was seeing double. 'I knew then that I was having a raging temperature, so I didn't go back on duty after that.'[26]

It was no better in the emergency hospitals, which might have only one attendant with professional nursing experience and the ability to make clinical judgements. As patients' conditions could rapidly worsen, she had to be constantly available. At the 20-bed Kaiapoi emergency hospital, for example, Lilian Emerson was in charge. Mr William Wharton, the North Canterbury Hospital Board secretary, noted that as she was the only trained nurse there, she 'had to be "on deck" all round the clock'. He was concerned that if they could not get relief for her soon, 'she would break down, and then they would be in trouble'. He sent a second trained nurse, but when she did not arrive, he discovered that the Health Department had commandeered her to nurse the Māori at Port Levy.[27]

The rate of infection among nurses was not due to ignorance or negligence. Nurses were aware of the precautions necessary when nursing a person with a highly infectious disease. A patient with diphtheria, for example, was usually isolated in a side room, and a single nurse was assigned to 'special' them on each shift. This meant she cared for no one else, partly to minimise the risk of cross-infection to other patients. She wore a special cap over all her hair and a gown over her usual uniform. Gloves were not worn – the nurse washed her hands and soaked them in a bowl of disinfectant solution. She wore a face mask only when giving the patient close personal care. In an epidemic of a disease such as scarlet fever, when an isolation ward

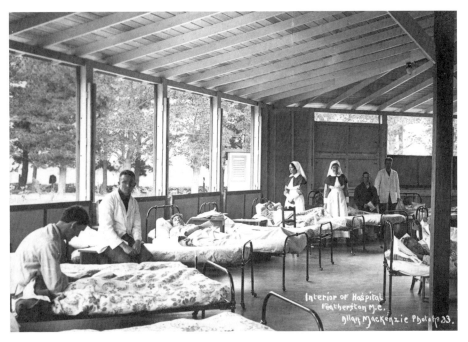

Military hospitals, as at the Featherston military camp in 1918, had octagonal isolation wards with large windows to provide ventilation and light. From the centre, nurses could easily see all the patients. Influenza ward, Featherston Military Hospital, 11-151-54, Wairarapa Archive, Masterton

might be full of patients with that single disease, cross-infection between patients was of less concern than the risk to nurses. The nurse still wore a gown and had time to take precautions like hand-washing between each patient. In the influenza pandemic, given the shortage of nurses and the pace of work, they were likely able to take only minimal precautions.

Lack of training and supervision was hazardous for probationers' health. Before the pandemic probationers worked with qualified nurses and others a year or two ahead of them in training, and were allocated tasks according to their level of experience. A ward sister oversaw all staff. This supervisory hierarchy worked well, particularly in the long, open wards of the time, providing a safe and structured environment in which probationers could learn. Senior nurses' and ward sisters' observation of what was happening in the ward offered another safeguard. In the pandemic, however, the supervisory hierarchy almost disappeared as senior probationers, staff nurses and ward sisters fell ill. A very junior probationer might be the only one on the ward with any professional training. She had to make decisions and carry out unfamiliar tasks, as well as organise and supervise the work of volunteers. She was therefore expected to cope well beyond the bounds of her usual role.[28] To make matters worse, new probationers would have lacked knowledge of protocols to avoid infection. At Dunedin Hospital, medical students who volunteered to help in the wards knew that the best place to learn was in the sick nurses' ward, as those patients knew exactly what should be done for them.[29] In all, 42 nurses died in the pandemic.[30]

In the culture of blame of the early 1900s, any nurse who caught her patient's infectious disease was considered to have brought her predicament on herself through incompetent nursing.[31] There were only three exceptions – infectious diseases caught when nursing in wartime, when nursing typhoid patients in remote fever camps, and in the 1918 pandemic.

Coping with an overwhelming number of patients required suspending accepted standards of nursing care, particularly in caring for patients with 'pneumonic influenza' or 'septic pneumonia'. Geoffrey Rice's analysis of pandemic death certificates showed that three-quarters of those who died in Auckland succumbed to the pneumonic form of the disease.[32] Before the pandemic, doctors and nurses acknowledged that only expert nursing care could bring a patient safely through the 'crisis' of pneumonia – the time when the fever peaked, usually on the seventh day of the illness. This was the point when either the patient died or their temperature dropped dramatically and they began the long process of recovery. In the pandemic, the pneumonic phase of the disease most often raced through to the crisis in three days.[33] There was little time to nurse the patient through the fever and few nurses left to do it.

With so many seriously ill patients, nurses struggled to provide even basic care like cold drinks and cool sponges to reduce the fever, starch-and-opium enemas to counteract the diarrhoea or nourishing fluids to boost strength. A volunteer would be given the task of keeping fluid jugs filled and cooled in a bath of cold water.[34] The fever could spike to 104 or 105 degrees Fahrenheit (about 40 degrees Celsius). It caused delirium, so nurses needed orderlies and male volunteers to help keep patients in bed. 'Frightful delirium,' Grace Widdowson remembered, 'they all seemed to be trying to get out of the windows, and we had a dreadful time.'[35] Anne Busch, also training at Christchurch Hospital, recalled: 'People became very excited, quite irrational, shouting out, calling out. In a few hours they'd be quite dark, almost black. And the condition was such that you couldn't believe it … It was a very drastic, very dreadful time.'[36] Nurses recognised the combination of delirium and the characteristic purple-black colouration from cyanosis as the portent of death. Even the best nursing skills could not save these patients.

In the absence of medical advice, nurses had to take control and make clinical decisions. When all the doctors between Whanganui and Hāwera were 'laid low with the malady', for example, the matron of Patea Hospital, Robina Lochhead, 'stepped in to the breach'. She did 'the work of two doctors', visiting homes 'and generally advising as to the best means to adopt to cope with the scourge'.[37]

Nurses outside hospitals also performed beyond their usual role. As an emergency health measure a town might be divided into 'blocks', each with a central 'depot' or 'bureau' where often a nurse was in charge, receiving telephone calls for help and organising appropriate responses, usually sending volunteers. Sometimes she could visit patients' homes herself, with a generous citizen conveying her by car or motorbike. The trained nurse who volunteered at the Riccarton depot, for example, had come 'back to the uniform' and not only 'capably directed the efforts of other volunteers' but made over 100 calls herself in three days.[38] Depot nurses trained volunteers to use a clinical thermometer to take and report patients' temperatures, thus enabling the nurses to monitor a patient's condition from a distance.[39] As the need for clinical thermometers outstripped the supply, dairy thermometers were used. One volunteer used a veterinarian's thermometer with a patient who was still well enough to retain his sense of humour – he 'hoped the instrument wouldn't make him hoarse'.[40]

Depot nurses were in short supply. The 'captains' in charge of Wellington's blocks noted this difficulty when they met to discuss progress in late November. When George Nathan of the Wadestown area happily boasted that they were doing so well they no longer needed their nurse, Mr McKenzie immediately snapped her up for Karori. Others also put in a claim but were too late. Peter Fraser, MP, overruled them by saying any available nurses were desperately needed in the hospital. The Wadestown nurse's health, as it turned out, did not allow her to 'stand the strain' of hospital work, but she was willing to serve in a district.[41]

Other nurses in community roles also worked beyond the scope of their usual responsibility. District nurses continued nursing their chronically ill patients but also cared for as many influenza patients as possible, too many to list in their monthly reports to their organisations.[42] Plunket nurses worked in emergency hospitals and set up temporary homes for the babies and children of mothers who were too ill to care for them or who had died.[43] Nurses in the health service for Māori continued doing the rounds of Māori settlements, providing or organising care for the sick. Others employed by hospital boards also attended Māori in their districts. Nurse Maine of Ōtorohanga, for example, reported that between 22 November and 31 December she had been responsible for the care of 250 European and 200 Māori influenza patients.[44]

Extra nurses were sent, or volunteered, where needed. Nurse Bulstrode was despatched from Wairoa to Mōhaka with orderlies, medicine and 'full equipment'.[45] Mereana Tangata, now Mrs Vincent Hattaway, despite having a large family to care for, 'worked very strenuously from the first', taking voluntary charge of the temporary hospital with 50 patients at a Māori settlement near Te Kūiti. And Sarah Polden, a highly experienced senior nurse, went from her home in Drury to nurse Māori in Kaikohe.[46] Lilian Alexander had just joined her missionary sister, Jessie, in the Nūhaka area as a mission nurse. According to Joan Rattray's 1961 account, Alexander arrived 'just in time to organize the health services of the whole district' during the pandemic and, with her helpers, 'conquered' it.[47] A perhaps more realistic picture of the nursing challenges came from Lady (Hēni) Carroll, who visited the area to encourage Māori to go into the temporary hospitals. She reported that there was only one nurse at Nūhaka, and she had not been able to restrain two delirious Māori patients from fleeing. Male assistance was therefore needed more than female help.[48]

Nurses' narratives of the pandemic are rare. The few existing accounts consistently focus on the grim time, the overwhelming work, patients' fevered delirium and the purple-black cyanosis. It was as though surviving the ordeal was sufficient. After the state final examination the following June, the examiner was surprised and disappointed that so few candidates had attempted the question on 'septic pneumonic influenza'. Nurses who had survived the pandemic were evidently exhausted with the topic. The 'best answer' to the question was a short, dispirited account of a fevered, cyanosed patient with intense thirst, diarrhoea, distressed breathing and copious, tenacious, blood-streaked sputum. He was delirious, restless and noisy. He showed no improvement and after a few days died 'practically of asphyxia'.[49]

New Zealand popular literature was similarly quiet on the subject. *Tides of Youth*, the second volume of Nelle Scanlan's extremely popular Pencarrow family saga, dealt with the influenza pandemic in a single paragraph.[50] Beryl McCarthy's tale of a Hawke's Bay family featured five paragraphs on the family's volunteering efforts in the pandemic, when people 'went down like flies before a Flit gun and were as difficult to revive'.[51]

Public references to nurses in the pandemic offered a paradoxical portrait of the trained nurse as a unique community asset – able to organise a block depot and run an emergency hospital – yet replaceable. Her lack was keenly felt, as at Methven, where the emergency hospital had to struggle to care for more than 30 patients without a trained nurse for a week.[52] Journalists reprimanded patients who employed a nurse for their sole benefit, because 'the need of the multitude [was] greater than the need of one person'. For every invalid who did this, there were 'dozens in distress, with no assistance at all'.[53] In addition, articles advised the public not to squander successful nursing care. Out of gratitude to those who had nursed them, convalescent patients should stay at home even when well enough to leave their beds rather than risk a relapse or spread the disease while still infectious. As one journalist noted: 'The world will go on for a few days without you.'[54]

When so many nurses were sick, however, substitutes were acceptable. An urgent call went out for volunteers – anyone who knew the 'rudiments of nursing', perhaps from caring for sick family members, but also anyone else who was prepared to help care for patients.[55] Willingness was all. For the duration of the pandemic, at least, nursing was seen as something anyone could do. And the bibbed white apron that symbolised nursing could be purchased at a local drapery for four shillings and sixpence.[56]

Other public references to nursing drew on the tropes of the quiet and devoted heroine and the self-sacrificing angel, especially in relation to nurses who died. An Ōtāne reporter said Dorothy Burgess had 'sacrificed her life to duty', and her parents could be proud that she had 'sacrificed herself nobly'.[57] She was buried at the Ōtāne Cemetery with a simple inscription on the granite cross above her grave. No memorial was erected to her at Napier Hospital where she had trained.

Ina Leech, the nurse who had volunteered while on holiday in the Hawke's Bay region, received a more elaborate farewell (perhaps because she was a registered nurse, a visitor and a volunteer, whereas Burgess was merely a local probationer doing what was expected of her). On her death, H. Ian Hislop, the mayor of Hastings, immediately set up a fund to commemorate Leech's 'brave deeds and to show our love and respect for a brave woman who died trying to save others'. He donated the first £3 and suggested that a monument on her grave might be suitable.[58] The Nurse Leech Memorial Fund raised at least £52, but her family requested that its name be changed instead to the Nurses and Orderlies Memorial Fund.[59] The mayor, apparently unwilling to forgo honouring Leech in some more personal way, gave the eulogy at her funeral, noting her 'devotion to duty'. He also acted as a pallbearer and gave one of the wreaths covering her coffin.[60] It is unclear how the fund was eventually used. Ina Leech was buried in a corner of the Hastings cemetery beside soldiers, and the inscription on her gravestone, placed by her widowed mother Evalina, ends with the words 'Steadfast in her duty'.[61]

Another quiet heroine was Minnie Dixon at the Hokitika hospital, one of 'a band of noble women' who 'laboured so untiringly in the great cause', who died on 29 November aged 21. She was from Kawhaka in the Arahura Valley.[62] Her colleague, Wilhelmina (Mina) Davies, had died six days earlier.[63] For a small rural hospital, the loss of two staff members was significant. When a memorial tablet to them was unveiled in a hospital corridor in August 1919, it also included the name of another influenza victim, Sister Ethel Taylor, who had trained at Hokitika but left in June 1918 to work in Hamilton.[64] These quiet heroines had 'all done their duty nobly'.[65]

The same tropes appeared in notices about the loss of three nurses at New Plymouth Hospital. According to the newspaper, Sister Agnes Taylor 'literally gave her life that others might live', and probationers Florence Austin and Phoebe Waite contracted influenza doing their 'sacred duty'.[66] The concept of a 'martyr to duty' was also prominent in the public perception of Sister Jessie Linton at Thames Hospital, who had 'sacrificed her life' doing 'more than her duty'.[67] Mrs C.H. Derrick told the *Thames Star* editor that Sister Linton had 'worked unceasingly' in a 'truly heroic service' and 'practically died on her feet'.[68]

Another who 'laid down her life' was Maud Manning. In the 10 years since she had trained at Christchurch Hospital she had been based at Paeroa, working as a mission nurse among Māori. With the outbreak of influenza, she volunteered to nurse Māori soldiers at the Narrow Neck camp near Auckland. Shortly afterwards she succumbed to the disease herself and died on 18 November.[69] Maud Mataira, who had trained at Wanganui Hospital and worked in the Māori health service until 1914, died on 22 November 1918 while nursing influenza patients at Hokianga.[70] She had been one of the nurses singled out in 1912 by the minister for public health, George W. Russell, for public recognition of their efforts in caring for Māori. In a prophetic remark, he had said Mataira's 'good work was doubtless inspired by the splendid example of her friend, Akenehi Hei, who died at the post of duty'.[71]

The frequent references to the heroism, self-sacrifice and martyrdom of nurses who died during the pandemic probably owed a great deal to the rhetoric surrounding war casualties.[72] The same tropes, along with that of the ministering angel, were also evident in reports of Ruth Drummond's death at Ohakune. Drummond had left her second year of training at Auckland Hospital because of poor health.

Nevertheless, when asked to help at Ohakune, not far from her parents' home in Rangataua, she went from house to house caring for the sick, organised the emergency six-bed cottage hospital there and cared for people in Raetihi. The heavy, relentless work took its toll, and she died of influenza on 15 November in the cottage hospital she had set up.[73] Dr Mitchell, who had been sent from Wanganui Hospital to organise the pandemic response in Ohakune, noted in his hospital board report that Ruth Drummond was a devoted and thorough nurse who 'exhibited nursing skill worthy of a much more highly-trained person' than a second-year probationer. He had trusted her sufficiently to leave the cottage hospital in her care and travel on to other parts of the Ohakune area.[74] He added that 'she died that others might live'. The board duly recorded its appreciation of 'the late Nurse Drummond's heroism'.[75] In a newspaper article about her death, an Auckland reporter pointed out to readers that visiting homes in Ohakune was 'quite a different thing to travelling in motor cars' (as nurses did in Auckland during the pandemic). On her rounds, Drummond had to 'walk through mud' to the point that 'her clothes were wet over her knees'. For her dedication, she was known as the 'Walking Angel'.[76]

Hester Maclean took a more prosaic tone in her notices of hospital nurses' deaths. She often noted simply that they contracted influenza 'in the course of their duty'. For probationers, she stated whether they had been due to sit the state final examination.[77] The terseness of these notices might be attributed to lack of information about probationers. In clear contrast, she warmly acknowledged the efforts of married and retired nurses who volunteered their services during the pandemic.[78]

In early 1919 a commission of inquiry considered what could be done to mitigate any future pandemic. A major concern among those who gave evidence was citizens' lack of even basic nursing skills. Sibylla Maude had headed the central Christchurch influenza depot in Cathedral Square while still managing her district nursing service. In her usual brusque way she said that she had been overwhelmed with people volunteering, but a great many were of little help, as they were appallingly ignorant of health, cleanliness and housekeeping. They could not take a temperature, and some could not even properly cook a potato.[79] Hester Maclean also found citizens' ignorance of the simplest measures of caring for the sick 'rather astonishing', considering the colonial woman's general adaptability and efficiency, but she was more generous in acknowledging their efforts.[80] Without the volunteer helpers, she said, the sick would have lain unattended. They had laboured night and day, doing their best to relieve terrible suffering. However, she adamantly resisted a suggestion that hospitals offer a short course in nursing to prepare women for any future emergency.

Such a proposal would lead to 'two grades of nursing' and undermine the status of probationers already sacrificing much to gain their qualification. Instead, she allocated trained nurses – particularly those returning from war – to different towns to teach home nursing courses, supplementing those run by St John and the Red Cross. Citizens initially flocked to these courses, but after just two years interest waned, attendance dropped and they were ended.[81]

The 1931 Hawke's Bay earthquake

The Hawke's Bay earthquake was a more sudden and localised disaster than the pandemic but dramatic in the devastation it wrought. That morning, a ward sister at Napier Hospital, who happened to be on the verandah looking out to sea, 'noticed a curious upheaval of the ocean'. She ran back to the ward, called for all possible patients to get up and go out to the grounds, and started getting helpless patients out. 'In a minute the crash came, but all were safe outside.'[82]

The noise and heaving of the ground was terrifying. The earthquake reduced much of Napier's centre to piles of rubble, and then a fire 'swept through what the earthquake left'.[83] The 'dull booming' of gas explosions in Napier and aftershocks continued during the night. More than 500 aftershocks were felt throughout the region in the next two weeks.[84] In all, the Hawke's Bay death toll was 256.[85]

The patients at Napier Hospital were evacuated to the nearby Botanical Gardens and to a tent hospital erected at the Greenmeadows racecourse. Casualty stations were also set up at McLean Park and Nelson Park. In Hastings, the new Fallen Soldiers Memorial Hospital was small and catered mainly for maternity cases, so an emergency tent hospital was erected at the racecourse. Small towns like Waipawa and Waipukurau also suffered, and there was hardly a chimney left standing between Waipukurau and Napier. In Wairoa the hospital was badly damaged and an emergency one erected. Isabel Banks, a Māori district health nurse at Frasertown, inland from Wairoa, reported a remark by an old man, Wiremu, who was riding by on his horse at the time of the quake: 'Pakeha sneaking into heaven – you can't get in that way.'[86]

Contemporary newspaper reports and nurses' own recollections, preserved in memoirs and oral histories, reveal the emergence of a folklore about nurses and nursing following the earthquake. Newspaper accounts combine the familiar tropes of the nurse as the quiet heroine and self-sacrificing angel. In contrast, the nurses' recollections emphasise the virtues of adaptability, pragmatism, resourcefulness, duty and resilience.

With Napier Hospital damaged in the 1931 earthquake, nurses cared for patients in emergency camps in parks and racecourses, including the town's Botanical Gardens, shown here. 1/2-060975-F, Alexander Turnbull Library, Wellington

The focus of many of these accounts was the destruction of the three-storey nurses' home at Napier Hospital, which 'collapsed like a pack of cards'.[87] The tragedy was symbolised by the 'pathetic pile' of rubble and broken concrete slabs that remained.[88] The fatalities in the nurses' home underscored the fact that nurses, admired for their selfless caring of vulnerable others, were themselves vulnerable to the quake's destructive power. According to a report in the *Auckland Star*, one rescuer in the relief party from the steamer *Taranaki* found a nurse dying in the ruins, who told him to go to others in greater need. Soon after, another girder fell and crushed her head.[89] Other accounts focused on the plight of the night nurses peacefully asleep on the quiet top floor,[90] ignoring the fact that other nurses were also in the home that morning. Even the New Zealand novelist Nelle Scanlan, who usually referred to national events just as a way to mark the passage of time in her Pencarrow saga, could not resist mentioning the night nurses in her third volume, *Winds of Heaven*.[91] The nurses in the greatest danger were in fact those on the lower floors.

Both newspaper accounts and nurses' narratives also highlighted the theme of the miraculous escape, a staple feature of disaster reportage, dramatically contrasted with the 'ghastly incidents' of some nurses' deaths. Mr E.T. Rees, who guided Margo Thorne-George to safety, then rescued a nurse who was hanging upside down, her legs trapped under debris. He climbed a fallen concrete slab, grabbed her by the armpits and pulled her free.[92] A dozen men spent three hours freeing a nurse pinned under a concrete slab and another trapped under a stairway behind her. The two nurses 'stoically endured the long suspense, crushed in discomfort and pain' and 'suffered severely' when the sledgehammers were used. Easing slabs with crowbars provided some relief.[93] Sister Beryl Nielsen was buried under rubble for 12 hours before an apparent looter heard her cries. She sustained a crushed shoulder and wrist.[94]

Other miraculous escapes required no rescuers. Sister Mary Wellock, ironing in the nurses' home laundry, was trapped by falling rubble, but a second shock opened up the tile roof above her, enabling her to scramble out.[95] Two night nurses had 'lucky escapes' when they decided to go to their family homes to sleep, as they had the next night off. Maisie Wilson's escape in this way became an enduring part of the family folklore.[96] Dorothy Scammell, a trainee nurse based at Wairoa Hospital, was gaining her required experience at the larger Napier Hospital and had come off the final shift of her stint of night duty there. She caught an early service car and arrived in Wairoa feeling 'a bit fagged by the hot dusty trip', so she was sitting in the shade on the riverbank eating an ice cream when the earthquake struck. In the pandemonium and 'kaleidoscope of din', with the ground cracking open in wide fissures, she managed to get to the hospital. Night nurses ran screaming from the Wairoa nurses' home, 'their night dresses drenched to transparency by water from overturned rain water tanks'. When news trickled through after five days, she was horrified to hear that so many of the nurses she had worked with in Napier had died.[97]

One often-repeated story, always portrayed as an 'amazing' or 'miraculous' escape, was that of Elaine Hamill, a second-year nurse at Napier Hospital. When she came off night duty friends invited her to have morning tea with them, but she decided to relax in a bath instead. When the earthquake struck, she remembered her mother's advice to stand in a doorway. She leapt from the bath and had just reached the doorway when the bathroom collapsed into rubble behind her. Her friends having morning tea in the sitting room were crushed. Soon after completing her training, Elaine became an internationally successful film and stage actor.[98] She happily told the bath story in publicity for films and stage performances. (No doubt her father, the proprietor-editor of the *Taihape Times*, had taught her the value of a good story.) The tale was then picked up by Sheilah Graham, one of Hollywood's

The story of the collapse of the nurses' home at Napier Hospital in the 1931 earthquake focused on the deaths of sleeping night nurses. 1/1-037340-F, Alexander Turnbull Library, Wellington

'Unholy Trinity' of gossip columnists, who told it in her widely syndicated column. The *Auckland Star* used Graham's account when Elaine appeared in Ivor Novello's play *Fresh Fields* in June 1936.[99] When the play went to Dunedin in July, however, perhaps the reporters there felt the story needed more decorum for the city's readers: in their version, Elaine managed to find a wrap to cover herself before making her escape.[100] She later played a role as a nurse – fully clad in uniform – in the 1939 American film *The Outsider*.[101]

Another theme in the folklore was that of nurses' pragmatism in coping with a world shaken upside down. Patients were transferred to tents. Nurses improvised supplies as they attended to casualties with 'crushed limbs, burns, scalds and haemorrhages'. After initial rescue efforts in Wairoa, 'the first thing everyone wanted was a cup of tea', so Dorothy Scammell helped dig through the rubbish for old tins that could be washed and boiled to replace broken crockery. In the ensuing weeks, the nurses became 'quite good' at cooking porridge and stews in kerosene tins.[102]

Nurses from outside the area offered pragmatic assistance. On the day after the quake, around 100 nurses in North Island towns had volunteered and were on their way to Hawke's Bay.[103] Mary Lambie, working for the Department of Health before taking up her role as instructor in the postgraduate course that year, was sent to Napier the day of the quake. After a 12-hour car journey she arrived there at 3.30am 'on a hot night with a full moon' to assist with the organisation of the racecourse emergency hospital. An operating theatre had been set up in the grandstand lunchroom, with cars shining their headlights against the windows to provide sufficient light. Within two hours health inspectors had organised water connections, lanterns and privies. During the morning marquees were set up for wards, equipment arrived and the emergency hospital took shape. Elizabeth Myles, matron of Wanganui Hospital, sent linen and uniforms, including two of her own, which Lambie gratefully wore. The only problem was that they had 44 buttons down the front – 'a source of amusement and great worry'.[104]

Margaret Macnab had set out from Whanganui the same day and arrived at 4am at the racecourse hospital, where 'improvisation was the order of the day'. It was 'not unusual to see wounds soaking in kerosene tins of antiseptics as nothing else was available'. Late that evening a loudspeaker announcement advised that a marquee had been set up for nurses, and they could collect groundsheets and blankets when off duty. When Margaret and two others finally finished work at 10pm, they found groundsheets but only one blanket left. Determined to change from the clothes she had worn for two days, Margaret stripped in the dark, put on her pink silk pyjamas and huddled with the others under their single blanket. In the morning light they saw a 'huge male figure with enormous walrus moustachios' erupting from a blanket. He was a cook from the *Diomede* (a cruiser bringing emergency supplies, doctors and nurses to Napier) who had been first to claim a sleeping space by the marquee's central pole, unaware that it was accommodation for nurses. They had not noticed him as they stumbled into the marquee in the dark. The nurse nearest to him, 'a wispy little person with her hair in little pigtails turned on him like a virago for thus endangering her reputation'.[105] Mary Lambie told the story from the point of view of the cook, who had apparently consumed 'a fair amount of liquor' before he stumbled into the marquee: when he woke to find himself surrounded by women, he thought he must be suffering from DTs.[106]

Meanwhile, Margaret Macnab had the problem of where to get dressed. She wandered the racecourse in her pink silk pyjamas with her bundle of clothes under her arm, gathering 'ribald remarks' about the dangling stocking suspenders. The next night, nurses were given the Totalisator building as their quarters. Disturbed by the frequent tremors, they pulled their beds out under the trees, only to have birds make 'unwelcome contributions' on their heads. One nurse was glad to wrap even a stiff grey blanket over herself, but found in the morning that it was stiff with congealed blood.[107]

Another practical problem was what to do with the 120 hens killed by the local poultryman and donated to the hospital. Mary Lambie was glad to receive them as food was needed not only for the hospital patients and staff but also for up to 800 evacuees. She set a party of men to prepare them for cooking, but they neglected to scald them before plucking. 'It was an extremely hot day,' she said, 'with a strong wind blowing, and suddenly I saw a cloud of feathers descending on the grounds. Everywhere there were feathers – on the ground, in the tents and on the grandstand.' When she heard that Lord and Lady Bledisloe were arriving that afternoon she immediately organised a team of small boys to pick up all the feathers, and she was grateful when the governor-general was delayed and did not arrive until after dark.[108]

The extraordinary circumstances required nurses to depart from their usual high standards of practice. A reporter described the scene at the racecourse hospital in the first few hours after the quake. As casualties were brought in and examined, dead bodies had to be simply placed on the floor and moved away when opportunity allowed. Throughout the night, as nurses tended patients in the double row of tents about 100 yards long, the reporter said that it gave 'an indescribable feeling' to repeatedly hear them give two low whistles to summon sailors to carry away the bodies of patients who had died. Equally 'nerve-wracking,' he said, was hearing people passing up and down between the tent rows, calling their missing relatives' names in the hope of hearing a reply. 'It was terribly like animals calling their young.'[109]

Managing the bodies of the dead was also a problem in Hastings, where Sister H. Dillon was in charge. By the end of the first day, nearly 50 bodies lay in clean sacks in rows on the gymnasium floor. She asked a reporter to assure the public that anyone handling the dead showed a 'fine depth of courtesy, gentleness, and reverence', but they needed to understand that 'some bodies were beyond possibility of identification'.[110] Besides bodies, the Napier morgue had 15 benzene packing-cases storing charred remains.[111] At the end of the long day transferring patients from the hospital, nurses went back to the mortuary to identify their friends' bodies.[112]

Nurses also accompanied patients transferred from Hawke's Bay to hospitals elsewhere. As rail transport between Napier and Hastings was disrupted by the quake, patients were loaded in their beds onto lorries and driven to Hastings, where their beds were placed in closed goods vans on a train bound for Palmerston North.

The beds were battened down to stop them rolling on the journey. Each patient had their particulars pinned onto their clothing, written on a sale price tag taken from a demolished drapery store, and spare dressings were tied in brown paper bags on bedrails. A nurse accompanied each lorry and railway van, but an observer said that many could not be distinguished from patients as they too had bandaged wounds.[113]

The public perception of nurses during the earthquake disaster exhibited the familiar tropes of quiet heroism and devotion to duty. Nurses' immediate efforts to rescue patients from the hospital were portrayed as acts of 'great heroism'. They 'dashed into the rocking buildings to rescue patients', even though their 'noble efforts' meant they might themselves have been trapped.[114] Hester Maclean said she was proud to know that nurses 'maintained their courage and rushed to the rescue of their patients at the risk of their own lives, two at least being sacrificed'. Her greatest praise, however, as in the pandemic, was reserved for nurses who volunteered from other towns: she cited their 'splendid response' and 'spirit to serve' and their willingness to work day and night.[115]

The public saw all nurses in the emergency hospitals as devoted to their duty. They 'worked until they dropped'.[116] Mrs C. Boyle, visiting from Auckland, noted that the McLean Park nurses, including some 'who had broken hearts', were doing 'noble and devoted work'. Her niece Eileen Williams had been killed in the nurses' home.[117] Recognition also came from far across the empire. In a cable to the New Zealand prime minister just five days after the quake, the Johannesburg Hospital Board chairman noted that 'one great fact' emerging from the meagre cable news was that 'many nurses perished', some of them 'displaying great heroism in trying to rescue patients'. It increased their 'very great respect and admiration' for nurses 'throughout the world', as it was evidence of the 'wonderful spirit of self-sacrifice and devotion to duty' that animated them.[118]

In the month after the earthquake Dr A.C. Biggs, the Napier Hospital medical superintendent, captured all these elements in a speech acknowledging everyone's 'splendid work'. He singled out a few doctors and nurses for special mention, including Sisters Marjorie Read and Lily Bull and Nurse Freda Chesterman. In particular, Sister Queenie Lowe, after a 'nerve-wracking experience' and 'heroic efforts' rescuing patients from the hospital's Robjohns Ward when it collapsed, had worked almost without ceasing for 36 hours at the racecourse hospital. Sister Mary Wellock had shown devotion to duty at McLean Park while suffering from a head wound that had not been detected for three days.[119] Eleanor Roy, the matron, simply noted in the hospital's register of sisters that Lowe and Bull 'managed well during the earthquake'.[120]

Nursing authorities were well aware of the earthquake's emotional toll. Catharine Drummond, the matron at Waipukurau, after long hours organising the earthquake response, drove great distances to help nurses get news of home and family.[121] Mary Lambie learned that besides organising an emergency hospital it was also important, once everything was under control, to organise recreation for staff. (There was a potential problem in the 'large number of men at a loose end in the evenings' and easily available liquor.)[122] And as soon as possible, nurses were given leave so that they could get away from the disaster areas. In her last weeks as matron of Wairoa Hospital, Lettie Croft reported that she could now allow nurses to take turns having a few days' leave 'to counteract the strain' on them from the earthquake.[123] At Napier, hospital and school nurses were also granted leave. Staff Nurse Gwen Hadfield had a few days with family in Wellington before returning to the Napier emergency hospital.[124] Lambie sent any staff members who had suffered severe shock to the Motuihi Health Camp in Auckland for a rest.[125]

Addressing material needs, nurses from around New Zealand donated clothing to Napier colleagues who had lost theirs in the demolished nurses' home, and citizens also contributed to funds – Gisborne residents alone quickly raised £161 5s 3d.[126] New Zealanders also offered other resources to help nurses recover. Mrs Charles Gray of Pukerua Bay near Wellington made her cottage available for nurses who had been through the earthquake disaster, 'for a recuperative period'. It was well supplied to accommodate six nurses at a time.[127]

As Hawke's Bay would be under emergency conditions for some months, special measures were needed to transfer trainee nurses to other hospitals. Rose Macdonald, who had retired as Napier Hospital's matron in June 1930, helped by compiling records of each trainee's experience, examinations and ward reports that could be sent to their next hospital.[128] Jessie Bicknell, nearing the end of her term as the chief nurse, organised the transfers. On 5 March she wrote to notify Valda Turley, a 22-year-old farmer's daughter from Pukehou in Hawke's Bay, who had started training the year before, that Dunedin Hospital had offered her a place starting in five days' time. She strongly advised her to take it as they were having 'much difficulty in placing so many nurses'. The southern climate was difficult for Turley, who suffered from rheumatism, but she completed her course with good marks. In November 1933, when the Dunedin Hospital matron Edith Tennent wrote her usual report on state final examination candidates to Mary Lambie, the next chief nurse, she noted that Turley's allegiance still lay with Napier Hospital. She had therefore not fitted in at Dunedin as she might have done. (Tennent greatly valued loyalty to

Dunedin Hospital.) However, Tennent's general testimonial for Turley in June 1934 described her as 'quiet and dignified', with a 'very pleasant manner with patients'. She was capable and reliable, and in the previous four months as a staff nurse she had kept the Casualty Department in good order. And (as high praise) she was 'ready in emergency'.[129] Perhaps her earthquake experience had been good training.

In March 1933 Lord Bledisloe opened Napier's rebuilt hospital and nurses' home and unveiled a memorial to the nurses who had died.[130] The simple brass tablet commemorated the nurses who were killed or injured in the earthquake and paid tribute to 'the subsequent noble work of those who survived'.[131] It was donated by the father of one of the dead, Marjorie Insull.[132] The others who were killed were Sister Ruth Mitchell and Nurses Joan Keddell, Lucy Stone, Winifred Staines, Nancy Thorne-George and W. Eileen Williams. Joan Keddell had started training only 28 days before the quake.[133] A second plaque also listed the names of nurses who died and similarly carried a tribute to 'the splendid devotion to duty' shown by staff to patients and the injured in the disaster.[134]

***

The narratives of nursing in the two disasters were distinctly different. As nurses struggled with the overwhelming number of patients in the influenza pandemic, there was no time to record experiences and little will to reflect on events later. It was enough to have survived. In contrast, the Hawke's Bay earthquake generated a strong folklore, created in part by the press and in part by nurses' vivid recollections of their personal experiences. The public perception of nurses in both disasters featured the tropes of the quiet heroine and self-sacrificing angel, devoted to duty and doing noble, sacred work. As usual, these portrayals were spurned by nurses, whose accounts focused on getting on with the job. Both disasters entailed working exhausting hours and performing beyond the scope of their usual roles. As Arlene Keeling and Barbara Mann Wall point out in their study of nursing in historical international disasters, the blurring and overlapping of professional roles is common in such situations.[135] Their analysis also shows the impact on nurses who become disaster victims. This impact was certainly felt in New Zealand, with the deaths of 42 nurses in the pandemic and seven in the earthquake.

However, hospital authorities at the time gave scant attention to the draining effect of nursing during the pandemic. Little could be done to offer them relief. In contrast, during and after the earthquake, authorities made efforts to provide nurses with rest and recreation.

Keeling and Wall note that after a disaster, people have often recognised that nurses should be better trained in preparation for future disasters. This did not happen in New Zealand. After the pandemic, even the effort to train citizens in basic nursing skills petered out after two years. No changes in nurse training resulted from either disaster.

Although New Zealand's location did not protect it from the pandemic, its proximity was valuable for Australia. The pandemic was 'scarcely over' in New Zealand when the government of Victoria urgently asked for 50 nurses to be sent to help there. Maclean could not spare that number, but she found 25 volunteers who went under the charge of Sister Sarah Polden to nurse influenza patients in the temporary hospital in Melbourne's Exhibition Hall.[136] To reach their sleeping quarters in the picture gallery and sculpture rooms, they passed through exhibits of stuffed seals and monkeys and the gallery of Egyptian mummies, which was soon dubbed the 'Mortuary'.[137]

Mary Lambie's experience of organising the temporary hospital at Cheviot during the pandemic no doubt stood her in good stead in Napier immediately after the earthquake. Despite the shortages of equipment, crowds of evacuees, the unexpected cloud of poultry feathers and a 'large number of men at a loose end in the evenings',[138] she did exceptional work. Dr A.C. Biggs, the Napier medical superintendent, included her in his public acknowledgements in March.[139] The same month, she was appointed as chief nurse in the position of director of the Division of Nursing.

CHAPTER 9

Contesting 'the modern nurse'

In August 1890, at the Dunedin Resident Magistrates Court, four nurses from the hospital gave evidence at a commission of inquiry into Dr Ferdinand Batchelor's complaints to the hospital trustees that insanitary conditions had caused septicaemia in two of his gynaecological patients. One had died and the other was seriously ill. The complaints were the culmination of general dissatisfaction among several of the senior honorary medical staff about hospital conditions. Batchelor had stirred up the unrest and championed the cause. He wanted reform and his own hospital ward (already supported by Dunedin women's public fundraising), which the trustees had refused to grant him. He and most of his colleagues gave detailed testimony of insanitary conditions.

The nurses – Mary Fraser, Caroline Shaw, Mary Waymouth and Ellen (Nellie) Monson – were nearly the last of the 25 witnesses examined. If the lawyer acting for Batchelor had expected the nurses to quietly concur with the various doctors' opinions about hospital conditions and the circumstances surrounding Batchelor's patients, he was disappointed. They refused to agree with doctors' testimony about hospital conditions, and they staunchly kept to their own version of surgical and postoperative events. At the end of one woman's operation, a glass drainage tube kept filling with blood, but Mary Waymouth heard Batchelor say he would 'chance it' that the bleeding had stopped. A few hours after the patient returned to the ward, Nellie Monson discovered that the woman's bed had become soaked with blood. A second operation fixed the bleeding, but the patient died. Batchelor denied any wrongdoing. He blamed his other patient's death from septicaemia partly on the foetid air that he believed contributed to wound sepsis. Nurses detailed their management of ventilation and draughts, but Dr Daniel Colquhoun, a consultant based at the university, contended that the lack of ventilation had made the hospital atmosphere so oppressive that an hour's work in it fatigued him more than a whole day's work outside. In contrast, Mary Fraser said she worked 12 to 16 hours a day. Someone coming in from outside might smell the tow (fibre dressing) or iodoform, but otherwise she could not account for his comment. Caroline Shaw was more direct. She had done a good deal more than an hour's work there and had never felt the slightest fatigue. If the doctor had experienced the atmosphere as stifling, it must have related to how he exerted himself, otherwise she did not know how he managed it.[1]

The commissioners agreed with the doctors' complaints and stipulated a number of recommendations for reform. While the nurses' testimony might not have swayed the commission about ward ventilation or surgical mishaps, they had held firm to what they had observed and believed, despite badgering by lawyers and the possibility of doctors' displeasure at their views. The case shows how nurses at this early time in New Zealand 'modern nursing' set a precedent for professional strength and integrity. But nurses' understanding and opinions of what a modern nurse should be and do sometimes rasped against those of others. These opinions varied even within the profession.

Public perception of the modern nurse

In the 1880s the public perception of the modern nurse began with the premise that nurses were 'born, not made'.[2] This view set up the argument that effective nursing depended on innate qualities and that professional training was unnecessary and possibly harmful, and it also made the capacity to nurse a gendered quality. It reflected Florence Nightingale's famous comment, often reiterated to probationers at St Thomas's Hospital: 'To be *a good Nurse* one must be *a good woman*.'[3] However, Nightingale was not asserting that only women could be nurses; rather she was emphasising womanly qualities and the need for continual self-improvement. The public perception was based on the idea that women embodied the qualities needed in a good nurse. According to an article in the *Evening Star*, 'The mothering instinct which is in every normal woman finds its natural outlet here ... They feel towards humanity a maternal instinct which yet never dissolves their good common sense.'[4]

At this point in the argument, ideas about nurse training diverged. In New Zealand, as elsewhere, hospital reforms of the 1880s and 1890s had achieved the shift to a female nursing workforce based on doctors' confidence that this would improve patients' health outcomes.[5] But whether these improvements arose from female nurses' innate qualities or from their training was still open to question. On the one hand, some observers saw training as beneficial. Charles Dickens' character Sairey Gamp – a nurse-midwife portrayed as degenerate, dishevelled and drunk – was often invoked in arguments about the deficiencies of untrained nurses.[6] Whether she was a caricature or a fair representation of nurses before the establishment of trained nursing in Britain is still debated.[7] However, training did not necessarily take 'all the old "gampishness" out of the modern nurse'.[8] As one observer said: 'There are odds in deacons as well as dogs. So there are in nurses.'[9]

On the other hand, detractors believed a professional nurse could become too 'scientific' and hardened through training,[10] whereas untrained women relied on their caring instincts and common sense. 'To be a good nurse it is not necessary to be hospital trained and to proclaim knowledge by special uniform,' said one commentator. 'Unfortunately, many of those who have entered the ranks of professional nurses have no natural ability for the duties that devolved upon them. The woman who has gained her experience on less pretentious lines, but has the quick sympathy that guides initiative is a better nurse than these misfits.'[11]

Counteracting the risks of becoming hardened through training required a sense of vocation. Nurses should take up the profession not just as a means of making a living or with romantic notions and dreams of marriage, but as a noble pursuit.[12] Many, noted one commentator, drifted into the profession without a vocation, especially 'the giddy sort' who was in a hurry to get off duty and 'gad about'.[13] A nurse with a true vocation could embody the patient's longing for a ministering angel, a self-sacrificing and devoted attendant who brought hope with her caring touch. As one journalist commented after being a patient, the nurse entered the sick room 'radiating peace and confidence' and 'bringing a kind of benediction'. She 'mediated the divine'.[14]

During the 1910s and 1920s another view emerged. Trade unionists wanted the ministering angel fairly recompensed. She was overworked and needed better conditions and pay.[15] In some instances, thundered the socialist *Maoriland Worker*, nursing was no better than sweated labour.[16] In 1913 the newspaper urged nurses to form a union and 'start an immediate crusade against sweating'.[17] When one nurse observed that some nurses had got the sack for trying to form one, he told his readers that the ministering angels did not get a 'square deal' but a 'round baton'.[18]

The idea was slow to gain traction. In the 1940s Sonja Davies raised support among her colleagues at Wellington Hospital for the idea of a union, but before she could 'brave the Trades Hall' to find out how to start one, she was summoned to the matron's office. She could not think of any misdemeanour she might have committed on the ward to warrant a reprimand. From her friends she 'gathered together sufficient crackling starched items, non-holey stockings and a belt with buttons', anchored her hair under her cap and set off with newly whitened shoes. The matron fixed her 'with a cold glance', informed her that she had heard about the union, and tartly reminded her that nursing was a profession, a vocation, and associating it with personal gain was unthinkable. If she wanted to be in a union, she should join a factory where 'that sort of thing' was acceptable. Once back in the nurses' home, the consensus was to 'back off'.[19] (Davies later became a notable trade unionist and member of parliament.)

Whatever views nurses held of unionism, they were irritated by the common and enduring stereotype of nurses as devoted, self-sacrificing angels, which contradicted their self-image as well-trained professionals. Florence Nightingale's comment on the matter was invoked in Britain's *Nursing Times* and New Zealand's *Kai Tiaki* in 1926, four decades after she made it to probationers at St Thomas's Hospital: 'A woman who takes a sentimental view of nursing, which she calls "ministering", as if she were an angel is, of course, worse than useless. A woman possessed of the idea that she is making a sacrifice will never do.'[20] At the 1925 New Zealand Trained Nurses' Association (NZTNA) annual meeting, a nurse quoted this remark in arguing against the angelic trope. She also reflected, however, on the disappearance of a religious base to professional nursing, and the emergence of a different kind of nurse from a new generation who sought 'more the pleasures of life'.[21]

In general, nurses tended to regard those of any previous generation as more self-sacrificing than they were; conversely, older nurses viewed the new modern nurse as career-oriented and commercially minded. As early as 1916, one nurse commented that on dark days she thought the profession had 'gone to the dogs', as nurses had lost the 'old-fashioned qualities of gentleness, thoughtfulness, unselfishness, and self-sacrifice' and were 'only out to make money and have a good time'. Even on good days, when she did not believe the profession had deteriorated, she still recognised that 'a strong commercial spirit [was] creeping in'.[22] Even so, nurses were quick to criticise novels like Louise Gerard's *Days of Probation* (published by Mills and Boon in 1917) that portrayed nurses as frivolous. As the reviewer said in *Kai Tiaki*, jealousy, intrigue, the romantic pursuit of doctors, dining out and theatre-going 'do NOT play a large part' in nurses' lives.[23] For Caroline Stewart, who had been matron of Gisborne Hospital from 1890 to 1909, the problem with the modern nurse in the 1930s was her style of dressing, particularly her bathing costume.[24]

Advertisers, however, were clear in their understanding of nurses' commercial value and the need to appeal simultaneously to their professionalism and the code of virtues of the nursing culture. When Hester Maclean started *Kai Tiaki* in 1908, she turned to advertising to help cover the costs. In turn, advertisers saw the nursing profession as a new and potentially lucrative market of women with disposable income and influence in the health field.[25] The journal therefore carried advertisements for hospital equipment, ladies' dresses, corsets, uniforms, comfortable shoes and health remedies.

Nurses in private practice were especially targeted, both as consumers and as intermediaries between product and patient, or between 'bad health and good', as Elaine Thomson notes.[26] Between 1908 and 1930, *Kai Tiaki* carried numerous advertisements for tonics – syrups, foods, beverages and additives for milk claiming to have restorative or health-protective powers.[27] Tonics were vigorously advertised to the public in newspapers and magazines, and recommended in domestic health guides that supported lay carers. The *Kai Tiaki* advertisements advised nurses that administering the right tonic could help their patient's recovery. Modern scientific discoveries, such as vitamins, were strongly featured in the changing tonic advertisements in the 1920s, aligning them with changes in the scientific basis of nurse training.[28]

Advertisements for Ceregen in 1916 were targeted at 'the run-down nurse'. Not only should she give the tonic to patients, she should take it herself.[29] In 1925 an advertisement warned that the nurse risked her health daily, so she should keep fit and up to 'nursing pitch' by taking Glax-Ovo, a tonic beverage.[30] Later advertisements for this product drew on professional nursing virtues. If nurses did not take care of their own health, they would be 'useless'.[31] Nurses must 'never fail on duty' – Glax-Ovo would rescue them by making them 'alert and quietly poised for any emergency'.[32] This was more than a recognition of the demands of nursing work: it evoked a fear of failure and inability to cope. While Thomson notes that British nursing journal advertisements targeted the nurse as the intermediary between 'bad health and good',[33] in these *Kai Tiaki* advertisements the distinction was between bad *nurse* and good.

Advertisements aimed at the general public featured the nurse as health adviser. The Australian Clements Tonic, for example, often used Australian nurses' testimonials in New Zealand newspaper advertisements, and in 1918 they included an endorsement by Nurse Ellen Everitt of Wellington, a 'specialist in nerve work and neurasthenia', who claimed that it was one of the 'best "nerve" foods' she recommended to her many patients.[34] In the 1940s an anonymous nurse proclaimed that she 'felt a different person' after taking Bidomak Tonic.[35] The testimonials might have been fictitious; or nurses, like consumers in this era, might have written them for payment or in the hope of receiving free samples. Laurie Lee, in his memoir *Cider with Rosie*, tells how his mother received five shillings for an unsolicited testimonial, and thereafter bombarded the market with 'ecstatically phrased' letters 'boasting miraculous cures' from products she had never used.[36]

Challenges, conflicts and 'hospital troubles'

The changing perceptions and roles of nurses were reflected in professional conflicts. Hester Maclean disliked 'hospital troubles', especially when nurses publicly grumbled about conditions. She was disturbed by the 'lack of esprit de corps' evident at Dunedin and Napier Hospitals in 1911, where a 'small section of the staff, discontent with existing conditions' had 'voiced their grievances in the public ear'. The proper way to seek remedy and reform was for nurses to go first to their matron. Often, she continued, their discontent was superficial: when 'put to the test', few could come up with 'a definite or legitimate cause for grumbling'. Moreover, nurses should expect some discomforts: 'We seem to think that because we are working in the cause of sick humanity, we must not in our own bed have even a crumpled rose-leaf; we must not be subjected to the ordinary vicissitudes of life.'[37]

More significantly, hospital trustees and boards often used the nurse as a currency of power. In 1901 Dr Duncan MacGregor, the inspector of hospitals, decried hospital trustees' 'unjustifiable interference' in the selection and promotion of nurses, favouring their own friends.[38] Hester Maclean complained in 1911 that when girls used 'influential friends' to gain a convincing recommendation, unless the matron was 'very strong in her conviction', it was difficult to avoid giving them a trial 'even against her own judgment'.[39] Several matrons struggled with boards to exercise the right to appoint or dismiss probationers and nurses. The issue was whether the matron had the right, as representative of the nursing profession and head of the nursing school, to decide who should be considered fit and proper to enter the nursing profession. The hospital boards considered that this authority rested with them: when applicants signed on as probationers, they became servants of the board. This technical argument disguised the board's real concern: the challenge to its control over all hospital affairs.

These issues are evident in the conflict at Dunedin Hospital in March 1916. The matron, Margaret Myles, with the agreement of the medical superintendent and the support of the hospital committee, recommended to the hospital board the dismissal of Irene Collie and Elsie Connelly, trainees who were still in the trial period before they could sign on as probationers. Despite a month's extension to the usual three-month trial, their work had continued to be unsatisfactory. The board rejected the recommendation. Although it couched its reason as giving the nurses 'every opportunity of proving their capabilities', personal connections appeared to play a part. Alfred Quelch told his fellow members that Collie 'had scarcely had a fair run' and had had 'a somewhat rough time of it'. She had given up 'a good situation with her sisters' to become a nurse. If dismissed, the nurses would not gain employment in any other hospital.[40] When newspapers reported the decision, public outcry included the stern comment from Annie Borrie, secretary of the NZTNA's Dunedin branch, that it placed the matron in 'a false position' and would affect the hospital's status as a training school.

Dr Thomas Valintine, the inspector-general of hospitals, told the board that he greatly regretted its decision and reminded it that under the hospital's own by-laws, approved by the minister, and the Nurses Registration Act 1901, the matron was the 'responsible officer' for nurse training. 'If the high standard of our nurses is to be kept up,' he said, 'it is absolutely necessary that she should have the power of deciding upon the fitness and suitability or otherwise for training of probationers on trial.' He expected the board to review its decision. Dr H. Lindo Ferguson, chairman of the deputation of honorary consultant medical staff at the board's next meeting, pointed out that the board's decision was 'as unjustifiable as if they were to order the dispenser to continue to use drugs which three months' trial had proved to be worthless'. Finally, a member of the board, Mary Ferguson (Lindo Ferguson's wife), moved to rescind the resolution. 'I question the right of any board to act in defiance of its own by-laws as to the training of nurses. What do a body of laymen and women know about nursing or the suitability of nurses in the hands of our responsible officers – the medical superintendent and the matron – otherwise what are they there for?' But the majority held firm.[41]

The Department of Hospitals then took action. Hester Maclean listened to outraged nurses' complaints, which resulted in 60 nurses signing a petition to the board stating that they had 'absolute trust' in the matron, relied completely on her 'judgment and justice' and strongly protested against her 'position being made untenable'. At a special board meeting, Valintine reasserted his position, observing that the board's decision was 'calculated to undermine the future discipline and satisfactory management of the nursing staff' because it had 'virtually expressed a lack of confidence' in the medical superintendent and matron. He praised Myles' work in glowing terms. As the board had already signed on the two nurses for four years, he said that its only course was to make a public statement confirming its confidence in the matron and medical superintendent and regretting the circumstances leading to its decision. A watered-down version of the statement, omitting any expression of regret, was passed without dissent but not without harrumphing from board members. Chairman James Walker still held to the view that the board's decision had been right and hinted darkly at inside knowledge. He then made the startling admission that the board had similarly rejected the matron's recommendations in the past; the only difference was that this time the decision had been made public.[42]

The public nature of a nurse's complaint had presented an even greater challenge to one hospital board in 1890. Margaret Arnaboldi was a nineteenth-century whistle-blower.[43] She had been a probationer at Auckland Hospital for nine months when she laid a complaint against the medical superintendent, Dr Floyd Collins, for neglect and unskilful treatment in two cases. Joseph Berry, a 56-year-old man from Birkenhead, had shattered his left hand when a gun exploded. He arrived at the hospital before 11am on 23 September, cold and collapsed from bleeding. Collins placed two pieces of cork against the main arteries and bandaged them in place. Berry continued bleeding through the day and night, continually soaking a large lump of tow (fibre dressing) and eight thicknesses of sheet through to the mackintosh protecting the bedding beneath. The nurses tending him reported the continued bleeding but no medical action was taken until a consulting surgeon was brought in at 11pm, and he and Collins amputated the hand. Berry died three hours later.

The second patient, Duncan McKenzie, aged 28, had crushed his leg between two logs, breaking it in three places near the ankle. A local doctor dressed the open fractures using iodoform, and he was brought down from Whangārei by steamer. He arrived in great pain at the hospital at 8pm on 30 October, about 18 hours after the accident. Collins examined the leg without removing the dressings and fixed it on three pillows, with a cage over it to support the weight of the bedclothes. Through the night McKenzie was restless and the prescribed morphia did not relieve his pain, but Collins would not come when requested. The next morning he splinted the leg and the nurses, as instructed, kept the wound damp with disinfectant. McKenzie continued to deteriorate until 8 November when Collins consulted two surgeons and the leg was amputated. It was gangrenous to the knee. McKenzie died three days later.

Nurse Arnaboldi thought it her duty to report these cases to the inspector of hospitals when he visited Auckland Hospital. MacGregor helped her write out a measured statement and forwarded it to the hospital board. Board members were furious. They asked Collins for a response to the charges and consulted the surgeons, but not the attending nurses Arnaboldi had named. Collins's venomous reply was a personal and professional attack on Arnaboldi. Either people had taken advantage of her ignorance, he said, or she had been motivated by a degree of 'persistent malignity' that could hardly be credited. 'Probationer Arnaboldi has broken the golden rule which is supposed to be a nurse's first lesson in all hospitals. I refer to the rule which enjoins strict obedience and strict silence. The teaching of silence refers, of course, to the very thing Probationer Arnaboldi has been guilty of, namely, criticism of those in authority over her.' The board dismissed the charges against him and censured Arnaboldi.[44]

Strongly worded newspaper articles throughout the colony, public outcry and a petition to the government forced a commission of inquiry in January 1891, led by a lawyer, Sir Maurice O'Rorke, and Dr Rudolf von Mirbach.[45] It found that Berry had died of haemorrhage, not shock as Collins had claimed, and that delaying both amputations for so long was unjustified. Arnaboldi's claims were motivated not by malice but by a sense of duty. As a doctor, however, Mirbach could not resist a final comment. Although Arnaboldi's actions had exposed 'an unfortunate state of affairs', the precedent they set was nevertheless a bad one, as it was 'subversive of necessary discipline; and espionage by subordinates is quite destructive of confidence on the part of responsible officials [doctors] and of the respect due to them by their assistants [nurses]'.[46]

The public had other ideas. The *Auckland Star* editor denounced the hospital board's actions and Mirbach's use of the word 'espionage' in his verdict. It was the colony's verdict, the editor proclaimed, that Miss Arnaboldi had acted courageously and 'in the unostentatious and conscientious manner in which a good woman would have done it'.[47] Members of the public contributed to a testimonial and gift of money for Arnaboldi, who had already left the hospital.[48] She did private case nursing for a while, then opened a small private hospital in Waihī, where she had the ironic satisfaction of successfully nursing a man injured in a gelignite explosion in the gold mine and another whose leg was crushed by logs in a bush sawmill.[49]

Nurses also sometimes opposed doctors in private practice. Eleanor Pascoe, who ran a private hospital in Rotorua, had good relations with local doctors, except for Dr Herbert Bertram, whom she found increasingly overbearing. In turn, he accused her of professional shortcomings. In 1914 the situation deteriorated to the extent that he removed a patient from her care and made openly derogatory remarks about her hospital, her nursing and herself. 'I do not trust Nurse Pascoe. She neglects her patients. She is not fit to be a nurse. She is the type of woman I loathe. I abhor and detest her. Two or three of the wealthiest people in Rotorua would like to get her out of town.'[50]

Pascoe sued Bertram for slander. During the trial it emerged that he had previously promised to help another nurse, Grace Castle, when she was ready to open a private hospital in Rotorua. The time had come. But as the pressure on Bertram increased, and questions arose about incidents in his previous work in Auckland, on the eighth day of trial the case was unexpectedly settled when Bertram issued a statement that Pascoe's 'skill and capacity as a surgical, medical and midwifery nurse is unquestioned'.[51]

Hester Maclean was thrilled with the result. She praised Pascoe's courage and expressed the hope that other nurses would take similar action. 'Nurses often shrink from publicity and allow many unjust actions and mis-statements to pass rather than undergo the ordeal of bringing a case to court.' She published Bertram's statement in full.[52] Despite this vindication, Pascoe left Rotorua to become matron of Timaru Hospital in 1916. And when Rotorua's isolation and cottage hospitals closed, citizens were advised that any of Dr Bertram's urgent cases were to go to the private hospital owned by Grace Castle.[53]

Doctors also took action against nurses' statements. In 1930 Dr Richard Richards of Wellington sued the Temperance and General Mutual Life Assurance Society for the slander by one of its nurses, Mabel Blathwayt. She had 'spoken falsely and maliciously about him' to a patient, allegedly saying, 'Oh, him. Like a few more of his cases. I have never had the pleasure of meeting Dr Richards, but when I see him I will tell him what I think of him.' She advised the patient to go to hospital.[54] Blathwayt denied the allegations. The judge noted the 'sharp conflict of evidence'. Although the conversation was a privileged one between patient and nurse, the question was whether the nurse spoke with malice. The jury believed she had.[55]

Professional etiquette, drilled into nurses during training, demanded loyalty and silence. Blathwayt had transgressed by disparaging a doctor to a patient. Arnaboldi had set in train a formal, public process that questioned a doctor's skill and clinical judgement. Although the commission supported her complaint and the public applauded her action, she left her hospital position. In contrast, when Pascoe sued a doctor for his public remarks, Maclean acclaimed her courage as an example to other nurses. Clearly, a doctor's public humiliation of a nurse outweighed any expected professional loyalty.

The modern nurse in the public spotlight: social and cultural drama

Public inquiries that involved modern nurses, like Arnaboldi's whistle-blowing, created a social drama, a dynamic social process arising from conflict.[56] A later example was the 'hospital trouble' in Gisborne between 1916 and 1918. Cook Hospital (formerly Gisborne Hospital) was the centre of a drama in two acts.[57] In October 1915 Sister Stella Barr resigned on the grounds that Dr Fritz Kahlenberg, the medical superintendent, had bullied her in the operating theatre. A group of nurses took action, complaining to a special committee that unless he resigned, they would. Kahlenberg resigned. So did the matron, Eva Godfray, and several sisters, again showing the nursing staff's tendency to form factions. Dr William A. Bowie became medical superintendent, and the new matron was Edith Tait, an Australian nurse who had held senior positions at Melbourne Hospital and other institutions. She started in December 1915.

With this new cast of characters in place, the drama began with disputes over the disciplining of a probationer, Amy Higgins. Tait had received multiple complaints about Higgins from Sister Matilda Maclellan, but she had 'tried to smooth things over'. However, early in January 1916 she herself twice observed Higgins, who was then on duty in the isolation ward, breaching isolation regulations by talking to other nurses at close quarters. When she spoke to Higgins about these regulation breaches, Higgins denied them.[58]

After hearing additional complaints about Higgins from Ruth Mitchell, an acting ward sister, Tait sent for Higgins and Mitchell. The outcome of their conversations was that Tait offered to help Higgins get into another hospital to finish her training, on condition that she submitted her resignation. Tait paid Higgins the salary she was owed, and she left.[59]

Higgins' lawyer then rang Tait to say the resignation had been obtained under pressure and that he was referring the issue to the hospital board chairman. At this point, Hester Maclean became involved when Sister May, Higgins' aunt, who had known Maclean a long time, wrote to Maclean on 21 January to complain that her niece had been unfairly treated and then 'forced to resign, which is tantamount to a dismissal'. She felt Tait was acting with 'unnecessary severity' against nurses, including Higgins, who had been prominent in the inquiry into Kahlenberg. She requested a departmental inquiry, or else she would have to appeal to the Supreme Court over wrongful dismissal. She ended, 'Matron, I do hope you will not think I am taking any liberty through my friendship. You understand hospital administration far better than I do, and I sadly need the counsel of a strong mind just now.'[60]

The matter split the hospital board into opposing factions and became the subject of impassioned newspaper coverage and correspondence. After conferring with Dr Thomas Valintine, the inspector-general of hospitals, and mindful of potential legal action, Maclean went to Gisborne to conduct an inquiry. After interviewing the matron and all others involved in the case, she concluded that the dismissal was 'quite unjustified' and tried to give Tait 'a way of climbing down from the position she had taken up without loss of dignity'.[61] Tait, however, wrote to Valintine complaining that Maclean had made up her mind before investigating matters, and Valintine travelled to Gisborne to intervene. He instructed Maclean to arrange Higgins' transfer to another training school. Higgins transferred to Palmerston North Hospital, where she passed her final examination in December 1917.[62]

Continued hospital unrest, factional disputes and outside interference led to a petition from the honorary medical staff to the hospital board in 1917 and began the second act of the drama. The petitioners identified a general breach in discipline and a breakdown in the relations between the department, board and staff. The unrest had culminated, they said, when the board passed a resolution, afterwards rescinded, asking the matron to resign. A degree of improvement had resulted from removing some board members who were 'a drag on the institution', but unless the causes were ascertained and rectified, the 'old trouble would reassert itself'. The main cause, they said, was still on the board – Dr J. Clive Collins.[63]

Collins was an Irish-trained doctor who had qualified in Dublin in 1893 and came to New Zealand in 1902 to be medical superintendent of Auckland Hospital. He resigned in 1904 when a commission of inquiry found him guilty of causing a patient's death. When the medical association subsequently disputed his appointment as surgeon of the Northern Wairoa Hospital, he resigned from the association and moved to Gisborne.[64] He was a member of the Cook Hospital Board from 1910 and was well known for championing the cause of individual nurses. He had vigorously challenged the board's decision, in his absence, to uphold the matron's decision that Higgins should go. Higgins had been 'forced to resign' and had had no chance to seek advice. He successfully argued that the board should give her a testimonial and a month's salary to mitigate the cost of transferring to another hospital.[65]

Friction followed, factions formed, heated discussions raged and public opinion festered and erupted. Eventually 6000 Gisborne residents sent a petition to the government to investigate the hospital troubles. The response was a magisterial commission of inquiry, led by H.W. Bishop, who comprehensively supported Tait. She was a 'most capable and efficient woman', he asserted, who 'realised the necessity for strict discipline and that the matron's authority should be supreme in her department'. Commenting on 'the extraordinary difficulties' she had faced as the new matron, he declared that 'few women would have had the courage and the grit to have seen it through'. She could bring the hospital to a 'high state of efficiency', but to do that 'she must have backing'. A matron and medical superintendent had to work harmoniously together. Although Bishop did not want to criticise Bowie too severely because of his ill-health arising from overwork, he believed his 'attitude and conduct generally' were open to criticism and he considered 'a change of some sort' was needed. Referring to the Higgins affair, he said that although 'local criticism was cast' at Maclean's inquiry, the transfer of the nurse had resolved it 'satisfactorily to all parties'.[66]

This should have ended the matter, but six months later Tait left the hospital. Maclean, as *Kai Tiaki* editor, commented that there had 'unfortunately, been much unrest at this hospital, and during the last three years many inquiries'. In her opinion the commission of inquiry 'failed to recognise the cause of the constant trouble'.[67] She later noted in her memoir that when Tait was appointed, she knew something of her (presumably from her Melbourne days) and had 'considered she would not be suitable'. She was not surprised when the matron's 'rather stormy career ... was terminated abruptly'. When the board chairman telegraphed to say Tait had been dismissed, he asked her to send another matron immediately. Maclean sent her assistant, Jessie Bicknell, for six weeks, as well as other nurses to replace departing sisters.[68] In the next seven years the hospital had four matrons.[69]

The commission of inquiry was an example of a cultural drama – a theatrical contestation of meaning. The inquiry contested what it meant to be a modern nurse, and who had the right to decide. Its theatricality lay in its very public, highly structured format; its cast of magistrate, lawyers and witnesses; its dramaturgical elements, highlighting revelations, humour, characters and action; its keen audience of spectators; and its script, made available to the public each day in newspaper verbatim reports of testimony. The January heat added to the drama,[70] as did the large supporting cast. Inside the court, one journalist reported, the 'scene was almost without parallel' as it was 'crowded with interested lady spectators' in the 'dress circle' of the jury box, many flapping fans to fight the heat. A 'bevy of young ladies' was sitting on one of the mantel-shelves and a 'well-known insurance agent had made himself comfortable' on the witness-stand floor.[71] Flashes of humour were brief counterpoints to the serious debates. Dr Kahlenberg said that the matron's cocker spaniel 'trotted round the wards almost daily'. He got the board chairman to tell the nurses not to let it in the wards and he had put up a notice 'to keep this particular dog out'. 'Apparently it had taken no notice of it,' quipped the lawyer Mr Myers. The audience laughed appreciatively.[72]

The testimony revealed conflicting conceptions of the modern nurse. Doctors asserted that nurses should be disciplined, punctual, tactful, sympathetic and able to keep the secrets of the operating theatre. They believed, however, that the best judges of a nurse's ability were the ward sister and matron.

Patients also had their say. The inquiry heard that a group of parents whose children were in the hospital suffering from infantile paralysis had petitioned the board regarding their care, and their action resulted in a change of ward sister. They too felt a right to be involved in defining and overseeing nursing care.[73]

Hospital board members, whether they supported the matron or individual nurses, certainly saw it as their right to control appointments. Nurses should get along with doctors, and the matron with the medical superintendent.[74] The matron and her assistant, in turn, saw their positions as requiring excellent administrative ability, tact, judgement and the backing of the medical superintendent and hospital board. Nurses in their charge should be respectful, truthful and competent.

The actions of nurses themselves showed they believed they had the right to complete their training, complain of bullying and take action against those who thwarted their sense of fairness or right. The magistrate's final monologue, praising Tait as epitomising the virtues of the modern nurse in charge of a hospital, revealed his view: she should be highly competent and demonstrate courage and grit in the face of trouble.[75]

***

Other narratives of upsets in the nursing world also involved conflicts between a matron and the hospital board over the disciplining of individual nurses. In one incident in 1916, however, it was the matron herself whose conduct was called into question. Jean Todd, the matron of Timaru Hospital, was accused of misappropriating goods from the hospital store. The honorary medical staff declared she was not only 'incapable of doing anything dishonest, but incapable of even thinking it',[76] and Dr Thomas Valintine took her part. A government expert's analysis of the storeroom-book handwriting conclusively exonerated her, but she felt she could no longer work for the board and resigned. The sisters resigned en masse in support.

A great number of Timaru residents and the nursing and medical staff subscribed to a public testimonial and gift for her. In 1926 the hospital secretary committed suicide, and it was discovered he had for many years been 'carrying out a system of dishonest dealings'.[77] To redress the wrong done to Todd and her reputation, the board named the hospital's new maternity ward after her and granted her an annual pension of £50.[78]

In 1934 it was Annie Pattrick, director of Plunket nursing, who suffered. After long and exemplary service, she was at the nexus of a power struggle between Plunket professionals and voluntary members of the executive committee of the central council. Despite her proven leadership and many years of exhausting work travelling the country to direct the expanding Plunket service, the central council claimed her frequent ill-health led to inefficiency in the service. Members questioned her loyalty and obedience to the council and demanded her resignation. The subsequent outcry among Plunket branches and a special conference attesting to her loyalty and ability made little difference, and she left the service.[79] The figure of the modern nurse was contested in political struggles among individuals and groups outside the profession as well as within it.

CHAPTER 10

Building a nursing community and culture

On 9 April 1912 Rae Neils married George Adams in St Marks Church, Remuera, Auckland. An account of the wedding appeared in the July 1912 issue of *Kai Tiaki*, along with the personal and professional doings of 70 other nurses.[1] It notes that Neils was attended by a bridesmaid and two little nieces as flower girls. She wore white satin with silver trimmings and a veil with orange blossom, carried a lovely bouquet and looked very winsome. After a reception at Rothesleith, the bride wore a tailor-made grey mole poplin going-away outfit, with a grey hat with cherries, and the happy couple left amid showers of rice, confetti and good wishes to go on a motor tour through the North Island.

The regular 'gossip column' of the journal, with its blurring of professional and personal spheres, was part of Hester Maclean's effort to make the journal a means of 'keeping all in touch with one another instead of drifting apart more and more every year, after parting on the threshold of our training schools'.[2] The same issue gave readers news from branches of the New Zealand Trained Nurses' Association (NZTNA), discussed superannuation, reported on the latest state final examination and commented on serious trouble at Auckland Hospital. There were articles on mental nursing, Wellington's new children's hospital, the new health service for Māori at Te Araroa, and school medical inspection. In her editorial, Hester Maclean indignantly protested against a New York newspaper's use of the word 'nurse' in describing a hospital kitchen worker who had put oxalic acid into babies' feeding bottles. State registration was not enough to protect the title, she said, particularly when a number of unqualified women used the uniform. Besides these professional topics, articles recounted a New Zealand nurse's work in California, another's travel in the Pacific, North America, Japan and China, and a holiday excursion to Franz Josef Glacier. An older nurse reminisced on training in a large London hospital, and a semi-regular column on books for study and leisure hours recommended a nursing textbook on hygiene, an English nurse's memoir and a romance novel that could be 'read with great pleasure'.[3]

The journal blended professional items, scholarly articles, editorial opinion and interests beyond the hospital, reflecting Maclean's goal of making it a 'bond of union, a common interest, a means of communication, a mutual help and a road to improvement [in nurses'] professional work and knowledge'.[4] *Kai Tiaki* was critical in sustaining the scattered New Zealand nursing community and reinforcing its culture.

Claiming specialised knowledge

All occupational cultures lay claim to specialised knowledge. Distinguishing nursing from medical knowledge was a continual and sometimes contested process of delineation. Some writers have argued that the medical profession controlled nursing knowledge.[5] However, once nursing was recognised in New Zealand as a profession with the passing of the Nurses Registration Act 1901, its distinct sphere of knowledge was defined by the first chief nurse, Grace Neill. She wrote the first nursing syllabus, which was implemented in all training hospitals from 1902. It specified the practical capability and knowledge that a candidate for registration should be able to demonstrate. The general nursing section listed the skills needed for patient care. While the syllabus incorporated elements of medical knowledge, such as an understanding of anatomy, physiology, diseases and conditions, it drew a clear distinction between doctors' and nurses' work.[6] The state final examination in December that year focused mainly on the nursing management of a range of conditions and on knowledge of practical skills such as how to peptonise milk to aid its digestion, give a hot-air bath, and administer threadworm, nutrient and starch-and-opium enemas.[7]

Although doctors initially set and marked state final examination questions and sometimes chided nurses for verging into the doctor's province,[8] it was the chief nurse who controlled nurse training and the examination process. She was quick to note any deviation from subject matter considered appropriate for nursing. Hester Maclean complained in 1910 that younger doctors giving lectures were 'often too keen to impart their knowledge to the nurse in a much larger degree than is at all necessary for her work'.[9] And Jessie Bicknell, the chief nurse from 1923 to 1931, similarly said that lectures to nurses were often given by a house surgeon who did not have sufficient experience to understand the difference between the medical and nursing provinces and, in addition, relied on lecture notes from his student days.[10]

Nurse leaders were certainly politically astute enough to engage medical colleagues to teach the scientific and medical underpinning of the syllabus (called a curriculum from the 1930s), and appreciated doctors' lectures to the NZTNA branches, which were published in the nursing journal. The specialised knowledge of the profession, however, was defined and circumscribed through the teaching of nursing by nurses: lectures and demonstrations by matrons and tutor sisters, bedside instruction by ward sisters, and senior nurses' increasing involvement in examinations. Senior nurses had always been co-examiners in the state final oral and practical examinations, and nurse examiners began setting written questions in the 1930s.[11] The instructional format of the case study or 'nursing study', implemented in the late 1930s, focused the student nurse's attention on the patient as an individual with a family and life beyond the hospital.[12] Colleen Turbet, training at Auckland Hospital from 1949, considered these assignments a challenge but 'very useful and enjoyable, especially getting to know a patient better; they were quite flattered to be the object of so much attention'.[13]

Home nursing books and courses blurred the boundary between professional and lay nursing knowledge. From the 1920s, some home nursing manuals were written by nurses. Isabel Haresnape's manual was intended for the 'average woman in the house' who was either 'absolutely untutored in the rudiments of nursing' or had only 'scratch' knowledge from other 'unreliable sources'. She aimed to give 'minute instructions', modified for 'practical home application', in how to perform routine treatments.[14] Bridget Ristori's advice to lay carers, serialised in the *New Zealand Woman's Weekly* and published as a book in the late 1940s, was similarly practical.[15]

Books and courses for lay carers lacked the explicit scientific underpinning that supported professional nursing knowledge. Home nursing courses were short and focused on basic skills. However, lay carers remained essential, and into the 1920s the St John Ambulance Association's home nursing manual showed a steady increase in the complexity and depth of information and topics covered.[16] During the 1920s the reliance on lay care decreased as confidence in hospital care strengthened and hospitals made more beds available. In the 1930s district nursing services increased to care for those remaining at home, and in the 1940s these became free to all.

The sphere of nursing knowledge expanded with practice changes, nursing scholarship and research. Some tasks and equipment that had once been firmly in the medical sphere were transferred to nurses. By the 1880s they were using clinical

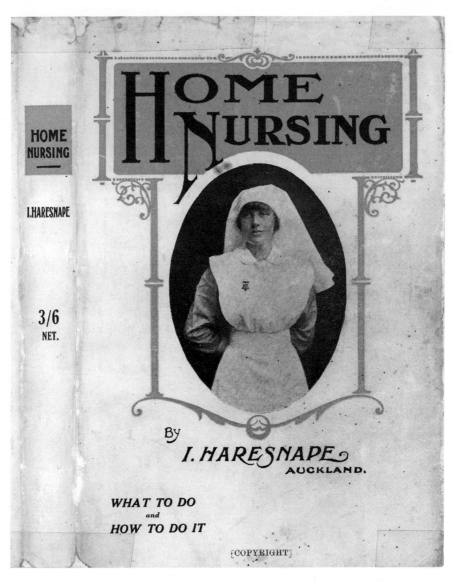

Manuals like Isabel Haresnape's *Home Nursing* showed that nurses were willing to share their knowledge with laypeople caring for sick family members.

Isobel Haresnape, *Home Nursing* (Auckland: Unity Press, 1923), photo Jeremy Bright

Registered nurses continued their studies at the Post Graduate School for Nurses in Wellington, established in 1928. In this 1939 class photograph, Mavis Attree is in the front row, far right. Mabel Mangakāhia is in the middle row, fourth from left.
Mavis Attree album, author's collection

thermometers and by the 1930s sphygmomanometers (for measuring blood pressure)[17]. The stethoscope, however, remained the doctor's tool and symbol. A state final candidate in 1937 particularly annoyed the medical examiner by describing the physical signs of disease she would hear through one.[18]

Mary Lambie led the NZTNA Nursing Education Committee's annual series of surveys on nursing procedures to substantiate best nursing practice. The professional association ran a student essay competition that encouraged scholarship, and the professional journal published these and other nurses' articles. The first formal nursing research study was conducted in 1933, when a group of nurses trialled different methods of dealing with conditions they commonly treated in the community – scabies, impetigo (a bacterial skin infection) and pediculosis (head lice and nits).[19] New Zealand did not, however, have enough nurses to support a journal dedicated to nursing research, as American nurses did from 1951.[20]

The sphere of nursing knowledge and practice continued to expand throughout the twentieth century, particularly with the growth of public health services. These included school nursing, venereal disease and tuberculosis clinics, children's health camps, Plunket nursing, antenatal care, industrial nursing, infant life protection and district health nursing in rural and urban areas. Nurses interested in public health nursing undertook the short preparatory course or the full postgraduate nursing diploma course, and many trained in Plunket and maternity nursing or midwifery. In the 1940s when she had finished her general training, Audrey Dawson sat on her bed on a Sunday afternoon and applied to 43 places for maternity training. Some wrote back about their long waiting lists, but the matron of Masterton Hospital said, 'Can you start on 20 November?' So she did.[21] Mabel Kewene chose Gisborne Hospital because it was one of two offering free uniforms.[22] Irene Cornwell trained as a Plunket nurse in the late 1940s when 'pooh parties' were a daily feature. Nurses gathered round a table where the matron unfolded dirty nappies saved by the night nurse. 'We'd examine it and say whether we thought the baby had been breast- or bottle-fed. It depended on the colour of the babies' bowel motions.'[23] With nurses continually training and gaining further qualifications, the chief nurse had a versatile workforce – and, owing to the disciplined nursing culture, a biddable one, willing to go where directed.

A disciplined hierarchy of power

The chief nurse could direct nurses in the government service, such as those returning from wartime nursing, on where they would go and what duties they would perform. Hester Maclean had nurses teach home nursing courses after the influenza pandemic of 1918 and serve as emergency replacements for matrons, as in the disarray at Gisborne Hospital.[24] Beyond her immediate sphere of authority, the chief nurse also advised emerging nursing leaders on their career progression, thus exerting influence over appointments for senior hospital positions. Maclean urged Edith Lewis, for instance, not to apply for the matron's position in Gisborne, where knowledge of her previous role as a private case nurse might undermine her authority, but to apply instead to Wairau Hospital in Blenheim, where she would be known only as the matron. 'There was nothing more to do,' said Lewis, 'but accept the advice of a very wise woman, who knew her nurses and what was best for them.'[25] When Mary Lambie advised Marjorie Chambers to apply for the matronship at Ōamaru Hospital, the suggestion 'took her breath away'.[26] Lambie also sent nurses under her direct control to district health positions in remote areas. Several had to ask colleagues or consult maps to locate their new base.[27] And when nurses returned from the Post Graduate School for Nurses, matrons could unexpectedly allocate them to their hospital's tutorial staff. This practice created 'accidental tutors' who had never considered teaching in a school of nursing and were surprised to find themselves doing so.[28]

A nurse could choose a steady progression up the career ladder, advancing to the positions of ward sister, supervising sister and assistant matron, perhaps eventually becoming a hospital board's matron-in-chief or a nurse inspector in the Department of Health. The public understood this hierarchy, and it appeared in girls' vocational novels. The American Sue Barton series, published between 1936 and 1952 and popular in New Zealand, followed the central character from student nurse to superintendent in charge of a nursing school. She made brief career detours to work as a district and rural nurse, but in this, her choices reflected Florence Nightingale's own professional interests.[29] On the other hand, the Cherry Ames vocational series, also American and broadly read, followed the main character as she undertook a wide range of nursing specialities, solving mysteries as she went. This series presented nursing as a diverse and fascinating career rather than a steady progression through the hospital ranks. In comparing the two series, the media scholar Julia Hallam argues that the Cherry Ames books were 'more entertaining, less pedantic in tone' and contained more information about actual nursing work but 'were nevertheless quickly discarded, a less valued cultural product'. She bases this assertion on the books' 'virtual disappearance' from public libraries and considers the greater longevity of the Sue Barton books a sign of their popularity with children's librarians.[30] It could also have been due to their portrayal of the traditional nursing virtues, which endured in the public mind. In the same way, the 1940s recruitment process, which presented nursing as a varied career, was unsuccessful partly because it spurned these values.

Within the profession, many nurses decided after qualifying that they wanted to concentrate on one specialty – surgical nursing – which they saw as dramatic and exciting. Surgical patients were hospitalised for a shorter time than medical patients, so the more rapid turnover of the ward population ensured a variety of cases. In consequence, chief nurses and matrons struggled to staff wards for medical or chronically ill patients. In 1942 Mary Lambie complained that emergency and country hospitals and sanatoria were short-staffed because nurses were interested only in surgical nursing or acute care. Invoking the ideal of wartime service, she wrote, 'Surely in times such as we now live in it is everybody's duty and pleasure to help where the need is most urgent and not just where personal preference exists.

Service in its deepest and sincerest aspect should be the ideal of our profession and unless it is more truly shown our profession is failing in its duty to its country.'[31]

Other nurses chose a pathway outside the hospital hierarchy, working as private case nurses. The nurse as businesswoman did not necessarily square with the public view of the devoted, self-sacrificing angel. In the nineteenth century, both untrained women who advertised as 'sick nurses' and professionally qualified nurses worked as private case nurses. To find patients, both relied to a great extent on doctors' recommendations. From 1902, nursing registration gave doctors and the public a reliable measure of a nurse's ability, which restricted untrained women's opportunities for work but made private case nursing a preferred career choice for the majority of registered nurses until the 1930s. Between attending cases in patients' homes, nurses could live at the local residential nurses' club, which also acted as a business bureau. The bureau also offered its referral services to nonresident nurses for a monthly fee.[32] For those who worked independently, a business sense was crucial. Many left business cards with local doctors and surgeons.[33] And Hester Maclean advertised an account form in *Kai Tiaki* that 'systematic and business-like' private case nurses could use, which gave patients the nurse's details for future reference and was an 'infinitely more pleasing' receipt than a slip of paper.[34]

During the 1920s and 1930s the demand for private case nurses lessened. Maclean ascribed this trend to the higher cost of living that mandated higher fees, better general health because of public health measures, fewer people having operations at home, and doctors grouping their patients in private hospitals to save on the number of individual visits they had to make.[35] During the Depression of the 1930s, nurses resisted lowering their fees but charged on a sliding scale. They still had to earn enough to tide them over times without cases and save for their old age.[36] Good working relationships with doctors were imperative, as doctors could influence private patients in their choice of nurse and even offer to appoint a nurse to a case. When one nurse asked a gruff Scots doctor why he always chose Dorothy Scammell, he replied: 'She's reliable and she takes anything, any time.' 'Which I did,' said Dorothy. 'Some nurses refused to go out on Sundays or to lay out dead people.'[37]

Despite these demands of the job, Bridget Ristori portrayed private case nursing as rather glamorous, exciting and adventurous in her career advice to potential nurses in the 1940s. 'Kings and Prime Ministers need nursing just as much as the chimney sweep,' she said. 'Rich people fall ill in luxurious hotels, palatial yachts, as well as in their own homes, and have even been known to take a nurse with them to the other side of the world at a few minutes' notice.'[38]

Owning a small private hospital offered a more secure financial footing, and many nurses did so. Some of these hospitals had an operating theatre and provided postoperative care, while others took surgical patients once they had been discharged from a public hospital. Others concentrated on medical cases or provided just convalescent care. Marian Thorp joined one on Hospital Hill in Napier, then bought it from her friends during World War I. 'It was certainly a busy life, but we were our own mistresses and we liked it.'[39]

Creating cultural traditions

Once nursing had achieved professional status, nurses reinforced it through cultural traditions. Graduation ceremonies, awards and prizes, farewell ceremonies and obituaries not only honoured nursing achievements but became traditions that publicised and celebrated the profession. A prize-winning entry in the 1939 centennial competition for a New Zealand nurses' anthem highlighted nurses' skills and knowledge and their calling to minister to the needs of the suffering without regard to material gain: it was service to humanity.[40] Traditions reinforced the code of virtues that was drilled into nurses during training.[41] And obituaries in newspapers and *Kai Tiaki* not only honoured nurses for their qualities but also reminded others of the expected virtues.

The obituaries were a special form of nursing narrative, a literary genre that followed particular conventions.[42] They were similar in tone to general obituaries in newspapers, but they tended to be much shorter, omitted some conventional features (such as most demographic facts) and added details of interest or value to those in the profession. Obituaries in the two Australian professional journals followed a similar format but were less informative and appeared less frequently than those in New Zealand's journal.

Obituaries drew on the familiar list of nursing virtues and were often idealistic in tone. The highest accolade was that the nurse was much loved by her patients. Matrons were sometimes obliquely criticised for strict discipline, but even these remarks were tempered. Isabella Fraser, who had been matron at Dunedin Hospital, was described as mixing a 'kindly motherliness' with a 'touch of asperity'.[43] The obituary for Jessie Ewart, matron at Southland Hospital for 24 years, observed that 'while ensuring strict discipline she was always sympathetic, kind and just, and her patients and staff were always happy'.[44]

Special note was made in an obituary if a nurse had died in training or soon after. Dorothy Bryham, for example, died in May 1929 aged 22, just into her third year of training at Auckland Hospital. She had been ill for only two days. The obituary noted that a service was held in the chapel with 100 nurses attending; many formed a guard of honour as the coffin was carried to the gate, and her classmates followed her body to the graveside.[45] Poignant obituaries of this kind decreased significantly in number through the decades, although nurses still died in training from scarlet fever and tuberculosis in the 1930s and 1940s.

Obituaries to nurses well beyond their training days chronicled their careers. Those who worked in remote rural places tended to have longer obituaries, perhaps because their careers were outside the conventional pattern and therefore offered novelty to readers. In acknowledging the pioneering nature of the nurse's work, this type of obituary served the professional agenda of proving nurses' fitness for new, expanded roles within the health system.[46]

Obituaries frequently mentioned nurses' sisters and close female friends. Emma Jane Margetts, who died in 1932, was the 'eldest of a band of three sisters' who trained at Auckland Hospital in the 1890s. She ran a private maternity hospital with her sisters Helen and Muriel, then lived with Helen in retirement.[47] It was commonly noted that the nurse had been cared for with devotion by her friend, or that the journal sent sympathy to the friend, as in the case of Miss Gladys Kidner, who had lived with Sister Elizabeth L.R. Fergusson in the Far North.[48] The nature of these friendships is unclear, but several appear to have been life partnerships. It is noteworthy that the profession recognised them as important and named the bereaved friends.

Indulging nurses' professional curiosity, some obituaries gave quite specific clinical comments on the nurse's illness and death. Nearly half gave the cause of death;[49] in the period 1908–20, more than two-thirds identified it. Just over half noted the length of the nurse's illness, always at one extreme or another – painfully long or brief and acute.

As the profession grew in the 1930s and 1940s, obituaries were published only for nurses who had held key roles, had notable achievements or linked the profession to its pioneering past.[50] By the end of the 1940s, obituaries were usually published only for international nurse leaders like Mrs (Ethel) Bedford Fenwick and Adelaide Nutting.[51]

Another cultural tradition was the farewell ceremony for nurses leaving a position to take up another appointment, or to travel, marry, study or retire. These were secularised rituals, similar to farewells outside the profession but often having a particular nursing touch. Local newspapers reported community farewells to Plunket nurses (with babies in attendance), whereas the professional journal published farewells to nurses leaving hospitals and other services.[52] These accounts typically described in detail the decorations of venues – hall, nurses' home sitting room or private residence – along with the 'delicious' or 'dainty' afternoon tea or supper.[53] The first farewell published in *Kai Tiaki* was for the first New Zealand registered nurse, Ellen Dougherty, matron of Palmerston North Hospital. The journal reported in 1908 that a 'very delicious afternoon tea was served, the table being prettily decorated with bowls of sweet peas and foliage'.[54] A departing matron was often given a formal farewell by the hospital board and another organised by her nurses or friends. Accounts of these events significantly declined in number from the end of the 1920s and disappeared almost entirely in the 1940s.

The formal ritual comprised speeches, the presentation of gifts, shared food, musical items and the collective singing of 'Auld Lang Syne' and the national anthem. Speeches were not usually reported in full except in newspaper accounts. Addresses by public dignitaries reinforced traditional nursing virtues and used the familiar tropes of the devoted and self-sacrificing nurse.[55] Variations on the ritual, especially on less formal occasions and farewells for nurses rather than matrons, included recitations, dancing, games, guessing competitions and even fortune-telling.[56] Elizabeth Rothwell's farewell after 25 years as matron of Waikato Hospital was hosted by Mrs Douglas, who, 'in a gown of purple floral voile, received her guests, and initiated them into the mysteries of a brain-racking competition under the shade of a large tree'.[57] A few farewells took the form of a progressive euchre evening, a 'coon can' competition (a card game similar to gin rummy), a croquet tournament or a fancy-dress party. Those for nurses leaving to marry could have the familiar theme of a 'linen tea', 'handkerchief afternoon' or 'kitchen tea'.[58] Some farewells ended with the nurses singing 'For She's a Jolly Good Fellow' or giving three cheers. When Helen Inglis left her position as matron of the Wellington St Helens Hospital, the nurses invited her to join them for a final afternoon tea. Much to her surprise, 'some of the senior nurses then carried her shoulder high along the corridor to her office'.[59]

Parting gifts ranged from framed portraits and illuminated testimonials to practical household items. Ellen Dougherty received a framed arrangement of individual photographs of the hospital's four nurses and three doctors and the hospital board chairman and secretary, surrounding an image of herself.[60] She might have preferred one of the traditional commemorative silver items – tea services, mirrors, hairbrushes, pots, vases, bowls, dishes, picture frames, inkstands, manicure sets and trinket boxes. The West Coast communities were particularly generous with jewellery. When Maude Hayward left Westport Hospital in 1908 after nine years as its matron, residents gave her a pearl spray brooch and a gold bangle set with rubies and diamonds.[61] The same year, when Matron Mabel Thurston left Greymouth Hospital, the mayor presented her with a gold watch and chain, and the local women gave her a pearl pendant in a silver casket.[62] Gold or silver wristwatches were frequent gifts throughout the decades, but other jewellery was rarely given. Māori communities gave nurses gifts of greenstone or woven mats.[63] Sometimes patients contributed as well. Those in Ward 3 at Napier Hospital in 1912 gave the departing matron, Katherine Berry, a silver case containing a glove stretcher, shoe horn and buttonhook.[64] The fashionable gift of a silver tea service gradually gave way to practical travelling items; suitcases and rugs were particularly popular from the 1920s onward. In 1926 Rose Macdonald, matron of Napier Hospital, received a travelling rug along with a leather cushion and a leather camp stool that folded into a small case to accompany her on her trip to India.[65] When Sister Jean Ingram left for war service in 1915, her colleagues had thought about practical matters: they gave her a Bible, a case of nursing instruments, an eiderdown and a thermos. Her patients gave her a silver brandy flask. The editor sniffed that the patients 'needless to say were men', and the flask was 'presumably for use for her future patients'.[66] From the 1930s onward the gift was often a simple bouquet.

It was well known that nurses, even those in senior positions, did not earn a sufficient amount to support them in adversity or retirement. Throughout the period nurses frequently received gifts of money, often described as 'a purse of sovereigns'. Maude Hayward of Westport received not only jewellery from residents but also a purse of 25 sovereigns from the hospital board.[67] And in 1923, when Sarah Polden was forced to resign her position as matron of Thames Hospital, the outraged community gave her a purse of 100 sovereigns.[68]

Farewell gifts such as jewellery or money were often public and intended to portray the contributors as well-to-do, or generous despite limited means.[69] And some gifts, such as the Thames community's purse of sovereigns to Sarah Polden, were intended to recognise injustice.[70] Farewell gifts to nurses could therefore represent conscience money as well as debts of gratitude.

Preserving nursing history

As New Zealand nurses developed a professional identity through training and traditions, they also sought to acknowledge the history of the profession through both formal and informal means. In 1932 the Nurses and Midwives Registration Board prescribed a six-hour series of lectures on nursing history.[71] This was later extended to 10 hours and supplemented in refresher courses, postgraduate studies and branch meetings of the Trained Nurses' Association.[72] Sister Pride gave a lecture on nursing history at a meeting of the South Canterbury branch in 1931.[73] During recruitment campaigns, association branches could borrow the collection of dolls representing historical nursing figures to display in a shop window as a 'cavalcade of nursing'.[74] But in 1950 the nursing history component of the postgraduate course became optional.[75]

From 1908 to 1950 the nursing journal featured numerous historical articles. As nursing historians Barbara Mortimer and Sioban Nelson have both pointed out, the early histories written by American nurse historians were celebratory, triumphalist and progressivist in character, creating a grand narrative that helped nurses identify themselves as members of a worthy profession. The histories inspired nurses in professional struggles, fostered a sense of tradition and valorised nursing's contribution to society and health care.[76] In the same way, articles on New Zealand nursing history served to legitimise the profession of nursing and secure its status in a new country, both by linking it with international nursing history and by building a local tradition. The articles were progressivist and celebratory, showing how nursing had developed significant professional markers such as state registration and a professional journal and association. They also noted the emergence of new areas of service. And by honouring pioneer nurses, these articles contributed to a grand narrative of New Zealand nursing.[77] By knowing their history, nurses could better understand the present.

Cultural symbols

Features of a professional nurse's appearance, such as the uniform's apron, cap or veil, as well as the untrained or volunteer nurse's red cross, symbolised nursing in the public mind. For the profession, however, there were two other, more distinctive symbols of nursing: the registered nurse's medal and the Florence Nightingale lamp. Nurses' uniforms varied across hospitals, but all New Zealand registered nurses wore the five-pointed star medal.[78] Its design is attributed to Grace Neill at the time of the Nurses Registration Act 1901. Its meaning was repeatedly explained in *Kai Tiaki* and sometimes even in newspapers.[79] It was linked to the temple of Isis in ancient Egypt and the admission of initiated men to its priesthood. The five points of the star represent the hand (extended to the sick and suffering to offer help, comfort and relief), the foot (not faltering, lingering or loitering when alleviating suffering), the knee (bowed in supplication for aid in relieving the sick), the breast (a safe and sacred repository of any secret entrusted or divulged during sickness or delirium), and the head (constantly pursuing and exercising knowledge to benefit the sick and suffering). The medal has enamel bands of red (representing compassion) and deep blue (signifying loyalty), with a central red cross on a white background (symbolising purity).[80] The cross also aligned with Christianity, the religion of most New Zealanders and most nurses in the nineteenth and early twentieth centuries, as shown, for example, in the records of nurses training at Dunedin Hospital and in narratives of church and commemorative services within the profession.[81] The star medal featured as a design in recruitment campaigns and even in a float in a Queen Carnival parade in 1951. Colleen Turbet and her colleagues poked thousands of hydrangea heads into the wire netting covering their truck to depict the medal on each side, and rode in it in front of 30,000 cheering Aucklanders.[82]

The association of a lamp with Florence Nightingale emerged from her portrayal as the 'Lady with the Lamp' during the Crimean War. This was the first war to have an on-site journalist sending reports back to a London newspaper.[83] His accounts of Nightingale's work captured the public imagination. Henry Wadsworth Longfellow's 1857 poem 'Santa Filomena' immortalised the image of soldiers kissing her shadow as she passed through the wards bearing a lamp. Illustrations and paintings based on Longfellow's poem portrayed her gliding between the wounded soldiers' beds holding a 'genie'-style lamp – a small, shallow lamp with a central flame and a handle at one end. In fact, the lamp Nightingale used at the Scutari hospital was cylindrical, with a collapsible translucent shade, carried by a handle at its top.[84] Nevertheless, the fanciful image of Nightingale's lamp endured – even in her statue in Waterloo Place in London – and became a widely recognised symbol of nursing.[85] It was used as the basis of the award for the NZRNA's annual student essay competition – a silver lamp mounted on a native beech base, with a koru for its handle and a lid of greenstone.[86]

The lamp as a symbol of courage and leadership, handed from one person or generation to another, was readily understood by the public. A children's newspaper column in 1922 emphasised that although Nightingale was known as 'an angel of mercy', her most notable quality was her determination and courage in standing up to the generals at Scutari to win her point.[87] The nursing profession also connected the lamp with leadership – a quality needed as much today, said one article in 1938, as when Nightingale 'stepped out of the ranks'. It was 'a satisfaction to us to feel that our leaders still carry her symbolic lamp to light our way'.[88] In presenting the essay-competition lamp for the first time in 1939, to Mary Sheehan from Waikato Hospital, Cecilia McKenny, the association's dominion president, said, 'Take this lamp, the symbol of the protection of the flame of life. May you carry the torch of enlightenment as worthily as the great women we are happy to follow.'[89]

Commemorating nursing

Rituals of commemoration enabled New Zealand nursing to join in the traditions of a larger, longer-established and international professional community and thereby claim a place within it.[90] To those outside the profession, memorials to nurses who died drew attention to the nurses' exemplary service; to nurses themselves, they offered encouragement to emulate their forebears' achievements.

Memorials took many forms – simple markers of a nurse's existence; mementoes and memorabilia; and markers of exemplary service, often in extraordinary circumstances. Obituaries inscribed a nurse's life in their readers' memory, but brass plaques in churches, chapels and hospital corridors formed permanent reminders. Sometimes a nurse was memorialised with a tree. In 1950 the NZRNA called for nurses throughout New Zealand to search for any nursing memorials in their hospitals. Miss Eileen M. Bascand, matron of Dannevirke Hospital, commented wryly that she could not find any trace of nursing memorials except for 'a few trees' planted by former members of the medical and nursing staff. She doubted they could be called 'suitable memorials', though, as one doctor had planted a monkey puzzle tree and a nurse had planted a Judas tree.[91]

More personal forms of memorialisation include photographic displays and collections of mementoes, such as framed certificates, embroideries and paintings. In hospitals, displays of photographs of past matrons preserve their physical images. The glass-doored Jessie Bicknell Cabinet at the New Zealand Nurses' Organisation headquarters not only commemorates the third chief nurse but also contains memorabilia such as nurses' photographs, albums and medals, along with symbols of the profession. Margaret Gunn's lace-edged handkerchief, which she embroidered with the five-pointed star medal in a corner, is a tangible link with her own handcraft. The cabinet also displays instruments used by one of the Crimean nurses and a probe purportedly used by Florence Nightingale herself.

The majority of nursing memorials are markers of exemplary service or extreme personal sacrifice. The organisation's presidential insignia, commissioned in 1952, commemorates the professional leadership of its founder and first president, Hester Maclean. The gold and silver centrepiece has a representation of the nursing medal and cherubim depicting 'the spiritual aspect of nursing'.[92] Beatrice Campbell trained and worked at New Plymouth Hospital for 40 years, serving as matron from 1917 to 1940. Her lengthy service was marked with a brass plaque inscribed: 'In affectionate memory and appreciation of her guidance and example.' Augusta Wilson Godfrey, who served as matron of Wellington Hospital from 1889 to 1898, represented stability after a period when the hospital went through eight matrons in 15 years. Her brass plaque was 'erected by her nurses in affectionate remembrance'.[93] Exemplary service was also commemorated by naming a classroom, building, ward or hospital bed after the person. Marian Little's service as matron at Hokitika from 1909 to 1922 was more prosaically marked by an entrance light.[94]

The idea of a 'living memorial' was often important. In discussions on the best way to commemorate Grace Neill, the first chief nurse, proposals included a new St Helens Hospital in Christchurch, a professorial chair of nursing at Otago University, a tuberculosis shelter, a hospital bed for sick nurses, a bursary and even a 'nice tablet placed in all nurses' sitting-rooms with Mrs Neill's ideals expressed on it'.[95] Grace Neill's son wrote to the organising group that his mother 'disliked, in general, monuments of the tombstone order'.[96] Perhaps swayed by this, in the end the group decided to establish the Grace Neill Memorial Library at the Post Graduate School for Nurses in Wellington.[97] Some matrons, like Isabella Fraser and Frances Keith Payne, at Dunedin and Wellington Hospitals respectively, were commemorated with a medal and prize awarded to a top student in each graduating class who also demonstrated excellence in a practical or professional capacity.[98]

Memorials to nurses who died in wartime service were more common than to those who died in the influenza pandemic or the Hawke's Bay earthquake. Local community war memorials note the names of Margaret Rogers at Akaroa, Marion Brown and Mabel Jamieson at Palmerston North, and Nora Hildyard (recorded as Nona) at Lyttelton, who all died when the *Marquette* sank in October 1915. Hospital plaques record other names, such as those of the Dunedin Hospital nurses Mary Rae and Catherine Fox (also *Marquette* victims); Esther Tubman, who died from illness

The roundel on the Wellington cenotaph shows a nurse, with the symbols of cape, veil and scissors in her pocket, feeding a soldier-patient. Photograph Clare Ashton

on wartime service overseas; and Elsie Loudon, Jessie McRae, Eva Cooper and Mary Watson, who died as a result of nursing during the influenza pandemic.[99] At Kumara, the *Marquette* nurses Helena Isdell and Mabel Jamieson had hospital beds named in their memory, and the *Marquette* Ward at the Waimate Hospital honoured Isabel Clark, Mary Gorman and Catherine Fox. Isabel Clark is also memorialised by a tree planted in her hometown of Ōamaru. More generally, nurses who died in World War I are commemorated by the Nurses' Bell in the carillon of the national war memorial in Wellington and a roundel on the city's cenotaph, depicting a nurse with scissors in her pocket feeding a soldier-patient.

The Christchurch Hospital Nurses' Memorial Chapel, completed in 1928, was designed as a singular and significant memorial to the hospital's three nurses who died in the *Marquette* tragedy (Nora Hildyard, Lorna Rattray and Margaret Rogers) and to Grace Beswick and Hilda Hooker, who died in the 1918 influenza pandemic. It appears to be the only New Zealand building dedicated to women who died in the line of duty in either World War I or the 1918 pandemic.[100] It is an example of what historian Katie Pickles has called a 'strongly parochial remembrance' within an 'imperial framework'.[101]

Over time, additions and alterations to the chapel gave it a broader commemorative function. The chapel windows, designed by the prominent English stained-glass artist Veronica Whall and installed before 1950, are dedicated to individual nurses associated with Christchurch Hospital but do not depict them directly. The window titled 'Angel of Charity and a Waif' commemorates Mary Ewart, matron at Christchurch from 1898 to 1908. A Madonna-like portrayal of a woman and a bandaged child is a memorial to Sibylla Maud, another former matron. 'Christ and Children' commemorates Annie Pattrick, the director of Plunket nursing, who trained at the hospital. In 1953 Whall's fourth window, 'The Angel of Hope', was completed and installed in memory of pioneer nurses more generally.[102] Symbols throughout the chapel that predate 1950 represent general notions of charity and sacrifice, such as a carved pelican pecking blood from its chest to feed its young. The only symbol specifically associated with nursing was in a nursing medal carved on a collection box by the chaplain Henry Williams.[103]

The living memorial for World War I nurses was the Nurses' Memorial Fund, set up in 1917 to provide help to any nurse in straitened circumstances resulting from either sickness or old age. This was particularly important before a sickness benefit and superannuation were available. Nurses in training learned in their history lectures that Hester Maclean donated all profits from *Kai Tiaki* to the fund.[104] Nurses made individual subscriptions and organised fundraising events. A 'very pleasant afternoon' and sale of work at the Queen Mary Hospital at Hanmer Springs in 1928, for example, had 'brisk business' at the stalls selling 'useful and pretty artistic articles' made by the staff.[105] The following year, nurses at Thames Hospital decided not to give each other Christmas presents but instead sent 'a nice cheque' to the treasurer.[106] Nurses held bazaars, garden fêtes, concerts, plays and other entertainments, street collections and even a guessing competition with a lace tablecloth as a prize that raised £34 5s for the fund.[107]

The Nurses' Memorial Fund actively represented nursing's core value of caring for others. Speeches from religious and public figures at services for nurses on *Marquette* Day (23 October) and Anzac Day also reinforced nursing's code of virtues but emphasised the public image of the devoted, self-sacrificing nurse. These services were recurring rituals that bound local nurses with one another and their community.

Memorials emphasised carrying on the valuable traditions and accomplishments of the past.[108] At the dedication of Frances Keith Payne's memorial plaque in 1926, Mabel Thurston reminded nurses that they had been 'content to accept and take for granted all the good so strenuously fought for' by their predecessors. It was 'right and fitting' to honour them and 'leave a lasting memorial of their deeds' that would 'build up the tradition and history' of nurses and the New Zealand profession. Those seeing the memorial in the future would 'envisage all that has been accomplished, and set their faces towards higher endeavours, nobler ideals, and determination to add their share in the progress of the nursing profession.'[109]

Nursing memorials therefore included small, vernacular examples, such as an embroidered handkerchief, and grander official monuments, such as war memorials.[110] Nurses appreciated these public tributes, even if they did not create them. In turn, they contributed to the national war memorial by raising funds for the Nurses' Bell in its carillon.

A sense of community

Although widely dispersed across the country, with a number working in remote areas, nurses developed a sense of community that was supported by both formal and informal mechanisms. When Hester Maclean established *Kai Tiaki* in 1908, one of her aims was to keep nurses in touch with each other once they had dispersed from their training hospitals. The journal maintained this role after being renamed the *New Zealand Nursing Journal* in 1930. In parallel, from 1909 the NZTNA (renamed the NZRNA in 1932) was a professional organisation that gave nurses direction and voice.[111] The Nurses' Christian Union (NCU), proposed by Marion Grant and Emma Williams in 1922 and founded by them with other nurses the following year, held Bible study groups and public meetings and conferences, and its members remained connected through a travelling secretary.[112] From 1932, the NCU formed Scattered Nurses' Groups in the main cities for nurses who had left their training hospitals and taken up other work.[113] These official organisations, groups and journals created and sustained a sense of professional community.

Nurses developed intense loyalties to their hospital and to each other, beginning in their training days and expressed in later years through reunions, publications and personal correspondence. In the 1930s, nurses at some hospitals started annual magazines to celebrate or comment on events and changes and keep in touch. As one nurse said: 'The thoughts that will stir our inmost natures will be those of personal relationships with other nurses – of the bond of fellowship in which we felt ourselves – of lifelong friendships held together by the bond of unity of purpose in life. These are the values that count – the memories that last.'[114] The magazines commonly featured letters and news of engagements, marriages and births, as well as poems and stories, news of events and travels, accounts of annual concerts or dances, fundraising, club activities and sports, the occasional puzzle and cartoon, humorous articles and inevitably one pondering 'What shall I write?' from someone coerced into contributing.[115] Nurses Sidney Wilding and Donella Dalton coedited the *New Plymouth Hospital Nurses Christmas Magazine* when it began in 1939.[116] The cover of the *Wellington Hospital Nurses' Journal*, first issued in 1932, had a coat of arms topped with a pair of open scissors and featuring a bucket, scrubbing brush and soap, the nursing medal and the motto 'Labor Perpetuus' (unceasing toil).

Kai Tiaki included one section dedicated to sustaining a sense of community: the gossip column. Its four or five pages at the end of each issue represented a tenth of its content. It continued in the *New Zealand Nursing Journal* under Hester Maclean's editorship until 1932 but trailed off as the profession grew in the 1930s and 1940s. Maclean urged nurses to send news about holiday trips, especially visits to other countries, and extracts from letters from nursing friends abroad. She assured them that any news from the most distant place in New Zealand was of as much interest as news from the centres. She asked matrons to send news of staff changes, resignations, promotions, marriages and births among former nurses, and obituary notices with any 'little biographical notes of interest to nurses', hospital alterations, new equipment and accounts of festivities. All would be welcome and help make the journal interesting.[117]

In the January 1912 journal, nurses read that Annie O'Callaghan, an Australian nurse working in the New Zealand backblocks service, had resigned her position at Urutī to start a private hospital in Hastings. Her sister Nellie would live with her and carry on her work as a Plunket nurse from their home. Jessie Kennedy, matron of Cromwell Hospital, would take up Annie's position at Urutī for six months. And Leonora (Nora) Kelly, a Dunedin Hospital sister, was now doing her six months' midwifery training at St Helens Hospital Christchurch.[118] In the July issue they read

Building a nursing community and culture

A nurses' magazine with playful depiction of nursing symbols – scissors, bucket, scrubbing brush and soap – and a motto, 'Labor Perpetuus', meaning 'unceasing toil'.
Wellington Public Hospital Nurses' Journal 1, no. 7, 1932, p. 1

that Jessie Kennedy had gone to work at Miss Tombe's private hospital in Dunedin, and Nora Kelly had taken up the backblocks work at Urutī.[119] Two years later, however, nurses read that Kelly had resigned and meant to take a long holiday.[120]

Brief accounts appeared of holidays with a friend or a sister, enjoying the favourite spots of Rotorua, Waikaremoana, Queenstown and the southern glaciers. Nina Black, matron of Coromandel Hospital in 1914, had 'spent a good deal of her time motoring, which was a great treat', as there were 'no cars in Coromandel and everyone must walk'.[121] News came of colleagues working or studying overseas, sometimes with brief excerpts from their letters. Nurses travelled to Britain, South Africa, the USA and Canada, to missions in India and China, for work in Samoa (when New Zealand was responsible for its health service), and to Australia – a favourite destination for work, travel and midwifery training.

Spells of illness were briefly reported. These items, with typical attention to professional details, often described the nurse's illness, how it was contracted and the nurse's likely time away. Dora Holmes and Daisy Anderson used their time as recovering patients in tuberculosis sanatoria to attend lectures and gain their certificates in tuberculosis nursing. They took up this specialty when well again.[122]

The gossip column was important in building group identity. Unlike a newspaper gossip column, it did not offer scurrilous or malicious rumours but conveyed personal information in a time when nurses often lacked regular contact with old friends or professional activities.[123] It was an appropriate inclusion in a professional journal. As the historian Joel Wiener has noted, editors of Victorian newspapers circulated gossip not to set one group against another but to convey a moral lesson and be entertaining.[124] *Kai Tiaki*'s gossip column entertained readers with news of people and events. Its moral lesson was that members of this small, newly professionalised occupation should maintain close ties even when scattered throughout the land.

Nurses' illness narratives and cultural folklore

Several nurses who contracted particular diseases, especially through nursing, later recounted their experience of illness to either a general or nursing audience.[125] These stories, which blended a personal story with professional insight, formed a particular component of the nursing folklore. From the professional perspective, the tale of the sick nurse portrayed shocking vulnerability; from the personal perspective it showed suffering, fear, courage and resilience.

Many nurses contracted tuberculosis either from working in a sanatorium without a mask or from a patient with undiagnosed tuberculosis on a medical ward. The tale typically started with both the nurse and the medical officer responsible for nurses' health ignoring a persistent cough, tiredness, weight loss and even a positive X-ray or Mantoux test for tuberculosis. The medical officer was aware of the need (and pressure) to maintain staffing levels, and the nurse had a natural fear of the diagnosis or blithely waved away the symptoms as due to overwork.[126] It was often not until a nurse coughed up blood that action was taken. The diagnosis brought shock, fear and also shame, because of the stigma associated with the disease. Sonja Davies said, 'I had heard of people's worlds falling apart and now I knew what that meant ... It suddenly occurred to me that like the leper, I was unclean. That was hard to accept.'[127]

Nurses with tuberculosis spent months or years in a sanatorium or isolation ward. Before effective medication became available in the 1950s, the standard treatment was complete rest, fresh air, sunshine and good food. Nurses' stories all told of living on a verandah or in a 'shack' with its sliding door always open to all elements. 'We were all very hardy and tough and slept with our shack fronts wide open. One morning I woke up to see snow on my blanket. We slept this way right through the winter, banked by two or three scalding hot water bottles. The spartan existence actually seemed to help quite a lot of people.' But they felt isolated and were haunted by the prospect of 'horror of horrors, the uncontrolled spurting blood of an haemoptysis'.[128] Progress was slow. As patients gained weight and energy, they were encouraged to do more for themselves. Any setback in a fellow patient's recovery plunged them into concern for their own. Each step toward recovery – even a small gain at the weekly weigh-in – was greeted with pride and delight. Like Dora Holmes and Daisy Anderson, nurses could attend lectures while convalescing and pass a specialty course, and many did.[129]

This form of nursing folklore was not unique to New Zealand. Many nurses in other countries brought the same personal understanding of tuberculosis nursing into their illness narratives.[130] One, published in the *Nursing Times* in Britain and reprinted in the *New Zealand Nursing Journal* in 1940, was structured in stages: the nurse's reaction on receiving the diagnosis, her time in the sanatorium, her convalescence and her reflections on what the disease had taught her. Her greatest surprise was that from the patient's perspective, efficiency was not the prime virtue of nursing: a less efficient nurse's personality could 'shine through the clumsiness and lack of method' and 'cheered and heartened' her in a way that her 'more skilful co-workers failed to do'. Such a nurse was 'a most delightful and stimulating help in getting well'.[131]

Graphic accounts of haemorrhaging and nursing details brought drama and credibility to the tale. The same applied to stories of other sickness, such as rheumatic fever, with vivid accounts of completely restricted movement during a long hospitalisation.[132] Some of these tales took the form of retrospective narratives in memoirs and oral histories.[133] The folklore reflected the emerging interest in illness narratives in popular literature, such as New Zealander June Opie's experience with poliomyelitis in *Over My Dead Body* and the American author Betty Macdonald's story of her time in a tuberculosis sanatorium in *The Plague and I*.[134]

Tales of memorable patients offered a counterpoint to nurses' own illness narratives. These stories recalled people with conditions or circumstances outside the nurse's usual experience, which connected with nurse and patient in a personal way or were distinctive for some other reason. Colleen Turbet offered a poignant recollection of a tuberculosis patient: 'The sadness of the disease hit me when a young woman ... died on my duty and was given the last rites by her priest; I can still see her face after all these years and remember how awful it was to see her slip away – she was not much older than I was.'[135] Bridget Ristori recounted a tale, often repeated, of the death of a patient with diabetes in the early 1920s, just before insulin was discovered. 'Our diabetics died slowly of starvation,' she said. 'I shall never forget one poor old man who had been practically living on air. On a certain afternoon he was to be allowed a thin slice of bread and butter.' At tea time when she was putting this out on the plates, he called out to her: 'Don't forget I can have a piece, Nurse.' She said, 'I'm bringing it now,' and turned to take it to him. 'But the excitement had proved too much, for whilst I was crossing the few yards which separated his bed from the tea trolley, he died. I did hope he found a good tea waiting for him on the other side.'[136]

Other versions of the tale told of women suffering from septicaemia after backstreet abortions or who had been abused by their husbands. Joan Loeber recalled that in the 1930s, with the economic depression, women were too proud or frightened to report abuse but 'sometimes, when you were sponging them, they would tell you some of the things that had happened to them'. The 'worst case of sexual abuse' she saw was in 1934. The woman's husband returned after a long period at sea. 'And he had literally raped her continuously, how long I don't know ... He didn't actually physically injure her, there were no open wounds. That woman slept for 36 hours. And nobody wakened her. She just stayed asleep in the hospital bed. She was safe, she was warm, she was comfortable.'[137]

Building a nursing community and culture

***

From early in the twentieth century, when nursing gained official recognition as a profession through legislation, examination and regulation, its leaders strove to build a professional culture and community. Grace Neill, with the first nursing syllabus, claimed a specialised sphere of knowledge distinct from medicine and, from the 1930s onward, under Mary Lambie's leadership nurses continued to refine their skills through surveys of best practice. Nurses were willing, however, to teach lay carers basic nursing skills and provide them with home nursing manuals. Hester Maclean, who had seen the value of professional nursing journals and organisations in Australia, established both in New Zealand within three years of her appointment as chief nurse in 1906. She ensured that these institutions were overseen by nurses. The NZTNA (and later the NZRNA) provided professional leadership, and *Kai Tiaki* (and later the *NZNJ*) kept nurses professionally up-to-date. *Kai Tiaki*, in particular, built a sense of community through its gossip column. Successive chief nurses exerted authority and powerful influence in shaping the profession and directing nurses' careers.

Creating cultural traditions, preserving nursing history, cherishing cultural symbols and commemorating significant nurses and events all bound nurses together, developed a professional identity, and fostered public recognition of the value of nursing. Even in their personal illness narratives, nurses took the opportunity to advise colleagues of best practice from the patient's perspective. New Zealand nurses developed and enjoyed a sense of community and a shared understanding of the realities of nursing.

CHAPTER 11

Nursing at the southern edge of empire

In 1908 Britain's *Nursing Mirror* published an article on the imperial spirit in nursing. 'The days have gone by when the march of empire brought mainly in its wake the whisky bottle and the rifle. Today the conquered races get their first glimpse of the benefits of British rule from the medical missionary, and their first lessons in the benevolent despotism of English civilisation at the hands of the mission Nurse.' The writer's view of nursing's role was staunchly imperialist and clear. 'Notable pioneer work among native races is being carried on by Nurses wherever the flag has penetrated,' she said. 'As English-women, we are proud that this country is the birthplace of modern nursing … and we rejoice as we look around and behold in how many quarters of the Empire the best traditions of the English training schools have taken root, and are showing vigorous growth.' She included New Zealand in her list. Trained nurses were proving themselves a 'high force' in these nations' development because of their 'true Imperial spirit'. The same imperial spirit, she said, had inspired Nightingale when she created the nursing profession.[1] Her viewpoint was distinctly from the empire's centre, looking outward to the spread of imperial power and influence throughout the world. New Zealand nurses had a different view. Not only was it from the edge of empire, it was of its own sphere of influence.

Empire and the New Zealand nursing culture

As children raised in New Zealand in the late nineteenth and early twentieth centuries, nurses were enculturated with the sense of empire. It permeated British culture and British children's books, widely read in New Zealand, in which the empire's colonies were frequently the setting. Empire, associated with a code of behaviour and values, was held up as natural and good for children well into the twentieth century. It then gradually became encoded as nostalgia for a more ordered way of life.² In books by local writers for young New Zealand readers, this imperialistic ethos was intertwined with the development of a national identity. They portrayed New Zealanders as citizens of empire with distinctive characteristics.³

From 1907 the *School Journal* carried the same messages. George Hogben, inspector-general of schools and a Liberal imperialist who initiated the journal, believed the empire was 'a civilising force with a high moral duty'. The journal met this purpose by exhorting all New Zealand schoolchildren to be 'loyal and dutiful citizens of the British Empire'. Hogben's views aligned with new educational movements designed to foster a love of country, starting with what was 'local and familiar and expanding outwards to the development of an imperial patriotic spirit'. In 1914 Hogben made the *School Journal* compulsory reading in all state schools. Robust celebrations of Empire Day (24 May) reinforced schoolchildren's understanding of their place in the empire. After World War I, when the myth-building around New Zealand's national identity focused on Gallipoli, observation of Empire Day was replaced by Anzac Day.⁴

Florence Nightingale featured in the *School Journal* as a model of a brave and dutiful citizen, sacrificing herself for soldiers, country and empire. This series of articles appealed to children, especially aspiring nurses, by portraying her as a young girl bandaging her dolls and her dog, then as a heroic nurse in the Crimean War who 'stood forth as England's Angel of Pity' as she organised her nurses at Scutari. With graphic sentimentality the journal asked: 'Can you not imagine the relief that came over the poor soldiers when they found themselves tended in smooth and comfortable beds by gentle women, and felt tender hands, which shrank from causing the smallest pain, lovingly fastening the bandages about their throbbing wounds?' It evoked the 'Lady with the Lamp' image and alerted children to the anagram her name formed: 'Flit on, cheering angel'.⁵ When the first of these articles was about to be printed in September 1910, news arrived that she had died on 14 August. Her death was briefly noted in that issue, and the October article summed up her life and character in a typically sentimental tone. The City of London had awarded Nightingale the Freedom of the City in 1908 – 'the greatest honour the capital of the Empire could bestow' – but for the elderly invalid, 'nothing was dearer to her heart than the work to which she had given herself as a little girl with her dolls'.⁶

The stories of Nightingale and other heroic figures of the empire, particularly from Britain, connected the empire's periphery and centre. Likewise, travel narratives brought the empire to life and made it familiar. Historian Felicity Barnes has shown how a fictive image of a New Zealander (initially a Māori) on London Bridge was invoked in nineteenth-century British writing whenever 'the metropole needed a symbol of the primitive periphery to contrast with its own civilised state'.[7] By the start of the twentieth century, the New Zealander was present in the flesh, a visitor from a new and modern dominion, at home in the imperial metropolis. New Zealanders brought with them a familiarity with England (often referred to as the Old Country, the Mother Country or Home) shaped in childhood. This sense of familiarity began with the first exciting glimpse of England. Setting foot in London and exploring its geography and sights allowed them to possess their imagined metropolis and bring it more closely into New Zealand's cultural landscape.[8]

Erin Bennett wrote a lengthy travel narrative for *Kai Tiaki* that captured the excitement on first catching sight of a country she had heard about since childhood. As her ship passed the Eddystone Lighthouse in 1908 she could 'get glimpses of the land – pretty green hills and woods, here and there a castle or a lighthouse, and a little village in Cornwall'. Then, 'Plymouth at last! ... At last we had arrived in England! The Old Country whose history has been familiar from our earliest schooldays.' While many New Zealand visitors gave detailed accounts of London's sights, even in a rapid tour, Erin Bennett simply 'roamed about every day; visiting some old historical sights'. A list followed. She was more interested in London's social conditions, the clearing of East End slums, and children's access to parks and the sight of a tree. Like other New Zealand nurses, she was just as interested in meeting up with nurses and visiting hospitals as in seeing London's sights. St Thomas's and St Bartholomew's were favourite pilgrimage sites. And, always the pragmatic nurse, she jotted down concrete facts. On a trip north: 'Left London at 10 a.m. by express from Kings Cross, distance 300 miles, fare 25s return, time, four hours.' On her return, her image of London was tempered by the disappointing reality. Instead of the empire's metropolis rising dramatically and gloriously as the train approached, it was shrouded in fog. Days of 'thick yellow ones' forced her to stay inside and miss visiting some of the hospitals she had wanted to see.[9]

Professional nursing journals evoked the idea of empire in editorials and articles. In 1889 the *Nursing Record* (which became the *British Journal of Nursing*) carried a letter from Kate Marsden. She had just returned to Britain after four years in New Zealand, where she was lady superintendent of Wellington Hospital from 1885 to 1886. Like most writers extolling the virtues of colonial emigration, Marsden focused on opportunities for work in New Zealand where a 'large field' was open to nurses. Given the overcrowding of the profession in Britain, she invited qualified nurses who might consider going to New Zealand to discuss possible arrangements with her.[10] The empire received a boost from another source when Martha Myers, an American-born journalist, playwright and novelist who lived in England, addressed the NZTNA's Auckland Branch in 1909. She applauded the saluting of the Union Jack in every school, as it reinforced the idea that each child was a 'unit in the Empire'. (She missed the fact that New Zealand had had its own official flag from 1902.) They needed 'to make that unit as fine, as healthy, as straight in body and in morals' as possible. 'Teach hygiene and health along with patriotism, and you will evolve a healthy, useful citizen. Hygiene and patriotism make a pretty good work-a-day religion.'[11]

New Zealand nursing's place in the empire

For some nurses, the all-encompassing idea of empire chafed against the sense of New Zealand as a distinct entity. A nurse's travel narrative in 1911 showed her irritation with Sir George Quick's speech on board the ship on Empire Day, in which he referred only to the English. During the speech someone had corrected him by calling out 'British' (which was clearly seen as including the empire), and he used the term once, then relapsed. 'He spoke of Australia, but New Zealand was not in it. We were told afterwards that these two incidents – British, and the omission of New Zealand – kept two men in the smoke-room going hot for two hours.'[12] However, at the Empire Exhibition in London in 1925 when New Zealand nurse Janet Moore overheard a woman, who was viewing depictions of New Zealand's scenic features, wonder 'if it is really like that boiling mud at all', she proceeded to describe Rotorua and 'presently found a crowd around her listening intently'.[13]

Evocations of empire featured in the pages of the professional journal during Hester Maclean's time as editor and then faded. This shift aligned with New Zealand's evolving self-image as a modern, self-governing country that was also part of both the empire and the commonwealth. It was Maclean's predecessor as chief nurse, Grace Neill, who had earlier defined New Zealand nursing's role as distinctive and as leading not only the empire but the wider nursing world.

Despite the British nurse's triumphalist claim in 1908 of the imperial spirit, which had ensured that the best traditions of English nursing had taken root around the world, this was not how New Zealand nurses saw matters.[14] They were well aware that many professional innovations had originated in New Zealand. They saw New Zealand as its own centre of influence in the empire and beyond. In 1895 Grace

Neill became the world's first chief nurse – a leader in a central government department who had responsibility for all nursing matters in the country. Britain did not appoint one until 1948, even though nurse leaders there had envied Neill's position and influence. In 1908 Mrs Bedford (Ethel) Fenwick commented that 'nothing could prove more conclusively the value … of a trained nurse to an official position in the Inspector General's department than the lucid and practical exposition' Hester Maclean had given in the department's annual report on legislation that affected nursing.[15] In addition, New Zealand was the first country to have nurse inspectors of hospitals. This was part of each chief nurse's role from 1895, captured in their formal title of assistant inspector of hospitals, and the role continued even with their new title of director of the Division of Nursing from 1920. Additional nurse inspectors were appointed to assist the chief nurse from 1907.[16] New Zealand's government scholarship scheme to support Indigenous women to train as nurses (see chapter 6) was another example of innovation.[17] New Zealand also led in the reduction of nursing shifts from 12 to 8 hours, which Wellington Hospital introduced in some form in 1887 and established securely from 1895 (although, partly because of opposition from Hester Maclean, the 1909 legislation applied only to nurses in training).[18]

Underlying all these innovations was the fact that from 1893, nurses, like all other women in New Zealand, were eligible to vote. It was 1918 before Britain introduced female franchise, and even then it was limited by age and financial status. The nursing leaders Ethel Fenwick (British) and Lavinia Dock (American) envied Grace Neill's enfranchised status and encouraged discussion on women's suffrage at the 1899 International Council of Women's conference in London.[19] When a journalist from the *British Journal of Nursing* interviewed the New Zealand nurse Janet Speed in 1902, she exclaimed that Speed was the first nurse she had met who was both a registered nurse and enfranchised woman, and it was an 'additional gratification that she belonged to one of our own colonies'. As she talked to Speed, she noted 'her keen appreciation and grip of both professional and public affairs [that showed] the educational value of according to women a self-respecting position in the State'.[20]

The state registration of nurses was another example of New Zealand global leadership. The Cape Colony in South Africa had established state registration of nurses 10 years earlier, but New Zealand was the first country to enact it through specific legislation: the Nurses' Registration Act of 1901, drafted by Grace Neill. Britain did not pass its Nurses Registration Act until 1919, after a long struggle among vested interests and without a clear mandate from the divided profession.[21] Ethel Fenwick had championed the cause of state registration for British nurses from the 1880s and established the Society for State Registration of Nurses in 1902. Frances Payne, the matron of Wellington Hospital, attended the Matron's Conference in Paris in 1907 in a party led by Fenwick, where delegates showed 'very keen interest' in New Zealand's system of state registration after three years' training, its eight-hour day and votes for women.[22] This and other achievements earned Grace Neill international renown. The *British Journal of Nursing*, which Fenwick had founded, acknowledged Neill's achievements in an 'appreciation' in 1924 and again after her death in 1926.[23]

New Zealand's leadership in nursing at the turn of the century was in keeping with international social commentators' view of New Zealand as the social laboratory of the world.[24] The profession was proud of its achievements. But this confidence was soon to falter over the issue of reciprocity of registration across countries. Hester Maclean was proud that New Zealand had been the first country to have specific legislation for nursing registration.[25] She fully supported British nurses' efforts to gain registration as she believed any measure affecting nurses there also affected nurses in New Zealand. Moreover, she expected that British registration would make it easier to evaluate the qualifications of British nurses who applied for registration in New Zealand, as some were 'not of the best type of nurse'.[26] But she began worrying in 1908 that Britain might not recognise New Zealand registration. She warned that New Zealand would have to 'look to it' to ensure that its standard of training would not debar its nurses from reciprocal recognition.[27] Their professional position should be 'unassailable all over the world, especially in the Motherland'.[28] In fact, New Zealand nurses working overseas found more similarities than differences in the work and standard of practice. Katherine Berry, a former matron of Napier Hospital, saw 'very little difference in the actual nursing' when she visited Manchester in 1912. She thought the newer hospitals in New Zealand compared 'very favourably'. Even in Napier they were 'carrying out the most recent treatments known'.[29]

After Britain passed nursing registration legislation in 1919, Maclean felt both slighted and superior. New Zealand's experience of implementing registration and its ensuing regulations had a lot to offer nursing leaders at Home, who in 1920, she sniffed, were still dawdling over this.[30] They had not sought her advice. When British authorities finally opened the nursing register in 1921 and agreed to reciprocity with New Zealand, Maclean was both relieved and gratified. She thanked those nurses who had served so well overseas in the war, as they had 'proved themselves as well trained, capable and resourceful nurses', thereby easing British acceptance of New Zealand registration.[31]

Empire and nurses' wartime service

New Zealand's involvement in the South African War caused citizens to champion the idea that New Zealand nurses should tend their own wounded. A Colonel Morris of Dunedin urged people to think what it would mean to soldiers in a hospital tent in that far-off land to see the faces of nurses they had known in New Zealand, instead of strangers. 'Why, it would be like a peep of home! Think what it means to the mothers in Dunedin to know their sons are in the hands of friends. Why, half the pangs of parting would be assuaged.' He had seen service and knew the reality of camp life. 'It is not all beer and skittles. When sick or wounded, the sight of a home face is simply heaven.'[32] A soldier's parent agreed, saying how pleased 'our boys are to have some nurses who know their friends and country, to share their troubles and sufferings alike, and make the dreary stay in hospital less dreary by their presence and assistance. We all know that the English nurse, too, is a ministering angel, but then she is not a colonial nurse, and not acquainted with their land and friends.'[33]

At the beginning of World War I, ceremonial farewells to nurses departing overseas showed a more complex sense of dominion and empire. James Allen, minister of defence, told the 'First Fifty' nurses who left in April 1915 that they were not going simply as a 'batch of New Zealand nurses': they were going as 'Empire nurses', to do whatever the British Army Council asked. Prime Minister William Massey presented them with their military badges, bordered with fern leaves in silver.[34] 'That will show where we come from,' said one of the nurses. (With typical nursing pragmatism she then added that the badge would 'also let anyone know who we are in case of accident, because each one bears an identification number.')[35]

Nurses going from Otago in 1915 were told they were 'in every way worthy to represent the province, and take their stand beside the nurses from any part of the world'. They had 'a much longer and more varied course of training than nurses did in the Old Country, and nursing organisation in the colonies was far more thorough and advanced than it was at Home'.[36] At a reception in Wellington for the surviving nurses of the *Marquette* tragedy, George Russell, minister of public health, said the war had displayed to the world 'many of the finer characteristics of the British race, and none finer than the womanly qualities which were the pride of our nation'. He admired the way they wanted to serve again. 'It was a fine thing for this country that its women were showing the same pertinacity and bull-dog courage as our heroes at the Dardanelles.' Colonel Valintine told them he knew that 'as the name

"Anzac" had been writ large in the history of the Empire so also would there be undying fame' of the *Marquette* nurses who had 'exhibited all that was noblest in British tradition'. He felt that the work of the New Zealand nurses would contribute greatly to the credit of the country of their birth.[37] Nurses were citizens of both a dominion and an empire. But being colonial was still an advantage. Clara Cherry, working at the British No. 21 General Hospital in Alexandria in 1916, believed the English people there were 'surprised and satisfied at our general colonial grit'.[38]

Both the South African War and World War I gave New Zealand nurses the chance to compare themselves with those from the Old Country and other parts of the empire. They quickly recognised that New Zealand training was equal to the best elsewhere, and they valued the system that had trained them to roll up their sleeves and care for patients directly instead of delegating tasks to orderlies. On her return from South Africa in 1900, Sarah Ross told a Dunedin audience that their Dunedin Hospital training made them 'quite as good as any of the English sisters who were there'.[39] New Zealand nurses in World War I likened themselves far more to nurses from Australia and Canada than to British nurses. Daphne Commons on the transport ship *Scotian* in June 1915 told her mother: 'I may mention in passing that the majority of English nurses on board have the most wonderful figures, we gaze at the size of their waists in amazement – how they manage to endure them & work hard I don't know'. They were apparently wearing corsets. On a more professional note, she added: 'As a whole (this in confidence) they didn't seem at all as superior a class of girls as our fifty are as a whole. The worst of it is we will naturally be classed together – people don't stop to see which are which.'[40]

As Anna Rogers has noted, New Zealand nurses in Cairo in World War II considered British nurses kind and helpful but also stern, and strict about routine and discipline. The more relaxed New Zealand approach did not easily fit the British army system. When Pat Williams waved back to a major, she was reported to the matron for being too familiar. There was 'so much tradition … we felt we'd like to get on with some nursing instead of waiting for the colonel's round'. The unfamiliar work routine emphasised how different it was from working with New Zealanders. It strengthened their 'love and loyalty to New Zealand'.[41]

New Zealand was proud when Hester Maclean became first nurse in the Southern Hemisphere to receive the Florence Nightingale Medal in 1920, the first year the International Committee of the Red Cross awarded these medals. Recipients were qualified nurses who had shown exceptional distinction in caring for the sick or wounded, in peace or war.[42] Maclean had already received the Royal Red Cross

Wartime service overseas gave New Zealand nurses a chance to compare their professional achievements with nurses from other countries in the empire. Here New Zealand nurses in Cairo in World War I are with Canadian, Australian and British nurses.
PH-ALB-398-p11-7, Auckland War Memorial Museum

award. At the reception held by the NZTNA in recognition of the medal, Maclean said the Florence Nightingale Medal might have been awarded to her, but it belonged to all New Zealand nurses who had 'done so splendidly in the war'.[43]

Plunket nursing and the idea of empire

One branch of New Zealand nursing particularly connected with the notion of empire was Plunket nursing. The Society for Promoting the Health of Women and Children started in 1907 and had an immediate connection with empire through its viceregal patronage and use of the name of Lady (Victoria) Plunket, wife of the governor-general of New Zealand.

Historian Linda Bryder has explained that this service was one of several initiatives in Western countries to improve future citizens' survival and fitness in the interests of 'national efficiency'.[44] At the beginning of the twentieth century, New Zealand was proud of its reputation for having the lowest infant death rate in the world, but the failure to further reduce it caused anxiety about the future of the nation and empire. Premier Richard Seddon said: 'In the younger colonies of the Empire population is essential and if increased from British stock the self-governing colonies will still further strengthen and buttress our great Empire.'[45]

As Bryder notes, advocates of the social-Darwinist eugenics movement believed social policy should aim to encourage the propagation of 'good stock'. But more prominent in progressivist thinking was the idea that changes to a child's environment could ameliorate its condition. From 1891 Seddon's Liberal government was willing to use the state's powers to intervene in individuals' lives for the greater good. The Infant Life Protection Act 1896, for example, responded to the 'baby-farming' scandal in which some people who were paid to look after children neglected them, and concealed or even caused their deaths.[46] The legislation was amended in 1907 to shift responsibility for infants in care from the police to the Education Department and appoint registered nurses as its officers. The Midwives Act 1904 brought in the state-subsidised St Helens hospitals, which trained midwives and provided a childbirth service for working-class women. This type of environmentalism had influential proponents, including Dr Frederic Truby King, who was then medical superintendent of the Seacliff Asylum, and Dr James Mason, the country's first chief health officer. Mason identified intestinal disease resulting from poor feeding as one of the leading causes of infant death. A related concern was a perceived decline in breastfeeding. Truby King became a 'fanatical enthusiast' on correct infant feeding and promoted 'humanised milk'[47] as an alternative if breastfeeding was not possible. Implementing his disciplined routine and feeding regime, Plunket nurses worked to help mothers and 'Save the Babies'.[48]

Nurses wanting to join the Plunket service were trained at the Karitane Hospital in Dunedin. Harriette Morgan, Nelson's first Plunket nurse, became the Karitane Hospital matron in 1915. At her farewell afternoon tea in Nelson, her speech of thanks for her gifts firmly connected nursing to economic and imperial interests. The society's aim, she said, was to help the British nation by building strong, healthy babies. During the next 10 years, 250,000 babies would be born in New Zealand, but through improper treatment 1500 would die each year. The number could be more than halved through competent nursing and teaching. Every healthy adult was worth £300 to the country. If children were given their birthright – being fed naturally or with humanised milk – the race would become a much finer one. Forty percent of men who had tried to enlist as soldiers had been found physically unfit and were rejected. This would have been avoided if they had been given their birthright. Much therefore rested with women for race improvement. She herself had not gone to the front as a nurse because by staying in her present work in New Zealand, she felt she was answering the call of the future empire.[49]

Morgan's statements aligned with a pamphlet written by the second chief health officer, Dr Thomas Valintine, in 1909. He, too, placed the value of a healthy young adult at £300. Morgan's statistic for rejected recruits was perhaps slightly elevated, however; in fact, 31 percent were rejected by the Army Medical Board.[50]

After the war Truby King was invited to set up a 'Babies of the Empire' mothercraft training centre in London, where Annie Pattrick became the matron. Publicity around him triggered some imperial rivalry. An English nurse, L.E. Sherliker, wrote to the *British Journal of Nursing* suggesting that Truby King's reputation as a 'babysaver' rested more on the 'skies, open spaces, healthy homes and conditions' of New Zealand than on medical expertise. She was clearly irked that the press had given him this title. She hoped that when he compared New Zealand figures and conditions with those in Britain, he would admit that it was British medical men who should be 'given the palm' for reducing the infant death rate, because they had 'improved the health of the race in spite of tremendous obstacles'. Maclean reprinted the letter in *Kai Tiaki*, noting that she admired 'the champion of the doctors and nurses who have had to fight against conditions undreamed of in New Zealand'.[51]

Infant welfare movements in Britain and the USA operated under medical authority, with services delivered by doctors, but the Plunket service was organised by women's voluntary committees and delivered by registered nurses.[52] To provide an effective service, however, Plunket nurses had to use their political acumen to maintain good relations with local doctors, as the medical response was mixed. In 1908 it was 'chilled indifference', although Walter Fell, editor of the *New Zealand Medical Journal*, supported the service, as his wife was involved.[53]

Part of the problem was negotiating the boundary between medical and nursing responsibilities. Although Plunket's focus was on caring for well babies, in the early years Plunket nurses also tended babies brought into the 'Plunket Rooms' (clinics) with diarrhoea, malnutrition and childhood illnesses. From 1917, *Kai Tiaki* articles about Plunket nursing placed less emphasis on the society's philosophy and mothers, and more on the development of a well-trained and experienced workforce that could care for sick infants.[54] Annie Pattrick provided leadership for this as director of nursing from 1920. In 1922 the Auckland Branch noted an 'exceptional number of very tiny and very ill babies brought into the rooms this year – real hospital cases – poor little scraps of humanity, with wee, wan faces and wasted bodies'. But in 1928 it reported: 'Twelve years ago almost every baby brought to the Plunket Nurses for the first time was suffering from acute malnutrition ... To-day we seldom see those terribly emaciated little wrecks that were all too often to be seen at our rooms in the past.'[55] New Zealand's infant death rate dropped from 40.57 per 1000 live births in the years 1906–10 to 9.5 by 1936–40. Factors such as reduced family size, girls' education, better nutrition and reduction in overcrowding all contributed, perhaps more, to this improvement, but the major credit was given to the work of the Plunket nurses.[56]

The Plunket nursing service focused mainly on Pākehā women and babies in towns, but from the 1920s an increasing number of Plunket-trained public health nurses provided the same service for rural Māori women. The division between the two services was not rigidly observed. While Iris Christofferson was working as a Plunket nurse in Raetihi in 1942, the district's public health nurse phoned to ask if she could visit a rural Māori woman who was cut off from her by the flood. Iris found the woman 'sitting in the kitchen crying her eyes out'. The baby was screaming, nobody was around, and the mother had no milk for the baby, no car and no money. Iris spotted a cow standing in the yard and learned that it belonged to the farmer who owned the property. Iris found a basin, managed to milk the cow (although terrified it would flick its tail into her face) and collected enough milk to make a mixture to feed the baby for 24 hours and give the mother a cup of tea. She set off to the farmer to admit she had milked his cow. He was 'an amiable fellow' who said the family could have the cow for the season, as long as they could 'strip it' properly. She then drove into Raetihi and asked the first person she met, a policeman, if he could milk a cow. Luckily he could, and he agreed to teach the family. They were delighted, and from that time the mother walked regularly into Raetihi to bring flowers to the Plunket nurse and help with cleaning and fundraising activities.[57]

Although Plunket nursing was only one of several infant welfare movements operating simultaneously in several countries, it had the reputation of being a world leader. A newspaper reporter who saw a historical nursing pageant staged at an international fair at the Auckland Town Hall in 1936 was impressed that it included the 'New Zealand innovation' of Plunket nursing. He linked it to the often-repeated claim that the country had the lowest infant mortality rate and said it revealed 'that in some respects at least this small Dominion can lead the world'.[58]

A global outlook

New Zealand nurses engaged with other nurses not only within the British Empire but around the world. Ironically, it was a nurse leader at the centre of empire, Ethel Fenwick, who introduced 'the international idea', sparked by her attendance at a women's congress at the 1893 Chicago World's Fair. In 1899 Fenwick invited nurses attending the International Council of Women's congress in London to meet afterwards in the matron's house of St Bartholomew's Hospital to discuss the formation of an international nurses' organisation. Grace Neill was one of the nurses elected to form a provisional committee. She and nurse leaders from Britain, the USA, Canada, Australia, Holland, South Africa and Denmark drew up a constitution and bylaws that were approved at the first official meeting of the International Council of Nurses (ICN) in London in July 1900.[59] It was the first international association of professional women.[60]

A country could join the ICN if it had a single professional nursing association that would represent it in the council. At the time of the second ICN congress in 1909, when Holland, Belgium and Finland were joining, New Zealand was ineligible because the separate nursing associations in Auckland, Wellington, Christchurch and Dunedin had not yet combined to form the NZTNA. Moreover, it saw itself firmly as a part of the empire and did not want to join the ICN as an independent country 'on the same basis as these foreign nations', as Maclean noted in *Kai Tiaki*. Instead, it wanted to be 'incorporated with nurses of the Mother Country' as a branch of the National Council of Trained Nurses of Great Britain and Ireland, which Fenwick had established in 1904.[61] The idea was discussed in British, Canadian and American nursing journals. The Canadian editor applauded Maclean's leadership in this and suggested that the organisation could be renamed the Imperial Association of British Nurses.[62] This seemed to run counter to the 'international idea' and showed the ambivalence sometimes apparent in New Zealand nurses' view of their place in the empire and the international nursing world.

The impulse to connect with the Mother Country was not always apparent. In 1877 Fenwick had founded another organisation, the British Nurses' Association (later the Royal British Nurses' Association, or RBNA). New Zealand nurses could join, but by 1909 only 120 had done so. Of these, 64 joined before New Zealand's state nursing register opened in January 1902, perhaps to gain some form of recognition for their training.[63]

New Zealand finally joined the ICN at its 1912 congress in Cologne. In the October issue of *Kai Tiaki* Maclean was able to say: 'We, in New Zealand, must feel proud that we now belong to this great body of women – a body which is collectively so strong that it must have influence on the future of mankind all over the world.' Annie Holgate, one of the New Zealand delegates, reported that the German nurses had 'entertained us royally in every way. What internationalism does! We know the German nation now as we should not know it in years in an ordinary way.' However, at the banquet a German doctor proposing the delegates' health named each country, including Lapland. Someone near her explained that he meant New Zealand.[64]

Nurses attended ICN congresses if they coincided with other overseas travel. Many nurses travelled for study and work. For midwifery training they favoured London, Dublin and Melbourne (although from 1905 they could train in New Zealand), and for postgraduate study they ventured to North American universities such as Toronto, McGill and Columbia, or Bedford College in London. New Zealand's 'first International Scholar' was Grace Webster, who was granted a Red Cross scholarship for the Bedford College course in 1921.[65] In 1935 the Florence Nightingale Memorial Committee awarded its first study scholarship to E. Ruth Bridges, who completed the Bedford College course and spent the rest of her 18 months overseas on a study tour of Britain, Europe and the United States. In the 1930s and 1940s, Rockefeller Foundation fellowships enabled nurse leaders like Mary Lambie and Flora Cameron to study developments in nursing in North America and Europe.[66]

Until it went into abeyance during World War II, the Bedford College course gave New Zealand nurses a chance to study, work and socialise with nurses from many countries. When the course came under the auspices of the League of Red Cross Societies, different member countries each decorated a room in the Manchester Square hostel in London. The name of the country was marked on the door, and pictures, cushions and needlework with scenic views and national emblems reminded the occupant of home. Janet Moore, studying at Bedford College in 1927, said: 'Just picture a welcome after a hard day's study combined with an excursion to see the housing conditions in the slums of London to return to the warmth and comfort of your own country portrayed in your room, it really puts new life into one.' Unfortunately, the New Zealand Red Cross had not decorated a room, and she hoped it would soon do so, as surely New Zealand was not poorer than Finland or Latvia.[67] But no dedicated New Zealand room had been organised by the 1933–34 academic year, when Bridget Ristori took the course. She was assigned to the Japan room, between Finland and Iceland.[38]

Nurses who worked while travelling usually stayed overseas for two to five years before returning. Clare Jordan wrote from Honolulu in 1912 to say that although it was very beautiful there and the nursing exceptionally easy in most cases, she was 'still loyal to New Zealand' and looked forward to her return.[69] A few stayed away permanently, catching up with news of home through the gossip column or nurses' visits. Agnes Barclay of Wellington Hospital wrote from Scotland in 1914 to say how much she enjoyed reading *Kai Tiaki*, 'with so many familiar names mentioned in it.'[70] Mission nurses worked in the Solomon Islands, Papua New Guinea, Fiji and China.[71] Others seeking to combine work and travel chose Australia, England, Scotland, South Africa, Samoa, Canada and America. Unfamiliar conditions could be a challenge. Katherine Berry, 'gaining an insight into nursing in England' by working in Manchester, missed the 'bright sunny days of New Zealand'. As there was 'so much smoke and dirt about … you never feel clean', she lamented. Manchester was 'the dirtiest town' she had ever been in.[72]

Despite New Zealand's remoteness, nurses at home could keep up to date with developments in international nursing. From the time Maclean started *Kai Tiaki*, she summarised or reprinted important articles from overseas nursing journals sent by other editors. They similarly reprinted *Kai Tiaki* articles. This sweeping gaze across the nursing world continued after *Kai Tiaki* became the *New Zealand Nursing Journal*.

Nurses could also observe and exchange views with others from overseas working in New Zealand. *Kai Tiaki* noted their arrivals. When the journal began in 1908, 11 percent of the 639 nurses on the New Zealand register had trained overseas.[73] By January 1925, with 3945 nurses on the register, this proportion had risen to nearly 15 percent.[74] During the 1920s 412 overseas nurses gained New Zealand registration, more than half of them from Britain.[75] Some visitors might have been surprised at their destinations. Margherita Peters, for example, came from the Bristol Royal Infirmary in 1912 to work at the tuberculosis shelters at the small rural settlement of Seddon.[76] Edith Hill arrived from England the same year to take charge of the Waiapu Hospital in Waipiro Bay on the remote East Cape – a stark contrast to St Bartholomew's in London where she had trained.[77] There were only eight patients there when the hospital inspector visited, most suffering from typhoid fever.[78] The hospital's small size and remote location were perhaps the reasons why she left within a year.[79] However, she would not have been alone in finding such work uncongenial. An *Auckland Star* reporter in 1925 relished the chance to point out that New Zealand nurses had been reluctant to take on the district nursing position in the Wellsford backblocks, even though it was 'the boast of the people of the Dominion that the training of the colonial girl is such that she is fitted to take up any kind of work under any conditions of life in our country'. He added wryly that it was probably only a coincidence that two Scottish nurses from Aberdeen had in succession 'taken up the arduous duties'.[80]

New Zealand nurses were interested in how nurses overseas perceived them. Visiting Toronto in 1912, Jeannie Sutherland was a little taken aback that Canadian nurses had an apparently 'very exalted opinion' of New Zealand, considering it 'the most well governed and most up-to-date country in the world'. Nurses asked 'how we ever managed to get State Registration so long ago'. In contrast, people she spoke to in the southern United States 'had never heard of New Zealand'. A clergyman's wife told her she 'could not imagine a lady so civilised' as Sutherland 'living in a little island away out in the Pacific Ocean'. 'I am sure they thought the island small enough for me to run all round it every day and that there was even danger of me falling off it into the water', she added. She was surprised at their lack of geographic clarity and by the fact that some of the people she spoke to had 'never even seen the sea'. Nevertheless, her contact with nurses in the USA and Canada showed her that New Zealanders were 'making a name' for themselves 'in many parts of the world as a very progressive country', especially in nursing.[81]

In the 1930s and 1940s, although journal announcements of nurses' travel waned, international engagement continued. In 1937 Jessie Bicknell, a former chief nurse, represented New Zealand at the ICN's board of directors meeting. Mary Lambie, the current chief nurse, attended the ICN congress with others, and four New Zealand nurses were elected to ICN standing committees.[82] At the congress Lambie presented the research she had been doing with the ICN on nurses' health.[83] The New Zealand Registered Nurses' Association actively engaged with Corso (the Council of Organisations for Relief Services Overseas), and some New Zealand nurses worked for UNRRA (the United Nations Relief and Rehabilitation Administration, founded in 1943). Alice Reid, for example, was with UNRRA in Germany, working with displaced people and running a refresher course for nurses from the Baltic countries. In 1946 Lambie was elected president of the Florence Nightingale International Foundation and the following year became the first vice-president of ICN. In 1950 she chaired the World Health Organisation's Expert Committee on Nursing. Its report profoundly influenced nursing worldwide. In a history of the ICN, Lambie's influence on nursing affairs was described as 'internationally recognised; through personal contacts, much travel and an extensive correspondence, and because of her breadth of vision, her guidance and wisdom, she has been claimed as a friend and counsellor by nurses the world over.'[84]

Nursing in the Pacific offered the pleasure and challenge of working in a new setting as well as a professional opportunity. These nurses are at the hospital in Rarotonga, Cook Islands, in the 1940s. Whites Aviation Ltd, WA-00986-G, Alexander Turnbull Library, Wellington

Nursing in the Pacific

At the start of the twentieth century Premier Richard Seddon had his own imperial ambitions. He was eager to expand New Zealand's power and governance into the Pacific and envisioned gaining control over a federation of several countries. Instead, perhaps to acknowledge New Zealand's assistance in the South African War, the British government allowed him to annex the Cook Islands and Niue.[85] At the outbreak of World War I, just 11 days after Britain declared war on Germany on 4 August 1914, six nurses sailed with New Zealand troops who were ordered to take over German-occupied Samoa. In Fiji they collected another nurse who had been stranded during her holiday, and reached Apia on 29 August. Samoa was smoothly taken. According to one of the nurses, this 'bloodless victory' caused 'absolute disgust' among the disappointed soldiers.[86]

The nurses worked at the main Apia hospital, where German doctors and nurses continued to work before being evacuated. While this was a largely peaceful military effort, it was the first Allied occupation of German territory in the war. It was also the first time that the military authority had specifically requested the engagement of New Zealand nurses. New Zealand's early efforts at administration in Samoa have been described as 'disgracefully inept',[87] but its imperial involvement in the Pacific continued.

New Zealand was responsible for supplying and supervising the Cook Islands nursing service from early in the twentieth century and in Western Samoa and Niue from 1920.[88] Winifred Waite went to Samoa in April 1920 with glowing testimonials. Her reference from Miss L.W. Stott, the Wellington matron, portrayed her as ideal to tackle the very different work in the Pacific.[89] When she resigned at the end of 1921, her testimonial from Dr S.G. Grail, the acting chief medical officer, confirmed that she had done her work well.[90] Conditions could be challenging. The first nurse on Niue in 1920 travelled the 40-mile (64km) coast by bicycle, with a horse and gig, or sometimes in a borrowed car with tyres that had to be stuffed with grass and bound tightly to the wheel.[91]

Some nurses worked in multiple areas of the Pacific. Amy Rickman served in Rarotonga from 1940, taking over from Beth Paora (who had warned her not to kill the big spider in the wardrobe that ate the mosquitoes). Rickman went to villages to see mothers and children, weigh babies and visit schools. When her two-year contract ended, she accepted the position of hospital matron at Niue. The hospital was 'rat infested, and there were ants by the million'. To deter these pests, food was stored in an icebox or on a table in a small store room. 'The table legs were kept in tins of water and smeared with Vaseline.' In addition, Rickman had unexpected duties. She wished she had been warned that she would be giving anaesthetics when the retired doctor, Ernest Hunt, pulled teeth. 'I had never done anything like that, and I had to give these wretched injections into their gums. Poor old Dr Hunt, who couldn't see, would pull the wrong tooth.' Fortunately, he had left Niue when she was asked to go back for a second term in 1946.[92]

The Department of Health was eager to find nurses to work in the Pacific. The *Kai Tiaki* gossip column carried regular news of nurses going to or returning from Pacific posts, though it printed no vivid accounts of the Pacific nursing experience that might have induced nurses to apply. Word of mouth was perhaps a more persuasive recruitment tool, as several nurses at the Pukeora Sanatorium in Waipukurau went in turn to Samoa.

From the outbreak of World War II in 1939, Mary Lambie reported that nurses were reluctant to work in the islands because they were hoping to go on active wartime service.[93] When Amy Rickman told her public health nurse inspector, Helen Comrie, that she would love to go to the islands, Comrie immediately said, 'Would you really? I'll ring Wellington at once, because I know they are desperate for people.' It was arranged very quickly.[94] Nurses' later stories show that working in the Pacific offered the excitement and challenge of nursing in a new setting and gaining experience caring for people with tropical diseases. Nurses enjoyed working with the Pacific people, were fascinated by the lush vegetation and different flowers and relished sightseeing and swimming in waterholes with tiny coloured fish, but found the hot, humid climate and insects trying. They saw their experience not as an imperial venture but as a Pacific adventure.

Unlike the work of Britain's Colonial Nursing Association (CNA), New Zealand nurses' work in the Pacific was part of a local administrative responsibility. Annie Stuart has argued that the impact of the influenza pandemic on Samoa was a catalyst for New Zealand's assumption of responsibility for the Samoan population's health and welfare. From the 1920s nurse training in Samoa was expanded, with recruits drawn mainly from a mission girls' school.[95] Successive New Zealand chief nurses also recruited New Zealand nurses to staff Pacific hospitals and supervise public health nursing ventures. In 1934 Mary Lambie was sent to Samoa to reorganise the nursing service. On her way back to New Zealand she visited Niue, where she also initiated changes. The Pacific effort then expanded. In 1935, when the Fijian government was finding it difficult to continue recruiting nurses from Australia, Lambie arranged for the secondment of New Zealand nurses. She sent one of her nurse inspectors to be matron, initially for three years. (This was Lucy Lea, who had had to dodge mistletoe advances from patients at Brockenhurst during World War I.) The next year the Fijian government asked Lambie to survey its nursing service. She recommended that New Zealand rather than Australia should continue to be actively involved in Fiji's nurse training and registration. In the 1940s she actively recruited nurses for the service through *New Zealand Nursing Journal* articles.[96] This was a specifically expansionist step in what was otherwise a 'neighbourly' involvement in Pacific nursing.

***

New Zealand nurses' view of the British Empire and their position in it contrasted significantly with views from the empire's centre. Triumphalist accounts depicted the influence of British nursing spreading outward across the empire. New Zealand nurses understood this attitude, having been raised as dutiful citizens of the empire, and had benefited from the nursing diaspora that brought competent matrons and the chief nurse Grace Neill. But for them this view was tempered with a strong sense of distinctive national identity. Between 1895 and 1909, New Zealand's remoteness released its nurses from the constraints hampering advances in British nursing. New Zealand nursing forged its own vision and direction, and its professional innovations were admired elsewhere in the empire. Neither passive nor peripheral, New Zealand nursing was the Mother Country's adult child showing its parent the way.

Historians Katie Pickles, Catharine Coleborn and colleagues have similarly challenged the view of New Zealand as simply an imperial outpost. In a number of areas, they argue, it was the centre of a local world.[97] This was evident particularly in nursing initiatives in the Pacific. Until Lambie's expansionist efforts in the later 1930s, this was not a professional imperial project but a practical acknowledgement of its administrative responsibilities.

Nevertheless, as Clare Midgley, Alison Twells and Julie Carlier have argued, the local and the global are mutually constituted.[98] The British endeavours to assure colonial Indigenous populations' welfare, along with new scientific and medical possibilities, were reflected in New Zealand's health policy and services in the Pacific.[99] Conversely, Plunket nursing connected New Zealand nursing with an imperial endeavour. Its success influenced mother and child care in Britain, Australia and other countries. The local and global shaped each other.

Moreover, New Zealand nurses identified themselves as independent of British nursing services and standards. Their overseas wartime service had shown them how they differed from British nurses. They likened themselves far more to Australian nurses, who were equally willing to roll up their sleeves and give direct care, and the feeling was mutual. As historians Jan Bassett, Ruth Rae and Kirsty Harris have each shown, Australian nurses recognised that colonial nurses in wartime hospitals did hands-on nursing as well as supervise orderlies and VADs, and were therefore highly sought after.[100] While British nurses might have believed themselves more skilled than their Dominion cousins, notes Harris, in practice the reverse was often true. British nurses were less flexible when adaptations were needed.[101] After the war Hester Maclean reported that her experience had shown that British nurses were not 'in any way superior to those trained in New Zealand hospitals'.[102]

New Zealand nurses travelled, worked and studied well beyond the borders of the empire, meeting nurses of many countries and engaging in international endeavours through ICN and other organisations. Later, Mary Lambie's efforts gained New Zealand further recognition for international nursing leadership. New Zealand nurses were confident that the edge of empire had something to teach the Old Country and the world.

Conclusion

When the nurse at Naseby Hospital on Christmas Eve 1911 was faced with choosing which flowers to use to decorate her ward and thought of Florence Nightingale, her thoughts reflected the strong link forged in the nursing profession between the empire's centre and its southern edge. In the 1880s and 1890s, New Zealand hospitals made the radical shift to a qualified female nursing workforce by recruiting nurses trained in the Nightingale system, whether in Britain or Australia, to be hospital matrons and direct schools of nursing. Isabella Fraser, for example, trained at the Edinburgh Royal Infirmary, where the Nightingale approach to nurse training had been in place since 1873, and was appointed matron of Dunedin Hospital in 1893.[1] As nursing graduates from these new schools took positions in other hospitals, disciplined, knowledgeable nursing practice spread through the country. The British nursing diaspora therefore initiated modern professional nursing in New Zealand.

Was a British nursing culture transplanted with this diaspora, or did a distinctly New Zealand nursing culture emerge? The training of New Zealand nurses was similar in intent and content to that of training in Britain. The curriculum consistently focused on three components – dirt, body and duty. Like their British counterparts, New Zealand nurses learned to eradicate all forms of visible dirt in a dreary round of drudgery, with mop, bucket, duster and bed bath. More senior nurses combatted invisible dirt – the microbe – when assisting with operations and dressing wounds. Nurses gained exposure to a wide range of conditions by the system of rotating through the wards. The aim was to produce an all-rounder nurse. Training also emphasised dedication to duty. Hospital etiquette, ethics and a code of ideal nursing virtues were made explicit in texts and lectures and reinforced through practical experience. The influence of British nursing culture was recognisable in all these aspects of New Zealand nurse training.

Yet New Zealand's position as the southernmost landfall of the nineteenth-century British nursing diaspora encouraged the development of a distinctive and largely autonomous nursing profession. By 1909, New Zealand had become the first country with a chief nurse in a central government department, a government scholarship scheme to support Indigenous women to train as nurses, a specific nursing registration act, an enfranchised nursing workforce, Indigenous registered nurses, nurse inspectors of hospitals, and an eight-hour day legislated for all nurses in training. These rapid innovations were in keeping with international social commentators' view of New Zealand as a site of social and political innovation.

Once the professional standing of New Zealand nurses had been established by the Nurses Registration Act 1901, their professional journal and association provided a vision and direction and sustained a community spirit. The nursing journal reported not only professional innovations but also news of colleagues' career moves, personal lives and deaths. Memorials commemorated nurses and stood as public reminders of their contribution. Like the folklore that arose around district, backblocks and hospital nursing, these were all significant elements in the New Zealand nursing culture. Public perceptions of nurses did not always align with their own view. Nurses were irritated with the public's insistence on viewing them as heroic, self-sacrificing, ministering angels when they saw themselves as well-trained professionals.

Within hospitals, nurses' conduct was governed by a code of virtues intended to shape an efficient, effective and biddable nursing workforce. Violations of this code led to incidents that illustrated the relationships and hierarchies that shaped the profession: the authority of the chief nurse, hospital matrons and ward sisters over nurses and probationers; the relationship between the nursing and medical professions; and the relative authority of the hospital matron and the hospital board. The social drama of 'hospital troubles', enacted in public inquiries, demonstrated that everyone – the public, journalists, authorities, patients and relatives, nurses, doctors and hospital board members – felt entitled to contest what a modern nurse should be and do. Nurses were not alone in deciding what it meant to be a New Zealand nurse.

Different practice settings demanded different and sometimes unexpected qualities in New Zealand nurses. District nurses needed flexibility and ingenuity to adapt their hospital-based skills to the care of the sick poor. Journalistic accounts of their work revealed the grim effects of an Old World evil – poverty – in the new. Journalists used nurses' stories in fundraising appeals to describe cases among the sick poor in a relentless rendering of wretchedness, and portrayed nurses as 'brightening sunless lives'. The myth portraying Sybilla Maude as the founder of district nursing emphasised the need for philanthropic support and provided a model for similar services throughout the country.

Nursing services for rural Māori and backblocks settlers made unique contributions to New Zealand's nursing culture. Young Māori women training as nurses had to cross and recross the cultural boundary between the traditional ways of the Māori world and the Pākehā-dominated health system, with its cultural biases and assumptions, but were also supported with scholarships and the opportunity to use te reo Māori in state examinations. The depiction of the first Māori registered nurse in New Zealand was based on inaccurate information, but it achieved its mythic function of explaining contradictions by showing that Māori women could succeed in a Pākehā-dominated health system. It also served as a charter for action by holding Ākenehi Hei as a role model for future Māori nurses.

The folklore of the Māori nursing service also reflected the experiences of the Pākehā nurses who were needed to help staff the service. These nurses had to overcome the challenges of long journeys to treat patients and nursing acutely ill patients in remote and scantily equipped fever camps. Pākehā nurses also sometimes struggled with the teachings and practices of tohunga and religious movements, while Māori nurses struggled with giving advice against that of their elders or working in an iwi different from their own. Stories of nursing in marae meeting houses and patients' homes showed that cross-cultural learning was continuous and shared.

The backblocks nursing folklore likewise emphasised the virtues of versatility, resourcefulness and resilience and also portrayed the nurse as an intrepid adventurer in new geographic and professional territory. This folklore aligned with New Zealand's sense of its pioneering spirit and worthy place in the empire. Nurses' dramatic stories reflected women's travel writing and the emerging nationalist literature of the New Zealand bush.

Did nurses' engagement in the backblocks and Māori health services make them agents of empire? They did not regard themselves as such. Backblocks nurses believed they were helping fellow citizens who were isolated from hospitals and doctors. However, their folklore does show that they were aware of settlers' actions in clearing native bush and turning it into farmland. Like the settlers themselves, they saw this as progress – proof of New Zealand's value to the empire. In nursing Māori, they certainly did not see themselves as 'smoothing the pillow of a dying race' but rather as bringing Western health measures to Māori in order to safeguard and improve their health. In that role, they saw themselves as contributing to New Zealand's image as a modern, productive and humanitarian dominion.

Were nurses agents of empire when they engaged in wars overseas? Their work in South Africa at the turn of the century and overseas in World War I certainly supported the British imperial effort. Nurses themselves, however, generally regarded wars as 'ghastly' and simply wanted to help 'their boys'. They identified with empire to the extent of comparing themselves with nurses from Britain and other dominions. They proved themselves to be highly capable, willing, resourceful and hard-working. The folklore of wartime nursing reveals a sense of adventure as well as stoicism and endurance to cope with the emotional labour of tending sick, wounded and dying soldiers.

Early Plunket nurses contributed to the dominion's effort to keep New Zealand populated with 'British stock', as Seddon put it, rather than immigrants from other cultures, and so 'further strengthen and buttress our great Empire'.[2] The Plunket Society's contribution to the imperial project is perhaps epitomised by the establishment of the Plunket-based 'Babies of the Empire' mothercraft centre in London, managed by a New Zealander.

Finally, how did New Zealand nurses view themselves in relation to empire and the wider nursing world? From the late nineteenth century they seized the 'international idea'. Despite the time and cost associated with overseas travel, they studied as much in North America as they did in Britain. They also worked and travelled in Europe and North America, as well as in the Solomon Islands, New Guinea, Fiji and China. New Zealand nurses were part of a worldwide sorority of professional women earning a meagre living while serving their fellow citizens in sickness and health.

New Zealand nurses' study, conferences and contact with nurses elsewhere in the world linked them in a professional network and shaped practice and professional issues. From 1899, New Zealand nurses were well aware of international interest in their professional vision, direction and achievement. They actively engaged with the International Council of Nurses. Their attention also turned to the Pacific: they worked in the Cook Islands, Western Samoa and Niue. Nurses did not see this as a professional imperial endeavour but more as a personal and professional adventure in which they helped Pacific neighbours and fulfilled New Zealand's administrative responsibility for these islands' nursing services. But New Zealand's provision of nursing leadership, education and staff to Fiji in the 1930s can only be seen as steps toward a Pacific nursing 'empire'.

CONCLUSION

Over the decades the scientific basis of nursing knowledge was strengthened, and the profession paid increasing attention to evidence-based practice. The nursing journal narrowed its focus, eschewing book reviews and personal news in favour of clinical articles, career items and professional commentary. What remained constant throughout the period were, first, nurses' willingness to develop new forms of nursing expertise to respond to the country's changing health needs, and second, the essential nature of nursing practice – providing care for the sick and protecting and promoting health. And while the public continued to apply the tropes of the heroine and the self-sacrificing angel, nurses remained constant in their self-image as trained professionals.

Mary Lambie's 1950 version of her history of New Zealand nursing included a world-leading vision for the professional direction of nursing, the value placed on training Māori women to be nurses in their communities, nurses' crucial place in emerging services outside the hospital that served the sick and promoted public health, and the profession's growing sense of its place as a leader in the Pacific. New Zealand required a robust, adaptable nursing profession to address the Old World evils of poverty and sickness that reappeared in the new, to support backblocks settlers in order to secure its position as a valuable source of exports to the empire, to demonstrate its standing as a modern civilised country by improving the health of its Indigenous population, and to implement its vision for a strong, free health system. Without nurses, Lambie pointed out, none of this could have been achieved.

***

This book started and ends with flowers. The Naseby nurse and Florence Nightingale both acknowledged the place of flowers in creating a nurturing environment for the sick and infirm. Nightingale herself particularly valued the Scutari flowers that Emma Dent of Sudeley Castle had gathered and dried for her, and the Naseby nurse appreciated James Crawford's small flowers from his cottage garden.[3] And Edith Lewis and her nurses at Trentham at the end of World War II recognised the difference flowers could make. For the emaciated women who had been interned at Stanley Camp in Hong Kong, filling the wards with flowers provided 'a great uplift to a better life'.[4] Flowers were highly symbolic in the New Zealand nursing culture. They appeared in ceremonies, social events, welcomes and farewells, presentations to visiting dignitaries, room decorations for special events and fundraising sales. Edith Dunsford, who began nursing 1894, exhorted nurses in any country hospital to grow them. 'Get the right side of cook to put some soot into a bag for you,' she said. 'From the wards collect all rejected greenery and flowers, throw them all into a hole kept for the purpose. When rotten, they make beautiful mould. Patients and their friends soon become interested in nurse's plot and gladly contribute treasures.' Penny packets of seeds would also provide a mass of colour. 'There are often times when books or study clog, human companionship for the moment irritates, rather than soothes, then seek your garden.'[5]

From the beginning of 'modern nursing' in New Zealand, flowers were a symbol of caring. On his September 1884 inspection of Wellington Hospital, Dr George Grabham observed 'a profusion of cut flowers' in the wards each day.[6] A nurse on barge duty in France in World War I made sure that her barge was 'gay with lovely flowers and we keep them all arranged between trips, as when patients are on there is no time.'[7] Nurses in a tuberculosis sanatorium awarded a 'beautiful porcelain flower vase' in turn each week to the patient who had gained the most weight. 'The winner has this before him at meal times, filled with beautiful flowers until the next Sunday, when he must show cause, in bulk, why he should retain it.'[8] When Mabel Mander, the matron of Ashburton Hospital, was dying in September 1918, the nurses strewed her bed with flowers.[9] And Norah Carson, on active service overseas in World War II, visited a former patient now in a different military hospital and took flowers for the 'lad who has been there for months poor beggar'.[10]

Surgeon-General Robert Henderson, speaking at a fundraising event for the Nurses' Memorial Fund, told the audience that just as the brilliance and fragrance of the flowers surrounding them in the hall brought them light, comfort and gladness, so the sisters at the front in World War I brought 'joy and comfort, skilled sympathy, and a touch of home to the hearts of our wounded and sick boys in camps and hospitals'.[11] Even artificial flowers were used to supplement the fund. Wellington women made brightly coloured tulips for a 'Dutch garden' in the Town Hall. 'Persuasive saleswomen' encouraged the public to buy a tulip in a pot for a shilling. With the flower, they received a small gift planted at its root.[12]

In hospitals, it was usually the junior or night nurse's task to take all the flowers out of the ward or to the sluice room in the evening, because it was believed that they gave off unhealthy quantities of carbon dioxide or used up valuable oxygen during the night.[13] But knowledge and the practice culture could change, and a New Plymouth student nurse in 1939 relished debunking this practice. 'Believe it or not!', clamoured her headline in the *New Plymouth Hospital Nurses' Christmas Magazine*. 'Well! Well! Even in hospitals some things are done just because they have always been done. Flowers use just as much oxygen at night as they do in the daytime, and

Conclusion

Flowers often featured in nurses' stories of caring for the sick. These nurses in Wellington in 1951 have their arms full. *Evening Post*, 114/386/09-G, Alexander Turnbull Library, Wellington

that is about as much as one Micky Mouse. True, they breathe out carbon dioxide at night, but that is about as much as a mouse does too, and we hope you keep a window open!'[14] This new knowledge did not, however, alter the value of tending to the vases and bouquets. One nurse gave advice through the nursing journal from her experience of being a patient: 'Do let us take great care of our ward flowers – they represent to the patient, in most cases, memories of friends and loved ones … Be interested in them … The tender care bestowed on flowers is an indication of what that nurse is capable of to patients themselves.'[15]

Abbreviations

AES Auckland Evening Star
AG Ashburton Guardian
AJHR Appendices of the Journals of the House of Representatives
AJN American Journal of Nursing
ANZ Archives New Zealand
AS Auckland Star
ATL Alexander Turnbull Library
BA Bush Advocate
BJN British Journal of Nursing
BPT Bay of Plenty Times
EP Evening Post
ES Evening Star
FS Feilding Star
FT Franklin Times
GES Greymouth Evening Star
GH Gisborne Herald
GRA Grey River Argus
GT Gisborne Times
HBH Hawke's Bay Herald
HC Horowhenua Chronicle
HG Hokitika Guardian
HNS Hawera & Normanby Star
HS Hastings Standard
JDHHCA Journal of the Department of Health, Hospitals and Charitable Aid
KCC King Country Chronicle
KT Kai Tiaki

LT Lyttelton Times
ME Marlborough Express
MR Matamata Record
MS Manawatu Standard
MW Maoriland Worker
NA Northern Advocate
NEM Nelson Evening Mail
NZANS New Zealand Army Nursing Service
NZG New Zealand Gazette
NZH New Zealand Herald
NZMJ New Zealand Medical Journal
NZNJ New Zealand Nursing Journal
NZNO New Zealand Nurses' Organisation
NZRNA New Zealand Registered Nurses' Association
NZT New Zealand Times
NZTNA New Zealand Trained Nurses Association
ODT Otago Daily Times
OW Otago Witness
PBH Poverty Bay Herald
PM Patea Mail
SEP Stratford Evening Post
TH Timaru Herald
TS Thames Star
WC Wanganui Chronicle
WCT West Coast Times
WDT Waihi Daily Telegraph

Notes

Introduction

1. J.M. Brown, 'Naseby in the "Golden Age"', in *Tales of Pioneer Women, Collected by the Women's Institutes of New Zealand*, ed. Airini E. Woodhouse (Christchurch: Whitcombe and Tombs, 1940), pp. 293–94. I am very grateful to the Executive of the New Zealand Federation of Women's Institutes for their kind permission to include this story and to Colleen Dryden, executive officer, for her assistance.
2. 'Nursing echoes', *BJN* 81, July 1933, p. 183. Eva Lückes told her London Hospital probationers: 'I have spoken to you before about the importance of being very faithful over little things.' Eva E.C. Lückes, *Lectures on General Nursing* (London: Kegan Paul, Trench, 1888), p. 164. For articles drawing nurses' attention to doing small things well, see, for example, Isabel Hampton Robb, 'The quality of thoroughness in nurses' work', *AJN* 4, no. 3, 1903, pp. 168–77; Alice Lucas, 'Our duty in small things', *AJN* 5, no. 12, 1905, pp. 879–81; Cora McCabe Sargent, 'The hospital tray', *AJN* 15, no. 7, 1915, pp. 554–60.
3. Florence Nightingale, *Notes on Nursing: What it is and what it is not* (London: Gerald Duckworth, [1859] 1952), p. 70.
4. Diary of Emma Dent, Sudeley Castle, 3 December 1864; Florence Nightingale to Emma Dent, 24 December 1864, Archival collection, Sudeley Castle and Gardens, Winchcombe, UK. I am very grateful to Derek Maddock, the Sudeley Castle archivist, for his generous help in sending me this material during a difficult time (2020).
5. See, for example, the opening statement in Margaret Goldsmith's 1937 biography: 'Florence Nightingale was the founder of modern nursing.' Margaret Goldsmith, *Florence Nightingale: The woman and the legend* (London: Hodder & Stoughton, 1937), p. 9.
6. Annie Matheson, *Florence Nightingale: A biography* (London: Thomas Nelson, 1913), p. 18. For a recent and measured account of Nightingale, see Mark Bostridge, *The Life of Florence Nightingale: The making of an icon* (New York: Farrar, Straus & Giroux, 2008).
7. Sir Edward T. Cook, *The Life of Florence Nightingale*, 2 vols (London: Macmillan, 1913).
8. 'The Life of Florence Nightingale, second volume', Book review, *KT* 17, October 1914, p. 164. Maclean kept the biography for 14 years, then donated it to the Grace Neill Memorial Library in 1929, five years after her retirement as chief nurse. 'The Grace Neill Memorial Library', *KT* 21, July 1928, p. 137.
9. Edna Pengelly, *Nursing in Peace and War* (Wellington: Wingfield Press, 1956), p. 24.

10. E. Blackburn, 'Crimean nurses', Letter to the editor, *NEM*, 12 May 1913, p. 6.
11. 'Personal matters', *NEM*, 16 March 1910, p. 5.
12. 'One who experienced Miss Nightingale's kindness', *EP*, 17 August 1910, p. 2.
13. 'Discovery of grave', *EP*, 2 May 1944, p. 8.
14. Notes on the inside cover and the front page of the volume differ on whether it was compiled in 1953 or 1938. It is reasonable to assume that it was 1938, when Mary Lambie and Janet Moore, who received the letters from Lyons, were still working. Papers related to Nurse Lyons 1873–1877, School of Advanced Nursing Studies, New Zealand Nurses' Association records, 20/2/22, ANZ. See also 'Obituary', *KT* 22, July 1929, p. 124.
15. A.H. Reed, *Florence Nightingale*, 2nd edn. (Dunedin: A.H. & A.W. Reed, 1966), p. 4.
16. 'Snow statues', *EP*, 19 August 1939, p. 27.
17. 'Nightingale bricks', *BJN* 84, August 1936, p. 212.
18. 'A treasured brick', *EP*, 30 April 1943, p. 6; Audrey Gilbert (née Dawson), oral history interview with Pamela Wood, 9 August 2005.
19. See Judith Godden, *Lucy Osburn, a Lady Displaced: Florence Nightingale's envoy to Australia* (Sydney: Sydney University Press, 2006).
20. Most studies of this diaspora have examined it from the viewpoint of the empire's centre, particularly through the experience of nurses sent by the Colonial Nursing Association or by religious missions as part of an imperial project related to Indigenous peoples. See, for example, Anne-Marie Rafferty, 'The seductions of history and the nursing diaspora', *Health and History* 7, 2005, pp. 2–16; Helen Sweet, '"Wanted: 16 nurses of the better educated type": Provision of nurses to South Africa in the late nineteenth and early twentieth centuries', *Nursing Inquiry* 11, no. 3, 2004, pp. 176–84. In contrast, New Zealand developed its own nursing service for Māori.
21. 'Pioneer nurses', *ODT*, 24 August 1926, p. 7; 'Memoir of M.H. Fraser', Pioneer Women's Hall, Dunedin, 1934.
22. 'The conference room of the International Council of Nurses, Geneva', *KT* 19, April 1926, p. 70; 'Notice', *KT* 6, April 1913, p. 82; 'International Nurses' Library', *KT* 3, July 1910, p. 121; 'Notice', *KT* 11, April 1918, p. 60.
23. 'The International Council of Nurses', *KT* 19, January 1926, p. 18; 'New Zealand Trained Nurses' Association Annual Report', *KT* 19, October 1926, p. 152.
24. See, for example, the argument in Maxine Alterio, 'Memoirs of First World War nurses: Making meaning of traumatic experiences', PhD thesis, Victoria University of Wellington, 2013.
25. For a detailed discussion of nursing folklore and narratives of personal stories in backblocks nursing, see Pamela J. Wood, 'The nurse's odyssey: The professional folktale in New Zealand backblocks nurses' stories, 1910–1915', *Nursing Inquiry* 16, no. 2, 2009, pp. 111–21.
26. See Lauri Honko, 'The problem of defining myth', *Scripta Instituti Donneriani Aboensis* 6, 1972, pp. 7–19.
27. 'Nursing sister, world traveller, writer, renews acquaintances with Dannevirke', *Dannevirke Evening News*, 3 May 1958, n.p.; 'Legion of Friends greet Bridget Tothill', *Northland Age*, 13 May 1958, n.p., Bridget Madge Isobel Francois, 1902–1992: Diaries and Papers–Scrapbook–MSY–6766, ATL. Bridget Ristori's married names were Tothill and Francois. She wrote under her original name, Ristori. In addition to bristling at errors in newspaper articles, she was annoyed when she received her autobiography, *Patients in My Care*, from the London publisher, as they had changed the title, and their other changes had caused 40 'silly errors'. Bridget Ristori,

'Talk given to coffee and book morning, August 1968', Bridget Madge Isobel Francois, 1901–1992; Diaries and Papers, Loose material removed from MSY–6766, MS–Papers–9556–1, ATL.

28. 'The imperial spirit in nursing', *Australasian Nurses' Journal* 6, October 1908, pp. 353–54.

29. Clare Midgley, Alison Twells and Julie Carlier, eds, *Women in Transnational History: Connecting the local and the global* (Abingdon: Routledge, 2016), p. 4.

30. See, for example, James T. Patterson, 'How do we write the history of disease?', *Health and History* 1, 1998, pp. 5–29.

31. The history of New Zealand psychiatric nursing has been addressed by other scholars. See, for example, Kate Prebble and Linda Bryder, 'Gender and class tensions between psychiatric nurses and the general nursing profession in mid-twentieth-century New Zealand', *Contemporary Nurse* 30, no. 2, 2008, pp. 181–95.

32. For a detailed history of Plunket services and nursing, see Linda Bryder, '"Babies of the Empire": The evolution of infant welfare services in New Zealand and Britain in the first half of the twentieth century', in *The Practice of Reform in Health, Medicine, and Science, 1500–2000: Essays for Charles Webster*, eds M. Pelling and S. Mandelbrote (Abingdon: Routledge, 2017), pp. 247–62.

33. Ākenehi Hei, 'Nursing amongst the Maoris', *KT* 3, July 1910, pp. 103–4.

34. 'More needed, trained male nurses', *EP*, 2 August 1945, p. 3.

35. Margaret Brown, Diana Masters and Barbara Smith, *Nurses of Auckland: The history of the general nursing programme in the Auckland School of Nursing* (Auckland: Margaret Brown, Diana Masters and Barbara Smith, 1994), p. 129.

36. As the history of the professional organisation has already been addressed by others, this book explains its work only in relation to the nursing culture. See, for example, Margaret Gibson Smith and Yvonne T. Shadbolt, *Objects and Outcomes: New Zealand Nurses' Association, 1909–1983* (Wellington: New Zealand Nurses' Association, 1984); Mary Ellen O'Connor, *Freed to Care, Proud to Nurse: 100 years of the New Zealand Nurses Organisation* (Wellington: Steele Roberts, 2010).

37. For more comprehensive histories of wartime nursing, see, for example, Anna Rogers, *While You're Away: New Zealand nurses at war, 1899–1948* (Auckland: Auckland University Press, 2003); Sheryl McNabb, *100 Years New Zealand Military Nursing: New Zealand Army Nursing Service; Royal New Zealand Nursing Corps, 1915–2015* (Hawke's Bay: Sheryl McNabb, 2015); Kay Morris Matthews, *Recovery: Women's overseas service in World War I* (Gisborne: Tairāwhiti Museum, 2017).

Chapter 1. Narrating a history

1. See Mary Lambie, 'The prevention of endemic goitre in New Zealand by a public health nurse', *Canadian Nurse* 21, no. 9, 1925, pp. 464–66.

2. Dominika Pietzcker, M. Berg-Domas and Mary I. Lambie, 'Report of the Health Statistics Committee presented at the Congress in London, July 1937', International Council of Nurses, London, 1937.

3. Mary Lambie, *My Story: Memoirs of a New Zealand nurse* (Christchurch: N.M. Peryer, 1956); *AJHR*, H-31, 1939, pp. 56–72. In contrast to Lambie, the director of the Division of Public Hygiene, T.R. Ritchie, wrote only three brief paragraphs.

4. Lambie's 1939 account was an official report to the government. Three years earlier, she had described the role of the first three chief nurses in a published article. See M.I. Lambie, 'The work of a

nurse in a Government Department: The Nursing Division of the Department of Health, New Zealand, 1936', typescript, in SANS papers, 24/1/11, ANZ. At the end of this typescript is a notation in red ink: 'Extract from "The International Nursing Review", Vol X No 4 1936'. Hester Maclean, the second chief nurse (1906–23) had written a historical account of New Zealand nursing for an international book and a 'history and reminiscences' when she had been retired for nine years. Hester Maclean, 'New Zealand', in *A History of Nursing*, vol. 4, ed. L. Dock (New York: G.P. Putnam's Sons, 1912), pp. 189–222; Hester Maclean, *Nursing in New Zealand: History and reminiscences* (Wellington: Tolan, 1932).

5. [Mary Lambie], *Historical Development of Nursing in New Zealand, 1840–1946* (Wellington: Department of Health, 1946); [Mary Lambie], *Historical Development of Nursing in New Zealand, 1840–1950* (Wellington: Department of Health, 1950), in SANS papers, 20/2/30, ANZ.
6. 'A wealth of information: Facts relating to our nursing history which every nurse should know', *NZNJ* 53, no. 7, July 1960, pp. 8–17.
7. *AJHR*, 1939, H-31, p. 57.
8. Catherine Bishop, *Women Mean Business: Colonial businesswomen in New Zealand* (Dunedin: Otago University Press, 2019).
9. As one example among many, see Advertisement, *HBH*, 17 October 1868, p. 1.
10. Advertisement, *ES*, 20 January 1879, p. 3.
11. Advertisement, *AS*, 2 March 1888, p. 1.
12. See, for example, Advertisement, *ES*, 22 February 1879, p. 3.
13. See, for example, Advertisement, *ES*, 4 June 1877, p. 3; Advertisement, *ES*, 21 December 1877, p. 3.
14. 'The hospital wardsman', *Taranaki Herald*, 19 June 1899, p. 2; Untitled, *Taranaki Herald*, 13 June 1899, p. 2.
15. Untitled, *Taranaki Herald*, 22 May 1894, p. 2; Untitled, *Taranaki Herald*, 14 September 1895, p. 2.
16. D. Macdonald Wilson, *A Hundred Years of Healing: Wellington Hospital, 1847–1947* (Wellington: A.H. & A.W. Reed, 1948), p. 22.
17. John Angus, *A History of the Otago Hospital Board and its Predecessors* (Dunedin: Otago Hospital Board, 1984), p. 82.
18. See, as just one example, the correspondence and editorial comment relating to a wardsman at Dunedin Hospital, starting with a letter to the editor from William Gay, 'The Dunedin Hospital', *ODT*, 31 January 1889, p. 3.
19. *AJHR*, 1939, H-31, p. 56.
20. See, for example, reports of Dunstan and Greymouth Hospitals for reports of good care, and Wellington Hospital for a report of rough care. *AJHR*, 1883, H-3a.
21. *AJHR*, 1884, H-7a, p. 1.
22. *AJHR*, 1887, H-19, p. 23.
23. It appears that Mrs Bernard Moore's qualifications for the position were two home nursing certificates, gained in London.
24. Emily Lloyd Lees became matron at Napier Hospital in 1888; Lilian Heath at Masterton in 1893; Ellen Dougherty at Palmerston North in 1897; Frances Payne at Christchurch, Southland, then Christchurch again in 1898 (a position she held until 1900 and again from 1904 to 1906); Ellen Gosling at Reefton in 1902 and Nelson in 1909; Edith Rennell at the Rotorua Sanatorium in 1905; Cecilia McKenny at Whanganui in 1906; Jean Todd at Timaru in 1906; and Elizabeth (Katherine) Berry at Napier in 1909. Augusta Godfrey stayed at Wellington and was its matron from 1889 to 1998. Laurie H. Barber and Roy J. Towers, *Wellington Hospital 1847–1976* (Wellington: Wellington Hospital Board, 1976), pp. 139–45.
25. Angus, *History of the Otago Hospital Board*. See also Anne Smillie, 'The end

of tranquillity? An exploration of some organisational and societal factors that generated discord upon the introduction of trained nurses into New Zealand hospitals, 1885–1914', MA (Applied) research paper, Victoria University of Wellington, 2003, pp. 39–41.
26. Patricia A. Sargison, 'Gender, class and power: Ideologies and conflict during the transition to trained female nursing at two New Zealand hospitals, 1889–95', *Women's History Review* 6, no. 2, 1997, pp. 183–200.
27. 'Female nursing in hospitals', *ODT*, 10 April 1890, p. 3; Dr Grace's opinion and *Press* comment reported in 'Hospital nurses', *ME*, 22 April 1890, p. 3.
28. Angus, *History of the Otago Hospital Board*.
29. Sargison, 'Gender, class and power', pp. 183, 188.
30. Rosemary Weir, *Educating Nurses in Scotland: A history of innovation and change, 1950–2000* (Penzance: Hypatia Trust/Royal College of Nursing Archive, 2004), p. 5.
31. Angus, *History of the Otago Hospital Board*.
32. This description of the conditions of probationer training is based on Angus, *History of the Otago Hospital Board*, pp. 88–89, 94.
33. Susan McGann, *The Battle of the Nurses: A study of eight women who influenced the development of professional nursing, 1880–1930* (London: Scutari Press, 1992), p. 9.
34. 'The Private Hospital', *The Cyclopedia of New Zealand, Wellington Provincial District* (Wellington: Cyclopedia, 1897), p. 493. For a discussion of Eva Godfray as a historical figure, see Pamela J. Wood, 'Understanding and evaluating historical sources in nursing history research', *Nursing Praxis in New Zealand* 27, no. 1, 2011, pp. 25–33.
35. 'Local and general', *HS*, 6 February 1897, p. 2. The hospital was originally named for its county and hospital board district, Waipawa, which was also a town, but the hospital was located in the neighbouring town of Waipukurau and eventually took that town's name. The name used in official reports is used here.
36. *AJHR*, 1898, H-22, p. 32.
37. J.O.C. Neill, *Grace Neill: The story of a noble woman* (Christchurch: N.M. Peryer, 1961).
38. *AJHR*, 1895, H-22, p. 2; *AJHR*, 1939, H-31, p. 57.
39. Neill, *Grace Neill*, pp. 1–2. The comment about the hat is from 'An appreciation', *KT* 20, April 1927, p. 71. A piece by Agnes Bennett, 'Tribute, an excerpt from the *International Nursing Review*, 1927', was included in material provided by the New Zealand Registered Nurses' Association to schools of nursing for an essay competition on the subject of Grace Neill in 1945.
40. Maclean also noted the swiftness of change that was possible in New Zealand. See Maclean, *Nursing in New Zealand*, p. 42. On factions in British nursing, see McGann, *The Battle of the Nurses*.
41. Grace Neill, 'The professional training and status of nurses', *Nursing Record and Hospital World* 23, 15 July 1899, p. 47.
42. See Lavinia Dock's comments in 'Discussion', *Nursing Record and Hospital World* 23, 15 July 1899, pp. 48–49.
43. Sargison, 'Gender, class and power', p. 194.
44. Matron's Annual Letter, April 1914, p. 4, RLH/LH/N/7/1/21, Royal London Hospital Archives. See also McGann, *The Battle of the Nurses*, p. 33.
45. 'An appreciation', p. 71.
46. Grace Neill, letter to Agnes Bennett, 16 February 1909, Agnes Bennett papers, MS–Papers–1346, folder 211, ATL; also cited by Margaret Tennant, 'Grace Neill', in *The Book of New Zealand Women*, eds C. Macdonald, M. Penfold and B. Williams (Wellington: Bridget Williams Books, 1991), pp. 468–69.

47. S.E. Maude, 'District nursing', *KT* 1, October 1908, pp. 118–19.
48. E. Somers Cocks, *A Friend in Need: Nurse Maude, her life and work* (Christchurch: Nurse Maude District Nursing Association, 1950).
49. Maude, 'District nursing', p. 118.
50. Untitled, *KT* 6, January 1913, p. 11.
51. On the question of poverty in the New World, see, for example, 'Sunless lives', *EP*, 15 June 1904, p. 5. As James Belich has explained, many settlers were lured by 'colonising crusaders' and migrated to New Zealand to escape poverty and maximise their chance of a better life in the colony. James Belich, *Paradise Reforged: A history of the New Zealanders from the 1880s to the year 2000* (Auckland: Allen Lane/Penguin, 2001), p. 21. Settlers regarded the emergence of poverty, especially in the Long Depression of the 1880s and 1890s, as an Old World evil reproduced in the New.
52. *AJHR*, 1939, H-22, p. 57.
53. Anna Rogers, *While You're Away: New Zealand nurses at war, 1899–1948* (Auckland: Auckland University Press, 2003), p. 16.
54. 'Local and general', *HS*, 26 February 1900, p. 2; 'Napier Borough Council', *HBH*, 4 October 1900, p. 4.
55. 'Waipawa', *HBH*, 9 March 1900, p. 3; 'Waipawa', *HBH*, 20 March 1900, p. 4.
56. *Star*, 13 August 1900, p. 1.
57. *TH*, 18 September 1900, p. 3.
58. 'Waipawa Hospital Board', *HBH*, 5 March 1904, p. 4.
59. *Waipukurau Hospital Centennial, 1879–1979, Souvenir Booklet* (Waipukurau: Waipawa Hospital Board, 1979), p. 29.
60. *AJHR*, 1939, H-22, p. 58.
61. *AJHR*, 1939, H-31, p. 59.
62. Maclean, *Nursing in New Zealand*, p. 54.
63. Ibid., pp. 39–40.
64. 'New appointment in the Hospitals and Charitable Aid Department', *KT* 1, July 1908, p. 80.
65. *AJHR*, 1939, H-22, p. 59.
66. *AJHR*, 1898, E-2, p. 12. For a more detailed description of the scholarship scheme, see Pamela J. Wood, 'Efficient preachers of the gospel of health: The 1898 scheme for educating Maori nurses', *Nursing Praxis in New Zealand* 7, no. 1, 1992, pp. 12–21. See also A.H. McKegg, '"Ministering angels": The government backblock nursing service and the Maori health nurses, 1909–1939', MA thesis, University of Auckland, 1991; A.H. McKegg, 'The Maori health nursing scheme: An experiment in autonomous health care', *New Zealand Journal of History* 26, no. 2, 1992, pp. 145–60.
67. Hāmiora Hei, 'Maori girls and nursing', Papers and addresses read before the Second Conference of the Te Aute College Students' Association, December 1897, Napier, 1898, pp. 30–31.
68. Wood, 'Efficient preachers'.
69. *AJHR*, 1899, E-2, p. 14.
70. *AJHR*, 1905, E-2, p. 14.
71. Hēni Whangapirita had previously been at Napier Hospital under the day-pupil scholarship scheme. Ākenehi Hei also worked there from 1901.
72. Marie Burgess, 'Pritchard, Ethel', from the Dictionary of New Zealand Biography: www.teara.govt.nz/en/biographies/5p38/pritchard-ethel. See also Kay Morris Matthews, *Recovery: Women's overseas service in World War One* (Gisborne: Tairāwhiti Museum, 2017).
73. *AJHR*, 1939, H-22, p. 59.
74. The society was initially known as the Society for Promoting the Health of Women and Children but became more familiarly known as the Plunket Society.
75. *AJHR*, 1939, H-22, p. 59.
76. 'The health of the Maoris, measures being taken', *KT* 4, July 1911, p. 108; 'Notes from the hospitals and personal items', *KT* 4, July 1911, p. 136.
77. *AJHR*, 1939, H-22, p. 58.
78. On Ethel Taylor, see Burgess, 'Pritchard,

Ethel'. On Williams, see Flora Straessle, 'Agnes Wood, one of the First Fifty', *Nursing Praxis in New Zealand* 13, no. 1, 1998, pp. 47–49. Both are also described in Morris Matthews, *Recovery*.
79. 'Notes from the hospitals and personal items', *KT* 7, April 1914, pp. 99–103, item on p. 100.
80. *AJHR*, 1939, H-22, p. 59.
81. Geoffrey Rice identified 37 nurses who died in New Zealand during the pandemic. This was also the figure given in contemporary accounts. See Geoffrey W. Rice, *Black November: The 1918 influenza pandemic in New Zealand*, 2nd edn. (Christchurch: Canterbury University Press, 2005). However, further research has identified five more. This does not include those described as nurses in newspaper lists of deaths, unless their professional status could be verified from other sources.
82. For a detailed account of this proposed scheme, see Pamela J. Wood, 'Managing boundaries between professional and lay nursing following the influenza pandemic, 1918–1919: Insights for professional resilience today?' *Journal of Clinical Nursing* 26, 2017, pp. 805–12. The comment about 'two grades of nursing' came initially from Dr Thomas Valintine, the inspector-general of hospitals and chief health officer, who disliked the notion. See 'Nursing the sick, the woman's part, modern ignorance deplored', *EP*, 12 March 1919, p. 3. Maclean's objections can be seen in 'Training of nursing aids on home service', *KT* 12, April 1919, pp. 73–81.
83. *AJHR*, 1939, H-22, p. 61. The same comment held in the later editions of the report.
84. For an account of nursing at this hospital, see Michael Belgrave, *The Mater: A history of Auckland's Mercy Hospital, 1900–2000* (Palmerston North: Dunmore Press, 2000).
85. See, as just one example, the farewell to Isabella Fraser at Dunedin Hospital: 'Farewell and presentation to Miss Fraser', *KT* 4, April 1911, pp. 86–87.
86. 'Nurses' superannuation', *ODT*, 3 September 1924, p. 4.
87. Beryl Smedley, 'Ricky's story: The memoirs of Amy Rickman', MS–Papers–4404, ATL, p. 14.
88. Bishop, *Women Mean Business*. In the twentieth century, nurses who bought or established private hospitals were astute businesswomen catering expertly to a market need.
89. Straessle, 'Agnes Wood'.
90. Smedley, 'Ricky's story', pp. 18, 20, 21, 24.
91. In the 1930s nurses in training were often called *pupil nurses*. In the 1940s the term *student nurse* was sometimes used.
92. For a detailed description of the response to the nursing shortage, see Victoria Cullens, 'Not just a shortage of girls: The shortage of nurses in post World War II New Zealand, 1945–1955', MA (Applied) thesis, Victoria University of Wellington, 2001.
93. *AJHR*, 1939, H-31, p. 64.
94. [Lambie], *Historical Development of Nursing in New Zealand, 1840–1950*, p. 24.
95. Smedley, 'Ricky's story'.
96. Rogers, *While You're Away*, p. 200.
97. [Lambie], *Historical Development of Nursing in New Zealand, 1840–1950*, p. 32.
98. For a detailed discussion of the evolution of research in nursing, see Pamela J. Wood and Katherine Nelson, 'Striving for best practice: Standardising New Zealand nursing procedures, 1930–60', *Journal of Clinical Nursing* 22, nos. 21–22, 2013, pp. 3217–24; Pamela J. Wood and Katherine Nelson, 'The journal *Kai Tiaki*'s role in developing research capability in New Zealand nursing, 1908–1959', *Nursing Praxis in New Zealand* 29, no. 1, 2013, pp. 12–22.

99. [Lambie], *Historical Development of Nursing in New Zealand, 1840–1950*, p. 35.
100. Smedley, 'Ricky's story'.
101. Ibid.
102. [Lambie], *Historical Development of Nursing in New Zealand 1840–1950*, p. 35.
103. Marjorie Chambers, *My Life in Nursing: Christchurch Hospital, 1936–1966* (Tauranga: Moana Press, 1988), p. 80.
104. Lawrence Jones, 'Myth and anti-myth in literary responses to the centennial', in *Creating a National Spirit: Celebrating New Zealand's centennial*, ed. William Renwick (Wellington: Victoria University Press, 2004), pp. 207–09.

Chapter 2. Nurse training

1. Geoff Conly, *A Case History: The Hawke's Bay Hospital Board, 1876–1989* (Napier: Hawke's Bay Area Health Board, 1992), pp. 36–37.
2. Colleen Williams, *All for a Medal: The nursing memoirs of Colleen Turbet Williams* (Auckland: Self-published, 2006), pp. 9, 15. I am very grateful to Colleen Williams for her generous permission to quote and relate stories from her book.
3. Williams, *All for a Medal*, p. 78.
4. As there was interest in what was happening in New Zealand, Neill sent the first syllabus to the International Council of Nurses meeting in 1904, and it was then published in Britain. The state final examination in December 1902 was published in Australia. 'Nursing education in New Zealand', *BJN* 33, 10 September 1904, pp. 209–10; 'State registration of nurses', *Una* 1, no. 1, pp. 8–9. Jan Rodgers incorrectly states that the first state final examination was held in December 1903, perhaps because copies of the 1902 examination do not seem to be extant in New Zealand. Jan A. Rodgers, 'Nursing education in New Zealand, 1883–1930: The persistence of the Nightingale ethos', MA thesis, Massey University, 1985, p. 31.
5. Waikato Hospital was the first in New Zealand to adopt the block system. D.I. Buchanan, 'The "block" system of teaching', *NZNJ* 32, February 1939, pp. 48–49; E.R. Bridges, 'The block and study day systems of organising practical and theoretical work', *NZNJ* 40, no. 1, 1947, pp. 7–10.
6. 'Pioneer nurses', *ODT*, 24 August 1926, p. 7.
7. 'The Auckland Hospital Commission', *NZMJ* 3, no. 12, 1904, pp. 443–592.
8. *AJHR*, 1905, H-22, p. 4.
9. Rosemary I. Weir, 'The lecture notes of two pupil nurses of the preliminary training school at Glasgow Royal Infirmary', *International History of Nursing Journal* 1, no. 4, 1996, pp. 49–60; Susan McGann, *The Battle of the Nurses: A study of eight women who influenced the development of professional nursing, 1880–1930* (London: Scutari Press, 1992).
10. Untitled, *ODT*, 19 April 1907, p. 4.
11. *AJHR*, 1919, H-33, p. 10.
12. Cited in Margaret McDougall and Annette Stevenson, 'The interdependence of nurse training and nursing service', in *New Countries and Old Medicine*, eds L. Bryder and D. Dow (Auckland: Pyramid, 1995), pp. 285–90. On teacher training at that time, see Roger Openshaw and Teresa Ball, 'New Zealand teacher education: Progression or prescription?' *Education Research and Perspectives* 33, no. 2, 2006, pp. 102–23.
13. Dorothy Alice Ford, *Journey from Stranger's Rest* (Wellington: Daphne Brasell Associates, 1989), p. 108.
14. H. Maclean, 'The conditions of nursing in New Zealand', *Australasian Nurses' Journal* 5, no. 9, 1907, p. 274. This was the journal of the Australasian Trained Nurses' Association. Despite the name, it was a Sydney-based association that covered all Australian states except Victoria and did not include New Zealand.
15. In her account of New Zealand nursing history for a book compiled by the

American nurse leader Lavinia Dock, Maclean doubted the value of the eight-hour day. Dock commented in a footnote, 'As overwork in hospitals is a grave problem in many countries, it seems a pity that this fortunate land should find its nurses critical of the eight-hour hospital day. It probably only needs some modification as to change of shifts.' Hester Maclean, 'New Zealand', in *A History of Nursing*, vol. 4, ed. L. Dock (New York: G.P. Putnam's Sons, 1912), p. 220.
16. As just two of many examples, see Ford, *Journey from Stranger's Rest*, p. 113; Bridget Madge Isabel Francois [Ristori], 1902–1992, Diaries, MS–Papers–10108-004, ATL.
17. See for example, comments by the Hon. C.J. Parr, minister of public health in 1921, in 'One day off per week', *KT* 14, April 1921, p. 97; 'Conference of hospital matrons', *KT* 16, July 1927, pp. 137–41.
18. See for example, 'Training of nurses', *KT* 12, April 1919, pp. 85–87; 'Probationary period of nurses in training', *KT* 20, January 1927, p. 30.
19. See, for example, 'A criticism of the training of nurses', *NZNJ* 29, March 1936, pp. 6–10. See also the flurry of letters in response.
20. See, for example, Bridges, 'The block and study day system'.
21. Isabella Fraser suggested an extension of the contract to the Dunedin Hospital Trustees. 'Hospital trustees', *ODT*, 18 April 1907, p. 2. It was introduced in the early 1920s when Edith Tennent was matron. See Nurses' personal records, Dunedin Hospital, DAHI records, D262, 9189, Dunedin Office, ANZ.
22. 'The nursing service', *NZNJ* 31, March 1938, pp. 61–69.
23. Williams, *All for a Medal*, p. 39.
24. Mary Douglas, *Purity and Danger: An analysis of concepts of pollution and taboo* (London: Routledge & Kegan Paul, 1966); Mary Douglas, *Implicit Meanings: Essays in anthropology* (London: Routledge & Kegan Paul, 1975); Julia Kristeva, *Powers of Horror: An essay on abjection* (New York: Columbia University Press, 1982); Pamela J. Wood, *Dirt: Filth and decay in a New World Arcadia* (Auckland: Auckland University Press, 2005).The term *matter out of place* is often attributed to Douglas, but it was well-known in the nineteenth century.
25. F. Gill, 'The practical teacher, ward sisters as teachers', *KT* 22, October 1929, pp. 181–85, quotation on p. 184.
26. J.K. Watson, *A Handbook for Nurses* (London: Scientific Press, 1899), p. 61. The same statement also appeared in later editions.
27. Margaret Macnab, cited in Helen Campbell, *Looking Back: A history of the Christchurch School of Nursing, 1891–1987* (Christchurch: Nursing History Christchurch Charitable Trust, 1997), p. 15; Helen Gilmour-Jones, 'Reintroducing Miss Margaret Macnab', *Nursing Praxis in New Zealand* 7, no. 3, 1992, pp. 40–42.
28. Mary Clark, 'Nursing – as it was in my day', *Auckland-Waikato Historical Journal* 62, April 1993, p. 26.
29. Marjorie Chambers, *My Life in Nursing: Christchurch Hospital, 1936–1966* (Tauranga: Moana Press, 1988), p. 14.
30. Chambers, *My Life in Nursing*, p. 21.
31. Macnab, cited in Campbell, *Looking Back*, p. 15.
32. J.G. Furness, *Wairau Hospital: 100 years of caring* (Blenheim: Marlborough Hospital Board, 1978), p. 64.
33. 'Probationer nurses', letter to the editor, *ODT*, 27 January 1924, p. 5.
34. Bridget Ristori, 'Even nursing changes', *New Zealand Dairy Exporter*, 1 June 1957, p. 100. Bridget Madge Isobel Francois [née Ristori], 1902–1992: Diaries and Papers–Scrapbook–MSY–6766, ATL.
35. Macnab, cited in Campbell, *Looking Back*, p. 19; Gilmour-Jones, 'Reintroducing Miss Margaret Macnab'.

NOTES: CHAPTER 2. NURSE TRAINING

36. Sandra Main, 'My nursing days at Waikato Hospital, 1929–1934', *Auckland-Waikato Historical Journal* 54, April 1989, p. 20.
37. Ford, *Journey from Stranger's Rest*, pp. 106–07.
38. Sonja Davies, *Bread and Roses: Sonja Davies, her story* (Masterton: Fraser Books, 1984), p. 50. I am grateful to Ian F. Grant and Diane Grant of Fraser Books, Masterton, for their generous permission to quote and relate stories from this book.
39. Ford, *Journey from Stranger's Rest*, p. 114.
40. Williams, *All for a Medal*, p. 57.
41. Ford, *Journey from Stranger's Rest*, p. 124.
42. For an earlier discussion of this topic, see Pamela J. Wood, 'Supporting or sabotaging the surgeon's heroic efforts: Portrayals of the surgical nurse's role in preventing wound sepsis, 1895–1935', *Journal of Clinical Nursing* 18, 2009, pp. 2739–46. For a transnational description and detailed explanation, see Pamela J. Wood, 'Pus, pedagogy and practice: How "dirt" shaped surgical nurse training and hierarchies of practice, 1900–1935', in *Germs and Governance: The past, present and future of hospital infection, prevention and control*, eds A.M. Rafferty, M. Dupree and F. Bound Alberti (Manchester: Manchester University Press, 2021), pp. 81–103.
43. Wood, *Dirt*. On the olive-green colouring of the urine as a sign of carbolic acid poisoning, see, for example, Watson, *A Handbook for Nurses*, p. 171.
44. T.M. Group and J. Roberts, *Nursing, Physician Control, and the Medical Monopoly: Historical perspectives on gendered inequality in roles, rights, and range of practice* (Bloomington: Indiana University Press, 2001); J.A. Ashley, *Hospitals, Paternalism, and the Role of the Nurse* (New York: Teachers College Press, 1976); B. Melosh, 'The Physician's Hand': Work culture and conflict in American nursing* (Philadelphia: Temple University Press, 1982). For an overview and critique of such historical interpretations, see Julie Fairman, '"Not all nurses are good, not all doctors are bad ...", essay review', *Bulletin of the History of Medicine* 78, 2004, pp. 451–60.
45. A. Miles, *Surgical Ward Work and Nursing: A handbook for nurses and others* (London: Scientific Press, 1921), pp. 191, 31.
46. A.N. McGregor, *A System of Surgical Nursing* (Glasgow: David Bryce, 1905), p. 17.
47. 'The surgical nurse', *Australasian Nurses' Journal* 21, 1923, p. 264.
48. R. Howard, *Surgical Nursing and the Principles of Surgery for Nurses* (London: Edward Arnold, 1908), p. vii; H.J. Paterson, 'Lecture: The preparation for and after-treatment of abdominal operations', *BJN* 85, March 1937, pp. 68–69.
49. 'Operating room procedures for nurses', *BJN* 85, March 1937, p. 80.
50. The most collegial view was evident in a textbook by a Sydney surgeon. H.C. Rutherford Darling, *Surgical Nursing and After-Treatment: A handbook for nurses and others* (London: J. & A. Churchill, 1917) and later editions. Another surgical nursing textbook used in New Zealand omitted any mention of the nurse's role: F. Wilson Harlow, ed., *Modern Surgery for Nurses* (London: William Heinemann, 1948). No textbooks on surgical nursing written by New Zealand doctors appeared until 1952, with the publication of John Cairney, *Surgery for Students of Nursing* (Christchurch: N.M Peryer, 1952).
51. 'Second lecture delivered before Wellington Branch, N.Z.T.N.A., by J. McNaughton Christie, M.D.', *KT* 7, January 1914, pp. 7–18.
52. Ford, *Journey from Stranger's Rest*, p. 109.
53. Louisa Corkill to Miss Kimbell, recollecting her training, 2 November 1964, Hawke's Bay District Health Board Library, Hastings.
54. See, for example, Sidney Wilding, notebook, 1937–1940, ARC2008–136,

Puke Ariki; Nurse's notebook, Wellington Hospital, 1939–1942; Dr Max Herz, 'Asepsis', *KT* 1, July 1908, pp. 85–86.
55. Pamela J. Wood, 'The enduring issue of assessing nursing knowledge: Surgical nursing final examinations in Australia and New Zealand, 1905–1930', *Contemporary Nurse* 32, nos. 1–2, 2009, pp. 109–22.
56. 'An investigation concerning nursing technique', *NZNJ* 27, July 1934, pp. 105–06. Biniodide of mercury and perchloride of mercury (corrosive sublimate) were irritating to the hands and could cause eczema. If absorbed through raw surfaces, they were poisonous. Signs of perchloride of mercury poisoning included bloodstained diarrhoea and copious saliva. Nurses were still advised to use it in the 1920s and, as with Lambie's study, in the 1930s. See Darling, *Surgical Nursing and After-Treatment*, p. 133; A. Millicent Ashdown, *A Complete System of Nursing* (London: J.M. Dent & Sons, 1939), p. 46. However, Ashdown, a nurse, recommended that nurses use a hand cream and gave the ingredients for one.
57. Alison Robinson, ed., *Stratford Hospital Memories* (Stratford: Thurlstone Press, 2001), p. 12.
58. 'An investigation concerning nursing technique'.
59. 'Wound dressing technique: Research by the Education Committee of the New Zealand Registered Nurses' Association', *NZNJ* 35, February 1942, pp. 39–41.
60. Nursing Education Committee, New Zealand Registered Nurses' Association, 'Report on the survey undertaken re septic fingers (nursing staff)', c. 1945–46, New Zealand Nurses' Association records, 79–032–09/9, ATL.
61. 'Handwashing technique', *NZNJ* 41, February 1948, pp. 8–9.
62. A minimum height was not specified in regulations. However, Edna Hall was not accepted for training at Dunedin Hospital in 1931 as her height was only 4′ 11¾″ (151cm). She reapplied in 1934, when her height was 5′ 1″, but was again declined. Meanwhile, she had gained experience working at Dunstan and Middlemarch hospitals. When she reapplied in 1935, the Dunedin matron said that if Hall worked well at Middlemarch for a year, she would consider giving her a trial. Hall proved her worth and successfully trained at Dunedin Hospital from November 1936. Nurses' personal records, Dunedin Hospital, DAHI records, D347, 9189, Dunedin Office, ANZ.
63. 'Preliminary school', *Wellington Hospital Nurses' Journal* 1, no. 5, 1936, p. 25. See also Dr A.R. Thorne, medical superintendent, Wellington Hospital, report to the Policy and Finance Committee, June 1938, History of Nursing – Wellington Hospital folder, Wellington Hospital Nursing Archive, Capital and Coast District Health Board, Wellington.
64. Even with curriculum changes in the 1930s and 1940s, psychology was not included, mainly because of the difficulty of finding suitable lecturers and lack of curriculum time available. It was felt that the effects of illness on behaviour could be learned 'in the daily round of the ward'. 'The nursing curriculum', editorial, *NZNJ* 38, August 1945, pp. 179–81. However, social and preventive aspects of disease were introduced with the curriculum review in 1945. See Pamela J. Wood, 'Nursing the patient, the room and the doctor: Assessing New Zealand nurses' practical capability, 1900–1945', *Nurse Education Today* 31, 2011, pp. 140–44.
65. Williams, *All for a Medal*, p. 30.
66. Nurse's answer in the elementary nursing and hygiene examination, May 1948, untitled collection of howlers, 1945–55, History of nursing – Wellington Hospital folder, Wellington Hospital Nursing Archive, Capital and Coast District Health Board.

67. Nurse's notebook, Wellington Hospital, 1939–1942.
68. State examination papers, *KT* 8, July 1915, p. 151.
69. Quoted in Ashdown, *Complete System of Nursing*, p. 181.
70. Williams, *All for a Medal*, p. 38.
71. M.S. Smith, 'Introducing Louisa Dixon', *Nursing Praxis in New Zealand* 14, no.1, 1999, p. 48.
72. Williams, *All for a Medal*, p. 35.
73. Ford, *Journey from Stranger's Rest*, pp. 117, 118.
74. Ford, *Journey from Stranger's Rest*, pp. 114, 117.
75. Robinson, ed., *Stratford Hospital Memories*, p. 173.
76. Williams, *All for a Medal*, p. 41.
77. Furness, *Wairau Hospital*, p. 40.
78. Anne L. McDonald and C. Tulloch, *Wellington Hospital: Educating nurses for more than a century 1883–1991* (Wellington: Wellington Hospital Nurses' Reunion Committee, c. 1992), p. 10.
79. Robinson, ed., *Stratford Hospital Memories*, p. 14.
80. David Scott, ed., *Middlemore Memories: The first 50 years of Middlemore Hospital* ([Manukau]: South Auckland Health, 1997), p. 21.
81. Ashdown, *A Complete System of Nursing*, p. 3.
82. This was a common assertion. For one example, see Bridget Ristori, 'My 36 years of nursing', (New Zealand) *Mirror*, February 1957, pp. 12–13, 71, in Bridget Madge Isobel Francois [née Ristori], 1902–1992: Diaries and Papers–Scrapbook–MSY–6766, ATL.
83. An analysis of medical papers in the state final examinations from 1907 to 1949 shows that questions on pneumonia represented 17 percent of all questions.
84. Ashdown, *A Complete System of Nursing*, p. 250.
85. Ford, *Journey from Stranger's Rest*, p. 115.
86. 'Nursing in the 1930s', *Spectrum* #800, 1993, Radio New Zealand.
87. Watson, *A Handbook for Nurses*, 1899, p. 111. This statement was repeated in successive editions.
88. Davies, *Bread and Roses*, p. 47.
89. Ford, *Journey from Stranger's Rest*, p. 114.
90. These preventive measures were detailed in textbooks and nurses' notebooks. See, for example, Ashdown, *A Complete System of Nursing*, pp. 16–17; Sidney Wilding, notebook, 1937–40, ARC2008–136, Puke Ariki; Nurse's notebook, Wellington Hospital, 1939–1942.
91. Ashdown, *A Complete System of Nursing*, pp. 17–18.
92. Evelyn C. Pearce, *A General Textbook of Nursing* (London: Faber & Faber, 1942), p. 107.
93. 'Nursing education in New Zealand', *BJN* 33, 10 September 1904, pp. 209–10; Rodgers, 'Nursing education in New Zealand', p. 108.
94. Rodgers, 'Nursing education in New Zealand'. The thesis' subtitle was 'The persistence of the Nightingale ethos'.
95. Chambers, *My Life in Nursing*, p. 9.
96. Nurse's notebook, Wellington Hospital, 1939–42.
97. Wellington Hospital, Notices, unnumbered memo, c. 1940s, History of Nursing – Wellington Hospital folder, Wellington Hospital Nursing Archive.
98. Main, 'My nursing days', p. 22.
99. Ford, *Journey from Stranger's Rest*, pp. 106, 108–09.
100. Campbell, *Looking Back*, p. 17.
101. This was an internationally accepted definition. For example, it appeared in a speech by Dr Kirkpatrick, Registrar of the Royal College of Physicians in Ireland, which was published in the *Journal of the American Medical Association*, 13 February 1915, and reprinted in *KT* five months later: 'Nursing ethics', *KT* 8, July 1915, p. 148.
102. 'Nursing ethics', *KT* 15, November 1922,

pp. 214–15; Ashdown, *A Complete System of Nursing*, p. 1; Anna C. Maxwell and Amy E. Pope, *Practical Nursing: A textbook for nurses* (New York: G.P. Putnam's Sons, 1914), pp. 16–18.
103. 'State examination of nurses', *KT* 14, October 1921, pp. 171–78, quotation on p. 173; 'Nursing ethics', *KT* 18, January 1925, p. 27.
104. Clark, 'Nursing – as it was in my day', p. 27.
105. Chambers, *My Life in Nursing*, p. 22.
106. Campbell, *Looking Back*, p. 69.
107. 'Nursing in the 1930s'.
108. Ford, *Journey from Stranger's Rest*, p. 107.
109. Bridget Ristori, *Nursing as a Career* (Kawakawa: Northland Gazette, 1947), p. 20.
110. Bridget Ristori, *Patients in My Care: The autobiography of a nurse* (London: Elek, 1967), p. 38.
111. 'Pioneer nurses', *ODT*, 24 August 1926, p. 7; Ristori, *Patients in My Care*, p. 39; Bridget Madge Isabel Francois [Ristori], 1902–1992, Diaries, MS–Papers–10108–004.
112. 'Address to nurses at the Wellington Hospital', *KT* 19, April 1926, p. 72.
113. This analysis was based on four editions of Watson, *A Handbook of Nursing*, 1899–1934; Maxwell and Pope, *Practical Nursing*, 1914; Ashdown, *A Complete System of Nursing*, 1934; and W.T. Gordon Pugh, *Practical Nursing*, 12th edn. (Edinburgh: William Blackwood, 1940). They were also recorded in nurses' notebooks. See, for example, Sidney Wilding, notebook, ARC2008-136, Puke Ariki.
114. This is based on an analysis of letters of reference supporting applications for training at Dunedin Hospital. Nurses' personal records, Dunedin Hospital, 1909–50, DAHI, D262 and D347, 9189, Dunedin Office, ANZ.
115. Agnes Innes, 'Nurses' examinations', *KT* 22, January 1929, p. 13.
116. Register of sisters, Napier Hospital, in Register and papers, Napier Hospital, Rose Macdonald, 68039a, Box ARI540, MTG Archive, Napier.
117. 'A criticism of the training of nurses', *NZNJ* 29, March 1936, pp. 6–10, quotation on p. 6.
118. Nurse's answer in the elementary nursing and hygiene examination, November 1948, untitled collection of howlers, 1945–55, History of nursing – Wellington Hospital folder, Wellington Hospital Nursing Archive.
119. 'Supplementary remits', *KT*, 22, April 1929, p. 55. Tennent might have been using Lavinia L. Dock and Isabel M. Stewart, *A Short History of Nursing from the Earliest Times to the Present Day* (New York: G.P. Putnam's Sons, 1920).
120. Sidney Wilding, notebook 1937–40, ARC2008–136, Puke Ariki; Nurse's notebook, Wellington Hospital, 1939–1942.
121. Sidney Wilding, notebook 1937–40, ARC2008–136, Puke Ariki; Nurse's notebook, Wellington Hospital, 1939–1942. See also M. Adelaide Nutting and Lavinia L. Dock, *A History of Nursing*, 4 vols (New York: G.P. Putnam's Sons, 1907–12).
122. 'The nursing curriculum', editorial, *NZNJ* 38, August 1945, pp. 179–81, quotation on p. 80.
123. 'The historic pageant and masque', *KT* 4, April 1911, pp. 71–74; 'The historic pageant and masque', *KT* 4, July 1911, pp. 103–07.
124. As just one example of each, see 'Hospital nurses', *NZH*, 16 February 1938, p. 5; 'Pageant of nursing', *GH*, 5 April 1944, p. 4; 'Nursing through the ages', *Press*, 1 April 1940, p. 2.
125. 'Recruiting appeal for nurses', *NA*, 23 January 1943, p. 2.
126. 'Evolution of nursing', *NZH*, 12 September 1936, p. 6 (Supplement).

Chapter 3. Becoming a nurse

1. Nurses' personal records, Dunedin Hospital, DAHI records, D262, 9189, Dunedin Office, ANZ.
2. Nurses' personal records, Dunedin Hospital, DAHI records, D347, 9189, Dunedin Office, ANZ.
3. This overview of reasons is based on an analysis of a sample of unrestricted nurses' personal records, Dunedin Hospital, DAHI records, 1905–1940s, Dunedin Office, ANZ.
4. Nurses' personal records, Dunedin Hospital, DAHI records D262, 9189, Dunedin Office, ANZ. For a World War II example, see Ruth Crawford, 'Elizabeth McIlwrick (formerly Wayte), née Crawford: Nursing in the 1940s', *Nursing Praxis in New Zealand* 12, no. 3, 1997, pp. 31–33.
5. Nurses' personal records, Dunedin Hospital, DAHI records D262, 9189, Dunedin Office, ANZ.
6. Register, Napier Hospital Applications Book, VN [82506], MTG Archive, Napier.
7. 'Reminiscences of nursing in New Zealand: Script of talk given by Janet A. Moore on 14 August 1950 as part of the "Mid-century Review" series in the Women's Hour Session on Station 2ZB', *KT* 43, October 1950, pp. 187–89, quotation on p. 187.
8. Edna Pengelly, *Nursing in Peace and War* (Wellington: Wingfield, 1956), p. 12.
9. Sandra Main, 'My nursing days at Waikato Hospital, 1929–1934', *Auckland-Waikato Historical Journal* 54, April 1989, p. 20.
10. Lynette Low, 'Phillys Streeter (née Wright) RGN, maternity nurse', *Nursing Praxis in New Zealand* 12, no. 1, 1997, pp. 29–30.
11. Deborah Montgomerie, 'Man-powering women: Industrial conscription during the Second World War', in *Women in History 2*, eds B. Brookes, C. Macdonald and M. Tennant (Wellington: Bridget Williams Books, 1992), pp. 184–204; Melanie Nolan, *Breadwinning: New Zealand women and the state* (Christchurch: Canterbury University Press, 2000), pp. 225–28.
12. Audrey Gilbert, oral history interview with Pamela Wood, 9 August 2005.
13. Yvonne Shadbolt, 'Re-introducing Mabel Mahinarangi Kewene, MBE, QSO', *Nursing Praxis in New Zealand* 16, no. 3, 2000, pp. 50–53.
14. Clive A. Lind, *Step by Step: The history of nursing education in Southland* (Invercargill: Southland Hospital Nurses Reunion Committee, 1982), p. 51.
15. Marian M. Thorp, *The Long, Long Trail: An autobiography* (Hastings: Hart Printing House, 1971), p. 20.
16. In her autobiography Ristori gives the required age as 21 and her age then as 19, but her diary entry for 21 February 1920 said, 'Sad to relate you've got to be 20 so I s'pose I'll have to forfeit two years of my life & miss being 18 & 19'. Bridget Ristori, *Patients in My Care: The autobiography of a nurse* (London: Elek, 1967), p. 31; Bridget Madge Isabel Francois [Ristori], 1902–1992, Diaries (while training as a nurse) MS–Papers–10108–004, ATL.
17. Mary Clark, 'Nursing – as it was in my day', *Auckland-Waikato Historical Journal* 62, April 1993, p. 26 and p. 27.
18. Dorothy Ford, *Journey from Stranger's Rest* (Wellington: Daphne Brasell Associates, 1989), p. 21.
19. Ristori, *Patients in my Care*, 32; Bridget Madge Isabel Francois [Ristori], 1902–1992, Diaries (while training as a nurse) MS–Papers–10108–004, ATL. Years previously, as the widowed Mrs Hutchinson, Mabel Beetham had become a surrogate 'auntie' to Bridget Ristori in England for two years when Ristori was orphaned.
20. Pengelly, *Nursing in Peace and War*, p. 13.
21. Marjorie Chambers, *My Life in Nursing: Christchurch Hospital, 1936–1966* (Tauranga: Moana Press, 1988), p. 9.
22. Colleen Williams, *All for a Medal: The nursing memoirs of Colleen Turbet*

Williams (Auckland: Self-published, 2006), pp. 11–12.
23. *AJHR*, 1906, H-22, p. 3.
24. Notices, Wellington Hospital, 1940s, History of Nursing –Wellington Hospital folder, Wellington Hospital Nursing Archive.
25. 'Hair and caps', editorial, *NZNJ* 36, April 1943, pp. 75–76.
26. Helen Campbell, *Looking Back: A history of the Christchurch School of Nursing, 1891–1987* (Christchurch: Nursing History Christchurch Charitable Trust, 1997), p. 15.
27. Ford, *Journey from Stranger's Rest*, p. 102.
28. Chambers, *My Life in Nursing*, p. 12.
29. 'Nursing in the 1930s', *Spectrum* #800, 1993, Radio New Zealand.
30. Beryl Smedley, 'Ricky's story: The memoirs of Amy Rickman', MS–Papers–4404, ATL, p. 13.
31. This was a review of Horace Annesley Vachell's novel *The Paladin, as Beheld by a Woman of Temperament*. The reviewer complained that the nurse-heroine had apparently received her certificate after serving for three years in a private nursing home. 'If this picture of a nurse's career is drawn from life', said the reviewer, 'it emphasizes the need of a uniform standard of training, such as is being worked for by the most progressive British nurses'. 'Books for study and leisure hours', *KT* 3, April 1910, p. 67.
32. James Johnston Abraham, *The Night Nurse*, 3rd edn. (London: Chapman & Hall, 1913). For the review, see 'Some new books', *KT* 6, July 1913, p. 100.
33. Bridget Madge Isabel [Ristori] Francois, 1902–1992, Diaries (while training as a nurse) MS–Papers–10108–004, ATL.
34. Chambers, *My Life in Nursing*, p. 16.
35. Williams, *All for a Medal*, p. 32.
36. Edith M. Lewis, *Joy in the Caring* (Christchurch: N.M. Peryer, 1963), pp. 5–6.
37. Lind, *Step by Step*, p. 59.
38. Ford, *Journey from Stranger's Rest*, pp. 125–26.
39. Henry Jellett, an Irish consultant in gynaecology and obstetrics, who served as an advisory obstetrician to the New Zealand Department of Health, wrote a midwifery textbook for nurses that was first published in 1901. He continued to update it after coming to New Zealand. The ninth edition was published the year before his collaboration with Marsh. Henry Jellett, *A Short Practice of Midwifery for Nurses* (London: J. & A. Churchill, 1933).
40. 'Exit Sir Derek', *Press*, 2 October 1935, p. 2.
41. Dame Ngaio Marsh, *Exit Sir Derek*, two versions–MS–Personal Papers–1397–4/-8, Series IV, Folder 8, ATL.
42. Joanne Drayton, *Ngaio Marsh: Her life in crime* (Auckland: Harper Collins, 2008), p. 63.
43. Audrey Gilbert, oral history interview with Pamela Wood, 9 August 2005.
44. Margaret McDougall, 'Discovering our past through exploring a register from Wellington Hospital, 1916–1925', in *Looking Back, Moving Forward: Essays in the history of New Zealand nursing and midwifery*, eds N. Chick and J. Rodgers (Palmerston North: Department of Nursing and Midwifery, Massey University, 1997), pp. 23–32.
45. Nurses' personal records, Dunedin Hospital, DAHI records, 9189 D262 and D347, Dunedin Office, ANZ.
46. Main, 'My nursing days', p. 19.
47. Ristori, *Patients in my Care*, pp. 32–33.
48. Ford, *Journey from Stranger's Rest*, p. 103.
49. Williams, *All for a Medal*, p. 56.
50. Sonja Davies, *Bread and Roses: Sonja Davies, her story* (Masterton: Fraser Books, 1984), p. 55.
51. Elizabeth Woodward, oral history interview with Pamela Wood, 25 June 2004.
52. Williams, *All for a Medal*, p. 24.
53. Davies, *Bread and Roses*, p. 43.

NOTES: CHAPTER 3. BECOMING A NURSE

54. Ibid., p. 46.
55. Williams, *All for a Medal*, p. 52.
56. Sue Greenstreet, *A Nursing Odyssey: An account of the beginning of registered nursing in New Zealand* (Wellington: First Edition, 2007), p. 20.
57. Williams, *All for a Medal*, p. 25.
58. 'Helpful hints to student nurses', *Wellington Public Hospital Nurses Journal* 1, no. 5, 1936, pp. 5–6, quotation on p. 5.
59. Main, 'My nursing days', p. 20.
60. Lind, *Step by Step*, p. 55. Joyce Speirs was the Southland Hospital Board's chief nurse from 1979 to 1984.
61. Anne McDonald, oral history interview with Pamela Wood, 22 November 2005.
62. Davies, *Bread and Roses*, p. 42.
63. See Nurse's notebook, Wellington Hospital, 1939–42; Sidney Wilding, notebook, 1937–1940, ARC2008-136, Puke Ariki.
64. Williams, *All for a Medal*, p. 25.
65. Ibid., p. 74.
66. Ford, *Journey from Stranger's Rest*, pp. 121–22.
67. This was mentioned by Mavis Hunter (née Borthwick) in *Stratford Hospital Memories*, ed. Alison Robinson (Stratford: Thurlstone Press, 2001), p. 13.
68. Geoff Conly, *A Case History: The Hawke's Bay Hospital Board, 1876–1989* (Napier: Hawke's Bay Area Health Board, 1992), pp. 36–37.
69. Williams, *All for a Medal*, p. 45.
70. Campbell, *Looking Back*, p. 25.
71. For a more detailed discussion, see Pamela J. Wood, 'Sickening nurses: Fever nursing, nurses' illness, and the anatomy of blame, New Zealand 1903–1923', *Nursing History Review* 19, 2011, pp. 53–77; Pamela J. Wood, 'Nurses' occupational health as a driver for curriculum change emphasising health promotion: An historical research study', *Nurse Education Today* 34, 2014, pp. 709–13.
72. 'Up the fire escape', *EP*, 27 November 1925, p. 6.
73. 'Fire escape incident', *AS*, 19 December 1925, p. 14.
74. 'Discipline', editorial, *KT* 19, January 1926, pp. 1–2.
75. Campbell, *Looking Back*, p. 24.
76. Cooking corn cobs was mentioned by Dawn Dresser in Robinson, *Stratford Hospital Memories*, p. 85. The remaining functions were from Campbell, *Looking Back*, pp. 87, 91–92.
77. Ford, *Journey from Stranger's Rest*, pp. 100, 121.
78. Woodward, oral history interview.
79. Chambers, *My Life in Nursing*, pp. 21–22.
80. Davies, *Bread and Roses*, p. 32.
81. Williams, *All for a Medal*, pp. 60–61.
82. Ibid., p. 74.
83. Nurses' personal records, Dunedin Hospital, DAHI records, D262, 9189, Dunedin Office, ANZ.
84. Nurses' personal records, Dunedin Hospital, DAHI records, D262, 9189, Dunedin Office, ANZ. On this case see also Patricia Sargison, 'The wages of sin: Aspects of nurse training at Dunedin Hospital in the 1920s and 1930s', *Women's Studies Journal* 11, no. 1–2 August 1995, pp. 165–78.
85. This is based on an analysis of pass rates for the period 1909–32.
86. Pamela J. Wood, 'Nursing the patient, the room and the doctor: Assessing New Zealand nurses' practical capability, 1900–1945', *Nurse Education Today* 31, 22011, pp. 140–44; Pamela J. Wood, 'The enduring issue of assessing nursing knowledge: Surgical nursing final examinations in Australia and New Zealand, 1950–1930', *Contemporary Nurse* 32, no. 1–2, 2009, pp. 109–22.
87. Kay Morris Matthews, *Recovery: Women's overseas service in World War One* (Gisborne: Tairāwhiti Museum, 2017), p. 114.
88. Ford, *Journey from Stranger's Rest*, p. 134.
89. 'Nursing in the 1930s'.
90. Ristori, *Patients in my Care*, p. 39; Diary entry for 5 July 1923, Bridget Madge Isabel

Francois [Ristori], 1902–1992, Diaries (while training as a nurse) MS–Papers–10108–004, ATL.

91. C.M. Lepper, secretary of the Taranaki District Hospital and Charitable Aid Board, to Winifred Waite, 24 July 1915. Winifred Ellen Waite, ARC2005–187, Puke Ariki.
92. Chambers, *My Life in Nursing*, p. 50.
93. Lewis, *Joy in the Caring*, p. 6. Joan Loeber's experience is recounted in 'Nursing in the 1930s'. Bet McMillan (later Sinclair) in Southland in the 1930s also received her medal by post, packed in a tobacco tin. See Lind, *Step by Step*, p. 40.
94. 'Training school of nurses', *ODT*, 12 May 1924, p. 3.
95. 'Nursing in the 1930s'; see also Chambers, *My Life in Nursing*, p. 50.
96. Geoffrey Yeo, *Nursing at Bart's: A history of nursing service and nurse education at St Bartholomew's Hospital, London* (Stroud: Alan Sutton Publishing, 1995), p. 32.
97. Jane Thomas, 'A glance back in time: The nursing notes of Edwina Perkins', *International History of Nursing Journal* 7, no. 2, 2003, p. 22.
98. For Britain, see, for example, Claire Laurent, *Rituals and Myths in Nursing: A social history* (Barnsley: Pen & Sword Books, 2019). For Australia, see, for example, Isabel Gill, *The Lamp Still Burns: Nursing in Victoria, 1936–1981; An autobiographical account* (Bendigo: Bendigo College of Advanced Education, 1989).

Chapter 4. District nursing

1. Annie Sexton and Mirian Macandrew, 'The St John Ambulance Association District Nursing Guild: Some notes on district nursing in Wellington', *KT* 1, July 1908, pp. 59–60. Sexton was born Omra Regan in England around 1849 of Irish parentage. She worked as a trained military nurse at Aldershot, served in India and South Africa, and later came with her husband to New Zealand because of his ill-health. She took charge of a hospital on Somes Island in Wellington Harbour for invalided soldiers returning from the South African (Boer) War, who presented her with a gold watch and chain in gratitude. 'Women in print, Obituary', *EP*, 27 January 1930, p. 15. Sexton could have been nursing soldiers with measles and one with suspected smallpox on Somes Island in 1902. See 'Serious outbreak of smallpox, Former epidemics', *EP*, 14 January 1904, p. 6. Mirian Macandrew trained at Wellington Hospital and was then matron of Ashburton Hospital. See her obituary, 'Nurse Marion [*sic*] Macandrew', *KT* 19, January 1926, p. 27; 'Local and general', *EP*, 6 March 1906, p. 4.
2. S.E. Maude, 'District nursing', *KT* 1, October 1908, pp. 118–19.
3. Sexton and Macandrew, 'The St John Ambulance Association District Nursing Guild', pp. 59–60.
4. For a description of this co-construction of the sick poor by Wellington journalists and district nurses from 1900 to 1920, see Pamela J. Wood and Kerry Arcus, '"Sunless lives": District nurses' and journalists' co-construction of the "sick poor" as a vulnerable population in early twentieth-century New Zealand', *Contemporary Nurse* 42, no. 2, 2012, pp. 145–55.
5. See, for example, 'A praiseworthy project', *EP*, 9 December 1901, p. 4.
6. Jessie Munro, *The Story of Suzanne Aubert* (Auckland: Auckland University Press, 1996), p. 247.
7. Edith Somers Cocks, *A Friend in Need. Nurse Maude: Her life and work* (Christchurch: Nurse Maude District Nursing Association, 1950).
8. 'Prison Gate Mission', *Press*, 11 July 1888, p. 6.

9. 'City Mission Home', *Press*, 6 April 1894, p. 3.
10. 'City Mission Home', *Press*, 11 October 1888, p. 6.
11. 'City Mission Home', *Press*, 11 November 1890, p. 6; 'City Mission Home', *Press*, 13 January 1891, p. 6; 'City Mission Home', *Press*, 16 June 1894, p. 8; 'City Mission Home', *Press*, 3 May 1895, p. 6.
12. 'A nurse for the poor', *Press*, 8 May 1895, p. 6.
13. *AJHR*, 1891, H-7, pp. 14–15. Lloyd Lees' salary was listed in *AJHR*, 1889, H-3, pp. 14–15.
14. 'News of the day', *Press*, 17 August 1895, p. 7.
15. 'News of the day', *Press*, 19 June 1895, p. 5; 'News of the day', *Press*, 16 July 1895, p. 4.
16. 'City Mission Home', *Press*, 4 April 1896, p. 9.
17. 'Relief in Christchurch', *Press*, 28 August 1896, p. 5.
18. 'Obituary', *Press*, 31 March 1897, p. 6; 'City Mission Home', *Press*, 1 April 1897, p. 5. See also 'To the editor', *Press*, 1 April 1897, p. 5.
19. As one example, see 'Advertisement', *KT* 1, October 1908, p. ix.
20. 'Nurse Lloyd Lees', *Press*, 18 August 1911, p. 9; 'Obituary', *KT* 4, October 1911, p. 163.
21. Geoffrey Rice, *Heaton Rhodes of Otahuna: The illustrated biography* (Christchurch: Canterbury University Press, 2008).
22. For a detailed description of this philanthropic support for district nursing, see Pamela J. Wood and Kerri Arcus, 'Poverty, philanthropy, and professionalism: The establishment of a district nursing service in Wellington, New Zealand, 1903', *Health and History* 13, no. 1, 2011, pp. 44–64.
23. Margaret Tennant, *The Fabric of Welfare: Voluntary organisations, government and welfare in New Zealand, 1940–2005* (Wellington: Bridget Williams Books, 2007), p. 41.
24. Ibid., p. 91.
25. Wood and Arcus, 'Poverty, philanthropy, and professionalism', p. 53; *NZG*, 1903, p. 195; 'St John Ambulance Nursing Guild', *EP*, 7 October 1903, p. 2. Sibylla Maude left the Middlesex Hospital in November 1892. See Cocks, *A Friend in Need*, p. 28.
26. 'District nursing', *ES*, 8 December 1905, p. 4; 'District nursing', *ODT*, 11 December 1905, p. 4.
27. For example, Nurse E.T. Barclay visited in 1905 before starting the Dunedin St John service. Agnes Falconer, who sponsored Dunedin's Roslyn service, and its first nurse, Harriet Kinmont, visited in 1934. 'District nursing', *ODT*, 7 May 1934, p. 9.
28. 'Women's corner', *Press*, 23 October 1926, p. 2.
29. This was the caption to her photograph in the *AS* noting her OBE award, 4 January 1934, p. 12. On her death the following year, the newspaper noted her role as 'founding the district nursing movement in New Zealand'. 'Women in 1935', *AS*, 31 December 1935, p. 12. The caption to a photograph in the Christchurch *Press* noted that 'many thousands of citizens lined the route' of her funeral procession. 'Death of Nurse Maude', *Press*, 15 July 1935, p. 20.
30. Elizabeth Barclay was born in Inverness in 1870 and came to New Zealand as a three-year-old child. She started training at Dunedin Hospital in 1894, worked there for six years, and then became matron of Greymouth Hospital. At the time of her appointment as district nurse she was a private nurse in Dunedin. She retired in 1936 after 30 years in district nursing, interrupted by military service. 'St John Ambulance Association', *ODT*, 6 March 1906, p. 8; 'St John Ambulance Association', *ODT*, 13 March 1906, p. 3; 'Years of service', *ODT*, 20 March 1936, p. 6; 'Obituary', *ES*, 26 April 1946, p. 8.
31. Jessie Torrance trained at Dunedin Hospital. She qualified in December

1908 after achieving fourth-equal place, with her classmate Jean Cormack, out of 51 candidates sitting the examination in New Zealand. She was one of the earliest Plunket nurses, working in the north end of the city. Her appointment as the Knox Church nurse, at a salary of £150, was made possible by a bequest from Miss Jessie Dalglish. 'State Examinations', *KT* 2, January 1909, p. 18; Knox Church Deacon's Court minutes, 12 April 1919, Presbyterian Research Centre (Archives); 'Otago Branch', *KT* 12, July 1919, p. 106; 'Knox Church', *ES*, 1 September 1919, p. 2; 'Knox Church', *ODT*, 4 August 1942, p. 4; 'Knox Church', *ODT*, 10 August 1943, p. 4; 'Personal', *ODT*, 12 August 1943, p. 4; Untitled, *Outlook*, 25 January 1950, p. 8. See Lyndall Hancock, 'Torrance, Jessie (1874–1949)', in *Southern People: A dictionary of Otago Southland biography*, ed. J. Thomson (Dunedin: Longacre Press, 1998), p. 516.

32. 'Country girls' week', *ES*, 1 September 1938, p. 11. This policy was confirmed in the Knox Church Annual Report 1920, Presbyterian Research Centre (Archives), p. 18. Although employed by a church, Torrance was not a 'parish nurse'. Sibylla Maude had pointed out that untrained women were often employed as parish nurses. See 'District nursing', *ES*, 8 December 1905, p. 4.

33. In 1923, the Colonial Mutual Life Assurance Company employed an English nurse, Florence Heany, for a six-month trial of a district nursing service for its policyholders in Wellington, after successfully initiating services around 10 years earlier in Australia. The company paid Heany a fixed retaining salary and a fee for each case attended, as well as travelling expenses from the Nurses' Club, where she lived. *NZG*, 1925, p. 406; 'Nursing under an insurance company', *KT* 16, July 1923, p. 109. For more details of insurance nurses' work, see 'Five minute papers', *KT* 20, July 1927, p. 118; 'Insurance nurses', *KT* 20, July 1927, p. 149. See also a mention of insurance nurse Gertrude E. Cheek in 'Notes from the hospitals and personal items', *NZNJ* 23, November 1930, pp. 331–44, see p. 344. Little information is available about the T&G nurses. The company's centenary booklet, *T&G: 100 years* (Wellington: T&G Mutual Life Assurance Society, 1976), does not mention the nursing service. Nurses' work in these Australasian insurance companies is described in Helen Vicars Foote, 'Nursing services of life assurance societies in Australia and New Zealand', *International Nursing Review* 8, nos. 1–4, 1933, pp. 89–91. See also 'Insurance company nursing', *Una* 9, April 1911, pp. 30–31. *Una*, established in 1903 as the journal of the Victorian Trained Nurses' Association, is held in the State Library of Victoria.

34. *Ariki Toa* was the CML in-house publication, irregularly but frequently sent to all its agents, usually exhorting them to canvass more and win in the agents' league tables. The publication is held in the ATL. See 'A word about the nursing service', *Ariki Toa* 2a, no. 6, 27 October 1926, p. 1; 'More canvassing levers', *Ariki Toa* 3a, no. 2a, 7 March 1927, p. 1; 'The nursing service', *Ariki Toa* 3a, no. 4, 5 July 1927, p. 4; 'Your friend the nurse', *Ariki Toa*, 15 May 1947, p. 3; 'Nursing and welfare services', *Ariki Toa*, 15 June 1947, p. 4.

35. 'South Otago Hospital', *ODT*, 13 August 1921, p. 12; 'South Otago Hospital Board', *ES*, 9 December 1925, p. 10.

36. 'Nurses without work', *NZH*, 15 May 1931, p. 12. The Auckland branch of the Trained Nurses Association opened an hourly nurse register for unemployed nurses. The association discussed the scheme at its conference that year and urged its extension. In 1933, however, the nurses' journal reported that only a small proportion of nurses in the country were working as hourly nurses. 'Trained nurses',

ODT, 3 October 1931, p. 12; 'Hourly nursing', NZNJ 26, November 1933, pp. 195–96. In Dunedin in 1947, just one nurse was advertising as an hourly nurse: see 'Trained nurse', advertisement, ES, 19 January 1947, p. 2. A number must have been nursing in this way throughout the country, though, as the matrons' conference in Napier in April 1949 discussed appropriate hourly nursing fees. 'News of the day', ODT, 2 March 1949, p. 4.

37. 'District nursing', ES, 18 April 1934, p. 5; 'District nursing', ODT, 7 May 1934, p. 9. Harriet Kinmont qualified as a nurse in Dunedin in July 1918, then worked in Auckland and Dunedin in private hospital and case nursing. In 1920 she took over from Maude Hayward as matron of the Te Terata Private Hospital at 58 Royal Terrace, Dunedin. 'State examinations', KT 11, July 1918, pp. 120–24; 'Personal', ODT, 11 September 1920, p. 9; Untitled, ODT, 30 October 1914, p. 4. Maude Hayward resigned her position as matron of the Westport Hospital in 1908 to open her own private hospital there. In 1910 she became matron of Masterton Hospital, a position she left in 1914 to convert the Royal Terrace house into a private hospital. After her marriage in 1920, Kinmont became its matron. See 'Presentation', KT 8, January 1915, p. 55.

38. In her first six months in the position in 1934, she paid over 500 visits to patients' homes, and 260 calls were made at her rooms at 104a Highgate for treatment or advice. 'District nursing', ES, 14 November 1934, p. 16; 'Busy hours', ODT, 16 November 1934, p. 15.

39. See, for example, 'District nursing', ODT, 7 May 1940, p. 5; 'Home nursing', ODT, 20 November 1941, p. 8.

40. Mary Lambie, 'District nursing in NZ: How it is organised and how it is planned,' lecture, 4 June 1934, in Notebook, Miss Cameron Public Health Nursing, SANS records, 8/1/6, ANZ.

41. 'Ambulance Saturday', WC, 2 July 1909, p. 5. The letter to the editor from M.I. Fraser gave a strange rationale for the service: obtaining a good soldier meant having a man physically worth training, which required good conditions in childhood, which needed well-tended mothers, which required a maternity/district nurse.

42. 'Nurse Beatrice Walton explains her resignation', WC, 14 September 1911, p. 8. Her sister, Clara, who was a midwife but not a nurse, also worked for the service; she too resigned. She eventually became Plunket nurse in Hastings. 'Women's corner', Press, 10 September 1917, p. 2.

43. For examples of letters supporting the nurse, see 'The district nurse', WC, 15 August 1911, p. 3; 'Wanganui District Nursing League', WC, 17 August 1911, p. 3; 'The district nurse', WC, 17 August 1911, p. 3. For examples supporting the League's position, see 'The district nurse', WC, 18 August 1911, p. 6; 'Observations by the man on the lookout', WC, 19 August 1911, p. 2.

44. Patricia Sargison, '"Essentially a woman's work": A history of general nursing in New Zealand, 1830–1930', PhD thesis, University of Otago, 2001.

45. As one example of 12-hour days and heartache, see 'The district nurses', WC, 6 March 1913, p. 4.

46. 'St John Ambulance district nursing', KT 10, October 1917, pp. 209–12, quotations on p. 210.

47. 'Short story of the growth of district nursing in Dunedin', SANS, 20/2/29, ANZ, p. 3.

48. 'St John Ambulance district nursing', p. 211.

49. William Rathbone instituted training for district nurses in England. See also Helen Sweet with Rona Dougall, Community Nursing and Primary Healthcare in Britain in the Twentieth Century (London: Routledge, 2008).

50. See, for example, 'New Zealand Trained Nurses' Association Wellington', KT 4,

Notes: Chapter 4. District nursing

January 1911, p. 4; 'Home nursing', *AS*, 12 April 1933, p. 14.
51. 'St John Ambulance district nursing', p. 210.
52. Bridget Ristori, *Nursing as a Career* (Kawakawa: Northland Gazette, 1947), p. 35.
53. Bronwyn Labrum, 'The material culture of welfare in Aotearoa/New Zealand: A case study of clothing', *History Australia* 2, no. 3, 2005, 81.1–81.12.
54. 'Books for study and leisure hours', *KT* 3, April 1910, p. 67; Amy Hughes, *Practical Hints on District Nursing* (London: Scientific Press, 1898), p. 4.
55. Margaret Tennant, *Paupers and Providers: Charitable aid in New Zealand* (Wellington: Allen & Unwin, 1989), p. 124.
56. 'District nursing for Auckland city', *KT* 13, January 1920, p. 43.
57. Sexton and Macandrew, 'The St John Ambulance Association District Nursing Guild', p. 59.
58. When Jessie Torrance began work as the Knox Church district nurse, she was allocated an additional £12 for this purpose, the equivalent of 8 percent of her salary.
59. Knox Church Annual Report 1920, p. 18, Presbyterian Research Centre (Archives), Dunedin.
60. 'Lantern lecture', *ODT*, 28 July 1921, p. 7; 'Lantern lecture', *ODT*, 3 August 1921, p. 7.
61. Bazaar, programme pamphlet, St John Ambulance District Nursing Guild, Wellington, 1904, St John Ambulance Association records, ATL, cited in Kerrin J. Arcus, 'Often wearisome, sometimes saddening, but always interesting: A hundred years of district nursing in Wellington, 1903–2003', MA (Applied) in Nursing thesis, Victoria University of Wellington, 2004.
62. 'St John Ambulance Association', *ODT*, 9 July 1920, p. 8; 'St John Ambulance Association', *ES*, 9 July 1920, p. 3; 'District nursing', *ODT*, 4 May 1938, p. 14; 'District nursing', *ES*, 4 May 1938, p. 18.
63. 'St John Association', *ES*, 22 May 1924, p. 9.
64. 'Poverty and pain', *AS*, 2 March 1932, p. 12.
65. 'Hard times', *EP*, 22 April 1908, p. 2.
66. 'Wanganui District Nursing League', *WC*, 31 May 1912, p. 7. Grace Nobbs completed her training at Auckland Hospital in 1901 and did private nursing in Auckland, Sydney and Whanganui. She was district nurse in Whanganui from September 1911 to November 1912, matron of the Cook Hospital in Rarotonga from 1913 to 1916 and employed by the British Red Cross until 1919. She died in Honolulu in November 1923. Margaret Brown, Diana Masters and Barbara Smith, *Nurses of Auckland: The history of the general nursing programme in the Auckland School of Nursing* (Auckland: M. Brown, D. Masters & B. Smith, 1998), p. 210; 'Notes from the hospitals and personal items', *KT* 6, January 1913, p. 38; 'Notes from the hospitals and personal items', *KT* 9, October 1916, p. 246; 'Resignations, appointments, etc', *KT* 12, October 1919, p. 197; 'Obituary', *KT* 17, April 1924, p. 89.
67. 'District nursing', *ES*, 8 December 1905, p. 4.
68. 'Short story of the growth of district nursing in Dunedin', p. 3.
69. 'District nursing in a country town', *KT* 3, October 1910, p. 163.
70. 'Hard times', *EP*, 22 April 1908, p. 2.
71. Maude, 'District nursing', p. 119.
72. 'Short story of the growth of district nursing in Dunedin', p. 4.
73. 'More tributes to the nursing service', *Ariki Toa* 6, no. 3, 8 September 1930, p. 4.
74. 'The nursing service – how policyholders regard it', *Ariki Toa* 10, no. 11, 7 December 1934, p. 3.
75. 'District nursing', *ODT*, 4 May 1938, p. 14; 'District nursing', *ES*, 4 May 1938, p. 18.
76. Knox Church Annual Report 1920, Presbyterian Research Centre (Archives), p. 18.
77. Frank Prochaska, 'Body and soul: Bible nurses and the poor in Victorian London',

Historical Research 60, no, 143, 1987, p. 346.
78. Sexton and Macandrew, 'St John Ambulance Association District Nursing Guild'.
79. 'Busy hours', *ODT*, 16 November 1934, p. 15.
80. 'St John Ambulance District Nursing', p. 212.
81. 'District nursing for Auckland city', *KT* 13, January 1920, p. 43.
82. 'Sunless lives', *EP*, 15 June 1904, p. 5; 'In the shadow', *EP*, 23 April 1908, p. 6.
83. 'In the shadow'.
84. Robin Law, 'On the streets of southern Dunedin: Gender and transport', in *Sites of Gender: Women, men and modernity in southern Dunedin, 1890–1939*, eds B. Brookes, A. Cooper and R. Law (Auckland: Auckland University Press, 2003), pp. 258–84.
85. Wood and Arcus, 'Poverty, philanthropy and professionalism'; Pamela J. Wood, *Dirt: Filth and decay in a New World Arcadia* (Auckland: Auckland University Press, 2005).
86. Mark Peel, 'Charity, case work, and the dramas of class in Melbourne 1910–1940', *History Australia* 2, no. 3, 2005, 83.1–83.15.
87. Wood and Arcus, 'Poverty, philanthropy and professionalism'.
88. A New Zealand nurse working in London's East End felt her uniform gave her a 'mantle of safety'. Joan Rattray, *Great Days in New Zealand Nursing* (London: George G. Harrap, 1961), p. 14.
89. 'St John Ambulance District Nursing', p. 211.
90. Alan Mayne, *Representing the Slum: Popular journalism in a late nineteenth-century city* (Parkville, VIC: University of Melbourne, 1990); Alan Mayne, *The Imagined Slum: Newspaper representations in three cities, 1870–1914* (Leicester: Leicester University Press, 1993).
91. 'In the shadow'.
92. 'A noble work', *EP*, 23 October 1906, p. 4.
93. Katherine Mansfield, 'The Garden Party', in *The Best of Katherine Mansfield's Short Stories* (Auckland: Vintage, 1998), pp. 227, 231.
94. Maude, 'District nursing', p. 119.
95. 'St John Ambulance District Nursing'.
96. Maude, 'District nursing', p. 119.
97. 'With the district nurse', *KT* 2, January 1909, pp. 23–24.
98. 'To-day's appeal', *WC*, 1 June 1912, p. 4.
99. 'Order of St John', *EP*, 25 October 1928, p. 15.
100. 'Timely help', *AS*, 25 July 1936, p. 11; 'Knox Church', *ES*, 10 August 1937, p. 14; 'District nursing', *ODT*, 4 May 1938, p. 14.
101. 'District nursing', *ODT*, 7 May 1940, p. 5; 'District nursing', *ES*, 3 May 1944, p. 8.
102. Untitled, *The Outlook*, 25 January 1950, p. 8.
103. His survey was published in separate volumes. See, for example, Charles Booth, ed., *Life and Labour of the People of London*, vol. 1, *East, Central and South London* (London: Macmillan, 1892). For an example of a newspaper reference to it, see 'Notes and comments', *NZH*, 7 September 1908, p. 4. It was referred to again in the 1930s, when the London School of Economics started a similar survey. See, for example, 'Notes and comments', *NZH*, 7 September 1928, p. 10; 'Notes and comments', *NZH*, 10 January 1933, p. 8; 'The poverty line', *NZH*, 13 March 1934, p. 9.
104. 'Sunless lives'. Tom Brooking, Seddon's biographer, pointed out that Seddon, while on a trip to Britain in 1897, actually stated that there were 'no extremes in New Zealand. They had no millionaires and from poverty a man could uplift himself.' Further, it was New Zealand newspapers that represented this statement as a denial of poverty in New Zealand. Tom Brooking, *Richard Seddon, King of God's Own: The life and times of New Zealand's*

longest-serving prime minister (Auckland: Penguin, 2014), p. 339. However, Seddon clearly liked the journalists' paraphrasing and used it himself in speeches in London and Cape Town in 1902. 'New Zealanders in London', *EP*, 19 June 1902, p. 5; 'New Zealand dinner', *OW*, 25 June 1902, p. 15; 'The week', *OW*, 25 June 1902, p. 47; 'Mr Seddon at Capetown', *EP*, 28 June 1902, p. 2; 'Anglo-colonial notes', *EP*, 6 October 1902, p. 2.
105. John Stenhouse, 'Religion and society', in *The New Oxford History of New Zealand*, ed. G. Byrnes (South Melbourne: Oxford University Press, 2009), pp. 323–56.
106. Prochaska, *Body and Soul*.
107. Tennant, *Fabric of Welfare*; 'The City Mission Home', *Press*, 6 April 1894, p. 4.
108. 'Poor relief', *EP*, 2 November 1910, p. 3.
109. 'In the shadow'.
110. As just three examples, see 'A praiseworthy project', *EP*, 9 December 1901, p. 4; 'Nursing the poor', *ODT*, 1 September 1906, p. 4; 'St John Ambulance Association', *ODT*, 13 March 1906, p. 3.
111. 'District nurses', *ODT*, 24 November 1917, p. 5; 'St John Ambulance Association', *ODT*, 9 July 1920, p. 8; 'St John Ambulance Association', *ES*, 9 July 1920, p. 3; 'District nursing', *ODT*, 4 May 1938, p. 14.
112. 'A noble work', *EP*, 23 October 1906, p. 4.
113. 'In the shadow'; 'Pitiful poverty', *EP*, 17 July 1914, p. 8; 'St John Ambulance District Nursing'.
114. 'St John Ambulance District Nursing'. A Beatrice stove was a cast-iron and enamel stove fuelled by oil or paraffin.
115. 'St John Ambulance Association', *ODT*, 9 July 1920, p. 8; 'District nursing', *ODT*, 4 May 1938, p. 14.
116. 'Five minute papers', *KT* 16, July 1927, pp. 115–29, quotation on p. 119.
117. 'With the district nurse', *KT* 2, January 1909, pp. 23–24.
118. See, for example, 'Poverty and pain', *AS*, 2 March 1932, p. 12; 'District Nursing Association' *ES*, 14 November 1934, p. 16.
119. 'District nursing', *ES*, 8 December 1905, p. 4.
120. Ristori, *Nursing as a Career*, p. 35.
121. 'With the district nurse', *KT* 2, January 1909, pp. 23–24, quotation on p. 23.
122. 'Nursing the poor', *ODT*, 1 September 1906, p. 4; 'With the district nurse'.
123. 'District nurses', *ODT*, 24 November 1917, p. 5.
124. 'St John Ambulance District Nursing'. See also 'District nurses', *ODT*, 24 November 1917, p. 5.
125. See, for example, 'Busy hours', *ODT*, 16 November 1934, p. 15; 'Timely help', *AS*, 25 July 1936, p. 11; 'With the district nurse', *NZNJ* 31, August 1938, pp. 206–07.
126. 'A noble work', *EP*, 23 October 1906, p. 4.
127. 'The district nurses', *WC*, 6 March 1913, p. 4.
128. 'District nursing', *ODT*, 11 December 1905, p. 4.
129. 'Nursing the poor', *ODT*, 1 September 1906, p. 4.
130. 'St John Ambulance Association', *ES*, 28 May 1909, p. 2; 'St John Ambulance Association: Annual meeting', *OW*, 9 June 1909, p. 18.
131. 'The district nurse: Some notes by Florence Nightingale', *KT* 4, April 1911, p. 76.
132. 'District nursing', *ODT*, 4 May 1938, p. 14.
133. 'Faithful service', *ES*, 20 March 1936, p. 8.
134. 'District nurse', *EP*, 18 October 1935, p. 3.
135. 'Home nursing', *AS*, 12 April 1933, p. 14; 'District nursing', *ODT*, 4 May 1938, p. 14; 'Home nursing service', *AS*, 16 May 1934, p. 17.
136. Maude, 'District nursing', p. 119.
137. Carrie Howse, '"The reflection of England's light": The Instructive District Nursing Association of Boston, 1814–1914', *Nursing History Review* 17, 2009, pp. 47–79. See also Karen Buhler-Wilkerson, *No Place Like Home: A history of nursing and home care in the United States* (Baltimore: Johns Hopkins University Press, 2001).

138. Hester Maclean, *Nursing in New Zealand: History and reminiscences* (Wellington: Tolan, 1932).
139. See, for example, Monica Bayly, *A History of the Queen's Nursing Institute* (London: Croom Helm, 1987).
140. Sweet with Dougall, *Community Nursing*.
141. Sweet with Dougall, *Community Nursing*; Bayly, *A History of the Queen's Nursing Institute*; Margaret Dannant, 'District nursing: Professional skills and knowledge in domestic settings; Linking national and local networks of expertise', PhD thesis, University of Leicester, 2005; Carrie Howse, '"The ultimate destination of all nursing": The development of district nursing in England, 1880–1925', *Nursing History Review* 15, 2007, pp. 65–94.

Chapter 5. The 'intrepid nurse'

1. Amelia 'Bagley, 'The nurse's larger sphere', *KT* 5, January 1912, p. 21; 'New Zealand Trained Nurses' Association, Wellington', *KT* 4, April 1911, p. 47.
2. 'District nursing', *KT* 5, April 1912, p. 25. Jessie Kennedy registered in December 1905, having trained at Wellington Hospital. She worked at Hawera Hospital in 1909 and was then matron of Cromwell Hospital until 1910. She became the Uruti nurse in 1912 and later worked in private nursing. *NZG*, 1915, p. 423. Charlotte Parker trained at Kingston Union Infirmary in Britain from 1902 to 1905. On coming to New Zealand in 1906, she registered and worked at Greytown Hospital until 1909. The following year she completed her midwifery training at the Dunedin St Helens Hospital before taking up private nursing. In 1911 she took on the Waipiro Bay position. *NZG*, 1912, p. 395.
3. 'Personal notes', *GT*, 2 October 1912, p. 4.
4. 'Obituary', *KT* 5, October 1912, p. 131.
5. 'New Zealand Trained Nurses' Association', *KT* 6, January 1913, pp. 3–9, quotation on p. 7.
6. Joan Rattray, *Great Days in New Zealand Nursing* (Wellington: A.H. & A.W. Reed, 1961), p. 39.
7. Valintine's initiation of the service is well documented. It is acknowledged in Maclean's memoir, along with her own role. Hester Maclean, *Nursing in New Zealand: History and reminiscences* (Wellington: Tolan, 1932), p. 86.
8. 'District nursing', *KT* 3, July 1910, pp. 100–02, quotations on p. 100.
9. See, for example, Pamela J. Wood, 'Historical imagination and issues in rural and remote area nursing', *Australian Journal of Advanced Nursing* 27, no. 4, 2010, pp. 54–61; Cynthia Toman, Jayne Elliott and Meryn Stuart, eds, *Place and Practice in Canadian Nursing History* (Vancouver, BC: University of British Columbia Press, 2008); Myra Rutherdale, ed., *Caregiving on the Periphery: Historical perspectives on nursing and midwifery in Canada* (Montreal, QC: McGill Queen's University Press, 2010); Ina Bramadat and Marion Saydak, 'Nursing on the Canadian prairies, 1909–1930: Effects on immigration', *Nursing History Review* 1, 1993, pp. 105–17; Diane J. Dodd, Jayne Elliott and Nicole Rousseau, 'Outpost nursing in Canada', in *On All Frontiers: Four centuries of Canadian nursing*, eds C. Bates, D. Dodd and N. Rousseau (Ottawa, ON: University of Ottawa Press, 2005), pp. 139–52; Nicole Rousseau and Johanne Daigle, 'Medical service to settlers: The gestation and establishment of a nursing service in Quebec, 1932–43', *Nursing History Review* 8, 2000, pp. 95–116; Helen Sweet with Rona Dougall, *Community Nursing and Primary Healthcare in Britain in the Twentieth Century* (London: Routledge, 2007).
10. 'District nursing', *KT* 3, July 1910, pp. 100–02, quotation on pp. 100–01.
11. 'District nursing in Pongaroa', *KT* 6, April 1913, p. 65. Esther Gates registered in May 1903 following her training at Timaru

Hospital, where she remained for a year. She then alternated private nursing with work in Waimate Hospital in 1905 and the Cambridge Sanatorium from 1908 to 1909. *NZG*, 1912, p. 381.
12. F. McDonald, 'Backblocks nursing – my first experience', *KT* 7, July 1914, pp. 123–24.
13. Rattray, *Great Days in New Zealand Nursing*, pp. 40–41. Sara Somerville trained at the Glasgow Western Infirmary from 1879 to 1882, worked at the Simpson Memorial Hospital in Edinburgh from 1882 to 1883 and gained her midwifery diploma and worked for the West of Scotland Nursing Association from 1883 to 1888. She registered in New Zealand in February 1902 and was backblocks district nurse on Stewart Island from 1912 until 1917. *NZG*, 1920, p. 651.
14. Gladys Swain, *Stewart Island Days: A district nurse looks back* (Dunedin: Whitcombe & Tombs, 1970), p. 24. The fisherman who towed Sara Somerville to shore, George Swain, later married Gladys Peters.
15. Beryl Smedley, 'Ricky's story: The memoirs of Amy Rickman', MS–Papers–4404, ATL, p. 20.
16. 'Nurse's adventures', *NZH*, 19 May 1937, p. 14.
17. Helen Mackie, *A Nursing Journey* ([Wellington]: Helen Mackie, 1990), p. 1.
18. 'District nursing in Pongaroa'.
19. 'District nursing and Native Health nursing', *KT* 7, January 1914, p. 46.
20. 'Appointments vacant', *KT* 13, July 1920, p. 125.
21. 'Late locals', *HG*, 22 October 1920, p. 3.
22. 'A nurse's New Year's Day', *KT* 14, April 1921, p. 81. Mabel Baker (later Gunn) trained at Guy's Hospital, London, and Waihī Hospital and registered in January 1920. She was South Westland's nurse from November 1920 until 1924. *NZG*, 1925, p. 402.
23. *AJHR*, 1915, H-31, p. 6.
24. 'Back-blocks district nursing', *KT* 4, January 1911, pp. 30–31, quotation on p. 31. Annie O'Callaghan trained at Perth Hospital, Western Australia, from 1897 to 1902, was in private nursing for three years and then worked for a year at Laverton Hospital. She qualified as a midwife at Melbourne Women's Hospital. She registered in New Zealand in May 1908 and did private nursing until 1910 when she joined the Backblocks Nursing Service. In 1912 she set up her own private hospital in Avenue Road, Hastings. *NZG*, 1930, p. 434.
25. 'A nurse in a country hospital', *KT* 15, July 1922, p. 112.
26. Smedley, 'Ricky's story, 'p. 30. The photograph was apparently published in Ross Ewing and Ross Macpherson, *The History of New Zealand Aviation* (Auckland: Heinemann, 1986).
27. 'District nursing in Pongaroa'.
28. Mary Lambie, nurse instructor, to Dr Turbott, medical officer of health, Gisborne, 16 November 1928, in District Nurses – Reports of Inspection – 1928–1943, H1–23/6/3, Department of Health records, ANZ; Alexandra McKegg, '"Ministering Angels: The government Backblock Nursing Service and the Maori Health Nurses, 1909–1939', MA thesis, University of Auckland, 1991.
29. Untitled, *KT* 7, April 1914, p. 68.
30. *AJHR*, 1911, H-31, pp. 77–78.
31. *AJHR*, 1914, H-31, p. 7.
32. Swain, *Stewart Island Days*, p. 44.
33. Mackie, *A Nursing Journey*, p. 2.
34. District nursing, *KT*, July 1911, pp. 94–95.
35. 'A tough year in the backblocks', *KT*, July 1913, p. 113. This was a reprint from the *Dominion* newspaper.
36. 'Nursing in the backblocks', *KT*, January 1922, pp. 27–28, quotations on p. 28.
37. Mackie, *A Nursing Journey*, p. 15.
38. M.A. Burgess, 'Cod liver oil treatment of wounds', *NZNJ* 31, January 1938, p. 20.
39. Smedley, 'Ricky's story', p. 28.

Notes: Chapter 5. The 'intrepid nurse'

40. See, for example, 'Accident at Otira Tunnel', *WCT*, 3 May 1910, p. 4. Olive Drewitt trained at the Royal Portsmouth Portsea and Gosport Hospitals and worked at the Stamford and Rutland General Infirmary, the Park Fever Hospital in London, the Royal Portsmouth again and finally the Sidlaw Sanatorium before coming to New Zealand, where she registered in December 1908. She worked at Greymouth Hospital from 1908 to 1910. *NZG*, 1915, p. 411.
41. 'Fell 260 feet over cliff', *SEP*, 14 August 1934, p. 4; 'Trains collide', *SEP*, 18 December 1934, p. 5. Doris May Workman trained at Taumarunui Hospital and registered in January 1932. *NZG*, 1933, p. 1033.
42. 'Long trip', *AS*, 6 February 1939, p. 4.
43. *AJHR*, 1912, H-31, p. 19; Maclean, *Nursing in New Zealand*, pp. 101–02.
44. Alexandra McKegg found that of the 46 backblocks nurses who were working between 1909 and 1930, 10 lasted in the position for only a year, 15 for up to two years, 9 for up to five years, 10 for up to 10 years, and 2 for between 15 and 20 years. McKegg, 'Ministering Angels', p. 185.
45. 'District nursing and Native Health nursing', *KT* 7, January 1914, p. 46.
46. 'District nursing in Pongaroa'.
47. 'Backblocks District Nursing Scheme', *KT* 3, January 1910, pp. 28–29, story on p. 28.
48. For a detailed description of this folktale, see Pamela J. Wood, 'The nurse's odyssey: The professional folktale in New Zealand backblocks nurses' stories, 1910–1915', *Nursing Inquiry* 16, no. 2, 2009, pp. 111–21.
49. The test, for instance, is a classic folktale motif. See Vladimir Propp, *Morphology of the Folktale*, trans. Laurence Scott (Austin: University of Texas Press, [1927] 1971); Stith Thompson, *The Folktale* (New York: Holt, Rinehart & Winston, 1946).
50. It therefore met Jack Santino's criteria for occupational 'hero' folktales, providing insight into physical challenges and problems of responsibility, status and authority. Jack Santino, 'Characteristics of occupational narratives', *Western Folklore* 37, 1978, pp. 199–212.
51. 'Back-blocks district nursing', *KT* 4, January 1911, pp. 30–31, story on p. 30. Sarah Warnock trained at Christchurch Hospital and registered in May 1905. She undertook private case nursing and worked in Farleigh, a private hospital, until 1909, when she became a Plunket nurse in New Plymouth. She qualified as a midwife in 1910, was a backblocks nurse from 1910 to 1911 and was submatron of a St Helens hospital until 1912. She then worked in a Geraldine private hospital before taking up district nursing again in 1913. *NZG*, 1915, p. 445.
52. Hester Maclean, 'New Zealand', in *A History of Nursing*, vol. 4, ed. Lavinia Dock (New York: G.P. Putnam's Sons, 1912), p. 211.
53. 'Back-blocks district nursing', *KT* 4, January 1911, pp. 30–31.
54. N. Kelly, 'A ride in the backblocks', *KT* 7, January 1914, pp. 21–22. Leonora (Nora) Kelly registered in December 1906 after training at Timaru Hospital. She was a sister at Dunedin Hospital from 1906 to 1910, gained her midwifery certificate in 1912, and worked at Uruti from 1912 to 1914. *NZG*, 1915, p. 423. See also Patricia Radford, 'Calamity Kate, the galloping chestnut: An historical investigation into three major areas of nursing in New Zealand during the period 1911–1935, explored through the career of Leonora Flight Kelly, registered nurse and midwife', MA (Applied) research report, Victoria University of Wellington, 2000.
55. See, for example, Untitled, *Press*, 20 July 1934, p. 11; 'In nurse's arms', *AS*, 17 July 1934, p. 5.
56. Smedley, 'Ricky's story', p. 29; 'Double poisoning tragedy in far north', *NA*, 16 October 1936, p. 6. At that time, sheep dip could contain chemicals such as arsenic. 'Characteristics of sheep-dip

contamination', Ministry for the Environment: www.mfe.govt.nz. Gladys Peters on Stewart Island encountered a similar situation with a fisherman who mistook A.B.C. liniment for a cough mixture. The liniment contained aconite, belladonna and chloroform. On a doctor's advice, she counteracted the poisoning with a stomach washout of bismuth and soda, followed by Epsom salts. Swain, *Stewart Island Days*, pp. 60–61.

57. 'Back-blocks district nursing', *KT* 4, April 1911, pp. 74–75, quotation on p. 74.
58. Placenta praevia is a condition in which the placenta is attached near the opening of the uterus and detaches as the uterus stretches or as the uterine opening (the os) dilates during labour.
59. 'Back-blocks district nursing', pp. 74–75.
60. 'District nursing', *KT* 4, July 1911, pp. 94–95, quotations on p. 95.
61. 'Nurse's duty', *EP*, 13 December 1930, p. 14; 'Nurse's duty', *GT*, 20 December 1930, p. 12 Supplement. This was a reprint of Mary Lambie's article 'Rural nursing in New Zealand' from what was described as the official journal of the US public health nurses' organisation. This was cited as *The Public Health Nurse* but was probably *Public Health Nursing*. F.J. Cameron, 'A day in the country with the district health nurse', *NZNJ* 39, January 1946, pp. 6–9. This was a reprint from the *Public Service Journal*, November 1945.
62. Mabel Vos trained at Auckland Hospital and registered in January 1917. After gaining her midwifery qualification, she worked as a Native Health Nurse. *NZG*, 1930, p. 1325.
63. Ella Leslie registered in January 1922, having trained at Auckland Hospital. She gained her maternity certificate and then her midwifery certificate at the Auckland St Helens Hospital and became a district health nurse in November 1922. *NZG*, 1930, p. 124.
64. Ngapori Naera registered in January 1915, having trained at Auckland and Te Kopuru Hospitals. She gained a midwifery qualification at the Auckland St Helens Hospital in 1916, and was a Native health nurse until 1923. She then lived at Waitomarama in Hokianga. *NZG*, 1930, p. 1281.
65. Amy Jewiss trained at Whangārei Hospital, registering in January 1917, and gained her midwifery certificate at Wairau Hospital in Blenheim. She was charge nurse at Rāwene Hospital in 1917, then a sister at Hāwera Hospital until 1919. *NZG*, 1930, p. 1245. In 1935 she was working as a district health nurse, based first at Ōpunake and then at Manaia in Taranaki. See, for example, Amy Jewiss to Mary Lambie, 27 April 1935, in District Nurses – Manaia, H1, 23/21/39, ANZ. Mabel Te Aowhaitini Mangakāhia was born at Whangatoua on the Coromandel Peninsula, attended Victoria School in Auckland and trained at Auckland Hospital with a government scholarship. She registered in July 1923 and gained her midwifery certificate at the Auckland St Helens Hospital in 1928. From June 1925 until 1929 she was assistant district nurse at Rāwene, and then she opened the Lake Taupō district centre at Tokaanu. She later worked at Te Araroa, East Cape, and finally in the South Auckland district with Waikato Māori. *NZG*, 1920, p. 1270; 'Notes from the hospitals and personal items', *NZNJ* 23, January 1930, pp. 40–44; 'Obituary', *NZNJ* 33, September 1940, pp. 303–4. She is said to have been the first Māori nurse to gain four qualifications – nursing, midwifery, Plunket nursing and the postgraduate diploma in nursing. Rattray, *Great Days in New Zealand Nursing*, p. 47.
66. Mary Hall registered in July 1920 with an Auckland Hospital certificate and gained her midwifery certificate at the Women's Hospital, Melbourne, and the Auckland St Helens Hospital. *NZG*, 1930, p. 1229.

67. 'With the Maori Health Nurses in the North Auckland District', *NZNJ* 22, July 1929, pp. 130–31.
68. 'Notes from the hospitals and personal items', *NZNJ* 24, July 1931, pp. 193–96, account on p. 194.
69. 'Early nursing history of East Cape Health District', MS–Papers–7072–6, ATL.
70. Robert Dixon, *Writing the Colonial Adventure: Race, gender and nation in Anglo-Australian popular fiction, 1875–1914* (Cambridge: Cambridge University Press, 1995); Maria Frawley, *A Wider Range: Travel writing by women in Victorian England* (Rutherford, NJ: Fairleigh Dickinson University Press, 1994); Ulrike Brisson, 'Nineteenth-century European women's travel writings: Female heroes, danger, and death', PhD diss., Pennsylvania State University, 2000.
71. Mary Louise Pratt, *Imperial Eyes: Studies in travel writing and transculturation* (London: Routledge, 1992); Karen M. Morin, 'Peak practices: Englishwomen's "heroic" adventures in the nineteenth-century American West', *Annals of the Association of American Geographers* 89, no. 3, 1999, pp. 489–514; Frawley, *A Wider Range*.
72. Lydia Wevers, *Country of Writing: Travel writing and New Zealand, 1809–1900* (Auckland: Auckland University Press, 2002), pp. 159, 166.
73. Julian Kuzma, 'New Zealand landscape and literature, 1890–1925', *Environment and History* 9, no. 4, 2003, pp. 451–61. The bush landscape was also represented as a silent source of depression and terror, a romantic manifestation of the sacred, and an evoker of religious response.
74. Jane Stafford and Mark Williams, 'Fashioned intimacies: Maoriland and colonial modernity', *Journal of Commonwealth Literature* 37, 2002, pp. 31–48; Jane Stafford and Mark Williams, *Maoriland: New Zealand literature, 1872–1914* (Wellington: Victoria University Press, 2006).
75. Blanche Baughan, 'An early morning walk', in B. Baughan, *Brown Bread from a Colonial Oven, Being Sketches of Up-Country Life in New Zealand* (Christchurch: Whitcombe & Tombs, 1912), p. 124; 'Blanche Baughan, A bush section, (1908)', in *The Auckland University Press Anthology of New Zealand Literature*, eds Jane Stafford and Mark Williams (Auckland: Auckland University Press, 2012), p. 103.
76. Stafford and Williams, 'Fashioned intimacies', p. 37.
77. 'District nursing in Pongaroa'.
78. Patricia Sargison, '"Essentially a woman's work": A history of general nursing in New Zealand, 1830–1930', PhD thesis, University of Otago, 2001.
79. Ruth Fry, *It's Different for Daughters: A history of the curriculum for girls in New Zealand schools, 1900–1975* (Wellington: New Zealand Council for Educational Research, 1985).
80. Radford, 'Calamity Kate'.
81. Dr T.H.A. Valintine, 'Proposed amendment of Hospitals and Charitable Institutions Acts', Hospital Boards Conference, Wellington, 9–11 June 1908, *AJHR*, 1908, H-22a, p. 13.
82. H.B. Turbott, 'East Cape Health District, New Zealand', *International Nursing Review* 8, nos. 1–4, 1933, pp. 65–70.
83. Lambie to Turbott, 16 November 1928. Her memo criticised the inattention to preventive work, lack of consistent standards in maternity work, and spasmodic health teaching. The memo did not include comments on each nurse, but Turbott's response shows that these had been made, probably verbally.
84. H.B. Turbott, medical officer of health, District Health Office Gisborne, memo to director-general of health, 7 January 1929, re District nurses, East Cape District, in District Nurses: Reports of Inspection–1928–43, H1-23/6/3, Department of Health records,

ANZ. Susie Trewby trained at St Bartholomew's Hospital, London, and registered in New Zealand in 1925. She completed her maternity and midwifery training at the St Helens Hospital Wellington in 1927, started rural district nursing in 1928 and in 1933 was based in Whangārei. *NZG*, 1933, p. 1015.
85. M.H. Watt, acting director-general of health to Dr Turbott, medical officer of health, Gisborne, 11 March 1929, in District Nurses – Reports of Inspection – 1928–1943, H1–23/6/3, Department of Health records, ANZ.
86. H.B. Turbott to director-general of health, 18 March 1929, re Miss Banks, district nurse, Frasertown, in District Nurses: Reports of Inspection – 1928–1943, H1–23/6/3, Department of Health records, ANZ. Derek Dow notes that Turbott's manner could be 'combative'. Derek A. Dow, *Safeguarding the Public Health: A history of the New Zealand Department of Health* (Wellington: Victoria University Press, 1995), p. 155.
87. As a further example, the nurse at Mōkau was the centre of a struggle between two hospital boards and later between the medical officer of health and the Department of Health. Pamela J. Wood, 'Professional, practice and political issues in the history of New Zealand's remote rural "backblocks" nursing: The case of Mokau, 1910–1940', *Contemporary Nurse* 30, no. 2, 2008, pp. 168–80.
88. See, for example, 'Westland Hospitals and Charitable Aid Board', *HG*, 28 August 1919, p. 4; 'Appointments vacant', *KT* 13, July 1920, p. 125; 'Westland Hospitals and Charitable Aid Board', *HG*, 27 July 1920, p. 4; Untitled, *HG*, 26 August 1920, p. 2.
89. Untitled, *HG*, 6 September 1921, p. 2.
90. 'Westland Hospital Board', *HG*, 13 December 1921, p. 4.
91. 'Correspondence', *HG*, 19 January 1922, p. 4.
92. 'Correspondence', *HG*, 10 February 1922, p. 4.
93. Ibid.
94. 'Westland Hospital Board', *HG*, 28 February 1922, p. 1.
95. 'Correspondence', *HG*, 19 April 1924, p. 2.
96. Rosemarie Smith, 'Women's Division Federated Farmers, 1925 –', in *Women Together: A history of women's organisations in New Zealand*, ed. A. Else (Wellington: Daphne Brasell Associates, 1993), pp. 392–95; R. Lynette Russell and Judith A. Cornell, *A Vision for the Bush: The NSW Bush Nursing Association 1911–1974* (Burwood, NSW: Australian College of Nursing, 2012); Susan Priestly, *Bush Nursing in Victoria, 1910–1985: The first 75 years* (Melbourne: Victorian Bush Nursing Association, 1986); Marita Bardenhagen, 'Professional isolation and independence of bush nurses in Tasmania, 1910–1957: "We were very much individuals on our own"', PhD thesis, University of Tasmania, 2003; Wood, 'Historical imagination and issues in rural and remote area nursing'. For one Tasmanian visitor's comment on the difference between the New Zealand and Tasmanian systems, see 'In Tasmania', *EP*, 1 February 1930, p. 10.
97. 'In the country', *EP*, 4 June 1927, p. 10. Catherine Blackie trained at Dunedin Hospital and registered in January 1910. She did private nursing and then joined the Native Health Service in 1912. *NZG*, 1915, p. 403. Blackie served with the NZANS in World War I and survived the sinking of the *Marquette* in October 1915. After the war, in poorer health, she did light duties as matron of the Ōtaki Cottage Hospital. She was appointed as the Māori health nurse at Tolaga Bay in 1926 and as the WDFU bush nurse the following year. See, for example, Untitled, *KT* 19, July 1926, p. 141; 'Appointments', *KT* 21, April 1928, p. 102.
98. 'Farmers' Union', *ES*, 24 July 1930, p. 1.
99. 'District nursing in New Zealand: How it is organised and how it is planned', lecture

by M. Lambie 4.6.34, Miss Cameron Public Health Nursing Notebook, n.d., SANS, 8/1/6, ANZ.
100. See, for example, the two stories in 'The bush nurse', *KT* 12, April 1919, p. 89.
101. Bridget Ristori, *Patients in My Care: The autobiography of a nurse* (London: Elek, 1967). Mary Breckinridge, the director of the Frontier Nursing Service, wrote the foreword for Ristori's book.
102. A. Wickham, '"She must be content to be their servant as well as their teacher": The early years of district nursing in Ireland', in *Care to Remember: Nursing and midwifery in Ireland*, ed. G. Fealy (Cork: Mercier Press, 2005), pp. 101–21.
103. Jessica Howell, 'Nursing and empire: Travel letters from Africa and the Caribbean', *Studies in Travel Writing* 17, no. 1, 2013, pp. 62–77.
104. 'A tough year in the backblocks'.
105. 'District nursing in Pongaroa'.

Chapter 6. Nursing Māori, Māori nurses

1. 'A district nurse's work in a northern district', *KT* 15, July 1922, pp. 127–30. Mary Cartwright trained at Christchurch Hospital and registered in July 1917. *NZG*, 1920, p. 592.
2. In the published version of this story, the nurse uses these words, but spells *neehi* as 'naahi' and *kei te pai* as 'kaitapai', presumably recording them in the way she heard them.
3. Raeburn Lange, *May the People Live: A history of Maori health development, 1900–1920* (Auckland: Auckland University Press, 1999).
4. D. Ian Pool, *The Maori Population of New Zealand, 1769–1971* (Auckland: Auckland University Press, 1977); D. Ian Pool, *Te Iwi Maori: A New Zealand population past, present and projected* (Auckland: Auckland University Press, 1991).
5. Lange, *May the People Live*, p. 55. See also Jane Stafford and Mark Williams, *Maoriland: New Zealand literature, 1872–1914* (Wellington: Victoria University Press, 2006).
6. Lange, *May the People Live*; James Pope, *Health for the Maori: A manual for use in native schools* (Wellington: George Didsbury, Government Printer, 1884).
7. These three paragraphs summarise the explanation given in Lange, *May the People Live*, pp. 17–166. I am very grateful to Dr Raeburn Lange for generously allowing me to include this summary.
8. Jessie Munro, *The Story of Suzanne Aubert* (Auckland: Auckland University Press/ Bridget Williams Books, 1997).
9. *AJHR*, 1912, H-31, p. 20. For an account by a registered mission nurse and midwife, see 'Letter from a mission district nurse', *KT* 11, July 1918, p. 51.
10. Lange, *May the People Live*, pp. 36, 43–44.
11. Pamela J. Wood, '"Efficient preachers of the gospel of health": The 1898 scheme for educating Maori nurses', *Nursing Praxis in New Zealand* 7, 1 1992, pp. 12–21. Hāmiora Hei presented a paper on this topic, 'Maori Girls and Nursing', at the conference of former Te Aute College students at Gisborne in December 1897, published the following year. See 'Papers and Addresses read before the Second Conference of the Te Aute College Students' Association, Napier, 1898', pp. 30–31. See also Alexandra McKegg, 'The Maori Health Nursing Scheme: An experiment in autonomous health care', *New Zealand Journal of History* 26, no. 2, 1992, pp. 145–60.
12. *AJHR*, 1906, E-2, p. 16. This comment was from William W. Bird, inspector of Native schools.
13. In addition to the scholarship scheme, Premier Richard Seddon proposed in 1906 to give hospital boards £25 per year for each new probationer in order to address a nursing shortage, and encouraged them to give some of the places to Māori applicants. Views were mixed.
14. In 1907 James Mason, the chief health

officer, in trying to persuade the matron of the Waikato Sanatorium to take Māori probationers, suggested providing a separate cottage for them in case Pākehā probationers objected to sleeping in the same room. McKegg, 'The Maori Health Nursing Scheme', p. 151.

15. 'Native nurses', *WC*, 18 February 1915, p. 3. Eventually the board agreed to put her name on the waiting list but not to employ her while the two other Māori nurses were still at the hospital. For examples of different hospital board members' views, see 'Maori hospital nurses', *PBH*, 26 July 1904, p. 2; 'Hawera Hospital Board', *HNS*, 20 March 1906, p. 5; 'Maori girls as nurses', *ODT*, 1 September 1906, p. 8; 'Maoris as nurses: Hospital Board discussion', *NZH*, 28 July 1911, p. 4; 'Maoris as nurses: Colour no deterrent; Qualified applicants welcome', *AS*, 13 June 1912 p. 4.

16. Hester Maclean, 'The conditions of nursing in New Zealand', *Australasian Nurses' Journal* 5, no. 9, 1907, pp. 272–75.

17. *AJHR*, 1936, H-31, p. 47.

18. Diana S. Masters, 'Mereana Tangata, the first Maori registered nurse', *Nursing New Zealand* 7, no. 8, 2001, p. 27. Her obituary in the name of Mrs Marianne Hattaway in the *NZNJ* said that 'she belonged to both races'. 'Obituary', *NZNJ* 23, January 1930, p. 36.

19. John Tombleson, 'Whataupoko: The land, its people', p. 29, Tairāwhiti Museum, Gisborne. I am very grateful to Eloise Wallace, director, and Christine Page, archivist, for providing material relating to Kate Wyllie.

20. Hospital trustees, *PBH*, 14 April 1898, p. 3.

21. Kate Wyllie material, Tairāwhiti Museum, Gisborne. The hospital certificate is dated 18 December 1901. As her three-year training would have finished well before this, it could have been a 'just in time' certificate to enable her to apply for registration as soon as the register opened the following month.

22. *NZG*, 1925, p. 479. The entry shows that all her experience from 1894 to 1901 was counted as evidence for her registration. A copy of her registration certificate is dated April 1902. Certificates are dated later than nurses' actual registration because nurses had to apply after registration for their certificate and medal.

23. The first nurse to register was Ellen Dougherty, matron of the Palmerston North Hospital. For more on Caroline Stewart, see Marie Burgess, *Nursing Remembered* (Gisborne: Cook Hospital Nurses' Reunion Committee, 2010).

24. 'Wedding bells', *GT*, 1 May 1902, p. 2; Tombleson, 'Whataupoko', p. 29; Sir Robert Hall, papers, Box 1, File 25, p. 4, Tairāwhiti Museum, Gisborne. Flora Stevens trained at Auckland Hospital, registering in June 1929. *NZG*, 1930, p. 1313. No information could be found on Tui Stevens' training or registration.

25. As just three examples, see 'Personal', *Bush Advocate*, 30 November 1910, p. 8; 'Personalia', *NZT*, 30 November 1910, p. 6; 'Personal', *MS*, 1 December 1910, p. 5.

26. For a longer account that also includes the idea of a charter for action, see Untitled, *PBH*, 29 November 1910, p. 4. It said that Hei's lead 'has already induced others to follow in the same useful work'. Ākenehi Hei was the first Māori to complete both nursing and midwifery qualifications. A prestigious Te Ākenehi Hei Memorial Award, instituted by Te Rūnanga o Aotearoa, is conferred every two years through the New Zealand Nurses Organisation for significant contribution to Māori health.

27. 'Akenehi Hei, nursing amongst the Maori', *KT* 3, July 1910, p. 16.

28. See, for example, 'Nurses' training', *AS*, 19 March 1937, p. 15; 'Shortage of nurses', *AS*, 9 February 1939, p. 7.

29. *AJHR*, 1937, H-31, p. 45. Entering the preliminary training school rather than having an initial preparatory year in

hospital meant that full general training with proper supervision was possible from the beginning.
30. 'Scholarships for registered Maori nurses', *NZNJ* 39, January 1946, p. 5.
31. *AJHR*, 1912, E-3, preceding p. 11.
32. *AJHR*, 1912, H-31, p. 21.
33. Mary Purcell completed her training at Wellington Hospital in 1903 and her midwifery qualification at St Helens Hospital Wellington in 1905. After stints as a private case and private hospital nurse, in 1911 she became the first nurse appointed to the Native Health Nursing Service. In 1912 she became a Plunket nurse in Hastings. *NZG*, 1914, p. 471. Cicely Beetham started training at Auckland Hospital in 1898 and registered in February 1902. She gained her midwifery certificate in Melbourne in 1904, was matron of Manganui Hospital in 1909, did private nursing in 1910, and joined the Native Health Service in 1911. *NZG*, 1915, p. 402.
34. McKegg, 'The Maori Health Nursing Scheme', pp. 184–85. See also Ann M. McKillop, 'Native health nursing in New Zealand, 1911–1930: "A new work and a new profession for women"', MA thesis, Massey University, 1998.
35. See, for example, *AJHR*, 1934, H-31, p. 44; *AJHR*, 1935, H-31, p. 56; *AJHR*, 1939, H-31, p. 64; *AJHR*, 1947, H-31, p. 26.
36. Ann McKillop noted that only five Māori nurses worked in the Native or Māori Health Nursing Services. McKillop, 'Native health nursing in New Zealand, 1911–1930', p. 3. She rightly excludes Ākenehi Hei and Hēni Whangapirita from this calculation, as they did not work for these services. However, additional Māori nurses who worked in these services have now been identified.
37. Maud Mataira trained at Wanganui Hospital and registered in June 1911. *NZG*, 1917, p. 675.
38. *AJHR*, 1912, H-31, p. 20.
39. In a hospital inquiry in 1911 investigating, among other issues, why so many nurses were leaving Napier Hospital, Eva Wi Repa said that she had resigned because she had not been appointed sister and that another nurse, who was from Blenheim Hospital and only recently qualified, had been appointed sister over her. Her colleague Grace Reed had resigned for the same reason. 'Hospital Inquiry', *HS*, 1 November 1911, p. 3.
40. Ellen Taare trained at Palmerston North Hospital and registered in April 1913. *NZG*, 1915, p. 443.
41. 'Resignations, appointments, etc', *KT* 15, April 1923, p. 87. Ngapori Naera trained at Auckland and Te Kopuru Hospitals, registering in January 1915. She gained her midwifery certificate at St Helens Hospital Auckland in 1916. She remained in the Māori health service until 1923. *NZG*, 1930, p. 1281.
42. 'Obituary', *KT* 5, July 1912, p. 124. Concert advertisements and accounts of performances appeared in the *ST* during 1918 and 1919. Her first was described in Entertainments, *ST*, 28 October 1911, p. 7. Rena Te Au was a day pupil at Napier Hospital before training as a probationer at Southland Hospital, which she completed in December 1913.
43. Untitled, *KT* 11, July 1918, p. 163. Ngaro Ngapo trained at Waikato Hospital, passing the state final examination in June 1915. *NZG*, 1925, p. 440. The work of nurses Mataira, Wi Repa, Taare, Naera, Te Au and Ngapo is also described in Lange, *May the People Live*, pp. 174–76.
44. Marie Burgess, 'Pritchard, Ethel', from the Dictionary of New Zealand Biography: www:teara.govt.nz/en/biographies/5p38/pritchard-ethel; 'Notes from the hospitals and personal items', *KT* 16, October 1923, pp. 187–96, see p. 193; 'Sister Pritchard, a Pen Portrait', typescript, Tairāwhiti Museum.
45. Rangi Wereta trained at Palmerston North

Hospital, registering in December 1922 and gaining her midwifery certificate the following year from the Wellington St Helens Hospital. *NZG*, 1925, p. 474.
46. Joan Rattray, *Great Days in New Zealand Nursing* (Wellington: A.H. & A.W. Reed, 1961), p. 47.
47. McKegg, 'The Maori Health Nursing Scheme', pp. 150, 153–54.
48. *AJHR*, 1911, H-31, p. 183.
49. *AJHR*, 1914, H-31, p. 7.
50. McKegg, 'The Maori Health Nursing Scheme', pp. 150, 153–54.
51. 'News from the hospitals and personal notes', *KT* 4, October 1911, pp. 164–65, see p. 164; 'Resignations, appointments and presentations', *KT* 6, July 1913, pp. 127–30, see p. 128. Lilian (Lily) Dawson qualified at the Launceston General Hospital in 1897 and completed her midwifery training in London in 1903. She worked at Pretoria Hospital in South Africa, various Australian hospitals and then Talbot Hospital in Timaru before joining the Native Health Service. *NZG*, 1915, p. 410. In 1920 she was in India. *NZG*, 1920, p. 598.
52. The persistence of this idea until the 1930s was noted in James Belich, *Making Peoples: A history of the New Zealanders from Polynesian settlement to the end of the nineteenth century* (Auckland: Penguin, 1996), p. 174, citing Angela Ballara, *Proud to be White? A survey of Pakeha prejudice in New Zealand* (Auckland: Heinemann, 1986), p. 86.
53. *AJHR*, 1912, H-31, p. 76.
54. Lange, *May the People Live*, p. 64.
55. *AJHR*, 1912, H-31, p. 20. See also 'Natives district nursing', *KT* 7, October 1914, p. 158.
56. *AJHR*, 1912, H-31, p. 21. Ann McKillop notes that one of the distinctive aspects of Māori health nursing was nurses living in close association with Māori communities in a social role not previously considered part of nursing. McKillop, 'Native health nursing in New Zealand, 1911–1930', p. 3.
57. Māori provided supplies and assistance to nurses in fever camps or nursing individual patients in remote areas, and supported their efforts in kainga by word of mouth or by raising funds for cottages and cars. Support for nurses' public health work continued into the 1940s. Beth Paora commented on the value of Māori women's committees and groups, as well as the co-operation of Pākehā schoolteachers in Native schools. Elizabeth Paora, 'Public health and other problems of a Maori health district and suggestions for improvement', *NZNJ* 33, September 1940, pp. 285–86.
58. Linda Bryder, '"They do what you wish; they like you; you the good nurse!": Colonialism and Native Health nursing in New Zealand, 1900-40', in *Colonial Caring: A history of colonial and post-colonial nursing*, eds H. Sweet and S. Hawkins (Manchester: Manchester University Press, 2015), p. 99.
59. 'District nursing', *KT* 3, July 1910, pp. 100–02.
60. 'Nurses for the Maoris', *KT*, 5, October 1912, p. 99.
61. *AJHR*, 1932, H-31, p. 35; *AJHR*, 1934, H-31, p. 36.
62. 'Native health nursing', *KT* 10, April 1917, p. 70. Bertha Whittaker trained at Waikato Hospital and registered in August 1914. She gained her midwifery certificate at the St Helens Hospital Christchurch in 1915 and then joined the Native Health Service. *NZG*, 1920, p. 660.
63. 'A health caravan on tour', *KT* 12, April 1919, p. 75. Elizabeth Fergusson trained and worked at the Bristol Royal Infirmary from 1894 to 1897, gaining her midwifery certificate as well in 1897. She did private nursing until 1900, served in the Army Nursing Reserve in South Africa from 1900 to 1902, and then came to New Zealand, where she registered in November. After working as a private

63. (cont.) hospital nurse in Whanganui from 1902 to 1907, she worked in the Ruanui Maternity Hospital from 1907 to 1912. She was matron of Kawakawa Hospital until November 1914, when she joined the Native Health Service. *NZG*, 1920, p. 603.
64. A. Bagley, 'A visit to the Far North', *KT* 13, April 1920, pp. 87–91.
65. Helen Gilmour-Jones, 'Reintroducing Miss Margaret Macnab', *Nursing Praxis in New Zealand* 7, no. 3, 1992, pp. 40–42.
66. See, for example, 'Maori nursing – Te Araroa', *KT* 5, July 1912, pp. 74–76; 'Native health nursing', *KT* 10, April 1917, p. 70; 'Letter from a mission district nurse', *KT* 11, July 1918, p. 51; Frances Hayman, *King Country Nurse* (Auckland: Blackwood & Janet Paul, 1964), p. 74; Beryl Smedley, 'Ricky's Story: The memoirs of Amy Rickman', p. 26, MS–Papers–4404, ATL.
67. 'Maori Health Nurses', *KT* 21, July 1928, pp. 139–40. Jane Minnie Jarrett completed her training at Newcastle-upon-Tyne Infirmary in 1899 and gained her midwifery certificate. She registered in New Zealand in December 1915 and joined the Native Health Service in February 1916. *NZG*, 1920, p. 618.
68. Lilian Ada Hill, oral history interview with Ailsa McCutcheon, 5 May 1983, OHI–0014/073, New Zealand Nursing Education & Research Foundation Oral History collection, ATL.
69. Smedley, 'Ricky's Story', p. 26.
70. Helen Mackie, *A Nursing Journey* ([Wellington]: H. Mackie, 1990), pp. 10–11.
71. Barbara Ancott-Johnson, *Nurse in the North: With Dr G.M. Smith in the Hokianga* (Christchurch: Whitcombe & Tombs, 1973), p. 33.
72. 'Native health nursing in Auckland District', *KT* 7, January 1914, pp. 47–49, quotation on p. 47.
73. 'District nurse's notes', *KT* 6, October 1913, p. 155.
74. Mackie, *A Nursing Journey*, p. 6.
75. Hayman, *King Country Nurse*, pp. 55, 88, 96.
76. Gilmour-Jones, 'Reintroducing Miss Margaret Macnab', p. 41.
77. 'A district nurse's work in a northern district', *KT* 15, July 1922, pp. 127–30, quotation on p. 127.
78. 'Prevention is better than cure', *KT* 13, April 1920, pp. 70–72.
79. 'Nursing Maoris (by Nurse Street)', *KT* 4, July 1911, p. 110; 'Nursing under the Maori health scheme', *KT* 5, January 1912, p. 25; 'Maori health nurses', *KT* 21, July 1928, pp. 139–40; 'With the Maori health nurses in the North Auckland district', *KT* 22, July 1929, pp. 130–31; F.J. Cameron, 'A day in the country with the district health nurse', *NZNJ* 39, January 1946, pp. 6–9.
80. Paora, 'Public health and other problems of a Maori health district', p. 285.
81. Public Health Nursing Committee, 'The Story of Public Health Nursing in New Zealand', New Zealand Registered Nurses Association, Wellington, 1955, p. 13.
82. 'The camp in the north', *KT* 6, July 1913, pp. 110–12.
83. Gill identifies it as being at Pakaraka near Ōhaeawai. The first account did not name the location but Gill's description of it, and details of the camp, match. Florence Gill, 'Some camp hospital experiences', *KT* 6, October 1913, p. 146.
84. Ibid.
85. 'Active service in the back blocks', *KT* 9, January 1916, p. 38.
86. 'More camp hospital experiences', *KT* 6, October 1913, pp. 152–53.
87. 'The smallpox campaign', *KT* 7, April 1914, pp. 82–86.
88. 'An emergency hospital', *KT* 6, April 1913, pp. 80–81, quotation on p. 81.
89. 'The health of the Maoris, measures being taken', *KT* 4, July 1911, pp. 108–10.
90. Ancott-Johnson, *Nurse in the North*, pp. 14–15.
91. Ibid., p. 20.
92. Ibid., p. 18.

93. Ibid., pp. 39–41.
94. Hei, 'Nursing amongst the Maori', p. 16.
95. See, for example, 'Maori nurses', *KT* 2, October 1909, p. 157; 'Native Health Nurses', *KT* 6, April 1913, pp. 73–74; 'Natives district nursing', *KT* 7, October 1914, pp. 158–60; 'Natives district nursing', *KT* 8, April 1915, pp. 87–88; 'The district nurse', *EP*, 14 November 1932, p. 7, reprinted as 'The district nurse: Helping the Maoris', *NZNJ* 25, January 1933, pp. 311–12, and in 'The story of public health nursing in New Zealand', *NZNJ* 49, August 1956, pp. 151–55.
96. 'Natives district nursing', *KT*, 8, April 1915, p. 87. The writer is unidentified. The usual nurse at Te Teko, Janie North, was away on holiday. It could have been Kate Wright, the nurse based at Rotorua who visited Te Teko in her absence. In 1862 Te Ua Haumene based his Pai Mārire or Hauhau religion on the principles of goodness and grace, but it was sometimes subverted by violent elements who came to be known as Hauhau.
97. 'Early nursing history of East Cape Health District', pp. 5–6, MS–Papers–7072–6, ATL.
98. Lange, *May the People Live*, pp. 223–24.
99. 'Early nursing history of East Cape Health District', p. 6.
100. 'Tuberculosis among the Maoris', *KT* 22, November 1929, pp. 196–200, see p. 197.
101. Public Health Nursing Committee, 'The Story of Public Health Nursing in New Zealand', p. 12.
102. Ibid.
103. Lilian Ada Hill, oral history interview with Alisa McCutcheon, 5 May 1983.
104. Mary (Molly) O'Meara, oral history interview with Nancy Kinross, 12 October 1993, 0014/128, Nursing Education & Research Foundation Oral History collection, ATL.
105. Hayman, *King Country Nurse*, p. 66; Smedley, 'Ricky's Story', p. 27.
106. Hayman, *King Country Nurse*, p. 66.
107. 'Nursing Maoris (by Nurse Street)', p. 110.
108. 'District nurse's notes', *KT* 6, October 1913, p. 155.
109. 'Early nursing history of East Cape Health District', pp. 3, 5.
110. 'Native district nursing', *KT* 9, October 1916, p. 220.
111. 'Maori Health Nurses', *KT* 21, July 1928, pp. 139–40, quotation on p. 139.
112. 'Native Health Nurses', *KT* 6, April 1913, p. 38. Marky Minto Tait gained her nursing certificate at the Western Infirmary in Glasgow in 1909 and her midwifery certificate at the Glasgow Maternity Hospital in 1912. She came to New Zealand the same year, registering in August 1912, and was appointed as a Native Health Nurse. *NZG*, 1920, p. 654. When she completed her year's contract, she and her friend, Nurse Angus, planned to go to India, where Tait was to marry and Angus was to join Lady Minto's Nursing Association in Bombay. 'Te Araroa', *KT* 6, July 1913, p. 97. It seems these plans were set aside. The two nurses gave up nursing for a time and successfully ran a poultry farm in Britain, which they had to sell at a loss when recalled as Territorial nurses. Because of reports of German atrocities, instead of going to the front they were sent to their old hospital, the Western Infirmary in Glasgow. 'From a nurse at Home', *KT* 8, January 1915, p. 38. Other nurses also commented on the need to work beyond their usual scope. See, for example, the section on Edith Fletcher, the Whangamōmona district health nurse from 1945 to 48, in *Stratford Hospital Memories*, ed. Alison Robinson (Stratford: Thurlstone Press, 2001), p. 24.
113. 'Nurses for the Maoris', *KT* 5, October 1912, p. 99.
114. 'Letters translated from the Maori', *KT* 6, October 1913, p. 151.
115. 'Splendid work of a nurse', *PBH*, 4 April 1914, p. 6. This was reprinted in 'A tribute to a nurse', *KT* 7, July 1914, p. 124.

116. *AJHR*, 1921, H-31, p. 33. Amy Jewiss completed her training at Whangārei Hospital, sat the state final examination in December 1916 and registered in January 1917. She was charge nurse that year at Rāwene Hospital, then sister at Hāwera Hospital from 1917 to 1919. She gained her midwifery certificate at Wairau Maternity Hospital. *NZG*, 1930, p. 1245.
117. Mary Lambie, Wellington, to Amy Jewiss, Auckland, 19 December 1933, in District Nurses: Manaia, H1, 23/21/39, ANZ.
118. Amy Jewiss, Ōpunake, to Mary Lambie, 27 April 1935, in District Nurses: Manaia, H, 23/21/39, ANZ; Amy Jewiss, Ōpunake, to Mary Lambie, 30 April 1935, in District Nurses: Manaia, H1, 23/21/39, ANZ.
119. Memos between Dr M. Watt, director-general of health, and Dr F.S Maclean, medical officer of health, Wellington, November 1936, in District Nurses: Manaia, H1, 23/21/39, ANZ.
120. Dr M.H. Watt, memo to Janet Moore [acting director, Division of Nursing], 21 September 1937, in District Nurses: Manaia, H1, 23/21/39, ANZ.
121. Janet Moore, acting director, Division of Nursing, memo to Mr Drake, chief clerk, Department of Health, 4 October 1937, in District Nurses: Manaia, H1, 23/21/39, ANZ.
122. Dr Frederick Dawson, medical officer of health, New Plymouth, to director-general of health, 18 September 1939, in District Nurses: Manaia, H1, 23/21/39, ANZ.
123. J.W. Brimblecombe, inspector (buildings), to medical officer of health, New Plymouth, n.d. [August 1944]; acting resident engineer, Public Works Department, memo to medical officer of health, New Plymouth, 16 August 1944, in District Nurses: Manaia, H1, 23/21/39, ANZ. Heath Robinson was an English cartoonist and illustrator, whose images characteristically depicted complicated machines that performed simple functions.
124. See, for example, Sweet and Hawkins, *Colonial Caring*; Jane Howell, 'Nursing and empire: Travel letters from Africa and the Caribbean', *Studies in Travel Writing* 17, no. 1, 2013, pp. 62–77.
125. McKegg, 'The Maori Health Nursing Scheme', pp. 154–55.
126. Bryder, '"They do what you wish"', pp. 98–99.
127. Mary Mahoney became the first African American trained nurse in 1879, but registration did not start in Massachusetts, the state where she trained, until 1910.
128. Untitled, *PBH*, 24 February 1915 p. 2.

Chapter 7. Caring in conflict

1. This war of 1899–1902 is variously called the Boer War, the South African War, and the Second Anglo-Boer War. New Zealand newspapers of the time called it the Transvaal War.
2. Joan Woodward and Glenys Mitchell, eds, *A Nurse at War: Emily Peter, 1858–1927* (Christchurch: Te Waihora Press, 2008), pp. 92–93.
3. 'Local and general', *GES*, 31 August 1916, p. 2. Christian Maclean completed her training at Wanganui Hospital in December 1913 and her midwifery training at the St Helens Hospital Auckland in 1914, becoming its submatron the following year. *NZG*, 1915, p. 427.
4. Joyce Macdonald, *Away from Home* (Christchurch: Bookroom, 1945), p. 12.
5. Elsie Isabella Leipst, oral history interview with unidentified interviewer, n.d., Hawke's Bay Knowledge Bank, Hastings.
6. Sonja Davies, *Bread and Roses: Sonja Davies, her story* (Masterton: Fraser Books, 1984), p. 45.
7. Anna Rogers explains the difficulty of calculating the number. Anna Rogers, *While You're Away: New Zealand nurses at war, 1899–1948* (Auckland: Auckland University Press, 2003), p. 16.
8. 'The Transvaal war', *ES*, 20 June 1900, p. 3.

9. The numbers are difficult to confirm, particularly as nurses served with different organisations. Sherayl McNabb includes 626 nurses and masseuses in her list of NZANS personnel on her comprehensive website, New Zealand Military Nursing, www.nzans.org. In contrast, John Studholme named just 518 in his list in 1928. See Lt Col John Studholme, *New Zealand Expeditionary Force, Record of Personal Services during the War of Officers, Nurses, and First-Class Warrant Officers; and other facts relating to the N.Z.E.F., Unofficial but based on official records* (Wellington: W.A.G. Skinner, Government Printer, 1928), pp. 321–55. These lists do not include New Zealand nurses serving overseas with other organisations.
10. Arlie Hochschild, *The Managed Heart: Commercialization of human feeling* (Berkeley: University of California Press, 1983).
11. Rogers, *While You're Away*, p. 3.
12. 'A pioneer nurse', *Press*, 1 February 1901, p. 5. 'The dreaded enteric raged everywhere,' she said, 'and no wonder, with no sanitary arrangements whatever; animals lying dead everywhere, water bad, buildings covered black with flies, and patients covered with vermin.'
13. 'The troubles of our nurses', *ES*, 26 June 1900, p. 5.
14. 'An army nurse', *Press*, 24 January 1901, p. 5.
15. 'A pioneer nurse', *Press*, 1 February 1901, p. 5.
16. 'At a base hospital', *KT* 8, October 1915, p. 173.
17. 'News from No. 1 New Zealand Stationary Hospital, B.E.F., France', *KT* 10, January 1917, p. 11.
18. 'The Hospital Ships', *KT* 9, October 1916, pp. 201–22, quotation on p. 201.
19. See, for example, 'Life on board a hospital ship', *KT* 8, April 1915, pp. 106–07, quotation on p. 107.
20. 'At a base hospital', *KT*, 8, October 1915, p. 173.
21. 'Transport duty', *KT*,11, April 1918, pp. 67–69, quotation on p. 68.
22. 'News of our nurses in Egypt', *KT* 9, January 1916, pp. 43–44, quotation on p. 43.
23. 'Letters from our nurses abroad', *KT* 9, July 1916, pp. 139–47.
24. The term gangrene refers to tissue death, often resulting from lack of blood supply, pressure or infection. With gas gangrene, a specific bacterium, *Clostridium perfringens* (formerly known as *Bacillus welchii*), destroys the tissue and creates pockets of gas underneath the skin. If the skin is tapped, it sounds like paper.
25. 'Extracts from nurses' letters', *KT* 8, October 1915, pp. 170–74, quotation on p. 170. Lily Eddy trained at Thames Hospital and registered in March 1911. *NZG*, 1915, p. 412.
26. Basil Hughes, Capt. RAMC (TF), 'Early treatment of compound fracture of the long bones of the extremities', *British Medical Journal*, 3 March 1917, pp. 289–92, quotation on p. 290.
27. 'Letter from Hospital Ship "Maheno" (first commission)', *KT* 9, January 1916, pp. 18–19, quotation on p. 19. This is signed 'J.M.', and the author is probably Jean Muir.
28. 'Notes from Balmer Lawn, Brockenhurst, BIPP treatment', *KT* 11, April 1918, p. 82. The comment about pain and sleep came from Jeanne Sinclair at Balmer Lawn, a hotel in Brockenhurst converted into part of the Brockenhurst hospital. 'News from our nurses abroad', *KT* 11, January 1918, pp. 9–13, see p. 9.
29. Orthopaedic surgeon William McCaw believed BIPP was 'the greatest blessing of all' and that it 'completely changed the clinical picture'. William C. McCaw, 'Modern antiseptics', *KT* 15, January 1922, pp. 5–8, quotations on p. 6. For a description of the Carrel-Dakin wound

irrigation process, see H.C. Rutherford Darling, *Surgical Nursing and After-Treatment: A handbook for nurses and others* 2nd edn. (London: J. & H. Churchill, 1923), pp. 121–23. Dakin's solution contained sodium hypochlorite.

30. 'Diary and observations of a hospital ship's sister', *KT* 9, April 1916, pp. 75–79, quotation on p. 75. Margaret Tucker registered in August 1913, having trained at Christchurch Hospital. She then became a sister at Ashburton Hospital and worked there until July 1915, when she joined the NZANS, serving until November 1919. *NZG*, 1920, p. 656.

31. 'With the Army Nursing Service', *PBH*, 1 October 1915, p. 4. Clara Cherry trained at Auckland Hospital, registering in August 1913. After the war, she became a school nurse based at Te Awamutu. *NZG*, 1925, p. 377.

32. 'The troubles of our nurses', *ES*, 26 June 1900, p. 5.

33. 'Caring for the wounded', *Press*, 16 June 1900, p. 10.

34. 'Letter from a member of Queen Alexandra's Nursing Service', *KT* 8, January 1915, p. 33. Laura James trained at Wellington Hospital and placed Top of the Dominion in the state final examination in June 1909. She joined the QAIMNS and worked at the Millbank Military Hospital. *NZG*, 1920, p. 617.

35. Letter from the New Zealand General Hospital, Brockenhurst, England, 14 July 1916, Commons Family: Papers–Letters from Daphne to her family–MS–Papers–1582–12, ATL. (There is some indication that Daphne Commons preferred to be called Rona, but the name Daphne is used here to align with official records.) Ethel Lewis had completed her training at the Bristol General Hospital in England in 1905 and registered in New Zealand in May 1911. After working as a private case nurse, she became the Native Health nurse for Ōtaki in 1912. She served in Serbia in 1915, joined the NZANS in 1917 and returned to Native Health nursing in July 1919. *NZG*, 1920, p. 623.

36. Christine E. Hallett, *Containing Trauma: Nursing work in the First World War* (Manchester: Manchester University Press, 2009), pp. 158–59.

37. Otherwise, she noted, they were sent to Codford and Hornchurch, which were 'usually only stopping places on their way to Sling ... and then – back to France'. Letter from the No. 1 New Zealand General Hospital, Brockenhurst, England, Commons Family: Papers–Letters from Daphne to her family–MS–Papers–1582–12, ATL. New Zealand soldiers convalesced at Hornchurch and were 'hardened' at Codford. Sling was the 'unloved, bleak, and lonely' training camp of wooden huts on the Salisbury Plain. Lt H.T.B. Drew, 'The New Zealand camps in England', in *The War Effort of New Zealand*, ed. H.T.B. Drew (Auckland: Whitcombe & Tombs, 1923), pp. 266, 248.

38. 'Letters from our nurses abroad', *KT* 10, April 1917, pp. 74–77, quotation on p. 74. 'Blighty' was military slang for England. Kate Barnitt registered in July 1909 after training at the New Plymouth Hospital, and worked as a sister there until 1915. She then served with the NZANS until 1919. *NZG*, 1920, p. 583.

39. 'News from our nurses in Egypt', *KT* 9, April 1916, pp. 83–86, quotation on p. 86. Mabel Kittlety completed her training at Greymouth Hospital in June 1910. After registering the following month, she worked as a staff nurse at Christchurch Hospital before joining the NZANS. *NZG*, 1915, p. 424.

40. 'Transport duty', *KT* 11, April 1918, pp. 67–69, quotation on p. 68.

41. 'Welcome to Miss Ross', *ES*, 2 November 1900, p. 6. Sarah Ross had 'never seen men so ill in her life as she did there'. She was responsible for six marquees and sometimes had 20 sick men lying on the

floor of just one of them. The audience was probably relieved to applaud when she finished by saying she would go back tomorrow if she had the chance.

42. 'Caring for the wounded', *Press*, 16 June 1900, p. 10.
43. This letter was probably from Bessie Hay. 'The nurses who went from Dunedin', *ES*, 19 May 1900, p. 2.
44. Letter from the New Zealand General Hospital, Pont de Koubbeh, Cairo, 25 April 1916, Commons Family: Papers–Letters from Daphne to her family–MS–Papers–1582–11, ATL.
45. *Ghastly* was the word nurses used most frequently in letters to describe the war and its impact. Pamela J. Wood, '"This ghastly war": Emotional glimpses in New Zealand nurses' published letters in World War I', paper presented at the History of Emotions Conference, Stout Centre, Victoria University of Wellington, Wellington, 3–5 September 2015.
46. 'Extracts from nurses' letters', *KT* 8, October 1915, pp. 170–74, quotation on p. 171.
47. 'Letters from our nurses abroad', *KT* 10, January 1917, pp. 6–15, quotation on p. 11.
48. 'Casualty clearing station: Letter from a New Zealand sister', *KT* 11, April 1918, pp. 76–77.
49. 'News from the hospitals and personal items', *KT* 8, October 1915, pp. 201–02, see p. 202; 'News from our nurses in Egypt', *KT* 9, April 1916, pp. 83–86, see p. 84; 'News from our nurses abroad', *KT* 12, July 1919, pp. 107–09, see p. 108; 'Obituary', *KT* 13, October 1920, p. 193.
50. Sister Grace Calder on the *Galeka* was delighted to receive her mail in December 1915. 'I got such piles of letters yesterday I did not know where to start reading them it was nearly two months since I had any.' 'Extracts from nurses' letters', *KT* 9, January 1916, pp. 20–30, quotation on p. 22. It was five months before she got the next batch, as her ship's run changed. 'It was most exciting when they all arrived in the end.' The bundle had nearly 80 letters and 50 papers as well as parcels. 'I did not know where to start with them all.' 'Letters from our nurses abroad', *KT* 9, October 1916, pp. 189–98, quotation on p. 194.
51. Occasional weddings occurred overseas, such as Sister Mildred Ellis's marriage to Captain Salt. 'Wedding bells', *KT* 9, July 1916, p. 177.
52. 'Life in Bloemfontein: Letter from Nurse Teape', *Press*, 4 July 1900 p. 6. Bessie Hay had a surprise visit from someone she identified only as 'B' and enjoyed fussing over him. 'A nurse's letter', *ES*, 13 July 1900, p. 4.
53. 'Twenty months in France with the New Zealand Stationary Hospital and an English casualty clearing station', *KT* 11, July 1918, pp. 136–39, quotation on pp. 136–37.
54. Letter from the New Zealand General Hospital, Brockenhurst, England, 14 June 1916, Commons Family: Papers–Letters from Daphne to her family–MS–Papers–1582–12, ATL.
55. Letters from the Citadel Military Hospital, Cairo, Egypt, 17 June 1915; Heliopolis House Hotel, Cairo, Egypt, 7 July 1915; New Zealand General Hospital, Pont de Koubbeh, Cairo, Egypt, 2 January 1916, 18 March 1916; Balmer Lawn, Brockenhurst, England, 13 July 1916, Commons Family: Papers–Letters from Daphne to her family–MS–Papers–1582–09, 1582–11 and 1582–12, ATL.
56. The soldier who told her this said he did not think Kenneth was a prisoner, as 'he would die fighting first'. Letter from the Heliopolis House Hotel, Cairo, Egypt, 7 July 1915, Commons Family: Papers–Letters from Daphne to her family–MS–Papers–1582–09, ATL.
57. One nurse at the No. 1 General Hospital in the leafy Wynberg suburb of Cape Town described the masses of arum lilies at the foot of Table Mountain that had to be mown with a scythe. She had

pressed a few little star-like flowers that were scattered in the undergrowth. 'The Transvaal war', *ES*, 9 June 1900, p. 3. See also 'A nurse's letter', *ES*, 9 July 1900 p. 4.
58. 'A nurse's letter', *ES*, 9 July 1900, p. 4; 'The Transvaal war', *ES*, 20 June 1900, p. 3.
59. See, for example, 'Extracts from Egyptian letters', *KT* 9, April 1916, pp. 84–86.
60. This was Edna Pengelly's description in 'A nurse's impressions of work in Egypt', *KT* 9, January 1916, p. 21.
61. Edith M. Lewis, *Joy in the Caring* (Christchurch: N.M. Peryer, 1963), p. 41.
62. 'News from our nurses abroad', *KT* 11, October 1918, pp. 171–76, quotation on p. 174. On the beautiful English countryside, see, for example, comments by Emily Curtis, Edna Pengelly and Grace Calder, 'Letters from our nurses abroad', *KT* 9, October 1916, pp. 189–98, see pp. 189, 192, 193.
63. 'Letters from our nurses abroad and at sea', *KT* 10, October 1917, pp. 193–96, see p. 196.
64. 'Rest home for nurses', *KT* 9, April 1916, p. 98. A photograph of the house appeared in *KT* 10, January 1917, p. 23.
65. Sister Violet Barker wrote a detailed account of the house, named Pilland, and the trees, flowers, walks and other recreational activities possible. 'Letters from our nurses abroad and at sea', *KT* 10, October 1917, pp. 193–96, see pp. 194–95.
66. In her limited spare time at Amiens, Ida Willis enjoyed 'walks, hitching rides in army trucks, visits in the town to see the beautiful cathedral, the old city walls and fortifications, and enjoy in one of the inns an occasional meal of omelette and French bread. We found pleasure in boating on the river Somme or on one of the many canals on the banks of which stood the attractive weekend homes of Parisians.' L. Ida G. Willis, *A Nurse Remembers: The life story of L. Ida G. Willis* (Lower Hutt: A.K. Wilson, 1968), p. 40.
67. 'News from our nurses abroad', *KT* 11, October 1918, pp. 171–76, see p. 171. Unfortunately, as Maclean noted, the German advance since Eva Brooke had written the letter meant 'there will be no time for gardening or such occupations'. 'News from our nurses abroad', *KT* 11, July 1918, pp. 126–28, quotation on p. 127. Maclean had summarised Brooke's letter in this issue and printed it in full in the October issue.
68. Work relationships with doctors raised few comments. Although Emily Peter thought the British army medical system needed drastic reform, other nurses in South Africa generally thought well of the doctors serving with them. Dora Harris, for example, thought they were 'all awfully nice', and Bessie Teape at Bloemfontein was pleased when two doctors she had worked with at Rondebosch in Cape Town were transferred there. 'The Transvaal war', *ES*, 20 June 1900, p. 3; 'Life in Bloemfontein: Letter from Nurse Teape', *Press*, 4 July 1900, p. 6. Occasional comments from nurses in World War I showed they appreciated the chance to work with doctors in England when it meant seeing new treatment methods. See, for example, 'Surgical Work: Alexandria', *KT* 9, January 1916, p. 30.
69. 'An army nurse', *Press*, 24 January 1901 p. 5.
70. 'Caring for the wounded', *Press*, 16 June 1900 p. 10.
71. 'The Transvaal war', *ES*, 9 June 1900, p. 3. The writer is likely either Janet Williamson or Isabella Campbell, as she mentions a Dunedin Hospital ward. The other nurse at the No. 1 General Hospital at Wynberg was Dora Peiper from Southland Hospital. Dora Harris felt the same about orderlies: 'Some are very good, and some no good at all.' 'The Transvaal war', *ES*, 20 June 1900, p. 3.
72. 'The troubles of our nurses', *ES*, 26 June 1900, p. 5.

73. 'Welcome to Miss Ross', *ES*, 2 November 1900, p. 6.
74. Willis, *A Nurse Remembers*, p. 40. See also Daphne Commons' comment when 30 of her orderlies were moved on. 'We are so sorry, we shall miss them very much. Their places are to be taken by some new ones (more training to be done) who arrived by the *Marama*.' Letter from the New Zealand General Hospital, Pont de Koubbeh, Cairo, Egypt, 10 January 1916, Commons Family: Papers–Letters from Daphne to her family–MS-Papers–1582-11, ATL.
75. Letter from the No. 1 New Zealand General Hospital, Brockenhurst, England, 27 September 1916, Commons Family: Papers–Letters from Daphne to her family–MS-Papers–1582-12, ATL.
76. Hester Maclean, *Nursing in New Zealand: History and reminiscences* (Wellington: Tolan, 1932), p. 205.
77. Ettie Rout also turned her alarm at the high rate of venereal disease among soldiers to practical efforts, providing free kits of condoms and the antiseptic Condy's crystals (potassium permanganate) and organising brothel inspections. See Jane Tolerton, *Ettie: A life of Ettie Rout* (Auckland: Penguin, 1992).
78. Jan Rodgers discusses this issue in '"A Paradox of Power and Marginality": New Zealand nurses' professional campaign during war, 1900–1920', PhD thesis, Massey University, 1994.
79. Her article appeared in the London *Daily Chronicle* and was reprinted in New Zealand. 'Butterfly sisterhood', *EP*, 4 September 1915 p. 13; 'Women's column', *MW*, 13 October 1915, p. 8.
80. Christine Hallett, '"Emotional nursing": Involvement, engagement, and detachment in the writings of First World War nurses and VADs', in *First World War Nursing: New perspectives*, eds A.S. Fell and C.E. Hallett (New York: Routledge, 2013), pp. 87–102.
81. Hallett has also noted that both nurses and VADs could express admiration and respect for each other, as well as frustration and resentment, in their letters and diaries. See Christine Hallett, *Veiled Warriors: Allied nurses of the First World War* (Oxford: Oxford University Press, 2016), p. 14.
82. 'Notes from the hospitals and personal items', *KT* 9, January 1916, pp. 59–62, quotation on p. 61.
83. 'News from our nurses abroad', *KT* 11, January 1918, pp. 9–13, quotation on p. 9.
84. Willis, *A Nurse Remembers*, p. 41.
85. Maud Haste and Louise Brandon set up a practice in Willis St, Wellington. 'Resignations, appointments, etc', *KT* 13, July 1920, p. 153. 'Orthopaedics and massage training for trained nurses', *KT* 11, April 1918, p. 59.
86. Richard E. Rawstron, *A Unique Nursing Group: New Zealand Army nurse anaesthetists of WWI* (Christchurch: Rawstron, 2005). See also 'Waikato', *JDPHHCA* 2, no. 11, 1919, p. 338.
87. Maclean, *Nursing in New Zealand*, p. 232.
88. 'Nurses' complaints', *NZH*, 21 January 1920 p. 8.
89. 'Found drowned', *AS*, 12 May 1927, p. 9. The story was carried by several newspapers around New Zealand.
90. Under the Discharged Soldiers' Settlement Act 1915 the government purchased suitable land. Returned soldiers and others (including nurses) could apply for a particular section of land. If there were several suitable applicants, the allocation was decided by ballot.
91. 'Resignations, appointments, etc', *KT* 13, January 1920, pp. 49–54, quotation on p. 53.
92. 'Ruakura state farm', *KT* 13, January 1920, p. 46. See also 'Notes from the hospitals and personal items', *KT* 21, April 1928, pp. 102–05, quotation on p. 105.
93. Kathy Wilson, 'Nursing on the home front during World War II: An essential service

in New Zealand', in *Looking Back, Moving Forward: Essays in the history of New Zealand nursing and midwifery*, eds N. Chick and J. Rodgers (Palmerston North: Department of Nursing and Midwifery, Massey University, 1997), pp. 67–79, see p. 70.
94. 'Service at home', editorial, *NZNJ* 33, May 1940, p. 133.
95. 'Ward 8 in Wartime', *Spectrum* #807, 1993, Radio New Zealand; 'Nurse', in L. Edmond, ed., *Women in Wartime: New Zealand women tell their story* (Wellington: Government Printing Office Publishing, 1986), pp. 238–43. Although the author of this piece is not identified, the content is the same as 'Ward 8 in Wartime' and therefore indicates it is by Joan Loeber.
96. VAs had to complete a home nursing course and a first aid course and, if accepted for overseas service, a set number of hours in a hospital to gain basic experience. From 1942, 300 VAs served overseas with the 650 NZANS nurses. Wilson, 'Nursing on the home front during World War II', p. 73. After World War II, VAs could be granted a one-year concession if they went on to train to become registered nurses. This was the same concession available to registered nursing aids, though aids had already completed a two-year training for that registration. The training of registered nursing aids began in 1939.
97. 'Voluntary aids in hospitals: as others see us', *NZNJ* 36, January 1943, p. 8.
98. 'To the editor, Voluntary aids in hospitals', *NZNJ* 36, February 1943, p. 38.
99. 'Nurse', in *Women in Wartime*, p. 241.
100. 'Ward 8 in Wartime'.
101. Davies, *Bread and Roses*, p. 45.
102. Ruth Crawford, 'Elizabeth McIlwrick (formerly Wayte), née Crawford, nursing in the 1940s', *Nursing Praxis in New Zealand* 12, no. 3, 1997, p. 31.
103. Davies, *Bread and Roses*, p. 45.
104. 'General Observations Applying during an Air Raid or Other Emergency: Re Nursing Staff; Wellington Hospital', Notices, unnumbered memo, 5 March 1942, History of Nursing – Wellington Hospital folder, Wellington Hospital Nursing Archive.
105. Yvonne Shadbolt, 'Re-introducing Mavis Helena ('Pat') Paton', *Nursing Praxis in New Zealand* 14, no. 3, 1999, p. 48.
106. 'Hair and caps', editorial, *KT* 36, April 1943, pp. 75–76.
107. Notices, Wellington Hospital, 1940s, History of Nursing – Wellington Hospital folder, Wellington Hospital Nursing Archive.
108. 'Nurse', in *Women in Wartime*, p. 242.
109. Letter from the New Zealand General Hospital, Balmer Lawn, Brockenhurst, 22 December 1916, Commons family: Papers–Letters from Daphne to her family–MS–Papers–1582–12, ATL.
110. A typical account of a Christmas celebration, though it occurred on a hospital ship, was one from the *Maheno* in 1915. 'Christmas on the "Maheno"', *KT* 9, April 1916, p. 74.
111. Willis, *A Nurse Remembers*, p. 41.
112. Lewis, *Joy in the Caring*, p. 61.
113. Willis, *A Nurse Remembers*, p. 41.
114. 'Christmas on the "Maheno"'.
115. Willis, *A Nurse Remembers*, p. 41.
116. 'Nursing in France', *KT* 9, April 1916, p. 90.
117. This was a form of Jacques Godbout and Alain Caille's notion of the 'gift to strangers', whereby giving is its own reward. Jacques T. Godbout and Alain C. Caille, *World of the Gift* (Montreal: McGill-Queen's Press, 1998), cited in Mark Osteen, 'Introduction: Questions of the gift', in *The Question of the Gift: Essays across disciplines*, ed. M. Osteen (London: Routledge, 2002), p. 22.
118. 'Letters from our nurses abroad and at sea', *KT* 10, July 1917, pp. 133–43, quotation on p. 136. Judging by Kate Stephenson's remarks, the gifts certainly achieved Russell Belk's view of the essential capacity

of the gift – to surprise and delight. See Osteen, 'Introduction', p. 22.

119. Ideas in this paragraph have been previously discussed as part of the importance of food more generally in nurses' experience of war. Pamela J. Wood and Sara Knight, 'The taste of war: The meaning of food to New Zealand and Australian nurses far from home in World War I, 1915–18', in *Histories of Nursing Practice*, eds G.M. Fealy, C.E. Hallett and S.M. Dietz (Manchester: Manchester University Press, 2015), pp. 35–51.

120. 'Christmas on the "Maheno"'. This is an example of the way 'food-talk' cements cultural identity in a foreign place. Andrea Pető, 'Food-talk: Markers of identity and imaginary belonging', in *Women Migrants from East to West: Gender, mobility and belonging in contemporary Europe*, eds L. Passerini, D. Lyon, E. Capusotti and I. Laliotou (Oxford: Berhahn Books, 2010), pp. 152–64.

121. Of the 22 digitised annual volumes of *KT*, only three are without an account of Christmas at a hospital: 1910, 1917 and 1919. Twelve volumes carry more than one account, and the volumes for 1912, 1921, 1925 and 1927 include five accounts each. The journal also published Christmas recipes. See, for example, 'Christmas cake', *KT* 16, October 1923, p. 182; 'Recipes', *KT* 15, January 1922, p. 25.

122. The dead prisoner was said to be a nephew of General Piet Cronje. 'The troubles of our nurses', *ES*, 26 June 1900, p. 5.

123. 'Letters from nurses at the front', *KT* 8, April 1915, pp. 82–85, quotation on p. 82.

124. 'Ward 8 in Wartime'.

125. Davies, *Bread and Roses*, p. 44.

126. This passage is drawn from several narratives published in *KT*, mostly in the January and April 1916 issues, and from my address given at the National War Memorial in 2001 to commemorate New Zealand nurses who died in wartime or humanitarian service. See Pamela J. Wood, '*Marquette* Memorial Service for Nurses', *Nursing Praxis in New Zealand* 18, no. 3, 2002, pp. 62–64. The quotation in this passage is from 'The loss of the "Marquette"', *KT* 9, January 1916, pp. 9 –13, quotation on p. 10. For one example of nurses grieving at the news of *Marquette* colleagues' deaths, see Minnie Jeffery's war diaries, MS–2934, Jeffery, Garry: Jeffery family papers relating to World War I, Hocken Collections, University of Otago. Nora Hildyard was occasionally known as Nona, but the Register of Nurses, official wartime and war graves records, and the Christchurch *Press* and *Lyttelton Times* use the name Nora. The Lyttelton war memorial lists her as Nona, but the Auckland War Memorial Museum and others use the name Nora.

127. See, for example, 'Late news', *Dominion*, 12 November 1915, p. 5. Hester Maclean initially reprinted this version in *KT* under its subtitle. '"Take the fighting men first!"', *KT* 8, October 1915, p. 198. Newspapers later clarified what had happened. See, for example, 'Bravery, but no melodrama', *Dominion*, 17 April 1916, p. 6.

128. Sarah Christie, 'Gender, remembrance, and the sinking of the *Marquette*', *Women's Studies Journal* 30, no. 1, 2016, p. 31.

129. 'The "Marquette" disaster', *KT* 9, April 1916, p. 70. Soldiers also disliked the story, as they felt it reflected poorly on them. See, for example, 'Nurses bore up bravely', *EP*, 15 April 1916, p. 5.

130. Katie Pickles, 'Mapping memorials for Edith Cavell on the colonial edge', *New Zealand Geographer* 62, 2006, pp. 13–24; Katie Pickles, *Transnational Outrage: The death and commemoration of Edith Cavell* (Basingstoke: Palgrave Macmillan, 2015).

131. Maclean, *Nursing in New Zealand*; Hester Maclean, 'New Zealand Army Nurses', in Drew, ed., *The War Effort of New Zealand*, pp. 87–104.

132. 'Around the schools', *ES*, 27 April 1936, p. 5.

133. Lewis, *Joy in the Caring*, pp. 291–94. The experiences of women in the Stanley Internment Camp are detailed in Bernice Archer and Fedorowich Kent, 'The women of Stanley: Internment in Hong Kong, 1942–45', *Women's History Review* 5, no. 3, 1996, pp. 373–99. The women interviewed commented that for many, their determination to survive and be useful while enduring camp life made them resilient. Two New Zealand nurses were also interned there: Margaret North, a missionary nurse in China, and Kathleen Thomson, with the QAIMNS. Others were interned in Sumatra, Banka Island, Changi Prison in Singapore, Malaya and Shanghai. Joan Rattray, *Great Days in New Zealand Nursing* (Wellington: A.H. & A.W. Reed, 1961), pp. 165–69. Eight of these nurses who returned to New Zealand were granted £25 each to address their immediate needs by the Nurses' Memorial Fund. New Zealand Nurses' Memorial Fund: Records, ARC–0547–#9, Hocken Collections, University of Otago. For firsthand accounts of grim conditions during internment, see those by Maisie Uniacke, who was interned at Changi Prison: 'First to return: New Zealand nurse Interned in Singapore', *AS*, 21 September 1945 p. 6; 'They "made do": Women of Singapore; N.Z. nurse gets home', *AS*, 22 September 1945, p. 9.

134. See Jane Potter, *Boys in Khaki, Girls in Print: Women's literary responses to the Great War, 1914–1918* (Oxford: Clarendon University Press, 2005), pp. 15, 225–26. The Christchurch *Press* also carried a story for children. 'Hospital Jean', *Press*, 26 May 1900, p. 3.

135. Carol Mutch, Rosemary Bingham, Lynette Kingsbury and Maria Perreau, 'Political indoctrination through myth building: The New Zealand School Journal at the time of World War I', *Curriculum Matters* 14, 2018, pp. 102–28.

136. Mutch et al., 'Political indoctrination through myth building', p. 103.

137. 'At Anzac in a hospital ship', *School Journal*, part 3, 10, no. 5, 1916, p. 159. This was a reprint from *The Navy*. The nurse is writing about August 1915, but as she mentions that she was also there in May 1915 (before New Zealand nurses were at Gallipoli) and is writing for a British publication, she is likely to have been a British nurse. Nevertheless, very similar accounts written by New Zealand nurses were published in *KT* and New Zealand newspapers.

138. 'The war in South Africa', *LT*, 15 August 1900, p. 5.

139. Potter, *Boys in Khaki, Girls in Print*, p. 34. 'The Rose of No Man's Land' was produced again in 1945. It portrays the Red Cross nurse.

140. See also Hallett, *Veiled Warriors*.

141. See, for example, 'The King's Theatre', *EP*, 3 March 1916, p. 3. A critic was unimpressed, saying the film 'lowers one of the most moving tragedies of the war to a level of an incident in the love affair of an obscure Belgian lieutenant, and makes the betrayal of Nurse Cavell an act of pure jealousy on the part of an utterly ridiculous spy of the most stagey type'. 'King's Theatre', *EP*, 7 March 1916, p. 3.

142. Rebecca West, *War Nurse: The true story of a woman who lived, loved and suffered on the Western Front* (New York: A.L. Burt, 1930); Vera Brittain, *Testament of Youth* (London: Victor Gollancz, 1933).

143. *War Nurse* was presented as a true story about an American volunteer nurse. For an excellent discussion of the mystery surrounding its origins, see Christine E. Hallett, *Nurse Writers of the Great War* (Manchester: Manchester University Press, 2016), pp. 179–86. The book *War Nurse* was later made into a film of the same name.

144. Sharon Ouditt, *Fighting Forces, Writing Women: Identity and ideology in the First World War* (London: Routledge, 1994), p. 29. See also Christine Hallett's comment

that VAD Enid Bagnold's accounts revealed her 'disdain for her professional colleagues'. Hallett, *Containing Trauma*, p. 201.
145. Hallett, 'Emotional nursing'.
146. Nelle M. Scanlan, *Tides of Youth* ([Christchurch]: Whitcombe & Tombs, [1933] 1958).
147. The *Otago Daily Times*, for example, featured a regular column on books that were in demand by readers at Dunedin's Athenaeum Library. See, for example, 'Books in demand', *ODT*, 11 November 1933, p. 4; 'Books in demand', *ODT*, 11 August 1934, p. 4. See also the declaration that 'forty odd reviewers can't be wrong!' in an advertisement for Brittain's *Testament of Youth* in 'Book news', *ODT*, 8 November 1933, p. 1. One reviewer, however, said, 'I was the duck's back and it was the water. Result, nil.' 'I've struck some plums', *Press*, 17 April 1937, p. 17. The booksellers Whitcombe & Tombs in Christchurch also suggested it as a Christmas gift in 1939. 'Some suggestions', *Press*, 9 December 1939, p. 1. And in August 1943 they promoted it in the same list as Adolf Hitler's *Mein Kampf*. 'Various books', *Press*, 14 August 1943, p. 1.
148. Letter to the editor from Guy Farrell, *KT* 9, January 1916, p. 32.
149. Len Hart to his family, 1 January 1916, MS–Papers–2157–4, ATL, cited in Kate Hunter and Kirstie Ross, *Holding on to Home: New Zealand stories and objects of the First World War* (Wellington: Te Papa Press, 2014), p. 196.
150. 'An echo of the Crimea', *KT* 9, July 1916, p. 48; Letter from the No. 1 New Zealand General Hospital, Brockenhurst, England, 27 September 1916, Commons Family: Papers–Letters from Daphne to her family–MS–Papers–1582–12, ATL.
151. Letter from the New Zealand General Hospital, Pont de Koubbeh, Cairo, 25 April 1916, Commons Family: Papers–Letters from Daphne to her family–MS–Papers–1582–11, ATL.
152. Maclean, *Nursing in New Zealand*, p. 165.
153. 'Letters from our nurses abroad', *KT* 9, July 1916, pp. 139–47, quotation on p. 144.
154. 'Editorial', *KT* 11, January 1918, p. 1.
155. 'Nurses' Memorial Fund', *KT* 11, January 1918, pp. 19–20, quotations on p. 19.
156. Lewis, *Joy in the Caring*, p. 34.
157. Letter from the New Zealand General Hospital, Pont de Koubbeh, Cairo, 2 January 1916, Commons Family: Papers–Letters from Daphne to her family–MS–Papers–1582–11, ATL.
158. 'In a military hospital in time of war', *PBH*, 7 March 1900, p. 3.
159. 'Ex-P.O.W. and army nurse answer some pertinent questions', *AS*, 2 November 1945, p. 4.

Chapter 8. Virus and tremor

1. 'Education Board', *HS*, 9 March 1909, p. 5. Ōtāne, established in the 1870s, encompassed the previous and neighbouring small township of Kaikora.
2. 'Personal', *HS*, 12 February 1918, p. 6.
3. Geoff Conly, *A Case History: The Hawke's Bay Hospital Board, 1876–1989* (Napier: Hawke's Bay Area Health Board, 1992), p. 83.
4. 'Influenza', *HS*, 18 November 1918, p. 3; 'Influenza', *HS*, 2 December 1918, p. 5.
5. 'Women's corner', *Press*, 2 December 1918, p. 2.
6. 'The schools', *GT*, 18 December 1917, p. 6; 'Obituary', *GH*, 29 April 1944, p. 4. Their grandfather Seymour Thorne-George was a politician and later mayor of Parnell, Auckland. His wife was connected to Governor George Grey.
7. 'Survivor's story', *BPT*, 5 February 1931, p. 3; 'The death roll', *EP*, 5 February 1931, p. 14; 'Outstanding tragedies', *GT*, 5 February 1931, p. 5.
8. 'Wreck of a nurses' home', *BPT*, 14 February 1931, p. 3.

9. 'Death roll now 220 dead', *AS*, 7 February 1931, p. 10.
10. 'Notes from the hospitals and personal items', *NZNJ* 23, January 1930, p. 40; 'The disastrous earthquake', *KT* 22, July 1929, p. 125.
11. 'Report of the Influenza Epidemic Commission', *AJHR*, 1919, H-31a, appendix A, Influenza Pandemic, p. 29. Geoffrey Rice estimated that 6091 Pākehā and 2060 Māori died in New Zealand during the pandemic. Adding soldiers who died from influenza overseas raises the total number of New Zealand deaths to 8573. Geoffrey Rice, *Black November: The 1918 influenza pandemic in New Zealand* (Christchurch: Canterbury University Press, 2005), p. 18. Rice has subsequently adjusted the estimate of Māori deaths to as many as 2500, for a total of 8591. Geoffrey W. Rice, *Black Flu 1918: The story of New Zealand's worst public health disaster* (Christchurch: Canterbury University Press, 2017), p. 68.
12. Rice, *Black November*, p. 17.
13. Hester Maclean identified the health impact on the profession. See *AJHR*, 1919, H-31, p. 10.
14. 'Minister in reply', *EP*, 19 June 1919, p. 3.
15. *AJHR*, 1919, H-31a, p. 24.
16. Rice, *Black November*, p. 113.
17. 'Health officers', *EP*, 25 March 1919, p. 8.
18. 'Masks and influenza', *EP*, 2 April 1919, p. 8.
19. 'Influenza epidemic', *GT*, 18 December 1918, p. 6.
20. 'Influenza epidemic', *KT* 12, January 1919, p. 13.
21. Hester Maclean, *Nursing in New Zealand: History and reminiscences* (Wellington: Tolan, 1932), p. 226.
22. Mary Lambie, *My Story: Memoirs of a New Zealand nurse* (Christchurch: Whitcomb & Tombs, 1956), pp. 18–19.
23. 'Influenza at Paeroa', *AS*, 6 December 1918, p. 6; 'Influenza epidemic', *KT* 12, January 1919, p. 13.
24. A more comprehensive accounting of deaths among untrained volunteers is still needed. The proportion of volunteers who died, however, appears smaller than that of hospital nurses, who had close continuous care of patients with the most virulent form of influenza.
25. Grace Widdowson, oral history interview with Helen Campbell, 27 January 1983, OHI–0014/176, Nursing Education & Research Foundation Oral History collection, ATL. See also Marie Burgess, compiler, 'We Wanted to Nurse', audiotape, New Zealand Nurses' Organisation, Wellington, for edited excerpts from these oral history interview recordings.
26. Sophia Maria Dorothy Reyburn (née Palmer), oral history interview with Yvonne Shadbolt, 14 April 1983, OHI–0014/138, Nursing Education and Research Foundation Oral History collection, ATL.
27. 'In the country', *Press*, 2 November 1918, p. 7. Lilian A. Kissel trained at Christchurch Hospital and registered in December 1908. Early in 1914 she married Percy 'Tiny' Emerson, who had earned his nickname as the smallest member of the First South African Contingent in the South African War, and because of his 'pluck and good humour'. In World War I he served with the Wellington Mounted Rifles and was killed in action at Gallipoli. Lilian Emerson had also gone to England in September 1914 and offered her services to the War Office. She served in hospitals in Egypt and England. 'Personal notes', *Press*, 15 June 1915, p. 9. After the war she worked for the Department of Health as a school nurse in Christchurch. 'School nurses', *KT* 14, April 1921, p. 58.
28. This was the case in Dunedin Hospital, where Matron Margaret Myles had to urgently engage more probationers. They became ill almost immediately and did not return until the end of December. Judith A. Roddick, 'Delirium and fever in the

antipodes: Nursing and the 1918 influenza epidemic in Dunedin Hospital, New Zealand', *Journal of Research in Nursing* 11, no. 4, 2006, p. 364.

29. Roddick, 'Delirium and fever in the antipodes', pp. 363–64.
30. The figure of 42 nurses' deaths is based on an analysis of death notices and obituaries in newspapers and the *New Zealand Nursing Journal*. Nine can be confirmed as probationers, and a further five were also likely to have been still in training.
31. Pamela J. Wood, 'Sickening nurses: Fever nursing, nurses' illness and the anatomy of blame, New Zealand 1903–23', *Nursing History Review* 19, 2011, pp. 53–77.
32. Rice, *Black November*.
33. Ibid.
34. Widdowson, oral history interview with Helen Campbell, 27 January 1983.
35. Widdowson, oral history interview with Helen Campbell, 27 January 1983.
36. Anne Elizabeth Busch, oral history interview with Yvonne Shadbolt, 15 December 1982, OHI–0014/021, Nursing Education and Research Foundation Oral History collection, ATL.
37. 'A pleasing function', *PM*, 7 March 1919, p. 2; 'The epidemic', *PM*, 22 November 1918, p. 3. Robina Lochhead trained at Timaru Hospital, registered in January 1912 and worked as a sister there until 1916. She was then matron of Kumara Hospital until 1917, before going to Pātea. *NZG*, 1918, p. 712.
38. 'District reports', *LT*, 22 November 1918, p. 6.
39. As one example, see 'Influenza', *LT*, 18 November 1918, p. 5.
40. 'Influenza bureau incidents', *ES*, 30 November 1918, p. 6.
41. 'General notes', *Dominion*, 21 November 1918, p. 6.
42. As one example, see 'St John Ambulance', *ES*, 14 December 1918, p. 5.
43. On Plunket nurses working in emergency hospitals, see, for example, '2000 cases at Lower Hutt', *EP*, 10 December 1918, p. 7; 'Influenza epidemic', *KT* 12, January 1919, p. 13. On homes set up by Plunket nurses, see, for example, 'Plunket Society', *Press*, 21 December 1918, p. 2; 'Plunket Society', *ES*, 17 May 1919, p. 2.
44. 'Influenza epidemic', *AS*, 17 January 1919, p. 2.
45. 'Influenza', *HS*, 13 December 1918, p. 5.
46. 'Influenza epidemic', *KT* 12, January 1919, p. 13. See also Diana S. Masters, 'Mereana Tangata: The first Maori registered nurse', *Nursing New Zealand*, 7, no. 8, 2001, pp. 14–15, 27. (In fact, Mereana Tangata was not the first Māori registered nurse: see chapter 6 of this volume.) Sarah Polden completed her three years' training at St Bartholomew's Hospital in London in 1897, and worked in senior positions in various hospitals in London and Bath before coming to New Zealand, where she registered in November 1910. She was matron of the Infectious Diseases [Fever] Hospital in Wellington until 1915, then of the Te Waikato Sanatorium until 1916. *NZG*, 1918, p. 726.
47. Joan Rattray, *Great Days in New Zealand Nursing* (Wellington: A.H. & A.W. Reed, 1961), pp. 25–26.
48. 'Influenza', *Dominion*, 11 December 1918, p. 6.
49. 'State examinations', *KT* 12, July 1919, pp. 131, 133.
50. Nelle M. Scanlan, *Tides of Youth* (Christchurch: Whitcombe & Tombs, [1933] 1958), pp. 277–78.
51. Beryl McCarthy, *Castles in the Soil* (Dunedin: A.H. & A.W. Reed, 1939), p. 315. This novel of a 'sheepy paradise' came third equal in the literary competition celebrating the New Zealand centennial and was the only work to be subsequently published. Lawrence Jones, 'Myth and anti-myth in literary responses to the centennial', in *Creating a National Spirit: Celebrating New Zealand's centennial, 1940*, ed. W. Renwick (Wellington:

Victoria University Press, 2004), p. 209.
52. 'Methven's handicap', *AG*, 10 December 1918, p. 4.
53. 'At exhaustion point', *AS*, 18 November 1918, p. 2.
54. 'Influenza epidemic', *KCC*, 19 November 1918, p. 5; 'The epidemic', *MR*, 28 November 1918, p. 3.
55. As just one example, see 'Fighting influenza', *Dominion*, 14 November 1918, p. 6.
56. One Wellington advertisement noted that the nurse's bibbed apron, 'as used in the London hospitals', could be purchased at Cole's Drapery in Cuba St. 'Red Cross nurse aprons', *EP*, 19 November 1918, p. 1.
57. 'Otane', *HS*, 3 December 1918, p. 6. She had a 'very kindly and retiring disposition' and 'endeared herself to all'.
58. 'Hastings', *HS*, 28 November 1918, p. 5.
59. 'Influenza fund', *HS*, 2 December 1918, p. 6; 'Influenza', *HS*, 10 December 1918, p. 6. Edward (Jerry) Gigg, who had volunteered as an orderly, also died. 'Deaths', *HS*, 28 November 1918, p. 4; 'The influenza epidemic', letter to the editor signed 'Citizen', *HS*, 29 November 1918, p. 6.
60. 'Women's corner', *Press*, 4 December 1918, p. 2.
61. A photograph of the inscription is available in the Cemetery Database, Hastings District Council. The stone cross above the grave might have been erected through the memorial fund. I am grateful to Dr Judith Clare, who sent me a fuller photograph showing the whole grave with its cross and the information that Leech is buried in the soldiers' section of the cemetery.
62. 'Influenza', *GES*, 30 November 1918, p. 5.
63. 'Influenza', *GES*, 25 November 1918, p. 5.
64. 'Hokitika notes', *GES*, 18 August 1919, p. 7. On Taylor's appointment to train as a probationer, see 'Personal notes', *GES*, 9 May 1913, p. 5.
65. 'Memorial to nurses', *HG*, 18 August 1919, p. 4.
66. 'Personal', *Taranaki Herald*, 22 November 1918, p. 2; Untitled, *Taranaki Herald*, 18 December 1918, p. 2.
67. 'Martyrs to duty', *TS*, 12 December 1918, p. 2.
68. 'A good cause', *TS*, 19 August 1922, p. 4; 'Late Sister Linton', *TS*, 14 September 1922, p. 5.
69. 'Passed away', *AS*, 19 November 1918, p. 3. Alice Maud Manning trained at Wellington Hospital from 1897 to 1900, registering in March 1902. She was number 91 on the register. *NZG*, 1918, p. 717.
70. 'Obituary', *KT* 12, January 1919, p. 45. Maud Mataira trained at Wanganui Hospital, registering in June 1911. She was a Native Health nurse from 1911 to 1914. *NZG*, 1917, p. 675.
71. 'The health of the people', *NZH*, 25 April 1912, p. 9.
72. As a particular example, see 'Nurses memorial service', *GRA*, 28 October 1919, p. 2.
73. 'A martyr to duty', *AS*, 26 November 1918, p. 5.
74. 'Influenza epidemic', *WC*, 19 December 1918, p. 5.
75. Ibid.
76. 'A martyr to duty', *AS*, 26 November 1918, p. 5.
77. 'Obituary', *KT* 12, January 1919, p. 45; 'Nurses' memorial tablet', *KT* 15, January 1922, p. 24.
78. 'Influenza epidemic', *KT* 12, 1, January 1919, p. 13.
79. 'Influenza inquiry', *AG*, 26 March 1919, p. 5.
80. *AJHR*, 1919, H-31, p. 10.
81. For a detailed account of this proposed scheme, see Pamela J. Wood, 'Managing boundaries between professional and lay nursing following the influenza pandemic, 1918–1919: Insights for professional resilience today?' *Journal of Clinical Nursing* 26, 2017, pp. 805–12. The comment about 'two grades of nursing'

came initially from Dr T.H.A. Valintine, the inspector-general of hospitals and chief health officer, who disliked the notion. See 'Nursing the sick, the woman's part, modern ignorance deplored', *EP*, 12 March 1919 p. 3. Maclean's objections can be seen in 'Training of nursing aids on home service', *KT* 12, April 1919, pp. 73–81.

82. 'Incidents and anecdotes of the earthquake', *NZNJ* 24, May 1931, p. 108.
83. 'Survivor's story', *BPT*, 5 February 1931, p. 3.
84. 'Harrowing story', *EP*, 5 February 1931, p. 15.
85. Conly, *A Case History*, p. 115.
86. Janet Takarangi, 'Reintroducing Miss I. Banks', *Nursing Praxis in New Zealand* 1, no. 1, 1985, p. 47. Isabel Banks was a Māori nurse who did psychiatric nurse training at Porirua Hospital in 1919 before her general training at Wellington Hospital from 1920 to 1924. She was district health nurse at Frasertown from 1926 and in Ruatōria from 1935.
87. See, for example, 'Survivor's story', *BPT*, 5 February 1931, p. 3; 'Doctors and nurses', *EP*, 5 February 1931, p. 15; 'The death roll', *EP*, 5 February 1931, p. 14; 'Outstanding tragedies', *GT*, 5 February 1931, p. 5.
88. 'Wholesale destruction of town', *EP*, 5 February 1931, p. 13.
89. 'The first few hours', *AS*, 6 February 1931, p. 9.
90. See, for example, 'Doctors and nurses', *EP*, 5 February 1931, p. 15; 'The death roll', *EP*, 5 February 1931, p. 14; 'Outstanding tragedies', *GT*, 5 February 1931, p. 5.
91. Scanlan said, 'In Napier the roof of the Nurses' Home had fallen in and crushed to death the night nurses who were still sleeping.' Nelle M. Scanlan, *Winds of Heaven* (Christchurch: Whitcombe & Tombs, [1934] 1958), p. 272. She gave a short but vivid description of the earthquake's destruction and impact on people.
92. 'Wreck of a nurses' home', *BPT*, 14 February 1931, p. 3.
93. 'The nurses' home', *EP*, 5 February 1931, p. 13; 'Survivor's story', *BPT*, 5 February 1931, p. 3.
94. From the text of a framed memorial with her photograph and medal, on the wall of the foyer outside the chapel at the Hawke's Bay Hospital, Hastings. The foyer was initially the entranceway to the Fallen Soldiers Memorial Hospital.
95. Conly, *A Case History*, p. 115.
96. Barbara Joan Haywood, oral history interview with Erica Tenquist, 16 October 2017, Hawke's Bay Knowledge Bank, Hastings. Maisie Wilson was her aunt.
97. Dorothy Alice Ford, *Journey from Stranger's Rest* (Wellington: Daphne Brasell Associates, 1989), pp. 128–30, 132.
98. After the earthquake, probationers were relocated to other training hospitals. Elaine Hamill completed her training at Dannevirke Hospital. She had always wanted to be an actor, so when the notable actor Dame Sybil Thorndike visited Dannevirke with her son, Hamill boldly asked her advice about acting. Thorndike warned her that it meant hard work and disappointment, but as Hamill was adamant in her ambition, Thorndike recommended that she contact a Sydney repertory company director. See 'A New Zealand actress', *NA*, 28 March 1936, p. 6. This piece was also published in the *CC*, *HC*, *FT* and *SEP*. Elaine trained in acting at the Cinesound academy and worked mainly for the J.C. Williamson Ltd film and theatre company.
99. See, for example, 'Peeping at filmdom', *AS*, 13 June 1936, p. 5, Supplement.
100. 'Personal and social', *ODT*, 23 July 1936, p. 18; 'Stage folk', *ES*, 25 July 1936, p. 6.
101. A photograph of Elaine Hamill in *The Outsider* role appears in the *NZH*, 2 September 1939, p. 14 (Supplement). Although she is playing the role of an American nurse, she is wearing her New

Zealand five-pointed star medal, just visible in the photograph.
102. Ford, *Journey from Stranger's Rest*, p. 131.
103. 'Appalling earthquake', *GT*, 4 February 1931, p. 5. Along with doctors, 15 nurses came from Auckland, 23 from Wellington, 14 from Gisborne, 23 from towns between Palmerston North and Napier and 24 from other places.
104. Lambie, *My Story*, p. 68.
105. Margaret Duirs Macnab, 'Account of experiences following the Napier earthquake', MS–Papers–3838, ATL.
106. Lambie, *My Story*, pp. 68–69.
107. Macnab, 'Account of experiences following the Napier earthquake'.
108. Lambie, *My Story*, 69.
109. 'Harrowing story', *EP*, 5 February 1931, p. 15.
110. 'Hastings sanitation', *EP*, 9 February 1931, p. 10. One body was finally assumed to be that of Rex Fredsberg, a 14-year-old schoolboy killed in Roach's department store where he had gone to buy a school cap. M.B. Boyd, *City of the Plains: A history of Hastings* (Hastings: Victoria University Press for Hastings District Council, 1984), p. 270; 'Earthquake horror', *GT*, 6 February 1931 p. 5; 'Hastings death toll', *DT*, 16 February 1931 p. 7. Sadly, Rex Fredsberg's name does not appear on the Hastings earthquake memorial.
111. 'Total death roll 230', *ES*, 12 February 1931, p. 8.
112. 'Exodus', *AS*, 5 February 1931, p. 8.
113. 'Removal of injured', *GT*, 10 February 1931, p. 3.
114. 'Scenes of ruin', *EP*, 4 February 1931, p. 10; 'Outstanding tragedies', *GT*, 5 February 1931, p. 5; 'Doctors and nurses', *EP*, 5 February 1931, p. 15.
115. 'Editorial', *NZNJ* 24, March 1931, pp. 51–52.
116. 'Harrowing story', *EP*, 5 February 1931, p. 15.
117. 'Fires all around them', *AS*, 5 February 1931, p. 9. Eileen's brother Sidney Williams, of Gisborne, was the shipping manager for the Williams and Kettle Company. 'Personal items', *GT*, 6 February 1931, p. 6.
118. 'Incidents and anecdotes of the earthquake', *NZNJ* 24, May 1931, p. 108.
119. 'Splendid workers', *AS*, 7 March 1931, p. 12. Mary Wellock trained at Napier Hospital, registering in July 1928. *NZG*, 1930, p. 1330.
120. Register of Sisters, Napier Hospital, 68039a, Box AR1540, MTG archive, Napier. This register also shows that Eleanor Camilla Roy trained at Auckland Hospital, registering in 1905. She worked at Nelson and Hamilton and then at the Melbourne Fever Hospital before her appointment as a sister at Napier Hospital in December 1915, aged 38. She became matron in June 1930 on Rose Macdonald's retirement.
121. *Waipukurau Hospital Centennial, 1879–1979, Souvenir Booklet* (Waipukurau: Waipawa Hospital Board, 1979), p. 29. Catharine Isabel Drummond trained at Wellington and Waipawa Hospitals, registering in December 1905. She interspersed private nursing with being in charge of the Victoria and Seddon Wards (1910–12), acting matron at Waipawa Hospital at Waipukurau (1913) and matron of Bowen Street Private Hospital in Wellington (1915–16). She served in the New Zealand Army Nursing Service overseas from October 1916 to February 1921 before becoming matron of Waipukurau Hospital. *NZG*, 1930, p. 1208.
122. Lambie, *My Story*, p. 69.
123. 'Wairoa Hospital', *GT*, 12 March 1931, p. 3.
124. 'Personal notes', *EP*, 23 February 1931, p. 13. For school nurses, see 'Notes from the hospitals and personal items', *NZNJ* 24, March 1931, pp. 94–96.
125. Lambie, *My Story*, pp. 69–70.
126. 'Provision for nurses', *EP*, 14 February 1931, p. 10; 'Hospital nurses', *AS*, 17 February 1931, p. 8; 'H.B. disaster', *GT*, 17

February 1931, p. 5; 'Earthquake relief', *GT*, 24 February 1931, p. 5.
127. 'Provision for nurses', *EP*, 14 February 1931, p. 10.
128. Lambie, *My Story*, p. 71.
129. Nurses' personal records, Dunedin Hospital, DAHI records, 9189 D262, Dunedin Office, ANZ.
130. Untitled, *AS*, 21 January 1933, p. 6.
131. The tablet was initially placed in a Napier Hospital corridor, but now that the hospital has been demolished, it is in the original foyer (outside the chapel) of the Fallen Soldiers' Memorial Hospital, now called the Hawke's Bay Hospital, in Hastings.
132. Conly, *A Case History*, p. 124.
133. Napier Hospital Applications Register, VN [82506], MTG archive.
134. This plaque is also in the Hawke's Bay Hospital chapel foyer.
135. Arlene W. Keeling and Barbara Mann Wall, eds, *Nurses and Disasters: Global, historical case studies* (New York: Springer, 2015). Keeling and Wall's conclusions are based on an analysis of these case studies.
136. Maclean, *Nursing in New Zealand*, pp. 228–29.
137. S.E. Polden, 'N.Z. nurses and influenza in Australia', *KT* 12, October 1919, p. 161.
138. Lambie, *My Story*, p. 69.
139. 'Splendid workers', *AS*, 7 March 1931, p. 12.

Chapter 9. 'The modern nurse'

1. Report of the Dunedin Hospital Inquiry Commission, *AJHR*, 1891, H-1, pp. 227–34; Pamela Wood, *Dirt: Filth and decay in a New World Arcadia* (Auckland: Auckland University Press, 2005), pp. 207–08.
2. As one example, see the comment of George Fisher, parliamentary representative for Wellington Central, in Jottings, in 'Parliamentary news and notes', *EP*, 16 August 1901 p. 5. In a discussion of whether men or women were better nurses, the key point was that nurses were 'born, not made'. 'Women in print', *EP*, 13 March 1923, p. 9.
3. See, for example, Rosalind Nash, ed., *Florence Nightingale to Her Nurses: A selection from Miss Nightingale's addresses to probationers and nurses of the Nightingale School at St Thomas's Hospital* (London: Macmillan, 1914), p. 5.
4. 'From a suburban balcony', *ES*, 7 November 1925, p. 2.
5. New Zealand senior medical men argued for this shift, having themselves observed the difference female nurses made in hospitals in Australia, Britain and the United States of America, or having heard firsthand accounts from colleagues at intercolonial and other medical conferences or read them in medical journals.
6. As just four examples, see 'Parliamentary news and notes', *EP*, 16 August 1901, p. 5; 'Nurses for the country', *AS*, 3 January 1910, p. 4; 'In praise of nurses', *ES*, 8 March 1924, p. 2; 'Red Cross', *ES*, 11 September 1926, p. 16. The last example was an account for young readers.
7. For a good discussion of this, see Carol Helmstadter, 'A third look at Sarah Gamp', *Canadian Bulletin of Medical History* 30, no. 2, 2013, pp. 141–59. Sairey Gamp appears in Dickens' 1844 novel *The Life and Adventures of Martin Chuzzlewit*.
8. This was a comment about a private case nurse in a fictional story by Florence Stagpoole, serialised in a New Zealand newspaper. 'The uninvited guest', *ES*, 22 June 1907, p. 3.
9. 'In praise of nurses', *ES*, 8 March 1924, p. 2.
10. As one example, see 'From a suburban balcony'. A disgruntled doctor reviewing a nursing textbook in 1908 also grumbled: 'The modern nurse has too much science to be able to cook, and knows too much to be able to make her patient comfortable.'

'Reviews', *NZMJ* 6, no. 25, 1908, p. 47.
11. 'Nurses and nursing', *FS*, 5 August 1916, p. 1.
12. See, for example, 'In praise of nurses'.
13. 'Women in print', *EP*, 13 March 1923, p. 9.
14. 'In praise of nurses'; 'From a suburban balcony'.
15. 'Overworked', *Press*, 26 November 1925, p. 7.
16. 'The position of the nurse', *MW*, 4 December 1918, p. 7; 'Sweating of nurses', *MW*, 1 September 1920, p. 6.
17. 'News and views', *MW*, 15 August 1913, p. 1.
18. 'One big union', *MW*, 1 December 1915, p. 8.
19. Sonja Davies, *Bread and Roses: Sonja Davies, her story* (Masterton: Fraser, 1984), p. 51.
20. 'News and notes', *KT* 19, April 1926, p. 52. This item noted the *Nursing Times*' publication of extracts from Nightingale's writing.
21. 'Nurses of a period: The tradition of Florence Nightingale', *KT* 18, October 1925, p. 176.
22. 'Are we losing our ideals?' *KT* 9, July 1916, p. 171.
23. 'Nursing novels', *KT* 11, April 1918, p. 104.
24. 'Registered nurse', *NZH*, 6 November 1937, p. 26.
25. See marketing historian Elaine Thomson's study of advertisements in historical British nursing journals: '"Beware of worthless imitations": Advertising in nursing periodicals, c. 1888–1945', in *New Directions in the History of Nursing: International perspectives*, eds B. Mortimer and S. McGann (Abingdon: Routledge, 2005), p. 166.
26. Thomson, '"Beware of worthless imitations"', p. 166.
27. For a detailed discussion of *KT* advertisements for tonics, see Jayne Krisjanous and Pamela J. Wood, '"For quiet nerves and steady poise": A historical analysis of advertising to New Zealand nurses in the *Kai Tiaki* journal, 1908–1929', *Journal of Historical Research in Marketing* 12, no. 1, 2019, pp. 19–52. Our research identifies 242 tonic advertisements in *KT* between 1908 and 1929.
28. Advertisement for Glax-Ovo, *KT* 21, January 1928, p. ii; 'What to eat: Advice by Dr Clark', *KT* 20, July 1927, p. 110.
29. Advertisement for Ceregen, *KT* 9, April 1916, p. 108.
30. Advertisement for Glax-Ovo, *KT* 18, October 1925, p. ii.
31. Advertisement for Glax-Ovo, *KT* 19, April 1926, p. ii.
32. Advertisement for Glax-Ovo, *KT* 19, July 1926, p. ii.
33. Thomson, '"Beware of worthless imitations"', p. 166.
34. 'In special appointment to Lord Islington', advertisement, *EP*, 26 September 1918, p. 11. Although identified as a Wellington nurse, Ellen Everitt does not appear in the *NZG* register of nurses.
35. 'The amazing case of Nurse "X"', advertisement, *EP*, 21 April 1941, p. 3.
36. Laurie Lee, *Cider with Rosie* (Harlow: Longman, 1976), p. 105.
37. 'Hospital troubles', *KT* 4, January 1911, p. 1.
38. *AJHR*, 1901, H-22, p. 3.
39. 'Selection and training of probationers', editorial, *KT* 4, April 1911, pp. 43–45, quotation on p. 44.
40. 'Hospital and Charitable Aid Board', *ODT*, 18 February 1916, p. 8.
41. 'Hospital nurses', *ODT*, 17 March 1916, p. 2.
42. 'Hospital and Charitable Aid Board', *ODT*, 29 March 1916, p. 2.
43. Her name was actually Margarita Dorothea Arnaboldi, but at the hospital she went by Margaret.
44. 'Our hospital', *AS*, 16 December 1890, p. 2.
45. See, for example, 'Hospital Inquiry', *AS*, 26 January 1891, p. 4; 'The hospital inquiry', *AS*, 19 February 1891, p. 5.
46. 'The hospital charges', *AS*, 3 March 1891, p. 5.

47. Editorial, *AS*, 19 March 1891, p. 4.
48. 'The hospital inquiry', *AS*, 21 April 1891, p. 2; Editorial, *AS*, 21 April 1891, p. 4; 'Arnaboldi testimonial', *AS*, 22 April 1891, p. 8.
49. 'Accident at Waihi', *AS*, 3 February 1896, p. 3; 'Shocking accident', *AS*, 2 July 1901, p. 5; 'The Waihi accident', *AS*, 3 July 1901, p. 4; 'Accident at Waihi', *AS*, 21 April 1903, p. 5. After many years in Waihī, and doing 'splendid work, in her quiet unostentatious way' during the influenza pandemic of 1918, Arnaboldi died at Auckland Hospital in 1921, leaving her 12-roomed hospital and contents, which sold for £800, and a cottage on an acre of land. 'Local and general', *WDT*, 16 March 1921, p. 2; 'Local and general', *WDT*, 11 February 1921, p. 2.
50. 'Doctor and nurse', *NZH*, 24 March 1914, p. 8.
51. 'Withdrawn from court', *NZH*, 1 April 1914, p. 10.
52. Untitled, *KT* 7, April 1914, p. 91.
53. For a detailed description of this case, see Kathryn Wilson, *Angels in the Devil's Pit: Nursing in Rotorua, 1840–1940* (Wellington: Karo, 1998), pp. 15–17, 173.
54. 'Doctor's claim', *EP*, 13 August 1930, p. 12. The case was mentioned in the professional journal. 'A court case for insurance nurse', *NZNJ* 23, September 1930, p. 242.
55. 'Slander proved', *EP*, 15 August 1930, p. 15. The next year Richards sued the newspapers that had covered the case, winning one case for libel and losing another. 'Newspaper reports', *EP*, 9 February 1931, p. 12; 'Sequel to libel action', *EP*, 25 February 1931, p. 4. See also 'A court case for insurance nurse', *KT* 23, September 1930, p. 242.
56. Anthropologist Victor Turner described the phases of social drama as a breach of social relations that are usually governed by norms, a crisis leading to different factions grappling with the issues in public, and redressive action ranging from personal advice to public ritual, ending with either reintegration of the social group or an irreparable schism. Victor Turner, *Schism and Continuity in an African Society: A study of Ndembu village life* (Manchester: Manchester University Press, 1957); Victor Turner, *On the Edge of the Bush: Anthropology as experience* (Tucson, AZ: University of Arizona Press, 1985).
57. This account is based on an analysis of numerous newspaper reports from 1916 to 1918, which included verbatim transcripts of official documents, and a retrospective account by Hester Maclean in her memoir. Only sources for specific quotations and items of information are included in the notes.
58. 'Hospital inquiry', *GT*, 19 January 1918, p. 5.
59. This account of events is from a verbatim report of Tait's written statement to the hospital board. 'Dismissal or resignation?' *GT*, 8 February 1916, p. 5.
60. Maclean described Sister May as a professional rather than private friend, as she had been on her staff in Melbourne. 'Hospital inquiry', *GT*, 23 January 1918, p. 5.
61. Hester Maclean, *Nursing in New Zealand: History and reminiscences* (Wellington: Tolan, 1932), p. 75. Maclean does not name the hospital, matron or nurse in her memoir, but from its details the story is now easily identifiable.
62. 'State examination of nurses', *KT* 11, January 1918, p. 7.
63. 'Alleged unrest at hospital', *GT*, 17 January 1918, p. 6.
64. Rex Wright-St Clair, *Historia Nunc Vivat: Medical practitioners in New Zealand, 1840 to 1930* (Christchurch: Rex Wright-St Clair, 2003).
65. 'Dismissal or resignation?' *GT*, 8 February 1916, p. 5; 'Nurse Higgins' resignation', *GT*, 18 March 1916, p. 5.
66. 'The hospital inquiry', *GT*, 25 February 1918, p. 5.

67. 'Gisborne Hospital', *KT* 11, October 1918, p. 217.
68. Maclean, *Nursing in New Zealand*, p. 75; 'Gisborne Hospital', *KT* 11, October 1918, p. 217.
69. Frances (Fanny) Price, Nancie McArdle, Minnie Walsh and Bertha Nurse successively held the matron's position between 1918 and 1925, when Kate Benjamin took over and remained for seven years. Marie E. Burgess, *Nursing Remembered* (Gisborne: Cook Hospital Nurses' Reunion Committee, 2010).
70. 'I remember the terrible heat!' said Maclean in her memoir. Maclean, *Nursing in New Zealand*, p. 75.
71. 'A novel court scene', *GT*, 22 January 1918, p. 4.
72. 'Hospital inquiry', *GT*, 18 January 1918, p. 5.
73. 'Hospital inquiry', *GT*, 21 January 1918, p. 6.
74. 'Hospital inquiry', *GT*, 18 January 1918, p. 5.
75. This account is drawn from numerous newspaper articles covering the inquiry testimony and magistrate's final report. For his comment on courage and grit, see 'Hospital inquiry', *GT*, 18 January 1918, p. 5.
76. 'Timaru Hospital', *KT* 9, April 1916, p. 108.
77. 'Timaru Hospital', *KT* 18, April 1925, p. 56.
78. Untitled, *KT* 19, April 1926, p. 69.
79. Linda Bryder, 'Pattrick, Anne', from the Dictionary of New Zealand Biography: www: teara.govt.nz/en/biographies/4p5/pattrick-anne

Chapter 10. Building a community and culture

1. 'Notes from the hospitals and personal items', *KT* 5, July 1912, p. 88.
2. 'The purpose of the journal', editorial, *KT* 1, January 1908, pp. 1–2, quotation on p. 2.
3. 'Books for study and leisure hours', *KT* 5, July 1912, p. 72.
4. 'The purpose of the journal', p. 1.
5. See, for example, Patricia Sargison, '"Essentially a woman's work": A history of general nursing in New Zealand, 1830–1930', PhD thesis, University of Otago, 2001.
6. Because of the international interest in New Zealand's system of nurse training and state registration, Grace Neill sent the syllabus to the International Congress of Nurses meeting, and it was also published as 'Nursing education in New Zealand', *BJN* 33, 10 September 1904, pp. 209–10. The general nursing section of the syllabus also included invalid cookery, household hygiene, the required nursing qualities (virtues) and hospital etiquette. Practical skills included bed-making; washing and bathing a patient; preventing and treating bedsores; monitoring a patient's temperature, pulse and respiration; reporting cases; and administering food, medicine, enemas, packs, blisters, strapping, poultices, fomentations and leeches.
7. The conditions covered in the question on symptoms and nursing management included diabetes, herpes-zoster [shingles], cerebral meningitis and gastric ulcer. Other questions asked candidates about signs of arsenic and morphia poisoning, the healing of fractures, drugs and dose calculation, infant feeding, and preparing a patient and instruments for skull trephining surgery. Candidates also had to define inflammation, rigor, hectic, dyspnoea, Cheyne-Stokes breathing, antitoxin, nystagmus, meconium, stertor and menorrhagia. Again, in response to international interest in New Zealand's process of state registration, the questions for this state final examination were reported in the professional nursing journal of the Victorian Trained Nurses Association, Australia. 'State registration of nurses', *Una* 1, July 1903, pp. 8–9.

8. 'Medical nursing examination: Comments by the examiner', *KT* 18, April 1925, p. 86.
9. *AJHR*, 1910, H-22, p. 9.
10. 'Post-graduate course for registered nurses, Paper read by Miss Bicknell', *KT*, 17, October 1924, p. 156.
11. Pamela J. Wood, 'Nursing the patient, the room and the doctor: Assessing New Zealand nurses' practical capability, 1900–1945', *Nurse Education Today* 31, 2011, pp. 140–44.
12. 'Nursing care', *NZNJ* 32, June 1939, pp. 201–04; 'The nursing study', *NZNJ* 32, June 1939, pp. 237–40. Nurses had to choose a patient they had nursed, review their chart, interview them and reflect on what they had learned. At least two studies were required each year. Some were published in the *NZJN*. See, for example, D. Thompson, 'A case study: A nursing treatment of a tuberculosis spine', *NZNJ* 33, October 1940, pp. 317–20.
13. Colleen Williams, *All for a Medal: The nursing memoirs of Colleen Turbet Williams* (Auckland: Self-published, 2006), p. 65.
14. Isabel Haresnape, *Home Nursing: What to do and how to do it* (Auckland: Isabel Haresnape, 1923), preface. Louisa Corkill, who worked at Wairoa Hospital under Haresnape when she was Sister Isabel Tozer, before her marriage, thought she was 'a grand nurse' with 'journalistic ability'. Louisa Corkill, Foxton Beach, to Miss Kimbell, 2 November 1964, Hawke's Bay District Health Board Library, Hastings. A reviewer thought the instructions were 'clear and practical'. 'New books for study and leisure hours', *KT* 17, April 1924, p. 60. The only question is why she included treatment for snakebite in a New Zealand book. Perhaps she hoped for an international readership?
15. Bridget Ristori, *Nursing in the Home* (Whangārei: Northern Publishing, 1949). Ristori notes in her foreword (p. 2) that the book was based on her series of articles published in the *New Zealand Woman's Weekly* and that she had received several letters requesting them to be published as a book. Cuttings of the articles, from August to November 1945, are held in Bridget Madge Isabel [née Ristori] Francois 1902–1992: Diaries and papers, Scrapbook, MSY–6766, ATL.
16. Susan L. Robins, 'Keeping the homes fires burning: The history of home nursing in New Zealand, 1900–1925', MA (Applied) in Nursing thesis, Victoria University of Wellington, 2002.
17. As a patient needed to be supervised for up to 8 minutes while their temperature was taken, by the 1880s hospital doctors were relinquishing the task to nurses. In describing the process to her probationers, Eva Lückes, the London Hospital matron, warned nurses that 'many doctors are reluctant to admit that nurses are capable of taking the temperature of the patient'. Eva C.E. Lückes, *Lectures on General Nursing* (London: Kegan Paul, Trench, 1888), p. 163. Doctors' increasing use of the sphygmomanometer led one doctor in the United States to declare in 1910 that 'it has become necessary that every nurse should be able to take accurate blood pressure observations in order that she may follow her cases intelligently'. See 'The estimation of the blood pressure', *BJN* 44, 11 June 1910, pp. 467–68, quotation on p. 468. However, the use of this instrument by nurses was not widely described in nursing textbooks until the 1930s. See, for example, Evelyn C. Pearce, *A General Textbook of Nursing: A comprehensive guide* (London: Faber & Faber, 1938), p. 37.
18. 'Nurses' and Midwives' Registration Board, State Examinations, December, 1937', *NZNJ* 31, March 1938, pp. 86–90.
19. H.B. Turbott, 'Treatment of scabies, impetigo and pediculosis', *NZNJ* 26, January 1933, pp. 316, 318, 320. The nurses are identified in the article as Janie North (nurse inspector) and Nurses Cox (school

nurse), Uniacke (district health nurse at Tikitiki) and Hill (district health nurse at Whakatāne). The latter two are likely to be Geraldine Uniacke, who trained at Wanganui Hospital, registered in February 1926, and gained her maternity certificate at Masterton Hospital in 1927 and a Postgraduate Diploma in 1928; and Lillian Hill, who trained at Auckland Hospital, registering in July 1923, gaining a midwifery certificate at Franklin Memorial Hospital, Waiuku. *NZG*, 1930, pp. 1236, 1324. Nurse Cox could not be identified. The article was published under the name of the medical officer of health, Dr H.B. Turbott.

20. For detailed discussion of the development of nursing research, see Pamela J. Wood and Katherine Nelson, 'Striving for best practice: Standardising New Zealand nursing procedures, 1930–60', *Journal of Clinical Nursing* 22, nos. 21–22, 2013, pp. 3217–24; Pamela J. Wood and Katherine Nelson, 'The journal *Kai Tiaki*'s role in developing research capability in New Zealand nursing, 1908–1959', *Nursing Praxis in New Zealand* 29, no. 1, 2013, pp. 12–22.

21. Audrey Gilbert (née Dawson), oral history interview with Pamela Wood, 9 August 2005.

22. Yvonne Shadbolt, 'Re-introducing Mabel Mahinarangi Kewene, MBE, QSO', *Nursing Praxis in New Zealand* 16, no. 3, 2000, p. 51.

23. Irene Cornwell, 'Fresh air and regular habits', in *Plunket Pioneers: Recollections of Plunket nurses from 1940 to 2000*, ed. J. Powell (Auckland: Heritage Press, 2003), p. 21.

24. See, for example, 'Gisborne Hospital', *KT* 11, October 1918, p. 217.

25. Edith M. Lewis, *Joy in the Caring* (Christchurch: N.M. Peryer, 1962), pp. 94–95.

26. Marjorie Chambers, *My Life in Nursing: Christchurch Hospital, 1936–1966* (Tauranga: Moana Press, 1988), p. 88.

27. In 1948 Audrey Dawson was finishing her Plunket training when she was appointed as district health nurse at Mangakino. No one in her class knew where it was. The public works camp had been set up there just two years before. Audrey Gilbert, oral history interview with Pamela Wood, 9 August 2005.

28. Marjorie Chambers was one such tutor. When she returned to Christchurch Hospital in 1944, she suddenly found herself teaching nursing history, hygiene, bacteriology and materia medica. She felt very tentative at first but then 'found her feet'. Chambers, *My Life in Nursing*, p. 85.

29. Julia Hallam, 'Nursing an image: The Sue Barton career novels', in *Image and Power: Women in fiction in the twentieth century*, eds S. Sceats and G. Cunningham (London: Longmans, 1996), pp. 91–102.

30. Hallam, 'Nursing an image', p. 97.

31. M.I. Lambie, 'Shortage of nurses', *NZNJ* 35, August 1942, p. 192.

32. See, for example, 'Notes from the hospitals and personal items', *KT* 1, July 1908, pp. 90–92, see p. 91. The nurses' clubs were the forerunners of the New Zealand Trained Nurses Association branches but continued as bureaus. In 1929 the main nurses' clubs were in Auckland at Mountain Road, Epsom; in Wellington at 1 Kensington Street; in Christchurch at 104 Salisbury Street; and in Dunedin at 169 York Place (and previously at 45 Royal Terrace). See, for example, Untitled, advertisements, *KT* 22, November 1929, p. iii.

33. As just one example, see 'The B.M.A. boycott', *AS*, 19 December 1908, p. 7.

34. See, for example, 'To the readers of "Kai Tiaki"', advertisement, *KT* 8, January 1915, p. 54.

35. *AJHR*, 1921, H-31, p. 21; 'The future of private nursing', editorial, *KT* 17, April 1928, pp. 61–62.

36. 'Nurses' fees', *EP*, 15 June 1932, p. 13.

37. Dorothy Alice Ford, *Journey from Stranger's Rest* (Wellington: Daphne Brasell Associates, 1989), p. 137.
38. Bridget Ristori, *Nursing as a Career* (Kawakawa: Northland Gazette, 1947), p. 39.
39. Marian M. Thorp, *The Long, Long Trail: An autobiography* (Hastings: Hart, 1971), p. 39. According to one source, in 1943 there were 450 private hospitals. Ten years later this number had dwindled to fewer than 160. Eva Bradley, *The History of Royston Hospital* (Hastings: Royston Hospital Trust Board, 2007), p. 33. Not all would have been owned by nurses; some were owned by doctors who hired nurses to manage them.
40. 'The New Zealand nurses' anthem', *NZNJ* 33, February 1940, pp. 54–55; Nurses' Anthem, 82495a and b, MTG archive, Napier.
41. See, for example, 'Graduation ceremony', *Press*, 18 February 1943, p. 2. From the 1930s, the Bertram Eli Hamilton Memorial Prize was awarded annually to a nurse of any rank who demonstrated the essential nursing qualities of sympathy, patience, skill, industry, and knowledge of human nature and the profession. The range of seniority was seen in the awards: in 1934 it was awarded to Nurse M. Kensington, in 1935 to Sister Naomi Garner, in 1937 to Staff Nurse E. Gidding, and in 1938 to Sister M.F. Barnett, the assistant matron, who was about to leave to become matron at Masterton Hospital. 'News for women', *Press*, 11 October 1934, p. 2; 'Prize awarded to nurse', *Press*, 25 October 1935, p. 9; 'Eli Hamilton Prize', *Press*, 12 October 1937, p. 2; 'Current notes', *Press*, 7 October 1938, p. 2.
42. The following description is based on an analysis of 340 obituaries in *KT* and the *NZNJ*, 1910–50. See Pamela J. Wood, 'Nursing mortubiography: New Zealand nursing obituaries, 1910–1940', paper presented at the 10th History of Nursing Research Colloquium, 'International history of nursing: Theoretical interpretations and approaches', Wellcome Unit for the History of Medicine, Oxford University, Oxford, UK, 11 March 2005; Pamela J. Wood, 'Threading the dead in the professional collective memory: Nursing obituaries, 1910–1939', paper presented at the Australian College of Nursing Inaugural History Conference, Nurses' Memorial Centre, Melbourne, 15–16 November 2012.
43. 'Miss Isabella Frazer: A notable record', *NZNJ* 26, January 1933, pp. 314–16.
44. 'Obituary', *NZNJ* 33, October 1940, p. 339.
45. 'Obituary', *KT* 22, July 1929, p. 124.
46. See, for example, the 1930 obituary of Sister E.L.R Fergusson, who 'passed away suddenly in the train on her way to her home in Wanganui'. It described her achievements in the Boer War and pioneering services in Taihape and the far north. 'Obituary', *NZNJ* 23, March 1930, pp. 60–61.
47. 'Obituary. Nurse E.J. Margetts', *NZNJ* 25, March 1932, p. 88; 'Notes from the hospitals and personal items', *KT* 2, July 1909, pp. 117–24, see p. 121.
48. 'Obituary', *NZNJ* 23, March 1930, pp. 60–61.
49. Overall, half the deaths were caused by infectious diseases. In fact, this was the cause of two-thirds of nurses' deaths in the years 1908–20.
50. See, for example, the obituary for Margaret Bilton, the first nurse in the Backblocks Nursing Service. 'Obituary', *NZNJ* 27, November 1934, p. 204. See also the obituary for Jessie Ewart, who started training at Christchurch Hospital in 1895, was appointed matron of Southland Hospital in 1900 and held that position for 24 years. 'Miss Ewart's death severs yet another link with our nursing pioneers who so courageously worked for the progress of nursing in New Zealand.' 'Obituary', *NZNJ* 33, October 1940, p. 339.

Another obituary commemorates Mabel Te Aowhaitini Mangakāhia, the first Māori nurse to hold four qualifications. 'Obituary: Mabel Mangakahia', *NZNJ* 33, September 1940, pp. 303–04.

51. 'Obituary: Ethel G.B. Fenwick', *NZNJ* 40, June 1947, pp. 115–16; 'Obituary: Adelaide Nutting', *NZNJ* 42, April 1949, p. 59. Adelaide Nutting was an eminent American nurse leader.
52. Public farewells to matrons were often also published in newspapers.
53. These were very common descriptors. This account of farewells is based on an analysis of 137 reports of farewells in *KT* and the *NZNJ* from 1908 to 1950.
54. 'Notes from the hospitals and personal items', *KT* 1, April 1908, pp. 50–52, quotation on p. 52.
55. See, for example, the speech at the farewell to Sarah Polden, matron of Thames Hospital, in which the mayor acclaimed her 'gracious, untiring, self-sacrificing service'. 'Valedictory', *TS*, 30 November 1923, p. 5, reprinted as 'Farewell to Miss Polden', *KT* 17, January 1924, p. 23.
56. See the accounts of farewells to Sister Fitz-Gibbon, theatre sister at Christchurch Hospital. 'Au revoir', *KT* 18, April 1925, p. 64, and Edith Tennent, assistant matron of Wellington Hospital, when she left to become matron at Dunedin Hospital. At Tennent's farewell, nurses ate a 'delicious tea' handed round in one room; 'in another room various mysteries were unfolded by an Eastern occultist'. 'Farewells and presentations', *KT* 18, April 1925, p. 52. This was a reprint from the *Dominion*.
57. 'Matron Rothwell honoured', *KT* 14, July 1921, p. 130. Dr Hugh Douglas had been medical superintendent of Waikato Hospital.
58. For a progressive euchre competition example, see 'Notes from the hospitals and personal items', *KT* 10, April 1917, pp. 123–24, see p. 124. For an example of a 'coon can' card evening, see 'Valedictory, Nurse Jessie Aitken', *KT* 16, July 1923, p. 119. For an example of a croquet tournament, see 'Valedictory', *KT* 5, April 1912, pp. 23–24, see p. 23. For a fancy dress example, see 'Presentation to Miss Brown', *KT* 6, April 1913, pp. 164–65. When Miss Brookes (RRC and bar) left after four years as matron of the Rannderdale Home for ex-service patients in order to marry, she was honoured by several functions and gift parties, including both a 'linen tea' and a 'kitchen tea'. 'Notes from the hospitals and personal items', *KT* 18, July 1925, pp. 149–63, see pp. 149–50. For a 'handkerchief afternoon', see 'Appointments and resignations', *KT* 6, October 1913, p. 180.
59. 'Farewell to Miss Inglis', *KT* 16, April 1923, p. 60.
60. 'Notes from the hospitals and personal items', *KT* 1, April 1908, pp. 50–52, see p. 52.
61. Untitled, *KT* 1, July 1908, p. 70. Maude Hayward trained and worked at Christchurch Hospital from 1895 to 1899, was matron at Westport Hospital from 1899 to 1908, worked in a private hospital from 1908 to 1910, and was matron at Masterton Hospital from 1910 to 1913. *NZG*, 1920, p. 613.
62. 'Presentations to Miss Thurston', *KT* 1, October 1908, p. 123. Mabel Thurston trained at Wellington Hospital and registered in December 1904. She was matron of Greymouth Hospital from 1906 to 1908, Christchurch Hospital from 1908 to 1916 and Walton-on-Thames military hospital from 1916 to 1917. She then served as matron-in-chief of the NZANS overseas from 1917 to 1920. On her return to New Zealand she was matron of the military hospitals in Rotorua (1920), Trentham (1920–23) and Hanmer (Queen Mary Hospital, 1924). She was matron of the Pukeora Sanatorium at Waipukurau in 1927. *NZG*, 1930, p. 1321.

63. Nurse McDonald at Pōrangahau received 'a very fine kiwi feather mat' from local Māori. 'Notes from the hospitals and personal items', *KT* 18, July 1925, pp. 149–63, see p. 155.
64. 'Farewell to Miss Berry at Napier Hospital', *KT* 5, January 1912, p. 43. The patients also gave her a testimonial that recorded her untiring efforts and thoughtfulness. She had resigned following disruptions among the nursing staff and a consequent public inquiry led by Dr T.H.A. Valintine, inspector-general of hospitals.
65. 'Presentation', *KT* 19, October 1926, p. 163.
66. 'Notes from the hospitals and personal items', *KT* 8, April 1915, p. 111.
67. Untitled, *KT* 1, July 1908, p. 70.
68. 'Farewell to Miss Polden'. When the hospital board decided to add a maternity annex to the hospital, it also decided that Sarah Polden could no longer hold the position as matron as she did not have a maternity or midwifery qualification. (This difficulty could have been resolved by appointing a midwife to oversee the annex.) The community's response was clearly an acknowledgement that what they regarded as an injustice needed to be remedied. See, for example, 'Public meeting', *TS*, 10 November 1923, p. 5.
69. For scholarly views of the idea of 'the gift', see Mark Osteen, 'Introduction: Questions of the gift', in *The Question of the Gift: Essays across disciplines*, ed. Mark Osteen (London: Routledge, 2002), pp. 1–42.
70. In this respect the gift suggests Lee Anne Fennel's idea of gift-giving as 'empathetic dialogue'. Fennel is describing personal gifts between individuals, but her idea of 'empathetic dialogue' shows the meaning that a gift can carry beyond a commodity of exchange. Lee Anne Fennel, 'Unpacking the gift: Illiquid goods and the empathetic dialogue', in Osteen, *The Question of the Gift*, pp. 85–102.
71. 'Notes concerning the Nurses' and Midwives' Registration Board meeting', *NZNJ* 25, September 1932, pp. 210–11. The lectures covered the history of nursing from ancient times, changes brought about by staffing hospitals with nurses, Nightingale's life and works, the development of modern nursing and specialist fields, the history of the four main New Zealand hospitals and their introduction of systematic nurse training, and the history of state registration and the professional association. Reference works were to be Lavinia Dock and Isabel Stewart's *A Short History of Nursing*, Edward Cook's *The Life of Florence Nightingale* and Hester Maclean's forthcoming reminiscences.
72. 'Nursing education', *KT* 16, October 1923, pp. 153–54; 'Post-graduate course for registered nurses', *KT* 17, October 1924, pp. 156–58; 'University of Otago Diploma in Nursing', *KT* 18, January 1925, p. 33.
73. 'History of nursing', *NZNJ* 24, September 1931, pp. 220–24.
74. 'Recruitment campaign', *NZNJ* 36, February 1943, p. 45; 'Nursing Education Committee, Report of business of meetings held on 15 December and 11 May', *NZNJ* 36, July 1943, pp. 161–62.
75. 'Curriculum of Post-graduate Course', Nursing Education Committee, NZRNA, [?1950]; Nursing Education Committee, NZRNA, Minutes of Meetings (1941–54); both in New Zealand Nurses Association records, 79–032–09/11A, ATL.
76. Barbara Mortimer, 'The history of nursing: Yesterday, today and tomorrow', in *New Directions in the History of Nursing: International perspectives*, eds B. Mortimer and S. McGann (Abingdon: Routledge, 2005), pp. 1–21; Sioban Nelson, 'A history of small things', in *Advanced Qualitative Research for Nursing*, ed. J. Latimer (Oxford: Blackwell Science, 2003), pp. 211–29.
77. This description of nurses' history narratives is based on an analysis of 422 articles in *KT* and the *NZNJ* from 1908

to 1950 referring to or devoted to nursing history.
78. After an Amendment Act in 1920, the medal was given only to nurses who had trained and qualified in New Zealand and not to those who qualified overseas and then registered in New Zealand. See 'The Nurses' Registration Amendment Act, 1920', *KT* 14, January 1921, p. 20.
79. The first description in *KT* was 'The origin of the five-point star', *KT* 9, January 1916, p. 42. Additional descriptions appeared throughout the period. For an example of a newspaper account, see 'New Zealand trained nurses' badge', *ES*, 11 September 1926, p. 16.
80. Grace Neill claimed in 1923, however, that the five points had 'no other special meaning' than representing the New Zealand flag – an explanation that remains obscure. See Hester Maclean's response to a correspondent inquiring about the 'special meaning' of the five points, in *KT* 16, July 1923, p. 123.
81. Until 1920, more than 90 percent of New Zealanders identified as Christian. The percentage dropped only slightly between 1920 and 1950.
82. Williams, *All for a Medal*, p. 26.
83. This was (later Sir) William Howard Russell, writing for *The Times*.
84. Lamps of this kind can be seen, for example, at the Florence Nightingale Museum in London and the Royal College of Nursing Archive in Edinburgh. In the background of the stained-glass window in the Timaru Hospital chapel, Florence Nightingale is holding the cylindrical style of lamp.
85. A stylised version forms the symbol of the International Council of Nurses.
86. 'Award to nurse', *EP*, 1 February 1939, p. 11; 'Dominion nurses', *EP*, 20 February 1940, p. 7. The essay competition lamp was designed by James Johnston of Christchurch. In sending the design to the NZRNA secretary, he said, 'I also thought I would set a piece of greenstone on the lid if I could secure a suitable piece. It is usually difficult to get greenstone in a shape & size to suit one's requirements & to have it made specially is costly – anyway I will do what I can.' Letter from James Johnston, Christchurch, to Miss Clark, n.d., New Zealand Nurses' Association records–Essay Competition–79–032–12/7, ATL.
87. 'Mum's letter', *MW*, 6 September 1922, p. 12.
88. 'Leadership', *NZNJ* 31, December 1938, p. 341.
89. 'The Florence Nightingale Lamp awarded to Waikato Hospital', *KT* 32, March 1939, pp. 96–97.
90. For an expanded discussion of nursing commemoration, see Pamela J. Wood, 'Commemorating nursing: An exercise in historical imagination', *Nursing Praxis in New Zealand* 21, no. 2, 2005, pp. 47–57.
91. Letter from E.M. Bascand, Dannevirke Hospital, to NZRNA, 10 October 1950, Memorials to New Zealand Nurses file, NZNO library, Wellington. See also 'Memorials to New Zealand nurses', *NZNJ* 43, December 1950, p. 226. Eileen Bascand trained at Christchurch Hospital and completed her training in June 1927. 'State examination of nurses', *KT* 20, July 1927, p. 164.
92. On the commissioning, see Margaret Gibson and Yvonne T. Shadbolt, 'NZNA: Structure and function, 1909–1983', in *Objects and Outcomes: New Zealand Nurses' Association, 1909–1983*, eds M. Gibson and Y.T. Shadbolt (Wellington: New Zealand Nurses' Association, 1984, p. 9. On the quotation, see the caption for the cover photograph, *NZNJ* 53, April 1960, p. 3.
93. Beatrice Campbell trained at New Plymouth Hospital and registered in December 1906. She continued working there and was matron from November 1917. *NZG*, 1920, p. 591. Augusta Godfrey

nursed at Wellington Hospital from 1885 to 1890 and was then matron there from 1890 to 1898. *NZG*, 1905, p. 328. Another memorial plaque was created for Frances Keith Payne's service of more than 20 years at the same hospital, including as matron from 1898 to 1900 and 1904 to 1916. In 1926, a plaque was funded by nurses who wanted 'to have her memory kept alive'. 'Memorial to the late Miss Payne', *KT* 20, January 1927, p. 27.

94. Marian Little trained and worked at Christchurch Hospital 1892–1905, registering in May 1902. She then did private nursing until 1908, when she became matron of Ashburton Hospital. In 1909 she took the matron position at Hokitika Hospital. *NZG*, 1920, p. 623.

95. See, for example, 'Mrs Grace Neill memorial', *KT* 20, January 1927, pp. 29–30.

96. Letter from J.O.C. Neill to the NZTNA, 29 November 1926, Memorials to New Zealand Nurses file, NZNO library, Wellington.

97. This initiative received international attention. See 'The Grace Neill Memorial Library', *BJN* 76, April 1928, pp. 94–95. The library continued to benefit nurses until the school was disestablished in the 1970s.

98. See, for example, 'The Fraser Medal', *KT* 4, April 1911, p. 87; 'Frances Keith Payne Memorial Medal', *NZNJ* 22, July 1929, p. 133.

99. 'Nurses' memorial tablet: Unveiling ceremony at Nurses' Home, Dunedin', *KT* 14, January 1921, p. 31. The plaque is now in the hospital chapel.

100. This description of the chapel is drawn mainly from Fiona Ciaran, 'Christchurch Hospital's threatened shrine', *Historic Places*, December 1986, pp. 8–11; Fiona Ciaran, *The Architectural Heritage of Christchurch, vol. 7, Nurses' Memorial Chapel* (Christchurch: Christchurch City Council Planning Policy Unit, 1990); Fiona Ciaran, *Stained Glass Windows of Canterbury, New Zealand* (Dunedin: Otago University Press, 1998). The chapel was restored following the 2010 and 2011 earthquakes.

101. Katie Pickles, 'Mapping memorials for Edith Cavell on the colonial edge', *New Zealand Geographer* 62, 2006, p. 20. See also Katie Pickles, *Transnational Outrage: The death and commemoration of Edith Cavell* (Basingstoke: Palgrave Macmillan, 2007).

102. This was a precursor to what Katie Pickles has noted as the chapel's more recent shift toward becoming a national rather than regional memorial. Pickles, 'Mapping memorials', 21.

103. Later chapel windows, often made in the 1960s at Miller Studios, Dunedin, have clear nursing symbols. A window at the Timaru Hospital chapel portrays a uniformed nurse with apron and veil, the nursing medal and, in the background, Florence Nightingale holding a (historically correct) lamp. At the now-demolished Wellington Hospital chapel, separate depictions portrayed the archetypal nurse Fabiola, the nursing medal, a cap, a cape, red cross and nurses' hands, as well as flames and nails representing sacrifice. For a detailed description of the Wellington Hospital chapel windows, see Annette Stevenson, *Wellington Hospital Nurses Memorial Chapel* (Wellington: Wellington Hospital Nurses Memorial Chapel Committee, 2001). See also Wellington Hospital Nurses Reunion and Chapel Association records, AP001, Wellington City Council Archives, Wellington. Annette Stevenson made a great effort to prevent the chapel being demolished, particularly as it had been funded largely by nurses' donations, but was unsuccessful. The chapel windows were installed in the new hospital.

104. See, for example, Sidney Wilding, nurse's notebook, [?1937], ARC2008–136, Puke Ariki. See also the general announcement

in 'Notice to Subscribers', *KT* 17, January 1924, p. 2.
105. 'An effort for the Nurses' Memorial Fund', *KT*, 22, January 1929, p. 14. It raised £18 10s.
106. 'Nurses' Memorial Fund', *KT* 22, April 1929, p. 58.
107. 'Auckland Branch', *KT* 12, April 1919, p. 59.
108. At the unveiling of the Dunedin Hospital memorial in 1920, a nurse's relative said he hoped it would serve 'not only as a lasting memorial to those brave women' but also as an 'incentive to good and noble deeds' for those who came after them. 'Nurses' memorial tablet', *KT* 14, January 1921, p. 33. And Mr J.A. Murdoch, the mayor of Kumara, said on the dedication of the Kumara nurses' memorial that he hoped their lives would be 'a beacon guide for others'. 'Memorial to Nurses Isdell and Jamieson', *KT* 9, April 1916, p. 72.
109. 'Memorial to the late Miss Payne', *KT* 20, January 1927, pp. 28–29.
110. John Bodnar, *Remaking America: Public memory, commemoration and patriotism in the 20th century* (Princeton, NJ: Princeton University Press, 1992).
111. For the history of the professional organisation, see Gibson Smith and Shadbolt, *Objects and Outcomes*; Mary Ellen O'Connor, *Freed to Care, Proud to Nurse: 100 years of the New Zealand Nurses Organisation* (Wellington: Steele Roberts, 2010).
112. Joan Rattray, *Great Days in New Zealand Nursing* (Wellington: A.H. & A.W. Reed, 1961), p. 79.
113. 'Correspondence', *NZNJ* 25, May 1932, p. 109; 'Nurses' Christian Union', *NZNJ* 37, March 1944, p. 72.
114. 'Hospital days', *Wellington Public Hospital Nurses Journal* 1, no. 7, 1939, p. 15.
115. As one example, see I.M. Beechy, 'The trials of the amateur journalist', *Wellington Public Hospital Nurses Journal* 1, no. 5, 1936, p. 13.
116. Sidney Wilding, ARC2008–136, Puke Ariki. The co-editor, Nurse Dalton, is listed in the magazine as N.D. Dalton. However, inside the cover of Sidney Wilding's notebook, Wilding has listed the names of all her classmates, and Dalton's first name is noted as Donella.
117. As an example of this regular plea, see 'Business notices', *KT* 12, July 1919, p. 150.
118. 'Notes from the hospitals and personal items', *KT* 5, January 1912, p. 45.
119. 'Notes from the hospitals and personal items', *KT* 5, July 1912, p. 88.
120. 'Notes from the hospitals and personal items', *KT* 7, April 1914, p. 99.
121. Ibid., p. 103.
122. 'Notes from the hospitals and personal items', *KT* 13, April 1920, p. 99 and *KT* 14, April 1921, p. 105.
123. Patricia Meyer Spacks, *Gossip* (New York: Knopf, 1985); M.R. Alfano and Brian Robinson, 'Gossip as a burdened virtue', *Ethical Theory and Moral Practice* 20, no. 3, 2017, pp. 473–87. Acceptance of the term 'gossip' for this kind of column in nursing journals is demonstrated, for example, in an Australian journal: see 'Gossip notes', *The Lamp* 12, no. 7, August 1955, pp. 15–16.
124. Joel H. Wiener, 'Edmund Yates: The gossip as editor', in *Innovators and Preachers: The role of the editor in Victorian England*, ed. Joel H. Wiener (Westport, CT: Praeger, 1985), p. 262.
125. Nurses' illness narratives were similar to pathographies. See, for example, Anne H. Hawkins, 'Pathography: Patient narratives of illness', *Western Journal of Medicine* 171, no. 2, 1999, pp. 127–29; Anne H. Hawkins, *Reconstructing Illness: Studies in pathography* (West Lafayette, IN: Purdue University Press, 1999); Kay Torney Souter, 'Narrating the body: Disease as interpersonal event', *Health and History* 1, 1998, pp. 35–42. See also J. Wiltshire, 'Biography, pathography, and the recovery of meaning', *Cambridge Quarterly* 29, no. 4, 2000, pp. 409–22.

126. See, for example, 'Hospital inquiry', *EP*, 31 July 1928, p. 10; 'Death of nurse', *EP*, 30 July 1928, p. 10; Alison Robinson, ed., *Stratford Hospital Memories* (Stratford: Thurlstone, 2001), pp. 14–15; Sonja Davies, *Bread and Roses: Sonja Davies, her story* (Masterton: Fraser Books, 1984), pp. 55–56, 61–62; Deborah Dunsford, 'Tuberculosis and the Auckland Hospital nurse, 1938–1948', in *New Countries and Old Medicine*, eds L. Bryder and D. Dow (Auckland: Pyramid, 1995), pp. 291–97.
127. Davies, *Bread and Roses*, pp. 61–62. Davies' health was severely compromised when she contracted tuberculosis, so she had to leave her nurse training.
128. Davies, *Bread and Roses*, p. 66.
129. 'Notes from the hospitals and personal items', *KT* 13, April 1920, p. 99, and *KT* 14, April 1921, p. 105.
130. See, for example, Stephanie Kirby, 'Sputum and the scent of wallflowers: Nursing in tuberculosis sanatoria, 1920–1970', *Social History of Medicine* 23, no. 3, 2010, pp. 602–20.
131. 'A nurse-patient looks at tuberculosis', *NZNJ* 33, May 1940, p. 144.
132. Williams, *All for a Medal*, pp. 38–39.
133. See, for example, 'Pauline's Story', n.d., part of the Home Truths section of the Immunisation Advisory Centre's Piercing Memories project: www.immune.org.nz
134. June Opie, *Over My Dead Body* (London: Methuen, 1957); Betty Macdonald, *The Plague and I* (Seattle, WA: University of Washington Press, [1948] 2000).
135. Williams, *All for a Medal*, pp. 56–57.
136. Bridget Ristori, 'My 36 years of nursing', (New Zealand) *Mirror*, February 1957, pp. 12–13, 71; Bridget Ristori, 'Even nursing changes', *New Zealand Dairy Exporter*, 1 June 1957, p. 100, both in Bridget Madge Isobel [née Ristori] Francois, 1902–1992: Diaries and Papers–Scrapbook–MSY–6766, ATL.
137. Joan Loeber, 'Nursing in the 1930s', *Spectrum* #800, 1993, Radio New Zealand.

Chapter 11. Nursing at the southern edge of empire

1. 'The imperial spirit in nursing', *Australasian Nurses' Journal* 6, no. 10, 1908, pp. 353–34 reprinted from *BJN*.
2. M. Daphne Kutzer, *Empire's Children: Empire and imperialism in classic British children's books* (London: Routledge, 2002). See also Michelle Smith, *Empire in British Girls' Literature and Culture: Imperial girls, 1880–1915* (London: Palgrave Macmillan, 2011); Michelle J. Smith, Kristine Moruzi and Clare Bradford, *From Colonial to Modern: Transnational girlhood in Canadian, Australian, and New Zealand children's literature, 1840–1940* (Toronto: University of Toronto Press, 2018).
3. Betty Gilderdale, *A Sea Change: 145 years of New Zealand junior fiction* (Auckland: Longman Paul, 1982); Louise Clark, '"Making its own history": New Zealand historical fiction for children, 1862–2008', PhD thesis, University of Waikato, 2010.
4. Carol Mutch, Rosemary Bingham, Lynette Kingsbury and Maria Perreau, 'Political indoctrination through myth building: The *New Zealand School Journal* at the time of World War I', *Curriculum Matters* 14, 2018, pp. 103–04, 108–09.
5. 'Florence Nightingale', *School Journal*, part 2, vol. 4, no. 8, September 1910, pp. 119–21; 'Florence Nightingale', *School Journal*, part 2, vol. 4, no. 9, October 1910, pp. 130–31.
6. 'Florence Nightingale', *School Journal*, part 2, vol. 4, no. 9, October 1910, p. 132.
7. Felicity Barnes, *New Zealand's London: A colony and its metropolis* (Auckland: Auckland University Press, 2012), p. 1.
8. Barnes, *New Zealand's London*, especially chapter 1.
9. 'Holiday rambles of a New Zealand nurse', *KT* 2, January 1909, pp. 25–29.
10. 'Nursing in New Zealand', *Nursing Record* 3, 22 August 1889, p. 119.

11. 'Woman's work: A wider outlook', *KT* 2, October 1909, p. 149; 'Obituary', *AS*, 5 May 1945, p. 9.
12. 'Some extracts from the diary of a nurse on her travels', *KT* 4, October 1911, p. 173.
13. 'Notes from the hospitals and personal items', *KT* 18, July 1925, p. 163.
14. 'The imperial spirit in nursing', *Australasian Nurses' Journal* 6, no. 10, 1908, pp. 353–54.
15. 'Nursing in New Zealand', editorial, *BJN* 41, 17 October 1908, p. 305.
16. The additional nurse inspectors were Amelia Bagley and Jessie Bicknell. The *BJN* carried an article on their appointment and also noted that Western Australia had appointed its first nurse inspector. 'Assistant Inspector', *BJN* 41, 12 September 1908, p. 209; 'Nurse-Inspector of Hospitals', *BJN* 41, 12 September 1908, p. 209.
17. Grace Neill, 'The professional training and status of nurses', *Nursing Record and Hospital World* 23, 15 July 1899, p. 47. See also Lavinia Dock, 'Discussion', *Nursing Record and Hospital World* 23, 15 July 1899, pp. 48–49. Dock entirely ignored the barely descriptive paper by the nurse representing the Cape Colony, who spoke after Neill, and concentrated completely on Neill's.
18. The lack of a definitive date is due to two reports referring to an eight-hour day. The inspector of hospitals, Dr George Grabham, mentions in 1887 that assistant nurses worked eight hours a day, and Dr Duncan MacGregor, in that role in 1895, refers to the benefit likely to accrue from the introduction of the eight-hour daily duty under Matron Augusta Godfrey. D. Macdonald Wilson, *A Hundred Years of Healing: Wellington Hospital, 1847–1947* (Wellington: A.H. & A.W. Reed, 1948), p. 79. Christchurch Hospital also claimed to be the first to introduce a system of three eight-hour shifts. See 'Eight hour day', *NZNJ* 28, May 1936, pp. 94–95.
19. See Dock, 'Discussion'.
20. 'Personal notes from London', *EP*, 27 November 1902, p. 9.
21. See, for example, Susan McGann, *The Battle of the Nurses: A study of eight women who influenced the development of professional nursing, 1880–1930* (London: Scutari Press, 1992).
22. 'Some notes from the conference of matrons and nurses at Paris', *KT* 1, January 1908, p. 19.
23. Neill's achievements were noted in 'Mrs Grace Neill', *KT* 18, January 1925, p. 20; 'An appreciation', *KT* 20, April 1927, p. 71. She was also named on the banner of a memorial to international nurse leaders displayed at the Royal College of Nursing in London. In 1946, the British journal noted with 'profound interest' the winning entry of the New Zealand professional association's student essay competition on 'Mrs Grace Neill: Her life and work and her contribution to nursing in New Zealand'. The journalist added, 'She was a wonderful woman to whom we owe a great gratitude for past services'. 'Nursing echoes', *BJN* 94, September 1946, p. 99.
24. Michael King describes New Zealand being, in Premier Richard Seddon's term, 'God's Own Country', with commentators visiting to see its social innovations for themselves, including Beatrice and Sidney Webb, Mark Twain and others. King says this view was encouraged by Liberal politicians and writers and was linked to the notion that New Zealand was 'one of the most loyal – if not *the* most loyal – of Britain's children'. Michael King, *The Penguin History of New Zealand* (Auckland: Penguin, 2003), p. 282.
25. See, for example, Hester Maclean, *Nursing in New Zealand: History and reminiscences* (Wellington: Tolan, 1932), p. 28.
26. 'State registration of nurses', *KT* 7, October 1914, p. 14.; *AJHR*, 1911, H-31, p. 78. Although some nurses who came to New

Zealand after the British system was established were already registered in Britain, the New Zealand records do not show evidence of this. The process still noted the specifics of their training – the hospital, the length of training and the fact they had gained a certificate – rather than simply acknowledging their British registration.

27. 'Progress of state registration of trained nurses', *KT* 1, October 1908, p. 94.
28. *AJHR*, 1909, H-22, p .9. Maclean was concerned that New Zealand's comparatively small population meant that many nurses had to train in smaller hospitals than their British counterparts. See, for example, 'What is a training school?', *KT* 9, October 1916, p. 239. This topic was discussed more widely in H. Maclean, 'Training of nurses in small hospitals', *JDHHCA* 1, no. 13, 1918, pp. 212–14; 'Training of nurses in small hospitals', *JDHHCA* 2, no. 12, 1919, pp. 361–62.
29. 'Notes from the hospitals and personal items', *KT* 5, April 1912, p. 87.
30. 'Editorial', *KT* 13, July 1920, 106.
31. 'Reciprocity between the Dominion of New Zealand and the General Nursing Council of England and Wales', editorial, *KT* 16, January 1923, pp. 1–2.
32. Colonel Morris's views were reported in a Christchurch newspaper. 'Topics of the day: Nurses for the Transvaal', *Press*, 14 October 1899, p. 7. The *NZH* and the Christchurch *Press* had considered Colonel Morris as a potential war correspondent, but he provided expert military commentary on the war from New Zealand. Allison Oosterman, 'New Zealand war correspondence before 1915', *Pacific Journalism Review* 16, no. 1, 2010, pp. 133–52.
33. 'Nurses for the war', *EP*, 21 February 1902, p. 7.
34. New Zealand's attachment to the silver fern as an emblem is discussed in Molly Duggins, '"The world's fernery": New Zealand, fern albums, and nineteenth-century fern fever', in *New Zealand's Empire*, eds Katie Pickles and Catharine Coleborn (Manchester: Manchester University Press, 2016), pp. 102–24.
35. 'Departure of New Zealand nurses for the front', *KT* 8, April 1915, p. 67.
36. 'Otago nurses for the front', *ES*, 27 March 1915, p. 5.
37. 'Arrival of the transport "Tahiti"', *KT* 9, January 1916, p. 31.
38. 'Woman's world', *Dominion*, 19 February 1916, p. 12.
39. 'Welcome to Miss Ross', *ES*, 2 November 1990, p. 6.
40. Commons Family: Papers–Letters from Daphne to her family–MS–Papers–1582–09, ATL.
41. Anna Rogers, *While You're Away: New Zealand nurses at war, 1899–1948* (Auckland: Auckland University Press, 2003), pp. 200–01.
42. Jill Caughley, 'Humanitarian, international nursing and the New Zealand recipients of the Florence Nightingale Medal, 1920–1999', MA (Applied) thesis, Victoria University of Wellington, 2001.
43. 'Reception to Miss Maclean, R.R.C.', *KT* 13, July 1920, p. 108.
44. Linda Bryder, *A Voice for Mothers: The Plunket Society and infant welfare, 1907–2000* (Auckland: Auckland University Press, 2003).
45. 'Early Plunket', AG7–27, Plunket Society Archive, Hocken Library, Dunedin, cited in Bryder, *A Voice for Mothers*, p. 1.
46. See, for example, Lynley Hood, *Minnie Dean: Her life and crimes* (Auckland: Penguin, 1994).
47. Humanised milk was cow's milk modified according to a strict formula, including the addition of lactose (milk sugar), to approximate the composition of mothers' milk. See Bryder, *A Voice for Mothers*, pp. 13, 14.

48. Bryder, *A Voice for Mothers*, see especially foreword and chapter 1, quotation on p. 8.
49. 'Departure of Nurse Morgan', *NEM*, 21 June 1915, p. 6. Morgan was given a handsome bouquet, a travelling clock, a rug with straps, and a bound set of letters of appreciation from the mothers. Despite her declared dedication to New Zealand nursing, she served overseas from January 1917 to 1920. *NZG*, 1920, p. 634.
50. Bryder, *A Voice for Mothers*, p. 2.
51. 'Babies of the Empire', *KT* 11, October 1918, p. 192.
52. Bryder, *A Voice for Mothers*; Linda Bryder, 'More than educators: New Zealand's Plunket nurses, 1907–1950', *Nursing History Review* 26, 2018, pp. 83–96.
53. Bryder, 'More than educators', p. 86.
54. Christine Andrews, 'Developing a nursing specialty – Plunket nursing, 1905–1920', MA (Applied) in Nursing research paper, Victoria University of Wellington, 2001, pp. 41–42.
55. Cited in Bryder, 'More than educators', p. 87.
56. Bryder, *A Voice for Mothers*, p. x.
57. Iris Christofferson, 'Keep pumping those brakes, Nurse!', in *Plunket Pioneers: Recollections of Plunket nurses from 1940 to 2000*, ed. Joyce Powell (Auckland: Heritage Press, 2003), p. 25.
58. 'Evolution of nursing', *NZH*, 12 September 1936, p. 6 (Supplement).
59. Joan E. Lynaugh, 'Inventing international nursing: The first decade (1899–1910)', *International Nursing Review* 46, no. 1, 1999, pp. 9–12.
60. E. Beatrice Salmon, 'The international idea', in *Objects and Outcomes: New Zealand Nurses' Association, 1909–1983*, eds. M.G. Smith and Y.T. Shadbolt (Wellington: New Zealand Nurses' Association, 1984), pp. 118–38.
61. 'The International Congress of Nursing', 1909, *KT* 2, January 1909, p. 32.
62. 'An Imperial British Nurses Association', *KT* 2, July 1909, p. 85; Salmon, 'The international idea', p. 122.
63. These figures are based on an analysis of all entries in the RBNA Pioneer Nurses database: www.kingscollections.org. Some British nurses were accepted into the RBNA without strong evidence of any qualification.
64. 'The International Congress of Nurses', *KT* 5, October 1912, p. 101.
65. 'The international scholars', *KT* 16, April 1923, p. 65. See also 'Items from correspondents', *KT* 15, January 1922, p. 36.
66. See, for example, Mary Lambie's report after visiting the USA, Canada, Britain, Poland, Finland and Sweden. 'The nursing service', *NZNJ* 31, March 1938, pp. 61–69.
67. 'Home for international studies', *KT* 20, July 1927, p. 149.
68. Bridget Ristori, *Patients in My Care: The autobiography of a nurse* (London: Elek, 1967), p. 76.
69. 'Notes from the hospitals and personal items', *KT* 5, July 1912, p. 89.
70. 'Notes from the hospitals and personal items', *KT* 7, January 1914, p. 52.
71. Joan Rattray, *Great Days in New Zealand Nursing* (Wellington: A.H. & A.W. Reed, 1961), pp. 88–90.
72. 'Notes from the hospitals and personal items', *KT* 6, April 1913, p. 87.
73. *NZG*, 1908, pp. 170–86.
74. These figures are based on an analysis of the Register of Nurses, published in the *NZG* as an annual cumulative list. Nurses came from Britain and Ireland (332), Australia (229), Fiji (8), the US (5), South Africa (3), Switzerland (1) and Finland (1). *NZG*, 1925, pp. 357–480.
75. These figures are based on the Register of Nurses analysis. In 1908, 71 nurses had trained overseas. In 1925, 579 (14.67 percent) had done so. After 1933, the *NZG* no longer published this list. Some information on overseas-trained nurses was occasionally given in the chief nurses' annual report in the *AJHR*.

76. 'Notes from the hospitals and personal items', *KT* 5, July 1912, p. 90. Peters' official registration information, however, shows her working as a charge nurse at Wellington Hospital in 1912, and then in private case nursing. *NZG*, 1913, p. 434.
77. 'Notes from the hospitals and personal items', *KT* 5, April 1912, p. 39.
78. *AJHR*, 1913, H-31, p. 92. A typhoid camp hospital had also been set up at Tūpāroa.
79. The nursing register after 1913 lists no address for Hill and shows no record of nursing work at any other place beyond Waiapu Hospital. She had perhaps married or left New Zealand. See, for example, *NZG*, 1914, p. 455; 1915, p. 419; 1916, p. 352. In 1913 Agnes Allan, who had trained at Auckland Hospital but had experience working as a sister in a small rural hospital, was appointed matron in her place and stayed for 15 years. *AJHR*, 1913, H-31, 92; *NZG*, 1913, 405; Notes from the hospitals and personal items, *KT* 21, October 1928, p. 200.
80. 'Nursing in the north', *AS*, 24 April 1925, p. 12.
81. 'Some impressions in Canada and United States, being extracts from letter written by Miss Jeannie Sutherland', *KT* 6, July 1913, pp. 105–06.
82. Shadbolt, 'The international idea', p. 125.
83. Mary I. Lambie, 'The maintenance of high standards of health in the nursing community', *International Council of Nurses Congress Papers 1937*, section 2, session 3, International Council of Nurses, London, pp. 67–69.
84. Shadbolt, 'The international idea', p. 127. For nurses' involvement in UNRRA, see, for example, S. Udell, 'UNRRA nurses in Europe', *NZNJ* 39, June 1946, pp. 154–55; 'N.Z. nurses with UNRRA', *NZNJ* 39, June 1946, pp. 155–57.
85. King, *The Penguin History of New Zealand*, p. 292.
86. 'From letters from our nurses at Samoa', *KT* 7, October 1914, p. 182.
87. King, *The Penguin History of New Zealand*, p. 323. See also Patricia O'Brien, 'From Sudan to Samoa: Imperial legacies and cultures in New Zealand's rule over the Mandated Territory of Western Samoa', in Pickles and Coleborn, *New Zealand's Empire*, pp. 127–46.
88. Mary Lambie, *My Story: Memoirs of a New Zealand nurse* (Christchurch: Whitcombe & Tombs, 1956), p. 83.
89. Memo from Matron L.W. Stott, Wellington Hospital, 7 June 1920, Winifred Ellen Waite records, ARC2005–187, Puke Ariki, New Plymouth.
90. Testimonial, S.G. Grail, acting chief medical officer, Medical Department, Clinical Division, Administration of Western Samoa, Apia, Samoa, 19 November 1921, Winifred Ellen Waite records, ARC2005–187, Puke Ariki, New Plymouth. See also *NZG*, 1922, p. 400.
91. Rattray, *Great Days in New Zealand Nursing*, p. 91.
92. Smedley, 'Ricky's Story', pp. 41–45.
93. *AJHR*, 1940, H-31, p. 30.
94. Smedley, 'Ricky's story', p. 33.
95. Annie Stuart, 'Parasites lost? The Rockefeller Foundation and the expansion of health services in the colonial South Pacific, 1916–1939', PhD thesis in history, University of Canterbury, 2002, pp. 190–91.
96. Lambie, *My Story*, pp. 83–89. For her recruiting efforts through the *NZNJ*, see, for example, 'Tropical nursing service', *NZNJ* 35, April 1942, p. 119; Mary I. Lambie, 'The South Pacific Nursing Service', *NZNJ* 39, February 1946, pp. 29–30.
97. Katie Pickles and Catharine Coleborn, 'Introduction: New Zealand's empire', in *New Zealand's Empire*, eds Pickles and Coleborn, pp. 1–12.
98. Clare Midgley, Alison Twells and Julie Carlier, eds, *Women in Transnational History: Connecting the local and the global* (Abingdon: Routledge, 2016), p. 4.

99. Stuart, 'Parasites lost?', p. 10.
100. Jan Bassett, *Guns and Brooches: Australian Army nursing from the Boer War to the Gulf War* (Melbourne: Oxford University Press, 1992), pp. 66–67; Ruth Rae, *Scarlet Poppies: The army experience of Australian nurses during World War One* (Burwood, NSW: College of Nursing, 2004), p. 232; Kirsty Harris, *More than Bombs and Bandages: Australian Army nurses at work in World War I* (Newport, NSW: Big Sky, 2011), pp. 151–53.
101. Harris, *More than Bombs and Bandages*, p. 154.
102. *AJHR*, 1921, H-31, p. 21. In 1911 Maclean had already voiced her concerns that British nurses who came to New Zealand were not the best type and not thoroughly trained. *AJHR*, 1911, H-31, p. 78.

Conclusion

1. See, for example, 'Miss Isabella Fraser', in *The Cyclopedia of New Zealand, Otago and Southland Provincial Districts* (Christchurch: Cyclopedia Company, 1905), pp. 146–47; Pioneering Nurses, Royal British Nurses' Association records, King's College London Archives: www.kingscollections.org
2. Cited in Linda Bryder, *A Voice for Mothers: The Plunket Society and infant welfare, 1907–2000* (Auckland: Auckland University Press, 2003), p. 1; Tom Brooking, *Richard Seddon, King of God's Own: The life and times of New Zealand's longest-serving prime minister* (Auckland: Penguin, 2014), p. 380.
3. J.M. Brown, 'Naseby in the "Golden Age"', in *Tales of Pioneer Women, collected by the Women's Institutes of New Zealand*, ed. Airini E. Woodhouse (Christchurch: Whitcombe and Tombs, 1940), pp. 293–94; Florence Nightingale, *Notes on Nursing: What it is and what it is not* (London: Gerald Duckworth, (1859) 1952), p. 70; Emma Dent, Sudeley Castle, diary entry 3 December 1864; Florence Nightingale to Emma Dent, Christmas Eve 1864, Archival collection, Sudeley Castle and Gardens, Winchcombe, UK.
4. Edith M. Lewis, *Joy in the Caring* (Christchurch: N.M Peryer, 1962), p. 290.
5. E.M. Dunsford, 'Recreation for nurses in country hospitals', *KT* 6, January 1913, p. 2. Edith Dunsford trained at Timaru Hospital from 1894, registering in October 1902. After a period as matron of Hāwera Hospital from 1904 to 1907, she did private case and private hospital nursing. She gained her midwifery certificate at the Dunedin St Helens Hospital in 1909. In 1911 she became matron of Westport Hospital. *NZG*, 1930, p. 1209.
6. *AJHR*, 1885, H-18a, p. 17.
7. 'Barge duty in France', *KT* 10, October 1917, p. 208.
8. 'Life in a sanatorium', *KT* 11, April 1918, p. 93.
9. 'Obituary', *KT* 12, October 1919, p. 179.
10. Norah Carson, letter, 25 January 1941, MS–Papers–4713-1, ATL.
11. Nurses' Memorial Fund, *KT* 11, January 1918, pp. 19–20, quotation on p. 20.
12. 'Table talk', *OW*, 28 November 1917, p. 49.
13. See, for example, Colleen Williams, *All for a Medal: The nursing memoirs of Colleen Turbet Williams* (Auckland: Self-published, 2006), p. 24.
14. 'Believe it or not!', *New Plymouth Hospital Nurses' Christmas Magazine*, December 1939, n.p.; Sidney Wilding, ARC2008–136, Puke Ariki, New Plymouth. This first volume was cyclostyled and stapled and had no page numbers.
15. 'Reflections of a nurse patient', *NZNJ* 23, March 1930, pp. 99–102, quotation on p. 101.

Bibliography

Primary sources

OFFICIAL RECORDS

Appendices to the Journals of the House of Representatives
[Lambie, M.I.] *Historical Development of Nursing in New Zealand, 1840–1946* (Wellington: Department of Health, 1946)
[Lambie, M.I.] *Historical Development of Nursing in New Zealand, 1840–1950* (Wellington: Department of Health, 1950)
New Zealand Parliamentary Debates
Register of Nurses, *New Zealand Gazette*

ARCHIVES

Alexander Turnbull Library (ATL)

Bennett, Agnes: Papers, MS–Papers–1346, folder 211
Carson, Norah: Papers, MS–Papers–4713-1
Commons Family: Papers, Letters from Daphne to her family–MS–Papers–1582
Early nursing history of the East Cape District, MS–Papers–7072–6
Francois, Bridget Madge Isobel [née Ristori], 1902–1992: Diaries and Papers, MSY–6766; MS–Papers–4690; MS–Papers–9556; MS–Group–0195; MS–Papers–10108
Marsh, Dame Ngaio: MS–Personal Papers–1397–4/08, Series IV, Folder 8
Macnab, Margaret Duirs: 'Account of experiences following the Napier earthquake', MS–Papers–3838
New Zealand Nurses Association: Records, MS–Group–0241; 79–032
Smedley, Beryl, 'Ricky's Story: The memoirs of Amy Rickman', MS–Papers–4404

Archives New Zealand (ANZ)

Department of Health, District Nurses: Manaia–H1–23/21/39
Department of Health, District Nurses: Reports of Inspection–1928–43, H1–23/6/3
Nurses' personal records, Dunedin Hospital, DAHI records, 9189 D262
School of Advanced Nursing Studies, Series 16377, SANS 8; Series 16389, SANS 20; SANS 24

Miscellaneous archives

Corkill, Louisa, letter, Hawke's Bay District Health Board Library, Hastings
Dent, Emma, Diary and Letters, Archival Collection, Sudeley Castle and Gardens, Winchcombe, UK
Hall, Sir Robert, Papers, Box 1, File 25, Tairāwhiti Museum, Gisborne
History of Nursing – Wellington Hospital folder, Wellington Hospital Nursing

Archive, Capital and Coast District Health Board, Wellington

Jeffery, Minnie, war diaries, MS–2934, Jeffery, Garry: Jeffery family papers relating to World War I, Hocken Collections, University of Otago, Dunedin

Knox Church: Deacon's Court Minutes; Annual Reports, Presbyterian Research Centre (Archives), Dunedin

Matron's Annual Letters, RLH/LH/N/7, Royal London Hospital Archive, London

'Memoir of M.H. Fraser', 1934, Pioneer Women's Hall, Dunedin

Memorials to New Zealand Nurses file, New Zealand Nurses' Organisation Library, Wellington

Napier Hospital Applications Register, VN [82506], MTG Archive, Napier

Napier Hospital Register of Sisters, Register and Papers, Napier Hospital, Rose Macdonald, 68039a, Box ARI540, MTG Archive, Napier

New Zealand Nurses' Memorial Fund: Records, ARC–0547–#9, Hocken Collection, University of Otago, Dunedin

'Nurses' Anthem', 82495a and b, MTG Archive, Napier

Nurse's notebook, Wellington Hospital, 1939–42, author's personal collection

Powley, Violet, material, 2012/42/1–41, MTG Archive, Napier

'Sister Pritchard, a Pen Portrait', typescript, Tairāwhiti Museum, Gisborne

Tombleson, John, 'Whataupoko: The land, its people', Tairāwhiti Museum, Gisborne

Waite, Winifred Ellen, material, ARC2005–187, Heritage Collection, Puke Ariki, New Plymouth

Wellington Hospital Nurses Reunion and Chapel Association records, AP001, Wellington City Council Archives

Wilding, Sidney, ARC2008-136, Heritage Collection, Puke Ariki, New Plymouth

Wyllie, Kate, material, Tairāwhiti Museum, Gisborne

JOURNALS

Australasian Nurses' Journal, 1902–50
British Journal of Nursing, 1902–50
Journal of the Department of Public Health, Hospitals, and Charitable Aid, 1917–19
Kai Tiaki: The Journal of the Nurses of New Zealand, 1908–29
New Zealand Nursing Journal, 1930–50
Ladies' Mirror, 1922–26
Nursing Gazette, 1951
Nursing Record, 1888–1901
Una, 1903–50

NEWSPAPERS

Ashburton Guardian, 1880–50
Auckland Star, 1880–1945
Bay of Plenty Times, 1880–1949
Clutha Leader, 1880–1920
Dominion, 1907–20
Evening Post (Wellington), 1880–1945
Evening Star (Dunedin), 1900–45
Free Lance, 1900–20
Gisborne Times, 1901–37
Greymouth Evening Star, 1901–20
Hastings Standard, 1896–1920
Hawera and Normanby Star, 1880–1924
Hawke's Bay Herald, 1880–1904
Hokitika Guardian, 1919–24
Lyttelton Times, 1880–1920
Manawatu Standard, 1990–45
Maoriland Worker, 1910–24
Marlborough Express, 1880–1920
Nelson Evening Mail, 1880–1937
New Zealand Herald, 1880–1945
New Zealand Times, 1910
North Canterbury Gazette, 1932–39
NZ Truth, 1906–30
Otago Daily Times, 1880–1950
Otago Witness, 1880–1920
Poverty Bay Herald, 1880–1939
Press, 1880–1945
Star (Christchurch), 1880–1920
Stratford Evening Post, 1911–36
Taranaki Herald, 1890–1920

Thames Star, 1923
Timaru Herald, 1880–1928
Waihi Daily Telegraph, 1921
Wairarapa Age, 1906–20
Wanganui Chronicle, 1880–1919
West Coast Times, 1880–1916

ORAL HISTORY INTERVIEWS

Bakewell, Margaret, OHI–0014/009, 25 January 1983, Nursing Education and Research Foundation Oral History Collection, ATL, Wellington

Bayly, Gladys, ARC2007–197, Heritage Collection, Puke Ariki, New Plymouth

Burgess, Marie, compiler, 'We wanted to nurse', New Zealand Nurses Organisation, edited excerpts from oral history interviews, Nursing Education and Research Foundation Oral History Collection, OHI–0014, ATL, Wellington

Busch, Anne, OHI–0014/021, 15 December 1982, Nursing Education and Research Foundation Oral History Collection, ATL, Wellington

Gilbert, Audrey (née Dawson), 9 August 2005, author's personal collection

Haywood, Barbara Joan, oral history interview, 16 October 2017, Hawke's Bay Knowledge Bank, Hastings

Hikaka, Veronica, ARC2005–292, Heritage Collection, Puke Ariki, New Plymouth

Hill, Lilian, OHI–0014/073, 5 May 1983, Nursing Education and Research Foundation Oral History Collection, ATL, Wellington

Holderness, Mary, OHI–0014/075, 25 August and 5 September 1982, Nursing Education and Research Foundation Oral History Collection, ATL, Wellington

Leipst, Elsie Isabella, n.d., Hawke's Bay Knowledge Bank, Hastings

McDonald, Anne, 22 November 2005, author's personal collection

O'Meara, Mary (Molly), OHI–0014/128, 12 October 1983, Nursing Education and Research Foundation Oral History Collection, ATL, Wellington

Reyburn, Sophia Mary Dorothy (née Palmer), OHI–0014/138, 14 April 1983, Nursing Education and Research Foundation Oral History Collection, ATL, Wellington

Widdowson, Grace, OHI–0014/176, 27 January 1983, Nursing Education and Research Foundation Oral History Collection, ATL, Wellington

Woodward, Elizabeth (née Will), 25 June 2004, author's personal collection

PUBLISHED WORKS

Ashdown, A. Millicent, *A Complete System of Nursing*, 12th edn (London: J.M. Dent, 1939)

'At Anzac in a hospital ship', *School Journal*, part 3, 10, no. 5, 1916, 154–59

Baughan, Blanche, 'An early morning walk', in Blanche Baughan, *Brown Bread from a Colonial Oven, Being Sketches of Up-Country Life in New Zealand* (Christchurch: Whitcombe & Tombs, 1912), 124

Baughan, Blanche. 'Blanche Baughan, A bush section, (1908)', in *The Auckland University Press Anthology of New Zealand Literature*, eds Jane Stafford and Mark Williams (Auckland: Auckland University Press, 2012), 103–06

Baughan, Blanche, 'Burnt Bush', in Blanche Baughan, *Shingle-Short and Other Verses* (Christchurch: Whitcombe & Tombs, 1908)

Bedggood, N., 'Method of preparation of cod liver oil Vaseline dressings', in *Medical Advice from a Backblock Hospital*, ed. George M. Smith (Wellington: Progressive Publishing Society, 1943), 58

Beechy, I.M., 'The trials of the amateur journalist', *Wellington Public Hospital Nurses Journal* 1, no. 5, 1936, 13

Booth, Charles, ed., *Life and Labour of the People of London*, vol. 1, *East, Central and*

South London (London: Macmillan, 1892)
Brittain, Vera, *Testament of Youth* (London: Victor Gollancz, 1933)
Brown, J.M., 'Naseby in the "Golden Age"', in *Tales of Pioneer Women, collected by the Women's Institutes of New Zealand*, ed. Airini E. Woodhouse (Christchurch: Whitcombe & Tombs, 1940), 290–95
By-Laws for Nurses 1927, Wellington Hospital Board, Wellington, 1927
Cairney, John, *Surgery for Students of Nursing* (Christchurch: N.M. Peryer, 1952)
Cook, Sir Edward T., *The Life of Florence Nightingale*, 2 vols (London: Macmillan, 1913)
Darling, H.C. Rutherford, *Surgical Nursing and After-Treatment: A handbook for nurses and others* (London: J. & A. Churchill, 1917)
Darling, H.C. Rutherford, *Surgical Nursing and After-Treatment: A handbook for nurses and others*, 2nd edn (London: J. & A. Churchill, 1923)
Darling, H.C. Rutherford, *Surgical Nursing and After-Treatment: A handbook for nurses and others*, 4th edn (London: J. & A. Churchill, 1932)
Dock, Lavinia L., and Stewart, Isabel M., *A Short History of Nursing from the Earliest Times to the Present Day* (New York: G.P. Putnam's Sons, 1920)
Dock, Lavinia, 'Discussion', *Nursing Record and Hospital World* 23, 15 July 1899, 48
Dock, Lavinia, ed., *A History of Nursing*, vol. 4 (New York: G.P. Putnam's Sons, 1912)
Drew, Lt. H.T.B., 'The New Zealand camps in England', in *The War Effort of New Zealand*, ed. H.T.B. Drew (Auckland: Whitcombe & Tombs, 1923), 244–74
'Florence Nightingale', *School Journal*, part 2, vol. 4, no. 9, October 1910, 129–33
'Florence Nightingale', *School Journal*, part 2, vol. 4, no. 8, September 1910, 119–21
Foote, Helen Vicars, 'Nursing services of life assurance societies in Australia and New Zealand', *International Nursing Review* 8, nos. 1–4, 1933, 89–91

Goldsmith, Margaret, *Florence Nightingale: The woman and the legend* (London: Hodder & Stoughton, 1937)
'Gossip notes', *The Lamp* 12, no. 7, 1955, 15–16
Haresnape, Isabel, *Home nursing. What to do and how to do it* (Auckland: Isabel Haresnape, 1923)
Harlow, F. Wilson, ed., *Modern Surgery for Nurses* (London: William Heinemann, 1948)
'Helpful hints to student nurses', *Wellington Public Hospital Nurses Journal* 1, no. 5, 1936, 5–6
Hei, Hamiora, 'Maori girls and nursing', Papers and addresses read before the second conference of the Te Aute College Students' Association, December 1897, Napier, 1898, 30–31
'Hospital days', *Wellington Public Hospital Nurses Journal* 1, no. 7, 1939, 15
Howard, Russell, *Surgical Nursing and the Principles of Surgery for Nurses* (London: Edward Arnold, 1908)
Hughes, Amy, *Practical Hints on District Nursing* (London: Scientific Press, 1898)
Hughes, Basil, 'Early treatment of compound fracture of the long bones of the extremities', *BMJ*, 3 March 1917, 289–92
Jellett, Henry, *A Short Practice of Midwifery for Nurses* (London: J. & A. Churchill, 1933)
Lambie, Mary I., 'The maintenance of high standards of health in the nursing community', International Council of Nurses Congress Papers 1937, section 2, session 3, International Council of Nurses, London, 67–69
Lambie, Mary, 'The prevention of endemic goitre in New Zealand by a public health nurse', *Canadian Nurse* 21, no. 9, 1925, 464–66
Lucas, Alice, 'Our duty in small things', *AJN* 5, no. 12, 1905, 879–81
Lückes, Eva E.C., *Lectures on General Nursing* (London: Kegan Paul, Trench, 1888)

Macdonald, Joyce, *Away from Home* (Christchurch: Bookroom, 1945)

Maclean, Hester, 'New Zealand Army Nurses', in *The War Effort of New Zealand*, ed. H.T.B. Drew (Auckland: Whitcombe & Tombs, 1923), 87–104

Maclean, Hester, 'New Zealand', in *A History of Nursing*, ed. Lavinia L. Dock (New York: G.P. Putnam's Sons, 1912), 4:189–222

Maclean, Hester, *Nursing in New Zealand: History and reminiscences* (Wellington: Tolan, 1932)

Matheson, Annie, *Florence Nightingale: A biography* (London: Thomas Nelson, 1913)

Maxwell, Anna C., and Pope, Amy E., *Practical Nursing: A text-book for nurses* (New York: G.P. Putnam's Sons, 1914)

McCarthy, Beryl, *Castles in the Soil* (Dunedin: A.H. & A.W. Reed, 1939)

McGregor, A.N., *A System of Surgical Nursing* (Glasgow: David Bryce, 1905)

Miles, Alexander, *Surgical Ward Work and Nursing: A handbook for nurses and others* (London: Scientific Press, 1921)

'Miss Isabella Fraser', in *The Cyclopedia of New Zealand, Otago and Southland Provincial Districts* (Christchurch: Cyclopedia Company, 1905), 146–47

'More canvassing levers', *Ariki Toa* 3a, no. 2a, 7 March 1927, 1

'More tributes to the nursing service', *Ariki Toa* 6, no. 3, 8 September 1930, 4

Nash, Rosalind, ed., *Florence Nightingale to Her Nurses: A selection from Miss Nightingale's addresses to probationers and nurses of the Nightingale School at St Thomas's Hospital* (London: Macmillan, 1914)

Nightingale, Florence, *Notes on Nursing: What it is and what it is not* (London: Gerald Duckworth, [1859] 1952)

Nurse Maude's Household Book, Nurse Maude for the District Nursing Association, Christchurch, n.d.

'Nursing and welfare services', *Ariki Toa*, 15 June 1947, 4

Nursing ... as a Career, Wellington Hospital Board, n.d. (c. 1940s–50s)

'The nursing service', *Ariki Toa* 3a, no. 4, 5 July 1927, 4

Nutting, Adelaide M., and Dock, Lavinia L., *A History of Nursing*, vols 1–4 (New York: G.P. Putnam's Sons, 1907–12)

Pearce, Evelyn C., *A General Textbook of Nursing: A comprehensive guide* (London: Faber & Faber, 1938)

Pearce, Evelyn C., *A General Textbook of Nursing: A comprehensive guide to the final state examinations* (London: Faber & Faber, 1942)

Pietzcker, Dominika, Berg-Domas, M., and Lambie, Mary I., Report of the Health Statistics Committee presented at the Congress in London, July 1937, International Council of Nurses, London, 1937

Pope, James, *Health for the Maori: A manual for use in native schools* (Wellington: George Didsbury, Government Printer, 1884)

'The Private Hospital', *The Cyclopedia of New Zealand, Wellington Provincial District* (Wellington: Cyclopedia Company Ltd, 1897), 493

Public Health Nursing Committee, 'The story of public health nursing in New Zealand', New Zealand Registered Nurses Association, Wellington, 1955

Pugh, W.T. Gordon, *Practical Nursing*, 12th edn (Edinburgh: William Blackwood, 1940)

Ristori, Bridget, *Nursing as a Career* (Kawakawa: Northland Gazette, 1947)

Ristori, Bridget, *Nursing in the Home* (Whangārei: Northern Publishing, 1949)

Robb, Isabel Hampton, 'The quality of thoroughness in nurses' work', *AJN* 4, no. 3 1903, 168–77

Sargent, Cora McCabe, 'The hospital tray', *AJN* 15, no. 7, 1915, 554–60

Scanlan, Nelle, *Tides of Youth* ([Christchurch]: Whitcombe & Tombs, [1933] 1958)

Scanlan, Nelle, *Winds of Heaven* (Christchurch: Whitcombe & Tombs, [1934] 1958)

Somers Cocks, E., *A Friend in Need: Nurse Maude, her life and work* (Christchurch: Nurse Maude District Nursing Association, 1950)

Studholme, Lt. Colonel John, *New Zealand Expeditionary Force, Record of Personal Services during the War of Officers, Nurses, and First-Class Warrant Officers; And other facts relating to the N.Z.E.F., Unofficial but based on official records* (Wellington: W.A.G. Skinner, Government Printer, 1928)

Turbott, Henry B., 'East Cape Health District, New Zealand', *International Nursing Review* 8, nos. 1-4, 1933, 65–70

Waikato Hospital, Hamilton, New Zealand: A pictorial record and survey, 1887–1948 (Hamilton: Waikato Hospital, 1948)

Watson, J.K., *A Handbook for Nurses* (London: Scientific Press, 1899)

West, Rebecca, *War Nurse: The true story of a woman who lived, loved and suffered on the Western Front* (New York and Chicago: A.L. Burt, 1930)

Wilson, Macdonald D., *A Hundred Years of Healing: Wellington Hospital, 1847–1947* (Wellington: A.H. & A.W. Reed, 1948)

'A word about the nursing service', *Ariki Toa* 2a, no. 6, 27 October 1926, 1

'Your friend the nurse', *Ariki Toa*, 15 May 1947, 3

Secondary Sources

Alfano, Mark R., and Robinson, Brian, 'Gossip as a burdened virtue', *Ethical Theory and Moral Practice* 20, no. 3, 2017, 473–87

Alterio, Maxine, 'Memoirs of First World War nurses: Making meaning of traumatic experiences', PhD thesis, Victoria University of Wellington, 2013

Ancott-Johnson, Barbara, *Nurse in the North: With Dr G.M. Smith in the Hokianga* (Christchurch: Whitcombe & Tombs, 1973)

Andrews, Christine, 'Developing a nursing specialty – Plunket nursing, 1905–1920', MA (Applied) research report, Victoria University of Wellington, 2001

Angus, John, *A History of the Otago Hospital Board and Its Predecessors* (Dunedin: Otago Hospital Board, 1984)

Archer, Bernice, and Kent, Fedorowich, 'The women of Stanley: Internment in Hong Kong 1942–45', *Women's History Review* 5, no. 3, 1996, 373–99

Arcus, Kerrin J, 'Often wearisome, sometimes saddening, but always interesting: A hundred years of district nursing in Wellington, 1903–2003', MA (Applied) thesis, Victoria University of Wellington, 2004

Ashley, Jo Ann, *Hospitals, Paternalism, and the Role of the Nurse* (New York: Teachers College Press, 1976)

Barber, Laurie H., and Towers, Roy J., *Wellington Hospital, 1847–1976* (Wellington: Wellington Hospital Board, 1976)

Bardenhagen, Marita, 'Professional isolation and independence of bush nurses in Tasmania, 1910–1957: "We were very much individuals on our own"', PhD thesis, University of Tasmania, 2003

Barnes, Felicity, *New Zealand's London: A colony and its metropolis* (Auckland: Auckland University Press, 2012)

Bassett, Jan, *Guns and Brooches: Australian Army nursing from the Boer War to the Gulf War* (Melbourne: Oxford University Press, 1992)

Bayly, Monica, *A History of the Queen's Nursing Institute* (London: Croom Helm, 1987)

Belgrave, Michael, *The Mater: A history of Auckland's Mercy Hospital, 1900–2000* (Palmerston North: Dunmore Press, 2000)

Belich, James, *Making Peoples: A history of the New Zealanders from Polynesian settlement to the end of the nineteenth century* (Auckland: Penguin Books, 1996)

Belich, James, *Paradise Reforged: A history of the New Zealanders from the 1880s to the year 2000* (Auckland: Allen Lane/Penguin, 2001)

Bishop, Catherine, *Women Mean Business: Colonial businesswomen in New Zealand* (Dunedin: Otago University Press, 2020)

Bodnar, John, *Remaking America: Public memory, commemoration and patriotism in the 20th century* (Princeton, NJ: Princeton University Press, 1992)

Bostridge, Mark, *The Life of Florence Nightingale: The making of an icon* (New York: Farrar, Straus & Giroux, 2008)

Boyd, M.B., *City of the Plains: A history of Hastings* (Hastings: Victoria University Press, 1984)

Bradley, Eva, *The History of Royston Hospital* (Hastings: Royston Hospital Trust Board, 2007)

Bramadat, Ina, and Saydak, Marion, 'Nursing on the Canadian prairies, 1909–1930: Effects on immigration', *Nursing History Review* 1, 1993, 105–17

Brisson, Ulrike, 'Nineteenth-century European women's travel writings: Female heroes, danger, and death', PhD diss., Pennsylvania State University, 2000

Brooking, Tom, *Richard Seddon, King of God's Own: The life and times of New Zealand's longest-serving prime minister* (Auckland: Penguin, 2014)

Brown, Margaret, Masters, Diana, and Smith, Barbara, *Nurses of Auckland: The history of the general nursing programme in the Auckland School of Nursing* (Auckland: M. Brown, D. Masters & B. Smith, 1998)

Bryder, Linda, '"Babies of the Empire": The evolution of infant welfare services in New Zealand and Britain in the first half of the twentieth century', in *The Practice of Reform in Health, Medicine, and Science, 1500–2000: Essays for Charles Webster*, eds Margaret Pelling and Scott Mandelbrote (Abingdon: Routledge, 2017), 247–62

Bryder, Linda, 'More than educators: New Zealand's Plunket nurses, 1907–1950', *Nursing History Review* 26, 2018, 83–96

Bryder, Linda, 'Pattrick, Anne', from the Dictionary of New Zealand Biography: www: teara.govt.nz/en/biographies/4p5/pattrick-anne

Bryder, Linda, '"They do what you wish; they like you; you the good nurse!": Colonialism and Native Health nursing in New Zealand, 1900–40', in *Colonial Caring: A history of colonial and post-colonial nursing*, eds Helen Sweet and Sue Hawkins (Manchester: Manchester University Press, 2015), 84–103

Bryder, Linda, *A Voice for Mothers: The Plunket Society and infant welfare, 1907–2000* (Auckland: Auckland University Press, 2003)

Buhler-Wilkerson, Karen, *No Place Like Home: A history of nursing and home care in the United States* (Baltimore: Johns Hopkins University Press, 2001)

Burgess, Marie E., *Nursing Remembered* (Gisborne: Cook Hospital Nurses' Reunion Committee, 2010)

Burgess, Marie, 'Pritchard, Ethel', Dictionary of New Zealand Biography: www.teara.govt.nz/en/biographies/5p38/pritchard-ethel

Campbell, Helen, *Looking Back: A history of the Christchurch School of Nursing, 1891–1987* (Christchurch: Nursing History Christchurch Charitable Trust, 1997)

Campbell, Sister, 'Nursing homes in the Paeroa area', *Ohinemuri Regional History Journal* 5, no. 2, 1968, 19–20

Caughley, Jill, 'Humanitarian, international nursing and the New Zealand recipients of the Florence Nightingale Medal, 1920–1999', MA (Applied) thesis, Victoria University of Wellington, 2001

Cemetery Database, Hastings District Council: www.hastingsdc.govt.nz/services/

Chambers, Marjorie, *My Life in Nursing: Christchurch Hospital, 1936–1966* (Tauranga: Moana Press, 1988)

Christie, Sarah, 'Gender, remembrance, and the sinking of the *Marquette*', *Women's Studies Journal* 30, no. 1, 2016, 30–46

Christofferson, Iris, 'Keep pumping those brakes, Nurse!', in *Plunket Pioneers: Recollections of Plunket nurses from 1940* to 2000, ed. Joyce Powell (Auckland: Heritage Press, 2003), 24–25

Ciaran, Fiona, *The Architectural Heritage of Christchurch*, vol. 7, *Nurses' Memorial Chapel* (Christchurch: Christchurch City Council Planning Policy Unit, 1990)

Ciaran, Fiona, 'Christchurch Hospital's threatened shrine', *Historic Places*, December 1986, 8–11

Ciaran, Fiona, *Stained Glass Windows of Canterbury, New Zealand* (Dunedin: Otago University Press, 1998)

Clark, Louise, '"Making its own history": New Zealand historical fiction for children, 1862–2008', PhD thesis, University of Waikato, 2010

Clark, Mary, 'Nursing: As it was in my day', *Auckland Waikato Historical Journal* 62, April 1993, 26–28

Conly, Geoff, *A Case History: The Hawke's Bay Hospital Board, 1876–1989* (Napier: Hawke's Bay Area Health Board, 1992)

Cornwell, Irene, 'Fresh air and regular habits', in *Plunket Pioneers: Recollections of Plunket nurses from 1940 to 2000*, ed. Joyce Powell (Auckland: Heritage Press, 2003), 17–23

Crawford, Ruth, 'Elizabeth McIlwrick (formerly Wayte), née Crawford, Nursing in the 1940s', *Nursing Praxis in New Zealand* 12, no. 3, 1997, 31–33

Cullens, Victoria J., 'Not just a shortage of girls: The shortage of nurses in post–World War II New Zealand, 1945–1955', MA (Applied) thesis, Victoria University of Wellington, 2001

Damian, Sister Mary, *Growl You May but Go You Must* (Wellington: A.H. & A.W. Reed, 1968)

Dannant, Margaret, 'District nursing: Professional skills and knowledge in domestic settings: Linking national and local networks of expertise', PhD thesis, University of Leicester, 2005

Davies, Sonja, *Bread and Roses: Sonja Davies, her story* (Masterton: Fraser Books, 1984)

Dixon, Robert, *Writing the Colonial Adventure: Race, gender and nation in Anglo-Australian popular fiction, 1875–1914* (Cambridge: Cambridge University Press, 1995)

Dodd, Dianne D., Elliott, Jayne and Rousseau, Nicole, 'Outpost nursing in Canada', in *On All Frontiers: Four centuries of Canadian nursing*, eds Christina Bates, Dianne Dodd and Nicole Rousseau (Ottawa, ON: University of Ottawa Press, 2005), 139–52

Douglas, Mary, *Implicit Meanings: Essays in anthropology* (London: Routledge & Kegan Paul, 1975)

Douglas, Mary, *Purity and Danger: An analysis of concepts of pollution and taboo* (London: Routledge & Kegan Paul, 1966)

Dow, Derek, *Safeguarding the Public Health: A history of the New Zealand Department of Health* (Wellington: Victoria University Press, 1995)

Drayton, Joanne, *Ngaio Marsh: Her life in crime* (Auckland: Harper Collins, 2008)

Duggins, Molly, '"The world's fernery": New Zealand, fern albums, and nineteenth-century fern fever', in *New Zealand's Empire*, eds Katie Pickles and Catharine Coleborn (Manchester: Manchester University Press, 2016), 102–24

Dunsford, Deborah, 'Tuberculosis and the Auckland Hospital nurse, 1938–1948', in *New Countries and Old Medicine*, eds Linda Bryder and Derek Dow (Auckland: Pyramid Press, 1995), 291–97

Fairman, Julie, '"Not all nurses are good, not all doctors are bad …", essay review', *Bulletin of the History of Medicine* 78, 2004, 451–60

Fennel, Lee Anne, 'Unpacking the gift: Illiquid goods and the empathetic dialogue', in *The Question of the Gift: Essays across disciplines*, ed. Mark Osteen (London: Routledge, 2002) 85–102

Ford, Dorothy Alice, *Journey from Stranger's Rest* (Wellington: Daphne Brasell Associates, 1989)

Frawley, Maria, *A Wider Range: Travel writing by women in Victorian England*

(Rutherford, NJ: Fairleigh Dickinson University Press, 1994)

Fry, Ruth, *It's Different for Daughters: A history of the curriculum for girls in New Zealand schools, 1900–1975* (Wellington: New Zealand Council for Educational Research, 1985)

Furness, J.G., *Wairau Hospital: 100 years of caring* (Blenheim: Marlborough Hospital Board, 1978)

Gibson Smith, Margaret, and Shadbolt, Yvonne T., 'NZNA: Structure and function, 1909–1983', in *Objects and Outcomes: New Zealand Nurses' Association, 1909–1983*, eds Margaret Gibson and Yvonne T. Shadbolt (Wellington: New Zealand Nurses' Association, 1984), 1–21

Gibson Smith, Margaret, and Shadbolt, Yvonne T., *Objects and Outcomes: New Zealand Nurses' Association, 1909–1983* (Wellington: New Zealand Nurses' Association, 1984)

Gilderdale, Betty, *A Sea Change: 145 years of New Zealand junior fiction* (Auckland: Longman Paul, 1982)

Gill, Isabel, *The Lamp Still Burns: Nursing in Victoria, 1936–1981; An autobiographical account* (Bendigo: Bendigo College of Advanced Education, 1989)

Gilmour-Jones, Helen, 'Reintroducing Miss Margaret Macnab', *Nursing Praxis in New Zealand* 7, no. 3, 1992, 40–42

Godden, Judith, *Lucy Osburn, a Lady Displaced: Florence Nightingale's envoy to Australia* (Sydney: Sydney University Press, 2006)

Greenstreet, Sue, *A Nursing Odyssey: An account of the beginning of registered nursing in New Zealand* (Wellington: First Edition, 2007)

Group, T.M., and Roberts, J., *Nursing, Physician Control, and the Medical Monopoly: Historical perspectives on gendered inequality in roles, rights, and range of practice* (Bloomington: Indiana University Press, 2001)

Hallam, Julia, 'Nursing an image: The Sue Barton career novels', in *Image and Power: Women in fiction in the twentieth century*, eds Sarah Sceats and Gail Cunningham (London: Longmans, 1996), 91–102

Hallett, Christine E., *Containing Trauma: Nursing work in the First World War* (Manchester: Manchester University Press, 2009)

Hallett, Christine, '"Emotional nursing": Involvement, engagement, and detachment in the writings of First World War nurses and VADs', in *First World War Nursing: New perspectives*, eds Alison S. Fell and Christine E. Hallett (New York: Routledge, 2013), 87–102

Hallett, Christine E., *Nurse Writers of the Great War* (Manchester: Manchester University Press, 2016)

Hallett, Christine E., *Veiled Warriors: Allied nurses of the First World War* (Oxford: Oxford University Press, 2016)

Hancock, Lyndall, 'Torrance, Jessie (1874–1949)', in *Southern People: A dictionary of Otago Southland biography*, ed. Jane Thomson (Dunedin: Longacre Press, 1998), 516

Harris, Kirsty, *More than Bombs and Bandages: Australian Army nurses at work in World War I* (Newport, NSW: Big Sky Publishing, 2011)

Hawkins, Anne H., 'Pathography: Patient narratives of illness', *Western Journal of Medicine* 171, no. 2, 1999, 127–29

Hawkins, Anne H., *Reconstructing Illness: Studies in pathography* (West Lafayette, IN: Purdue University Press, 1999)

Hayman, Frances, *King Country Nurse* (Auckland: Blackwood & Janet Paul, 1964)

Helmstadter, Carol, 'A third look at Sarah Gamp', *Canadian Bulletin of Medical History* 30, no. 2, 2013, 141–59

Hochschild, Arlie, *The Managed Heart: Commercialization of human feeling* (Berkeley: University of California Press, 1983)

Home Truths, Piercing Memories project, Immunisation Advisory Centre: www.immune.org.nz

Honko, Lauri, 'The problem of defining myth', *Scripta Instituti Donneriani Aboensis* 6, 1972, 7–19

Hood, Lynley, *Minnie Dean: Her life and crimes* (Auckland: Penguin, 1994)

Howell, Jessica, 'Nursing and empire: Travel letters from Africa and the Caribbean', *Studies in Travel Writing* 17, no. 1, 2013, 62–77

Howell, Jessica, Rafferty, Anne Marie, and Snaith, Anna, '(Author)ity abroad: The life writing of colonial nurses', *International Journal of Nursing Studies* 48, no. 9, September 2011, 1155–62

Howse, Carrie, '"The reflection of England's light": The Instructive District Nursing Association of Boston, 1814–1914', *Nursing History Review* 17, 2009, 47–79

Howse, Carrie, '"The ultimate destination of all nursing": The development of district nursing in England, 1880–1925', *Nursing History Review* 15, 2007, 65–94

Hunter, Kate, and Ross, Kirstie, *Holding on to Home: New Zealand stories and objects of the First World War* (Wellington: Te Papa Press, 2014)

Jones, Lawrence, 'Myth and anti-myth in literary responses to the centennial', in *Creating a National Spirit: Celebrating New Zealand's centennial 1940*, ed. William Renwick (Wellington: Victoria University Press, 2004), 207–21

Keeling, Arlene W., and Wall, Barbara Mann, *Nurses and Disasters: Global, historical case studies* (New York: Springer, 2015)

King, Michael, *The Penguin History of New Zealand* (Auckland: Penguin, 2003)

Kirby, Stephanie, 'Sputum and the scent of wallflowers: Nursing in tuberculosis sanatoria, 1920–1970', *Social History of Medicine* 23, no. 3, 2010, 602–20

Krisjanous, Jayne, and Wood, Pamela J., '"For quiet nerves and steady poise": A historical analysis of advertising to New Zealand nurses in the *Kai Tiaki* journal, 1908–1929', *Journal of Historical Research in Marketing* 12, no. 1, 2019, 19–52

Kristeva, Julia, *Powers of Horror: An essay on abjection* (New York: Columbia University Press, 1982)

Kutzer, M. Daphne, *Empire's Children: Empire and imperialism in classic British children's books* (London: Routledge, 2002)

Kuzma, Julian, 'New Zealand landscape and literature, 1890–1925', *Environment and History* 9, no. 4, 2003, 451–61

Labrum, Bronwyn, 'The material culture of welfare in Aotearoa/New Zealand: A case study of clothing', *History Australia* 2, no. 3, 2005, 81.1–81.12

Lambie, Mary, *My Story: Memoirs of a New Zealand nurse* (Christchurch: Whitcombe & Tombs, 1956)

Lange, Raeburn, *May the People Live: A history of Maori health development, 1900–1920* (Auckland: Auckland University Press, 1999)

Laurant, Claire, *Rituals and Myths in Nursing: A social history* (Barnsley: Pen & Sword Books, 2019)

Law, Robin, 'On the streets of southern Dunedin: Gender and transport', in *Sites of Gender: Women, men and modernity in southern Dunedin, 1890–1939*, eds Barbara Brookes, Annabel Cooper and Robin Law (Auckland: Auckland University Press, 2003), 258–84

Lee, Laurie, *Cider with Rosie* (Harlow: Longman, 1976)

Lewis, Edith M., *Joy in the Caring* (Christchurch: N.M. Peryer, 1962)

Lind, Clive A., *Step by Step: The history of nursing education in Southland* (Invercargill: Southland Hospital Nurses Reunion Committee, 1982)

Low, Lynette, 'Phillys Streeter (née Wright) RGN, Maternity Nurse', *Nursing Praxis in New Zealand* 12, no. 1 1997, 29–30

Lynaugh, Joan E., 'Inventing international nursing: The first decade (1899–1910)',

International Nursing Review 46, no. 1, 1999, 9–12

Macdonald, Betty, *The Plague and I* (Seattle: University of Washington Press, [1948] 2000)

Mackie, Helen, *A Nursing Journey* ([Wellington]: Helen Mackie, 1990)

Main, Sandra, 'My nursing days at Waikato Hospital, 1929–1934', *Auckland–Waikato Historical Journal* 54, April 1989, 19–22

Mansfield, Katherine, *The Best of Katherine Mansfield's Short Stories* (Auckland: Vintage, 1998)

Masters, Diana S., 'Mereana Tangata: The first Maori registered nurse', *Nursing New Zealand* 7, no. 8, 2001, 14–15 and 27

Mayne, Alan, *The Imagined Slum: Newspaper representations in three cities, 1870–1914* (Leicester: Leicester University Press, 1993)

Mayne, Alan, *Representing the Slum: Popular journalism in a late nineteenth-century city* (Parkville, VIC: University of Melbourne, 1990)

McDonald, Anne L., and Tulloch, C., *Wellington Hospital: Educating nurses for more than a century, 1883–1991* (Wellington: Wellington Hospital Nurses' Reunion Committee, c. 1992)

McDougall, Margaret, 'Discovering our past through exploring a register from Wellington Hospital, 1916–1925', in *Looking Back, Moving Forward: Essays in the history of New Zealand nursing and midwifery*, eds Norma Chick and Jan Rodgers (Palmerston North: Department of Nursing and Midwifery, Massey University, 1997), 23–32

McDougall, Margaret, and Stevenson, Annette, 'The interdependence of nurse training and nursing service', in *New Countries and Old Medicine*, eds Linda Bryder and Derek Dow (Auckland: Pyramid, 1995), 285–90

McGann, Susan, *The Battle of the Nurses: A study of eight women who influenced the development of professional nursing, 1880–1930* (London: Scutari Press, 1992)

McKegg, A.H., '"Ministering angels": The government backblock nursing service and the Maori health nurses, 1909–1939', MA thesis, University of Auckland, 1991

McKegg, Alexandra H., 'The Maori Health Nursing scheme: An experiment in autonomous health care', *New Zealand Journal of History* 26, no. 2, 1992, 145–60

McKillop, Ann M., 'Native health nursing in New Zealand, 1911–1930: A new work and a new profession for women', MA thesis, Massey University, 1998

McNabb, Sheryl, *100 Years New Zealand Military Nursing: New Zealand Army Nursing Service: Royal New Zealand Nursing Corps, 1915–2015* (Hawke's Bay: Sheryl McNabb, 2015)

Melosh, Barbara, *'The Physician's Hand': Work culture and conflict in American nursing* (Philadelphia, PA: Temple University Press, 1982)

Midgley, Clare, Twells, Alison, and Carlier, Julie, eds, *Women in Transnational History: Connecting the local and the global* (Abingdon: Routledge, 2016)

Montgomerie, Deborah, 'Man-powering women: Industrial conscription during the Second World War', in *Women in History 2*, eds Barbara Brookes, Charlotte Macdonald and Margaret Tennant (Wellington: Bridget Williams Books, 1992), 184–204

Morin, Karen M., 'Peak practices: Englishwomen's "heroic" adventures in the nineteenth-century American West', *Annals of the Association of American Geographers* 89, no. 3, 1999, 489–514

Morris Matthews, Kay, *Recovery: Women's overseas service in World War I* (Gisborne: Tairāwhiti Museum, 2017)

Mortimer, Barbara, 'The history of nursing: Yesterday, today and tomorrow', in *New Directions in the History of Nursing: International perspectives*, eds Barbara Mortimer and Susan McGann (Abingdon: Routledge, 2005), 1–21

Munro, Jessie, *The Story of Suzanne Aubert* (Auckland: Auckland University Press, 1997)

Mutch, Carol, Bingham, Rosemary, Kingsbury, Lynette, and Perreau, Maria, 'Political indoctrination through myth building: The *New Zealand School Journal* at the time of World War I', *Curriculum Matters* 14, 2018, 102–28

'My war effort', in *Women in Wartime: New Zealand women tell their story*, ed. Lauris Edmond (Wellington: Government Printing Office Publishing, 1986), 49–52

Neill, J.O.C., *Grace Neill: The story of a noble woman* (Christchurch: N.M. Peryer, 1961)

Nelson, Sioban, 'A history of small things', in *Advanced Qualitative Research for Nursing*, ed. Joanna Latimer (Oxford: Blackwell Science, 2003), 211–29

New Zealand Army Nursing Service: www.nzans.org

Nolan, Melanie, *Breadwinning: New Zealand women and the state* (Christchurch: Canterbury University Press, 2000)

'Nurse', in *Women in Wartime: New Zealand women tell their story*, ed. Lauris Edmond (Wellington: Government Printing Office Publishing, 1986), 238–43

'Nursing in the 1930s', *Spectrum* #800, 1993, Radio New Zealand

O'Brien, Patricia, 'From Sudan to Samoa: Imperial legacies and cultures in New Zealand's rule over the Mandated Territory of Western Samoa', in *New Zealand's Empire*, eds Katie Pickles and Catharine Coleborn (Manchester: Manchester University Press, 2016), 127–46

O'Connor, Mary Ellen, *Freed to Care, Proud to Nurse: 100 years of the New Zealand Nurses' Organisation* (Wellington: Steele Roberts, 2010)

Oosterman, Allison, 'New Zealand war correspondence before 1915', *Pacific Journalism Review* 16, no. 1, 2010, 133–52

Openshaw, Roger, and Ball, Teresa, 'New Zealand teacher education: Progression or prescription?' *Education Research and Perspectives* 33, no. 2, 2006, 102–23

Opie, June, *Over My Dead Body* (London: Methuen, 1957)

Osteen, Mark, 'Introduction: Questions of the gift', in *The Question of the Gift: Essays across disciplines*, ed. Mark Osteen (London: Routledge, 2002), 1–42

Ouditt, Sharon, *Fighting Forces, Writing Women: Identity and ideology in the First World War* (London: Routledge, 1994)

Patterson, James T., 'How do we write the history of disease?', *Health and History* 1, 1998, 5–29

Peel, Mark, 'Charity, case work, and the dramas of class in Melbourne, 1910–1940', *History Australia* 2, no. 3, 2005, 83.1–83.15

Pengelly, Edna, *Nursing in Peace and War* (Wellington: Wingfield Press, 1956)

Pető, Andrea, 'Food-talk: Markers of identity and imaginary belonging', in *Women Migrants from East to West: Gender, mobility and belonging in contemporary Europe*, eds Luisa Passerini, Dawn Lyon, Enrica Capusotti and Ioanna Laliotou (Oxford: Berhahn, 2010), 152–64

Pickles, Katie, 'Mapping memorials for Edith Cavell on the colonial edge', *New Zealand Geographer* 62, 2006, 13–24

Pickles, Katie, *Transnational Outrage: The death and commemoration of Edith Cavell* (Basingstoke: Palgrave Macmillan, 2007)

Pickles, Katie, and Coleborn, Catharine, eds, *New Zealand's Empire* (Manchester: Manchester University Press, 2016)

Pool, D. Ian, *Te Iwi Maori: A New Zealand population past, present and projected* (Auckland: Auckland University Press, 1991)

Pool, D. Ian, *The Maori Population of New Zealand, 1769–1971* (Auckland: Auckland University Press, 1977)

Potter, Jane, *Boys in Khaki, Girls in Print: Women's literary responses to the Great War, 1914–1918* (Oxford: Clarendon Press, 2005)

Pratt, Mary Louise, *Imperial Eyes: Studies*

in travel writing and transculturation (London: Routledge, 1992)

Prebble, Kate, and Bryder, Linda, 'Gender and class tensions between psychiatric nurses and the general nursing profession in mid-twentieth-century New Zealand', *Contemporary Nurse* 30, no. 2, 2008, 181–95

Priestly, Susan, *Bush Nursing in Victoria, 1910–1985: The first 75 years* (Melbourne, VIC: Victorian Bush Nursing Association/Lothian, 1986)

Prochaska, Frank, 'Body and soul: Bible nurses and the poor in Victorian London', *Historical Research* 60, no. 143, 1987, 336–48

Propp, Vladimir, *Morphology of the Folktale*, trans. Laurence Scott (Austin: University of Texas Press, [1927] 1971)

Radford, Patricia M., 'Calamity Kate, the galloping chestnut: An historical investigation into three major areas of nursing in New Zealand during the period 1911–1935, explored through the career of Leonora Flight Kelly, registered nurse and midwife', MA (Applied) research report, Victoria University of Wellington, 2000

Rae, Ruth, *Scarlet Poppies: The army experience of Australian nurses during World War One* (Burwood, NSW: College of Nursing, 2004)

Rafferty, Anne-Marie, 'The seduction of history and the nursing diaspora', *Health and History* 7, 2005, 2–16

Rattray, Joan, *Great Days in New Zealand Nursing* (Wellington: A.H. & A.W. Reed, 1961)

Rawstron, Richard E., *A Unique Nursing Group: New Zealand Army nurse anaesthetists of WWI* (Christchurch: Rawstron Publishing, 2005)

Reed, A.H., *Florence Nightingale*, 2nd edn (Dunedin: A.H. & A.W. Reed, 1966)

Reverby, Susan, *Ordered to Care: The dilemma of American nursing, 1850–1945* (Cambridge: Cambridge University Press, 1987)

Rice, Geoffrey, *Black Flu 1918: The story of New Zealand's worst public health disaster* (Christchurch: Canterbury University Press, 2017)

Rice, Geoffrey, *Black November: The 1918 influenza pandemic in New Zealand* (Christchurch: Canterbury University Press, 2005)

Rice, Geoffrey, *Heaton Rhodes of Otahuna: The illustrated biography* (Christchurch: Canterbury University Press, 2008)

Ristori, Bridget, *Patients in My Care: The autobiography of a nurse* (London: Elek, 1967)

Robins, Susan L., 'Keeping the homes fires burning: The history of home nursing in New Zealand, 1900–1925', MA (Applied) thesis, Victoria University of Wellington, 2002

Robinson, Alison, ed., *Stratford Hospital Memories* (Stratford: Thurlstone Press, 2001)

Roddick, Judith A., 'Delirium and fever in the antipodes: Nursing and the 1918 influenza epidemic in Dunedin Hospital, New Zealand', *Journal of Research in Nursing* 11, no. 4, 2006, 357–70

Roddick, Judith A., 'When the flag flew at half mast: Nursing and the 1918 influenza epidemic in Dunedin', MN thesis, Otago Polytechnic, 2005

Rodgers, Jan, 'Nursing education in New Zealand, 1883 to 1930: The persistence of the Nightingale ethos', MA thesis, Massey University, 1985

Rodgers, Jan, '"A paradox of power and marginality": New Zealand nurses' professional campaign during war, 1900–1920', PhD thesis, Massey University, 1994

Rogers, Anna, *While You're Away: New Zealand nurses at war, 1899–1948* (Auckland: Auckland University Press, 2003)

Rousseau, Nicole, and Daigle, Johanne, 'Medical service to settlers: The gestation and establishment of a nursing service in Quebec, 1932–43', *Nursing History Review* 8, 2000, 95–116

Royal British Nurses' Association, Pioneer Nurses, King's College Collection: www.kingscollections.org

Royal College of Nursing, Special Collection, Historical Journals: www.rcnarchive.rcn.org.uk

Russell, R. Lynette, and Cornell, Judith A., *A Vision for the Bush: The NSW Bush Nursing Association, 1911–1974* (Burwood, NSW: Australian College of Nursing, 2012)

Rutherdale, Myra, ed., *Caregiving on the Periphery: Historical perspectives on nursing and midwifery in Canada* (Montreal, QC: McGill Queen's University Press, 2010)

Salmon, E. Beatrice, 'The international idea', in *Objects and Outcomes: New Zealand Nurses' Association, 1909–1983*, eds Margaret Gibson Smith and Yvonne T. Shadbolt (Wellington: New Zealand Nurses' Association, 1984), 118–38

Santino, J. 'Characteristics of occupational narratives', *Western Folklore* 37, 1978, 199–212

Sargison, Patricia A., '"Essentially a woman's work": A history of general nursing in New Zealand, 1830–1930', PhD thesis, University of Otago, 2001

Sargison, Patricia A., 'Gender, class and power: Ideologies and conflict during the transition to trained female nursing at two New Zealand hospitals, 1889–95', *Women's History Review* 6, no. 2, 1997, 183–200

Sargison, Patricia A, 'The wages of sin: Aspects of nurse training at Dunedin Hospital in the 1920s and 1930s', *Women's Studies Journal* 11, no. 1–2, 1995, 165–78

Scott, David, ed., *Middlemore Memories: The first 50 years of Middlemore Hospital* ([Manukau]: South Auckland Health, 1997)

Seymer, L., *Selected Writings of Florence Nightingale* (London: Macmillan, 1954)

Shadbolt, Yvonne, 'Re-introducing Mabel Mahinarangi Kewene, MBE, QSO', *Nursing Praxis in New Zealand* 16, no. 3, 2000, 50–53

Shadbolt, Yvonne, 'Re-introducing Mavis Helena ('Pat') Paton', *Nursing Praxis in New Zealand* 14, no. 3, 1999, 47–53

Smillie, Anne, 'The end of tranquillity? An exploration of some organisational and societal factors that generated discord upon the introduction of trained nurses into New Zealand hospitals, 1885–1914', MA (Applied) in Nursing research report, Victoria University of Wellington, 2003

Smith, M.S., 'Introducing Louisa Dixon', *Nursing Praxis in New Zealand* 14, March 1999, 46–49

Smith, Michelle, *Empire in British Girls' Literature and Culture: Imperial girls, 1880–1915* (London: Palgrave Macmillan, 2011)

Smith, Michelle J., Moruzi, Kristine, and Bradford, Clare, *From Colonial to Modern: Transnational girlhood in Canadian, Australian, and New Zealand children's literature, 1840–1940* (Toronto, ON: University of Toronto Press, 2018)

Smith, Rosemarie, 'Women's Division Federated Farmers 1925–', in *Women Together: A history of women's organisations in New Zealand*, ed. Anne Else (Wellington: Daphne Brasell Associates, 1993), 392–95

Souter, Kay Torney, 'Narrating the body: Disease as interpersonal event', *Health and History* 1, 1998, 35–42

Spacks, Patricia Meyer, *Gossip* (New York: Knopf, 1985)

Stafford, Jane, and Williams, Mark, 'Fashioned intimacies: Maoriland and colonial modernity', *Journal of Commonwealth Literature* 37, 2002, 31–48

Stafford, Jane, and Williams, Mark, *Maoriland: New Zealand literature, 1872–1914* (Wellington: Victoria University Press, 2006)

Stenhouse, John, 'Religion and society', in *The New Oxford History of New Zealand*, ed. Giselle Byrnes (South Melbourne: Oxford

University Press, 2009), 323–56

Stevenson, Annette, *Wellington Hospital Nurses Memorial Chapel* (Wellington: Wellington Hospital Nurses Memorial Chapel Committee, 2001)

Stonehouse, Eve A., *In the Name of Nurse Maude* (Christchurch: Nurse Maude District Nursing Association, 1972)

Straessle, Flora, 'Agnes Wood, one of the First Fifty', *Nursing Praxis in New Zealand* 13, no. 1, 1998, 47–49

Stuart, Annie, 'Parasites lost? The Rockefeller Foundation and the expansion of health services in the colonial South Pacific, 1916–1939', PhD thesis, University of Canterbury, 2002

Swain, Gladys, *Stewart Island Days: A district nurse looks back* (Dunedin: Whitcombe & Tombs, 1970)

Sweet, Helen, '"Wanted: 16 nurses of the better educated type": Provision of nurses to South Africa in the late nineteenth and early twentieth centuries', *Nursing Inquiry* 11, no. 3, 2004, 176–84

Sweet, Helen, with Dougall, Rona, *Community Nursing and Primary Healthcare in Britain in the Twentieth Century* (London: Routledge, 2008)

Sweet, Helen, and Hawkins, Sue, eds, *Colonial Caring: A history of colonial and post-colonial nursing* (Manchester: Manchester University Press, 2015)

T&G: 100 Years (Wellington: T&G Mutual Life Assurance Society, 1976)

Takarangi, Janet, 'Reintroducing Miss I. Banks', *Nursing Praxis in New Zealand* 1, no. 1, 1985, 47

Tennant, Margaret, *The Fabric of Welfare: Voluntary organisations, government and welfare in New Zealand, 1840–2005* (Wellington: Bridget Williams Books, 2007)

Tennant, Margaret, 'Grace Neill', in *The Book of New Zealand Women*, eds Charlotte Macdonald, Merimeri Penfold and Bridget Williams (Wellington: Bridget Williams Books, 1991), 468–69

Tennant, Margaret, *Paupers and Providers: Charitable aid in New Zealand* (Wellington: Allen & Unwin, 1989)

Thomas, Jane, 'A glance back in time: The nursing notes of Edwina Perkins', *International History of Nursing Journal* 7, no. 2, 2003, 21–28

Thompson, Stith, *The Folktale* (New York: Holt, Rinehart & Winston, 1946)

Thomson, Elaine, '"Beware of worthless imitations": Advertising in nursing periodicals, c. 1888–1945', in *New Directions in the History of Nursing: International perspective*, eds Barbara Mortimer and Susan McGann (Abingdon: Routledge, 2005), 158–78

Thorp, Marian M., *The Long, Long Trail: An autobiography* (Hastings: Hart, 1971)

Tolerton, Jane, *Ettie: A life of Ettie Rout* (Auckland: Penguin, 1992)

Toman, Cynthia, Elliott, Jayne and Stuart, Meryn, eds, *Place and Practice in Canadian Nursing History* (Vancouver: University of British Columbia Press, 2008)

Turner, Victor, *On the Edge of the Bush: Anthropology as experience* (Tucson: University of Arizona Press, 1985)

Turner, Victor, *Schism and Continuity in an African Society: A study of Ndembu village life* (Manchester: Manchester University Press, 1957)

Waipukurau Hospital Centennial, 1879–1979, Souvenir Booklet (Waipukurau: Waipawa Hospital Board, 1979)

'Ward 8 in Wartime', *Spectrum* #807, 1993, Radio New Zealand

Weir, Rosemary, *Educating Nurses in Scotland: A history of innovation and change, 1950–2000* (Penzance: Hypatia Trust, 2004)

Weir, Rosemary I., 'The lecture notes of two pupil nurses of the preliminary training school at Glasgow Royal Infirmary', *International History of Nursing Journal* 1, no. 4, 1996, 49–60

Wevers, Lydia, *Country of Writing: Travel writing and New Zealand, 1809–1900*

(Auckland: Auckland University Press, 2002)

Wickham, A., '"She must be content to be their servant as well as their teacher": The early years of district nursing in Ireland', in *Care to Remember: Nursing and midwifery in Ireland*, ed. Gerard Fealy (Cork: Mercier Press, 2005), 101– 21

Wiener, Joel H., 'Edmund Yates: The gossip as editor', in *Innovators and Preachers: The role of the editor in Victorian England*, ed. Joel H. Wiener (Westport, CT: Praeger, 1985), 260–69

Williams, Colleen, *All for a Medal: The nursing memoirs of Colleen Turbet Williams* (Auckland: Self-published, 2006)

Willis, L. Ida G., *A Nurse Remembers: The life story of L. Ida G. Willis* (Lower Hutt: A.K. Wilson, 1968)

Wilson, Kathryn, *Angels in the Devil's Pit: Nursing in Rotorua, 1840–1940* (Wellington: Karo Press, 1998)

Wilson, Kathy, 'Nursing on the home front during World War II: An essential service in New Zealand', in *Looking Back, Moving Forward: Essays in the history of New Zealand nursing and midwifery*, eds Norma Chick and Jan Rodgers (Palmerston North: Department of Nursing and Midwifery, Massey University, 1997), 67–79

Wiltshire, John, 'Biography, pathography, and the recovery of meaning', *Cambridge Quarterly* 29, no. 4, 2000, 409–22

Wood, Pamela J., 'The blurred boundary between professional and lay home nursing knowledge and practice in New Zealand, 1900–1935', *Home Healthcare Nurse* 31, no. 2, 2013, E1–E7

Wood, Pamela J., 'Commemorating nursing: An exercise in historical imagination', *Nursing Praxis in New Zealand* 21, no. 2, 2005, 47–57

Wood, Pamela, *Dirt: Filth and decay in a New World Arcadia* (Auckland: Auckland University Press, 2005)

Wood, Pamela J., 'Efficient preachers of the gospel of health: The 1898 scheme for educating Maori nurses', *Nursing Praxis in New Zealand* 7, no. 1, 1992, 12–21

Wood, Pamela J., 'The enduring issue of assessing nursing knowledge: Surgical nursing final examinations in Australia and New Zealand, 1905–1930', *Contemporary Nurse* 32, nos. 1–2, 2009, 109–22

Wood, Pamela J., 'A glimpse through the typhoid window: Connecting nursing care, medical treatment and the search for best practice, 1890–1920', in *Conference Proceedings, Waiora: Nursing research in Aotearoa/New Zealand: Evolving a shared sense of our future*, eds Paul Watson and Martin Woods (Palmerston North: Nursing Research Section, New Zealand Nurses Organisation, 1999), 106–15

Wood, Pamela J., 'Historical imagination and issues in rural and remote area nursing', *Australian Journal of Advanced Nursing* 27, no. 4, 2010, 54–61

Wood, Pamela J., 'Managing boundaries between professional and lay nursing following the influenza pandemic, 1918–1919: Insights for professional resilience today?' *Journal of Clinical Nursing* 26, 2017, 805–12

Wood, Pamela J., '*Marquette* memorial service for nurses', *Nursing Praxis in New Zealand* 18, no. 3, 2002, 62–64

Wood, Pamela J., 'The nurse's odyssey: The professional folktale in New Zealand backblocks nurses' stories, 1910–1915', *Nursing Inquiry* 16, no. 2, 2009, 111–21

Wood, Pamela J., 'Nurses' occupational health as a driver for curriculum change emphasising health promotion: An historical research study', *Nurse Education Today* 34, 2014, 709–13

Wood, Pamela J., 'Nursing mortubiography: New Zealand nursing obituaries, 1910–1940', paper presented at the 10th History of Nursing Research Colloquium, 'International History of Nursing: Theoretical Interpretations and Approaches', Wellcome Unit for the

History of Medicine, Oxford University, Oxford, UK, 11 March 2005

Wood, Pamela J., 'Nursing the patient, the room and the doctor: Assessing New Zealand nurses' practical capability, 1900–1945', *Nurse Education Today* 31, 2011, 140–44

Wood, Pamela J., 'Professional, practice and political issues in the history of New Zealand's remote rural "backblocks" nursing: The case of Mokau, 1910–1940', *Contemporary Nurse* 30, no. 2, 2008, 168–80

Wood, Pamela J., 'Pus, pedagogy and practice: How "dirt" shaped surgical nurse training and hierarchies of practice, 1900–1935', in *Germs and Governance: The past, present and future of hospital infection, prevention and control*, eds Anne Marie Rafferty, Marguerite Dupree and Fay Bound Alberti (Manchester: Manchester University Press, 2021), 81–103

Wood, Pamela J., 'Sickening nurses: Fever nursing, nurses' illness, and the anatomy of blame, New Zealand, 1903–1923', *Nursing History Review* 19, 2011, 53–77

Wood, Pamela J., 'Supporting or sabotaging the surgeon's heroic efforts: Portrayals of the surgical nurse's role in preventing wound sepsis, 1895–1935', *Journal of Clinical Nursing* 18, 2009, 2739–46

Wood, Pamela J., '"This ghastly war": Emotional glimpses in New Zealand nurses' published letters in World War I', paper presented at the History of Emotions Conference, Stout Centre, Victoria University of Wellington, Wellington, 3–5 September 2015

Wood, Pamela J., 'Threading the dead in the professional collective memory: Nursing obituaries, 1910–1939', paper presented at the Australian College of Nursing Inaugural History Conference, Nurses' Memorial Centre, Melbourne, 15–16 November, 2012

Wood, Pamela J., 'Understanding and evaluating historical sources in nursing history research', *Nursing Praxis in New Zealand* 27, no. 1, 2011, 25–33

Wood, Pamela J., and Arcus, Kerri, 'Poverty, philanthropy, and professionalism: The establishment of a district nursing service in Wellington, New Zealand, 1903', *Health and History* 13, no. 1, 2011, 44–64

Wood, Pamela J., and Arcus, Kerri, '"Sunless lives": District nurses' and journalists' co-construction of the "sick poor" as a vulnerable population in early twentieth-century New Zealand', *Contemporary Nurse* 42, no. 2, 2012, 2452–75

Wood, Pamela J., and Knight, Sara, 'The taste of war: The meaning of food to New Zealand and Australian nurses far from home in World War I, 1915–18', in *Histories of Nursing Practice*, eds Gerard M. Fealy, Christine E. Hallett and Susanne Malchau Dietz (Manchester: Manchester University Press, 2015), 35–51

Wood, Pamela J., and Nelson, Katherine, 'The journal *Kai Tiaki*'s role in developing research capability in New Zealand nursing, 1908–1959', *Nursing Praxis in New Zealand* 29, no. 1, 2013, 12–22

Wood, Pamela J., and Nelson, Katherine, 'Striving for best practice: Standardising New Zealand nursing procedures, 1930-60', *Journal of Clinical Nursing* 22, nos. 21–22, 2013, 3217–24

Woodward, Joan, and Mitchell, Glenys, eds, *A Nurse at War: Emily Peter, 1858–1927* (Christchurch: Te Waihora Press, 2008)

Wright-St Clair, Rex, *Historia Nunc Vivat: Medical practitioners in New Zealand, 1840 to 1930* (Christchurch: Rex Wright-St Clair, 2003).

Yeo, Geoffrey, *Nursing at Bart's: A history of nursing service and nurse education at St Bartholomew's Hospital, London* (Stroud: Alan Sutton Publishing, 1995)

Index

Bold denotes illustrations.

advertising, nurses in 211–22, 230
all-female nursing *see* female nursing, transition to
Ames, Cherry 229
amputations 78, 165, 169, 214, 215
Anderson, Cora 164
applicants/application process, nursing 26, 33, 47, 69–71, 76, 137, 228, 289n62
Arnaboldi, Margaret 214–15, 216, 331n49
Attree, Mavis **158, 227**
Aubert, Suzanne 136
Auckland Hospital 18, 47–48, 49, 50–51, 73–74, 114, 173, 214–15
Auckland Hospital Board 18, 114
Australia 34, 92, 110, 113, 130, 205, 211, 268

backblock nursing 37, 111–12
    attrition rate 120
    Backblocks Nursing Service 37, 111, 112, 113, 121, 130
    East Coast 128, **151**
    folklore 121–27, 273
    Gates, Esther 114, 116, 120, 127, 131
    horse, travelling by 43, 111, 114–15, **115**, 117, 122
    illness/death, nurses' 112
    Kai Tiaki (nursing journal) 111, 121–22, 124, 127
    letters, nurses' 111
    Maclean, Hester 112–14, 116, 117, 118–19, 121, 124
    Māori nurses/communities 133–34, 273
    Marlborough 122
    Northland 117–18, **118**, 119, 120, 125–26, **125**, 133, 144–45, 148
    perception, public/professional 128–31
    Stewart Island 114, 119
    Taranaki 37, 111, 117, 119, 120, 121, 122–23, 157
    West Coast 116–17, 120, 129–30
    work/culture 112–20
    see also district nursing
Bagley, Amelia 26, **27**, 35–36, 37–38, 111, **142**, 145, 153–54
Baker, Mabel 129
Banks, Isabel 128–29
Barclay, Elizabeth 96, 105, 107, 109, 296n30
Barton, Sue 228, 229
Batchelor, Ferdinand 207
Bay of Plenty **146, 147**, 154–55
bedsores 59–60
Beetham, Cicely 144, 322n141
Bennett, Erin 251
Berry, Joseph 214, 215
Berry, Katherine 254, 263, 337n64
Bertram, Herbert 215–16
Bicknell, Jessie 34–35, 39, 203, 224–25, 237, 264
Biggs, A.C. 202, 205
Bilton, Margaret 37, 121
Blathwayt, Mabel 216
Boer War *see* South African (Boer) War
Borthwick, Mavis 55, 58
Boyle, Joan *see* Loeber, Joan (née Boyle)
British Empire/imperialism
    anti-Empire feelings 252

colonial nursing 159, 267
Empire-centred view of nursing 16, 249–52, 268
influence on New Zealand nursing 271
New Zealand identity 16, 252–53, 268–69, 271–72, 274
see also Great Britain
British Journal of Nursing 65, 251, 253, 254, 259, 342n23
British nurses working in New Zealand 26–28
Bryder, Linda 144, 159, 257, 258

Cairney, John **60**
Canada 256, 264
career progression 228–31
Carston, Margaret 33
Cartwright, Mary Jane 133–34, 148
Cavell, Edith 180, 182, 322n141
ceremonies 65, 88, 160, 231, 232–34, 255
Chambers, Marjorie 51–52, 62, 72, 73, 74, 85, 88
Cherry, Clara 166, 170, 173, 256, 316n31
chief nurses 253
    Lambie, Mary 21, 50, 131, 174, 205, 229–30
    Maclean, Hester 34–36, **35**, 172, 187, 228, 247
    Neill, Grace **29**, 100, 224, 238
    roles/power 86, 110, 111, 203, 224, 228, 247, 252–53, 267, 272
Child Welfare Act 1907 37
Chisholm, Sandra 61, 70, 77, 79
Christchurch Hospital 82–83
    code of virtues violation 82–83, 84
    district nursing 32, 93–95, **103**
    influenza pandemic (1918–19) 187, 188, 195
    Maude, Sibylla 32, 95–96, **103**
    Nurses' Memorial Chapel 180, 240
    training 48, 51–52
    uniform, nurses' 72
Clark, Blanche 73, 175–76
Clark, Isabel 239
Clark, Mary 51, 62, 71
cleaning/cleanliness 51–53, 54–55, 59, 271
code of virtues 17, 63–64, 67, 68, 88, 211, 231, 241, 245–46

district nursing virtues 98–99, 101, 102, 117–18, 121, 127
Māori health nursing virtues 144
violating 82–87, 272
Coleman, Sue 78–79
Collins, Clive 49, 218
Collins, Floyd 214–15
Colonial Mutual Life Assurance Society 96, 97
Colonial Nursing Association 159, 267
Colonial Nursing Service 131, 159
commemorations/memorials 40, 180, 194, 204, 237–41, **239**, 321n126, 328n110, 339n93, 340n108, 342n23
commissions of inquiry 39, 195, 207–08, 215, 219
Commons, Daphne 166, 167, 168, 170, 171, 176, 183, 184, 256, 319n74
complaints against nurses 128–29, 207
complaints by nurses 174, 208, 213–16, 217–18, 220–21
Complete System of Nursing, A (Ashdown) 63
conflicts/complaints, hospital 212–21
    Dunedin Hospital 212–14
    hospital boards 84, 212–14, 215, 217–21, 272
    Maclean, Hester 212, 213, 216, 219
    matrons 212–14, 217–21
    newspaper coverage 84, 215, 218, 219–20
    probationers 217–19
    public perception of nurses/nursing 213, 214, 215, 216, 217–21
    sister nurses 220–21
    see also doctor–nurse relations
Cook Hospital 87, 138, **139**, 157, 217–20, 228
    see also East Coast
Cook Islands **265**
Cormack, Jean 146, 157, 160, 164
Crawford, James 11–12, 275
Cry Havoc (movie) 182
cultural traditions, nursing 231–34

Davies, Sonja 52, 78, 80, 85, 162, 175, 178–79, 209–10, 245
Dawson, Audrey 70, 76, 228, 334n27
Dawson, Lily 146
Days of Probation (Gerard) 210
death, dealing with 80–82, 163, 170

deaths/illnesses while nursing
   Hawke's Bay 1931 earthquake 193,
     194–95, 198, **199**, 204
   infectious diseases **83**, 112, 138, 185,
     187–88, 190, 193–95, 204, 244–46,
     285n81, 324n24
   memorials 238–40, **239**
   training 232
   wartime 172, 179–80
   see also health, nurses'; obituaries
Department of Health
   career progression 229
   conflicts, hospital 128
   inspectors/instructors 24, **125**
   instructors 40
   Māori health nursing 157–58
   minister(s) of public health 18, 187, 194,
     255
   nursing history, New Zealand 21
   organisation 39
   Pacific, nursing in 266
   recruitment 43
   see also Public Health Department
Department of Hospitals 29, 113, 136, 213
Department of Native Affairs 37
Depression, the 42, 96–97, 107, 230, 246
Dickens, Charles 65, 104, 109, 209
disasters *see* Hawke's Bay 1931 earthquake;
   influenza pandemic (1918–19)
district nursing
   Australia 92, 110
   Christchurch 32, 93–95, **103**
   development 92–96
   Dunedin 96–97, 99, 100–01, 102, 104,
     105, 107, 109
   folklore 92, 104–08
   fundraising 93, 100–01
   Great Britain 92, 110
   Herrick, Thomas 93–94
   hospital boards 93
   Kai Tiaki (nursing journal) 37, 91
   Lloyd Lees, Emily 94
   Macandrew, Mirian 91, 102
   Maclean, Hester 110
   Maude, Sibylla 32, 94–96, 101–02, **103**,
     107, 110
   Nightingale, Florence 92, 109

   pay/salary 299n58
   philanthropy 93, 95, 110, 273
   public perception 108–10
   Rickman, Amy 42–43, 44
   Ristori, Bridget 99, 107, 130
   services, delivering 96–98
   Sexton, Anne 91, 102, 104–05
   Torrance, Jessie 96, **97**, 99, 100, 102, 103,
     104, 105, 106–08, 109, 296n31, 299n58
   virtues 98–99, 101, 102, 117–18, 121, 127
   Whanganui 97–98, 101, 105, 109
   work/culture 98–103
   working hours/shifts 124
   see also backblock nursing
Dixon, Minnie 194
Dock, Lavinia 30, 122, 253, 287n15
doctor–nurse relations 53–54, 62, 207–08,
   214–16, 220
   see also conflicts/complaints, hospital
Dougherty, Ellen 31, 233–34
Drummond, Ruth 194–95
Dunedin Hospital **27**, 48–49
   all-female staff 24, 26
   conflicts, hospital 212–14
   drunkenness 23
   influenza pandemic (1918–19) 186, 187,
     190, 238–39
   nurses' behaviour 86
   reforms 24
   training 15, 26, **27**, 48–49, 67–68,
     203–04, 212–13
   see also Karitane Hospital
Dunsford, Edith 186, 275–76

East Coast 87, 118, 128, 138, **139**, **141**, **151**,
   157, 203, 217–20, 228
Education Department 36, 136, 141, 258
Egypt 161–62, 164, 166, **168**, 170, **257**
emergency/temporary hospitals 187, 188,
   191, 192, 193, 195, 196, 197, 205
essay competitions, nursing 45, 227, 231,
   236–37
ethics 62, 85, 271
etiquette 61, 71, 216, 271
Ewart, Jessie 231, 335n50

Fallen Soldiers Memorial Hospital (Hastings) 196
Farrar, Andrew 23
Featherston military camp **189**
female nursing, transition to 24–26
Fenwick, Bedford (Ethel) 30, 253–54, 261
Fergusson, Elizabeth 144–45, 232, 311n63, 335n46
Fiji 265, 267, 274
Florence Nightingale Medal 256–57
Florence Nightingale Memorial Committee 44, 262
flowers, importance of 11–12, 85, 181, 275–77, **277**
Fraser, Isabella 26, 231, 271, 287n21
Fraser, Mary 15, 207–08, 298n41
Fraser, Peter 191
Frasertown 116, 119, 146
Fresh Fields (Novello) 199
fundraising 88, 93, 100–01, 240, 272–73, 276
 see also philanthropy

Gates, Esther 114, 116, 120, 127, 131
Gill, Florence 51, 150–51
Gisborne Hospital 87, 138, **139**, 157, 217–20, 228
 see also East Coast
Godfray, Eva 27–28, **28**, 31, 33, 42, 217
Grabham, George 24, 276, 342n18
Great Britain
 British nurses/nursing culture 14, 24, 26–27, 102, 130, 159, 172, 180, 256, **257**, 263, 268
 code of virtues 88
 comparison between British and New Zealand nurses 256, **257**, 268, 274
 district nursing 92, 110
 influence on New Zealand nursing 16–17, 249–50, 252–53, 268, 271–72
 London 14, 29–30, 102, 105–06, 236, 250–51
 military hospitals 166, **167**, **169**
 paediatrics 259
 registration, nurses' 17, 30, 253–54
 training, nurse 49, 88, 271
 visits by New Zealand nurses 251
 see also British Empire
Gunn, Alick 129–30

Hallett, Christine 166, 172, 182
Hamill, Elaine 198–99, 327n98
Haresnape, Isabel 225, **226**, 333n14
Hastings 96, 185, 196, 201
Hāwera 23, 157–58
Hawke's Bay
 Hastings 96, 185, 196, 201
 Napier Hospital 47, 64, 185–86, 196–99, **197**, **199**, 203, 204, 234, 254, 310n39
 Waipukurau 28, 185, 196, 283n35, 328n121
 Wairoa Hospital 61, 71–72, 73, 74, 84, 187, 196, 198, 203
Hawke's Bay 1931 earthquake 42
 emergency hospitals 196, 197
 fatalities/casualties 196, 197, 198, 201–02, 204
 folklore 198–99, 204
 memorial 204
 Napier Hospital 186, 196–99, **197**, **199**, 203
 nurses' home 186, 187, 198–99, **199**, 203, 204
 post-quake assistance 199–201, 203
 public perception of nurses 202, 204
Health Act 1920 39
Health for the Maori (Pope) 135
health, nurses' 83, 211
 see also deaths/illnesses while nursing
Hei, Ākenehi 18, 36, 37, **138**, 139–40, 154, 273
Hei, Hāmiora 36, 136
Henderson, Robert 183–84, 276
Herrick, Thomas 93–94, 106
hierarchy, hospital 53–54, 62–63, 64, 82, 189–90, 212, 218, 228–31, 272
Higgins, Amy 217–19
Hildyard, Nora 179, 238, 240
Hill, Lilian 155–56, 334n19
Hogben, George 250
Holgate, Annie 95–96, 100, 104, 169, 262
Home Nursing (Haresnape) 225, **226**
horse, travelling by 43, 111, 114–15, **115**, 117, 122, 126, **146**
hospital boards
 Auckland Hospital Board 18, 114
 backblock nursing 113, 114, 116, 123, 129

conflicts, hospital 84, 212–14, 215, 217–21, 272
Cook Hospital Board 217, 218, 219
district nursing 44, 93
Dunedin Hospital Board 212–14, 215
examinations 87–88
Hospital Boards Association 40
influenza pandemic (1918–19) 195
Māori health nursing 137
Nurses and Midwives Board 45
Stratford Hospital Board 123
superannuation 40–41
Timaru Hospital Board 220–21
Wanganui Hospital Board 137, 195
Wellington Hospital Board 84
Westland Hospital Board 116
hospital inspectors/inspection *see* inspectors/inspection of hospitals, government
hospitals
    Auckland Hospital 18, 47–48, 49, 50–51, 73–74, 114, 173, 214–15
    Cook Hospital 87, 138, **139**, 157, 217–20, 228
    emergency/temporary hospitals 187, 188, 191, 192, 193, 195, 196, 197, 205
    Fallen Soldiers Memorial Hospital (Hastings) 196
    Gisborne Hospital 87, 138, **139**, 157, 217–20, 228
    Karitane Hospital 258
    military hospitals 166, **167**, 169, 171, 178, 180, **189**
    Napier Hospital 47, 64, 185–86, 196–99, **197**, **199**, 203, 204, 234, 254, 310n39
    Naseby Hospital 11, 271
    nurses' homes 44, 61, **71**, 73–74, 80, **81**, 83–84, 175, 186, 197, 198, **199**, 204
    private hospitals 34, 36, 41–42, 43, 69, 85, 215–16, 230–31
    St Helens hospitals 17, 34–35, 258
    Stratford Hospital 55, 57, 58, 82, 123
    St Thomas's Hospital 14, 208, 210
    Timaru Hospital 47, 220–21, 338n84, 339n103
    Waikato Hospital 77–78
    Waipawa Hospital **28**, 33, 185, 283n35
    Wairau Hospital 58
    Wairoa Hospital 61, 71–72, 73, 74, 84, 187, 196, 198, 203
    see also Christchurch Hospital; Dunedin Hospital; Wellington Hospital
Houhora 43, **118**, 123, 145

imperialism *see* British Empire/imperialism
infant death rate, New Zealand 257–58, 259, 260
Infant Life Protection Act 1896 258
infection (sepsis) 53, 54, 55, 83, 165
infectious diseases 47, **168**, 190, 335n49
    deaths/illnesses, nurses' **83**, 112, 138, 185, 187–88, 190, 193–95, 204, 245–46, 285n81, 324n24
    isolation wards 47, 58, 188–89, **189**, 217
    scarlet fever 58, **83**, 188–89
    tuberculosis 56, 77, 83, 232, 244–46, 276
    typhoid 133, 138, 140, **141**, 148–49, **151**, 152–53, 161, 163
influenza pandemic (1918–19)
    Australia 205
    caring for patients 187–92
    deaths, number of 42, 186, 190, 324n11
    emergency/temporary hospitals 187, 188, 191, 192, 193, 195, 205
    infection/death of nurses 39, 186–87, 188–89, 190, 193–95, 324n24
    isolation wards 188–89, **189**
    literature, popular 192
    Māori patients 192
    memorial 240
    nurses' accounts 192
    nurse shortage 187–88, 191–92
    probationers 185, 187, 189–90, 195
    public perception 193
    Samoa 267
    working hours/shifts 58, 187–88
innovations, New Zealand nursing 29, 34, 65–66, 119–20, 252–53, 260, 272
inspectors/inspections of hospitals, government
    Bagley, Amelia 35–36
    Bicknell, Jessie 34–35, 39
    career progression 229
    female inspectors 29, 31, 34, 35–36, 39
    Grabham, George 24, 276, 342n18

inspector-generals 34, 49, 112, 213, 218
Lambie, Mary 128
MacGregor Duncan 24, 28, 29, 31–32, 49, 72, 94, 106, 212, 214–15, 342n18
Moore, Janet 125–26, **125**
Neill, Grace 29, 31, 34
nursing innovation 253
Valintine, Thomas 34, 106, 112, 128, 143, 157, 213–14, 218, 259
International Council of Nurses 15, 21, 30, 261–62, 264, 274
isolation wards 47, 58, 188–89, **189**, 217

Jarrett, Jane 145, 156
Jordan, Clare 169, 262–63
journalism *see* newspaper coverage
journals, nursing
    British Journal of Nursing 65, 251, 253, 254, 259, 342n23
    New Zealand Nursing Journal 15, 21, 73, 241, 242, 245, 267
    Nursing Mirror 16, 249
    Nursing Times 210, 245
    see also Kai Tiaki (nursing journal); magazines, hospital/nursing

Kahlenberg, Fritz 217, 220
Kai Tiaki (nursing journal)
    advertising 211, 230
    backblock nursing 111, 121–22, 124, 127
    Bilton, Margaret 37
    conflicts, hospital 219
    district nursing 37, 91
    founding/history 15, 34, 42, 236, 241, 263
    'gossip column' 223–24, 233, 242–44, 247, 251, 266
    international nursing 261–63
    letters, nurses' 182
    Maclean, Hester 15, 34, 42, 211, 219, 223, 240, 261–62
    Māori health nursing 140, 148–51
    modern nursing 210
    Nurses' Memorial Fund 240
    nursing pageant script 65
    obituaries 231–32
    Plunket nursing 259
    poetry 127
    wartime nursing 162, 175, 182–83
    see also New Zealand Nursing Journal
Karitane Hospital 258
Keddie, Alexandra 77
Keeling, Arlene 204–05
Kelly, Nora 122–23, 127, 244
Kēnana, Rua 154–55
Kennedy, Jessie 111, 302n2
Kingsford-Smith, Charles 117, **118**
Kinmont, Harriet 97, 103, 298n37

Lambie, Mary **20**
    chief nurse 21, 50, 131, 174, 205, 229–30
    cleaning/cleanliness 54
    Department of Health instructor 40, **41**
    Director of the Division of Nursing (DDN) 42
    district/backblock nursing 97, 130
    education 21
    Hawke's Bay 1931 earthquake 200–01
    health, nurses' 83
    history, New Zealand nursing (1840–1900) 22–33
    history, New Zealand nursing (1900–19) 34–39
    history, New Zealand nursing (1920–35) 39–43
    history, New Zealand nursing (1935–50) 43–46
    influenza pandemic (1918–19) 187, 205
    International Council of Nurses 264
    nurse inspector 128
    Pacific, nursing in 267
    personality 46
    research 21, 227
    South African (Boer) War 33
    training, nurses' 40, 50
    World War II 174
Lange, Raeburn 134–35
Leech, Ina 193–94
legal cases/proceedings 207–08, 216, 219–20
legislation
    Child Welfare Act 1907 37
    Health Act 1920 39
    Infant Life Protection Act 1896 258
    Medical and Pharmacy Act 1891 30
    Midwives Act 1904 17, 34, 258

Nurses and Midwives Act 1945 18, 45, 258
Nurses and Midwives Registration Act 1925 18, 40
Nurses Registration Act 1901 30, 172, 213, 224, 236, 253, 272
Private Hospitals Act 1906 34
Public Health Act 1900 135
Social Security Act 1938 43, 44
Superannuation Act 1926 41
Tohunga Suppression Act 1907 154
women's franchise 29, 253
leisure time/entertainment 73–76, **75**, 83, 84
Leslie, Ella 126, 305n63
letters, nurses' 15–16, 111–12, 130–31, 162, 174, 184, 242
Lewis, Edith 74, 164, 167, 170, 176, 180–81, **180**, 228, 275
Lewis, Ethel 166
literature, nursing depicted in 76, 182, 210, 228, 229
Lloyd Lees, Emily 94
Loeber, Joan (née Boyle) 59, 63, 73, 87, 88, 174, 176, 246
Long Depression (1880s/1890s) 93, 94, 106

Macandrew, Mirian 91, 102
Macdonald, Joyce 161–62
MacGregor Duncan 24, 28, 29, 31–32, 49, 72, 94, 106, 212, 214–15, 342n18
Mackie, Helen 114–15, 119, 145, 146
Maclean, Christian 161, 162
Maclean, Hester
  backblock nursing 112–14
  chief nurse 34–36, **35**, 172, 187, 228, 247
  conflicts, hospital 212, 213, 216, 219
  Director of the Division of Nursing (DDN) 39
  district nursing 110
  early career 34
  Florence Nightingale Medal 256–57
  Hawke's Bay 1931 earthquake 202
  health, nurses' 83
  influenza pandemic (1918–19) 195–96
  Kai Tiaki/New Zealand Nursing Journal 15, 34, 42, 211, 219, 223, 240, 261–62
  leisure time, nurses' 83, 84
  Māori nursing 141–42, 143, 144
pay, nurses' 49
personality 34
registration 254
training, nurse 39
wartime nursing 162, 172, 173, 179–80, 183
working hours, nurses' 50
Macnab, Margaret 51, 62, 73, 145, 148, 200
magazines, hospital/nursing 63, 79, 119, 242, **243**, 276–77
  see also journals, nursing
male nurses/nursing 18, 45
  see also wardsmen
Mangakāhia, Mabel 126, 143, **227**, 305n65
Māori
  Department of Native Affairs 37, 138, 140–41
  government health policy 134–36
  Public Health Act 1900 135
  racism/discrimination towards 136–37
  te reo 134, 137, 156, 164, 273
Māori health nursing/nurses 18
  attrition rate 142
  backblock nursing 133–34, 273
  Bagley, Amelia 38, **142**, 145, 153–54
  British Empire 159–60
  Cartwright, Mary Jane 133–34, 148
  challenges/tensions 136–37, 139, 143
  fever camps 140–41, 142, 148–52, **151**
  folklore 148–54, 273
  Hei, Ākenehi 18, 36, 37, **138**, 139–40, 154, 273
  Kai Tiaki (nursing journal) 140, 148–51
  Maclean, Hester 141–42, 143, 144
  Māori communities, nursing in 37–38, 133–34, 140–48
  Māori culture/customs 153, 154–56
  McElligot, Nurse 140–42, **141**, **151**
  Native (Māori) Health Nursing Service 140–41, 142
  perception, public/professional 144, 157–59
  Plunket nursing 260
  registration 137–40
  scholarships 36–37, 136–37, 140–41, 160, 272, 273
  services, development of 140–43

Taylor, Ethel Watkins 37, 143, 164, 194
te reo Māori 134, 137, 156, 164, 273
Tohunga Suppression Act 1907 154
training 36–37, 136–37, 160
virtues 144
Whangapirita, Hēni 36–37, 138, 140–42, **141**, 284n71, 310n36
work/culture 144–48
working hours/shifts 152
Marquette (troopship) 38, 179–80, 238, 239, 255–56
Marsden, Kate 251
Martyrdom of Nurse Cavell, The (movie) 182
Mason, James 258, 309n14
maternity nursing 17, 40, 124, 145, 228, 258
matrons
    conflicts, hospital 212–14, 217–21
    inspections by 62
    pay/salary 23, 47, 94
    relations with nurses 62, 212, 213–14, 220
    reports, nurses' 67
    roles of 14, 26
    training by 24, 31, 212–13
    see specific individuals
Maude, Sibylla 22, 32, 94–96, 101–02, **103**, 107, 110, 195
Mawe, Edith 26
McElligot, Nurse 140–42, **141**
McKegg, Alexandra 136, 137, 142, 143, 159
McKenzie, Duncan 214
Medical and Pharmacy Act 1891 30
memorials/commemorations 40, 180, 194, 204, 237–41, **239**, 321n126, 328n110, 339n93, 340n108, 342n23
midwifery
    Midwives Act 1904 17, 34, 258
    Nurses and Midwives Act 1945 18, 45, 258
    Nurses and Midwives Registration Act 1925 18, 40
    Nurses and Midwives Registration Board (NMRB) 40, 235
    training 17–18, 34, 40, 262, 293n39
Midwives Act 1904 17, 34, 258
military hospitals 166, **167**, 169, 171, 178, 180, **189**, 275
minister(s) of public health 18, 187, 194, 255
modern nurse/nursing 208–12

Monson, Nellie 88, **165**, 207
Moore, Janet 39–40, **41**, 70, 125–26, **125**, 262
Morgan, Harriette 258, 259
movies/television, nursing depicted in 181–82, 198–99
Myles, Margaret 212–13, 324n28

Napier Hospital 47, 64, 185–86, 196–99, **197**, **199**, 203, 204, 234, 254, 310n39
Naseby Hospital 11, 271
National Council of Trained Nurses of Great Britain and Ireland 15, 261
Neill, Grace 22, 28–29
    chief nurse **29**, 100, 224, 238
    Grace Neill Memorial Library 238
    Midwives Act 1904 34
    personality 32
    registration, nursing 30, 224, 253–54
    star medal, nursing 236
    syllabus 61, 224, 332n6
    training 30–31
New Zealand Army Nursing Service 38, 162, 164, 172, 174, 307n97, 315n9, 320n96
New Zealand centennial celebrations 21
New Zealand nurses comparisons with other nurses 183–84, 256, **257**, 259, 264, 268, 271, 274
New Zealand nursing history
    1840–1900 22–33
    1900–19 34–39
    1920–35 39–43
    1935–50 43–46
    newspaper coverage 65
    preserving 64–65, 235
    training 64–65, 235, 240
New Zealand Nursing Journal 15, 21, 73, 241, 242, 245, 267
    see also Kai Tiaki (nursing journal)
New Zealand nursing style/culture 14
New Zealand Registered Nurses' Association 21, 42, 264, 283n39
New Zealand Trained Nurses' Association 15, 34, 40, 50, 62, 111, 210, 223, 227, 241
Newman, Nancy 68
newspaper coverage
    advertising 211
    conflicts, hospital 84, 215, 218, 219–20

district/backblocks nursing 92, 94–95, 104, 106, 107–08, 109, 124–25, 129, 263–64
farewells, nursing 233
fundraising 32
Hawke's Bay 1931 earthquake 198–99, 201
influenza pandemic (1918–19) 193, 195, 196
nursing history 65
nurses' pay 49
obituaries 231
Plunket nursing 260
poverty 32, 104, 105–06, 272–73
registration 253
unionism 209
wartime nursing 160, 162, 179–80
Nightingale, Florence 12–13, 250
   Crimean War 11, 13, 236–37, 250
   death 250
   district nursing 92, 109
   Florence Nightingale Medal 256–57
   Florence Nightingale Memorial Committee 44, 262
   flowers 11, 275
   influence 12–14, 61, 237, 271
   lamp 235, 236, 338n84, 339n103
   New Zealand, association with 13–14
   nursing system/philosophy 14, 24, 208, 210, 249, 271
   poetry 183
   School Journal 181, 250
   St Thomas's Hospital 14, 208, 210
Niue 45–46, 266
Nobbs, Grace 101, 299n66
Nordmeyer, Arnold 18
North, Janie 155, 156
Northland
   Far North 43, 44, 117, **118**, 119, 120, 125–26, **125**, 148–49, 153
   Hokianga 117, 119, 120, 125–26, 133, 142, 144–45
   Houhora 43, **118**, 123, 145
   Kaitaia 126
   Rāwene 119, 120, 125–26, 133
Nurses and Midwives Act 1945 18, 45, 258
Nurses and Midwives Board 45
Nurses and Midwives Registration Act 1925 18, 40

Nurses and Midwives Registration Board 40, 235
Nurses' Christian Union 241
nurses' homes 44, 61, **71**, 73–74, 80, **81**, 83–84, 175, 186, 197, 198, **199**, 204
Nurses' Memorial Fund 40, 183, 240–41, 276, 322n133
Nurses Registration Act 1901 30, 172, 213, 224, 236, 253, 272
Nursing Home Murder, The (Marsh) 76
Nursing Mirror (journal) 16, 249
Nursing Times (journal) 210, 245

O'Callaghan, Annie 117, 122, 123–24, 242, 303n24
obituaries 105, 231–32, 237
Ohakune 194–95
orthopaedic nursing 58

Pacific nations, nursing in 45–46, 265–69, **265**, 274
paediatric nursing/medicine 57, 156, 257–60
   see also Plunket Society/nursing
pageants 12, 65–66, 260
pandemic *see* influenza pandemic (1918–19)
Paora, Beth 45, 148, 311n57
Parker, Charlotte 111, 112, 302n2
Pascoe, Eleanor 215–16
patients' perspectives on nursing 11–12, 17, 245–46
Pattrick, Annie 221, 240
pay/salary, matrons' 23, 47, 94
pay/salary, nurses'
   19th century 23, 48–49
   district nursing 299n58
   gifts 234
   while training 47, 48, 49–50, 136
   see also superannuation
Pengelly, Edna **71**
Peter, Emily 161, 162, 163–64, 171, 318n68
Peters, Gladys 114, 119
philanthropy 93, 95, 110, 140, 273
   see also fundraising
plays, nursing depicted in 76, 199
Plunket Society/nursing 37, 65, 191, 221, 228, 257–60, 268, 274
pneumonia 56, 59, 85, 121, 190, 290n83

poetry 127, 183
Polden, Sarah 234, 325n46, 336n55, 337n68
Pope, James 36, 135, 136
Post Graduate School for Nurses 44–45, 65, 97, **227**, 229
poverty 32, 94, 101, 105–07, 272–73
Price, Katharine 82–83
private hospitals 34, 36, 41–42, 43, 69, 85, 215–16, 230–31
Private Hospitals Act 1906 34
private nursing 41, 42–43, 92, 94, 130, 211, 215, 230–31
probationers
    appointment/dismissal 212–13, 217–18
    conflicts, hospital 217–19
    deaths while training 195
    hierarchy, hospital 215
    influenza pandemic (1918–19) 185, 187, 189–90, 195
    Māori 137
    pay 49–50, 136
    private hospitals 36
    scholarships 136, 141
    training 24, **25**, 26, 48, 196
    working hours 50, 188
    see also training
Public Health Act 1900 135
Public Health Department 37, 43, 135, 142, 145, 157, 177, 188
    see also Department of Health
public hospitals, establishment of 23
public perception of nurses/nursing
    backblock nursing 128–31
    conflicts, hospital 213, 214, 215, 216, 217–21
    district nursing 108–10
    Hawke's Bay 1931 earthquake 202, 204
    hospital hierarchy 229, 230
    influenza pandemic (1918–19) 193, 194
    literature, nursing depicted in 76, 182, 210, 228, 229
    Māori health nursing/nurses 144, 157–59
    modern nursing 208–12
    movies/television, nursing depicted in 181–82, 198–99
    nurses' views 17, 272, 275
    obituaries 231

    patients' perspectives 11–12, 17, 245–46
    plays, nursing depicted in 76, 199
    songs, nurses' depiction in 181
    wartime nursing 38, 179–80, 181–84
Purcell, Mary 37–38, 310n33

Quick, George 252

racism/discrimination 136–37
Rātana movement 155
Rātana, Tahupōtiki 155
Rattray, Joan 112, 192
Rāwene 119, 120, 125–26, 133
recruitment campaigns 43, 65, 116, 120, 229, 235, 236, 266, 267
Red Cross 170, 177, 256, 262
Rees, E.T. 186, 198
reform, nursing 16, 24–25 (NZ), 26, 135, 208–09, 318n68
registration
    annual practising certificate 43
    examinations 62, 63, 64, 76, 87–88, 224, 225
    Great Britain 17, 30, 253–54
    Māori nurses 137–40
    New Zealand–Great Britain reciprocity 17, 254
    Nurses and Midwives Registration Act 1925 18, 40
    Nurses and Midwives Registration Board (NMRB) 40, 235
    Nurses Registration Act 1901 30, 172, 213, 224, 236, 253, 272
    star medal, nursing **31**, 88, 89, 164, 235–36, 238
religion 102, 106, 154–55, 236, 241
Renouf, Louise 47, 82
Rhodes family 95
Rhodes, Jessie 95
Rickman, Amy 41, 42–43, 44, 45–46, 73, 117, **118**, 266, 267
Ringatū Church 155
Ristori, Bridget
    Bedford College 262
    cleaning 52
    district nursing 99, 107, 130
    leisure time 74

private case nursing 230
scrapbooks 16
training 63, 71, 72, 74, 77, 87
tuberculosis 246
Rogers, Anna 162, 163
Rogers, Margaret 38
Ross, Sarah 163–64, **165**, 166, 168, 170, 171, 178, 256, 316n41
rural nursing *see* backblock nursing
Russell, George 187, 194, 255

Samoa 265–66, 267
Sargison, Patricia 24, 26, 30
Scammell, Dorothy
    cleaning/cleanliness 52–53
    doctors 63, 230
    examination 87
    Hawke's Bay 1931 earthquake 198, 199
    leisure time 74
    nursing experiences 57, 77, 78, 81–82, 84
    pay/salary 50
    pneumonia 59
    Wairoa Hospital 61–62, 71–72, 73, 84
scarlet fever 58, **83**, 188–89
scholarships 36–37, 44, 45, 136–37, 140–41, 160, 262, 272, 273
Scott, Nancy 67–68
Seddon, Richard 32, 106, 258, 265, 274, 300n104, 308n13
Sexton, Anne 91, 102, 104–05, 295n1
Shaw, Caroline 207, 208
shortages, nursing 43, 50–51, 174, 187, 229–30
sister nurses
    career progression 229
    conflicts, hospital 220–21
    home sisters 44, 61, 72, 73, 82
    influenza pandemic (1918–19) 189
    Māori nurses 137
    obituaries 232
    relations with nurses 61, 64, 73, 84, 85, 174
    roles 31, 44, 52, 62
    training 44, 48, 64, 67
    ward sisters 31, 48, 52, 62, 64, 68, 84, 189, 220
    wartime nursing 172–73, 276
Snell, Agnes Maud 83

Social Security Act 1938 43, 44
Society for Promoting the Health of Women and Children *see* Plunket Society/nursing
songs, nurses' depiction in 181
South African (Boer) War 33, 161, 162, 163–64, **165**, 178, 255, 295n1
Spanish flu *see* influenza pandemic (1918–19)
Speed, Janet 253
St Helens hospitals 17, 34–35, 258
St John Ambulance Association 95, 96, 100–01, 102, 103, 225
St Thomas's Hospital 14, 208, 210
star medal, nursing **31**, 88, 89, 164, 235–36, 238
sterilising 53, 79, 84
Stewart Island 114, 119, 305n56
Stratford Hospital 55, 57, 58, 82, 123
superannuation 40–41, 223
Superannuation Act 1926 41

Tait, Edith 217–19, 220
Tangata, Mereana 138, 192
Taranaki 23, 37, 111, 117, 119, 120, 121, 122–23, 157–59, **158**
Taylor, Ethel Watkins 37, 143, 164, 194
Teape, Bessie 163, 164, 166, 168, 169–70, 171, 318n68
Tennant, Margaret 95
Tennent, Edith 64, 67, 86–87, 203–04, 336n56
Testament of Youth (Brittain) 182
testimonials 22, 71, 204, 211–12, 215, 218, 221, 266, 337n64
textbooks/manuals 51, 59, 63, 135, 225, **226**, 288n50, 293n39
theatre *see* plays depicting nursing
Thomson, Elaine 211
Thorne-George, Margo 185–86, 198
Thorne-George, Nancy 185–86
Thorp, Marian 71, 231
Tides of Youth (Scanlan) 182, 192
Timaru Hospital 47, 220–21, 338n84, 339n103
Todd, Jean 220–21
Torrance, Jessie 96, **97**, 99, 100, 102, 103, 104, 105, 106–08, 109, 296n31, 299n58
trade unions 209–10, 241, 252
training
    attrition rate 18, 76, 120

Auckland Hospital 47–48, 49, 73–74
code of virtues 63–64, 67, 68, 88
cleaning/cleanliness 51–53, 54–55, 59, 271
deaths/illnesses, nurses' 232
Dunedin Hospital 15, 26, **27**, 48–49, 67–68, 203–04, 212–13
early (19th century) 24, 26
ethics 62, 271
etiquette 61, 71, 216, 271
examinations 26, 62, 63, 64, 76, 87–88, 224, 225
exercise classes 55–56, **57**
folklore 77–82
lectures 30, 47, 48–49, **60**, 63, 65, 84, 224–25, 235, 240
leisure time/entertainment 73–76, **75**
Māori 36–37, 136–37, 160
midwifery 17–18
Napier Hospital 47
nurses' homes 44, 61, 71, 73–74, 80, **81**, 175, 186, 197, 198, **199**, 204
nursing history 64–65, 235, 240
pay/salary 47, 48, 49–50, 136
postgraduate training 39–40, **41**, 44–45
Preliminary Training Schools 47–48, 49
reports 64, 67, 68, 86–87, 203–04
rotational training 57–58
syllabus/curriculum 30–31, 47–48, 61, 63, 64–65, 83, 224–25, 271, 289n64, 332n6
textbooks/manuals 51, 59, 63, 135, 225, **226**, 288n50, 293n39
Wellington Hospital 24, **25**, 55–56, **57**, 58, **60**, 76, 79
working hours/shifts 22, 26, 47, 48–49, 50
see also probationers
travel writing 126–27
Trentham military hospital 180, 275
Truby King, Frederic 258, 259
tuberculosis 56, 77, 83, 232, 244–46, 276
Tucker, Margaret 166, 183, 316n30
Turbet, Colleen 47–48, 72, 74, 77, 78, 79, 81, 82, 85–86, 225, 236, 246
Turbott, Harold 128–29
typhoid 133, 138, 140, **141**, 148–49, **151**, 152–53, 161, 163

uniforms 47, 58, 72–73, 162, 184, 235–36
unionism 209–10, 241, 252

Valintine, Thomas 34, 106, 112, 128, 143, 157, 213–14, 218, 259
virtues *see* code of virtues
Voluntary Aid Detachment 171–73, 174, 182
Vos, Mabel 125–26, **146**

Waikato Hospital 77–78
Waipawa Hospital **28**, 33, 185, 283n35
Waipukurau 28, 185, 196, 283n35, 328n121
Wairau Hospital 58
Wairoa Hospital 61, 71–72, 73, 74, 84, 187, 196, 198, 203
Waite, Winifred 266
Wall, Barbara 204–05
Walton, Beatrice 98
Wanganui District Nursing League 97–98
Wanganui Hospital Board 137
War Nurse (West) 182
wardsmen 23, 25–26
see also male nurses/nursing
Warnock, Sarah 122
wartime nursing
    casualties, nursing 179–78
    Christmas celebrations 176–78
    emotional effects 163–73, 184
    enemy encounters 178–79
    folklore 176–81
    leisure time/entertainment 170–71, 175
    letters to/from home 162, 164, 169–70, **169**, 174–75, 182, 184
    memorials 238–40, **239**
    military hospitals 166, **167**, **169**, 171, 178, 180, 189, 275
    New Zealand, representing 255–57
    New Zealand, returning to 173
    New Zealand, serving in 174–76
    orderlies/Voluntary Aid Detachment 171–73, 174
    perception, public/professional 179–80, 181–84
    qualities required 163, 165
    South African (Boer) War 33, 161, 162, 163–64, 178, 295n1
    see also World War I; World War II

Watt, Michael 42, 97, 158
Waymouth, Mary 207
Wellington Hospital
　chapel 339n103
　code of virtues violations 83–84
　inspection 72–73, 276
　nurses' home 71, **81**, 83–84
　training/lectures 24, **25**, 55–56, **57**, 58, **60**, 76, 79
　unionism 209–10
　World War II 175–76, 178–79
Wellock, Mary 198, 202
West Coast 13, 116–17, 120, 129–30, 186, 194, 234
Whanganui 97–98, 101, 105, 109, 137
Whangapirita, Hēni 36–37, 138, 140–42, **141**, 284n71, 310n36
Wharfe, P. **115**
Will, Elizabeth 77–78
Williams, Peggy 41–42
Willis, Ida 171, 172–73, 176–77, 318n66
women's franchise 253

working hours/shifts 22, 26, 47, 48–49, 50, 58, 124, 152, 187–88, 253
World War I
　Maheno (hospital ship) 161, 177–78, 182
　Marquette (troopship) 38, 179–80, 238, 239, 255–56
　New Zealand Army Nursing Service 38, 162, 164, 172, 307n97, 315n9
　nurses' experiences 161, 164–73, 176–78, 179–80, 181
　representing New Zealand 255–57, **257**
World War II
　New Zealand Army Nursing Service 174, 320n96
　New Zealand, serving in 174–76
　nurses' experiences 161–62, 174–76, 178–79, 180–81
　representing New Zealand 256
　volunteer nurses 45
wounds, treating 53, 54, 57, 60, 78, 120, 154, 161, 165–66, 207
Wyllie, Kate 138–39, **139**